In the Company of Others

IN THE
Company
OF Others

An Introduction to Communication

FIFTH EDITION

J. DAN ROTHWELL

CABRILLO COLLEGE, CALIFORNIA

NEW YORK   OXFORD
OXFORD UNIVERSITY PRESS

Oxford University Press is a department of the University of Oxford.
It furthers the University's objective of excellence in research,
scholarship, and education by publishing worldwide.
Oxford is a registered trademark of Oxford University Press
in the UK and certain other countries.

Published in the United States by Oxford University Press
198 Madison Avenue, New York, New York 10016,
United States of America
http://www.oup.com

Oxford   New York
Auckland   Cape Town   Dar es Salaam   Hong Kong   Karachi
Kuala Lumpur   Madrid   Melbourne   Mexico City   Nairobi
New Delhi   Shanghai   Taipei   Toronto

With offices in
Argentina   Austria   Brazil   Chile   Czech Republic   France   Greece
Guatemala   Hungary   Italy   Japan   Poland   Portugal   Singapore
South Korea   Switzerland   Thailand   Turkey   Ukraine   Vietnam

For titles covered by Section 112 of the US Higher Education
Opportunity Act, please visit www.oup.com/us/he for the
latest information about pricing and alternate formats.

Library of Congress Cataloging-in-Publication Data
Rothwell, J. Dan.
 In the company of others : an introduction to communication /
J. Dan Rothwell, Cabrillo College, California. -- Fifth edition.
     pages cm
 Includes bibliographical references and index.
 ISBN 978-0-19-045742-6
1. Communication. I. Title.
 P90.R665 2016
 302.2--dc23
                                                        2015027824

Printing number: 9 8 7 6 5 4 3

Printed in Canada
on acid-free paper

To my family,
MARCY, HILARY, GEOFF, BARRETT, AND CLARE

Brief Contents

Contents

CHAPTER 5   Nonverbal Communication   113

PART TWO: INTERPERSONAL COMMUNICATION

CHAPTER 13 Building Better Speeches   343

Preface

There are many good human communication textbooks available. If you compare just their Table of Contents (TOCs), it might seem that barely a whit of difference exists among the lot. What sets the fifth edition of *In the Company of Others* apart? Certainly not the TOC. Aside from the unique chapter on power and the two appendices (interviewing and special occasion speeches), it must appear to the casual observer that this fifth edition covers the same general topics as most other texts and is just a standard textbook. Surface appearances, however, can be deceiving.

Recognizing that students rarely read the preface because it is marginally relevant to them, I am specifically addressing instructors who might consider using *In the Company of Others* in their courses. It is unrealistic to expect you to peruse the cornucopia of competing communication texts and compare them to this new edition as though you have nothing better to do with your precious time. So let me highlight distinguishing features that make this textbook unique as a complete package.

Distinguishing Features

In the Company of Others covers in depth the standard topics found in every human communication textbook. Its special features, however, separate it from the crowd.

Unique Topic Selection or Coverage: Beyond the Standards

Every author wrestles with what to include and exclude from a textbook that covers a subject as broad as human communication. *In the Company of Others* provides substantial coverage of a multitude of topics that are excluded or given only cursory treatment by other authors:

1. Channel changing impact
2. Hindsight bias: answering the "only common sense" view of communication
3. Four types of communication noise (physical, physiological, semantic, and psychological)
4. Five elements of ethical communication (honesty, respect, fairness, choice, and responsibility) with applications
5. Hypercompetitiveness and communication climate
6. Ethics of hypercompetitiveness
7. Sensory limitations and sensation/perception subjectivity
8. Inattentional blindness and social media blunders
9. Excessive self-esteem
10. Contingencies of self-worth
11. Benevolent versus hostile sexism
12. Culture and gender linkages
13. Self-humbling and self-enhancement cultural differences
14. Power-distance and cultures
15. Ethnocentrism and cultural relativism versus multiculturalism
16. Acculturation strategies and intercultural communication
17. Gender similarities versus gender differences hypotheses
18. Female *and* male body image issues
19. The "beauty bias"
20. First impressions, accuracy and inaccuracy
21. Elements of language (structure, productivity, displacement, and self-reflexiveness)

22. Abstraction process (way beyond the "abstraction ladder")

23. The great texting debate

24. Sapir-Whorf hypothesis: the debate over whether you can you think without language

25. Signal reactions to words

26. Taboo language

27. Dead-level abstracting

28. False dichotomies

29. Mislabeling and stigma

30. Inferential errors

31. Street harassment of women (and some men)

32. Myths about nonverbal communication

33. Body shape and cultural perceptions of beauty

34. Touch taboos

35. Gated communities and territoriality

36. Personal space and prison designs

37. Comprehending phonemes (units of sound in language) and words (hearing is not listening)

38. Benefits of forgetting

39. Conversational narcissism

40. Competitive interrupting

41. Ambushing and listening

42. Critical listening: skepticism, cynicism, true belief, and the probability model

43. Open-mindedness and critical listening

44. Burden of proof

45. Confirmation bias and rationalization of disconfirmation

46. The Law of Very Large Numbers

47. Passive aggression (six types)

48. Sexual harassment

49. Violence and aggression in relationships and prevention strategies

50. Verbal and nonverbal indicators of power

51. Power resources

52. Types of power: dominance, prevention, and empowerment

53. Triangular theory of love (seven types)

54. Stages of relationships (coming together and coming apart): communication strategies

55. Opening lines (initiating relationships) and their effectiveness

56. Recognizing flirting signals

57. Communication approaches to intensifying relationships

58. Connecting bids and relationship maintenance

59. Defensive versus supportive communication: beyond a checklist

60. Negativity bias

61. Psychological reactance

62. Cross-sex friendships

63. Social media "addiction": myth versus reality

64. Cell phone and Internet etiquette

65. Online romance and dating

66. Intercultural romances

67. Serial arguments

68. Destructive versus constructive interpersonal conflicts

69. Dialectics within intimate relationships and with outsiders

70. Honesty in relationships: Always the best policy?

71. Contempt and the corrosion of relationships

72. Forgiveness in relationships

73. Culture and conflict management

74. Anger management of self and others

75. Workplace bullying

76. Grouphate and communication competence

77. Group synergy

78. Influence of group size on communication dynamics

79. Gender and ethnicity and leadership in groups

80. Teamwork and teambuilding in groups

81. Difficult group members ("bad apples")

82. Virtual groups

83. Reframing and creative group problem solving

84. Speech anxiety causes and solutions

85. Strategies for gaining *and* maintaining attention (see especially the humor section)

86. Extensive treatment of fallacies and evaluating supporting materials

87. Cooperative argumentation

88. Toulmin structure of argument

89. Competent speaking style

90. Attitude-behavior consistency and persuasive speaking

91. Social judgment theory

92. Elaboration Likelihood Model of persuasion

93. Fear appeals and persuasive speaking

94. Anger appeals and persuasive speaking

95. Identification and persuasive speaking

96. Source credibility and persuasive speaking

97. Contrast effect (door-in-the-face) strategy and persuasive speaking

98. Two-sided persuasion

99. Cognitive dissonance and persuasive speaking

100. Extensive models of both informative and persuasive speeches with applications of text material embedded

My apology to any authors whose books include some of these topics in extensive detail. I was not able to peruse each of the dozens of human communication textbooks available, only what I thought was a representative sample. *This list is not meant to be a criticism.* In my decades of writing textbooks and reading hundreds of reviews from bright, insightful colleagues, it has become abundantly clear that there is no one, incontrovertible view of how human communication should be taught and the subjects that should be included to enhance students' learning. I offer this list of topics as a potential aid in deciding whether *In the Company of Others* appeals to you as a textbook that extensively addresses topics that stretch beyond the standard offerings. There is no expectation that every topic will resonate with you as a "must cover" option.

Readability: Beyond the Ordinary

Samuel Johnson's comment, "What is written without effort is in general read without pleasure," guided the writing of this textbook. Readability is a vital concern to me, as I know it is to students. Textbooks are not meant to read like spy thrillers, but they don't need to read like an instruction manual for installing and setting up your new flat-screen TV. Similarly, an overly dense, theoretical text written in technical language can impede clarity and understanding for students. Consequently, I searched in obvious and not-so-obvious places for the precise example, the amusing illustration, the poignant event, and the dramatic instance to engage readers, enhance enjoyment, and improve clarity. Colorful language and lively metaphors are sprinkled throughout the text. Vivid heads and subheads (see, e.g., stages of relationship development in Chapter 8) help *In the Company of Others* seem less "textbooky." Humor is plentiful (see especially the introduction and "sharing meaning" segment in Chapter 1, the "semantics" and "displacement" segments in Chapter 4, the introduction to Chapter 5, the "active listening" segment in Chapter 6, and humor as attention strategy in Chapter 13 for concentrated examples). Reviewers have been generous with their praise about the readability of *In the Company of Others*. Students have likewise offered generous praise. Readability is often singled out as a distinctive characteristic that separates this textbook from others.

Scholarship: Beyond Opinion and Anecdotes

Too often mass-market books, and some textbooks, on human communication offer chirpy homilies encouraging readers to get along with others, be cooperative, improve self-esteem, listen intently, and the like. These are agreeable and worthwhile sentiments. Nevertheless, students can be forgiven if they find themselves perplexed by how to accomplish all of these worthwhile goals and more.

My own preference, both as a teacher and as a textbook author, is to provide detailed, practical ways, *supported by abundant research*, to address the myriad communication challenges each of us face in our complex lives. I look for insights, explanations, and practical solutions revealed by voluminous research that addresses issues uppermost in students' minds. If little had changed in this regard since the fourth edition of this text was published, I would feel content to leave well enough alone. Much has changed in our increasingly technocentered world, however, and much has been learned in the interim to help us meet the new challenges. The almost 1,700 references, most of them very recent, are a testament to my commitment to provide more than personal opinion based on anecdotes and observations. Students don't always appreciate the inclusion of scholarly research in a textbook, but we as academics take pride in practicing what we teach by providing evidence for our claims and advice. (See the introduction to the "leadership" section in Chapter 10 for elaboration of this point.) Otherwise, we might as well assign comedian Steve Harvey's mundane, anecdotal, and sexist advice book (*Act Like a Lady, Think Like a Man*) as required student reading.

Communication Competence Model: A Foundation for Students

The communication competence model is one of our discipline's unique contributions to understanding and improving human behavior. A premise of this book is that communication competence, whether in the arena of interpersonal relations, small-group work, public speaking, or communication technology, is critical to student success and achievement. The five components of the model—knowledge, skill, sensitivity, commitment, and ethics—for achieving communication effectiveness and appropriateness underscore the complexity of the communication process and provide direction and guidance for students. The model is integrated throughout the text (see the *Index*), not merely discussed in the first chapter and then dropped entirely or mentioned only briefly in later chapters. Most topics and issues in the text, including perception of self and others, intercultural and gender communication, language use, nonverbal communication, listening, transacting power, managing conflict, and using communication technologies, are analyzed from the model's perspective. In addition, *Developing Communication Competence* boxes are included to help students improve their communication.

Cooperation: A Recurring Theme

Cooperation is a recurring theme of this book. One of the great potential contributions of the communication discipline is that not only can we discuss cooperation theoretically, we can also provide specific, concrete advice on how to structure human transactions so cooperation can become a reality. Many textbooks in several disciplines pay lip service to the need for human cooperation, but they are noticeably devoid of informed, research-supported suggestions regarding how to make it happen. This does little more than frustrate students who are looking for practical guidance on working collaboratively. *In the Company of Others* thoroughly addresses the issue of cooperation in a variety of communication contexts. This book is based on the assumption that cooperation should be nurtured and cultivated.

Controversy: Embracing Disagreement

Communication theory separated from the realities of a complex and not always pleasant world can seem sadly irrelevant to students faced with vexing problems. Addressing important controversies directly can provide significant opportunities for student learning. Consider the white-hot issue of gender violence in relationships. Most human communication textbooks exclude any discussion of this enormously important issue (compare the indexes). The abundant, credible evidence I present, however, shows that violence from both men and women is prevalent in intimate relationships. So why exclude this topic from honest and open treatment? Communication is at the center of this "dark side" of intimate relationships. Power sharing and ways to communicate power balancing provide students important insights on how to prevent and address intimate aggression.

The aim of *Focus on Controversy* boxes is to show students how to weigh evidence and draw conclusions supported by research on important issues that spark disagreement. Additional examples of controversies addressed and worthy of class discussion include the ethics of hypercompetitiveness, absolute honesty in relationships, excessive self-esteem, verbal obscenity, texting and its effects on language skills, and plagiarism of public speeches. Every controversy receives a balanced treatment. Conclusions are drawn, and thought-provoking questions are posed. Treatment of relevant controversies will certainly spark interesting discussion in the classroom and, more important, trigger critical thinking by students.

Culture and Gender: Connected

Gender and culture are important themes because we live in a world of increasing diversity. *In the Company of Others* treats gender and culture as integral parts of the overall discussion of communication. Gender receives special attention early in the text, and culture and gender are the main subjects of Chapter 3. This material is thoroughly integrated in subsequent chapters. Topics related to gender and culture include cultural differences in perception and nonverbal meanings, the role of gender and culture in powerful/powerless language, cross-cultural friendships and romantic relationships, gender and cultural bias in the workplace, the effects of communication technologies on cultural transactions, leadership and the glass ceiling in groups, and many others.

Social Media: A Fresh Look at Communication Technologies

No one can doubt the enormous impact that communication technologies are having on our lives. How we cope with these technologies and the huge changes they bring are vital issues. Technological changes and advances are addressed in substantial detail throughout the text, but particular emphasis is given to the influence of technologies on social relationships (see especially Chapter 8). *In the Company of Others* provides the most extensive coverage of technology and its impact on our communication of any textbook on the market (see "technology" in the *Index*). Subjects include social online networks, student-teacher electronic communication rules, cyberdating and cyberlove, electronic marriage proposals, e-dumping, text messaging and language proficiency, nonverbal cues and electronic communication, social media distractions and listening, electronic technology and information overload, the "Google effect," halfalogues and cell phone intrusion, indiscriminate self-disclosure on Twitter and Facebook, cyberaddiction, cyberconflicts, virtual groups, cell phone and online etiquette, *Wikipedia*, Internet research and misinformation, and Power-Point uses and misuses, among others.

Power: Worthy of a Chapter

Power is inherent in every human transaction. "To be human is to be immersed in power dynamics" (Keltner, 2007). "There's only one path to intimacy. It runs straight through shared power in relationships" (Marano, 2014). It is perplexing that most textbooks give so little attention to the integral role power plays in all human relationships. If mentioned at all, power is usually treated more as an aside, or relegated to only a single specific topic or two, such as power and leadership in groups. The communication discipline has many valuable insights to offer on this essential subject that requires more than perfunctory, obligatory mention. Chapter 7 gives special focus and detailed analysis to the subject of power in relationships, and later chapters include additional discussions and applications. Such topics as the effects of power imbalances in relationships, the significance of sharing power in relationships, sexual harassment in the workplace, sources of personal power, strategies for transacting power competently and cooperatively, and ways to empower ourselves and others are addressed.

Critical Thinking: Open Minds Versus Closed Minds

Asking students to think critically and to determine which ideas and conclusions make sense may strike some students as promoting closed-mindedness. "Shouldn't all ideas be given an equal hearing?" *Chapter 6 explores skepticism and the probability model like no other textbook*, discussing the issue of open- and closed-mindedness in the process. Open-mindedness is explained as following where the evidence and reasoning lead, while closed-mindedness is accepting or rejecting an idea or conclusion despite what the evidence and reasoning suggest. Chapters 12, 13, 14, and 15 offer further coverage of critical thinking, with an emphasis on using sound reasoning and concrete evidence to build both informative and persuasive speeches. The *Focus on Controversy* boxes in each chapter also provide models for using sound reasoning and evidence to bolster claims.

Speech Anxiety and Attention Strategies: Extensive Treatment

In the Company of Others provides the most extensive treatment of speech anxiety of any human communication textbook. Speech anxiety is the most important concern on most students' minds when they are told that giving speeches will be a required activity in class. Also, no hybrid textbook on communication covers attention strategies for both gaining *and* maintaining it as thoroughly as *In the Company of Others*. Let's face the facts: no one wants to listen to boring speeches, and no one wants to present a speech that puts the audience in a stupor. Attention strategies are a vital part of any effective speech.

Film School Feature: Opportunity to Apply Communication Theory

The very popular *Film School Case Studies* at the end of every chapter identifies carefully selected movies on DVD or streaming video that illustrate key concepts. Instead of doing the work for students by analyzing each film and applying it to chapter material, I ask students to do this by answering critical thinking questions. More current films have been added to most chapter lists in this edition.

Carefully Composed Model Speeches: Applications

A major concern I had with general communication textbooks before I wrote *In the Company of Others* was the discrepancy between text descriptions and actual models of informative and persuasive speeches. Often the model speech even contradicted advice provided in the main text. Model informative and persuasive speeches have been carefully composed to illustrate the advice offered in this text.

New to this Edition

The proven organization of the text remains firm, but many significant improvements have been made.

Updates Throughout

- Almost 500 new references have been added and more than 500 older references have been deleted. Dozens of new studies, surveys, and statistics on a wide variety of topics have been included throughout the text. The scholarship has been thoroughly updated in every chapter.

- More than a hundred new examples, stories, jokes, anecdotes, and pop culture references have been added so that the material is contemporary, resonates with readers, and sparks reader interest.

- Many new photos, cartoons, and graphics have been added or have replaced previous illustrations. Custom cartoons drawn by Marcy Wieland appear in the public speaking chapters.

- Model informative and persuasive speeches have been thoroughly updated with more current research and statistics included, and the entire speeches have been edited for concision.

- The *Film School Case Studies* feature has been updated with many recent films included for analysis by students.

Additional Changes for This Edition

- New chapter openings have been provided for Chapters 3, 5, 7, 9, 12, and 13.

- Thirteen of the 15 chapters have been significantly condensed, saving substantial room for additional photos and cartoons while still shortening the text by 43 aggregate pages.

- Significant sections of Chapters 1, 2, 4, 5, 10, 11, 12, and 13 have been reorganized for improved clarity and impact. Some sections have been moved to different chapters to improve the organization (see especially Chapters 10,11,12, and 13).

- New captions have been provided for cartoons and photos, many asking multiple-choice or analytical questions.

- TED Talks and YouTube links now appear at the end of all four public speaking chapters (Chapters 12 to 15). These links provide students with opportunities to view excellent as well as not-always-good speeches for analysis and entertaining video presentations on key subject matter (e.g., delivery, organization, and cognitive dissonance).

Organization of the Text

In the Company of Others is divided into four parts. First, Chapters 1 to 6, on the fundamentals of communication, lay the groundwork for the rest of the book. Subjects include the communication competence model, the role of perception in human transactions, intercultural and gender communication, the use and misuse of language, nonverbal communication, and the listening process. Each of these subjects crosses into every area of communication. Second, Chapters 7 to 9, on interpersonal communication, discuss power in communication transactions, interpersonal dialectics, strategies for making relationships work, and conflict-management techniques. Third, Chapters 10 and 11, on group communication, explain the anatomy of small groups, teambuilding, and teamwork in groups and organizations. Fourth, Chapters 12 to 15, on public speaking, address preparing a first speech, presenting a more sophisticated speech to an audience, and constructing an effective informative or persuasive speech.

Supplements

A comprehensive support package accompanies the fifth edition of *In the Company of Others*:

For Students

- The **Companion Website** (www.oup.com/us/rothwellitcoo) offers a wealth of study and review resources, including: audio tutorials, chapter outlines, chapter summaries, key term flashcards, learning objectives, *Quizzes Without Consequences*, review questions, worksheets, speech preparation checklists, and speech topic ideas.

- *Now Playing 2016* **Student Edition** illustrates how communication concepts play out in a variety of situations, using a mass medium that is interactive, familiar, and easily accessible to students. Content can also be accessed via the Companion Website (www.oup.com/us/nowplaying).

For Instructors

- **Ancillary Resource Center** (ARC) at www.oup-arc.com is a convenient, instructor-focused website that provides access to all of the up-to-date teaching resources for this text—at any time—while guaranteeing the security of grade-significant resources. In addition, it allows Oxford University Press to keep instructors informed when new content becomes available. The following items are available on the ARC:

  - An **Instructor's Manual and Test Bank** with numerous, classroom-tested activities, video links, and multiple-choice and true-false questions; asterisked activities that rate extensively tested exercises, activities, demonstrations, and illustrations.

  - Newly revised **PowerPoint-based lecture slides** highlight key concepts, terms, and examples and incorporate images from each chapter.

- *Now Playing 2016* **Instructor's Edition** includes an introduction on how to incorporate film clips in class as well as even more film and TV examples, viewing guides and assignments, sample responses to the discussion questions in the student edition, and a full list of references.

Acknowledgments

I owe a special debt to the reviewers for their very helpful critiques:

Susan Opt
James Madison University

Kimberly Batty-Hebert
South Florida State College

Richard N. Benoit
Tarleton State University

Therese McGinnis
College of DuPage

Christy Sims
James Madison University

Windolyn Yarberry
Florida State College at Jacksonville

Paul Mabrey
James Madison University

Kenia Brown
Miami Dade College

Meryl J. Irwin
James Madison University

Rachel Martin Harlow
The University of Texas of the Permian Basin

Dan Schill
James Madison University

Jeffery L. Bineham
St. Cloud State University

Steve Stogsdill
Hardin-Simmons University

Deborah D. Ford
St. Petersburg College

Jaime Bochantin
DePaul University

Delwin E. Richey
Tarleton State University

Ashley Barden Alfaro
Tarrant County College

Tim Chandler
Hardin-Simmons University

Karley Goen
Tarleton State University

Lori Leonard Britt
James Madison University

John D. Stone
James Madison University

Ronald Jeffrey Ringer
St. Cloud State University

Lawrence MacKenzie
Community College of Philadelphia

I was often impressed by your insights and the eloquence with which you expressed your wisdom.

I would like to offer sincere thanks to my Oxford editors, Mark Haynes and Toni Magyar. I offer a heartfelt thank you to production editor Micheline Frederick for her careful oversight of the editing and production process, to art director Michele Laseau for developing an outstanding design, and to editorial assistant Paul Longo for ably managing the photo selections and ancillary program for this text.

Finally, to my wife, Marcy, a special thanks is due. She was unflagging in her support of me throughout this revision. Her support, love, and understanding during the hundreds of hours I spent isolated in my home office sustained me through many moments of frustration. Her talent for cartooning is also noteworthy and much appreciated, as it was when she provided all of the cartoons for my public speaking text, *Practically Speaking*, also published by Oxford University Press.

About the Author

J. Dan Rothwell is chair of the Communication Studies Department at Cabrillo College. He has a BA in American history from the University of Portland (Oregon), an MA in rhetoric and public address, and a PhD in communication theory and social influence. His MA and PhD are both from the University of Oregon. He has authored four other books: *In Mixed Company: Communication in Small Groups and Teams; Telling It Like It Isn't: Language Misuse and Malpractice; Interpersonal Communication: Influences and Alternatives* (with James Costigan); and *Practically Speaking*, a public speaking text with Oxford University Press. During his extensive teaching career, Dr. Rothwell has received more than two dozen teaching awards, including the 2014 Western States Communication Association Master Teacher award; a 2012 official resolution by the California State Senate acknowledging Dr. Rothwell's excellence in teaching; the 2011 National Communication Association Community College Educator of the Year award; the 2010 Ernest L. Boyer International Award for Excellence in Teaching, Learning, and Technology; and the 2010 Cabrillo College Innovative Teacher of the Year award.

Professor Rothwell appreciates feedback and correspondence from both students and instructors regarding *In the Company of Others*. Anyone so inclined may email him at darothwe@cabrillo.edu. Dr. Rothwell may also be reached by phone at 1-831-479-6511.

BY THE END OF THIS CHAPTER, YOU SHOULD BE ABLE TO:

1. Debunk common myths about communication.

2. Understand the transactional nature of human communication.

3. Diagnose communication problems using the communication competence model of effective and appropriate transactions—the theme of this text.

Competent Communication

WHAT MAKES US LAUGH illustrates the richness and complexity of human communication. A study called LaughLab sought to determine the world's funniest joke (British Association for the Advancement of Science, 2002). More than 350,000 people from more than 70 countries logged on to an Internet site, contributed 40,000 jokes, and then, from a random selection, rated the jokes on a scale from 1 to 5. Here's the joke that received the highest overall rating:

> Two hunters from New Jersey are out in the woods when one of them falls to the ground. He doesn't seem to be breathing. The other whips out his mobile phone and calls the emergency services. He gasps out to the operator: "My friend is dead. What can I do?" The operator in a calm soothing voice says, "Just take it easy. First let's make sure he's dead." There is silence, then a shot is heard. The guy's voice comes back on the line. He says, "Okay, now what?"

4. Understand the five global ways to achieve communication competence.

5. Recognize and create a cooperative, not a competitive, communication climate in a variety of contexts.

Humor is a matter of subjective perception. What is thigh-slappingly funny to one person may be offensive or lame to another. The LaughLab study found that men often favor jokes that put down women, involve sexual innuendo, or are aggressive (see also Nicholson, 2010). For example:

> **Texan:** Where are you from?
>
> **Harvard Graduate:** I come from a place where we do not end our sentences with prepositions.
>
> **Texan:** Okay, where are you from, Jackass?

Women often prefer jokes that are based on word play, such as "A man walks into a bar with a piece of tarmac under his arm. He says to the bartender: 'A pint for me, and one for the road.'"

Culture also influences what is perceived to be funny. Americans preferred this joke:

> A man and a friend are playing golf one day at their local golf course. One of the guys is about to chip onto the green when he sees a long funeral procession on the road next to the course. He stops in mid-swing, takes off his golf cap, closes his eyes, and bows down in prayer. His friend says, "Wow, that is the most thoughtful and touching thing I have ever seen. You truly are a kind man." The man replies, "Yeah, well, we were married 35 years."

The joke favored most by the British participants in the LaughLab study was this one:

> A woman gets on a bus with her baby. The bus driver says, "That's the ugliest baby that I've ever seen. Ugh!" The woman goes to the rear of the bus and sits down, fuming. She says to a man next to her, "The driver just insulted me!" The man says, "You go right up there and tell him off—go ahead. I'll hold your monkey for you."

The French liked this joke: "'You're a high-priced lawyer! If I give you $500, will you answer two questions for me?' The lawyer responds, 'Absolutely! What's the second question?'"

Using humor can be tricky business (Warren & McGraw, 2013). Jokes about religion, sex, and the underprivileged can cause deep offense in some circumstances (Kuipers, 2006). Jokes that rely on ethnic stereotypes and humor that disparages others are risky and can easily backfire (Wanzer et al., 2006). Some humor, such as slapstick, crosses cultural boundaries easily, but sick jokes and dark humor do not (Lewis, 1996).

Humor is largely a social event that bonds us with others (Nicholson, 2010). Typically, we like to laugh, and we like people who make us laugh. This is one reason we might email jokes at work. Humor, however, can be a dicey proposition, especially if it contains sexual content. One person receiving an emailed joke about sex might be amused, but another might file sexual harassment charges against the sender. A salacious joke told during a speech could provoke an awkward silence or a mass exodus by the audience.

We laugh louder and longer when a joke is told to us than when we merely read it (Provine, 2000). Often we laugh at a joke that doesn't seem funny because we don't want to embarrass the joke teller or because not laughing at a joke told by a more powerful person (e.g., your boss) can place you in an uncomfortable position (Myatt, 2012). How well you tell a joke also influences the response. This mostly involves nonverbal elements of facial expressions, eye movements, tone of voice, gestures, posture, and body movements.

Humor touches on virtually every main topic explored in this text—communication climate, perception, gender, culture, verbal and nonverbal communication, listening, power, conflict, relationships, groups, public speaking, and communication technologies. Knowing how to use humor well requires communication competence—the unifying theme of this text.

The purpose of this chapter is to explain the communication competence model. It serves as a map to guide your exploration of how to communicate well with others.

Benefits of Communication Competence

Communication is mostly what we humans do, often with the grace and clarity of an inebriated celebrity at an awards ceremony. You spend most of your time in college communicating. As the National Communication Association states, "Communication is the foundation of all disciplines" (Rhodes, 2010, p. 13). You listen to and ask questions of your professors; give oral reports and speeches in classes; debate controversial issues; engage in class discussions; talk to, text, and tweet fellow classmates and roommates; and form friendships through conversation that may even blossom into true love. The entire academic enterprise is largely a communication event. Anything that occupies so much of your time is certainly worth serious attention. This section discusses two general reasons to study communication: (1) the social, personal, and workplace benefits of communicating competently, and (2) the need to improve our communication with others.

Social Connection: Communicating with Others

We humans are "the social animal" (Aronson, 2012). Our brains "are wired to be social. We are driven by deep motivations to stay connected with friends and family. We are naturally curious about what is going on in the minds of other people" (Lieberman, 2013, p. ix).

Communication is the means by which we establish social connection and build relationships. Social media have exploded in popularity, permitting unprecedented social connection. Facebook, the world's most popular social networking site, for example, had 1.4 billion monthly "active users" and almost 900 billion "daily active users" in 2015 (C. Smith, 2015). Americans between ages 18 and 24 send and receive, on average, a prodigious 3,853 text messages per month. Female college students average 105 minutes per day texting, and male college students average 84 minutes per day (Roethel, 2014). Almost half of those 18 to 34 years old view texting as "just as meaningful . . . as an actual conversation on the phone" ("18-24-Year-Old Smartphone Owners," 2013). Then there is Twitter, Snapchat, and Instagram, among others, which contribute to our being awash in social media that connect us with others.

The depth of our social connections in the digital age, however, has come into question. For example, a reporter for *The New York Times*

Electronic devices can be socially connecting or disconnecting, and either result can begin surprisingly early. Francisco Sanchez, age 2, is thoroughly engrossed watching a YouTube video alone. He and his sister, Juliana, age 5, later sit side-by-side, but these siblings seem to be alone together.

observes that Facebook can too often be "a place of indiscriminate musings and minutiae, where people report their every thought, mood, hiccup, cappuccino, increased reps at the gym or switch to a new brand of toothpaste" (Ball, 2010). One study of Twitter tweets found that 41% of the tweets were "pointless babble" of the "I am eating a sandwich now" variety (Kelly, 2009).

All conversations, however, do not have to be deep and meaningful, and most are assuredly not wellsprings of wisdom and insight, but no matter. Sometimes we may need to talk about meaningless "stuff" just to connect for many reasons. One study found that everyday talk itself, whether face-to-face or on Facebook, helps maintain friendships and closeness, and when such talk decreases, it creates uncertainty and concerns that the friendship is in jeopardy (Ledbetter & Keating, 2015). The mere act of talking to others can create social connection.

The vital importance of social connection is perhaps even more obvious when you feel the sting of social rejection. The pain we experience from social rejection can be intense, and memories of social pain can be much more intense than those of physical pain (Lieberman, 2013). The pain from a broken leg usually fades relatively quickly; the pain from a "broken heart" can linger for a lifetime.

Consider further what your life would be like if you did not interact with another human being for a week, a month, or even a year. Stories of feral or "wild" children growing up without any apparent human contact and horrific instances of children imprisoned in closets or basements demonstrate how extreme the results of social isolation can be (Newton, 2002). Despite intensive training, however, these unfortunate children do not learn to communicate normally unless their plight is discovered within the first six years of life. After age 6, learning a language, any language, is very difficult, and shortly after puberty, the capacity to master a language virtually disappears if no language at all has been acquired (Kuhl et al., 2005).

Workplace Benefits: Positions, Performance, and Promotion

Communication skills are critical to landing a job, performing effectively, and receiving promotions in the workplace. A study of more than 400 employers conducted by the National Association of Colleges and Employers ranked communication skills as the *most important qualification* a candidate for employment can possess ("Top 10 Skills," 2013). Additional research arrives at the same conclusion (Hansen & Hansen, 2015b). Moreover, once people are hired, skillful communication is the determining factor in how well they perform on the job and their likelihood of promotion (Morreale & Pearson, 2008).

Communication Improvement: All Can Benefit

All of us can benefit from improving our communication with others, but not if we're convinced that no improvement is necessary. In one large study, team members' assessments of their group leaders were a whopping *50% lower* than the team leaders' self-assessments (LaFasto & Larson, 2001). Many studies report that college students vastly overrate their oral communication skills when compared to employers' assessments of them (Jaschik, 2015; Pinola, 2012).

No one is a perfect communicator, so studying communication can benefit everyone. This is why more than a thousand faculty members surveyed from a wide variety of academic disciplines and colleges identified these *essential skills* for every college graduate: *speaking, listening, problem solving, interpersonal skills, working in groups, and leading groups* (R. Diamond, 1997). That previews the general content of this text.

Communication Myths

American humorist Will Rogers once remarked, "It isn't what we don't know that gives us trouble; it's what we know that ain't so." As used here, a **myth** is a belief that is contradicted by fact. Communication myths can disrupt your ability to improve your communication knowledge and skills. If what you know about communication "ain't so," then what chance do you have to improve your communication competence? Because common misconceptions can interfere with your understanding of what communication is, let's first discuss what communication is not.

Myth 1: Communication Is a Cure-All

Relationships can't always be fixed by better communication. Sometimes communicating clearly reveals just how far apart individuals in a relationship have grown. Skillful communication may ease the pain of breaking up, but it may not sufficiently heal the wounds of a bruising relationship. Similarly, despite its importance to your employment future, improving your interviewing skills may not be sufficient to land a job. If the most challenging aspect of any job you've held involved asking, "Would you like fries with that?" then your chances of landing a high-skills managerial or technical position are about the same as a snail's safe passage across a freeway.

Research also reveals that some problems between individuals are not solvable (Fulwiler, 2012; Gottman & Silver, 1999). Your partner may never learn to enjoy events attended by large crowds. Your coworker may never develop a sunny disposition and a less cynical view of the world. Your boss may never be more than an imperious, narcissistic, inconsiderate tyrant. Your roommate may never become a tidy person. Competent communication can help us cope with our recurring disagreements and challenges, but it may not change people.

Communication is a very important tool. When employed skillfully, communication can help solve numerous problems. Communication, however, is a means to an end, not an end in itself. It is not the basis of all human problems. Thus, not all problems can be solved, even by textbook-perfect communication.

Myth 2: Communication Is Just Common Sense

Because all of us have communicated all of our lives, it is easy to think, as you read this text, "Oh, that's just common sense." This "I-knew-that-already" tendency is called the **hindsight bias** (Roese & Vohs, 2012). For example, everybody knows that opposites attract, correct? When psychologist David Myers (2002) told this to college students, most found the observation

to be unremarkable. Yet when another group of college students was told the *opposite* ("Birds of a feather flock together"), most also found this observation to be plain common sense. Sometimes what we know isn't so.

The proof for the claim that "I knew that already," of course, is whether you can provide the accurate information *before* you are told what the research says is true. I regularly quiz my students at the beginning of each term on their general knowledge of communication (see Box 1-1). I do not ask them technical definitions of concepts or query them about remote facts. The questions are kept within the average college student's communication experience. Thus, it is by far the easiest test of the term. Consistently, however, students do very poorly; most flunk the test. Such results are not unexpected, though, and certainly not cause for ridicule. One of your primary purposes for taking a communication course should be to learn new information, to gain new insights, and to unlearn the misinformation popular culture often disseminates.

If communication consists mostly of common sense, with no requirement for studying or training, then why do so many people exhibit inadequate communication knowledge and skills? Why is the divorce rate so persistently high, and why are breakups so often nasty, uncivilized battles? Why are most teams unsuccessful in achieving their desired goals and performing well (Coutu, 2009)? Why does it seem that public speaking is almost a lost art, as far too many politicians anesthetize us with bland, ghostwritten speeches? Why do so many Twitter users seemingly share every thought that enters their head only to realize too late that they have acted foolishly? Why have blogging sites so often become forums for "Internet trolls" to share abusive, bigoted comments?

As you read this text, note that what passes in the popular media for knowledge and insight about communication, and what may seem like common sense, is often pure myth. How do we know? *Because abundant research says so!*

Myth 3: Communication Quantity Equals Quality

"One of our culture's most cherished ideas is that when it comes to communication in

BOX 1-1 DEVELOPING COMMUNICATION COMPETENCE ▶▶▶

Hindsight Bias Test

Choose either TRUE or FALSE for each statement. Each correct answer is worth 2 points.

1. Research on communication between men and women shows that differences are so vast that women seem to be from Venus and men from Mars. ⊗ TRUE ○ FALSE

2. Personal relationships have a good chance of lasting and remaining strong as long as both partners balance negative, judgmental communication (criticism, blame) with an equal amount of positive, supportive communication (praise, recognition, affection). ○ TRUE ⊗ FALSE

3. Venting your anger (expelling it, not holding it in) so that it doesn't build up steam until you explode is usually a productive and effective way to manage your anger. ○ TRUE ⊗ FALSE

4. Females, far more than males, have body image concerns. ⊘ TRUE ⊘ FALSE

5. Relationships cannot thrive if there is any deception between partners. ⊗ TRUE ○ FALSE

6. The greater the fear appeal (e.g., scaring people about the health dangers of smoking), the likelier your audience members will be persuaded by your message to change their behavior (e.g., stop smoking). ○ TRUE ⊘ FALSE

7. Whenever we travel to another culture, we should attempt to be as direct, precise, and explicit in our communication as we can be to avoid misunderstandings. ⊗ TRUE ○ FALSE

8. Women rarely use violence against their male partners. ○ TRUE ⊘ FALSE

9. Most people can usually detect lying from others; college students, because of their general intelligence and education, are actually quite good at it. ⊗ TRUE ○ FALSE

10. Compromising is the most effective strategy for managing conflicts in relationships and groups because it is based on fairness. ⊗ TRUE ○ FALSE

11. Competition motivates the vast majority of individuals to give their very best performance. ⊗ TRUE ○ FALSE

12. Some stereotypes can be accurate depictions of groups in general. ○ TRUE ⊗ FALSE

13. Self-disclosure (communicating personal information about ourselves that others would not know unless we told them) should be plentiful on a first date to help determine whether a second date is desired. ○ TRUE ⊗ FALSE

14. Conflicts should not be avoided because this will only make things worse. ⊗ TRUE ○ FALSE

15. Parents should take every opportunity possible to praise their children because an individual can never have too much self-esteem. ○ TRUE ⊗ FALSE

16. First impressions are almost always inaccurate because they are based on very limited information. ○ TRUE ⊗ FALSE

17. You cannot think without language; just try thinking without words. ○ TRUE ⊗ FALSE

(continued)

(continued)

18. You can stop sending messages of any sort to other people if you want to, even when they are observing you. ⊗ TRUE ○ FALSE

19. No one is ever completely powerless. ⊗ TRUE ○ FALSE

20. Converting a person from one strong belief to a contradictory belief is very achievable if you know how to use persuasive strategies effectively. ⊗ TRUE ○ FALSE

See answers and how to score this test at the end of the chapter. Explanations occur throughout this text. Providing explanations here is premature and lacks context for understanding.

relationships, more is better" (Swann et al., 2003, p. 1104). Is this really the case, however? Relentless criticism is more communication, but it is hardly better communication. Persistently text messaging a boyfriend or girlfriend about a nasty argument may intensify the conflict, especially if the original argument centered on "smothering" with too much attention. If you have a disagreement with your professor about a grade, repeatedly approaching your teacher in the hope that persistence, or "nagging," might produce a favorable grade change will likely fail (Dunleavy et al. 2008). It may even harden your professor's resolve to stop listening to you. According to long-term studies of couples' communication, 69% of all marital conflicts never go away, and arguments about such conflicts recur year after year (Gottman & Gottman, 2006). These are called **serial arguments.** Couples who argue sometimes keep resurrecting points of contention, and like someone picking a scab, they reopen old wounds again and again. Finally, in a survey by LexisNexis of 1,700 white-collar professionals in five countries, almost 60% revealed that being constantly accessible via cell phone, email, and by other means was distracting and a serious interference with working effectively on tasks. More than half felt "demoralized" and close to a "breaking point" from information overload that resulted from easy access (Walsh & Vivona, 2010). *More communication isn't always better communication.*

Defining Communication

The *Oxford English Dictionary* (*OED*) takes about 1,200 words to define *communication*. Communication scholars and researchers have contributed more than a hundred different definitions of their own. There is no ideal, or sacred, definition of communication. Authors, scholars, and students of human communication offer definitions suitable to their perspectives on the subject.

The definition that best fits the perspective presented in this textbook is as follows: **Communication** *is a transactional process of sharing meaning with others.* Yet this seemingly simple, 10-word definition requires explanation. Be thankful that you won't be asked to memorize or explain the *OED*'s definition.

Communication Is Transactional: The Evolving Perspective

Many communication models have been developed over the years, and each attempts to describe communication in concrete terms. In this section, three communication models are discussed in the order of their development: linear, interactive, and transactional. Each of these models provides insights that explain how the communication process works.

LINEAR MODEL:
THE STRAIGHT-ARROW VIEW

The communication process has been described as a linear, one-way phenomenon. Communication, from this perspective, involves a **sender** (initiator and encoder) who sends a **message** (stimulus that produces meaning) through a **channel** (medium through which a message travels, such as oral or written) to a **receiver** (decoder of a message) in an atmosphere of **noise** (interference with effective transmission and reception of a message) (see Figure 1-1).

When the President of the United States addresses the nation on television, all the components of the linear model are present. The president is the sender who encodes the message (puts ideas into a spoken language). The message is composed of the ideas the president wishes to express (e.g., what this country should do about terrorism). The channel is the medium of television and is oral, aural (hearing), and visual. The receivers are members of the television audience who tune in to the address and decode the message (translate the president's spoken ideas). Noise might be the static in the television transmission or family members fighting over the remote control. *The linear model provides insight regarding the communication process, especially by highlighting the concepts of channel and noise.*

Channel Changing: The Medium Can Affect the Message The choice of channel can make an enormous difference in the way a message is received. Do you ask your partner to marry you, for example, by sending a text message? By proposing at a fancy restaurant with the engagement ring in a glass of champagne? Having an airplane pull a banner across the sky? Using a Jumbotron at an athletic event? Sending a registered letter with a prenuptial agreement attached (because nothing says "I love you" like a legal document that divides property)? Orchestrating a flash mob dancing to a sappy love song?

Conversely, channel choice can deeply affect the process of dumping your date or mate. In one study, 43% of women and 27% of men said they had been dumped by text messages ("Sex in the Digital Age," 2010). Dumping someone on Facebook or Twitter has also become quite common. How would you feel if you were dumped in such public, impersonal ways?

When it is especially important to remain civil in your communication with others, switching from electronic to face-to-face communication can be a more productive channel choice. Face-to-face communication is **channel rich**; it incorporates multiple channels besides words, such as gestures, facial expressions, tone of voice, posture, and other nonverbal cues. Text-only communication is **channel lean**; it provides only a single channel devoid of the richness of nonverbal cues available for understanding messages (Surinder & Cooper, 2003). Text-only, channel-lean communication can be **disinhibiting**—less restrained and more spontaneous but also impersonal, abrupt, and often offensive (Zornoza et al., 2002). Statements you would never say to a person face-to-face can be said easily and sent impulsively in text messages because the immediate reactions and consequences are not apparent. We seem to know this even though we may not always practice what we know. Ilana Gershon (2010) found that all but 4 of the 472 respondents she

FIGURE 1-1. Linear Model of Communication.

surveyed felt breaking up face-to-face is the "ideal way to end a relationship." Choosing the wrong medium to communicate bad news "can signal to others the initiator's cowardice, lack of respect, callousness, or indifference" (p. 3).

Types of Noise: Beyond the Jackhammer The linear model is also important because it broadens the definition of noise to include interference that goes beyond mere loud or irritating sounds. **Physical noise**, or external environmental distractions, such as startling sounds, poorly heated rooms, or the unfortunate periodic reappearance of bell-bottom pants and paisley ties, all divert our attention from the message sent by a source. **Physiological noise**, or biological influences, such as sweaty palms, pounding heart, and butterflies in the stomach induced by speech anxiety, or feeling sick or exhausted at work, can produce dramatic interference on both senders and receivers of messages. **Psychological noise**, in the form of preconceptions, biases, and assumptions, also interferes with effective message transmission and reception. For example, a huge global survey of 53,000 respondents from 102 nations conducted by the Anti-Defamation League found that more than a quarter of the world's population harbors intense prejudice toward Jews (Markoe, 2014). Another study showed that prejudice toward Muslim and Middle Eastern Americans has grown enormously in the United States since the 9/11 terrorist attacks on the Twin Towers and the Pentagon (Obeidallah, 2014). Such preconceived, dangerous biases make effective transmission and reception of messages between different ethnic and religious groups extremely difficult.

Semantic noise as reflected in word choice that is confusing, incomprehensible, or distracting also creates interference. Text messaging acronyms—for example, WTMI ("Way too much information") or YOYO ("You're on your own")—are noise if you can't translate the text lingo. Is the preferred term *African American* or *black* when referring to the relevant ethnic group? Should you use Native American or Indian? Hispanic or Latino? Different groups, even individuals within a group, prefer different terms. Choosing the "wrong" term can derail your message by drawing attention to

terminology disputes while submerging the content of your intended message.

Consider, for example, the kerfuffle ignited in January 2015 when British actor Benedict Cumberbatch commented on the complete absence of minority actors among that year's 20 Oscar nominees: "I think as far as colored actors go . . . that's something that needs to change" (quoted in Hicks, 2015). His reference to "colored" and his subsequent apology for using the term were headlined in the *San Jose Mercury News*: "Benedict Cumberbatch Sorry for Racist Remark." Cumberbatch apologized for "being an idiot" for causing "offense by using this outmoded terminology." Notice that Cumberbatch's original message was mostly lost when the focus in the media became his use of the term itself. Asserting that Cumberbatch's use of "colored" was racist seems misapplied, especially since the advocacy group the NAACP stands for the National Association for the Advancement of *Colored* People. Regardless, the choice of words can produce semantic noise, a distraction from the intended message.

Despite its insights, application of the linear model is quite limited. Its most glaring weakness is the absence of **feedback**—the receiver's verbal and nonverbal responses to a message.

INTERACTIVE MODEL: THE PING-PONG VIEW

The interactive model of communication includes feedback (see Figure 1-2). The addition of feedback clearly indicates that communication is not a one-way but a two-way process. Participants act as both senders and receivers of messages. The importance of feedback to the communication process cannot be overestimated. All of us constantly adjust our communication with others based on the feedback we receive. The inability to read feedback accurately and to make appropriate adjustments is a serious communication competence issue.

A second component of the interactive model missing from the linear version is **fields of experience**, which include our cultural background, ethnicity, geographic location, extent of travel, and general personal experiences accumulated over the course of a lifetime. You carry these fields of experience with

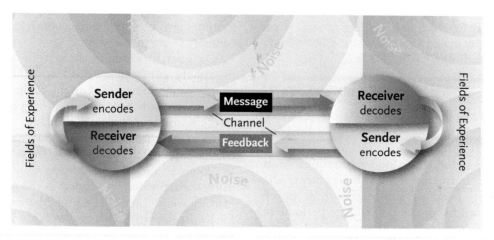

FIGURE 1-2. Interactive Model of Communication.

you to every communication event. Fields of experience between individuals may be poorly matched and consequently produce misunderstanding. Parents, who know from their own experience how important education was to their attainment of important goals, want the same for their children. Their kids, however, don't have equivalent experience that might give them the same perspective. Languishing in a math or chemistry class may seem to teenagers more like torment than a pursuit of life goals. The more experiences we have in common, the more likely it is that misunderstandings can be avoided.

Despite these improvements offered by the interactive model, some complexities of human communication are still not adequately depicted. Consequently, the transactional model was developed.

TRANSACTIONAL MODEL: THE SENDER-RECEIVER IMPACT VIEW

The transactional model, by definition, assumes that people are connected through communication; they engage in a transaction (see Figure 1-3). The transactional perspective recognizes that *communication influences all parties involved*. We are defined in relation to each other as we both send and receive messages, often simultaneously (sender-receivers), not as individuals separate from others. A teacher requires students. Parents require children. An interviewer must have an interviewee. A leader

must have followers. The roles we play in life result from how we are defined in relation to others. Thus, transactional communication is not merely two-way interaction. Something more than a mere exchange of information back and forth occurs when humans communicate. We continuously influence each other and develop a relationship one to the other as we communicate. We become interconnected.

We can see the influence we have on each other during communication more clearly by examining the two dimensions of every message: content and relationship (Watzlawick et al., 1967). The **content dimension** refers to what is actually said and done. The **relationship dimension** refers to how that message defines or redefines the association between individuals.

A college student might say, "Professor Tillson, I didn't like your test" or "Hey, Tillson, your test sucks." Both messages have the same essential content (unhappiness with the test), but the relationship dimension is different. The first statement exhibits respect. The second statement, by contrast, is disrespectful, even abrasive. Message content can also differ while the relationship dimension stays the same. "Will you please lend me 50 bucks?" and "Would you please help me study for my math final?" are messages that display different content but essentially the same relationship. Although the specific requests differ, respect is shown to the person receiving the request in both instances.

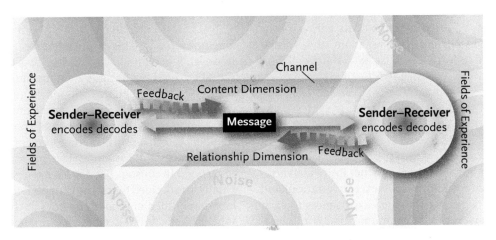

FIGURE 1-3. Transactional Model of Communication.

These illustrations show the content and relationship dimensions of messages, but they are not transactional. You don't see the reaction to the message and the impact it has on each party. Here is an example that shows transactional communication:

Student: Hey, Tillson, your test sucks.

Professor Tillson: Did you actually study for the exam?

Student: No. I figured you'd give an easy test, so I didn't need to study.

Professor Tillson: Perhaps you should take this class *more* seriously?

Student: Perhaps you should take me *less* seriously. I'M KIDDING. I studied hard for your test, but I was confused on several questions. I want to go over the exam with you.

Professor Tillson: Fine, but that'll cost you a five-point deduction on your exam score.

Student: WHAT?

Professor Tillson: JUST KIDDING!

Here the professor and the student are sparring with each other, defining their relationship as they converse. Will this be a formal relationship between teacher and student, or will this be an informal relationship between relative equals? The nature of the conversation and their relationship shifts once the professor realizes that the student is being glib but has a serious concern. The professor then makes an attempt at the end to match the informality of the student but also to reassert status.

This conversation, of course, could have progressed in many different ways. The professor could have chastised the student for the "test sucks" remark. This would have defined their relationship as a formal one of unequal power. The professor also could have chosen to end the conversation with an abrupt "Try studying next time" retort while walking away. This would likely produce an unfriendly, distant relationship between teacher and student. In each case, both parties are affected, not only by what is said (content) but also by how it is presented and its effect on the parties involved (relationship).

Communication Is a Process: The Continuous Flow

Communicating is a process of adapting to the inevitable changes that affect any relationship. The process view of communication recognizes "events and relationships as dynamic, ongoing, ever-changing, continuous" (Berlo, 1960, p. 24). In a relationship, "nothing never happens" (Johnson et al., 1974), or as the bumper sticker says, "Change is inevitable, except from a vending machine."

If you wanted to understand the ocean, you wouldn't just take a picture of a single wave or scoop up a cupful of water. The ocean can be understood only in terms of its entirety—the tides and currents, waves, plant and animal life, and so forth. Likewise, to understand communication, you need to focus not on single words, sentences, or gestures but on how currents of thoughts and feelings are expressed by both verbal and nonverbal means in the context of change.

Relationships can't be frozen in time, though our memories may be. Every conversation is a foothold on our next conversation, and we bring our accumulated experiences to each new conversation. Communication is an ongoing process, and each new experience influences future transactions.

Communication Is Sharing Meaning: Making Sense

The term *communication* is derived from the Latin word *communicare*, which denotes "to share." Sharing from this perspective does not mean merely exchanging information like one would exchange gifts. Communication is not just transferring "stuff" in our heads from one person to another, back and forth. We attempt, and often achieve, something deeper when we communicate with other humans. We attempt to share **meaning**, which is "the conscious pattern humans create out of their interpretation of experience" (Anderson & Ross, 1994, p. 73). You construct meaning by making connections and patterns in your mind that "make sense" of your world. You then attempt to share this constructed meaning with others, who in turn reconstruct your message to try to understand your meaning as you have constructed it in your mind.

There is never a perfect "meeting of the minds" regarding meaning. The meaning another person has for an experience, idea, relationship, concept, or symbol is an *approximation* of the meaning you have for the same thing. The closest we come to shared meaning *is when there are overlapping interpretations between individuals.* For example, when you view a relationship as a friendship and the other person sees it likewise, there is an overlap, and meaning is shared, approximately. The depth of that friendship, or even what constitutes friendship, however, is not identical between two people. There are always subtle differences.

We all attempt to share meaning both verbally and nonverbally. This is an imperfect process, however. Sometimes meaning doesn't get shared verbally even though words are transmitted from one person to another in a common language. For example, there is a story of a Catholic nun teaching religion to her third-graders and conducting standard catechism drills. She repeatedly asked her students, "Who is God?" Her students were to respond in unison, "God is a supreme being." Finally, she decided to test the fruits of her patient labor and called on one of the boys in the class. When asked "Who is God?" he promptly and proudly replied, "God is a string bean." Words were transmitted, but meaning was not shared. *Supreme being* was meaningless to the third-grader. *String bean* at least could be grasped, even if applying it to the divinity was a tad mysterious.

Sharing meaning between cultures poses its own unique problems. Electrolux, a Scandinavian manufacturer, discovered this when trying to sell its vacuum cleaners in the United States with the slogan "Nothing sucks like an Electrolux." In preparation for the 2008 Beijing Olympic Games, David Tool, a retired army colonel living in the Chinese capital, was hired to correct notoriously poor English on signs throughout the city. "Deformed Man Toilet" was thankfully replaced with "Disabled Person Toilet," and "Beijing Anus Hospital" was replaced with "Beijing Proctology Hospital" (Boudreau, 2007). Yet even when two people share the same language, but not the same culture, problems can emerge. For example, "The lorry driver taking kit to the football pitch was so knackered he pulled into the lay-by near the petrol station for a quick kip." Did you understand this message that includes abundant British figures of speech? The translation is "The truck driver delivering uniforms to the soccer field was so tired he pulled into the rest area near the gas station for a nap" (Wilson, 2012). George Bernard Shaw once remarked that England and America are two countries separated by the same language.

Sharing meaning nonverbally between cultures can be equally problematic (Cotton, 2013; Mancini, 2003). The "A-OK" gesture in the United States that forms a circle with the index finger and the thumb is obscene in Brazil, and it means "worthless" in France and "money" in Japan. Raising the index finger to signify "one" means

Common hand gestures can be offensive in many cultures. The "hook-em horns" gesture, a reference to the University of Texas Longhorns, displayed by George W. Bush when he was president is a salute to Satan in Norway. In Italy, it is an accusation of spousal infidelity.

"two" in Italy; the thumb is one. In Japan, however, the upright thumb means "five" (counting begins with the index finger, and the thumb is the last digit). Nodding the head up and down means "yes" in the United States, and shaking it side to side means "no." In Bulgaria, Turkey, Iran, and Bengal, however, it is the reverse. In Greece, tipping the head back abruptly means "no," but the same gesture in India means "yes." (Nod your head if you understand all of this.)

Communication is a transactional process of sharing meaning with others. We are senders and receivers trying to make sense of our dynamic, ever-changing relationships with others. These relationships define who we are and what roles we play in life.

Defining Communication Competence

Defining communication does not tell you how to communicate in a competent manner. So what does it mean to be a competent communicator? **Communication competence** *is engaging in communication with others that is perceived to be both effective and appropriate in a given context* (Spitzberg, 2000). This section explains this definition and its significant implications.

Effectiveness: Achieving Goals

Effectiveness is the degree to which you have progressed toward the achievement of your goals. It is a litmus test of communication competence. If your cynical humor provokes hostility from your roommate, for example, you may need to modify your humor.

DEGREES OF EFFECTIVENESS: FROM DEFICIENCY TO PROFICIENCY

You may be proficient at establishing intimate relationships with a few individuals, but you may feel awkward and ill at ease in large gatherings of strangers. You may relish the challenge of delivering a speech to a large audience, while others would rather bite off the head of a rattlesnake than give a public speech. Communication competence can vary by degrees from highly proficient to severely deficient depending on the circumstances. A person is more to less competent, not either competent or incompetent. Labeling someone a "competent communicator" makes a judgment of that individual's degree of proficiency *in a particular context,* but it does not identify an immutable characteristic of that person. Being a competent communicator is also not an idyllic state of perfection. Even the best communicators occasionally err.

WE-ORIENTATION: WE-FIRST, NOT ME-FIRST

Because communication is transactional, competence comes from focusing on "We" (what makes the *relationship* successful), not "Me" (what makes *me* successful). When you enter into an intimate relationship, for example, interdependence (a We-orientation) is primary, and independence (a Me-orientation) is secondary. A 20-year study of why marriages succeed and fail found that the more marriage partners, especially husbands, viewed their marriage as a joint undertaking, the more likely the marriage would succeed (Gottman & Silver, 1994). Problems for either partner were viewed as difficulties that affected both individuals together.

The "me-first" attitude also destroys teamwork in groups (Van Mierlo & Kleingeld, 2010). In fact, a collection of individuals doesn't function as a group at all if the members are more interested in individual accomplishment than in group achievement. Within organizations, the Me-orientation "must be avoided at all costs. It [creates] winners and losers. When that happens, the organization is always shortchanged" (LaFasto & Larson, 2001, p. 172).

Not all individual goals clash with relationship or group goals, and some individual goals, such as intimacy, can be accomplished only in a context of interdependence. Nevertheless, trying to achieve individual goals at the expense of relationship, group, or organizational goals usually produces unsatisfactory outcomes for both you and others.

Effectiveness is not the sole determinant of communication competence, however, because goals are not always achievable. Your lack of effectiveness may be due to forces beyond your control. A person can exhibit exemplary communication and still have relationships with family, friends, spouses, and coworkers fail (personality clashes perhaps). A public speech can be beautifully constructed and delivered, but listeners may still be unmoved because values and beliefs are not shared. Nevertheless, communication that often fails to achieve goals is probably deficient in some way.

Appropriateness: Communicating by the Rules

Appropriateness is behavior that "is viewed as legitimate for, or fitting to, the context" (Spitzberg, 2000, p. 375). Appropriateness can be determined only within a specific context. **Context** is the environment in which communication occurs: *who* (sender-receiver) communicates *what* (message) to *whom* (receiver-sender), *why* a message is sent (purpose), *where* (setting) it is sent, and *when* (timing) and *how* (channel) it is transmitted. We determine the appropriateness of our communication by analyzing all of these elements.

RULES: EXPLICIT AND IMPLICIT

Every communication context is guided by rules. A **rule** "is a prescription that indicates what behavior is obligated, prohibited, or preferred in a given context" (Shimanoff, 2009, p. 861). A family, for example, has many rules, such as who takes out the trash, who cooks the meals, who pays the bills, and so forth. There are also rules constraining and structuring communication transactions within the family unit, such as "We never go to bed angry," "Children will address a parent or stepparent in a respectful way at all times," and "Don't interrupt someone during dinner conversation."

Rules create expectations regarding appropriate behavior. Some rules are *explicitly* stated (directly expressed), such as "No shoes, no

This cartoon illustrates an:

○ **1.** Implicit rule of communication

○ **2.** Explicit rule of communication

Answers at end of chapter.

○ **3.** Linear model of communication

○ **4.** All of the above.

shirt, no service" and "No smoking." Social networking sites have explicit rules concerning text content and photos, and sometimes even the number of characters allowed. Most rules, however, are merely *implied* (indirectly indicated) by patterns of behavior. You don't have to be told directly what to do or not do. For example, it is unlikely that you will find signs in a grocery store that read "Don't eat cookies and put the half-empty bag back on the shelf," "Don't crash into other customers with your cart," and "Don't steal food from another person's cart." When you encounter a coworker or stranger who asks, "How ya doing?" you know better than to respond with a long-winded appraisal of your current state of affairs. Normally, you just say, "I'm fine, how are you?" Cultural greeting rules dictate that the question not be interpreted literally. Consequently, the greeting becomes ritualistic, even mindless, which is why I've caught myself on more than

one occasion asking, "How are you?" and receiving the response from the other person, "I'm fine, how are you?" whereupon I give the slightly embarrassing response, "I'm fine, how are you?" (Oops, already asked that—trapped in a feedback loop.)

A violation of an implicit rule often leads to an explicit statement of the rule. College instructors take for granted that students won't interrupt the flow of a lecture or discussion by talking inappropriately with fellow students or texting during class. On occasion, however, this implicit rule must be made explicit to students whose enthusiasm for casual conversation outweighs their ardor for the classroom task.

RULE VIOLATIONS: CONSEQUENTIAL EFFECTS

Communication becomes inappropriate if it violates rules when such violations could be averted without sacrificing a goal by choosing alternative

In a stunningly inappropriate act at the 2009 MTV Video Music Awards, Kanye West seized the microphone from Taylor Swift as she was about to give her acceptance speech after winning Best Female Video and touted a video by Beyoncé. The reaction to West's moment of hubris was swift (no pun intended) and vociferously negative from almost every circle. West repeated the inappropriate "Oh, look at me" stunt at the 2015 Grammy Awards, upstaging Beck, who beat Beyoncé for Album of the Year.

communication behaviors (Getter & Nowinski, 1981). Consider professor-student communication. One study found that college faculty are concerned about students communicating with them in too casual, careless, or cocky a manner (Duran et al., 2005). Another study asked college professors to assess an email message from a student that read "R U Able to Meat Me?" Professors especially disliked the casual "R U" acronym for "are you" and expressed strong dislike for using "meat" for "meet." There are implied rules about message formality, grammar, and spelling in student-teacher communication that, if violated, can produce very negative reactions. Messages such as the above made professors "like the student less, view them as less credible, have a lesser opinion of the message quality, and made them less willing to comply with students' simple email requests" (Stephens et al., 2009, p. 318). A professor, of course, can signal to a student in an email that common rules of formality may be loosened somewhat by constructing a message with texting acronyms and occasional slang (e.g., "ain't"). The higher status person, however, has the greater flexibility to loosen the rules.

Although rules for appropriate communication are determined by context, rules are not sacred. Some rules may need to be modified. When students share a dorm room or an apartment, rule modification is almost inevitable if communication is to remain competent. Difficulties living together will occur if one person expects a spotlessly clean, orderly environment and the other person is content with more casual surroundings. When rules clash, a modification of the rules will have to be negotiated unless one person is willing to accept the other's rules completely.

Achieving Communication Competence

Defining communication competence tells us what it is but not how to achieve it. There are five general ways the appropriateness and effectiveness of our communication can be improved. We can build *knowledge*, develop our communication *skills*, increase our *sensitivity*, enhance our *commitment*, and apply *ethics* to our communication choices (see Figure 1-4). Let's look at each of these in more detail.

Knowledge: Learning the Rules

Achieving communication competence begins with knowledge of the rules that create behavioral expectations and knowing what is likely

FIGURE 1-4. Communication Competence Model.

to work effectively given the rules of the situation. Communication can be inappropriate and ineffective (deficient in every respect), appropriate but ineffective (a desire to please others at your own expense or uncontrollable circumstances preventing achievement), inappropriate but effective (lying, cheating, intimidating, or coercing others to achieve goals), or appropriate and effective (goal achievement while following the rules relevant to a context). Which of these four possibilities is most likely largely depends on your knowledge of the rules and the communication strategies that work in particular communication situations.

Failure to know basic rules common in different cultures can produce embarrassment or even unpleasant international incidents. In South Korea, for example, men enter and exit through doors *before* women, and women assist men with their coats. In Zambia, you may go hungry at a dinner gathering unless you specifically ask for food. (It is deemed impolite for the dinner host to offer food before it is requested.) When American dignitaries and businesspeople travel to Japan, one source of awkward social interaction is the bowing ritual used as a social greeting. Roger Axtell (1998) briefly describes the Japanese bowing ritual with its list of rules. When bowing to "business inferiors," always permit them to bow lower and longer. When bowing to those of equal status, match bows. When bowing to "the top man" (and in Japan, it still usually is a man), "if he clearly outranks you, make sure you out bow him even if it takes your knuckles all the way to the floor. Also remember to keep your eyes respectfully lowered" (p. 44). Learning cultural rules helps you avoid serious misunderstandings and miscommunication.

Skills: Showing, Not Just Knowing

A **communication skill** is the ability to perform a communication behavior effectively and repeatedly. Clearly, fluently, concisely, eloquently, and confidently communicating messages are examples of skills. Knowledge about communication without communication skill will not produce competence. You can read stacks of

books about public speaking, but there is no substitute for skill gained by practice and experience speaking in front of an audience. The ability to communicate a message concisely and precisely is an important skill. Speaking with long pauses and vocal fillers (ums and ahs), however, can nullify your effectiveness despite an otherwise concise and precise message.

Conversely, *skill without knowledge is equally unproductive*. Learning to "express your feelings honestly" can be an important communication skill in many situations. Expressing your honest feelings indiscriminately, however, no matter what the likely consequences, mimics the act of an innocent child, not a mature adult. Confrontation—directly addressing a conflict with others—may be an appropriate and effective strategy for dealing with interpersonal conflict generally (see Chapter 9), but it is the worst strategy a stalking victim could choose because it feeds a stalker's desire for contact, any contact, with the victim (Wondrak & Hoffman, 2007). A one-size-fits-all skills package doesn't produce competent communication. *Being flexible and adaptive is essential to effective and appropriate (competent) communication.*

Sensitivity: Developing Receptive Accuracy

Can you accurately perceive the difference between a look of disgust, anger, playfulness, frustration, or contempt from a friend, stranger, or relative? Can you determine when a power struggle occurs by listening to a conversation? Can you detect flirtation? Deceit? Confusion? Discomfort? Can you sense when your audience doesn't like or is hostile to something you've said during a speech? Knowing what constitutes appropriate communication in a specific context and having the skill to communicate appropriately are great, but what if you don't have your antenna extended to pick up signals coming from others? How will you know which rules apply and how you should communicate?

Sensitivity is *receptive accuracy* whereby we can detect, decode, and comprehend signals in our social environment (Bernieri, 2001). Sensitivity can help us adapt our messages to a particular context in an appropriate and effective manner. Failure to recognize and to comprehend signals can severely limit our social effectiveness (Seubert & Regenbogen, 2012). If you are obviously angry but your partner doesn't have a clue that this is how you feel, you will easily perceive this cluelessness as insensitivity to your needs, and an argument will likely ensue. Competent communicators develop sensitivity to nuances and subtleties of communication transactions, and they respond to them. Those whose sensitivity receptors are inactive or malfunctioning act ineptly in social situations. These are the folks who might pull out their smartphones to check text messages during a moment of silence at a funeral service.

Sensitivity can be learned (Hall & Bernieri, 2001). One of the functions of this textbook is to help you become more sensitive to your social environment by identifying patterns of communication that cause problems in relationships and by learning how to analyze an audience before giving a speech.

A major aspect of sensitivity is being mindful, not mindless, about your communication and that of others. We exhibit **mindfulness** when "we think about our communication and continually work at changing what we do in order to become more effective" (Griffin, 2006, p. 432). For instance, we notice when friends or loved ones reach out to us for support and affection, and we respond in appropriate ways. We exhibit **mindlessness** when we're not cognizant of our communication with others and we put little or no effort into improving it.

John Gottman tells a story of a neurosurgeon he had as a client who exhibited mindlessness, not from any desire to be mean but from an emotional distance that served him well in his profession (Gottman & DeClaire, 2001). As a successful neurosurgeon, he practiced giving objective, clinical analyses of patients' afflictions. When he came home, he communicated with his wife in the same manner. His wife once asked him, "How do you think we're doing—as a couple?" He provided a long-winded, accurate analysis. His wife then burst into tears and ran from the room, leaving him flummoxed. He hadn't been mindful of what her question was actually seeking from him. She desired reassurance, support, and affection. Had he thought about why his wife would ask in a serious manner about the state of their relationship, surely he would have realized that she was not seeking an emotionally detached analysis. If you don't attend to the signals that indicate other people's emotional needs because you aren't looking, then you can't connect with those who can make life a joyful experience. This doesn't mean that you are obliged to connect with everyone you encounter daily, but you surely must connect with those individuals who are important influences on your life.

As email, text messaging, tweeting, and blogging are increasingly used to communicate with others, the channel-rich, nonverbal cues that you use to detect signals in your social environment are minimized. Consequently, your sensitivity is constrained. Think of the number of times that you've read an email or text message and mistaken the tone for irritation or hostility when the sender intended to communicate no such feeling. In one study of **virtual groups**, whose members communicate electronically and rarely, if ever, meet face-to-face, 94% of respondents found the "inability to read nonverbal cues" to be a significant problem (Solomon, 2010). Technological advances in communication pose new challenges to our sensitivity.

Commitment: Acquiring a Passion for Excellence

Knowledge, skills, and sensitivity are important ways to improve your communication competence. Communication effectiveness, however, also requires **commitment**—a passion for excellence: accepting nothing less than the best that you can be and dedicating yourself to achieving that excellence. You strive for excellence by identifying your communication weaknesses, learning constructive communication patterns, dedicating considerable effort toward changing bad communication habits to good patterns, and practicing your communication skills diligently.

To exhibit commitment, *attitude is as important as aptitude*. No one can force you to be a proficient communicator. You have to want to be proficient. In sports, athletes develop a high level of skills when they commit themselves to hard work, study, and practice. Academic success also does not come from lackluster effort. You must want to do well and be dedicated to making it happen. You make it a priority in your life. Sustaining love in an intimate relationship also requires commitment (Epstein, 2010). You have to want the relationship to remain successful, and you need to work hard to sustain that success. The same holds true for communication competence. You must want to improve, to change, and to grow more proficient in your communication with others.

Ethics: Determining the Right and Wrong of Communication

Competent communicators are concerned with more than just what works. As humans, we care about right and wrong behavior. Such concerns make us just a bit more interesting than your garden-variety slug. Lying, cheating, and backstabbing others to achieve personal goals violate ethical norms.

Ethics is a system for judging moral correctness by using an agreed-upon set of standards to determine what constitutes right and wrong behavior. The Credo of the National Communication Association identifies five ethical standards to guide our communication with others. These standards are:

1. *Respect.* "Some form of the Golden Rule is embraced by virtually all of the major religious and moral systems" (Jaksa & Pritchard, 1994, p. 101). A survey by the Josephson Institute of Ethics reported that 99% of respondents rated being shown respect by others as "very important" or "essential" to them, and treating others with respect received a similar response (Jarc, 2012).

2. *Honesty.* "There is no more fundamental ethical value than honesty" (Josephson, 2002). Honesty is a cultural expectation. All ethical systems condemn lying ("Lying Is Part," 1996).

3. *Fairness.* Prejudice has no place in the communication arena. Racism, sexism, homophobia, ageism, and all the other "isms" that plague the human spirit and divide

nations and peoples would diminish if we applied the standard of fairness in our communication with diverse groups. Fairness requires equal treatment. One study of community college students reported that fairness was perceived to be "very important" or "extremely important" by most respondents (Kidder et al., 2002)

4. *Choice.* Our communication should strive to allow people to make their own choices free of coercion (Jaksa & Pritchard, 1994). Persuasion allows free choice among available options. Coercion forces choice without permitting individuals to think or act for themselves.

5. *Responsibility.* We have a responsibility to consider the consequences of our communication on others. Responsibility means that ethical communication requires a We-orientation. Competent communicators must concern themselves with more than merely what works to achieve personal or group goals. A person may be quite effective at accomplishing individual goals (Me-orientation), but if these goals produce bad outcomes for others, their appropriateness must be questioned.

In the abstract, these standards may seem straightforward and uncontroversial, but almost nothing in human communication is absolute and clear-cut. Human communication behavior is so complex that any list of standards for judging the ethics of communication, applied without exceptions, is bound to run into difficulty. In some cases, two or more ethical standards may collide. Heckling a speaker, for example, is disrespectful, but is there never an instance in which heckling is the only available means of communicating dissension when the wealthy and powerful deny choice by controlling access to media and forums for debate? Conversely, when hecklers shut down a speaker's right to address an audience, they exhibit irresponsible behavior and may be removed coercively (security throws them out forcibly). Also, what if honesty shows disrespect and a lack of concern for another person's feelings ("Yes, you are fat and unattractive")? Despite such difficulties, however, all five of these ethical standards are strong values in our culture, and they serve as important guidelines for our communication behavior.

In summary, you can achieve communication competence in five general ways: building your knowledge, developing your skills, increasing your sensitivity to verbal and nonverbal cues, enhancing your commitment to achieving communication excellence, and applying ethics to your communication choices. These global ways of achieving communication competence are explained in far greater detail and complexity throughout this text. Achieving communication competence, however, occurs within the context of a communication climate that either encourages or discourages communication proficiency.

Creating a Communication Climate

A **communication climate** is the emotional atmosphere, the pervading or enveloping tone that we create by the way we communicate with others. Communication climate is integrally linked to communication competence. Some communication climates promote proficiency, and others promote deficiency, in goal attainment. The communication climate is critical to relationship effectiveness, team achievement, and organizational success (Ackerman et al., 2013). Even in the public speaking arena, the effectiveness of a speech is largely dependent on the communication climate that exists between speaker and listeners. Repeatedly attacking your audience's beliefs or values, for example, will likely provoke a counterattack in the form of heckling or audience members leaving the speech in disgust.

Types of Climates: Constructive and Destructive

A **constructive communication climate** is composed of two general elements: a pattern of **openness**, or a willingness to communicate, and a pattern of **supportiveness**, or a confirmation of the worth and value of others and a

willingness to help others succeed (LaFasto & Larson, 2001). At their core, openness and supportiveness are We-oriented, whereby our individual agendas are secondary to the relationship, group, or organizational agenda.

A **destructive communication climate** is composed of two general elements: a pattern of **closedness**, or an unwillingness to communicate with others, and a pattern of **defensiveness**, or a protective reaction to a perceived attack on our self-esteem and self-concept. The protective reaction usually takes three forms (Ellison, 2009):

1. You *deny* the validity or accuracy of the perceived attack. "I did *not* study halfheartedly for the exam; I studied hard" is an example of denial.

2. You *counterattack* the person whose communication diminishes your self-perception. "I did a whole lot better than you did" is one example.

3. You *withdraw.* This occurs when you psychologically and/or physically remove yourself from a threatening arena so that no further attacks can be launched against you. Hypercritical parents may not see you at holiday occasions, for example, because you wish to avoid their unsolicited abundance of evaluative remarks.

Individual instances of openness and supportiveness or of closedness and defensiveness do not typically constitute constructive or destructive communication climates. This is analogous to weather climates. When we say that a part of the country has a "temperate climate," we don't base this on a single 70-degree, sunny day. One critical comment, for example, is an *episode* that might provoke an immediate defensive response, but it doesn't create a destructive climate unless the episode is especially egregious. A *pattern* of criticism (several episodes) can create a destructive climate. Although examples offered in this and later chapters (see especially Chapter 8) to illustrate communication climates are by necessity just episodes, keep in mind that repetitive episodes of the same kind of communication create climates.

Communication Patterns and Climates: Competition and Cooperation

Competitive and cooperative communication patterns play a significant role in the creation of communication climates. These patterns permeate our daily communication with others. Before discussing the respective consequences to human relationships of these patterns, however, some seemingly straightforward terms need to be defined for conceptual clarity.

DRAWING CLEAR DISTINCTIONS: CONCEPTUAL CLARITY

Competition is a process of mutually *exclusive* goal attainment (MEGA); for you to win, others must lose (Kohn, 1992). The single inescapable fact that defines competition is that the system of rewards inherently benefits the victorious. Thus, examples of competitive communication include engaging in public debates; waging battles to win arguments with friends, spouses, or partners; arguing over material possessions and child custody during a divorce; and criticizing and diminishing others to look superior to rivals at work. In all of these acts, communication is a *winner-take-all* vehicle to defeat others and to establish oneself as best at others' expense.

Cooperation is a process of mutually *inclusive* goal attainment (MIGA); for me to achieve my goal, you must also achieve your goal. We sink or swim together. Examples of cooperative communication include negotiating problems to the mutual satisfaction of all parties in a conflict; engaging in teamwork to solve problems and make decisions; teaching those with inadequate skills to improve and become more capable; and expressing support to those who are discouraged. The essence of cooperation is a *winners-all* effort to raise everyone to a high standard, not drag anyone down to defeat for the sake of individual glory.

Competitive communication can be tumultuous, but cooperative communication also can be difficult, at times contentious, and even frustrating. *Cooperative communication is a process, not an outcome* (King et al., 2009). Parties in a conflict, for example, may communicate cooperatively yet still not reach an agreement because they seek very different outcomes. *The cooperative communication process also doesn't mean yielding to others.* Some may thank you for "being cooperative" when you capitulate to their demands, but that is not cooperation. That's surrender.

Individual achievement is the realization of personal goals without having to defeat an opponent. Giving a speech better the second time you perform it is an individual achievement. It becomes competitive when you try to outperform someone else, as in a speech contest or debate tournament. Saying that you "compete with yourself," as is so often heard, makes little conceptual sense. What would you deduce from someone saying, "I ran faster than myself"? *Competition is not a solitary undertaking; it is interactive* (Kohn, 1992). You can't be both the victor and the vanquished simultaneously. What we often call competing with ourselves is really striving for individual achievement.

HYPERCOMPETITIVENESS: ITS CONSEQUENCES

Competition itself is not inherently a problem for relationships. Verbal jousting with your intimate partner can be enjoyable and a cause for laughter. In some circumstances, a cooperative option may not exist. Interviewing for a job, for example, is unavoidably competitive whenever more than one applicant is vying for a single position. Encouraging individuals to hone their oral communication skills so that they might compete more effectively in such situations should be applauded.

It is the degree of competitiveness that can produce positive or negative consequences. **Constructive competition** occurs when competing against others produces a positive, enjoyable experience and promotes efforts to achieve victory without jeopardizing interpersonal relationships and personal well-being (Tjosvold et al., 2003, 2006). Friendly family rivalries, for example, can be a source of bonding. Some individuals, usually those who have the skills to win, thrive in competitive environments.

Research supports three conditions for constructive competition to occur (D. W. Johnson, 2003; Tjosvold et al., 2006). They are:

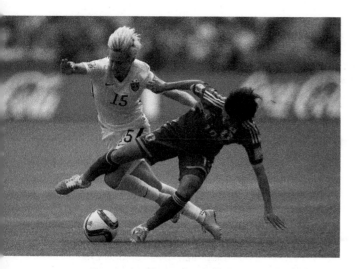

Competition can be constructive and enjoyable, unless hypercompetitiveness develops.

1. De-emphasis on winning
2. Competing against relative equals
3. Competing fairly

When these three conditions are violated by hypercompetitive communication, a destructive communication climate results.

Hypercompetitiveness is the excessive emphasis on beating others to achieve one's goals. One study of 198 elite athletes revealed that more than half would take a performance-enhancing drug if it would increase their chances of winning every competition for a five-year period. That probably doesn't surprise you, but here is the real stunner: these same elite athletes would take this drug even if they realized it would *kill them* at the end of the five years ("Superhuman Heroes," 1998). That's hypercompetitiveness.

The *winning-is-everything* attitude is widespread in American culture. Americans "manifest a staggering cultural obsession with victory" (Aronson, 2012, p. 258). This tendency toward hypercompetitiveness can produce a destructive communication climate in several ways. (see Box 1-2)

Interpersonal Relationships: Stress and Strain Competition is not structured to enhance interpersonal relationships. Trying to win an argument with your partner has "victory" as the goal, and "losing" an argument doesn't usually foster friendliness toward your antagonist. Even what may begin as playful verbal jousting can quickly deteriorate into a nasty hypercompetitive verbal battle if feelings are hurt.

As competitiveness increases, empathy decreases (Kohn, 1993). **Empathy** is "thinking and feeling what you perceive another to be thinking and feeling" (Howell, 1982, p. 108). When you have empathy, you experience another person's perspective. Trying to win at someone else's expense clouds your ability to empathize. Your focus is on yourself, not on the other person or on the damage that winning might produce. The more empathy you feel, the more difficult it becomes to view another person as a rival to be vanquished. Hypercompetitiveness can make empathy disappear.

This cartoon illustrates:
○ **1.** Individual achievement
○ **2.** Cooperation
Answers at end of chapter
○ **3.** Hypercompetitiveness
○ **4.** None of the above

BOX 1-2 FOCUS ON CONTROVERSY

Ethics and Hypercompetitiveness

Competent communication involves ethical considerations, and hypercompetitiveness raises serious ethical concerns. Lying and deception clearly violate the ethical criterion of honesty, and hypercompetitiveness encourages dishonesty (Callahan, 2004). Cheating, in addition to being dishonest, violates the ethical criterion of fairness because it gives an unfair advantage to the cheater. Unfortunately, cheating has become "astoundingly common" (Fang & Casadevall, 2013).

Another ethical standard, respect for others, is shown by communicating sportsmanship, empathy, and compassion. Hypercompetitiveness, which glorifies the victors with messages of praise and adulation and is indifferent to or even contemptuous of losers in a contest, teaches none of these elements of respect. As Alice Walker so eloquently notes, we live in a culture where "the only way I can bloom is if I step on your flower, the only way I can shine is if I put out your light" (quoted in Lanka, 1989, p. 24). Respect, not in the sense of being impressed by someone's talent as a potential rival but of valuing someone as a person,

doesn't blossom in a hypercompetitive climate in which being called "a loser" is a common experience for many.

This is all well and good, you may be saying, but we live in a hypercompetitive society. Just as we do, our children will have to face the disappointment of losing throughout their lives. They'll lose jobs because others gave better interviews; they'll lose arguments with parents and teachers; they'll lose speech contests; they may even lose in divorce proceedings because another lawyer did a more effective job. Is it not the responsibility of parents to teach children how to lose?

Teaching children how to lose with grace and dignity is an important communication lesson, but just as important is teaching them how to communicate cooperatively with others. Our children will be afforded many opportunities to practice losing without any encouragement from us. Doesn't it make more sense to offer cooperative experiences for our children to counterbalance the hypercompetitive exposure they most surely will face without our assistance?

Questions for Thought

1. Are the ethical questions raised here merely misplaced idealism that ignores the unavoidable realities of American society? Don't we have to deal with what our society is, not with what we might like it to be?

2. Are the ethical questions raised here an indictment only of hypercompetitiveness, or can the same questions be raised about competition in general?

Increasing levels of competitiveness can also incite increasingly hostile communication (Van Oostrum & Rabbie, 1995). In a survey of 60 high-school athletic associations, 76% of the respondents said increased verbal and nonverbal hostility are causing many officials of high-school sporting events to quit (Dahlberg, 2001).

Group Effects: Teamwork/Cohesiveness The degree of liking we have for members of a group, and the level of commitment to the group that this liking

produces, is called **cohesiveness**. Cohesiveness nurtures teamwork, and it is best enhanced by a cooperative communication climate of openness and supportiveness (LaFasto & Larson, 2001). Hypercompetitiveness, especially among group members, can destroy cohesiveness.

A common notion is that intergroup (between groups) competition promotes intragroup (within a group) cohesiveness and teamwork. This is primarily true, however, when intergroup competition is viewed as "all-out war" (Egas et al., 2013), and for winning teams. Losing teams typically fall apart as members look for someone to blame (Van Oostrum & Rabbie, 1995). Communication within the group often becomes hostile when defeat becomes common.

Teamwork requires cooperation, not competition (Johnson & Johnson, 2003; Wahr et al., 2013). The Me-orientation of competitiveness works against the We-orientation critical to teamwork. As former Los Angeles Dodgers manager Tommy Lasorda once said, "My responsibility is to get my 25 guys playing for the name on the front of the shirt and not the one on the back" (quoted in LaFasto & Larson, 2001, p. 100).

Achievement and Performance: Not What You Might Think There is a widely accepted belief in the United States that competition enhances achievement and performance in virtually every walk of life. A review of hundreds of studies in a variety of settings, however, points to an inescapable conclusion: *achievement and performance are typically best enhanced by a cooperative climate, not a competitive one* (Johnson & Johnson, 2005, 2009). Why? Rivals typically hoard resources to gain a perceived advantage over adversaries. Also, the vast majority who realize they have no chance to win (relative unequals) are unlikely to be motivated to perform optimally. They are more likely to want to quit,

TABLE 1-1 Effects of Cooperation Compared to Hypercompetitiveness

COOPERATION	HYPERCOMPETITION
Builds interpersonal relations	Damages interpersonal relations
Creates empathy	Creates hostility/aggression
Develops connection	Disconnects
Encourages trust	Encourages distrust
Develops teamwork/ cohesiveness	Teamwork increases when winning but not when losing
Improves achievement/ performance	Impedes achievement/ performance
Reduces incentive to cheat	Encourages cheating

and they often do (Emmons, 2005; Goodwin, 2010; Tjosvold et al., 2003).

Openness and supportiveness, the two components of a constructive communication climate, are discouraged by hypercompetitiveness because they give an advantage to your opponent. Encouraging greater cooperation in our communication with others merely calls for a better balance in a society awash in competition, not the impractical abolition of all competition and the substitution of some fairy-tale notion of total cooperation in a world of perfect harmony.

⊕ Summary

Communication is the transactional process of sharing meaning with others. The communication competence model acts as a map that can guide your transactions with others. Studying the human communication process increases your knowledge of how to behave appropriately and effectively in a specific context. Communication skill development allows you to use your knowledge of communication in useful ways. Knowledge and skills, however, don't automatically improve relationships. Being sensitive to your social environment by detecting, decoding, and comprehending signals increases effective communication. Sensitivity means monitoring your communication so that you can improve. Being committed to improving your communication by investing time, energy, feelings, thoughts, and effort is also necessary. The communication competence model of knowledge, skills, sensitivity, commitment, and ethics will serve as the map directing your journey into a variety of communication environments that will be explored in later chapters. Developing a constructive communication climate is a first step in this journey.

Answers for Critical Thinking captions:

ZITS (P. 16): #2

CATHY (P. 24): #3

Answers for Hindsight Bias Self-Test, Box 1-1

1. False	6. False	11. False	16. False
2. False	7. False	12. True	17. False
3. False	8. False	13. False	18. False
4. False	9. False	14. False	19. True
5. False	10. False	15. False	20. False

CALCULATING YOUR SCORING: *Each answer* is worth *2 points*.

YOUR SCORE: _____

Maximum 40 points (20 × 2)

36–40 = A
32–34 = B
28–30 = C
24–26 = D
Below 24 = F

Quizzes Without Consequences

Test your knowledge before your exam! Go to the companion website at www.oup.com/us/rothwell, click on the Student Resources for each chapter, and take the Quizzes Without Consequences.

Film School Case Studies

This activity section, found in every chapter, presents select films for you to analyze. A movie rating (PG-13, R, etc.) is included to assist you in deciding which films are appropriate. This is a critical thinking activity. A specific question or issue is raised that is relevant to each film listed. You are asked to explore this question or issue using chapter material for your analysis.

French Kiss (1995). Romantic Comedy; PG-13
Very amusing "relationship" movie with Kevin Kline and Meg Ryan turning in wonderful comedic performances. Notice the influence of culture on communication transactions. Where do you see examples of all four types of noise (physical, physiological, psychological, and semantic)?

I Am Legend (2007). Drama; PG-13
Will Smith is a man alone in New York City after a terrifying pandemic. Examine the influence of loneliness on one's well-being. Why is the death of his dog so traumatic?

Leatherheads (2008). Comedy; PG-13
Goofy comedy about the early days (1920s) of professional football starring George Clooney. Is the competition in all of its aspects depicted as constructive or destructive? Apply the three criteria for constructive competition.

Nell (1994). Drama; PG-13
The story of a socially isolated individual. Identify the powerful effects social isolation has on a person, especially in the main character's ability to communicate and establish connections with others.

Return to Paradise (1998). Drama; R
Underrated film about a harrowing moral dilemma. You'll be contemplating what you would do in the same circumstances. Analyze the film for communication ethics. You'll find much material to chew over.

The Hunger Games: Catching Fire (2013). Action-Adventure; PG-13
Katniss (Jennifer Lawrence) and Peeta (Josh Hutcherson) become enemies of the Capitol and must participate in a second Hunger Games pitting previous victors against each other. Apply the five criteria of ethical communication to analyze the ethics of the Hunger Games combatants.

1. Explain the three elements of perception: selecting, organizing, and interpreting.

2. Understand how self-concept is formed.

3. Recognize important issues associated with self-esteem.

Perception of Self and Others

PERCEPTION IS AN INHERENTLY SUBJECTIVE human process. There is no "immaculate perception" that can objectively convince everyone of the single correct interpretation of your experience. This is particularly striking when comparing cultures. Consider food choices across cultures, for example. The variety is astounding. One study analyzed 381 ingredients in 56,498 recipes worldwide (Ahn et al., 2011). Some varieties of cuisine are not universally embraced. The Scottish dish called haggis is a mixture of sheep innards blended with chunks of sheep fat, seasonings, and oatmeal, all cooked in the animal's stomach. It has little appeal to most Americans. Beetle grubs, which have the appearance of plump white worms, make most Americans gag at the thought of eating them, but they are a delicacy to the Asmat of New Guinea. The Inuit eat raw fish eyes like candy, and several East African tribes enjoy a tall drink of fresh cow's blood. To Americans, insects and raw animal blood don't

4. Determine when self-disclosure is appropriate and when it is not.

5. Recognize and combat errors in your perceptions of others.

6. Use specific strategies to improve your communication effectiveness and appropriateness given perceptual differences with others.

qualify as food. Other cultures, however, find some of our food choices equally revolting (Archer, 2000a). Many South Americans perceive our common peanut butter sandwich to be disgusting in taste, texture, and smell, and most people from India find our common practice of eating beef offensive.

Our culture teaches us what is food and what is inedible. This is largely a matter of learned expectation, not objective taste. If you are not told what you are eating, it may taste good until you are informed that it is lizard innards, at which point you may feel compelled to chuck your innards. Food preferences of all sorts can present communication challenges at mealtime, especially when you don't want to cause offense by declining to eat the meal presented but what is offered as food may be stomach churning.

The act of speaking also illustrates stark cultural differences in perception. Speaking is highly valued in the United States, and silence is not prized. Quiet individuals do not usually become leaders in groups (Bormann, 1990). Americans interpret silence mainly in negative ways, such as indicating sorrow, criticism, obligation, regret, indifference, rejection, or embarrassment (Martin & Nakayama, 2013). The silence of some men is often a source of frustration for their female partners. Women sometimes prod men to talk more. There's an old story about President Calvin Coolidge, who was renowned for his taciturnity. Two women approached him, and one said, "Mr. Coolidge, I just bet my friend that I could get you to say three words." Coolidge replied, "You lose." (Famed wit Dorothy Parker, upon hearing that Coolidge had died, remarked, "How can they tell?")

Some cultures, however, value silence and devalue speaking (Kim, 2010). The Thai culture values quietness as a sign of humility (Knutson & Posirisuk, 2006). There is a Chinese proverb: "Those who know do not speak; those who speak do not know." Asian students typically are hesitant to participate in class discussions, preferring to listen to the older, wiser teachers (Nataatmadja et al., 2007), while class participation is often encouraged, even required, as part of the grade in the United States. Students whose culture places little value on speaking are at a substantial disadvantage in U.S. classrooms. When you've been taught to value silence, speaking up is difficult, especially in a public forum.

Disagreements and conflicts are bound to emerge over perceptual differences, not just between diverse cultures but also within one's own ethnic group, family, and group of friends and even between intimate partners. A memorable scene from Woody Allen's Oscar-winning movie *Annie Hall* illustrates this point. When Annie's therapist asks her how often she and Alvy have sex, she replies, "Constantly. Three times a week." When Alvy's therapist asks him the same question, he responds, "Hardly ever. Three times a week." Imagine the difficulty two individuals like Annie and Alvy would have conversing about this issue. You can almost hear the argument: "You demand too much." "You want too little." "Too much." "Too little . . ."

Perception is not an unbiased process. Consequently, *the primary purpose of this chapter is to address how you communicate competently when your perceptions are inherently subjective and often markedly at odds with the perceptions of others.* We all behave as we do largely because of our perceptions of the world. Understanding the perceptual process is an important step toward improving our communication with others.

The Perceptual Process

Sight, sound, touch, taste, and smell are sensations, but *sensation and perception, although related, are not the same.* **Sensation** is the process by which our sense organs (eyes, ears, nose, skin, tongue) that contain sense receptors change physical energy (light, sound waves, chemical substances) into neural impulses that are sent to our brains. Perception is the processing of these neural impulses so that we go beyond merely sensing and begin to *make sense* of the impulses. Perception is how we build meaningful patterns (see Figure 2-1). "We sense the presence of a stimulus, but we perceive what it is" (Levine & Shefner, 1991, p. 1). Sound waves, for instance, are the raw materials of hearing, but they are not actual hearing. **Perception**, therefore, *is the process of selecting, organizing, and interpreting sensory data.*

In this section, the perceptual process is briefly explained. The three elements of perception—*selecting, organizing,* and *interpreting*—do not occur in isolation from each other. They all interact. Nevertheless, understanding the perceptual process requires that each element first be discussed separately.

Selecting: Forced Choices

The world is teeming with stimuli. We perceive what we can sense, but much of our world is hidden from us by the limitations of our senses. As discussed in this section, *perception is inherently subjective and selective.* Selecting which stimuli to notice begins the perceptual process. Your selection is determined by sensory limitations and selective attention.

SENSORY LIMITATIONS: WE'RE MOSTLY BLIND AND DEAF

What sensory data we select and how it will be organized and interpreted are influenced greatly by the capacity of our sensory receptors to be stimulated in the first place. Table 2-1

FIGURE 2-1. We may see movement where none exists when we stare at this image because our sensory receptors can be tricked. The interconnectedness of sensation and perception is a complex process.

TABLE 2-1   The Threshold of Human Senses

SENSE	STIMULUS	RECEPTORS	THRESHOLD
Vision	Electromagnetic energy	Rods and cones in the retina	A candle flame viewed from a distance of about 30 miles on a clear night
Hearing	Sound pressure waves	Hair cells on the basilar membrane of the inner ear	The ticking of a watch from about 20 feet away in a quiet room
Touch	Mechanical displacement or pressure on the skin	Nerve endings located in the skin	The wing of a bee falling on a cheek from one-half inch
Smell	Chemical substances in the air	Receptor cells in the upper part of the nasal cavity	One perfume drop diffused throughout a small apartment
Taste	Chemical substances	Taste buds on the tongue	About one teaspoon of sugar dissolved in two gallons of water

Source: Adapted from Galanter (1962).

indicates the average **threshold**, or minimum amount of energy, that triggers a sensation for each human sensory system. As sensitive as these receptors are, they have a limited capacity to receive stimuli. Vision is our primary sense, but we do not see ultraviolet rays, X-rays, gamma rays, or cosmic rays, nor do we see radar or long radio waves. There are as many microscopic creatures on our bodies (e.g., fungi, bacteria, and mites) as there are people on Earth. Fortunately, these are hidden from our view by the limitations of our eyesight.

Human hearing, like human vision, is sensitive yet limited. The frequency of sound waves hitting your ear registers from about 20 cycles per second to a maximum of about 20,000 cycles per second. Frequency is perceived as **pitch**—how low or high the sound is (e.g., how low or high a human voice is during conversation). Human hearing may seem impressive, but it is not when compared to a dog that can hear up to 50,000 cycles per second (very high-pitch sounds), a mouse that can hear up to 90,000 cycles per second, or a bat that can hear up to 100,000 cycles per second (Roediger et al., 1991). This tells us that we cannot sense a huge amount of the stimuli that envelops us each moment.

Sound also varies by **amplitude**, which is perceived as loudness. Normal conversation is 10,000 times louder than a human whisper, but have you ever been accused of mumbling? Cell phone conversations are typically a bit louder; they're sometimes referred to as the "cell yell"— or "cell hell" to those trapped in restaurants or planes unable to escape the high-decibel din. A passing subway train is 10 billion times louder than the minimum detectable sound to the human ear (Myers, 2012). Hearing loss occurs when you are exposed for a prolonged period to very loud sounds (e.g., a rock concert), reducing your already limited hearing acuity. When parents or grandparents have substantially diminished hearing, conducting a conversation with them can be enormously frustrating and a test of your compassion as they repetitively ask, "What did you say?" Watching television with them can also be an ear-splitting experience when volume is pumped to the maximum.

Individual differences in **sensory acuity**, which is the level of sensitivity of our senses, add another element to the subjective perception of our world. About 25% of the population are supertasters; they have six times more taste buds than those with the fewest (Rupp, 2014). If you are a supertaster, sugar seems twice as sweet as it does to average tasters, and bitter tastes can be overpowering (a reason Brussels sprouts are not everyone's favorite food). Arguments about something being "too sweet" or "not sweet enough" are wasted effort. Sensory acuity is an individual subjective difference.

Your sense of smell is about 10,000 times more sensitive than your sense of taste

("Smell," 2011). The issue of smell perception also can become a source of interpersonal conflict. I have observed some rather nasty verbal exchanges between people in movie theaters, on elevators, and in other public places that were triggered by one person wearing "offensive" perfume. Signs have even begun appearing in public facilities asking people not to wear strong-smelling perfumes or colognes that might provoke allergic reactions from some individuals. Some people with a clearly diminished sense of smell do not realize that marinating themselves in potent perfume, aftershave, or cologne and then leaving a vapor trail as they walk can be troublesome for others.

There can be vast individual differences in our abilities to see, hear, touch, smell, and taste because of the limitations and variations in the acuity of each of our senses. You subjectively perceive the world because your sensory experience doesn't identically match anyone else's, and it is only an approximation of the physical world.

SELECTIVE ATTENTION: BOMBARDED BY STIMULI

We don't process what we don't see, hear, taste, touch, or smell. What is available to our senses, however, is too voluminous for our brains to process. Attention is unavoidably selective. By one calculation, our five basic senses are bombarded with 11 million bits of information *each second*, but at best, we attend to only about 40 bits (Wilson, 2002). Our senses have the potential to receive a wide range of data, but the channel capacity of our senses is limited. Consequently, we must selectively attend to stimuli.

Selectively attending to stimuli involves two processes: (1) focusing on specific stimuli and (2) screening out other data (van der Heijden, 1991). You do both when you're talking intently to your date at a restaurant. You focus on that person and what your date says and does, and you screen out conversations occurring all around you (at least you do if you know what's good for you).

The results of these two processes working at the same time can produce **inattentional blindness**—lack of attention to an unexpected object. Research shows that we are easily victimized by this because we focus intently on one stimulus and are blind to a seemingly obvious, competing stimulus (Chabris & Simons, 2010). In a somewhat disturbing study of inattentional blindness, researchers asked 24 radiologists to view computed tomographic (CT) scans and perform a standard lung-nodule detection task. Unbeknownst to the radiologists, in the last of the CT scans examined, an image of a gorilla 48 times the size of an average nodule was inserted. A stunning 83% of the radiologists did not see the gorilla (Drew et al., 2013). Even observers, operating in their sphere of expertise, are vulnerable to inattentional blindness. If you are looking for a tumor, you may miss an aneurism or some other serious abnormality.

Inattentional blindness is a daily communication occurrence. Increasingly, people are becoming so focused on cell phone conversations and text messaging while walking that they run into street lamps, step off curbs into traffic, or trip and fall. They are blind to almost everything around them except for the focus of their attention. One woman was so intent on texting while walking in the Berkshire Mall in Reading, Pennsylvania, that she tumbled headfirst into a fountain. The security camera footage was subsequently posted on YouTube and viewed more than 2 million times ("Texting While Walking," 2011). A Pew Research Center study found that a quarter of cell phone users have actually bumped into another person or object while using their phone, and more than half of cell phone users ages 18 to 24 have done likewise (A. Smith, 2014).

The consequences of inattentional blindness can be more serious than embarrassment. An Ohio State University study discovered that more than 1,500 pedestrians visit emergency rooms annually because of injuries incurred while engaging in sidewalk texting or cell phone conversations, and this figure doesn't include pedestrians who were injured but went to personal physicians or who sought no medical treatment (Nasar & Troyer, 2013). Yet despite the common belief that most of us can adeptly do two things at once (multitasking), research shows the opposite. Texting while driving, for example, is six times more dangerous than driving while drunk (Wilms, 2012). Divided attention diminishes our ability to do either task well.

What we attend to at any given moment is influenced by the nature of the stimulus (Passer & Smith, 2011), a point that is explored in Chapter 13 when attention strategies for speeches are discussed. The *intensity* of the stimulus draws our attention without conscious effort on our part. For example, someone shrieking can snap our head around before we have a chance to think about what it means. It may be a child excitedly playing with a sibling, or it might be a person in serious trouble. *Novelty* invites attention. Perhaps that is one of the attractions of YouTube videos that show individuals acting weirdly or engaging in reckless behavior. *Movement* also draws attention. If a friend approaches you and feigns a punch to your stomach, you'll notice and reflexively protect yourself with your arms. *Repetition,* if it is irritating or annoying, triggers attention. If you're talking with someone at a party and they keep snorting when they laugh, you'll probably notice it if you find the noise bothersome. Finally, *contrast* provokes attention. When conversation at that same party suddenly stops, you'll notice the contrast. You may even feel anxious or concerned.

What we attend to is also influenced by internal factors peculiar to each individual. Hunger can make you notice a friend eating a large pepperoni pizza. *Fatigue* can screen out important stimuli, such as your partner's new hairdo or your teacher's announcement of an assignment due date. If your *interest* is riding horses, you will likely notice two people conversing about dressage. If you're fearful walking down a dark street at night because you've had an *experience* with a mugger, you'll likely notice strangers or anyone who might appear menacing.

Organizing: Creating Schemas

Perception does not operate apart from meaning, and we must organize selected stimuli to create meaning. **Schemas** are mental frameworks that create meaningful patterns from stimuli. The three types of schemas to organize perceptual stimuli discussed here are *prototypes, stereotypes,* and *scripts* (Wood, 2004).

PROTOTYPES: BEST CASE

Humans categorize persons, places, events, objects, phenomena, ideas, and so forth. Categorizing helps us make sense of our world. One way we categorize is by forming prototypes in our minds. A **prototype** is the most representative or "best" example of something. You have prototypes of a "boss from hell," a "best friend," an "ideal relationship," a "great movie," a "perfect date," or a "great communicator."

Poorly matched prototypes can be problematic. If one person's prototype of an "ideal date" is attending a ball game and munching on hot dogs but the other person's prototype is dressing elegantly and eating at a five-star restaurant, then a second date may not be in the offing. Yet a problem may also develop even if both parties share a similar prototype. The "made-in-Hollywood" prototype of a "perfect romance" may set an unreachable standard and inevitably lead to disappointment when your own relationship doesn't measure up.

STEREOTYPES: GENERALIZING ABOUT GROUPS

A **stereotype** is a generalization about a group or category of people. Stereotypes organize individuals according to categories such as ethnic origin, socioeconomic status, age, gender, sexual orientation, religious affiliation, and even body

Chongqing, a city in southwest China, has created two pedestrian lanes, one for those with and one for those without cell phones. Pedestrian collisions because of oblivious, multitasking cell phone users led to the lane division.

type, and they attribute common traits to all individuals in that group. For example, research comparing the American stereotype of the elderly as warm but incompetent is shared in six other countries studied (Cuddy et al., 2005). American stereotypes of Asians are consistent with media representations that they are academically successful but nerdy (Zhang, 2010).

Some stereotypes are positive ("Artists are creative, interesting people"), and some are negative ("College professors are stuffy and arrogant"). *Stereotyping isn't always bad.* Positive stereotypes of others—for example, "Most Hispanics are good-hearted and hardworking people"—can lead to cooperative transactions. Positive stereotypes are pervasive and can be quite powerful (Czopp et al., 2015). *Stereotypes are not necessarily completely incorrect, either.* (Lee et al., 1995). Sometimes they are mostly true and accurate, such as "College professors are intelligent and avid readers." Nevertheless, stereotypes can distort your perceptions and produce serious consequences, as discussed later in this chapter, because they allow for no individual differences within a group.

SCRIPTS: PREDICTABLE BEHAVIOR

A **script** is a predictable sequence of events that indicates what we are expected to do in a given situation. When you are sitting at a table in a restaurant and the server hands you a menu, you don't ask, "What's this?" You already know that you're expected to choose a meal from the menu. You have a "restaurant script." The more predictable the sequence of events, the more scripted it is.

A mental script operates the way a movie script works. The movie script tells you what to say and do. The script organizes your behavior into a sequence of activities. Your mental script does the same. We have scripts for greeting people, for expected behavior in classes, for asking someone for a date, and so on.

Scripts allow us to behave without having to think carefully. This can be positive and negative. When partners begin finishing each other's sentences, the script is well known to both individuals. Finishing your partner's sentences may be appreciated as "really knowing me." It may also be annoying because you are "too predictable." Partners may act out "conflict scripts" that repeat the same destructive behaviors. Without deviation from the script, the same ineffective arguing patterns get repeated, seemingly without end. Change the script if you want to change the outcome.

Interpreting: Making Sense of Stimuli

Two men were arrested in Scottsbluff, Nebraska, when, on a "triple-dog-dare" from a friend, they bought women's thong underwear at a Wal-Mart, changed in the store's bathroom, then walked through the store wearing only the thongs and T-shirts. Why did these men, ages 35 and 36, act so strangely?

We select stimuli and organize them, but we also interpret what they mean. We try to make sense of the stimuli that we've organized. Principally, we make sense of our own behavior and our transactions with others by making an **attribution**—assigning a cause to behavior. We attribute two principal causes to behavior: (1) the personal characteristics, or traits, of the individual (*dispositional causes*) and (2) the environment (*situational causes*).

Deciding the causes of our own behavior is a highly subjective process. Did we fail the exam because we didn't care enough, or was the exam too difficult for a lower division class? Some individuals assign personal reasons for their failure ("I'm not smart enough"), and others attribute situational causes ("There wasn't enough time to do my best on the exam").

Accurately attributing causes to the behavior of others is particularly difficult because we usually do not have enough information to make valid conclusions. This doesn't stop us, however. The *social desirability* of a behavior can influence whether you choose dispositional or situational attributions for the behavior of others. Usually, when a behavior will evoke disapproval, observers make a dispositional attribution (Gordon, 2012). You may think the two men who wore thongs in Wal-Mart did it because they are just weird individuals (dispositional attribution), but the explanation they gave suggests a strong influence from a friend's triple-dog-dare (situational attribution).

Person perception is not simply a linear, one-way process beginning with selecting, then organizing, and finally ending by interpreting stimuli. Our interpretations of self and others often double back and influence what data we continue to select and organize that in turn influence our self-perceptions and our view of others.

Perception of Self

From the moment you are welcomed into the world, you begin the process of becoming who you are, a person separate from others but defined in relation to others. This section discusses the perception of self and the role it plays in human communication.

Self-Concept: Influence of Others

Each one of you has a sense of who you are and what makes you a person distinct from others. This **self-concept** is the sum total of everything that encompasses the self-referential term *me*. It is your *identity* or *self-schemas*: perceiving yourself as athletic, intelligent, compassionate, attractive,

moody, awkward with others, or a host of other characterization.

Self-concept is also a central point of reference for your communication with others. If you see yourself as a person of integrity, you likely feel compelled to speak up when promises are broken and injustices based on deceit emerge. If you see yourself as attractive, you are more likely to flirt with a stranger than if you see yourself as unattractive. If you see yourself as compassionate and caring, you likely find it difficult to reject a homeless person's request for "spare change" when you have a pocketful of money. We communicate from the perspective of how we see ourselves. Your self-concept intrudes on every communication event of your life.

Your self-concept is not formed in isolation. *Self-concept is a social construction, a product of interpersonal communication.* "You find out who you are by meeting who you aren't" (Anderson & Ross, 1994, p. 116). Infants haven't formed a self-concept. Their self-concept gradually develops through communication with significant people over a long period of time. Parents, teachers, friends, relatives, coworkers, bosses, and even strangers are instrumental in shaping your concept of self. You think of yourself as humorous if others laugh at your jokes. You consider yourself as a leader if you notice that others follow you. You see yourself as quiet if others tell you that you're taciturn in social circumstances.

Your self-concept is relatively stable, especially once you reach adulthood (Bergner & Holmes, 2000). Self-concepts don't change easily even in the face of contradictory evidence. You may see yourself as shy because your parents, relatives, and teachers told you so when you were a child. In later life, this may no longer be as true, yet you may still cling to an outdated view of self. Self-concepts can change (English & Chen, 2007), but change comes from characterizations by others that are numerous and consistent (e.g., all your teachers say you're smart), the characterizations must come from those whom you see as competent and important sources (e.g., parents or romantic partners), and they can't be radically dissimilar to how you perceive yourself (e.g., outgoing instead of shy) (Bergner & Holmes, 2000).

Self-Esteem: Evaluating Your Personal Identity

Self-concept is the descriptive element of self-perception. **Self-esteem** is the evaluative element of self-perception (Myers, 2012). It is self-appraisal—the sum of all your self-schemas—your perception of self-worth, attractiveness, and social competence. "I am a quiet person" describes your perception of self without attaching an evaluation to the perception. "I'm *too* quiet," however, attaches an evaluation to the self-perception.

INFLUENCES ON SELF-ESTEEM: APPRAISALS, COMPARISONS, AND CONTINGENCIES

There are three primary influences on our self-esteem: *reflected appraisal, social comparison,* and *contingencies of self-worth.* **Reflected appraisal** refers to messages you receive from others that assess your self-concept. It is difficult for us to perceive ourselves as smart, for example, if every person important to us is saying that we are slow-witted or just average. Parents can have a particularly powerful effect on your self-esteem. They generally get the first crack at shaping your perception of self-worth. If parents persistently call you a failure, then feeling good about yourself is challenging. You'll need to turn to other significant people in your life (friends, siblings, other relatives, teachers, professional acquaintances) to counteract parental negativity.

Your self-esteem is also a product of **social comparison**—evaluating yourself by comparing yourself to other people. When we are in the presence of someone we perceive as impressive, even superior, our self-esteem tends to diminish. When we are in the presence of someone we perceive as unimpressive, however, our self-esteem tends to inflate (Pomery et al., 2012). Research shows that young women who regularly compare themselves to strikingly thin, professional models appearing in popular media develop negative images of their own bodies, which can lead to eating disorders (Han, 2003). Men also experience a similar dissatisfaction with their bodies when they view

Studies show conclusively that constant media images of women and men with "perfect" bodies foster body image dissatisfaction and negatively influence self-esteem because of social comparison. Shown here are models for Victoria's Secret and Abercrombie & Fitch

images of prototypically attractive, muscular men (Mulgrew et al., 2014).

Your self-esteem is also influenced by what is perceived as most important to you feeling good about yourself. This is called **contingencies of self-worth** (Crocker & Knight, 2005). Although people in general want to be perceived by others

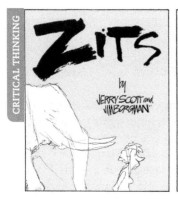 

Which influence on self-esteem is illustrated?

○ **1.** Reflected appraisal
○ **2.** Social comparison
Answers at end of chapter.

○ **3.** Contingencies of self-worth
○ **4.** None of the above

as attractive, smart, and capable, there are individual differences that add to the self-esteem equation. One study on Facebook postings of personal information found that women based their self-esteem on their appearance more than men did (Stefanone et al., 2011). "One person may have self-esteem that is highly contingent on doing well in school and being physically attractive, whereas another may have self-esteem that is contingent on being loved by God and adhering to moral standards" (Crocker & Wolfe, 2001). Making the first person feel highly moral and the second person feel highly attractive won't necessarily raise self-esteem for either. The reverse, however, likely will. Our self-esteem is contingent on what we value most and whether we succeed or fail in the pursuit of valued goals.

SELF-ESTEEM ISSUES: TOO LITTLE OR TOO MUCH?

Despite the common notion that low self-esteem is a serious problem in the United States (see Box 2-1), research reveals otherwise (Crocker & Carnevale, 2013). A global study of 17,000 respondents from 53 countries found that the United States ranked sixth among these nations on self-esteem. The United States scored especially high on self-competence, although not as strongly on self-liking (Schmitt & Allik, 2005).

Most of us feel quite accomplished, even more so than statistically makes sense (see Box 2-2). Only 1% of online daters rate their appearance as

---

BOX 2-1 DEVELOPING COMMUNICATION COMPETENCE

How's Your Self-Esteem?

Consider each of the following and rate yourself on a scale from 1 to 100, with 50 being the median (same number of others above you and below you.)

Compared to other people.

1. I rate my driving ability as   _____

2. My ability as a college student is   _____

3. My overall morality is   _____

4. My intellectual potential is   _____

5. My communication ability is   _____

6. My overall self-confidence is   _____

7. My physical attractiveness is   _____

8. My sense of humor is   _____

9. My compassion for others is   _____

10. My leadership abilities are   _____

So, how did you do? Any rating above 50 means that you are not suffering from low self-esteem. Any rating above 75 means that you see yourself as very strong in that area.

BOX 2-2 FOCUS ON CONTROVERSY

Self-Esteem: More Is Not Always Better

The *Final Report of the California Task Force to Promote Self-Esteem and Personal and Social Responsibility* (1990) asserted, "The lack of self-esteem is central to most personal and social ills plaguing our state and nation" (p. 4). It claimed, "People who esteem themselves are less likely to engage in destructive and self-destructive behavior, including child abuse, alcohol abuse, abuse of other drugs (legal and illegal), violence, crime, and so on" (p. 5). The conclusions of the task force were based on what to most people may seem to be self-evident truths. California Assemblyman John Vasconcellos, a member of the task force, had to admit, "We didn't claim to have proven it all. The science was not very far advanced" (Bauer, 1996). Nevertheless, the report became the best-selling state document of all time. Most of California's 58 counties formed self-esteem task forces as a result (Billingsley, 2010).

High self-esteem, so goes the reasoning of the task force, should provide a "social vaccine" that inoculates individuals against destructive communication that attacks self-concepts with criticism, insults, and demonstrations of disrespect. A review of more than 150 studies on self-esteem, however, contradicts this reasoning (Baumeister et al., 1996; see also Baumeister et al., 2003). The most aggressively violent individuals, whether neo-Nazi skinheads, terrorists, Ku Klux Klan members, juvenile delinquents, gang members, psychopaths, or spouse abusers, do not suffer from low self-esteem. Rather, they exhibit superiority complexes, and their "self-appraisal is unrealistically positive" (Baumeister et al., 1996, p. 28). Nazis thought of themselves as members of the "master race," and they vilified Jews as "vermin." The image of a Mafia godfather suffering from low self-esteem as he orders the assassinations of rivals is difficult to visualize. Bullies and psychopaths seem contemptuous of the unfortunate victims they torment.

Perhaps bullies, godfathers, gang members, and the like camouflage their low self-esteem, as is often asserted, beneath the veneer of bluster and aggressiveness. Maybe favorable self-appraisals mask deep-seated insecurities. If this sounds reasonable to you, then try arguing the reverse proposition: that timid, reticent individuals don't suffer from low self-esteem. They simply mask their enormous self-confidence and deep-seated security. Both claims require us to ignore persuasive evidence to the contrary without providing supportive evidence for the validity of the assertions. One study of 540 college students showed that those with the biggest egos were the most aggressive, and when criticized, they delivered three times the intensity of painful noise (retaliatory punishment) to a victim (Bushman & Baumeister, 1998). "Contrary to popular wisdom, aggressive people do not typically have low self-esteem . . . Thus, there are no compelling theoretical or empirical reasons to suggest that boosting self-esteem will be effective in reducing aggression" (Thomaes et al., 2009, p. 1536).

A major cause of aggression in human relations seems to be not low self-esteem, masked or otherwise, but "high self-esteem combined with an ego threat" (Baumeister et al., 1996, p. 8). In other words, aggression, with its emphasis on competitive, adversarial communication, results from a discrepancy between two views of self: favorable self-appraisal but an unfavorable reflected appraisal from others. When others do not communicate "proper respect" worthy of a "superior person"—and instead criticize, insult, or show disrespect—an aggressive response is likely (Thomaes et al., 2009). This is especially true for narcissistic individuals on Facebook who exhibit "self-absorption, vanity, and superiority" and who have "a sense of deserving respect." They respond very aggressively to derogatory comments made about them (Carpenter, 2012, p. 485). "The higher . . . the self-esteem, the greater the vulnerability to ego threats. Viewed in this light, the societal pursuit of high self-esteem for everyone may literally end up doing considerable harm" (Baumeister et al., 1996, p. 30).

Is our society's emphasis on bolstering self-esteem completely misguided? If we are looking

(Continued)

BOX 2-2 FOCUS ON CONTROVERSY

Self-Esteem: More Is Not Always Better (continued)

for a cure-all in raised self-esteem, the answer is "yes." In addition to having the potential for aggressiveness (Menon et al., 2007), those with inflated self-esteem are more likely than individuals with more moderate self-esteem to be obnoxious, interrupt more, and talk at others instead of listening carefully (Baumeister et al., 2003). When children's self-esteem is inflated by effusive praise for relatively trivial behavior ("Nice breathing"), the potential for later disillusionment, low frustration tolerance, and deflated egos increases (Crocker & Carnevale, 2013).

Nevertheless, ignoring low self-esteem in our children and even adults is not desirable. What good can possibly come from people feeling bad about themselves? Praising others for genuine performance, accomplishments, and effort, however, not for merely being themselves, is more likely to improve low self-esteem and to encourage socially beneficial behavior (Baumeister et al., 2003).

Questions for Thought

1. In your estimation, how much should improving self-esteem be emphasized in our schools?

2. Is it ethical to praise children or adults indiscriminately for completion of commonplace tasks knowing that this might lead to egomaniacal self-centeredness in some individuals?

"less than average" (Epstein, 2007). A robust 95% of respondents in close relationships think their romantic partner, a reflection on their own self-esteem, is above average in appearance, intelligence, warmth, and sense of humor (Gagne, 2004). Ninety-four percent of university professors believe they outperform their colleagues (cited in Reid et al., 2007). One survey even found that 79% of respondents thought Mother Teresa was at least "somewhat likely" to go to heaven, but 87% of respondents believed they themselves would make it there ("Oprah," 1997). Another national survey that asked participants "How would you rate your own morals and values on a scale from 1 to 100 (100 being perfect)?" found that 50% rated themselves 90 or above; only 11% rated themselves 74 or below (Lovett, 1997).

PERCEPTUAL DISTORTION: BODY IMAGE AND SELF-ESTEEM

Despite the common overestimation of one's competence on a variety of measures, body image is an area of self-esteem that veers from the norm in the United States. "Our body image does not constitute the whole of the self, but it is a highly significant aspect of it" (Hamachek, 1992, p. 159). Women have been socialized to equate body size with self-worth (Moncur et al., 2013), and more than three-quarters of women in the United States are dissatisfied with their bodies (Ross, 2012). Between 70% and 90% of women report dieting at some time, even though a large portion of these women do not need to lose weight for health or aesthetic reasons (Markey, 2005). Nevertheless, in one study, a majority of women (57%) had participated in at least one unhealthy diet (Markey, 2005).

Body image distortion is largely influenced by society's conception of an ideal body (prototype) and a bombardment of media images that present unrealistically thin models as the ideal (Lopez-Guimera et al., 2010). More than a quarter of female models presented in various media meet the medical definition for anorexia (Ross, 2012). These media images influence not only women in general but also peers, parents, coaches, and even physicians who then reinforce the "need" for women to be thin

(Lopez-Guimera et al., 2010). These perceptions of the "ideal female body" have encouraged Internet "fat shaming," especially of women (but sometimes men). Pink, Kelly Clarkson, and Selena Gomez, among many other celebrities, have been fat shamed. Despite these influential and distorting media images of the "ideal woman" as wafer thin (Levine & Murnen, 2009), most men prefer a woman to be heavier and more curvaceous ("Female Body Shape," 2015). Nevertheless, most women think men prefer very thin women (Gaulin & Lassek, 2012).

Body image distortion is also a problem for men. As one researcher concludes: "In our society, much is made of women's nagging anxieties about how they look. But if women ever really had a lock on such worries, those days are gone" (Pope, 2004). Cultural ideals for the male body communicated in the popular mass media have changed, alarming some researchers about distorted body images among boys and men (McCabe & Ricciardelli, 2004). More than 90% of college men are dissatisfied with their muscularity, and only 29% are satisfied with their level of body fat (Frederick et al., 2007). For men, however, the chief concern is how to become more muscular (Field et al., 2014). When college men from the United States, Austria, and France were asked to take the Body Image Test and choose the body they thought women prefer in a man, on average they chose one with *30 pounds more muscle* than their own body possessed (Pope et al., 2000). Not surprisingly, men, like women, feel worse about their own body's appearance and attractiveness the more they are exposed to media images of the "ideal male body" (Mulgrew et al., 2014).

Do women have the same "ideal body" image for men that men expect women to have? When American and Austrian college women were given the same Body Image Test as male college students, they chose a male body image with *15 to 20 pounds less muscle* than what the men thought women preferred (Pope et al., 2000).

The male concern about insufficient muscularity can lead to a disorder called **muscle dysmorphia**—a preoccupation with one's body size and a perception that, although one is very muscular, one actually looks puny (Thomas et al., 2011). Those with muscle dysmorphia perceive puniness when they look at themselves in a mirror, even when other people perceive massiveness (Waldron, 2015). One individual studied by researchers was 6 feet 3 inches tall, weighed 270 pounds, had a 52-inch chest, and sported 20-inch biceps. Despite his massively muscular physique, however, he confessed, "When I look in the mirror, I sometimes think that I look really small . . . You'd be amazed at how hard it is, sometimes, for me to actually convince myself that I'm big" (quoted in Pope et al., 2002, p. 83). These researchers estimate that more than 1 million men have this disorder. Muscle dysmorphia causes people to give up jobs, careers, and social engagements so that they can spend hours every day lifting weights to "bulk up." They may refuse to appear in public in a bathing suit, turn down dates, or avoid social gatherings fearing that people will see their bodies as tiny and out of shape. They also report checking themselves in the mirror an average of 9.2 times a day. They also average *325 minutes*—more than *5 hours per day*—worrying about their muscularity and body size.

SELF-SERVING BIAS: PROTECTING YOUR SELF-ESTEEM

Assigning causes (attribution) to our own behavior is not an objective process. We protect our self-concept and our self-esteem by exercising a **self-serving bias**—the tendency to attribute our successful behavior to ourselves (personal traits) but to assign external circumstances (situations) to our unsuccessful behavior (Major et al., 2003). Divorced individuals usually blame their partner for the marital split. Managers often blame poor worker performance on weak worker effort, but workers typically blame crushing workloads, ambiguous tasks, inadequate resources, or troublesome coworkers. Athletes tend to attribute their victories to personal prowess but blame their losses on bad officiating, weather conditions, or cheating by their opponents. Students who perform well on tests usually view exams as valid indicators of knowledge, whereas students who perform poorly on exams may see them as arbitrary, unfair measures of knowledge. Teachers may take credit for the success of their students but blame their students' lack of motivation, effort, or ability for their failures.

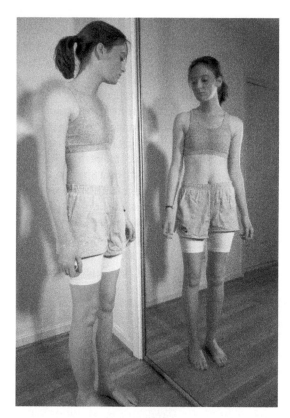

Most people see a massively muscled man and a wafer-thin woman. Those with muscle dysmorphia, however, perceive an embarrassingly scrawny man, and those with anorexia see an embarrassingly fat woman. Perception is strikingly subjective.

Our tendency to emphasize our accomplishments and downplay or deflect our shortcomings and failures is common. It is especially common in online virtual groups "where remote partners are unseen and ephemeral, [and] members are easy targets who can be blamed for the poor performances that an individual may have committed" (DeAndrea et al., 2011, p. 110). Unless we are mindful of this tendency to be self-serving, we are unlikely to learn new skills and gain new knowledge (Walther, 2008). Why seek to improve our communication skills if communication difficulties are usually perceived to be someone else's fault?

OPTIMAL SELF-ESTEEM: PURSUING GOALS, NOT SELF-ESTEEM

When we see professional athletes strutting and posturing before their fans, insisting that they receive thunderous applause and accolades for relatively insignificant athletic accomplishments, modesty and humility are missing. *Optimal self-esteem comes from significant accomplishments without expecting a coronation* (Kohn, 1993). Optimal self-esteem is unlikely to occur if you place yourself at the mercy of other people's appraisals (Crocker et al., 2006). Remaining in a relationship in which your partner persistently denigrates you, for example, can diminish self-esteem. Either your partner must be confronted and changes must occur, or your association with this negative influence should be curtailed or ended. Surrounding yourself with positive influences from warm and loving friends and partners is constructive.

Optimal self-esteem develops, paradoxically, when you don't strive to build self-esteem (Crocker, 2006). In fact, "actions designed to enhance self-esteem are motivated by a toxic preoccupation with self-judgment" (Crocker & Carnevale, 2013, p.33). Instead, concentrating on goals, especially compassionate ones such as "be supportive of my roommate" or "be aware of the impact my behavior might have on my roommate's feelings" (empathy), can boost a sense of self-worth (Crocker & Carnevale, 2013). Setting goals to learn new things can also build confidence. No one even has to know that you're learning a new language or studying economics, political science, or some other subject. Pursuing goals for self-improvement (internal reward), not for external rewards (e.g., grades, money, or social approval) is more likely to produce optimal self-esteem (Kernis, 2003). Concentrating on developing your talents and personal relationships with others is also productive (Crocker & Park, 2004).

Self-Disclosure: Revealing Your Self to Others

A principal way we reveal our self-concept and sense of self-esteem to others is through self-disclosure. Without self-disclosure, others are left inferring, outright guessing, who you are (self-concept) and how you feel about yourself (self-esteem). Without self-disclosure, you are essentially a stranger to other people. Revealing yourself to others is how friendships are born and intimacy blossoms.

Self-disclosure is the process of purposely revealing to others personal information about yourself that is significant and that others would not know unless you told them. *Self-disclosure is purposeful, not accidental, communication.* You may unintentionally demonstrate that you're clumsy at sports, but that is not self-disclosure. If you tell a friend that you are afraid to give public speeches and it is news to your friend, however, that is self-disclosure.

There are gender and cultural differences in self-disclosure. Women generally disclose more than men (Dindia, 2000; Sheldon, 2013). Women typically disclose more about themselves on Facebook, sharing more photos and spending greater time managing their profiles on social networking sites than men (Stefanone et al., 2011). Female-to-female self-disclosure is the most frequent, and male-to-male self-disclosure is the least frequent (Dindia, 2002).

CONSTRUCTIVE GOALS FOR SELF-DISCLOSURE

There are many possible goals for self-disclosing to others. Five primary constructive goals addressed here are *developing relationships, gaining self-knowledge, correcting misperceptions, eliciting reassurance,* and *creating impressions.*

Developing Relationships: Intimacy with Others Self-disclosure can be an important gateway to intimacy. Self-disclosure "fulfills fundamental needs for social connectedness and belonging and is intrinsically rewarding" (Bazarova & Choi, 2014, p. 2). When you limit your self-disclosure to another person, you have little that connects you to that person. *Self-disclosure is critical to the development of close personal relationships.*

Whether you and another person perceive each other as strangers, acquaintances, friends, or intimate partners depend largely on the breadth and depth of self-disclosure that takes place between the two of you (Altman & Taylor, 1973). **Breadth** refers to the range of subjects discussed. There may be several topics that you don't discuss with an acquaintance, but almost any topic is open for discussion with loved ones. **Depth** refers to how personal you become when discussing a particular subject. Intimate relationships usually have both breadth and depth, whereas impersonal, casual relationships usually have little of either. Breadth and depth of self-disclosure are critical factors in connecting with others.

Gaining Self-Knowledge: Self-Awareness Sharing information about yourself with others helps you to gain perspective. If you disclose to another person that you lack self-confidence, that person may point out several instances where you appeared very self-confident in front of others, which may cause you to revise your perception of self in this regard.

Correcting Misperceptions: Countering Inaccuracies Others may have misperceptions about you. They may perceive you to be unfriendly, for example. Revealing to them that you are shy, and explaining that engaging in conversation has always been challenging and anxiety producing for you, can open them to a different perception of you that is more accurate.

Eliciting Reassurance: Self-Validation When we have doubts about our body image, communication abilities, or other capabilities, disclosing these doubts often produces reassurance from others. Sometimes we just need to have others validate that we are a good and capable person (Bazarova & Choi, 2014).

Creating Impressions: The Image You Portray to Others We usually want others to like who we are. That's difficult to do if the other person knows little about you—your likes, dislikes, passions, goals, fears, and concerns. Self-disclosure is part of the process of creating favorable impressions.

COUNTERPRODUCTIVE GOALS FOR SELF-DISCLOSURE: INAPPROPRIATE ME-ORIENTATION

Two counterproductive goals for self-disclosure, *manipulation* and *catharsis*, are Me-oriented, not We-oriented. Both encourage incompetent communication.

Manipulation: You'll Disclose if I Disclose Research clearly shows that self-disclosure by one person induces self-disclosure by another (Dindia, 2000). Pretending to reveal important personal information about oneself merely to coax knowledge from another person that can be used against him or her is inappropriate and unethical communication. It may provide a competitive advantage—"So, Marissa doesn't like confrontation; how interesting"—but it is dishonest.

Using self-disclosure to deceive others is an ethical issue. Glenn Souther was a student at Virginia's Old Dominion University. He also was a Russian spy. He successfully deceived students and professors alike. Virginia Cooper (1994), a communication professor at the university, knew Souther well—or so she thought. Souther was a student of hers, her research assistant, and a frequent guest in her home. Curious how Souther could have deceived her so totally, she examined four hours of audiotape she had of him working with a group on a project. She discovered that Souther "was skilled in relationship deception due, in part, to his strategic disclosures that projected a plausible false image." Souther manipulated people into believing that he was trustworthy by disclosing large amounts of personal information. He

disclosed more personal information than any other group member. He seemed so "transparent" that no one suspected he was hiding an awful truth.

Catharsis: Getting Secrets Off Your Chest Spur-of-the-moment purging of personal information to "get it off your chest" or to relieve guilt is a poor reason to self-disclose. This is especially true if it is likely to damage the relationship you have with another person. Getting it off your chest may put it on the other person's chest. It also may create real problems for couples going through a divorce. The American Academy of Matrimonial Lawyers (AAML) notes that 81% of its members have used or faced evidence taken from social networking sites. More than 9 out of 10 AAML divorce attorneys note that use of evidence from text messages and smartphones used in divorce proceedings continues to increase as social media become ever more popular (Irvin, 2013). "The desire to talk trash is great" when a marriage runs aground, but "just blabbing things all over Facebook" when a marriage breaks up is "the worst possible time to share your feelings online" (Italie, 2010). Online disclosures can be used in court during child custody cases, property settlements, and other contentious issues. Social networking sites can make public what you may wish, upon reflection, to keep private.

APPROPRIATE SELF-DISCLOSURE: WHEN TO OPEN UP; WHEN TO SHUT UP

There are risks in self-disclosing to others. With the increasing popularity of social media, the line between public and private self-disclosure has blurred (Bazarova & Choi, 2014). Personal information (sexual preferences, symptoms of depression, relationship traumas) can be shared on Facebook beside innocuous information (restaurant or movie preferences). Unless careful attention is paid to restricting intimate information from a vast network of "friends" or followers both known and unknown on Facebook, LinkedIn, and other social media, real harm could result. Research shows that more than half of employers surveyed screen applicants' social media profiles when making hiring decisions, and 41% of these employers found objectionable material (e.g., provocative photos,

Twitter and other social media provide plentiful opportunities for indiscriminate and inappropriate self-disclosure. Be cautious when using social media.

revelations about drinking and drug use, or criticism of bosses or coworkers) on social media sites that resulted in rejection of the applicant (Grasz, 2015a). Another study revealed that individuals with low self-esteem found Facebook to be an appealing venue for self-disclosure, but the nature of their disclosures tended to be heavily negative (they didn't feel good about themselves), producing undesirable and even hurtful responses from others (Forest & Wood, 2012).

Several characteristics act as guidelines for appropriate self-disclosure. These include *trust, reciprocity, cultural appropriateness, situational appropriateness*, and *incremental disclosure*.

Trust: Can You Keep a Secret? When you self-disclose to another person, you risk being hurt or damaged by that person. Some of the risks involved with self-disclosure are indifference, rejection, loss of control, and betrayal. Disclosures we make to others may be used against us. Sometimes people betray our trust and reveal our secrets disclosed in confidence. Trusting another person to honor your feelings and to refrain from divulging the disclosure to anyone unless given permission says, "I value our relationship, and I trust that you will not hurt me."

Reciprocity: Two-Way Sharing Reciprocal, or mutual, self-disclosure demonstrates that trust and risk-taking are shared (Omarzu, 2000). If one person discloses but the other does not, the first person should be wary of further disclosures until reasons for the one-way self-disclosure become apparent. Perhaps the other

person is merely reticent and needs encouragement. Whatever the reason, however, one-way self-disclosure leaves you vulnerable and the other person protected, and that asymmetry can spell trouble. Therapy, of course, is one exception. Counselors need to hear about you; they don't need to self-disclose in return. Individuals also reveal intimate details about their sex lives to doctors who monitor sexually transmitted diseases, but they don't expect their doctor to reciprocate.

Cultural Appropriateness: Openness Is Not Universally Valued Appropriate self-disclosure in one culture may not be appropriate in another. Although self-disclosure is generally valued and encouraged in the United States, the Japanese and Chinese cultures, for example, exhibit greater hesitance to self-disclose because of concerns that it might be detrimental to the effectiveness of communication transactions (Xiao & Chen, 2009). Reasons for cultural differences in self-disclosure will be discussed in the next chapter.

<u>**Situational Appropriateness:**</u> **Considering Context** Public settings and private information are a poor fit. A public speech before a large audience is an awkward, uncomfortable setting for self-disclosure, as several political campaigns have demonstrated. The classroom also usually doesn't lend itself well to intimate self-disclosure.

A colleague of mine told of a surprising incident in her public speaking class that illustrates the importance of situational appropriateness. Students were assigned a four-minute speech in which they were to describe some event that had altered their lives in an important way. My colleague expected to hear speeches about trips taken abroad, geographic relocations, the college experience, and so forth. She did hear this—and more. A female student in her 30s began her speech by informing the class that she had never achieved sexual fulfillment until the previous weekend. She then proceeded to explain in awkward detail to her astonished classmates exactly what it was like. Such revelations might be appropriate in a professional counselor-client relationship whose purpose is to explore intimate issues in a comfortable setting. Such intimate self-disclosure might even be appropriate with certain close friends, but

Where Do You Draw the Line?

Consider each of the following opportunities for self-disclosure. Indicate whether you view each option for self-disclosure as appropriate or inappropriate for you.

1. Tell a friend what your favorite movie is.

2. Inform your parents that you've run out of money.

3. Indicate how much you earn annually to a stranger on a bus.

4. Tell your college class that you didn't vote in the last election.

5. Reveal to a friend of the opposite sex that you viewed a pornographic website.

6. Text message a friend that you have a crush on a teacher.

7. Identify on your Facebook page what you really dislike about one of your parents.

8. Tell a person you are very attracted to that you wish he or she were dating you and not your roommate.

9. Tell a classmate whom you barely know that you had a dream about him or her.

10. Reveal to the class what your GPA is.

There are no "right" answers, but this self-disclosure test should pose some issues for you: Do some revelations cross a line and become inappropriate? How do you decide what is appropriate to disclose and what is inappropriate? Identify the rules that you use to make such decisions. Does the means used to self-disclose (e.g., social network site, cell phone, or face-to-face) matter? Explain. If you considered all the situations listed as appropriate, what would you not reveal and to whom? Why?

Incremental Disclosure: Bit by Bit Overly zealous self-disclosure in which, for instance, you blurt out your whole life story in one sitting may overwhelm listeners and send them running to the nearest exit. This also may provoke a reflected appraisal: "You're creepy." Test the waters. Gradually disclose personal information to another person, and see whether it is reciprocated. There is no urgency required. A person usually needs to get to know someone before a proper perspective can be given to intimate revelations about self. "I've always hated guys like you" or "Women make me nervous" probably aren't very good openers. Once you get to know the person, these disclosures may seem funny. Initially, however, they might end the conversation and any potential for a relationship.

Most conversations concentrate on commonplace topics. Self-disclosure is important, especially during the initial stages of a relationship, but it isn't the principal focus of people's lives. There is only so much to disclose, and then your partner has heard it all. Even couples in intimate relationships spend relatively little time divulging personal information to each other (Duck, 1991).

Perception of Others

Perceptions of self influence our communication, but so do our perceptions of others. In this section, the impact our perceptions of others can have on our communication is explained. First impressions of others, attribution error, and the harm of stereotyping are discussed.

First Impressions: You Never Get a Second Chance

Speed dating is reducing the date-selection process to a quick first impression. In a few minutes, two strangers meet, conduct a quick conversation, and then check a box on a short form indicating interest in that person. If both parties check the box, the couple is notified within 24 hours, and email addresses are provided. Participants move from person to person, conducting instant interviews and potentially widening their dating pool. Malcolm Gladwell

not in front of relative strangers in a classroom where the main purpose is to hone public speaking skills. She needed to consider her audience and the obvious embarrassment she caused her listeners (see Box 2-3).

(2005) observed one such speed-dating event and heard a woman announce that she liked none of the dozen men she interviewed, remarking, "They lost me at hello" (p. 63).

Studies in which an image of an object or a face is flashed for an instant show that these images are evaluated as good or bad in as little as a *tenth of a second*, too quickly to think consciously about them (Olivola & Todorov, 2010; Willis & Todorov, 2006). This means *you cannot avoid virtually instantaneous impressions of others.* The human brain appears to be hardwired to make blink-of-the-eye judgments, probably because there is survival value in such quick determinations: "Which category do you fit, friend or foe?" (Krebs & Denton, 1997).

PRIMACY EFFECT: POWER OF FIRST IMPRESSIONS

First impressions can be lasting ones (Horan, 2012). If an initial positive impression is formed during a job interview, for example, that impression can act as a filter to excuse later revelations of potential concern ("Apparently, you learned from that disappointing failure") (Dougherty et al., 1994). College roommates who form positive first impressions of each other are likely to maintain positive relationships, manage their conflicts competently, and continue as roommates. Negative first impressions produce the opposite result (Marek et al., 2004).

Some first impressions can closely match impressions formed over lengthy periods of time (Gaschler, 2005). For example, participants in one study were shown three 10-second slices of Harvard University graduate students teaching undergraduates. These brief snippets ("thin slices") were sufficient for participants to match very closely the ratings given by students who observed these teachers for an entire semester (Ambady & Rosenthal, 1992, 1993). Even thinner slices—three 2-second clips—still produced only slightly less comparable ratings.

Although you cannot inhibit instant impressions of others because your brain makes them in a tenth of a second, you do not have to adhere steadfastly to the bias of the **primacy effect—the tendency to be more influenced by initial information about a person than by information gathered later.** Once aware of the primacy effect

Speed dating magnifies the expression "You never get a second chance to make a first impression."

and the automatic nature of initial impressions, you can make an effort to slowly, deliberately, and consciously consider more than the initial information about another person. This is especially true when people anticipate being held accountable for their impressions of others; they do not want to look foolish when they are asked to justify their judgments (Lerner & Tetlock, 1999).

ACCURACY OF FIRST IMPRESSIONS: IT DEPENDS

First impressions can be remarkably accurate in certain circumstances (Borkenau et al., 2004; Gaschler, 2005). A few minutes of thoughtful observations (type of clothes, hairstyle, speaking ability) and face-to-face conversation can lead to relatively accurate perceptions of others. Research shows that when a person reads for as little as three minutes out loud, mostly accurate perceptions of a person's intelligence can be discerned (Gaschler, 2005). Personality (openness and extroversion) and verbal skills also are quickly ascertained. A clean and tidy student apartment, for example, can quickly and accurately indicate that your roommate is a disciplined and dependable person. Quick glances and gut feelings, however, are not so accurate.

Thin slicing works fairly well on simple, broad impressions, but it is problematic on complex impressions. For example, the short, face-to-face job interview is a favorite method for hiring employees in institutions and organizations. Job interviews, however, usually require an assessment of more than one ability or attribute. You're not likely to deduce from a first impression whether an individual has integrity, conflict-management skills, and a strong work ethic. A thin slice of observed behavior, or even a half-hour face-to-face interview, is a less precise predictor of *job performance* than tests of job knowledge, peer ratings of prior job performance, aptitude tests, and samples of a candidate's work in previous positions (Kaplowitz, 1986; Schmidt & Hunter, 1998).

NEGATIVITY BIAS: AGILE, FUNNY, COMPASSIONATE, AND FAT

Broad first impressions can be quite accurate, but complex impressions are not so accurate. One factor that makes accuracy of first impressions sketchy is the **negativity bias**—our strong tendency to be influenced more heavily by negative than by positive information (Kiken & Shook, 2011). If I described someone to you as "outgoing, casual, fun-loving, articulate, and manipulative," would you want to be friends with that person? Would the single negative quality cause you to pause despite the four very positive qualities? Conversely, if I described someone as "abrasive, rude, domineering, closed-minded, and fun-loving," would the one positive quality even make a dent in the negative initial impression created by the first four qualities? Would you even want to meet such a person?

This negativity bias is actually built into your brain. As comedian Stephen Colbert once observed, "Mother Nature is on your side, keeping fear alive." Your amygdala, "the alarm bell of your brain," uses about two-thirds of its neurons to search for bad news. Why? Because negative information is potentially threatening to human well-being but positive information is merely pleasant, with little likely risk to human survival (Hanson, 2010). Even though most negative information ("You are fat") isn't an immediate threat to a person's survival, your brain doesn't make that nuanced assessment. Hesitation when faced with a real threat could prove fatal. It's best to be immediately on guard.

The negativity bias can be particularly strong during job interviews (Dougherty et al., 1994). In fact, negative information, especially if it is received early in the interview, is likely to lead to a candidate's rejection even when the total quantity of information about the candidate is overwhelmingly positive. In a hyper-competitive job market where differences in quality between candidates can be hard to discern, one poorly chosen phrase or inappropriate remark during an interview can negate a dozen very positive letters of recommendation. Sometimes the negative information, however, should outweigh the positive. Your roommate could have an abundance of positive attributes but also have a violent temper that risks your personal welfare.

The negativity bias can be overridden in much the same way as the primacy effect. Presenting an abundance of positive information that contradicts the negative can overcome negativity bias (Smith et al., 2006). Also, being mindful of the negativity bias can reduce it and increase positive judgments (Kiken & Shook, 2011).

A first impression can encourage further transactions with others when it is positive, and it can prevent any further contact with a person when the impression is negative. You never get to make a second first impression, so you want to begin on a positive note.

Attribution Error: Not So Kind to Others

There is a tendency to judge others more harshly than we judge ourselves. We have a strong tendency to commit the **fundamental attribution error**—overemphasizing personal traits and underemphasizing situations as causes of other people's behavior (Sherman, 2014). When you encounter panhandlers on the street begging for money, do you attribute bad luck as the cause of their plight, or do you attribute weak character or laziness? Recall the self-serving bias. Notice how kindly we interpret our own behavior, but how harshly we interpret the behavior of others. Our tendency is to find fault with others for bad behavior, but to find excuses for our own failings.

Marriage partners can experience difficulties because of attribution error. Partners are inclined to attribute relationship problems to personal traits rather than to situational forces

(Bradbury & Fincham, 1990; Gordon, 2012). A wife might complain that her husband does not help out sufficiently with the housework, leaves his clothes on the floor, and doesn't listen or pay attention to her. She then claims that her husband is lazy, sloppy, and uncaring, which are all personal traits. Her husband, however, is likely to assign situational causes, such as stress at work, exhaustion, or other factors beyond his control. If his wife is unmoved by such interpretations, he is likely to attribute her anger and frustration to "moodiness" or "irritability," also personal characteristics.

Attribution patterns of communication can indicate whether couples have a happy or an unhappy relationship (Gordon, 2012). Individuals in happy relationships, for instance, typically explain the nice behaviors of their partners as personal traits: "She did the grocery shopping after work because she is a caring, giving person." Negative behaviors are explained in situational terms: "He snapped at me because he's under a great deal of pressure." Individuals in unhappy relationships typically exhibit the reverse attribution pattern. Positive behavior is explained in situational terms: "She picked up my clothes at the laundry because she had nothing better to do with her time." Negative behaviors are explained in dispositional terms: "He was irritable with me because he is a very impatient person." Attribution patterns of communication do not automatically produce happy or unhappy relationships, but "the evidence supports the existence of a causal link between attributions . . . and relationship satisfaction" (Fletcher & Fincham, 1991, p. 14). *Attribution error can kill a relationship.* Conversely, preferring to see your partner's negative behavior as caused by bad situations, and his or her positive behavior as a reflection of strength of character, can reinforce a sense of happiness in a relationship (Fincham et al., 2000; Gordon, 2012).

It's not that traits are never the cause of bad behavior. Sometimes individuals just seem mean and disagreeable no matter what the circumstances. Attribution error, however, denies a person reasonable doubt. We begin by assuming character flaws explain antisocial communication patterns without adequately considering the influence of situational forces.

Stereotyping Others: The Dangers

This section discusses stereotyping and the role it can play in producing negative consequences. How to combat harmful stereotyping is also addressed.

UNINTENDED PREJUDICE: INSTANT DECISION MAKING

Stereotyping is natural and unavoidable. It permits rapid judgments when instant decisions are required ("Is this a Good Samaritan or a dangerous person?"), but it also can lead to serious mistakes (Jonas & Sassenberg, 2006). One study that used a video game simulation had African American and white participants make quick decisions to fire at armed targets and to withhold fire when targets were unarmed. Stereotypes of African Americans as "violent" triggered significantly greater errors (firing at unarmed targets) when the targets were African American than when they were white. Both African American and white participants made about the same number of errors, so mere knowledge of the stereotype may be sufficient to trigger errors (Correll et al., 2002). This could be one explanation for the spate of incidences where police officers, both white and black, have shot young, unarmed African American males. In one analysis, African Americans who were shot by police (and who were overwhelmingly male) were twice as likely to be unarmed as whites who were shot (Swaine et al., 2015). Stereotyping can be so automatic that a person's conscious intent or disagreement with the stereotype can be irrelevant (Devine, 1989).

BENEVOLENT SEXISM: THE FACADE OF POSITIVE STEREOTYPING

Benevolent sexism is a subtle form of discrimination that embraces the "positive" stereotype of women as "pure creatures" who deserve to be protected and shown affection, but only as long as they behave in the conventional manner (Tannenbaum, 2013). There are benefits to being protected, adored, and provided for, but people who have this view are likely to resist women's efforts to pursue education, careers, business opportunities, and full participation in the

A man knitting during a public meeting; "Only 4% of knitters are men" (Penn & Zalesne, 2007).

This photo illustrates which of the following?

○ **1.** Some stereotypes are mostly true

○ **2.** Stereotypes are negative generalizations about a group

○ **3.** Stereotypes don't allow for individual differences among group members

○ **4.** Stereotypes are always inaccurate depictions of members of groups

Answers at end of chapter

political life of the nation (Glick & Fiske, 2001). Challenging benevolent sexism would likely result in loss of benefits and could provoke **hostile sexism**—"antipathy toward women who are viewed as usurping men's power" (Glick & Fiske, 2001, p. 109). The seemingly positive stereotypes of women are not without their downside.

Men from diverse cultures tend to endorse benevolent sexism, and *women also tend to endorse it* (Glick & Fiske, 2001; Glick et al., 2004). Relinquishing the benefits is not always so easy, and it may appear that men are just being nice, not sexist. By rewarding women for maintaining a patriarchal, "chivalrous" status quo, however, benevolent sexism impedes gender equality (Becker & Wright, 2011). Men can treat women well without making the benevolence a reward for women who "know their place."

SELF-FULFILLING PROPHECIES: CREATING NEGATIVE CONSEQUENCES

Stereotyping can create a **self-fulfilling prophecy**—an erroneous expectation that produces an action that in turn causes the expected behavior and confirms the original impression. Hundreds of studies in a wide variety of circumstances and settings demonstrate the power of self-fulfilling prophecies (McNatt, 2000).

Self-fulfilling prophecies make inaccurate stereotypes appear valid (Snyder, 2001). If you expect an Asian student to be very quiet in group discussions (stereotype), you may ignore him or her whenever an attempt is made to contribute. When the student gives up trying to be heard by the group, the expectation is confirmed, even though this particular student may not typically be quiet in groups (individual difference). Those individuals who most expect to be negatively stereotyped tend to avoid opportunities that could counter prejudicial stereotypes (Pinel, 1999). Women who expect stigmatizing stereotypes, for example, behave more critically toward men who they expect to be sexist. Not surprisingly, such reactions to expected stereotypes trigger negative responses from men, making them appear sexist (Pinel, 2002).

COMBATING STEREOTYPES: COMMUNICATION SOLUTIONS

There are communication strategies that can combat negative stereotypes. First, confront the stereotypes head-on. Three studies show that both a hostile confrontation that accuses another person of being racist and a calm appeal for fairness ("They don't get equal treatment in our society") significantly reduce negative stereotyping and prejudiced attitudes (Czopp et al., 2006). Hostile confrontations, however, produce greater anger and irritation toward the confronter by those who are confronted than the less threatening appeal to fairness.

Second, **contact theory** predicts that interacting and becoming more familiar with members of stereotyped groups can diminish prejudice (negative attitude) and discrimination (behavior that manifests prejudice) resulting from stereotyping (Hodson, 2011). An analysis of 515 studies supports the general wisdom of this theory (Pettigrew & Tropp, 2006). Interacting works best under certain conditions: (1) contacts are more than just superficial, (2) status differences among group members are de-emphasized, (3) contact occurs between relative equals (e.g., skill and education levels), and (4) groups pursue a common, valued goal, preferably a **superordinate goal**—one that requires mutual effort by both groups to achieve a desired end (Pettigrew & Tropp, 2006).

Communication Competence and Perceptual Challenges

This final section explains competent communication strategies that overlap more than one perceptual problem or issue. These strategies will help you connect the discussion about perception of both self and others to an interrelated whole.

Monitor Perceptual Biases

Self-serving bias and attribution errors need to be carefully monitored. If you see yourself rationalizing your mistakes and taking credit for successes that may be more luck and good fortune than personal achievement, recognize your self-serving bias.

Resist attributing personal characteristics to the negative behaviors of others and situational causes to the positive behaviors of others. Practice the reverse. Try explaining the communication behaviors of your partner, coworker, friend, or relative that irritate or anger you with a situational attribution. Try explaining communication behaviors that please you with a personal characteristic attribution.

Recognize Cultural Differences

There is a cultural component to our self-appraisals. A common question during most job interviews in the United States is "Why should we hire you?" You are asked to promote yourself for the position. You are, after all, competing against other candidates, and the hiring committee is presumably looking for the best person.

In contrast, Asian cultures encourage the denial of self-importance. Reticence, not self-assertion, is valued. Promoting yourself is considered boastful. Your possible contribution to the group is important, as is your likely conformity to the norms of the group or organization (Brislin, 1993). Consequently, the self-serving bias is found far more in American culture than in Asian cultures (Anderson, 1999). Attribution error also occurs more often in American culture than in Asian cultures. (Na & Kitayama, 2011).

Manage Impressions

Create the impression you wish others to perceive. Of the many aspects of self, consider which you want to emphasize in a given situation. In a job interview, would you display your articulateness, friendliness, sense of humor, and dynamism, or would you display your irritability, cynicism, sarcasm, and interpersonal remoteness? These all may be aspects of your self-concept, but you can choose to display some aspects in a given situation and keep other aspects of yourself private. This is especially important given the power of the negativity bias.

This is not meant to encourage phoniness or dishonesty, only communication flexibility. When you are interviewed for a job, you make choices regarding which aspects of your self-image you wish to display. You put forward your best self to create a positive impression. This is not dishonest. It is adapting to the expectations of your audience. Communication is situational. We don't show the same self to strangers as we do to intimate partners—at least we don't if we know what's good for us.

Practice Empathy

You can counter attribution errors by practicing empathy, which has three dimensions (Goleman, 2013). The first is cognitive empathy, or *perspective taking*. Here you try to see as others see, to perceive as they perceive. You try on the viewpoint of another to gain understanding of his or her perspective. You don't have to accept the viewpoint of another to be empathic, just understand it. A second dimension is emotional empathy, or *emotional understanding*.

You participate in the feelings of others, experiencing their joy, anxiety, frustration, irritation, and so forth. The last dimension of empathy is compassionate empathy, or *concern for others*. You care what happens to others. When you view the behavior of others from their perspective, try to feel as they might feel given a specific situation. When you care what happens to others, attribution error is difficult to maintain.

Check Perceptions

Perhaps the most obvious, yet most often ignored, method for dealing with perceptual biases and distortions is **perception checking**. That is, we should not assume our perceptions of others are accurate without checking to see whether they are. The perceptual process of selecting, organizing, and interpreting is inherently subjective and prone to biases. Assuming that another person is angry, for example, can lead to misunderstanding.

Statements such as "You're so irritable" and "I know you're bored, but try to look interested" may assume facts not in evidence.

An effective perception check usually has three steps:

1. A behavior description
2. An interpretation of the behavior
3. A request for verification of the interpretation

Consider this example: "I noticed that you left the room before I was finished speaking (behavior description). You seemed offended by what I said (interpretation). Were you offended (request for verification)?" All three steps are present in this perception check. Sometimes an effective perception check is more abbreviated: "You looked very angry. Were you?" Here the behavior description is implied along with the interpretation, and the verification request follows.

Summary

Perception is the process of selecting, organizing, and interpreting data from our senses. This is an inherently subjective process with much potential for error both in the perception of self and the perception of others. Our self-concept and self-esteem are protected by the self-serving bias. Our perception of others is biased by the primacy effect, negativity bias, attribution error, and stereotyping. Our perception of self and others is a fundamental starting point of human communication. We reveal who we are to others by self-disclosing. To be a competent communicator, monitor your perceptual biases, recognize cultural differences, manage the impressions you make with others, practice empathy, and check your perceptions with others.

Answers for Critical Thinking captions:

ZITS (P. 38): #1

MAN KNITTING (P. 50): #1 and #3

Quizzes Without Consequences

Test your knowledge before your exam! Go to the companion website at www.oup.com/us/rothwell, click on the Student Resources for each chapter, and take the Quizzes Without Consequences.

Film School Case Studies

Before Sunset (2004). Romantic Drama; R
In this wonderful sequel to *Before Sunrise*, a tale of a young man and woman who meet by chance on a train traveling through Austria and share an intimate but brief romance, the two meet for a few hours in Paris nine years later. Explore the process of self-disclosure. Why do they hesitate to reveal feelings and experiences? What are the risks of opening up and the potential drawbacks of resisting self-disclosure?

Bridget Jones's Diary (2001).
Romantic Comedy; R

The somewhat underrated story of Bridget Jones (Renée Zellweger) and her battle with self-esteem issues. Analyze what influences her self-esteem most by applying concepts of reflected appraisal, contingencies of self-worth, and social comparison.

Brokeback Mountain (2005). Drama; R

Ennis Del Mar (Heath Ledger) and Jack Twist (Jake Gyllenhaal) tend sheep on Montana's Brokeback Mountain. They become friends and eventually lovers, keeping the secret from their wives and children. Examine how self-concept and self-disclosure interconnect. How do the two characters engage in impression management?

Catch Me If You Can (2002). Drama; PG-13

Leonardo DiCaprio plays a character who assumes several false identities and cons his way through life earning riches, respect, and admiration from others. In the process, however, he loses his own sense of identity. Analyze the cost of failure to self-disclose to others, to reveal one's true identity. Who pays the price?

City Island (2009). Comedy/Drama; PG-13

Andy Garcia is a prison guard who secretly wants to be an actor. In fact, just about everyone in the Rizzo family is keeping secrets. Examine this movie from the perspective of self-disclosure—when to open up and when to shut up.

Crash (2004). Drama; R

This intercultural clash of ethnicities provides gripping entertainment and poignant moments. Analyze the movie from the perspective of stereotypes.

I, Robot (2004). Drama; PG-13

Will Smith plays a suspicious cop of the future who does not trust the robot society being created to serve humankind. Analyze the many questions raised regarding what constitutes self-concept and personal identity.

McFarland, USA (2015). Drama/Sport; PG

A cross-country coach (Kevin Costner) in a small, poverty-stricken town composed mostly of Mexican residents transforms a rag-tag group of athletes into a state champion team. Analyze the stereotypes that are plentiful in this sweet movie. Consider contact theory. What influences the self-concepts and self-esteem of the athletes? How do cultural values play a part?

Precious (2009). Drama; R

Gabourey Sidibe plays Claireece "Precious" Jones, who is surrounded by abusive people. Analyze what parts reflected appraisal, social comparison, and contingencies of self-worth play in the formation and tenacity of her self-concept and self-esteem.

SMALL FACES

SMALL FACES

BY THE END OF THIS CHAPTER, YOU SHOULD BE ABLE TO:

1. Recognize the deep structural value differences among cultures that strongly affect communication.

2. Identify communication challenges and problems resulting from ethnocentrism, misunderstanding, and miscommunication.

3. Understand ways to address these cultural challenges.

Culture and Gender

SHOULD WOMEN BE ACCORDED equal rights with men?
Gender equality is a matter of cultural perspective. A Pew
Research Center study found that a majority in most cultures
surveyed believed, at least in the abstract, that there should
be gender equality ("Gender Equality," 2010). Between 97% and
99% of respondents in the United States, Britain, France,
Germany, and Spain supported gender equality. Indonesia
(64%), Jordan (61%), Egypt (60%), and Nigeria (45%) were far
less supportive. There was also a strong caveat: "When jobs
are scarce, should men have more right to a job than women?"
A vast majority of respondents from almost half of the cultures answered yes (e.g., Turkey [67%], China [73%], India
[84%], Indonesia [74%], Pakistan [82%], and Nigeria [77%]). Only
14% of U.S. respondents answered yes. When asked whether it
"is more important for a boy than for a girl" to receive a university education, most countries strongly disagreed with a
preference for educating males. The two most populous

4. Evaluate to what degree gender differences in communication exist.

5. Recognize the value of several perspectives that explain gender differences, large and small, in communication.

6. Choose effective and appropriate communication strategies to address gender differences in communication.

countries in the world, however, were not so supportive of providing a college education for women (48% of respondents in China preferred educating males and 63% in India).

As the results of this survey suggest, gender and culture are inextricably intertwined. **Gender** is "the cultural construction of beliefs and behaviors considered appropriate for each sex" (Lavenda & Schultz, 2015, p.11). The interconnectedness of culture and gender has important implications for communication. "Gender, culture, and communication are interlinked . . . What gender means depends heavily on cultural values and practices; a culture's definitions of masculinity and femininity shape expectations about how individual women and men should communicate" (Wood, 2014, p. 20). These gender role expectations vary across cultures from highly constraining to barely noticeable.

The principal purpose of this chapter is to explain how you can competently address the challenges of intercultural and gender differences in communication. Culture is discussed before gender because culture provides the broader context for gender similarities and differences in communication and permits a richer analysis.

Culture and Communication

You don't have to travel far to experience the challenges of cross-cultural transactions. Intercultural opportunities within the United States are wide and varied.

Intercultural Opportunities: It's a New World

Recent, vast demographic changes mean that the ever-mobile U.S. population is constantly exposed to diverse cultures and ethnicities. According to the U.S. Census, minorities comprised 35% of the population in the United States and 46% of children under 15 years old in 2010. By 2044, however, Latinos and Mexican Americans, African Americans, and Asian Americans will collectively constitute the majority of the population in the United States (Frey, 2014). The Census Bureau also notes that by 2018 the "minority population" of those age 18 and younger will become a numerical majority for that age group (Cordero-Guzman, 2014). International student enrollment in U.S. colleges and universities rose to an all-time high of almost 900,000 in 2014 (Witherall & Clayton, 2014). About 300,000 students from the United States study in other countries each year ("Trends in U.S. Study Abroad," 2015). Almost 60% of students in one survey said that they had dated someone from a different cultural group (Farrell, 2005). Despite some residual resistance to interracial dating and marriage in the United States, about 8% of marriages are mixed race (Yen, 2010). This doesn't include couples that are cohabiting. More than 90% of Americans aged 18 to 29 years approve of interracial dating, although these numbers drop significantly with older Americans (Burnley, 2015).

The development of electronic technologies has expanded opportunities for intercultural communication beyond anything our world has ever experienced. Where once a person had to travel for hours by plane or pay the prohibitive cost of international phone calls, the Internet and satellite transmission have made transactions with members of diverse cultures highly accessible. Online virtual groups allow members from diverse cultures to transcend time and space. Group members may represent many cultures and live in widely separate time zones. Electronic technologies have also expanded the opportunities for intercultural misunderstandings because, as you'll see, cultural values impact our communication with others (Hofstede & Hofstede, 2010).

Inescapable intercultural communication tells us why we need to know how to communicate competently with others from diverse cultural backgrounds. It doesn't explain why intercultural miscommunication occurs, however. Before discussing this, a few critical terms need defining. **Culture** is a learned set of enduring values, beliefs, and practices that are shared by an identifiable, large group of people with a common history. **Values** are the most deeply felt, generally shared view of what is deemed good, right, or worthwhile thinking or behavior. Values constitute a shared conception, not of what is, but of what ought to be. **Beliefs** are what a person thinks is true or probable. Two individuals may *value* human life, but one may *believe* that capital punishment preserves life by deterring homicides while the other may believe the contrary. Finally, a **co-culture** is any group that is part of a dominant culture yet often has a common history and shares some differences in values, beliefs, and practices from the dominant culture (Samovar et al., 2012). African Americans, Asian Americans, Native Americans, and Mexican Americans are some obvious examples of co-cultures within the United States, but the term can be applied even more broadly to the LGBT community, Jewish Americans, Muslim Americans, and even biker gangs.

Cultural Values: Deep, Not Surface, Differences

There can be hundreds of commonplace differences among cultures, from the utensils used for eating to forms of greeting and types of toilets available (some shockingly different from what Americans expect). The common practice of tipping after a meal at a restaurant is not universally accepted or appreciated. In cultures such as China, Japan, South Korea, New Zealand, and Costa Rica, there is no tipping, and Americans who do are perceived to be disrespectful. You're communicating the insulting message that the waitperson must be bribed to provide decent service. Tipping in Egypt, however, is tricky business. Most public restrooms are staffed by attendants, and especially at tourists sites, some attendants dole out toilet paper based on the size of the tip ("Tipping," 2015).

These practices are visible *surface differences* among cultures, and they can change, sometimes swiftly. Consider the vast changes that have occurred in virtually every culture on Earth with the advent of the Internet and numerous other communication technologies. You can observe members of the Bedouin tribe communicating by cell phone or rural Chinese farmers with satellite dishes mounted on rustic farmhouses. Email, text messaging, and Twitter have swept across the world with blinding speed.

Co-cultures are plentiful in the United States, as is seen here in San Francisco's Chinatown.

The rapid global changes in communication, as illustrated by these Masai tribesmen embracing electronic communication technology, underline how quickly surface differences among cultures can change.

Bedrock core values of a culture, however, are highly stable and resistant to change (Hofstede, 2012; Hofstede & Hofstede, 2010). What we "ought to do" becomes the hardened cement of our culture. It can be changed, but about as easily as jackhammering concrete. Perhaps this is because "cultural values and experiences shape neurocognitive processes," or put another way, "culture wires the brain" (Park & Huang, 2010). We see the world differently in part because culture has shaped the neural networks in our brains to perceive the world differently. **Value dimensions**—varying degrees of importance placed on those deeply felt views of what is right, good, and worthwhile— are the *deep structural reasons* why many cultural differences that provoke serious miscommunication and intense conflict exist.

Geert Hofstede conducted the largest cross-cultural survey ever attempted, eventually encompassing 50 countries and 3 geographic areas, to identify significant value dimensions that distinguish cultures from each other (Hofstede & Hofstede, 2010). Several value dimensions emerged from this abundance of data. Two have received considerable attention and substantial additional supporting research (Hofstede, 2012; see also Hofstede & Hofstede, 2010, for a summary). These two value dimensions are *individualism-collectivism* and *power-distance*.

INDIVIDUALISM-COLLECTIVISM: PRIME VALUE DIFFERENCE

The **individualism-collectivism dimension** is thought to be the most important of all value dimensions that distinguish cultures (Hui & Triandis, 1986). It clearly has received the most voluminous supportive research and interest (Oyserman & Uskul, 2008; Schimmack et al., 2005).

General Description: The Me-We Dimension An **individualist culture** has a "me" consciousness. Individuals see themselves as loosely linked to each other and largely independent of group identification (Hofstede & Hofstede, 2010; Triandis, 1995). They are chiefly motivated by their own preferences, needs, and goals. Personal achievement and initiative are stressed. Emphasis is placed on the self: self-help, self-sufficiency, self-actualization, self-disclosure, and personal growth. People communicate as individuals and

pay little heed to a person's group memberships. Decision making is based on what is best for the individual, sometimes even if this sacrifices the group's welfare. Words such as *independence, self, privacy,* and *rights* permeate cultural conversations. "I gotta be me; I gotta be free" is the anthem of the individualist. Finally, individualist cultures are characterized by an emphasis on a rational assessment of the benefits and drawbacks of relationships. Those that are perceived to be, on balance, disadvantageous are typically severed.

A **collectivist culture** has a "we" consciousness. Individuals see themselves as closely linked to one or more groups. Commitment to valued groups (e.g., the family or an organization) is paramount (Hofstede & Hofstede, 2010). People take notice of a person's place in the hierarchy of a group. Individuals often downplay personal goals in favor of advancing the goals of a valued group. The Chinese proverb "No need to know the

Children from collectivist cultures, such as most Asian cultures, are typically taught "the nail that sticks up gets hammered down" and are encouraged to blend into the group. Children from individualist cultures, such as the United States, are typically taught "the squeaky wheel gets the grease" and are encouraged to stand out from the group by being overtly expressive.

person, only the family" and the African adage "It takes a village to raise a child" express the collectivist perception. Words such as *loyalty, responsibility,* and *community* permeate collectivist cultural conversations. The decision regarding whom to marry must involve the wishes and preferences of family members and other interested parties.

All cultures vary in their emphasis on individualism and collectivism, and no culture is entirely one way or the other. Hofstede, however, was able to rank cultures on the basis of the relative importance placed on individualist or collectivist values (see Figure 3-1). In general, North American, Western European, and European-influenced cultures such as Australia, New Zealand, and South Africa are individualist, with the United States ranking number one among them. East Asian, North African, and most Latin American cultures are collectivist. Approximately 70% of the world's population lives in collectivist cultures (Triandis, 1990; see also Hofstede & Hofstede, 2010). The individualism-collectivism dimension also applies to co-cultures. The Mexican American co-culture, for example, expresses its collectivism in proverbs: "Better to be a fool with the crowd than wise by oneself" and "He who divides and shares is left with the best share" (Zormeier & Samovar, 2000).

Deep value differences between individualist and collectivist cultures can be seen in several ways. First, 131 businesspeople, scholars, government officials, and professionals in eight East Asian countries and the United States were asked, "Which of the following are critically important to your people?" (Simons &

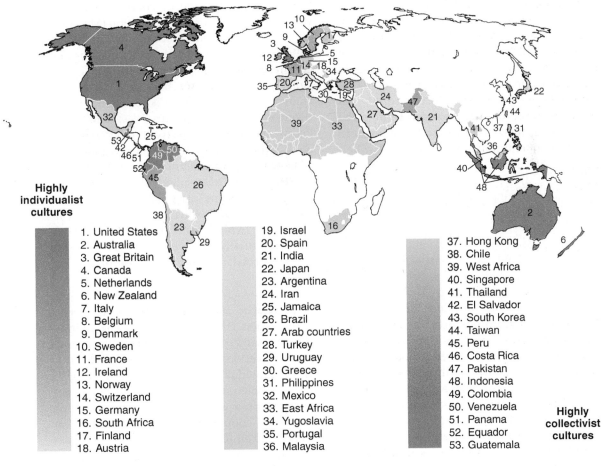

Highly individualist cultures

Highly collectivist cultures

1. United States
2. Australia
3. Great Britain
4. Canada
5. Netherlands
6. New Zealand
7. Italy
8. Belgium
9. Denmark
10. Sweden
11. France
12. Ireland
13. Norway
14. Switzerland
15. Germany
16. South Africa
17. Finland
18. Austria
19. Israel
20. Spain
21. India
22. Japan
23. Argentina
24. Iran
25. Jamaica
26. Brazil
27. Arab countries
28. Turkey
29. Uruguay
30. Greece
31. Philippines
32. Mexico
33. East Africa
34. Yugoslavia
35. Portugal
36. Malaysia
37. Hong Kong
38. Chile
39. West Africa
40. Singapore
41. Thailand
42. El Salvador
43. South Korea
44. Taiwan
45. Peru
46. Costa Rica
47. Pakistan
48. Indonesia
49. Colombia
50. Venezuela
51. Panama
52. Equador
53. Guatemala

FIGURE 3-1. Individualism-Collectivism Rankings for 50 Countries and 3 Regions. (Source: Based on rankings that appear in Hofstede & Hostede, 2010)

Zielenziger, 1996, p. A22). The results were as follows:

	Asians	Americans
1. An orderly society	70%	11%
2. Personal freedom	32%	82%
3. Individual rights	29%	73%

In line with these results, the 2011 U.S. Supreme Court decision *Snyder v. Phelps* starkly illustrates the deep structural (law) support given to individual rights, personal freedom, and less concern for an orderly society in the individualistic United States. A group of protesters from the Westboro Baptist Church demonstrated at hundreds of funerals for dead American soldiers killed in Iraq and Afghanistan. The demonstrators believed that God killed American soldiers as punishment for homosexuality and the nation's sinful policies. Picket signs were offensive slurs against gays and celebrations of dead soldiers. The demonstrations were peaceful but emotionally disruptive for mourners burying their dead sons and daughters. The group was sued for disrupting the funerals. Nevertheless, the Court ruled 8-1 that the Westboro protesters engaged in protected speech guaranteed by the First Amendment to the U.S. Constitution (Savage, 2011). A collectivist culture would likely arrest the demonstrators for disrupting the peace. Laws, rules, and historically ingrained practices reflect and support the deep structural value differences among cultures.

Second, deep value differences between individualist and collectivist cultures can be seen in attributions (causes) for behavior (dispositions/traits and situations; see Chapter 2). A tragic incident in November 1991 shows such differences in attributions between cultures. Gang Lu, who had recently received his doctorate in physics from the University of Iowa, methodically walked through two campus buildings shooting six people: the winner of a prestigious award that Lu felt he deserved, three physics professors, the associate vice president for academic affairs, and her receptionist. He killed five and then killed himself. *The New York Times* focused on dispositional causes of Lu's behavior ("very bad temper"; "deeply disturbed"; "psychological problems"). In stark contrast, reporters for the Chinese-language newspaper *World Journal* attributed Lu's behavior to situational causes ("isolated from the Chinese community"; "the availability of guns") (Morris & Peng, 1994). Collectivist cultural values with their focus on groups place greater emphasis on situational influences (Lu's isolation from the Chinese community), whereas individualist cultural values with their focus on individual uniqueness place greater emphasis on personal characteristics (Lu's psychological problems) (Mason & Morris, 2010). Clearly, people from individualist and collectivist cultures and co-cultures perceive the world in markedly different ways (Na & Kitayama, 2011).

People learn individualist or collectivist values from **socialization**—the communication of shared cultural practices, beliefs, and values from generation to generation (Maccoby, 1998). Socialization imbeds individualist or collectivist value systems into the marrow of a culture. Even so, *no culture's population is uniformly of one mind* (see Box 3-1). Within the United States, individualist tendencies are strongest in the Mountain West and Great Plains states, but collectivist tendencies are quite strong in the Deep South (Vandello & Cohen, 1999). An analysis of 35 studies involving thousands of respondents revealed that African Americans place significantly higher emphasis on individualism than European Americans (white participants), but that both are substantially more individualist than are collectivist Asian Americans (Oyserman et al., 2002).

Communication Differences: Self-Promotion Versus Group Support Differences in emphasis on individualism and collectivism create differences in communication. Useful communication skills in an individualist culture include getting to know people quickly, engaging easily in conversation on a wide variety of subjects, being interesting enough to make an impression on others, and employing public speaking skills in meetings (Samovar et al., 2010). Individualist cultures expect a person to initiate a job search and engage in personal promotion, called

BOX 3-1 DEVELOPING COMMUNICATION COMPETENCE

Be Ye Individualist or Collectivist?

How closely do you, personally, reflect individualist or collectivist values of your culture or co-culture? Consider the following statements, and using a scale from 1 (strongly disagree) to 9 (strongly agree), indicate your degree of disagreement or agreement with each statement.*

1. I prefer to be direct and forthright when I talk with people.
2. I would do what would please my family even if I detested that activity.
3. I enjoy being unique and different from others in many ways.
4. I usually sacrifice my self-interest for the benefit of my group.
5. I like my privacy.
6. Children should be taught to place duty before pleasure.
7. I like to demonstrate my abilities to others.
8. I hate to disagree with others in my group.
9. When I succeed, it is usually because of my abilities.
10. Before taking a major trip, I consult with most members of my family and many friends.

Total your score for all odd-numbered statements (1, 3, etc.), then total your score for even-numbered statements (2, 4, etc.). All *odd-numbered statements* reflect *individualism* and all *even-numbered statements* reflect *collectivism*. Which are you? Do you agree overall more with individualist statements (higher score on odd-numbered statements) than with collectivist statements (lower score on even-numbered statements)? If so, you reflect the prevailing individualist values of American culture. If not, can you explain why your values do not mirror those of mainstream U.S. culture? Are you influenced more by co-cultural influences? What communication challenges has this difference presented to you?

*For the entire 63-statement measuring instrument, see Triandis (1995).

self-enhancement (Ting-Toomey & Chung, 2012). You are expected to draw attention to your credentials, accomplishments, and special skills. You're largely on your own in social

Sideways glances, smiles, eye contact, brief touches, and a host of other nonverbal flirting cues can be acceptable in some cultures and extremely offensive in others.

interactions, and dating, flirting, and small talk play an important part in self-enhancement. In fact, receiving help from friends or family, such as getting set up with a blind date, can make you appear somewhat desperate and ineffectual. Selection of a mate is considered a personal choice. Parental approval is desirable but not necessary, and marriage will occur even in the face of parental disapproval.

Collectivist cultures do not require the same communication skills as individualist cultures. Self-enhancement is discouraged because it is competitive. Cooperative communication within valued groups is emphasized for its promotion of harmony and diminishment of conflict with others (see Box 3-2). Competitive self-enhancement can incite envy, jealousy, and friction within groups, and it is thought to divert energies away from the welfare of the group. Instead, **self-humbling**, which

BOX 3-2 FOCUS ON CONTROVERSY

Competition: Cultural Influence

In a highly competitive society such as the United States, it is easy to assume that intense competition is a natural part of being human. Seeing individuals from other cultures responding to competition in a way dramatically different from our own can help us understand the powerful influence of cultural values on exhibitions of competitive or cooperative behavior (Ehrlich, 2000). A story makes this point apparent:

> A newly trained teacher named Mary went to teach at a Navajo Indian reservation. Every day, she would ask five of the young Navajo students to go to the chalkboard and complete a simple math problem from their homework. They would stand there, silently, unwilling to complete the task. Mary couldn't figure it out . . .

> Finally, she asked the students what was wrong . . . It seemed that the students . . . knew that not all of them were capable of doing the problems . . . They believed no one would win if any students were shown up or embarrassed at the chalkboard. So they refused to compete with each other in public.

> Once she understood, Mary changed the system so that she could check each child's math problem individually, but not at any child's expense in front of classmates. They all wanted to learn—but not at someone else's expense. (Canfield et al., 1997, pp. 175–176)

In many cultures, the emphasis on being "the star" at someone else's expense is discouraged.

As Jules Henry (1963) explains, "To a Zuni, Hopi, or Dakota Indian, [besting another student] would seem cruel beyond belief, for competition, the wringing of success from somebody else's failure, is a form of torture" (p. 35).

Competitiveness is not an innate part of being human; it is socially constructed (de Waal, 2010). There is abundant evidence that American competitiveness is primarily a product of an individualist value system that is learned, not an evolutionary imperative common to all species (Chatman & Barsade, 1995; Maheshvarananda, 2012; Wright, 2000). Two studies compared people from cultures that vary widely on the individualism-collectivism dimension: Americans (extremely individualist) and Vietnamese (extremely collectivist). The first study showed that the Vietnamese "cooperated at an extraordinarily high rate." The Americans were inclined to be competitive. In the second study, Vietnamese subjects exhibited high rates of cooperation even when faced with competitive strategies from other participants. Americans showed far less cooperative and more competitive communication. The authors of these studies concluded: "The difference between the extremely individualistic and extremely collectivistic cultures was very large and consistent with cultural norms" (Parks & Vu, 1994, p. 712). When members of collectivist cultures perceive a threat from an outside group, however, they can be hypercompetitive in "protecting" their valued group (Ting-Toomey & Chung, 2012; Triandis, 2012).

Questions for Thought

1. Can you imagine a culture entirely free from competition? Would that be a desirable society? Could you avoid mass conformity in such a culture?

2. How might competitive and cooperative cultural environments affect the educational process? How might students address students and students address teachers?

3. How might you assess a group's comfort level with competitive transactions when you enter a new group? How would this assessment affect your communication behavior?

"emphasizes the importance of downplaying oneself via modest talk, restraint, hesitation and the use of self-deprecation message concerning one's performance and effort" (Ting-Toomey & Chung, 2012, p. 126), is encouraged. In exchange for loyalty to the group and contributions to the group's effectiveness, members of collectivist cultures receive help from influential members of the group or organization in finding jobs and making social contacts. Parents often arrange mate selection because family approval is important (Hofstede & Hofstede, 2010).

Edward Hall (1981) was the first to identify a specific difference in communication styles between individualist and collectivist cultures. *Individualist cultures typically use a low-context style, and collectivist cultures typically use a high-context style* (Ting-Toomey & Chung, 2012). The chief difference between the two styles is in verbal expression. A **low-context communication style** is verbally precise, direct, assertive, self-enhancing, and explicit. There is little assumption that others will be able to discern what you mean without precise verbal explanation. Self-expression and speaking ability are highly valued. Points of view are openly expressed, and persuasion is an accepted goal of speech (Ting-Toomey & Chung, 2012). "Say what you mean," "Tell me what you want," and "What's your point?" are statements that reflect a low-context communication style in individualist cultures. In collectivist cultures, however, the context, not the explicit message, is paramount. A **high-context communication style** uses indirect verbal expression. You are expected to "read between the lines." Significant information must be derived from contextual cues, such as the relationship, situation, setting, and time. Talk is tactful, diplomatic, and self-humbling (Ting-Toomey & Chung, 2012).

The contrast between the high- and low-context communication styles is aptly explained by a Japanese manager working in the United States: "When we say one word, we understand 10, but here you have to say 10 to understand one" (quoted in Kameda, 2003). For example, here is a seemingly confusing English message written by a Japanese manager: "Our office has moved to Kawasaki. I'm going to buy a Honda." To Americans, this likely seems to be two unrelated sentences. To the Japanese, however, the meaning is unmistakable: "Our office has moved to Kawasaki. It's too far from the station to walk, so I'll have to buy a car. I'm thinking of getting a Honda" (Kameda, 2003). "If you hear 'one' part of a message you are supposed to understand all the other unsaid 'nine' so that with 'one' part you must understand the whole 'ten' parts" (Kameda, 2007).

Harmony is highly regarded in collectivist cultures, and verbal messages tend to be vague to avoid causing offense. When a Japanese person says "maybe," it is a polite way of saying "no." "We will take that into consideration" also means "Sorry, but we have no interest" (Kameda, 2003). Imagine how American directness and in-your-face communication are perceived by cultures that value harmony between people. This can be very frustrating to Americans, who expect, with some exceptions (e.g., not "airing dirty laundry" in public), that everyone will speak openly and straightforwardly and who tend to view public agreement but private disagreement as deceptive or manipulative.

When cultural populations are quite similar, there is less need to be verbally explicit because there is historical understanding of the rules, roles, norms, and customary practices of the culture. Thus, *a high-context, implicit communication style is appropriate in collectivist cultures because they tend to have more homogeneous (similar) populations* (Samovar et al., 2010). Individualist cultures tend to have more heterogeneous (dissimilar) populations. With a culturally diverse population comes uncertainty. The rules, roles, norms, and customary practices are not immediately known by individuals from co-cultural backgrounds. There is a compelling need to be verbally explicit in individualist cultures to prevent misunderstanding and miscommunication. Thus, *a low-context, explicit communication style is appropriate in individualist cultures.*

POWER-DISTANCE: DOES BILL GATES DESERVE SPECIAL TREATMENT?

Cultures vary widely in their attitudes concerning the appropriateness of power imbalances. These variations in the *acceptability of unequal distribution of power* in relationships, institutions, and organizations are called the **power-distance dimension** (Hofstede & Hofstede, 2010). The extent to which members of a culture, both relatively powerful and powerless, *endorse* the society's overall level of inequality determines its place on the power-distance dimension (hereafter referred to as PD) (Hofstede, 2012).

General Description: Horizontal and Vertical Cultures
All cultures are **stratified**—divided into various levels of power that put distance between the haves and the have-nots. *The difference on the power-distance dimension lies in whether the culture tends to accept or reject stratification, even though it is a fact of life.* A **low PD culture**, or what

Triandis (2012) calls a *horizontal culture*, values relatively equal power sharing and discourages attention to status differences and ranking in society. Challenging authority, flattening organizational hierarchies to reduce status differences between management and employees, and using power legitimately are encouraged in a low-PD culture. Low-PD cultures do not expect power disparities to be eliminated. Nevertheless, in low-PD cultures such as the United States, Great Britain, Sweden, Denmark, Austria, Israel, and New Zealand (see Figure 3-2), norms that minimize power distinctions act as guides for appropriate behavior.

High PD cultures, or what Triandis (2012) calls *vertical cultures*, have a relatively strong

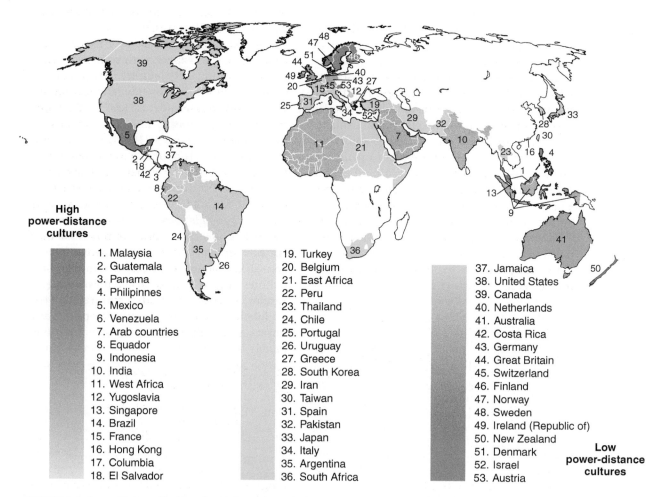

High power-distance cultures

1. Malaysia
2. Guatemala
3. Panama
4. Philipinnes
5. Mexico
6. Venezuela
7. Arab countries
8. Equador
9. Indonesia
10. India
11. West Africa
12. Yugoslavia
13. Singapore
14. Brazil
15. France
16. Hong Kong
17. Columbia
18. El Salvador

19. Turkey
20. Belgium
21. East Africa
22. Peru
23. Thailand
24. Chile
25. Portugal
26. Uruguay
27. Greece
28. South Korea
29. Iran
30. Taiwan
31. Spain
32. Pakistan
33. Japan
34. Italy
35. Argentina
36. South Africa

37. Jamaica
38. United States
39. Canada
40. Netherlands
41. Australia
42. Costa Rica
43. Germany
44. Great Britain
45. Switzerland
46. Finland
47. Norway
48. Sweden
49. Ireland (Republic of)
50. New Zealand
51. Denmark
52. Israel
53. Austria

Low power-distance cultures

FIGURE 3-2. Power-Distance Rankings for 50 Countries and 3 Regions (Source: Based on rankings that appear in Hofstede & Hofstede, 2010).

emphasis on maintaining power differences. The norms of cultures such as Malaysia, Guatemala, the Philippines, Mexico, India, Singapore, and Hong Kong encourage power distinctions (see Figure 3-2). Authorities are rarely challenged, the most powerful are thought to have a legitimate right to exercise their power, and organizational and social hierarchies are nurtured (Lustig & Koester, 2013). In Japan, for example, seeking a second opinion on a health issue is taboo; it is an affront to the primary care physician's expertise and power position (Ricks, 2000). In India, a massive 7.7-magnitude earthquake struck parts of the country on January 26, 2001, killing more than 20,000 people, injuring more than 165,000, and leaving about 1 million individuals homeless ("Historic Earthquakes," 2012). Yet the biggest impediment to the distribution of desperately needed aid to those afflicted wasn't the earthquake damage itself but India's traditional caste system—a social hierarchy, outlawed long ago but still strong in practice, with Brahmans at the top and "untouchables" at the bottom. As Catholic Relief Services worker Mayuri Mistry explained, "Whatever the distribution of aid, it first goes to the upper castes" (Coleman, 2001, p. 7A). Although the wealthy and privileged in America may, on occasion, receive preferential treatment, it is difficult to imagine a similar dispersal of emergency aid occurring in the United States during a natural disaster. Can you imagine the outcry that would ensue if such preferential treatment were to occur?

Communication Differences: With Whom May You Communicate? Communication in low-PD cultures reflects the minimization of power disparities. Workers may disagree with their supervisors; in fact, some bosses may encourage disagreement. Socializing outside the work environment and communication on a first-name basis between workers and bosses are not unusual. Students can question and disagree with their teachers. Some professors even encourage students to address them by their first names (Hofstede & Hofstede, 2010).

Communication in high-PD cultures reflects the desire to maintain power disparities.

Children raised in high-PD cultures are expected to obey their parents without question. Workers typically do not disagree with their bosses. Friendship between a worker and a boss would appear inappropriate. Students do not question or disagree with their teachers. Reticence to speak during class discussions unless asked to do so personally by the teacher underlines the acceptance of power disparities (Hofstede & Hofstede, 2010). The teacher is the expert. Students are in class to receive the wisdom of the instructor, not to challenge the more knowledgeable teacher or to show off their own knowledge (Samovar et al., 2010). Even a student admitting to a teacher that they "don't understand" something covered in a lecture is perceived as insulting the teacher. It implies that the teacher provided an inadequate explanation of the material.

Cultural differences on this dimension do not mean that high-PD cultures never experience conflict and aggression arising from power imbalances. Members of low-PD cultures, however, are more likely to respond to power imbalances with frustration, anger, and hostility than members of high-PD cultures. This occurs because low-PD cultures subscribe to power balance even though the reality of everyday life in such cultures may reflect significant power disparities. African Americans, Mexican Americans, and Native Americans in particular recognize this disparity between the "ideal" of power balance and the reality of socioeconomic disadvantage in the United States. In a low-PD culture, the battle to achieve the ideal of balanced power is more compelling, and the denial of power is likely to be viewed as more unjust and intolerable than in a high-PD culture, where power balance is seen differently.

RELATIONSHIP OF TWO DIMENSIONS: CONNECTING THE DOTS

Remembering all the details of value dimensions that distinguish cultures can seem daunting. When trying to condense all this material on cultural value differences, concentrate less on the details and more on two primary points. First, recognize that individualism-collectivism is probably "the crucial dimension of cultural variability" (Griffin, 2006, p. 425). Be particularly familiar with this dimension because it has the greatest support in cross-cultural research.

Second, there is a strong relationship between the individualism-collectivism and the power-distance dimensions (Hofstede & Hofstede, 2010). *High-PD cultures tend to be collectivist, and low-PD cultures tend to be individualist.* Thus, the United States, for example, being a highly individualist culture is also a low-PD culture. Duane Alwin, a sociologist at the University of Michigan, illustrates this combination in his study of parental values in the United States. Alwin found that parents placed the highest value on "thinking for oneself" as the quality that would best prepare children for life. Questioning authority (low-PD) also emerged as an important parental value (see Frerking, 1995). This exhibits an individualist, low-PD value system.

Intercultural Miscommunication

With differences in core values come numerous opportunities for miscommunication between members of differing cultures, making appropriate and effective intercultural communication a significant challenge. This section discusses basic intercultural miscommunication in the framework just presented of differences in core value dimensions (individualism-collectivism and power-distance).

Ethnocentrism: Intercultural Prejudice

Imagine two different ways to approach eating dinner. In the first version, the family believes dinner is a ritual that allows its members to put aside the diversions and distractions of the day. The focus should be on the family and what each person did that day—exciting things, happy experiences, problems, troubling issues, and the like. The family begins by saying grace before eating, thanking God for the bounty. Each person seated at the table formally requests that food be passed to him or her. They also say "Thank you" after the food is passed. No one reaches across the table and grabs anything. That

is considered rude. Conversation is encouraged. Silence is noticed and discouraged. No one leaves the table without first asking to be excused. When dinner is over, everyone busses their dishes and pitches in on cleanup.

In the second version, the family usually eats in front of the TV. On those rare occasions when dinner is eaten together at the table, everyone grabs for the food as though this were the final meal on Earth. No one asks for anything. Dinner is more a feeding frenzy, like sharks smelling blood in the water, than a relaxed, social affair. No one thanks anyone for passing food. Grace is not said. When dinner is over, the women take care of the dishes, and the men go about their business of relaxation or television watching.

Here we have two distinctly different ways of carrying out commonplace dinner activities. Do you deem the version closest to the way you were raised to conduct dinner to be superior and the other version to be inferior? If so, you have captured the fundamental essence of ethnocentrism: the way we do things is good, and the different way others do things is not so good.

ETHNOCENTRISM: CULTURAL SUPERIORITY COMPLEX

The term *ethnocentrism* is derived from two Greek words: *ethnos*, meaning "nation," and *kentron*, meaning "center" (Klopf, 1998). **Ethnocentrism** "means seeing our own culture as the center of the universe and seeing other cultures as insignificant or even inferior" (Ting-Toomey & Chung, 2012, p. 14). The degree of difference between your own and other cultures determines ratings on a superiority-inferiority scale. The bigger the difference found in a culture distinct from your own, the greater is the perceived inferiority of that culture.

All cultures are ethnocentric to some degree (Triandis, 2009). Ethnocentrism usually involves exalting one's own culture while disparaging other cultures. This ethnocentric bias is often shocking, even brutal, in its judgment of other cultures. Names of various tribes and groups sometimes reflect this bias. Kiowa means "real or principal people." Laplander means "human being." Greeks and Romans referred to outsiders as "barbarians" (Klopf, 1998). Immigrants to the United States are referred to as "aliens," legal or otherwise. Common definitions of alien include "strange," "unnatural," "repugnant," "outsider," and of course, "visitor from another galaxy."

Ethnocentrism is a learned belief. Experiencing another culture's customs, practices, and beliefs that are different from what we are accustomed to may seem weird and wrong. For example, the Masai of East Africa have a wedding tradition where the father of the bride blesses his daughter by spitting on her head and breasts (Droesch, 2013). Try that at an American wedding, and be prepared to duck.

I have visited Great Britain a half-dozen times over the years. Early visits revealed a frustrating lack of showers in my accommodations. I am not a bath person unless left with no alternative. I find sitting in a tub of water ("Dan soup," as my son refers to it), with a dirty oil slick formed on the surface of the tub water after washing, not to be particularly appealing. My first reaction to the shower scarcity was ethnocentric ("What a goofy culture"). I have since learned to relax my expectations and flow more with the difference-is-not-deficiency perspective (and lately, finding showers in Great Britain is not uncommon).

Consider differences in teaching and learning in schools (Samovar et al., 2010). In Russia, China, Japan, Korea, Vietnam, and Cambodia, learning is passive. Teachers read to their students. Students are mostly silent unless called on to answer questions or recite. Rote memorization is common. In Mexico, students are more active. They talk and learn through group work. In Germany, southern Italy, and the West Indies, students rise in unison when the teacher enters the classroom. In an Israeli kibbutz, students wander around the classroom, talk to each other, sharpen pencils, or get a drink without formal permission. They talk during lessons, even hum to themselves while working on an assignment. American classrooms are a mix of many of these practices, and they are less formal and more active places of learning than in most other cultures.

So which cultural communication practices are correct? Every culture believes the way it operates is preferable; otherwise, the practices would change (unless enforced by an authoritarian regime). Ethnocentrism is prejudice on a global scale.

CORE VALUES AND ETHNOCENTRISM: BEDROCK CULTURAL BIAS

The core value differences of individualism-collectivism and power-distance previously discussed highlight how markedly diverse cultures can be. Although even surface differences can provoke ethnocentrism, core value differences can easily serve as a bedrock foundation for ethnocentrism.

Consider arranged marriages. A high-PD culture such as India values the right of parents to arrange their children's marriages. According to UNICEF, about 90% of marriages in India are

A high power-distance country such as India values the right of parents to arrange their children's marriages. A low power-distance country such as the United States accords no such right to parents. What is your view of arranged marriages and cultures that promote them?

arranged ("Arranged Marriage," 2012). Usually, the bride and groom don't meet until the wedding. A low-PD culture such as the United States accords no such right to parents. So do you view a culture that promotes arranged marriages as just a little "strange" and not as "progressive" as the United States? It's difficult to resist judging cultures based on the core values of our own. Yet while high-PD cultures are different, they are not necessarily deficient. India, with its arranged marriages, has one of the lowest divorce rates in the world, and "the love experienced by Indian couples in arranged marriages appears to be even more robust than the love people experience in 'love marriages'" (Epstein, 2010, p. 31).

Consider also the Thai preference for what some researchers have called "unwillingness to communicate" (Knutson et al., 2002). Thais are slow to engage in conversation with strangers. To Americans, this may seem unfriendly. Research reveals, however, that Thais delay conversing with strangers to reflect carefully and choose communication that furthers social harmony and avoids giving offense (Knutson & Posirisuk, 2006). This exhibits a strong regard for sensitivity (receptive accuracy) in the communication competence model explained in Chapter 1. Thailand, the "Land of Smile," is a collectivist culture with unspoken rules that encourage modesty, humility, and harmony. Instead of seeing the Thai "unwillingness to communicate" as deficient from an American perspective, perhaps we could learn the potential value of listening more and talking less (see Chapter 6).

CULTURAL RELATIVISM: DIFFERENCES, NOT DEFICIENCIES

In an effort to combat ethnocentrism, anthropologists offered the cultural relativism viewpoint (Harrison & Huntington, 2000). **Cultural relativism** views cultures as merely different, not deficient (Lavenda & Schultz, 2015). From this viewpoint, "all phenomena can be assessed only from the perspective of the culture in which they exist" (Moghaddam, 1998, p. 506). We must respect all cultures and their inherent right to engage in practices, rituals, and communication behaviors that may appear strange, even repugnant. The "West is best" ethnocentrism should not be imposed on cultures that depart from the West's values. Men and women communicate openly with each other in Western cultures; they

are far more restricted in most Arab cultures. Americans usually expect to speak without interruption and are often irritated when not accorded this privilege. Arabs have no such expectation and will exuberantly join a conversation that to most Americans appears to be a chaotic shouting match (Lewis, 1996). Cultural relativism dictates that we respect these different cultural practices despite personal misgivings.

In the abstract, cultural relativism appears egalitarian and unprejudiced. The ethical and moral correctness of an act can only be judged within the value system of the culture in which it takes place. Confusion, however, can arise from the use of the term *relativism*, which seems to imply that there are no universal standards for judging cultural practices. There are practices in cultures around the world, however, that are condoned within the culture, but they contradict universal human rights. Female genital mutilation (female circumcision), denial of education and political participation to women, wife beating, "honor killings" (murdering women because they have "dishonored" the family by extramarital affairs, divorce, etc.), the selling of children, slavery, and myriad other practices are behaviors that some cultures and co-cultures condone (Mallicoat, 2015).

The United Nations Universal Declaration of Human Rights declares that every human being has certain basic rights, which include life, liberty, security, freedom of speech and belief, equal protection under the law, participation in the political process, a decent standard of living, necessary social services, and education (Harrison, 2000). Customs, practices, and communication behaviors that do not deny these human rights should not be rejected as inferior simply because they are different from our own ways of operating. Sexism, racism, homophobia, and all the "isms" that breed "ethnic cleansings" and genocidal wars, however, deserve no defense. Cultural relativists typically condemn these inhumane practices, which makes the term *cultural relativism* more confusing than clarifying.

MULTICULTURALISM: RECOGNITION OF HUMAN RIGHTS

An alternative to cultural relativism is *multiculturalism*. Flowers and Richardson (1996) define **multiculturalism** as a "social-intellectual movement that promotes the value of diversity as a core principle and insists that all cultural groups be treated with respect and as equals" (p. 609). Multiculturalism assumes universal human rights.

Multiculturalism incorporates the five ethical standards discussed in Chapter 1: *honesty, respect, fairness, choice,* and *responsibility.* To be a competent intercultural communicator, you must accept cultural diversity and eschew ethnocentrism, but always you are guided by these ethical standards. Inhumane behavior that degrades and diminishes others cannot be accepted with the justification "That's just the way they do things in their culture." Diversity is part of the colorful tapestry of humankind, but inhumanity is a stain on any culture's fabric.

Interpersonal Miscommunication: Not Knowing the Rules

Lustig and Koester (2013) provide a prime example of interpersonal miscommunication stemming from not knowing the rules of appropriate communication within a specific culture:

> Brian Holtz is a U.S. businessperson assigned by his company to manage its office in Thailand. Mr. Thani, a valued assistant manager in the Bangkok office, has recently been arriving late for work. Holtz has to decide what to do about this problem. After carefully thinking about his options, he decides there are four possible strategies:
>
> 1. Go privately to Mr. Thani, ask him why he has been arriving late, and tell him that he needs to come to work on time.
>
> 2. Ignore the problem.

3. Publicly reprimand Mr. Thani the next time he is late.

4. In a private discussion, suggest that he is seeking Mr. Thani's assistance in dealing with employees in the company who regularly arrive late for work, and solicit his suggestions about what should be done. (p.73)

If you were Holtz, what choice would you make? Which one is likely to be both appropriate and effective? The first choice is a typical American solution. It is direct and a typical response in an individualist culture with a low-context communication style. It would probably be effective in curbing Mr. Thani's tardiness. As already noted, however, an individual does not directly criticize another person in Thai culture. This causes a loss of face and threatens harmony (collectivist value). So the first choice would be very inappropriate, even embarrassing.

The second choice, ignoring the problem, would be appropriate but ineffective since Mr. Thani would likely continue arriving late to work. Mr. Holtz would view this as intolerable. Ignoring a problem is not direct and assertive.

The third choice, a public reprimand, would be neither appropriate nor effective. Mr. Thani, a valuable employee, would likely resign in shame. Public rebuke invites loss of face. It is aggressive and domineering.

Thus, the first three options, if chosen, would be examples of miscommunication that would likely aggravate the problem. The fourth choice, a problem-solving approach, is preferred because it is likely to be both appropriate and effective (Lustig & Koester, 2013). Mr. Thani can

Intercultural miscommunication is quite common.

receive the message indirectly that he must arrive at work on time without losing face. Mr. Holtz can comment to Mr. Thani that he needs his help solving a problem. "Tardiness has recently increased in the office." No specific person is identified. "I would be very pleased if you would help solve this problem." Mr. Thani can recognize that his tardiness is a problem without any public acknowledgment or humiliation, and he can "solve" the problem by changing his own behavior in the context of assisting his boss.

Interpersonal miscommunication can occur even in intercultural circumstances in which you might be attempting to be helpful or caring. Frequent interaction between supervisors and subordinates in work situations may be highly appreciated by members of some cultures but resented by others. In Japan, it is typically perceived as caring, but in the United States, it is often perceived as micromanaging or "spying" on workers to evaluate their performance. Close supervision of teenagers by parents is usually perceived by teens as showing love in collectivist cultures but as interference in individualist cultures (Triandis, 1995). Being an interculturally competent communicator is highly challenging.

Intercultural Communication Competence

Later chapters will delve into specific ways intercultural communication competence can be enhanced. In this section, general ways to develop appropriate and effective communication between cultures are discussed.

Become Mindful: Monitor Your Communication

Cultural values are so deep-seated, and communication that flows from these values is so automatic, we often take no notice. We see differences in the content of messages and the outcomes, but we often fail to see the communication process that separates members of diverse cultures.

One general way to take notice is to be mindful. As discussed in Chapter 1, mindfulness is thinking about our communication with others and persistently working to improve it. It is the process of exhibiting sensitivity in your communication with members of diverse cultures. When we are mindful, we recognize our ethnocentrism, and we resolve to correct our misperceptions.

We exhibit mindfulness in three ways (Langer, 1989). First, we make more careful distinctions. We aren't as prone to stereotype, and we look for information that contradicts stereotypes. Second, we are open to new information, especially that which focuses on the process, not the content, of communication. It is easy to identify disagreements over the content of messages—"You've asked for more office space, but we have none to spare." The disagreement on content of messages is usually so apparent that we often fail to examine the communication process that is essential to resolving differences. When individuals from diverse cultures communicate, a content-only focus can trigger ethnocentrism and misunderstanding. Third, we exhibit mindfulness when we recognize different perspectives. This is the essence of empathy, and it is critical to competent intercultural communication. Members of differing cultures perceive the world from their own cultural perspectives, and each person believes his or her perspective is reasonable and comfortable.

When we lock into our own cultural perspective, we respond to cultural differences in an unthinking, "mindless" way. Mindless communication is a universe away from competent communication. Remember, sensitivity is recognizing signals that can alert us to potential difficulties or possible solutions to problems. You have to extend your antenna. Mindfulness raises your antenna. Mindlessness keeps your antenna lowered.

Become Acculturated: Strangers in a Strange Space

Acculturation is the process of adapting to a culture different from one's own (Hofstede & Hofstede, 2010). When you engage another culture, two questions emerge: (1) should you seek a positive association with the dominant culture, and (2) is your native cultural identity valuable enough to maintain? How you answer these questions will result in a choice among four possible strategies of acculturation (Berry, 1994; Williams & Berry, 1991).

The first strategy is *assimilation*—the abandonment of the customs, practices, language, identity, and ways of living of one's heritage for those of the host culture. The original idea of the United States as a "melting pot" encouraged immigrants to assimilate and become Americans: to blend, not to stand apart. Recently, the idea of assimilation has been criticized as a way of eradicating co-cultures and destroying the unique heritages of diverse peoples.

The second strategy of acculturation is *separation*—maintaining one's ethnic identity and avoiding contact with the dominant culture. Individuals who separate may refuse to learn the language of the dominant culture, reside in homogeneous neighborhoods populated by others from the same ethnic heritage, and socialize predominantly with members of their own ethnic group.

A third strategy of acculturation is *integration*—maintaining one's ethnic identity while also becoming an active part of the dominant culture. For example, many Irish Americans, Asian Americans, Mexican Americans, and other groups celebrate their heritage with St. Patrick's Day parades, Chinese New Year street celebrations, and Cinco de Mayo activities, among other manifestations of ethnicity. At the same time, they express pride in their new culture by becoming American citizens, joining the military, and working in the outside community.

A fourth strategy of acculturation is *marginalization*—maintaining no ties to either one's native or new culture. These individuals experience feelings that they don't belong anywhere.

Which of these four strategies of acculturation is most effective? Berry (1997) concludes that "integration is usually the most successful; marginalization is the least; and assimilation and separation strategies are intermediate. This pattern has been found in virtually every study, and is present for all types of acculturation" (p. 24). Acculturation, however, in any form is more likely the longer the exposure to the dominant culture, and it is easier for those who are relatively young (Cheung et al., 2011).

St. Patrick's Day and Cinco de Mayo parades illustrate the integration strategy of acculturation.

Reduce Uncertainty: Egads, Nothing's the Same!

Uncertainty Reduction Theory posits that when strangers first meet, their principal goal is to reduce uncertainty and to increase predictability (Witt & Behnke, 2006). We are so motivated because uncertainty often produces anxiety. This is particularly true of intercultural communication (Neuliep, 2012). Managing uncertainty and its attendant anxiety (called *anxiety uncertainty management*) is an important part of competent intercultural communication (Gudykunst, 2005). It directly affects your communication effectiveness. You can see this most apparently when you reside in a culture distinctly different from your own. Initially, you will likely experience **culture shock**—the stressful transition stage after you move to unfamiliar cultural surroundings characterized by different rules, norms, and practices, with a corresponding challenge to adapt to these new circumstances. (Ting-Toomey & Chung, 2012). You may feel helpless, isolated, and even depressed because so much is different from what you are used to seeing and experiencing.

Uncertainty reduction can improve the effectiveness of your communication in unfamiliar cultural contexts. Engaging others in conversation and contact is an important aspect of uncertainty reduction. If your acculturative stress (culture shock) prods you into withdrawing from communication transactions with members of the unfamiliar culture, uncertainty will not be reduced. Merely spending time in another culture is not sufficient to counter acculturative stress and reduce uncertainty, but making friends with indigenous members of a culture is effective (Wood, 2004). Proceed cautiously, gently, and respectfully when interacting with individuals from other cultures.

Promote Convergence: Bringing Us Together

DeVito (1990) offers an apt example of the difficulties we face when trying to determine what is appropriate communication in an intercultural context:

> An American college student, while having a dinner party with a group of foreigners, learns that her favorite cousin has just died. She bites her lip, pulls herself up, and politely excuses herself from the group. The interpretation given to this behavior will vary with the culture of the observer. The Italian student thinks, "How insincere; she doesn't even cry." The Russian student thinks, "How unfriendly; she didn't care enough to share her grief with her friends." The fellow American student thinks, "How brave; she wanted to bear her burden by herself." (p. 218)

Here we see divergent interpretations of a single event. **Divergence** refers to differences that separate people. The American college student is insincere, unfriendly, or brave, depending on your cultural perspective. Ethnocentrism nourishes divergence. It makes difference a reason to dislike, hate, avoid, or feel contempt for individuals from other cultures.

Divergence widens the gap between cultures; convergence closes the gap. **Convergence** refers to similarities that connect us to others. Convergence doesn't erase, or attempt to change, core differences between cultures.

There are two primary ways to create convergence in intercultural transactions. First, *adjust your style of speaking.* Even minor adjustments can promote convergence. For example, more closely align your speaking rate, pitch, vocal intensity, frequency of pauses, and silences with those of the other person. The issue of speaking style can be controversial, however. Historically, relatively powerless groups (e.g., African Americans and Latinos) have been expected by the mainstream U.S. culture to shift their style of speaking to the mainstream speech style (Hecht et al., 1993). Sonia Weber (1994) cites an example. While she was lecturing to her class, a vocal black student began a "call and response," with encouraging "all right," "make it plain," and "teach" responses to her lecture. Soon, a few more black students joined. Startled white students, quizzed afterward, found the vocal responses disruptive, annoying, and rude. Social norms in mainstream American culture do not endorse "call and response" in college classrooms. Nevertheless, convergence requires effort from all parties, not just members of the mainstream culture or individuals from co-cultures.

Second, *find common ground.* Ask what interests members of other cultures. Let them introduce topics of possible mutual interest, and explore those topics with them. You are not trying to change people's interests; rather, you are attempting to share them. Interest in sports, religion, politics, history, and so forth may offer opportunities to find commonalities.

Gender and Communication

As previously explained, gender and culture intersect. Before exploring this intersection more fully, let's first clarify the difference between sex and gender. **Sex** is *biology* (female-male); it is genes, gonads, and hormones. One sex difference is that a male can impregnate a female and that a female can become pregnant. It doesn't work in the reverse. **Gender** is social role *behavior* (feminine-masculine) learned from communicating with others (Wood, 2015). The two terms are often used synonymously, and sometimes in ludicrous ways, such as a *People* magazine article claiming that pregnant Princess Kate of England did not "know the *gender* of baby No. 2'" before it was born (Perry & Tauber, 2014, p.22). Who would know the behavior of their unborn child? Is there a blood test for gender role expectations? Does amniocentesis inform a couple of the communication patterns of the unborn child?

Each culture's gender role expectations, what is perceived as appropriate behavior to be considered masculine or feminine, powerfully influence our communication with others (Lindsey & Zakahi, 2006). "It is through pervasive cultural value patterns—as filtered through family and media systems—that

persons define meanings and values of identities, such as gender . . ." (Ting-Toomey & Chung, 2012, p. 66).

Masculine-Feminine Dimension: Rigidity Versus Flexibility

The intersection of gender and culture serves as the basis for a third deep structural value called the **masculine-feminine dimension** (Hofstede & Hofstede, 2010). A **masculine culture** exhibits stereotypic masculine traits, such as male dominance, ambitiousness, assertiveness, competitiveness, and drive for achievement. *Gender roles are rigid and distinct in masculine cultures.* Cultures ranking high on masculinity include Japan, Austria, Venezuela, Italy, Switzerland, and Mexico. The United States also ranks relatively high on masculinity (see Figure 3-3).

A **feminine culture** exhibits stereotypic feminine traits, such as affection, nurturance,

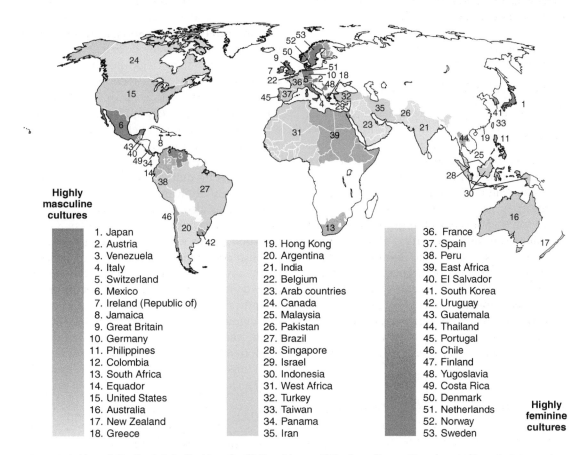

Highly masculine cultures

1. Japan	19. Hong Kong	36. France
2. Austria	20. Argentina	37. Spain
3. Venezuela	21. India	38. Peru
4. Italy	22. Belgium	39. East Africa
5. Switzerland	23. Arab countries	40. El Salvador
6. Mexico	24. Canada	41. South Korea
7. Ireland (Republic of)	25. Malaysia	42. Uruguay
8. Jamaica	26. Pakistan	43. Guatemala
9. Great Britain	27. Brazil	44. Thailand
10. Germany	28. Singapore	45. Portugal
11. Philippines	29. Israel	46. Chile
12. Colombia	30. Indonesia	47. Finland
13. South Africa	31. West Africa	48. Yugoslavia
14. Equador	32. Turkey	49. Costa Rica
15. United States	33. Taiwan	50. Denmark
16. Australia	34. Panama	51. Netherlands
17. New Zealand	35. Iran	52. Norway
18. Greece		53. Sweden

Highly feminine cultures

FIGURE 3-3. Masculinity-Femininity Rankings for 50 Countries and 3 Regions. (Source: Based on rankings that appear in Hofstede & Hofstede, 2010)

sensitivity, compassion, and emotional expressiveness. *In feminine cultures, however, gender roles are less rigid and more overlapping.* Sweden has a well-entrenched social support system of pregnancy leave, lengthy paid vacations, and time off to tend to sick children because a very high proportion of the workforce is composed of women. Cultures ranking high on femininity include Sweden, Norway, the Netherlands, Denmark, Costa Rica, Finland, and Chile.

In masculine cultures, men typically communicate in ways that will enhance their esteem (e.g., speak often, control the floor, and interrupt). Women in masculine cultures typically communicate in ways that will enhance relationships (e.g., express support, encourage, and listen well). In feminine cultures, both men and women communicate in ways that emphasize relationships over power. In Sweden, for example, management in organizations is democratic. Managers don't give orders to employees; they make suggestions or offer guidelines (Lewis, 1996). Nurturance and the creation of a caring society are paramount concerns.

It is important to note here that the rankings of cultures on the masculinity-femininity dimension are relative, not absolute. A high ranking on femininity doesn't mean that a culture treats women as well as men. No culture does (Hausmann et al., 2013). It simply means that feminine cultures have less rigid, stereotypic gender roles than masculine cultures with their distinctly different behaviors for males and females.

Given the masculine-feminine dimension of cultures, you might think gender differences in communication would be quite large. This is probably true when comparing a strongly masculine culture to a strongly feminine culture, but the size of gender differences in communication and the reasons for such differences, be they large or small, within the culture of the United States are both hotly debated issues, as you will see in the discussion that follows.

Gender Differences Hypothesis: Mars and Venus—Really?

When it comes to communicating, are women and men mostly similar or different? John Gray (1992) asserted that "men are from Mars and women are from Venus." He built a multimillion-dollar empire based on this metaphorical premise that men and women are dramatically different from each other. He's peddled this premise in books, seminars, audiotapes, DVDs, and even franchised counseling centers. His website sells "Mars Venus wellness solutions" composed of "super shakes, super minerals, and super cleanses" with, of course, separate ingredients for men and women. As Dindia (2006) says, he's proven that "not only does sex sell, but sex differences sell" (p. 13).

Are men and women really so different that they seem to exist in separate alien worlds? Deborah Cameron (2007) begs to differ in her book *The Myth of Mars and Venus*. Then again, Cameron hasn't sold 50 million copies of her book, as Gray has with his 20 books and counting (see Gray's current biography on Amazon. com), so her influence on popular conceptions of gender differences in communication is unfortunately minuscule compared to Gray's.

If you listen to stand-up comedians or consult numerous Internet sites, you would certainly think that Gray's depiction of vast gender differences is correct. Consider a few examples from the Internet. "Why does it take 1 million sperm to fertilize one egg? Because the sperm won't stop to ask for directions." "When do women stop advocating equality? When they have to kill large, hairy spiders." "Give a man an inch, and he thinks he's a ruler." "How do you impress a woman? Compliment her, cuddle her, caress her, love her, listen to her, support her, and spend money on her. How do you impress a man? Show up naked. Bring beer." Television series also repeatedly characterize men and women as hugely different beings.

Although the size and scope of gender differences in communication are certainly debatable issues, some large gender communication differences do exist that support the **gender differences hypothesis**—the assertion that men and women communicate in vastly divergent ways. Let's examine three significant examples that are well supported by research that concern some of the most important aspects of our lives: *sexual interest, social support,* and *negotiating for financial security.*

SEXUAL INTEREST: GETTING TO YES

"You know that look women get when they want sex? Me neither." Drew Carey is underlining the perceived difference between men and women regarding interest in sex. The stereotype is that men are sex hounds. Women, so goes this notion, have to resist the incessant overtures from men. They simply aren't as interested. Is there any truth to this popular gender stereotype? One review of studies on this question concluded that men do have more frequent and intense sexual desire than women (Baumeister et al., 2001). A more recent review came to the same conclusion (Sine, 2013). Men initiate sex about twice as often as women do (Byers & Heinlein, 1989; O'Sullivan & Byers, 1992), although this may be the communication expectation of both sexes. This gender difference has been validated across many cultures (Segall et al., 1990) and is true for straight and gay men alike (Bailey et al., 1994). It is also true for those over the age of 45 (Crary, 2010).

Men also have much greater difficulty maintaining platonic, "just friends," relationships with women than vice versa. "Although women seem to be genuine in their belief that opposite-sex friendships are platonic, men seem unable to turn off their desire for something more" (Ward, 2012). These, of course, are generalizations that do not apply to every man or woman.

In addition, research shows that women are about twice as likely as men to engage in **compliant sex**—having sexual intercourse when you don't want to, but your partner does, in circumstances that do not involve duress or coercion (Impett & Peplau, 2003). Compliant sex is not necessarily negative. It can communicate affection for your partner.

There are many potential communication problems associated with gender differences in sexual interest. First, there is greater pressure on women to engage in compliant sex out of fear that their partner will terminate their relationship or lose interest in them if they resist sexual overtures (Impett & Peplau, 2000). Second, conflict in relationships can be triggered by differential interest in sex. Individuals with the greater sexual interest may become angry when their partners are not compliant. Consenting to sex to prevent a partner's anger is associated with feelings of shame, fear, and anger (Impett & Peplau, 2003). Concerns that a partner might end the relationship or withhold love and affection if sexually rebuffed is associated with riskier sexual practices and unplanned pregnancies

(Cooper et al., 1998). Third, there may even be some association with sexual violence against women if a woman is less interested in sex and must "disappoint" her male partner (Impett & Peplau, 2003).

SOCIAL SUPPORT AND SOCIAL SKILLS: CARING ABOUT AND FOR OTHERS

We typically think of women as more supportive in times of stress and bereavement than men. This is among the largest gender differences in communication ever supported by research. A review of 30 studies revealed that men tend to "go it alone" in times of stress and emotional difficulty far more than women, whereas women draw on social-emotional support from family members, friends, and neighbors (Luckow et al., 1998). Women also provide help and comfort in such circumstances far more than men. This same pattern can be found cross-culturally (Belle, 1987, 1989; Taylor, 2002).

Men are also significantly more **emotionally restrictive**—"having difficulty and fears about expressing one's feelings and difficulty finding words to express basic emotions" (O'Neil et al., 1995, p. 176)—while women are more emotionally expressive (see also Wong et al., 2006). When it comes to the social skill of expressing how one feels, men generally are far more challenged than women (Burleson et al., 2005). One study found this to be true of the emotional expressivity of men and women on social networking sites such as Facebook and Twitter (Parkins, 2012).

This gender difference in emotional expressivity typically has a negative effect on the health of a romantic relationship (Rochlen & Mahalik, 2004). One important exception, however, involves display rules associated with emotional expressions. Men tend to express what are sometimes perceived to be negative emotions, such as anger or hatred, more easily than positive emotions, such as affection and joy. Women, conversely, have some difficulty expressing anger but little difficulty expressing positive emotions (Simpson & Stroh, 2004). When women do express anger, it tends to be through crying; men tend to express anger in outbursts, even rage (Domagalski, 1998; Girion, 2000). In fact, women generally cry about *five times more often* than men (Walter, 2006).

Republican Speaker of the House John Boehner has been teasingly dubbed "Weeper of the House" by some because of his well-known penchant for crying in public with seemingly little provocation. His behavior is surprising primarily because research shows that men typically are more emotionally restrictive and cry at work far less than women.

NEGOTIATING FOR SALARIES: DO YOU WANT A MILLION DOLLARS?

Women are vastly more hesitant than men to ask for higher starting salaries (Kay & Shipman, 2014). In a study of students graduating with master's degrees from Carnegie Mellon University, only 7% of the female students, but 57% of the male students, asked for higher starting salaries. Those students who asked for more money received, on average, $4,053 in additional starting compensation—the difference in average starting salaries between men and women generally (Babcock, 2002; see also Babcock & Laschever, 2009). Two professors of management, Robin Pinkley and Gregory Northcraft (2000), estimate that women who consistently accept whatever is offered as a starting salary will earn *$1 million less* by retirement than those who negotiate for a higher initial salary. Compounding the disadvantage, research shows that recognizing women's reluctance to ask for more money results in them often being offered less compensation because they are stereotyped as pushovers when negotiating (Bowles, 2012).

Why don't women typically ask for more money? A primary reason is that women are more inclined to believe that their individual circumstances are controlled by outside forces—"life happens." Men are more likely to believe that circumstances can be changed by individual action—"we make life happen" (Wade, 1996). In one study of salary negotiations, the male applicants were almost *six times more likely* than the female applicants to see their worth as determined by themselves, not by the company (Barron, 2003). This gender difference was found to be true not just in the United States but in 14 other diverse cultures as well (Smith et al., 1997). Another reason women usually don't ask for more money is that they are more than twice as likely as men to admit "a great deal of apprehension" about negotiating (Babcock et al., 2002). Women tend to see negotiation as an unpleasant conflict or contest that may disrupt interpersonal relations (Amanatullah & Morris, 2010; Babcock & Laschever, 2009). Men focus more on accomplishments and less on relationships with others when negotiations occur, whereas women focus more on relationships (Cross & Madson, 1997). Barron (2003) found that men were two-and-a-half times more prone than women to view a job negotiation as a means to advance their interests, but women were two-and-a-half times as likely to see a job negotiation as a method for furthering their acceptance by others.

There are other significant gender differences in communication besides sexual interest, social support, and salary negotiation. *Some of these additional significant differences will be highlighted throughout the rest of this text.*

Gender Similarities Hypothesis: United States and Canada

Some researchers don't think gender differences in communication are significant (Cameron, 2007). Janet Shibley Hyde (2005) calls this perspective the **gender similarities hypothesis**. According to this perspective, although a few large gender differences do exist, most are small. Instead of men and women being from different planets, it seems they are more Earth bound, like neighbors from similar adjacent nations, such as the United States and Canada.

Consider a few common examples. According to a Pew research study, in the United States 66% of males and 77% of females use Facebook; 24% of males and 21% of females use Twitter; and 28% of males and 27% of females use

LinkedIn. Only Pinterest showed significant differences, at 42% for females and 13% for males (Duggan et al., 2015). Although men are more likely than women to check their email over the weekend (69% to 62%) and in the middle of the night (44% to 36%), the gender differences are small according to a national survey (Conlon, 2007). Consider further some common communication activities while driving. A national survey of 502 U.S. drivers (251 males and 251 females) revealed that 24% of both males and females admitted to texting at least once a week while driving. Additionally, 43% of men and 41% of women used their car horn to express displeasure to another driver, and 50% of men and 43% of women admitted to using a rude gesture when expressing this displeasure (Burfeind & Witkemper, 2010). The gender communication differences here are small to nonexistent.

One review of a large number of studies on gender differences in communication found, in aggregate, that men and women are 99% similar and only 1% different (Canary & Hause, 1993), although some researchers dispute these results (Andersen, 2006; Wood, 1998). A more recent study of 13,301 individuals that analyzed 122 different characteristics found broad similarity between men and women (Carothers & Reis, 2013).

Assuming for the moment that gender differences in communication, for the most part, are small, please note that *even small differences can produce large effects* (Eagly, 1995). Chimpanzees and humans, for example, are almost 99% similar in chromosomes, yet consider the enormous differences in performance and behavior (not even counting looks). A computer simulation study of organizational hiring practices found that when gender accounted for a mere 1% difference in performance ratings that favored men over women, 65% of the highest-level positions in the organization were filled by men (Martell et al., 1996).

One review of research found 16 language features (e.g., use of personal pronouns and length of sentences) that distinguish male-female communication patterns. Each difference is small. Nevertheless, these "subtle language differences have substantial consequences in how communicators are evaluated. The inescapable conclusion is this: The language differences really do make a difference" (Mulac, 2006, p. 238).

Although gender differences in communication are mostly small, and men and women are far more similar than different in their communication patterns, that message hasn't been well publicized. **Gender role stereotypes** *magnify even small gender differences* (Lindsey & Zakahi, 2006). These stereotypes are important because they suggest not merely how men and women might differ, they specify how they *should* differ. For instance, historically, men's gender roles in most cultures have been the providers, protectors, and decision makers. Women's roles have been the nurturers, caregivers, and emotional supporters. Men have been dominant; women have been submissive. Stereotypic descriptions of men's positive characteristics relate to respect and power; stereotypic descriptions of women's positive characteristics relate to liking (Wojciszke

The gender similarities hypothesis is partially supported by the strong similarities in male and female use of communication technologies—for good or ill.

et al., 1998). These stereotypes may have reflected real, significant differences at one time, but they are far less credible as society changes. Thus, these gender differences have become smaller, but the stereotypes have lingered and nurtured the misperception that men and women still behave in markedly divergent ways.

In addition to stereotypes, context should be considered. Studies of interruptions during conversations have consistently shown that men far more than women interrupt intrusively to seize the floor or dominate a conversation in a variety of public settings (Anderson & Leaper, 1998). Despite the stereotype that women talk more than men, a review of 63 studies showed that men speak far more than women in committee meetings, classroom discussions, problem-solving groups, and other formal settings, and even in less formal contexts as well (Crawford & Kaufman, 2006). At home with their female partner, however, they may be far more taciturn because there is no one to impress (status enhancement).

Explaining Gender Differences: No Consensus

Clearly, there is no consensus among researchers and theorists regarding how numerous and how large the gender differences in communication are (see especially Dindia & Canary, 2006). It is also clear, however, that men and women do not communicate in identical ways, and in a few areas, there are very large differences. Why do these gender differences in communication exist? This section briefly discusses several perspectives.

STYLES PERSPECTIVE: STATUS VERSUS CONNECTION
Deborah Tannen (1990) popularized the different-styles perspective with her international bestselling book *You Just Don't Understand: Women and Men in Conversation*. She claims, as do others (Bruess & Pearson, 1996; Wood, 2015), that males and females learn *different communication styles* as the outgrowth of cultural expectations and socialization processes (see also Maccoby, 1998).

Every conversation has two dimensions: status and connection (Tannen, 2010). *Status* is hierarchical, and conversation perceived from this dimension is a "negotiation in which people try to

achieve and maintain the upper hand if they can" (Tannen, 1990, p. 24). When status is the focus, an individual asks, "Am I one-up or one-down?" *Connection* is nonhierarchical, and conversations perceived from this standpoint view talk between self and others as a "negotiation for closeness" (p. 25). When connection is the focus, an individual asks, "Are we closer or farther apart?"

Men and women are concerned with both status and connection, but *men typically give more focus and weight to status and women typically give more focus and weight to connection* (Eisenchlas, 2013; Kwang et al., 2013; Tannen, 2014). Note the supporting research, previously discussed on male and female patterns of negotiating salaries, in which men were far more prone than women to view a job negotiation as a means to advance their interests (status enhancing), whereas women were far more likely to see a job negotiation as a method for furthering their acceptance by others (connecting). Also, with strangers, men focus more on influencing the listener, while women focus more on affirming a connection with the listener (Leaper & Ayres, 2007). Women make phone calls and use instant messaging more for maintaining relationships, and they share more personal photos and maintain social networking sites more than men (Lacohee & Anderson, 2001; Ramirez & Broneck, 2009; Rosen et al., 2010).

If men and women often approach simple conversation from conflicting perspectives, then misunderstandings are likely to result. Conversation becomes a negotiation between individuals with two different perceptions. This negotiation can be a competitive, adversarial contest of wills that can threaten the very future of a relationship, or it can be a cooperative effort to find areas of agreement and to work out areas of disagreement.

DOMINANCE PERSPECTIVE: UNEQUAL POWER
Tannen's style-differences explanation for gender communication has been criticized for seriously underemphasizing the *dominance of men* (see Cameron, 2007; Freed, 1992; Talbot, 1998). "The fact that women are the outsiders, not that they have some universal conversational style, is what creates differences between the sexes" (Tavris, 1992, p. 300). Women communicate in ways typical of most people who are in a relatively powerless position, and men communicate in ways

typical of those with more power. These power disparities that disadvantage women result from cultural gender role expectations and the rigidity of these roles typical of a masculine culture.

There is evidence to support this dominance perspective. Because women have historically been in subordinate positions to men, they have been forced to use a communication style that is relatively noncompetitive, friendly, accommodating, and unassertive. When you have little status and authority, adopting the "male style," which emphasizes status, would be self-defeating. Bosses can order employees to perform certain tasks. Employees would be foolish if they tried the same with their bosses. When women are in positions of relatively equal power to men, however, they are likely to communicate in ways strikingly similar to men (Rosenthal & Hautaluoma, 1988; Sagrestano, 1992). For example, female college instructors, a relatively powerful position, do not typically exhibit nonverbal cues that would develop relational closeness with students any more or less often than male instructors (Miller, 2011).

Tannen (1990) does not ignore the obvious power differences between men and women. She simply offers the different-styles perspective as an additional view. She explains, "Male dominance is not the whole story. It is not sufficient to account for everything that happens to women and men in conversations—especially in conversations in which both are genuinely trying to relate to each other with attention and respect" (p. 18). As women increasingly gain power, communication differences are unlikely to disappear. The "men-are-dominant" perspective is also complicated by research on conflict. When one partner in a male-female relationship is dominant during a conflict (raises disagreements, insists on certain actions), *women are about twice as likely to be the dominant partner*, though not to gain a personal advantage but to resolve relationship troubles (Gottman, 1994). Research on leadership in groups and organizations also diminishes the men-are-dominant perspective on gender differences. "Rather than being less powerful, women may in fact be equally or more powerful than their male counterparts" because the typical leadership style of women, which is more interpersonally

friendly (connecting), is better suited to today's business and institutional environment than the typical male style (status enhancing) (Kalbfleisch & Herold, 2006; see also Eagly, 2007; Eagly & Carli, 2007). Finally, research on nonverbal communication shows inconsistent support for the dominance perspective (Hall, 2006b).

DEFICIENCIES PERSPECTIVE: COMMUNICATION INADEQUACIES

Some communication experts argue that, contrary to the different-styles or dominance-of-men perspectives, some gender differences can be better explained by *deficiencies in communication skills* (Kunkel & Burleson, 2006). They argue that if men and women have distinctly different communication styles, then men should prefer the "masculine style" and women should prefer the "feminine style." One's own gender style should be more familiar, more comfortable, and make better sense. Both men and women, however, prefer the female communication modes of providing comfort and emotional support. Thus, women are more often sought for comfort and emotional support by *both* men and women because women have been socialized, as part of cultural gender role expectations, to develop these skills. Men have not.

In contexts where persuasive skills are highly valued, however, such as in organizational meetings and legal proceedings, the female style might prove to be deficient. "Members of each sex tend to specialize in some skills while incurring deficits in other skills" (Kunkel & Burleson, 2006, p. 151). Thus, gender differences in communication reflect communication deficiencies encouraged by our culture's gender role expectations. The appropriate advice, then, would not be to accommodate gender style differences uncritically but to encourage skills development in areas where deficiencies exist.

Communication Competence and Gender

The issue of gender differences in communication is not settled. The magnitude of gender differences and their importance to communication competence are still hotly debated. *The research, however, does not support a conclusion that no important differences exist.* A couple of observations regarding how to approach gender differences in your communication with others can be offered.

Don't Magnify Gender Differences

John Gray's success with his Venus-Mars metaphor that argues a biological determinism, asserting that men and women are inherently and hugely different creatures, "does more than reflect gender stereotypes; he reproduces them (amplifies them to the level of intergalaxy differences) . . . His prescriptions are sexist . . . He provides an excuse for bad behavior" (Dindia, 2006, p. 13). For example, one stereotype he nurtures is that men need alone time to deal with stress at work and that women need to talk. He advises women to permit men to "go to their cave," to work out their feelings in private (Gray, 1992). Dindia (2006) notes, "I have asked thousands of women who work outside the home whether they would like to come home from work and 'go to their cave,' and they overwhelmingly say yes. This has nothing to do with whether you are a man or a woman" (p. 18). She continues, "When you have been interacting all day long with others, you want to come home and be left alone; when you have been home alone (or home with the kids) all day, you want

to engage in some (adult) interaction" (p. 18). Don't magnify gender differences in communication by nurturing gender role stereotypes.

Embrace the Value of Many Perspectives

There are some large, important gender differences in communication, and there are many small differences, some with potentially large effects. There are three primary explanations offered: *different communication styles, dominance of men,* and *deficiency in communication skills.* Picking any one of the three as the correct explanation ignores the insights the others provide. When power disparities exist between men and women, communication differences will likely emerge. Diminishing the power imbalances, a subject discussed in Chapter 7, will diminish communication differences. It will not eradicate them, however. Many such differences can be accurately explained as legitimate variation in styles. If, however, a clear skills deficiency exists (men are worse listeners; women are less assertive), then this may be the reason for communication differences. Skills training to diminish the gender differences would then be appropriate. So look to create power balance, correct skill deficiencies, and accommodate style differences that still account for some gender differences in communication.

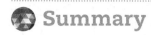 ## Summary

Intercultural communication is a fact of life. The United States is thoroughly multicultural. With cultural diversity comes new challenges. We tend to misunderstand individuals from other cultures and co-cultures because deep-seated cultural values differ. The main value dimensions are individualism-collectivism and power-distance. Cultures vary widely on these dimensions. These value differences and the communication patterns and styles that emerge from them can result in ethnocentrism, or the attitude that your own culture is the measure of all things and cultures that differ from your

own are deficient. This ethnocentric attitude can produce misunderstandings and miscommunication. Finding ways to become acculturated, to reduce uncertainty and create convergence while de-emphasizing divergence, can help produce competent intercultural communication.

Recognizing the interconnectedness of gender to culture is also important. Cultures can be ranked on a masculine-feminine dimension that reflects rigidity or flexibility of gender role expectations. Gender role expectations create stereotypes. These stereotypes occur within cultures. Although gender differences in communication clearly do exist, the magnitude and importance of these differences are still debated. Nevertheless, even small differences can produce large effects.

Quizzes Without Consequences

Test your knowledge before your exam! Go to the companion website at www.oup.com/us/rothwell, click on the Student Resources for each chapter, and take the Quizzes Without Consequences.

Film School Case Studies

Arranged (2007). Comedy/Drama/Romance; PG

A friendship between an Orthodox Jewish woman and a Muslim woman develops during their first year teaching at a public school in Brooklyn. Both are about to embark on arranged marriages. Analyze issues of divergence and convergence that center on this relationship.

Five to Seven (2014). Comedy/Drama/Romance; R

A young, aspiring novelist begins a relationship with an attractive, older French woman. The catch is that she is already married but has no problem meeting for intimacy from 5 to 7 each evening. Her husband knows about the affair and approves. Consider this film from the standpoint of cultural values and convergence versus divergence.

For Love of the Game (1999). Drama; PG-13

This charming film, ostensibly about baseball and a pitcher's swan song, is much more complex and multitextured than most sports movies. Identify gender differences in behavior, especially between the Kevin Costner and Kelly Preston characters. Applying the difference, dominance, and deficiency models of gender communication, what could these characters have done to make their relationship progress more smoothly?

Pride and Prejudice (2005). Romantic Drama; PG

A magnificent rendering of the Jane Austen novel. Analyze the gender role stereotypes and the verbal combat between the main characters of Elizabeth (a splendid Keira Knightley) and Mr. Darcy (Matthew Macfadyen) resulting from these stereotypes.

Spanglish (2004). Comedy/Drama; PG-13

This surprisingly touching film about a Mexican mother and her child who struggle to subsist in Los Angeles is an entertaining delight. Analyze the issue of assimilation versus multiculturalism in the context of ethnocentrism. Does this movie mostly support or challenge the desirability of assimilation? Provide arguments and evidence from the movie to defend your answer

The Joy Luck Club (1993). Drama; R

This film version of Amy Tan's critically acclaimed novel is a wonderful depiction of intercultural dynamics. See if you can identify all the instances of difficulties caused by the individualism-collectivism and power-distance dimensions of culture. Analyze this film for low-context and high-context communication patterns and their consequences. Does ethnocentrism play a part in the communication difficulties exhibited?

The Lunchbox (2013). Drama/Romance; PG

In this Indian film, Mumbai's famously efficient lunchbox delivery system for workers mistakenly connects a young housewife with an older man. Trading notes left in the lunchbox, the two create a fantasy world together. Identify both surface and deep structural cultural values that differ from U.S. culture.

The Namesake (2006). Drama; PG-13

Gogol Ganguli (Kal Penn), raised as an American by immigrant Bengali parents, is torn between Indian culture and modern Boston. Analyze assimilation and multiculturalism depicted in this film.

The Wedding Banquet (1993). Comedy; R

What happens when a New York real estate agent agrees to marry one of his tenants so that she can get a green card and he can stop his parents' attempt to find him the "perfect Chinese wife," all with the knowledge of the agent's male lover? Check out this very amusing film, and identify examples of convergence and divergence depicted in the movie.

CAUTION
PEDESTRIANS
SLIPPERY
WHEN
WET

BY THE END OF THIS CHAPTER, YOU SHOULD BE ABLE TO:

1. Explain the basic elements of language.

2. Describe the language abstraction process.

3. Understand and appreciate the power of language.

CHAPTER 4

Language

IMAGINE LIFE WITHOUT LANGUAGE. Individuals with Alzheimer's disease don't have to imagine because it is their reality (Ferris & Farlow, 2013). During the early phase of Alzheimer's disease, victims exhibit some difficulty retrieving appropriate words. For example, when asked to name a pen, a 77-year-old college graduate and former businessman afflicted with this disease replied, "A unit . . ." He substituted *pop* for watch, *sheet* for shoe, and *twice* for second floor (Clark et al., 2003). When trying to say his first name, Paul, he instead said "Parma" and later "Pisei." In the final phase of the disease, language ability all but disappears. Again, this same man at 79 years old could utter only a single meaningful sentence—"I'm going to die"—a few months before he did. Those afflicted with Alzheimer's, projected to be 16 million Americans by 2050, usually become extremely agitated by their inability to communicate coherent thoughts. Eventually, they withdraw from social contact and seek sad refuge in silence (Ferris & Farlow, 2013).

CHAPTER OUTLINE

- The Nature of Language
- The Abstracting Process
- The Power of Language
- Competent Language Use: Problems and Solutions

4. Recognize common sources of inappropriate and ineffective language use.

5. Understand ways to improve your use of language.

Although hopefully you will never personally experience this horrendous disease in your lifetime, surely you can empathize with its victims and understand the calamity such loss of language creates. Imagine how radically your life would change without the ability to communicate with language. A college education would no longer be an option. Try learning any subject without first understanding language. Students in American colleges whose native language is not English can certainly empathize with the struggle, and they haven't lost their language ability. Mastering a new language can be a difficult task with plenty of opportunities to feel perplexed, unable to comprehend even simple messages, as I so often experienced when taking Spanish classes in college.

Oliver Sacks (1990) calls deficiency in language "one of the most desperate of calamities, for it is only through language that we enter fully into our human estate and culture, communicate freely with our fellows, acquire and share information" (p. 8). Prior to the creation of sign language, the prelingually deaf were labeled as "dumb" and "mute" and treated outrageously by society, as little more than "imbeciles" incapable of learning beyond menial tasks (Sacks, 1990). Sign language freed the deaf community from its communication imprisonment.

Language facilitates human survival (Krauss, 2001). With language, you are not limited to direct experience, so you can learn from and avoid the fatal mistakes of others. You can also make requests, share your feelings, and get your needs met. Infants are limited mostly to crying and flailing their arms and legs to draw attention to their needs. Once language is learned in early childhood, you progress beyond flailing and wailing, although you may know folks who occasionally regress to such infantile communication. Without the ability to read, write, and speak a language, there would be no science, literature, history, or philosophy.

Even with language, humans often use this phenomenal communication tool ineffectively and inappropriately. *The primary purpose of this chapter is to explain how you can use language competently.*

The Nature of Language

Language is a structured system of symbols for communicating meaning. Without understanding this definition, recognizing and appreciating how we often use our language inappropriately and ineffectively will remain superficial at best. The fact that nonverbal communication is so commonly labeled as "body language" shows that most people have only the vaguest conception of what constitutes a language (see Chapter 5 for distinctions).

There are about 7,100 spoken languages in the world (Lewis, 2015). On the surface, they seem distinctly different from each other. If you are a native speaker of English, it would be difficult for you to mimic the sounds of Mandarin, Arabic, or Bengali without practice, much less understand what is said. Nevertheless, all languages share four essential elements: *structure, productivity, displacement,* and *self-reflexiveness.*

Structure: Saying by the Rules

Structure is the most essential element of any language and easily the most complicated. Without structure, you have no language. Every language has a **grammar**—the set of rules that specify how the units of language can be meaningfully combined—that provides this structure. Grammar is divided into *phonology, morphology, syntax,* and *semantics* (Krauss & Chiu, 1998).

PHONOLOGY: PATTERNS OF SOUND

The individual units of sound that compose a specific spoken language are called **phonemes**. These sounds correspond to consonants (such as *b*, *c*, *d*), vowels (*a*, *e*, *i*, *o*, *u*), and consonant combinations (such as *ch*, *th*). The human vocal apparatus is capable of producing many sounds, but no single language encompasses more than a fraction of the clicks, croaks, hisses, squeaks, snorts, and other noises—many of them considered rude, crude, or lewd—that people can produce. In fact, linguists have identified 869 phonemes in the almost 500 languages studied (Maddieson, 1984). The English language, however, has only 44 of this total, the Hawaiian language has 13, and some African languages have more than 100 (Crystal, 2005).

Phonology is a part of grammar that describes the patterns of sound in a language. Put another way, "[p]honology is the study of how we find order within the apparent chaos of speech sounds" (Crystal, 2005, p. 67). Phonemes cannot be strung together helter-skelter. They follow phonological rules. *Shirt* is a recognizable English word. *Shtri* is not, yet the exact same letters appear in both examples. No English word begins with the *shtr* phoneme combination. *English words can begin with up to three consonants, but no more, before a vowel becomes necessary* (e.g., *strap*) (Crystal, 2005). (In the word *crystal*, the *y* is considered a vowel—see Okrent, 2014.)

Every language has phonological rules indicating which sounds to use, how to pronounce these sounds, and how to combine these sounds in meaningful ways (Crystal, 2005). These rules may vary widely across different languages. For example, the Czech words *zmrzl* ("frozen"), *ztvrdl* ("hardened"), *blb* ("dimwit"), and *ctvrthrst* ("a quarter handful") have no vowels. The Czech language, unlike English, is notable for its vowelless words. Entire sentences can be constructed without any vowels, such as *strc prst skrz krk* ("stick a finger down your throat") ("Czech Translation," 2015).

MORPHOLOGY: TRANSFORMING PHONEMES INTO MEANINGFUL UNITS

Your ability to combine the 44 phonemes of the English language in highly complex ways permits your verbal communication to rise above the level of a primitive human being grunting, snorting, and pointing. You combine phonemes to create *morphemes*. A **morpheme** is the smallest unit of meaning in language. **Morphology** is the part of grammar that describes how morphemes are constructed meaningfully from phonemes. Morphemes are more than just words, however. A morpheme may be a stand-alone word (*friend*), called a **free morpheme**, or a unit of meaning, called a **bound morpheme**, that has no meaning until it is attached to a stand-alone word (e.g., prefixes such as *un-* in *unfriend* or suffixes such as *-ing* in *Facebooking*). *Bat* is a free morpheme composed of three phonemes (the *b*, *a*, and *t* sounds). Add an *s*, making *bats*, and there are two morphemes (one free and one bound) because the *s* means "more than one" when attached to the stand-alone word. Adding *-ly* to the word *loud* changes an adjective (the *loud* cry) into an adverb (he cried *loudly*). The suffix *-ly* by itself is meaningless.

Once morphemes are constructed from phonemes, you are faced with a challenging problem: multiple meanings. This is made apparent by a famous Groucho Marx quip: "Time *flies* like an arrow; fruit *flies* like a banana." Consider this example of multiple meanings: "The woman was *present* to *present* the *present* to her friend." Then there is this old joke: "A man walks into a bar, and so does a second man, but a third man didn't—because he ducked." There also is a big difference between a movie *buff* and seeing a movie in the *buff*. And a *booty call* can be a treasure hunt or a pursuit of a different sort.

The word *set* once held the record for the word with the most meanings in the English language, at 200. Lexicographer Peter Gilliver, however, has carefully calculated no fewer than *645 meanings* for the seemingly simple word *run* (Winchester, 2011). You can run a bath, run a race, run for office, run an app on your smartphone, and no, I'm not going to give all 645 meanings.

Some words are especially challenging because they can have contradictory meanings. *Sanction*, for example, can mean either "permit" or "forbid." *Fast* might denote "move quickly" or "stick firmly." A *blunt* instrument is dull, but a *blunt* remark is sharp and pointed.

Then there is the additional problem of the ambiguity of words, as actual newspaper headlines reported in several issues of the *Columbia*

This photo illustrates which of the following?

○ **1.** The multiple meanings for words that can produce confusion or misunderstandings

○ **2.** Grammatical rules of language are arbitrary conventions

○ **3.** The phonology of words

○ **4.** The structure of language

Answers at end of chapter

Journalism Review illustrate: "Kids Make Nutritious Snacks"; "Panda Mating Fails—Veterinarian Takes Over"; "Queen Mary Having Bottom Scraped"; "Juvenile Court to Try Shooting Defendant"; and "Prostitutes Appeal to Pope." Typically, we try to resolve the ambiguity in each case by interpreting from the context the correct meaning of the words. This is no small feat. Joshua Hartshorne (2011) notes in an article entitled "Where Are the Talking Robots?" that "language has proved harder to understand than anyone had imagined. Our ability to perform such tasks as choosing the correct meaning of ambiguous words is in fact the fruit of millions of years of evolution. And we accomplish these feats without knowing how we do so, much less how to teach the skill to an artificial being" (p. 46).

SYNTAX: WORD-ORDER RULES

Using single, isolated words is very limited and insufficient for complex communication to occur. That's why humans combine words into phrases ("the woman in the blue dress") and sentences ("She is the woman in the blue dress"). "Workers hoisted the iron girders" is a meaningful sentence, but "Hoisted girders workers iron the" is not. Why? There are rules, called **syntax**, that govern combining words into phrases and phrases into sentences. The article (*the*) and adjective (*iron*) come before the noun (*girders*), and the verb (*hoisted*) comes after the subject (*workers*). Subject-verb-object is, syntactically, the typical English word order. That is why the speech of Yoda, the Jedi Master in the *Star Wars* films, seems so strange. "Sick have I become" and "Your father he is" have an object-subject-verb order that is very unusual for English. Yodaspeak, in fact, is an unusual construction in all but a few rare languages (Crystal, 1997).

The English language is highly dependent on word-order rules for communicating meaning. For example, the sentence "Skateboarding is not a crime" has a far different meaning than "Not skateboarding is a crime." Word-order rules are a part of the grammar of language, but not all languages have the same word-order rules.

SEMANTICS: RULES OF MEANING

"Swift flowers smell noisy bells" is a syntactically correct sentence. It has a standard subject-verb-object order, with the modifiers placed immediately before the nouns. Nevertheless, the sentence is semantically incorrect. **Semantics** is the set of rules that governs the meaning of words and sentences. *Flowers* cannot be swift, and although they can emit a fragrance, they cannot actively smell anything. The meaning of the words, even though those appear in appropriate order, makes the sentence nonsensical. George W. Bush once urged listeners to put themselves in the role of a single mother "working hard to put food on your family" (see www.snopes.com). This is a semantic problem. Normally, we put food on the table, not on family members. (They seem to prefer it that way.) Bush also coughed up this linguistic hairball: "Families is where wings take dream" (see www.snopes.com). Here we see both a syntactic and a semantic problem. "Families is" violates subject-verb agreement because a plural subject requires a plural, not a singular, verb. The sentence is also semantically nonsensical because wings can't "take dream."

Each person constructs meaning from symbols that appear in the form of sounds, words, phrases, and sentences by interpreting those symbols in a context. **Symbols** are arbitrary representations of objects, events, ideas, or relationships. **Referents** are the objects, events, ideas, or relationships referred to by the words. For example, the referent for the word *table* is the physical object upon which we place the evening meal. Alfred Korzybski (1958) notes that *a word (symbol) is to a referent as a map is to a territory*. A map of New York City is obviously not the city of New York, only a representation of it. You would be viewed as more than a little odd if you spread a map of New York City in front of your car, then drove your car onto the map and happily announced your arrival in the "Big Apple." Similarly, the word *sandwich* won't take the edge off of anyone's hunger. Words are not their referents any

This sign exhibits a semantic problem. "Understanding" makes no sense as a warning sign. Presumably, "No Standing Under" (awkward phrasing to be sure) was the intended word order with corresponding meaning.

more than maps are their territories, a seemingly obvious point until we discuss verbal obscenity later (see Box 4-3).

Thus, a basic semantic rule is that *word origin is arbitrary, but word usage is conventional*. What we initially choose to call something, as long as it doesn't violate phonological rules, is arbitrary. A *house* could be called a *fadoydlehoffer* (but not a *zxchltz*, at least in English). Sniglets—words that are simply made up—also illustrate the arbitrariness of word origin (see Unwords.com). Here are a few examples: *arachnidiot* (a person who, having wandered into an "invisible" spiderweb, begins gyrating and flailing about wildly), *fornicorium* (a single man's apartment), *snowbooking* (constantly updating your status or post on Facebook during a snowstorm), *masogyny* (hatred of giving back rubs to women), *phonesia* (forgetting who you phoned when the person answers), and *downloafing* (surfing the net when you should be working). None of these "made-up words," however, will have meaning and become part of the English **lexicon**—the total vocabulary—without *conventionality*, common agreement to use these words with these specific meanings. Shakespeare invented more than 1,700 words (Bryson, 1990). *Barefoot, critical, leapfrog, monumental, excellent,*

This cartoon makes which of the following points about language?

○ **1.** Grammar is not a fixed set of rules

○ **2.** Language structure varies from language to language

○ **3.** Word origin is arbitrary, but word usage is conventional

○ **4.** Language has the capacity to be self-reflexive

Answers at end of chapter

summit, obscene, and *submerged* are just a few of his creations. Other made-up words of his, however, did not achieve common usage and fell into obscurity. Some examples are *barky, brisky, vastidity,* and *tortive.*

In summary, there are rules for which sounds may be included in a particular language (phonology), how these sounds may be linked into words (morphology), in what ways words and phrases may be ordered (syntax), and how words and sentences gain meaning (semantics). The next essential language element is productivity.

Productivity: Inventing Words and Expressing Thoughts

"There are hundreds of millions of trillions of thinkable thoughts" (Pinker, 1997, p. 118), yet in English, there are only a few dozen phonemes to communicate these thoughts. Even so, these phonemes can be transformed into at least 100,000 morphemes that can be combined into a lexicon of more than 1 million words, according to both Global Language Monitor and a Google/Harvard study ("Number of Words," 2014). English has the largest lexicon of any language.

This lexicon is forever expanding. Unlike sniglets, which do not make it into the accepted lexicon because of no shared usage, new words in English are added constantly, as reflected in the *Oxford English Dictionary.* In 2014, for example, words such as *neckbeard, douchebaggery, hot mess, humblebrag, mansplain, binge-watch, hate-watch,* and *live-tweet* were added, among others, and many more will be added annually ("Adorbs New Words," 2014). New words sprout up like mushrooms in loamy soil to accommodate new products, scientific discoveries, abstract concepts, and technologies. Again, according to Global Language Monitor, about 15 words in English are created each day. For example, the emergence of Twitter alone produced a growing lexicon, adding *twitterspeak: twitizens* (citizens in the *Twitterverse*—the universe of Twitter), *twitterpated* (a borrowed term from the Disney movie *Bambi* that meant infatuated but now also means getting addled by too many *tweets*), *twalking* (tweeting while walking), *tweeple* (Twitter people), and *twaffic* (traffic on Twitter) (Beal, 2014). You could even be a *twit* for tweeting too much.

This capacity of language to transform a small number of phonemes into whatever words, phrases, and sentences that you require to communicate your abundance of thoughts and feelings is called **productivity** (Crystal, 2005). This essential element of language allows you to express a virtually infinite number of thoughts and feelings in an amazing variety of ways. There are approximately 1 million grammatically correct 6-word sentences possible in the English language and an astounding *100 million trillion 20-word sentences possible* (Pinker, 1999). It is very likely that most sentences of about average length (10 to 15 words) that you might produce, aside from clichés and quotations, have never been spoken or written before, and they will never be randomly reproduced exactly by anyone in the future. When Shakespeare is the measure of human language potential, why settle for the commonplace? Be creative and unique with your language.

Displacement: Beyond the Here and Now

Your ability to use language to talk about objects, ideas, events, and relations that don't just exist in the physical here and now is called **displacement** (Lavenda & Schultz, 2015). You can talk about things that don't exist, such as unicorns, fairies, hobbits, and corporate responsibility. You can discuss past vacations or future adventures. You can ask questions about impossible things—"If I were 10 feet tall and weighed 450 pounds, would you consider me fat?"—and receive a response ("What's your body mass index?"). You can ponder abstract ideas, such as this bumper sticker "logic": "I'm nobody, nobody is perfect, therefore I'm perfect." The displacement capacity of language helps us all learn from past mistakes and consider potential solutions for anticipated future problems.

Displacement also allows humans to ponder abstract ideas, such as comedian Stephen Wright's questions: "If you are in a spaceship that is traveling at the speed of light, and you turn on the headlights, does anything happen?" or "So what's the speed of dark?" We can contemplate "Would I rather have a free bottle in front of me or a prefrontal lobotomy?" Language gives each of us the freedom to communicate about the past, present, or future; about things that may exist, don't exist, or can't exist; about the imaginary and ethereal as well as the concrete and physical.

Self-Reflexiveness: The Language of Language

Language has the capacity to be **self-reflexive**—the ability to use language to communicate about language (DeVito, 1970). All languages are self-reflexive. This chapter is an example of self-reflexiveness. We are using English to analyze and discuss both English and languages in general. A vocabulary has been created to identify and discuss the nature of languages (e.g., phonemes, morphemes, syntax, etc.). We use our language to reflect on how we might improve our use of it, which has the benefit of assisting us in solving life's problems by communicating clearly and effectively. The meaning we can communicate with language includes an analysis of language itself.

Considering all four elements—structure, productivity, displacement, and self-reflexiveness—must a language have the capacity to be spoken or written to qualify as a true language? For example, do sign languages qualify? Yes, they do. They have a structured system of symbols that can be expanded to accommodate any thought or feeling, concrete or abstract, immediate or far away, real or imaginary, and sign languages can use signs to discuss signs. Most signs, like words in spoken languages, are arbitrary representations of referents (Crystal, 2005). American Sign Language (ASL) and any of the more than 100 other sign languages, such as British (BSL) or Japanese (JSL) versions, are not mutually intelligible ("Is Sign Language the Same," 2015). Users of JSL or even BSL, for example, will not understand ASL users in conversation (see Figure 4-1). They require a translator. Any version of sign language is also not understandable to a nonsigner by observing the signs, which may appear to the nonsigner as mere pantomime. "Everyone can gesture; but few have learned to sign . . . It is not possible to tell a complicated story using everyday gestures. In sign language, it is routine" (Crystal, 2005, p. 163).

The Abstracting Process

All words are symbols, but all words do not reflect the same level of abstraction. *Comb, jacket,* and *hammer* are concrete words with clear physical referents. *Freedom, anarchy,* and *justice* are vague words with fuzzier referents. **Abstracting** is the process whereby we formulate increasingly vague, general conceptions of our world by leaving out details associated with objects, events, and ideas (Littlejohn & Foss, 2011).

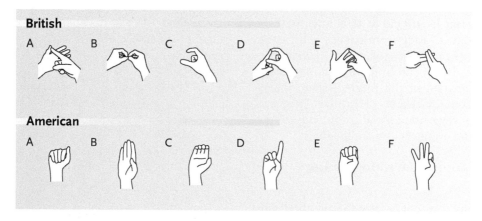

FIGURE 4-1. Comparison of Signs in British and American Sign Languages.

Abstracting permits displacement and self-reflexiveness. It allows our conversations to be more interesting and sophisticated than the communication efforts of average one-year-old children. *There are four levels of abstraction: sense experience, description, inference, and judgment.* Learning these different levels of abstraction permits you to understand some important common problems of language use discussed later in this chapter.

Sense Experience: Approximating Our Physical World

Abstracting begins with your sense experience of the physical world. Figure 4-2 illustrates the abstracting process. The parabola represents the world we live in, the territory (a reference to Korzybski's map-territory analogy). As discussed in Chapter 2, your sense experience with the physical world is inherently selective and limited. In your day-to-day existence, you do not perceive molecules, atoms, electrons, neutrons, protons, and quarks. These details are left out. Without language, your experiences would remain essentially private ones. With language, however, you are able to share your approximations of the world with others.

Description: Reporting the Approximation

The second level of the abstracting process is a description of your sense experience. **Descriptions** are *verbal reports* that sketch what you perceive from your senses. *Your description of the world is an approximation of the world as you perceive it, not an exact duplicate.* Something is always lost in the translation because you are describing to others what is in your head, not reality itself.

When your descriptions go from "I am in a committed, long-term relationship with Fran" to "I am in a committed relationship" and finally to "I am living with someone," you have become increasingly abstract. *The more general your description is, and the more details you leave out, the more abstract you are.* The potential for confusion and misunderstanding increases as we become more abstract in our use of language.

Inference: Drawing Conclusions

The third level of the abstracting process is the inferential stage. **Inferences** are conclusions about the unknown based on the known. They are *guesses*, educated or otherwise. Some inferences are more educated than others because their probability of accuracy is higher.

You can infer that a former boyfriend or girlfriend is dating someone new because you see the two of them around campus together, notice them at the local caffeine dispensary, and watch them engaging in animated conversation. This may be an accurate inference, a correct guess, but it is just an inference. It is a conclusion about the unknown (new boyfriend or girlfriend) based on the known (your observations of them). You have no

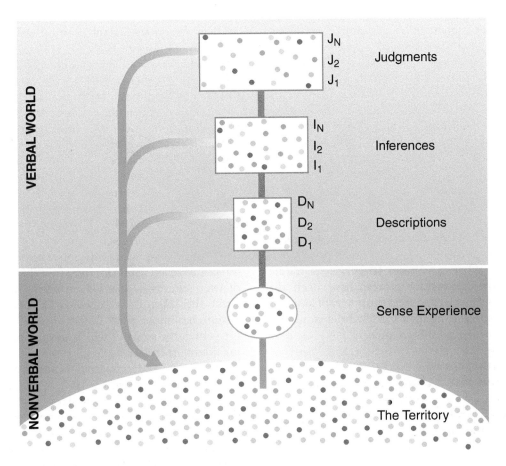

FIGURE 4-2. The Abstracting Process.

confirmation that they are dating. The inference may also be incorrect (an erroneous guess). The person seen with your ex may be an unfamiliar, visiting relative, a mere friend without "benefits," or a coworker engaged in work-related conversation.

Judgment: Conclusions That Assign Value

The fourth level of abstraction is making **judgments**—subjective *evaluations* of objects, events, or ideas. We attach a subjective positive or negative value, such as degrees of right or wrong, good or bad, ugly or beautiful, and so forth. "My partner is a generous person" is a judgment. It appears to be a description, but it is a subjective evaluation, not a factual report. Generosity is usually perceived as praiseworthy. Mark Lewis (2013), in a column entitled "Why I Hate Twitter," stated, "Twitter sucks you into small, petty battles." This statement by Lewis is a judgmental opinion, not a mere description of fact. The statement is also more than just an inference because it does more than draw an indifferent or neutral conclusion from what is known. "Petty" battles are to be scorned and avoided.

In review, let's comparatively illustrate the difference between a description (report), an inference (guess), and a judgment (evaluation):

(A report)	1. The woman is wearing a navy blue suit.
(A guess)	2. The woman wearing the navy blue suit wants to look professional.
(An evaluation)	3. The woman wearing the navy blue suit is a good employee.

The first statement is descriptive because it merely reports a simple observation. The second statement is inferential because it makes a guess based on the woman wearing a navy blue suit without assigning a value (some might see it as stuffy, others might see it as setting a good example, but neither is stated or implied). The third statement is judgmental because it expresses a positive opinion. It is more than just a guess (inference), and it's not a mere report (description). It's an evaluation.

The Power of Language

So far, what constitutes language, its nature, and the abstracting process have been discussed. Now let's address the power of language more specifically than the few brief comments that introduced this chapter.

Language and Thinking: Related But Different

Edward Sapir, an anthropologist, asserted in 1929 that human beings "are very much at the mercy of the particular language which has become the medium of expression for their society" (quoted in Mandelbaum, 1949, p. 162). He later argued that meanings are "not so much discovered in experience as imposed upon it, because of the tyrannical hold that linguistic form has upon our orientation in the world" (Sapir, 1931, p. 572). Sapir ignited a debate that has lasted for decades concerning the power of language to affect thought and perception.

SAPIR-WHORF HYPOTHESIS: LINGUISTIC IMPRISONMENT

It was left to Sapir's student Benjamin Whorf to be the principal advocate for what became known as the **Sapir-Whorf hypothesis**. There are two versions of this perspective. One claims we are the prisoners of our native language, unable to think certain thoughts or perceive in certain ways because of the grammatical structure and lexicon of our language (**linguistic determinism**). The other claims that the grammar and lexicon of our native language powerfully influence, but do not imprison, our thinking and perception (**linguistic relativity**).

Whorf noticed certain grammatical differences among languages. Some languages have few, if any, *tenses*—changes in the verb form to indicate time differences—such as *like* to *liked*. Other languages have many tenses. Do these tense differences determine our capacity to think in terms of time? No! "Whether a language has eleven tenses, three tenses, two tenses, or no tenses at all, its speakers have not the slightest difficulty in talking about any desired point in time, past, present, or future" (Trask, 1999, p. 62).

Whorf also claimed that the size of the vocabulary for various objects and concepts could determine how precisely a person can think about those objects and concepts. The Inuit language has seven words for *snow* (not the dozens or even hundreds asserted on many Internet sites), the Masai have 17 words for *cattle*, and Italian has more than 500 words related to types of *pasta*, some of which have unappetizing literal translations (e.g., *vermicelli* means "little worms" and *strozzapreti* means "strangled priests") (Bryson, 1990).

Is Whorf correct about the size of vocabulary and its deterministic influence on perception? It hardly seems so. In a September 2002 article in the Egyptian newspaper *Al-Ahram*, Egyptian businessman Tarek Haggy asserted that there is no Arabic word for *compromise*, giving the impression that if you have no word for compromise, how could you think the thought? The absence of a single word for compromise, however, doesn't mean Arabs can't, and don't, talk of "reaching a middle ground" (Nunberg, 2003). English has no handy single word that denotes the pleasure one takes in the misfortune of others, as the Germans have with the word *schadenfreude*. Does this mean that developers of Facebook could not think joyful thoughts about the precipitous, decreased popularity of Myspace as a social networking site during Facebook's popularity explosion? A limited vocabulary may make it more difficult to perceive subtle differences, but it doesn't make it impossible.

A principal problem with linguistic determinism is that it assumes thought is dependent on language, yet *we can think without language*. "If people had trouble thinking without language, where would their language have come from—a committee of Martians?" (Pinker,

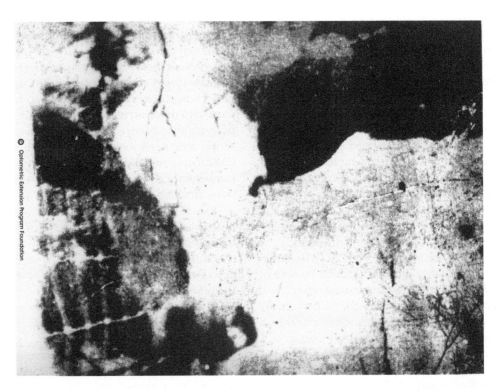

Look closely at this picture. Can you discern what it is? If you can't identify the image (it is unmistakable once you see it), ask a classmate or your instructor. Can you see it once it is labeled? Language labels help us see what may remain hidden without the label, validating the linguistic relativity view of language.

2007, p. 149). Does a child's thinking remain in a dormant stage until a first word is uttered, then BAM, the child's brain suddenly kicks into gear and thinking is activated? The simple answer is no (Damasio & Damasio, 1999). Finally, all of us have had the experience of not being able to express a thought in words, yet the thought exists. Thus, linguistic determinism is generally unsupported (Pinker, 2007).

GENDER BIASED LANGUAGE

Although linguistic determinism, the so-called "strong" version of the Sapir-Whorf hypothesis, has no merit, research does provide support for linguistic relativity, the "weaker" version of the hypothesis (Boroditsky, 2011; Gentner & Goldin-Meadow, 2003). Looking at just one avenue of research, studies on the influence of **masculine-generic gender references** in English reveal an easily understood instance of support for the linguistic relativity perspective. Consider the use of masculine nouns and pronouns to refer to both women and men (e.g., *man, mankind, he, him,*

and *his*). Sentences such as "*Man* is the master of *his* own destiny" and "A doctor should treat *his* patients compassionately" use masculine-generic language. The masculine-generic terms used in these sentences are far more likely than the inclusion of gender-neutral terms (e.g., *humankind* or *they*) to produce mental images of men to the exclusion of women (Stout & Dasgupta, 2011). Similarly, terms ending with the *-man* suffix (e.g., *chairman, businessman,* and *fireman*) promote gender-biased stereotyping, but gender-neutral terms (e.g., *chair, businessperson,* and *firefighter*) do not (Douglas & Sutton, 2014).

Gender-biased language makes women virtually invisible, and it tacitly brands them as less powerful and less important than men. Statements that use gender-biased language leave women guessing (having to make inferences) whether they are ever really included. Is this concern about gender-biased language merely "political correctness" run amok, as some have claimed? No! Research, not personal opinion or politics, shows that gender-biased language can lead women to feel excluded from groups, can produce a loss of motivation for women to apply for jobs advertised in gender-biased language, and can result in a diminished desire of employers to hire women (Budziszewska et al., 2014; Stout & Dasgupta, 2011). These are not inconsequential effects of gender-biased language.

There has been a concerted effort in recent years to address the problem by making small but important changes in language, such as *worker's* for *workman's* compensation and *husband* and wife for *man* and wife. In 2013, the state of Washington passed a law scrubbing gender-biased language from thousands of code sections in state laws (Nye, 2013). Unfortunately, sexist language continues to be widely used in a variety of important arenas (e.g., law and employment) (Chew & Kelley-Chew, 2007; Stout & Dasgupta, 2011). Research clearly shows that, although we are able to form images of women when gender-biased language is used (invalidating linguistic determinism), it is far more difficult (supporting linguistic relativity). Language may not create a mental prison from which there is no escape, but it certainly can narrow our thinking, making more expansive views of the world difficult to contemplate.

Although much discussion and research on the power of language have centered on grammatical and lexical differences between specific languages, the power of all languages to influence perception and behavior may provide a more compelling case for studying and improving language use (Ng, 2001).

Labeling: The Name Game

What's in a name? Research shows that people with highly unusual first names, such as Oder and Lethal, are more likely to be labeled psychotic than individuals with more common first names (Branan, 2007). The Reuters news agency reported that Germans with unflattering surnames, such as Dumm ("stupid"), Schwein ("pig"), Kotz ("vomit"), and Dreckman ("filth man"), admitted having problems as children because of their easily ridiculed names. Imagine a Dumm, Schwein, Kotz, and Dreckman law firm ("Go see stupid, pig, vomit, and filth man for legal advice"). Would you be

inclined to retain their legal services? Picture introducing Mr. Pig (Schwein) to Ms. Vomit (Kotz). Now there's an awkward social moment.

Advertisers and producers of myriad products know the importance of *labels*. A **label** is a name or a descriptive word or phrase, and it can powerfully influence perceptions. *Chinese gooseberries* didn't sell well until renamed *kiwi*. The California Prune Board approved a move to call prunes *dried plums* to escape negative connotations attached to this wrinkled fruit.

Labels can influence a subjective perception of smell. In one study, participants were asked to sniff a test odor (either isovaleric acid with cheddar cheese flavor or clean air) while it was described as "cheddar cheese" or "body odor." For both test odors, participants rated the smell as significantly more unpleasant when labeled "body odor" than when labeled "cheddar cheese" (de Araujo et al., 2005).

In 2013, the U. S. Census Bureau removed the term "Negro" from the "Black, African-American, or Negro" racial category on its surveys because of concern that the label might be offensive and outdated. A study comparing perception of the terms African American and black, however, discovered that whites view a person labeled as black to be of lower status, competence, and warmth. In addition, whites view a criminal suspect more negatively when identified as black than when the suspect is labeled African American (Hall et al., 2015). Labels matter!

The perceptual power of labels has become a huge issue regarding the name and mascot of the Washington *Redskins* NFL team. "The name of the Washington team is a racial insult, plain and simple. Once used to describe Native Americans' scalps sold for a bounty, it's no different from racial epithets used against African Americans, Latinos, Jews, or Asians" (Alejo, 2014, p. A7). One survey of Native Americans found that two-thirds considered the team's name "racist" and "disrespectful" (Fenelon, 2014). Should the name be banned and an alternative mascot be substituted? Rhetorical scholar Jason Black (2014), author of *American Indians and the Rhetoric of Removal and Allotment*, concludes: "It seems here that if a term for Native Americans is defined colloquially, historically, literarily, culturally, and politically as 'disparaging,' then the standard for a ban is satisfied" (Black, 2014, p. 17).

Besides perceptions, labeling can also strongly influence behavior. Labeling can produce prosocial (positive and helpful) behavior (Brownell et al., 2013). In one study, children were told that they were *kind* and *helpful*. These prosocial labels encouraged children to give prizes they received in the experiment to other children (Grusec et al., 1978). Even three weeks later, children labeled kind and helpful were more willing to aid others than children not so labeled (Grusec & Redler, 1980). Prosocial labels influence adults as well. New Haven, Connecticut, residents were more likely to give a donation to the Multiple Sclerosis Society when they were described as *generous* and *charitable* one to two weeks prior to the donation request (Kraut, 1973).

Framing: Influencing Choices

Two Catholic priests, Father O'Leary and Father Kelly, strongly disagreed with each other on the question of whether smoking and prayer are compatible behaviors. They each decided to write the Pope, plead their own case, and ask for his wisdom. When they received the Pope's reply, both priests were triumphant. Puzzled that the Pope could agree with both of them when only two contradictory choices seemed available, Father O'Leary asked Father Kelly, "What question did you ask the Pope?" Father Kelly responded, "I asked the Pope if it was permissible to pray while smoking. The Pope said that praying should always be encouraged no matter what you are doing." Father O'Leary chuckled to himself. "Well, I asked the Pope whether it is permissible to smoke while praying, and the Pope said that I should take praying very seriously and not trivialize it by smoking." The way each question was *framed* by the priests dictated the answer they received from the Pope.

A close associate of labeling, **framing is the influence wording has on our perception of choices**. Framing, more specifically than just labels, narrows our perceptions. It "captures a viewpoint" (Fairhurst & Sarr, 1996). Much like a photographer frames a picture to communicate a point of view, language frames choices and perceptions. When a photographer changes the

At an NFL football game between San Francisco and Washington, demonstrators protest the name of the Washington team: *Redskins*. Supporters of maintaining the team name, often members of other ethnic groups, might see things differently if the team name was a racist slur against them.

frame so that a person is no longer the center of interest but instead a mere bystander, our thoughts and perception of the picture change. The focus shifts. Likewise, changing language that describes or identifies our choices can change our focus and perception. As Fairhurst and Sarr (1996) explain, our "frames determine whether people notice problems, how they understand and remember problems, and how they evaluate and act upon them" (p. 4). Should you call it *partial-birth abortion* or *late-term abortion*? *Estate tax* or *death tax*? *Undocumented immigrants* or *illegal aliens*? *Income inequality* or *class warfare*? Is it *global warming*, allowing any cold spell or severe blizzard to be offered erroneously as refutation, or is it *climate change*? Framing matters (Bricker, 2014).

Studies abound showing the power of wording to shape our perception of choices. When subjects were presented with the option of treating lung cancer with surgery, 84% chose surgery when it was framed in terms of the odds of *living*, but only 56% chose surgery when this option was worded in terms of the chances of *dying* (McNeil et al., 1982). Most subjects thought condoms were an effective method of preventing AIDS when they were told that condoms have a 95% *success rate*, but a majority did not view

Framing "captures a viewpoint." Even acronyms can capture the viewpoint that gas prices are too high.

condoms as effective prevention when told that they had a 5% *failure rate* (Linville et al., 1992). In all instances, the two choices compared are about the same thing, but they are perceived differently because of how the wording frames them.

Clearly, language significantly influences our perception and behavior. It is important to remain aware of the power of framing and its capacity to alter perception and change behavior (Clark, 1996).

Identity: Languages R Us

The principal language that one uses to communicate can also mark an individual's or group's educational level, socioeconomic class, and ethnic and cultural identity. When India won its independence from Great Britain in 1947, an attempt was made to unify the Indian population by imposing the Hindi language on the entire country, in which 200 languages were spoken. Riots ensued, and many thousands were killed in years of conflict. A more benign language war has been waged in Canada, where Quebec has passed numerous laws making French the principal language of this province and restricting the use of English. "Language police" enforce the laws (Crystal, 1997).

America has not escaped the language wars, either. Following World War I, a wave of prejudice against immigrants produced laws in 35 states mandating English-only instruction in public schools (Crawford, 1996). Efforts continue to make English the official language of the United States (Crawford, 2012). *Washington Post* columnist Esther Cepeda (2015) relates an incident that occurred in a parking lot of a library. A man said to her, "We no speaky Spanish here." She retorted, "I have a graduate degree and I don't speaky stupid" (p. A19). For some, the English-only movement is a genuine attempt to unify an increasingly multicultural nation, but for others, it provides acceptable cover for ethnic prejudice.

The increasing globalization of business makes the choice of language to communicate within and among multicultural groups and organizations a significant issue. "Those who share a mother-tongue have a linguistic bond that differs from those who speak the same language as a second language" (Victor, 2007, p. 3). The choice of language to conduct business can directly affect teamwork and long-term business relationships for good or ill (Chen et al., 2006; Swift & Huang, 2004). If English, for example, is chosen as the preferred language of business, this can create an in-group/out-group dynamic between those who speak English easily and those who do not. When a group speaks a language not well understood by all of its members, as can occur in our increasingly multicultural workplaces, those left out of the conversation because of difficulties understanding the language spoken may feel ostracized and angry. This linguistic divide can reduce group productivity (Dotan-Eliaz et al., 2009).

Clearly, language is more than a mere neutral vehicle of information transmission (see Box 4-1). Language can help us improve the human condition by promoting tolerance and cooperation, or it can fan the embers of prejudice, ignite aggression, or fuel the flames of violence.

Competent Language Use: Problems and Solutions

The power of language makes it a vehicle for both positive and negative communication. In this section, several principal problems that

BOX 4-1 FOCUS ON CONTROVERSY

The Language of Texting: G9

Texting has become a hugely popular form of communication worldwide. Introduced to the world in 1992, texting has produced a substantial controversy, once again demonstrating that language is not a neutral vehicle of communication. Claims such as texting is destroying students' literacy and "fogs your brain like cannabis" are common. One columnist expressed "how texting is wrecking our language" with this over-heated

rhetoric: "It is the relentless onward march of the texters, the SMS (Short Message Service) vandals who are doing to our language what Genghis Khan did to his neighbors eight hundred years ago" (Humphrys, 2007). Really? In his book *Txtng: The gr8 db8*, David Crystal (2008), an internationally recognized linguist, comments: "It is the extraordinary antipathy to texting which has surprised me. I don't think I have ever come across a topic which has attracted more adult antagonism" (p. viii). He goes on to note: "All the popular beliefs about texting are wrong, or at least debatable" (p. 9).

Texting is not a new language or slang. "Texting is just another variety of language, which has arisen as a result of a particular technology" (p. 164). Texting language follows grammatical rules for Standard English. Claims that teens accustomed to frequent texting slip into using texting abbreviations when writing essays for composition classes are highly suspect (Crystal, 2008). Linguist Naomi Baron (2008) discovered from her research on college students that "abbreviations were rare, contractions were less common than expected, and that when it came to emoticons, students seemed to have a stunted vocabulary." She continued by noting that students usually realize the difference between writing essays and texting, and they typically respond appropriately except for an occasional slip-up.

The assertion that teens are becoming illiterate as a result of texting addiction is also highly dubious. A series of studies actually showed the opposite (Plester et al., 2009; Wood et al., 2014). There proved to be a strong positive relationship between use of texting language and success in use of Standard English (Kemp & Bushnell, 2011). Students "could not be good at texting if they had not already developed considerable literacy awareness" (Crystal, 2008, p. 162). As Crystal concludes: "Texting is one of the most innovative linguistic phenomena of modern times, and perhaps that is why it has generated such strong emotions . . . Yet all the evidence suggests that belief in an impending linguistic disaster is a consequence of a mythology largely created by the media" (p. 173). Texting is g9 (genius).

Questions for Thought

1. Is texting ever an appropriate communication medium in a college classroom?

2. Although texting itself is not merely slang, can there be slang in texting?

3. Are there any ideas or concepts that cannot be communicated in texting abbreviations?

occur when we use language ineffectively and inappropriately are discussed. Competent language usage for each problem is also explored.

Signal Reactions: Responding, Not Thinking

A **signal reaction** is an automatic, unthinking, emotional response to a symbol (Rothwell, 1982). In several experiments, participants reacted to "hot button" terms such as *affirmative action* and *death penalty* in about a quarter of a second (Lodge & Taber, 2005). This is too swift to process information relevant to these terms. Strong, swift, emotional reactions to verbal obscenity (see Box 4-3), vulgar language, ethnic slurs, pledges, oaths, slogans, ritualized greetings, chants, and buzzwords in advertising and politics are other instances of signal reactions to words.

SOURCE OF SIGNAL REACTIONS: CONNOTATIVE MEANING

The source of most signal reactions is connotative meaning. **Connotation** is personal meaning. It is the volatile, individual, subjective meaning of a word. Connotations have three dimensions (Osgood, 1969): *evaluation* (e.g., good/bad), *potency* (e.g., strong/weak), and *activity* (e.g., active/passive). Connotation changes from individual to individual, sometimes in barely perceptible shades of difference and sometimes in spectacular ways (see Box 4-2).

Connotative meaning is different from *denotative meaning*. **Denotation** is shared meaning. It is the objective meaning of words commonly agreed to by members of a speech community and usually found in a dictionary (although some words are left out of dictionaries, all have denotative meaning). The common denotation of *Rottweiler*, for example, is "a large breed of dog characterized by a short tail and short, black hair with tan markings." Connotations for the word, depending on your experience with such a dog, might vary from "cute" to "vicious" (evaluative), "powerful" to "indifferent" (potency), and "perpetual motion" to "sleepy" (activity).

Signal reactions to connotative meaning can launch individuals from their recliners and spring them into action with little thought about the consequences. Signal reactions can provoke offense, aggression, and violence (see Box 4-3). The U.S. Supreme Court recognized this decades ago in its precedent-setting 1942 decision *Chaplinsky v. New Hampshire*, which

---

BOX 4-2 DEVELOPING COMMUNICATION COMPETENCE

Measuring Connotative Meaning

Osgood (1969) originated the semantic differential to measure the varying connotative meaning between individuals. Individuals can be compared by asking each to respond to a word by assigning a number from 1 to 7 on a series of bipolar scales. For example,

TWITTER:

Good	○1 ○2 ○3 ○4 ○5 ○6 ○7	Bad
Hot	○1 ○2 ○3 ○4 ○5 ○6 ○7	Cold
Active	○1 ○2 ○3 ○4 ○5 ○6 ○7	Passive
Strong	○1 ○2 ○3 ○4 ○5 ○6 ○7	Weak
Pleasant	○1 ○2 ○3 ○4 ○5 ○6 ○7	Unpleasant

Try it yourself. Complete the semantic differentials for the word *Twitter*. Have a friend and a parent do likewise without them seeing your responses in advance. Now compare the results. Do you see any differences? You can do the same for any word (try *textbook* or *texting*).

BOX 4-3 FOCUS ON CONTROVERSY

Verbal Taboos: A Question of Appropriateness

One of my friends, whose daughter was four years old at the time, told this story. His daughter's name was Janie, and while playing with a boy of about her age in the neighborhood, she became very angry by something the boy did to her. Janie turned to the little boy and yelled, "I'm going to shit on your head!" Janie's mom heard this outburst and sternly admonished her daughter, "Janie, we don't talk like that." Janie paused, then turned to the boy and said, "I'm going to shit on your arm."

Janie's mom clearly had a signal reaction to Janie's use of an offensive word. Denotative meaning doesn't appear to be the real problem, however. The objectionable word was used for centuries in England without causing offense before becoming taboo in the early part of the 19th century (Bryson, 1990). Do you think Janie's mother would have been so alarmed and stern if Janie had said "I'm going to *toidee* on your head" instead? If denotative meaning is producing the signal reaction, why can a doctor ask you for a *feces* or *stool* sample without inviting reproach (even though mild embarrassment might accompany the request)? The denotation of all three terms for excrement is identical, yet the connotative meaning is not. It is the word itself that offends quite apart from its denotative meaning (the map becomes the territory). A signal reaction to "obscene words" is a learned behavior. Janie didn't seem to realize that she had uttered a "bad word." She apparently thought that the location of the threatened act was the problem (the head would indeed be a more objectionable target than the arm).

When we consider English words from Great Britain that incite similar signal reactions, it is even more apparent that denotation is not the source of the response. In England, *bloody* is a swear word as objectionable as Janie's offending term (Pinker, 2007). *Bloody* has no potency for Americans, however, and sparks no strong negative evaluation. We don't have the cultural associations that condition us to react negatively.

We denounce the use of "obscene and profane words" even though their denunciation may make little logical sense (Pinker, 2007). *Virgin, slut, tart, sex, virtuous,* and *bum* were all banned from U.S. newspapers and motion pictures until the second half of the 20th century. The famous line from the 1939 movie *Gone with the Wind*—"Frankly, my dear, I don't give a damn"—almost became the tepid and nonsensical "Frankly, my dear, I don't give a straw" because of objections to *damn* as a swear word (Dawn, 2014).

The prohibition on taboo words has relaxed in recent years, but despite the widespread and frequent use of taboo words among adults, and especially college students (Jay & Janschewitz, 2012), taboo words can still provoke negative responses. A Harris survey for CareerBuilder found that half of workers across America swear at work, 95% in front of other workers and 51% in front of their bosses, but rarely in front of clients. Men swear more than women, but only by a 54% to 47% margin. More importantly, 81% of employers believe that swearing at work is unprofessional, 71% believe it exhibits lack of control, and 68% view it as immature. Nevertheless, 25% of employers admit to swearing at their employees. A majority of employers (57%) said that they would be less likely to promote an employee who swears at work (Grasz, 2012). A Gallup survey of teens found that 75% agreed that "foul language" should be restricted in written assignments for a class (Ray, 2005).

Individuals, however, respond to taboo words in various ways. Some people find even relatively mild epithets completely objectionable—to be fighting words. Others are not bothered in the least even by the most outrageous obscenities or racist slurs. An Associated Press-MTV poll of 1,355 respondents ages 14 to 24 reported that half feel free to use racial epithets and offensive slang terms when texting on their cell phones or posting to sites such as Facebook. Most respondents perceived the slurs to be funny, not hurtful (Cass & Agiesta, 2011). Again, this underlines the connotative, personal

(continued)

BOX 4-3 FOCUS ON CONTROVERSY

Verbal Taboos: A Question of Appropriateness (continued)

meaning of taboo words. If the expectation is that coarse and vulgar language is permissible, even encouraged, in some situations (e.g., taverns or locker rooms), the reaction to it obviously would be quite different. The appropriateness or inappropriateness of verbal obscenity or other offensive terms is dependent on context (Jay & Janschewitz, 2012).

Questions for Thought

1. Is it ever appropriate to use obscene language? Should children be forbidden to use obscene and profane language? Why?

2. Are there ethical reasons to ban certain words? Which words would you ban, if any? Why?

3. Does the who, what, where, when, why, and how of communication contexts (see Chapter 1) influence our perception of verbal obscenity? Explain.

---

ruled that "fighting words" are not protected speech. More recently, "speech codes" banning "hate speech"—derogatory references to "race, sex, sexual orientation, or disability"—have emerged on college campuses, leading to court challenges and national debate over free speech (Lukianoff, 2013). The potential of hate speech to ignite signal reactions and tripwire explosions of violence is real.

COMPETENCE AND SIGNAL REACTIONS: DEVELOPING SEMANTIC REACTIONS

Here are two suggestions for avoiding problems of signal reactions and making your language usage appropriate and effective:

1. *Learn to follow signal reactions with semantic reactions.* A **semantic reaction** is a delayed, thoughtful response that seeks to decipher the user's intended meaning of a word, thus short-circuiting a behavioral response to the hair-trigger emotional reaction. A helpful way to delay your behavioral response until meaning has been confirmed is to ask the question "What do you mean?" or "Why are you saying that?" If someone calls you a racist, you can instantly react with verbal abuse or physical violence, or you can delay such behavioral responses by asking "What

do you mean by racist?" or "Why do you think I'm racist?" This encourages a thoughtful response to your questions. The initial response would occur too swiftly (a quarter of a second) to short-circuit the *emotional* response, but that does not prevent training yourself to delay your *behavioral* response (acting on your emotional response) until meaning has been clarified.

2. *Refrain from using words that will likely trigger signal reactions.* Verbal obscenity or fighting words may cause no signal reaction within certain groups, but they will likely trigger signal reactions in many contexts (see Box 4-3). Consequently, it is advisable to adapt your language use to the context, avoiding words that will likely provoke aggression and violence with certain individuals and groups.

Provoking a signal reaction isn't always undesirable. Shouting "Look out!" when someone is so engrossed in text messaging that he or she is about to step in front of an oncoming car, for example, should elicit an immediate response from the person texting; otherwise, that person is liable to end up as road kill. Nevertheless, there are relatively few instances when careful

CRITICAL THINKING

The NAACP burying "the N word." This photo illustrates which of the following?

○ **1.** Some words are inherently, naturally offensive

○ **2.** The source of signal reactions to "the N word" is its denotative meaning

○ **3.** Language can powerfully influence perceptions and behavior

○ **4.** "The N word" can never be used inoffensively no matter the context.

Answers at end of chapter

thought is not superior to immediate behavioral reactions.

Language of Abuse and Exclusion

Abusive language has severe consequences for targets of hurtful words. One study found that verbal abuse is comparable to "witnessing domestic violence or nonfamilial sexual abuse" (Teicher et al., 2006). Verbal abuse from peers is also equivalent to parental verbal abuse in producing anxiety, depression, hostility, and drug use (Teicher et al., 2010). Peer abuse has the added dimension of often appearing on the Internet, so "these very public insults and virtual assaults can 'go viral,' taking on lives of their own and persisting long after they would have otherwise lost their immediacy" (Putnam, 2010, p. 1422).

Verbal abuse of nurses by doctors is a serious national problem only recently recognized (Brewer et al, 2013). One survey of 2,100 doctors and nurses by the American College of Physician Executives found that 85% of respondents experienced degrading comments and insults, 73% yelling, and 50% cursing (C. Johnson, 2009). In one instance, a doctor said to a nurse "You don't look dumber than my dog. Why can't you at least fetch what I need?" In another case, a surgeon shouted that "monkeys could be trained to do what scrub nurses do" (C. Johnson, 2009, p. 8). Verbal abuse by doctors has consequences. The more that abuse is showered on nurses, the more likely they are to quit their jobs (Brewer et al., 2013; Grenny, 2009). Aside from the negative effects on nurses, patient care is also at risk. A study called "Silence Kills," conducted by VitalSmarts and the American Association of Critical-Care Nurses, showed that more than 20% of health care professionals have witnessed harm to patients because of disrespectful and abusive communication, mostly by doctors toward nurses (Maxfield et al., 2005).

As a result of these survey findings, hospitals across the country are instituting zero-tolerance policies to end such verbal abuse.

Language can also lead to feelings of social exclusion. "We all feel the pain of ostracism about equally, no matter how tough or sensitive we are" (Williams, 2011, p. 32). Sometimes we feel ostracized at work when coworkers speak Spanish but we speak only English, or vice versa. This social exclusion elicits a variety of negative outcomes, including hurt feelings, lowered self-esteem, and aggressive communication (Hitlan et al., 2006). This is life for many Latino baseball players who have joined major league teams (Davidson, 2014). Initially, most struggle with English, and many admit that it is the biggest obstacle in their career advancement. They often feel others perceive them as dumb when their initial attempts to speak English go awry.

Learning the language of connection and inclusion can be an effective antidote to poisonous language and ostracism, as discussed extensively in Chapter 8. The short version is to avoid abusive language. Treat people with respect as you would want them to treat you (remember the discussion of ethical communication in Chapter 1). Be sensitive to the feelings of exclusion that others may experience (pick up the signals) when the standard language spoken in groups and in the workplace is not a person's native language.

False Dichotomies: The Inaccuracy of Either-Or Framing

Advice columnist Ann Landers once raised a fuss when she coyly asked her female readers to answer this question: "Would you be content to be held close and treated tenderly and forget about 'the act'?" Landers was swamped with more than 90,000 responses. A stunning 72% of these respondents said they would prefer hugs to sexual intercourse ("Ann Landers Learns," 1985). The talk-show circuit went crazy. Experts, self-appointed and otherwise, all wanted to comment on the results. Typically, Landers' survey results were interpreted as proof that women are starved for affection from their insensitive lovers, and that they are willing to forego sexual consummation for tender caresses from their partners.

If you recognized that Landers asked a question that presented two choices as mutually exclusive alternatives (sex or hugs) when a third choice exists, congratulations! You just recognized a **false dichotomy**—using either-or language to frame a choice as though only two opposing possibilities exist when at least a third option is clearly available. How many women do you think would have answered "hugs only" if offered "both hugs and sexual intercourse" as a third choice?

If a thousand people were randomly chosen and plotted on a graph according to height, weight, or age, most of these individuals would bunch in the middle (average height and average weight), and only a few would fit the extremes (very tall or extremely short). This result is called a *bell-shaped curve*, or *normal distribution*. A dichotomy (*either* this *or* that) becomes false when our thinking and perception are focused on the extremes of the distribution while we ignore the vast middle.

Most people can't be accurately described as short or tall, fat or thin, smart or dumb, young or old, strong or weak. We fall somewhere in between. The issue of sexual orientation typically gets framed as "gay or straight," but psychologist Robert Epstein (2006) notes that it "lies on a continuum" from "exclusive same-sex attraction" to "mainly same-sex attraction" to "mainly opposite-sex attraction" to "exclusive opposite-sex attraction . . . It is not an all-or-nothing state" (p. 56).

False dichotomies can have a significant impact on how we think and act. Michael Huspek (2000) studied a riot at the Penitentiary of New Mexico that resulted in hundreds of serious injuries and 33 deaths. He concludes that *oppositional codes* "provided their respective users with diametrically opposed views of the world and ways of acting upon it" (p. 144). A "model prisoner" to the penitentiary's administration was a "punk" to inmates; a "trouble maker" to prison officials was a "bad ass" to prisoners; a "cooperative informant" to officials was a "snitch" to inmates; a "psychopathic personality" to officials was a "gladiator" to prisoners. Given the intractable oppositional codes (false dichotomies) prevalent in the prison, the riot was probably "inevitable." As the riot erupted, these oppositional codes provided agents representing the two sides "with increasingly few meanings that might have been

"Next question: I believe that life is a constant striving for balance, requiring frequent tradeoffs between morality and necessity, within a cyclic pattern of joy and sadness, forging a trail of bittersweet memories until one slips, inevitably, into the jaws of death. Agree or disagree?"

Imagine having only these two opposite choices, agree or disagree, to the complex question asked.

used effectively to derail the ever-escalating loco-motion of violence" (p. 157).

In some instances, a dichotomy is not false because there are only two opposing choices possible. Being "sort of pregnant," "almost a virgin," or "slightly dead" isn't a realistic third option, for example. Most dichotomous framing, however, inappropriately implies that the only possibilities are the two extreme choices when clearly this is not accurate.

There are two steps you can take to avoid false dichotomies:

1. *Think pluralistically.* When presented with a dichotomous choice, search for additional options. Ask the question, "Are these our only two choices?" This question reframes our thinking from dichotomous (considering only two contradictory choices) to pluralistic (expanding the choices).

2. *Recognize degrees of difference when using language.* To be appropriate and effective, your language should attempt to approximate reality closely, but false dichotomies allow for only gross approximations. The "always-never" dichotomy is one such example: "You always leave your dirty clothes on the floor for me to pick up, and you never put your tools away." Strive to use language more precisely. This means using terms such as *slightly, moderately, occasionally, rarely, sometimes, more often,* and *usually.* Note the different feel when replacing dichotomous language: "*Sometimes* you leave your clothes on the floor and your tools out. I'd appreci-ate it if you would pick up after yourself *more often.*" This is not the language of the wishy-washy fence straddler but the language of precision. The "always-never" dichotomy is usually an exaggeration, not an accurate depiction of events. Strive for improvement, not perfection.

Mislabeling: Inaccurate Descriptions

The power of labels can also produce significant problems if the labels are misapplied. In a clas-sic study, Ellen Langer and Robert Abelson (1974) showed therapists a videotape of an ordinary-looking man being interviewed. Half of the therapists were told in advance that the man was a "job applicant," and half were told he was a "psychiatric patient." Those therapists who thought they were watching a job interview described the man using terms such as *ingenious, open, straightforward, ordinary, candid,* and *up-standing.* Those therapists who thought they were observing a psychiatric patient described the man as *rigid, dependent, passive aggressive, im-pulsive,* and "frightened of his own aggressive impulses." Both groups of therapists saw exactly the same videotaped interview, but each group perceived a different reality. Labels can have a powerful biasing effect.

BIAS AND STIGMA: DISTORTING PERCEPTIONS

Labels can stigmatize and diminish people. The power of labels is particularly evident when mislabeling occurs. For example, eight individ-uals, none with any real psychiatric problems, gained admission to 12 psychiatric hospitals (some did it twice). This was the initial stage of a controversial study conducted by David Rosenhan (1973). These eight "pseudopatients" gained admittance under slightly false pretenses. They were instructed to complain to the admissions staff at each hospital that they heard voices that said "empty," "hollow," and "thud." Once admitted, none of the pseudopatients was to complain of these symptoms again. Eleven of the pseudopatients were diagnosed (mislabeled) as *schizophrenic*, and one was said to have *manic-depressive psychosis* (bipolar disorder). The pseudopatients had to remain in the hospital until the staff recognized the mistaken diagnosis or until they were simply freed. The stays in the hospital ranged from 7 to 52 days; the average was 19 days. Ironically, 35 of the 118 actual patients in the hospitals recognized the ruse of the pseudopatients and said so openly, but none of the staff ever questioned the initial diagnosis. Even when the pseudopatients were released, hospital records showed that their "psychiatric disorder" was merely "in remission," not cured or a mistaken diagnosis. Rosenhan replicated these disturbing findings in later studies (see Greenberg, 1981).

Psychiatric labels can stigmatize (Jacobson, 2014). They are particularly troublesome when misapplied. The stigma attached to these labels can linger even after full recovery from a real mental disorder. Individuals so labeled often become social lepers. Mislabeling mentally healthy individuals has the potential to ruin their lives. No one wants to be mislabeled, especially if the labels can stigmatize. Imagine how traumatic it would be if you were mislabeled as a child abuser, spouse abuser, rapist, or murderer.

The problem of mislabeling can be profoundly abusive. In one study, renowned speech pathologist Wendell Johnson purposely mislabeled children who exhibited no such speech problem as "stutterers." This mislabeling actually induced lifelong stuttering with ruinous consequences. The study was kept secret for 60 years and only discovered by an enterprising investigative reporter for the *San Jose Mercury News* (Dyer, 2001). Even though Johnson's purpose was laudable—to determine the cause of stuttering—the study was subsequently labeled

This is Mary Korlaske, victim of the "Monster Study" that made her a stutterer by labeling her as such when she was a child. This damaged her self-esteem, made her withdrawn, and caused her to be uneasy around people her entire life.

the "Monster Study" and correctly blasted as unethical.

COMPETENCE AND MISLABELING: OPERATIONAL DEFINITIONS

So how do you prevent the problem of mislabeling? Consider two steps:

1. *Operationally define significant labels.* An **operational definition** grounds a label by specifying which measurable behaviors or experiences are subsumed under the label and which are ruled out. When you ask someone to "be specific" or to "provide an example," you are asking them to operationalize their language. Operational definitions say, "For our purposes, an *'A' student* is anyone who scores 90% or above in the class." The Harvard School of Public Health operationally defines *binge drinking*, a behavior that almost half of the college students in the United States engage in, as "consuming five or more drinks at one sitting for men, and four or more drinks for women" (White & Hingson, 2013). Operational definitions clarify the meaning of labels to avoid misunderstanding and misapplication. You don't have to always agree with the operational definition, but at least you can understand what someone means when they use potentially confusing terms.

CRITICAL THINKING

This photo illustrates which of the following?

○ **1.** Mislabeling

○ **2.** Words can be too concrete to be useful

○ **3.** Operational definitions

○ **4.** Dead-level abstracting

Answers at end of chapter

2. *Apply the labels accurately once they have been operationalized.* Don't apply a label more broadly than the operational definition allows. Labeling older people *senile* simply because they have minor memory problems is inaccurate and inappropriate. Senility is not commonly defined as experiencing minor memory loss. The accuracy of any label depends on common agreement because word usage is conventional.

Dead-Level Abstracting: Ineffective Sense Making

The term **dead-level abstracting** (Johnson, 1946) refers to the practice of remaining stuck at one level of abstraction. As explained earlier, words operate at different levels of abstraction, from very vague to concrete or precise. Note the progression from high-level (vague) to low-level (concrete/precise) abstraction in the following statements:

George likes *sports.*

George likes *team sports.*

George likes *contact team sports.*

George likes *ice hockey and football.*

The first statement is fairly vague. The term *sports* includes many different kinds of sports. The second statement is more precise because it specifies "team" sports, but there are still many team sports from which to choose. The third statement is even more precise because "contact" identifies the specific type of team sports. Nevertheless, there are still many contact team sports. Finally, the last statement is the most precise and concrete because the particular team sports are indicated.

LANGUAGE INFLEXIBILITY: RIGID USE OF VAGUE OR CONCRETE WORDS

Dead-level abstraction occurs when we stick rigidly either to vague or to concrete words, thus making little sense. When politicians give speeches using vague, undefined terms such as *family values* or *patriotism*, voters can be forgiven for not knowing precisely what is meant. When they propose "comprehensive medical care for all," it's fair to ask, "What does that mean?" If they respond, "Really great coverage for every-one," you have dead-level abstracting. The response is as vague as the original statement. Research by Allan Paivio (1969) found that the degree of concreteness or vagueness of words could be the most important determinant of how easy or difficult it is to form mental images. Forming a clear image of a *horse, clown,* or *baseball* is easy. Forming a clear image of *truth, justice,* and the *American way* is difficult (although it may produce signal reactions). Concrete words produce concrete images; vague words can remain imprecise and fuzzy in our minds.

The solution to the problem of dead-level abstracting, however, does not lie in always speaking in concrete terminology and details. *Never rising above the level of the concrete and precise is also dead-level abstracting.* A professor who tells many jokes and stories may keep interest for a while, but eventually, students will ask, "What does this have to do with the class?" The details need to be tied to a higher level abstraction. All the jokes and stories need to be connected to concepts, principles, and generalizations. Otherwise, the professor is teaching trivia—unconnected factoids. Connecting the jokes and stories to the concepts and generalizations can produce learning.

COMMUNICATION COMPETENCE AND DEAD-LEVEL ABSTRACTING: THREE WAYS

To make your language use more effective, consider three suggestions for avoiding dead-level abstraction:

1. *Avoid by-passing.* When you assume that everyone assigns the same meaning to a word, without checking to see if it is true, you are by-passing. Vague, undefined words easily produce by-passing and consequent misunderstanding. If you by-pass, letting individuals remain in the fuzzy clouds of abstraction, there will be a lot of head-nodding affirmations among these individuals who are not aware that they sharply disagree.

2. *Operationally define abstract terms.* When a couple seeks help from a therapist, the therapist will likely request operational definitions frequently. If the husband says, "My wife and I are having a problem," the therapist undoubtedly will ask, "What specific

problem are you experiencing?" If the husband then responds, "We argue all the time," the therapist will pursue this abstraction by requesting, "What do you argue about?" "We argue about money," might be the response, whereupon the therapist might continue to ground the husband's language by further requesting, "Can you give me an example of a recent argument you had about money?" Each time, the therapist attempts to move the language from vague and abstract to precise and concrete. Thus, the husband moves from *problem* to *argument* to *argument about money* to a *specific behavioral example* of an argument about money.

3. Use *language flexibly.* Do not get stuck using either concrete or vague terms alone. Use both fluidly. When others get stuck at one level of abstraction, help them get traction and become unstuck by asking for examples or clearly identifiable behaviors that might clarify vague terms. If others remain frozen at the level of excessive concrete detail, ask them to clarify the significance or relevance of the detail.

Inferential Errors: Ineffective Guessing

There's a story of two women from the United States (a grandmother and her granddaughter), a Romanian officer, and a Nazi officer seated together in a train compartment. As the train passes through a dark tunnel, the sounds of a loud kiss and a slap are audible. When the train emerges from the tunnel, no words are spoken, but a noticeable welt forming on the face of the Nazi officer is observed by all. The grandmother muses to herself, "What a fine granddaughter I have raised. I have no need to worry. She can handle herself admirably." The granddaughter thinks to herself, "Grandmother packs a powerful wallop for a woman of her years. She sure is spunky." The Nazi officer, none too pleased by the course of events, ruminates to himself, "How clever is this Romanian. He steals a kiss and gets me slapped in the process." The Romanian chuckles to himself, "I am indeed clever. I kissed my hand and slapped a Nazi."

BOX 4-4 DEVELOPING COMMUNICATION COMPETENCE

The Uncritical Inference Test

Read the following story. For each statement about the story, choose **TRUE** if it can be determined from the information provided in the story that the statement is true, **FALSE** if the statement directly contradicts information provided in the story, or **?** if you cannot determine from the information provided whether the statement is either true or false. *Read the story only once,* and *don't check the story while answering the statements that follow.*

THE STORY: Pat Doyle was sitting behind the receptionist's desk typing rapidly on a computer. The executive director of the Atlantic Sports Equipment Company walked briskly by the receptionist and hurried into the office, grunting a hasty "Good morning" to Pat. A man with a briefcase, which had "Wilson's Sporting Goods" engraved on it, was leafing through a copy of *Wired* magazine while waiting in a chair. A few moments later, the director came out, made a beckoning motion, and said, "Hi, Jim! How's the sales racket?"

1. Pat, the executive director's receptionist, was typing rapidly on a computer.   ○ TRUE   ○ FALSE

2. Pat was sitting behind a desk while she typed rapidly.   ○ TRUE   ○ FALSE

3. Pat's boss walked briskly by the receptionist's desk.   ○ TRUE   ○ FALSE

4. Pat was sitting behind the desk when the executive director walked by and said, "Good morning."   ○ TRUE   ○ FALSE

5. The executive director hurried into his office.   ○ TRUE   ○ FALSE

6. A man with a briefcase was sitting in a chair.   ○ TRUE   ○ FALSE

7. A man was reading a copy of *Wired* magazine.   ○ TRUE   ○ FALSE

8. The man worked for Wilson's Sporting Goods.   ○ TRUE   ○ FALSE

9. The man was waiting to see the executive director.   ○ TRUE   ○ FALSE

10. The story involves only three people: a receptionist, the executive director of the company, and a salesman.   ○ TRUE   ○ FALSE

William Haney (1967) originally devised the "Uncritical Inference Test." The one above is a different version that I created. The correct answer for ALL of these statements is ?. Without exception, every statement is based on guesses (inferences) regarding what is likely, but not verifiably, true from the information provided. The reasons are as follows:

1. It can't be determined that Pat is the executive director's receptionist. Pat is merely sitting behind the receptionist's desk.

2. Is Pat a *she*? It can't be determined.

3. We don't know whether the executive director is Pat's boss.

4. Pat may not have been sitting behind the desk *when* the executive director walked by. Pat may have stood up (sign of respect?).

5. Is the executive director male ("his" office)? It can't be determined.

6. The man was "waiting" in a chair. May not have been sitting (ever see kids in a doctor's office?).

(continued)

BOX 4-4 **DEVELOPING COMMUNICATION COMPETENCE**

The Uncritical Inference Test (continued)

7. The man was "leafing through" *Wired* magazine. That may include some reading or not.

8. An engraved briefcase doesn't automatically mean that the man worked for Wilson's Sporting Goods any more than a "Harvard University" sweatshirt means that you actually attend that institution.

9. We don't know whom the man was waiting to see.

10. There is Pat, "a receptionist" who may or may not be Pat, an executive director, a man waiting in a chair, and someone named "Jim" who may or may not be the man in the chair. We don't know how many people there are.

NOTE: All statements are inferences, but some are better inferences than others. The man was very likely sitting in the chair because that is what most adults would do. That's a reliable inference. The executive director referred to as male, however, decades ago might have been a fairly reliable inference because most executive directors were male, but today, that is assuredly not the case. It's an unreliable inference.

This story illustrates **inferential error**—a mistaken conclusion that results from the assumption that inferences are factual descriptions of reality instead of interpretations of varying accuracy made by individuals (see Box 4-4). The facts reported are that the four characters in the story heard what sounded like a kiss followed by a slap. The Nazi officer had a welt on his face. Any conclusions drawn from these facts is an inference (a conclusion about the unknown based on the known). It was completely dark in the tunnel, and inferences were made that the sounds heard were that of a kiss and a slap. These are reliable inferences because we've all heard the sounds of a kiss and a slap many times. The visible welt on the face of the Nazi officer is further evidence for the reliability of the slap inference. Three people made an inferential error, however, because each leaped to a conclusion regarding who kissed and slapped whom based on superficial information. Only the Romanian knows the truth.

The Bush administration, based on faulty intelligence, inferred that Saddam Hussein possessed weapons of mass destruction (WMD). The inference turned out to be incorrect, but the United States went to war with Iraq using WMD as a prime justification (Daniel, 2008). The unfortunate practice of many law enforcement agencies in the United States to engage in "racial profiling"—making inferences typically based on superficial information (e.g., race, dress, or type of automobile)—produces many more inferential

errors than valid inferences (Lamberth, 1998). Nevertheless, a report by the American Civil Liberties Union (2009) concludes that "the practice of racial profiling by members of law enforcement at the federal, state, and local levels remains a widespread problem throughout the United States, impacting the lives of millions of people in African American, Asian, Latino, South Asian, and Arab communities." Many tragic incidences resulting in police killing unarmed minorities suggest racial profiling is a serious problem.

There are two ways to avoid inferential errors:

1. *Base inferences on a substantial quantity of information.* Limited information can lead to inaccurate inferences in the form of such practices as gossip and rumors.

2. *Base inferences on high-quality information.* Weak evidence produces weak inferences. You don't have to check every inference you make, but you should check important ones, especially if the quantity and quality of information on which the inference is based are limited or questionable.

Jargon, Euphemisms, and Slang: Promoting Misunderstanding

Language can promote clear thinking, or it can confuse and conceal. Sometimes the confusion is unintentional, and occasionally, concealment is warranted. Nevertheless, using words to confuse or conceal can produce ineffective communication.

Instead of achieving the important goal of understanding, you promote misunderstanding. Consider *jargon, euphemisms,* and *slang.*

JARGON: VERBAL SHORTHAND

Every profession and trade group has its specialized language called **jargon**. *Jargon is not inherently a poor use of language.* It is a kind of verbal shorthand. When lawyers use terms such as *prima facie case* and *habeas corpus,* they communicate to other attorneys and officers of the court very specific information without tedious, verbose explanation. "To the initiated, jargon is efficient, economical, and even crucial in that it can capture distinctions not made in the ordinary language" (Allan & Burridge, 1991, p. 201). Signal reactions, false dichotomies, dead-level abstracting, and inferential error are apt examples from this chapter.

Jargon, however, can pose problems for those who do not understand the verbal shorthand. When doctors use terms such as *bilateral periorbital hematoma* (black eye), *tinnitus* (ear ringing), *agrypnia* (sleeplessness), *cephalalgia* (headache), and *hyperemesis* (excessive vomiting), they communicate very specific conditions to medical staff, but they more than likely mystify patients and turn common conditions into dangerous diseases in the minds of the linguistically uninitiated (Wagner, 2011). The message is concealed when it should be revealed to those who most need to know.

Edspeak, the sometimes bewildering jargon of educators (Ravitch, 2007), can intimidate parents who may hesitate revealing their unfamiliarity with the jargon. Parents can be forgiven if they are flummoxed by jargon used to "explain" their child's strengths and shortcomings: *phonemic sequencing errors, phonological process delays, normed modality processing, morphosyntactic skills, scaffolding, hybrid learning, blended learning, psychometrics, deficit model, un-leveling, fitnessgram testing,* and *additive model,* to name just a few. To most parents, this bushel basket of buzzwords probably sounds closer to Klingon than any language they speak (Lithwick, 2013). Parents become the "outsiders," disconnected from teachers and administrators who "speak the language."

There are two guidelines for the competent use of jargon:

1. Cut the use of jargon when conversing with someone who is unfamiliar with it.

2. If jargon is necessary, operationalize terms unfamiliar to the receiver. Some school districts offer free jargon handbooks to parents.

EUPHEMISMS: LINGUISTIC NOVOCAIN

Businesses and corporations don't lay off workers anymore. They engage in *force management programs* and *duplication reduction,* or they give employees a *career-change opportunity.* The U.S. government didn't torture Iraqi prisoners; they engaged in *enhanced interrogation* such as waterboarding, a practice deemed torture by U.S. war crimes tribunals after World War II and among the charges that led to the executions of some of the Japanese perpetrators (Gorman, 2015). These are **euphemisms**—a form of linguistic Novocain whereby word choices numb us to or camouflage unpleasant or offensive realities. The word e*uphemism* is derived from the Greek *euphemismos,* meaning "to speak well of." It substitutes "kinder, gentler" terms for words that hurt, cause offense, or create problems for us. Euphemisms psychologically distance us from what may be painful or uncomfortable (McCallum & McGlone, 2011).

Not all euphemisms are inappropriate. Using *passed away* instead of *dead* is unlikely to cause harm to anyone, and it may cushion a devastating reality for grieving relatives and friends. Nevertheless, euphemisms can create mischief. When the nuclear power industry refers to out-of-control nuclear reactors simply going on *power excursions* or experiencing *rapid oxidation* (a major fire), the public is left in a fog. When *unplanned hypercriticality* (approaching a meltdown of the reactor core) can result in *spontaneous energetic disassembly* (a catastrophic explosion), the potential danger is hidden from us. When doctors refer to *therapeutic misadventures* (operations that kill patients), we have a clear case of inappropriate language use.

Here are two suggestions for dealing competently with euphemisms:

1. *Use euphemisms cautiously and wisely.* This is a judgment call. Substituting euphemisms for profanities and obscenities should cause few, if any, problems. Using euphemisms to confuse, however, can be more problematic. Normally, your communication goal

should be clarity, not confusion. Using language to confuse isn't always evil, but you wouldn't want to make it standard practice.

2. *Expunge dangerous euphemisms.* Euphemisms that simply lie to us to hide ugly, dangerous truths should be eliminated from our communication in all but the rarest instances.

SLANG: CASUAL LANGUAGE

Unless you are confident that your listeners will comprehend and identify with such casual speech, be very cautious using **slang**—the highly informal words not in standard usage that are employed by a group with a common interest. Slang acts as a means to identify those individuals who belong to a group and those who are outsiders. If you don't speak the slang, you don't belong. Using terms such as *warez* (pirated software, music, or movies copied from a friend or downloaded from the Internet), *off the*

hinges (outstanding or great), or *dot gone* (failed Internet company) may leave your listeners in a fog of confusion (check www.urbandictionary. com or SlangSite.com for translations and updates of constantly changing slang). Slang usually emerges and becomes popular among teens, college students, musicians, or marginalized groups in society (gays and lesbians; gangs).

It is typically inappropriate to use slang in formal speeches and presentations or at formal gatherings. Research shows, however, that creating a mildly informal classroom climate by using some positive slang (e.g., *awesome* or *props*) is well received by students and more effective than lectures entirely free of slang (Mazer & Hunt, 2008a, 2008b). Even so, using slang that is an awkward fit for you personally (e.g., an older person trying to sound young and "cool"), however, can be embarrassing. Slang also can become dated quickly, making you sound hopelessly "uncool."

 **Summary**

Language is a structured system of symbols for communicating meaning. It is our unique communication system. All languages have phonological, morphological, syntactic, and semantic sets of rules that allow us to share meaning with others. Every language has structure, productivity, displacement, and self-reflexiveness capabilities. Language influences thought, perception, and behavior in a wide variety of ways.

Language is a window to our minds and a catalyst of our behavior. It is our chief means of communicating with other human beings. As Pinker (1999) so nicely puts it, to notice the "deep parallels in the languages of the French and the Germans, the Arabs and the Israelis, the East and the West, people living in the Age of the Internet and people living in the Stone Age, is to catch a glimpse of the psychic unity of humankind" (p. 239). Language is our connection

to the world, and we pay dearly for misusing it. We need to replace gender-biased language with gender-neutral references, signal reactions with semantic reactions, abusive language with nonabusive terminology, false dichotomies with pluralistic thinking, dead-level abstracting with flexible language use, mislabeling with accurate operational definitions, inferential errors with more reliable conclusions based on high-quantity and high-quality information. And we need to use jargon, euphemisms, and slang clearly and carefully.

Answers for Critical Thinking captions:

"WHY" SIGN (P. 86): #1

CALVIN & HOBBES (P. 88): #3 and #4

BLURRY PHOTO (P. 93): a cow

NAACP (P. 101): #3

SIGN (P. 105): #4

Quizzes Without Consequences

Test your knowledge before your exam! Go to the companion website at www.oup.com/us/rothwell, click on the Student Resources for each chapter, and take the Quizzes Without Consequences.

Film School Case Studies

Doubt (2008). Drama; PG-13

Meryl Streep plays a Catholic nun who begins to suspect a highly popular priest (Philip Seymour Hoffman) of child molestation. Identify examples of uncritical inferences and euphemistic and evasive language.

Mean Girls (2004). Comedy/Drama; PG-13

The story of Cady Heron (Lindsay Lohan), raised by her zoologist parents in the African bush country and thrown into the unfamiliar environment of public high school in the United States. Examine Cady's experience with slang terminology to infiltrate "the Plastics" (high-status girl clique). How does language affect Cady's thoughts, perceptions, and behavior?

The N Word (2007). Documentary; Not Rated

This documentary explores the many uses and abuses of perhaps the most inflammatory word in the English language. Do you have signal reactions while watching? Are all uses of the word offensive to you? Do we give this word too much power by calling it "the N word"? Explain.

Still Alice (2014). Drama; PG-13

Alice (Julianne Moore in an Oscar-winning performance) is a brilliant linguistics professor who contracts early onset Alzheimer's disease and progressively loses her facility for language. Analyze this deterioration from the standpoint of the basic elements of language. Which parts of language degrade first? Note the loss of self-identity depicted and the close connection of language and our self-perception.

BY THE END OF THIS CHAPTER, YOU SHOULD BE ABLE TO:

1. Understand the power of nonverbal communication.

2. Compare and contrast nonverbal and verbal communication.

3. Recognize and understand the many channels of nonverbal communication.

Nonverbal Communication

AT THE 2014 ACADEMY AWARDS SHOW, actor John Travolta introduced Idina Menzel, the "Let It Go" singer from the animated movie *Frozen*, as Adele Dazeem (inexplicably sounding like a random choice bearing not even a slight resemblance to the singer's actual name). In an attempt to make light of the famous flub in front of millions of viewers, Travolta and Menzel were paired to make an Oscar presentation at the 2015 Academy Awards. Host Neil Patrick Harris introduced them to the audience with this quip: "Benedict Cumberbatch: It's not only the most awesome name in show business; it's also the sound you get when you ask John Travolta to pronounce 'Ben Affleck'" (Serico, 2015). On stage before presenting the Oscar, Menzel spoofed Travolta by presenting him as her "very dear friend, Glom Gazingo." Travolta then grabbed Menzel's chin while flashing a big smile (reportedly a planned stunt agreed to by both individuals). The audience laughed, and Menzel smiled broadly, but then Travolta

4. Improve your communication competence with nonverbal codes.

seemed incapable of letting go. He commenced to paw her face for what seemed to be the time it takes to gestate a baby. The Internet and Twitter went wild commenting on Travolta's "creepy face touching." Touching a person's face displays intimacy. It is normally off-limits for a stranger or an acquaintance (Chillot, 2013).

Touches, eye contact, dress, appearance, laughter, and a host of other nonverbal cues are exhibited daily, but we often don't recognize their impact until problems emerge. "When someone hisses at me, or makes those kissy smoochey noises, I hate that—that's my pet peeve," says American artist Tatyana Fazlalizadeh, who began the *Stop Telling Women to Smile* project in New York City. Fazlalizadeh paints posters and plasters them all over the city decrying the incessant street harassment of women by men. According to one national survey, 65% of women have experienced street harassment. Men are also harassed on the street (20% reported it in the survey), but most often the harassment of men is homophobic (Hess, 2014).

Women surveyed reported constant, aggressive street harassment from horn honking, wolf whistles, sexual grunts, animal noises, ogling, obscene gestures, and more. When women typically frown or look straight ahead, trying to "ignore" the unwelcomed sexist attention, male perpetrators of the nonverbal harassment often tell female targets to smile (Shearman, 2014).

As Soraya Chemaly (2013) observes, "Every woman wonders, no matter how briefly, about what could happen if she doesn't smile."

It is often difficult for men to appreciate the harassing nature of such unwanted attention from strangers on the streets of our cities. Their reaction frequently is "Stop taking everything so seriously. It's just a compliment" (Lang, 2015). That's a glib response to a serious problem, however. "After the thin veneer of flattery wears off, what is left is a sometimes-daily awareness of vulnerability, sexual objectification, shame at being targeted, and shame at not fighting back" (Chemaly, 2013). The 2014 documentary film *She's Beautiful When She's Angry* depicts, among many other feminist protest tactics, the 1970 Ogle-In on Wall Street, in which women lined the sidewalks and streets and, when brokers (almost entirely male) spilled out of the stock exchange, treated the men to catcalls, ogling, and other nonverbal (and some verbal) street harassment. The men were not amused (Yerman, 2015).

Nonverbal communication is an integral part of your daily communication with others. Much of what passes as insight about this important aspect of human communication, especially on the Internet and in social media, however, is misinformation. *The principal purpose of this chapter is to show how you might improve your nonverbal communication with others* based on research, not media speculation and unsupported supposition.

The Power of Nonverbal Communication

The city council of Palo Alto, California, once proposed a code of conduct that would ban elected officials from nonverbal expressions of disagreement, such as rolling their eyes, shaking their heads, or frowning, during discussions and debates. The proposal was meant to encourage civility at a time of great bickering during council meetings. The proposed code garnered national media coverage, worldwide attention, and no small amount of ridicule. Opponents defended their "right to frown" and wondered if the "demeanor police" might extend the code to include those who are caught "grinning too much." The proposal was subsequently dropped, but it underlined awareness of the power that nonverbal communication can have.

General Overview: Powerful, But Do Not Overstate

Nonverbal communication is central to emotional expression, impression management, and much of what facilitates healthy relationships (Giles & Le Poire, 2006). Eye contact, for instance, is especially important to social connection—documented in Chapter 1 as intrinsically necessary for human well-being (Lieberman, 2013). According to a study conducted by Quantified Impressions, a communications analytics company, emotional connection during conversations with others is established when eye contact is made during 60% to 70% of the conversation. The rise of multitasking on smartphones and other electronic devices, however, is reducing eye contact below this level (Gregoire, 2013). Daniel Sieberg, author of *The Digital Diet*, observes, "All too often we're like cornered animals with our eyes darting from device to human and back to device" (quoted in Gregoire, 2013). Note how often individuals don't even look up from their smartphones or laptops when conversing. Some people text message while supposedly engaging in conversation with someone right in front of them. Social connection is illusory when we are distracted (Goleman, 2013).

You can also determine nonverbally the socioeconomic status of individuals by observing people's level of *dis*connection when you speak to them. Those born into privilege may feel less need to foster a good first impression, so they exhibit disengagement by fidgeting, yawning, doodling, playing with social media, or otherwise showing disinterest. Mundane conversation may be viewed as "beneath them." Avoiding such nonverbal markers of disinterest typically indicates that one is likely not from the privileged class. Those of less fortunate means may feel more compelled to make a strong first impression, so they remain engaged even if bored with the conversation (Kraus & Keltner, 2009).

How important nonverbal communication is to the communication process in general, however, has been badly overstated in some

The increase in multitasking on smartphones and laptops while conversing is reducing the eye contact necessary for emotional connection between people.

instances. Some communication texts and numerous Internet sites misinterpret research by Albert Mehrabian and assert that 93% of all meaning in messages is communicated nonverbally (see Lapakko, 1997, for a detailed critique). Mehrabian (1971) never drew such a broad conclusion from his research. In fact, he repudiated it directly: "Clearly it is absurd to imply or suggest that the verbal portion of all communication constitutes only 7% of the message" (Mehrabian, 1995). He repudiated it for good reason, too—because it makes no sense. Turn off the sound when watching a movie scene of two characters quarreling and see if you can ascertain 93% of the meaning of their argument. Yes, you can know they are quarreling and even ascertain emotion (anger), but can you discern specific meaning? Travel to Paris without understanding French and observe Parisians in animated conversation. Can you understand more than a hint of the meaning in their transaction?

Another somewhat less extreme claim, based on limited research by Ray Birdwhistell (1970), is that communication is 65% nonverbal. The exact percentage is unimportant and certainly dubious for the same reasons already stated. Nonverbal communication, however, often does play a predominant part in communication with others (Giles & Le Poire, 2006). This is a remarkable conclusion considering the power of language to shape thought, perception, and behavior. The strength of your handshake can communicate degree of confidence. The intensity of your anger is exhibited mostly nonverbally (e.g., tone of voice, facial expressions, gestures, and posture). Anxiety is chiefly communicated nonverbally. As noted in Chapter 1, 94% of virtual group members found the "inability to read nonverbal cues" to be a significant problem (Solomon, 2010). If nonverbal communication were merely incidental to verbal messages, few would find this to be a problem. The power of nonverbal communication, regardless of the dubious percentages of import assigned to it, will be rendered obvious as this chapter unfolds.

Culture and Nonverbal Communication: Some Challenges

On November 14, 2009, President Barack Obama bowed to Japanese Emperor Akihito as a gesture of greeting. A controversy ensued. Former Vice-President Dick Cheney asserted: "There is no reason for an American president to bow to anyone. Our friends and allies don't expect it, and our enemies see it as a sign of weakness." Fox News anchor Steve Doocy asserted: "For 233 years of precedent dating back

President Obama greets Japanese Emperor Akihito. Note the accommodation both individuals make to ritual greetings in each man's respective culture: bowing in Japan and handshaking in the United States. Nevertheless, Obama was heavily criticized by some for bowing (perceived as showing subservience to the emperor). Imagine the uproar in Japan if the president had refused to bow.

to the very founding of this Republic, American leaders do not bow to leaders of other countries." Actually, Richard Nixon bowed to Chairman Mao of China, and Dwight Eisenhower bowed to French President Charles de Gaulle. George W. Bush even held hands and kissed Saudi Crown Prince Abdullah (Harris, 2009). Imagine the international incident that would have erupted had Obama refused to bow to the Japanese emperor. In deference to the president, Akihito shook hands with Obama to accommodate the standard American greeting ritual. Greeting rituals between cultures can be a source of social connection or disconnection, depending on how deftly they are handled.

Goleman (2013) provides another example of potential intercultural miscommunication. When Americans share business cards, it is usually a perfunctory nonevent with no special significance. In Japan, however, one does not merely pocket the card but instead takes it, holds it carefully in both hands, studies it for a while, and then puts it away in a special case. Doing otherwise is insulting because it communicates indifference to the importance of the gesture.

President Obama was the catalyst for yet another nonverbal controversy early in his presidency. In June 2009, an official White House photograph showed him talking on the phone to Israeli Prime Minister Benjamin Netanyahu with his feet propped on his Oval Office desk and the soles of his shoes prominently displayed. An article in *Haaretz*, a liberal-leaning Israeli daily, interpreted the photo this way: "As an enthusiast of Muslim culture, Obama surely knows there is no greater insult in the Middle East than pointing the soles of one's shoes at another person. Indeed, photos of other presidential phone calls depict Obama leaning on his desk, with his feet on the floor." The article also offered further interpretation: "The president is seen with his legs up on the table, his face stern and his fist clenched, as though he were dictating to Netanyahu: 'Listen up and write Palestinian state a hundred times'" ("Obama Shoe Photo," 2009). This constellation of nonverbal cues created an international incident. Nonverbal communication between cultures is tricky business, as this chapter will continue to explore.

Distinctions Between Verbal and Nonverbal Communication

Communication is a lot more than just words. "Actions speak louder than words" is a cultural cliché. **Nonverbal communication** is sharing meaning with others nonlinguistically. This definition excludes sign language and written communication but not vocal communication (e.g., sighs, tone of voice, and laughter). This definition also means that *body language* is a misnomer (Crystal, 2005). Despite some superficial similarities with language, characterizing nonverbal communication as "body language" is really a metaphor and not an accurate, literal description. This underlines the fact that verbal and nonverbal communication have important differences. Before these distinctions are explained, however, take the self-assessment test in Box 5-1 to get a glimpse of what you know about nonverbal communication.

Number of Channels: Single- Versus Multichanneled

Verbal communication is single-channeled, but nonverbal communication is multichanneled. You can express anger verbally by saying "I hate you" or "I hope you grow hair on your palms and your breath smells permanently like vomit." The statements change, but the channel (using words) is the same.

The same anger can be expressed nonverbally through multiple channels (channel-rich): shaking a fist, extending a middle finger, jumping up and down, glaring, screaming, or kicking a wall, to name just a few possibilities. The multichanneled nature of nonverbal communication can add impact and believability to a message. For instance, it's easy to lie with words as long as you can remember to keep your story consistent, but it is more challenging to lie convincingly in multiple nonverbal channels (Vrij, 2006). If the nonverbal channels reveal inconsistent messages, credibility is questioned. When you say "I'm telling the truth" but your nonverbal

---

BOX 5-1 DEVELOPING COMMUNICATION COMPETENCE

Nonverbal Communication Test

Answer the following questions either TRUE or FALSE.

1. Young people are significantly worse than older adults at both signaling emotions nonverbally and correctly interpreting them.
2. Averting one's eyes (looking away) is a strong indicator of lying.
3. Eye contact should be direct whenever conversing with someone, especially with a person of higher status.
4. Putting your hands behind your back is a gesture that clearly signifies power and status.
5. Folding your arms across your chest should be interpreted as a defensive gesture meaning "stay away" or "I'm not comfortable with you."
6. A smile is a sure sign of happiness.
7. There are no universal standards of beauty because beauty is in the eye of the beholder and therefore subjective.
8. All cultures have pretty much the same touch taboos.
9. There are no universal facial expressions of emotions; different cultures interpret facial expressions of emotion differently.
10. In a singles bar, when a woman smiles at a man she has never met, this is likely to be a sexual invitation.

ANSWERS: **End of chapter**. How did you do? If you did well, did you make lucky guesses? If you did poorly, don't fret. Much of what we "know" about nonverbal communication isn't so. The mass media are notoriously gullible purveyors of misinformation about nonverbal communication.

communication says "No, I am not," we tend to believe the nonverbal message. Because nonverbal communication is more spontaneous, is physiologically based, and has to be consistent in more than one channel, it seems more believable and genuine, even though it may not be.

Degree of Ambiguity: No "Reading a Person Like a Book"

Nonverbal communication is at least as ambiguous as language, and probably more so. Can you "read a person like a book," as is often asserted in the popular media? Consider deception detection. A review of 217 studies over a 60-year period involving tens of thousands of subjects showed participants correctly distinguish liars from truth tellers an average of only 55% of the time (Lock, 2004; see also Kim & Levine, 2011). That's only slightly better than chance (flipping a coin—"heads" you're lying, "tails" you're telling the truth). Even "experts" in deception detection (e.g., police and psychiatrists) do poorly when trying to determine truth tellers from liars (Ekman & O'Sullivan, 1991).

Psychologist Maureen O'Sullivan (2005) tested more than 13,000 individuals, and only 31 achieved 80% accuracy on detecting lying. She dubbed them "truth wizards." None was 100% accurate, however. Among the thousands of college students tested for truth wizardry, *not one* was found to be an exceptional lie detector. Subjects under 22 years of age were the least effective deception detectors (O'Sullivan, 2009). Some researchers question the existence of actual truth wizards (Bond & Uysal, 2007).

Jimmy Kimmel has his television crew regularly lie to people on the streets of Hollywood in the amusing segment "Lie Witness News." Reticent to admit that they are "not in the know" about pop culture and world events, respondents lie about their experience. If these individuals were at all capable of discerning when someone is lying to them, they would likely realize that they were being *punked* (lied to) on camera. In one segment shot in Austin, Texas, folks were asked about made-up music artists, such as Wiz Khalifa's little brother, Cheese Wiz Khalifa, and French artist DJ

Fictionelle. Respondents said that they were big fans. One person claimed to be a fan of DJ Gluten even though the interviewer said that "a lot of people say he's hard to tolerate." The person apparently didn't need to be gluten free because he claimed to have some of Gluten's music on his phone (Otterson, 2015).

Why are we such poor deception detectors? It is primarily because "there is no sign of deceit itself—no gesture, facial expression, or muscle twitch that in and of itself means that a person is lying" (Ekman, 1992, p. 80; see also Vrij, 2006). We think there is, however, and there lies the misperception. Two global studies of thousands of people from 75 countries found that the number-one answer to the question "How can you tell when people are lying?" was "Liars avert their eyes" (Bond & DePaulo, 2006; Porter & ten Brinke, 2010). Some cultures, however, consider maintaining direct eye contact during conversation as rude and eye aversion as polite, having nothing to do with lying (Vrij, 2000).

Your best shot to detect lying is by collecting a variety of nonverbal evidence over a period of days, weeks, or even months and by seeking information from third parties ("Did you see him with another woman?") (Park et al., 2002). There is also some evidence that liars provide fewer details than truth tellers when giving narratives (Vrij et al., 2010). The more details a liar provides while telling a story, the more opportunity to be exposed.

Despite a tendency toward overconfidence, *most of us don't read nonverbal cues very well.* Women, however, tend to be more accurate decoders of nonverbal messages than men, and middle-aged people tend to be better at reading nonverbal communication than younger people (Andersen, 2006; Hall, 2006b). So can we "read a person like a book"? It is unlikely, but we certainly can become more sensitive to nonverbal cues and improve our accuracy.

Discrete Versus Continuous: Stop and Go

Verbal communication has discrete beginnings and endings. We begin it when we start talking, and we end it when we stop talking. Nonverbal communication, however, has no discrete beginnings and endings. We continuously send messages for others to perceive, even when we may wish not to do so. Robert Noel was convicted of involuntary manslaughter as the owner of a Presa Canario (a breed of dog) that viciously mauled and killed Diane Whipple. Noel seemed oblivious to the continuous nature of nonverbal communication. After the trial, jurors in the case offered their impressions of Noel. They saw him as a man who seemed unremorseful and generally unpleasant in his demeanor. Staring stoically into space for most of the trial, Noel gave this assessment of the jurors' characterization of him: "I made up my mind not to react one way or another. I'm sitting there just watching what was going on, making notes for the attorneys . . . And it's just amazing that I could just sit there doing nothing and that gets twisted into, 'Oh, he's a cold-hearted son of a bitch'" (May, 2002, p. 18A).

Noel apparently believed that by sitting expressionless and "doing nothing," he would communicate nothing to a jury. We can't communicate "nothing," however, as long as others are observing us. Consider facial expressions, for example. Try not to display any facial expressions at all while another person looks at you. It can't be done. Even a blank stare may mean that you're introspective, or that you don't want to be bothered by anyone, or that you're inattentive, sullen, or disdainful.

Gestures and eye contact may seem to be discrete, not continuous, because a specific gesture begins and ends, and eye contact also begins and ends. Not gesturing, however, can indicate boredom, relaxation, or awkwardness. Lack of eye contact can indicate disinterest, intimidation, distraction, or a host of other messages.

Nonverbal communication is sometimes unintentional. We blush, blink our eyes rapidly, and shuffle our feet without necessarily intending to do so. Individuals standing before an audience giving speeches may want desperately to hide their nervousness. Nevertheless, their hands may shake, their voices may quaver, and perspiration may form on their brows. Nonverbal communication is continuous.

Interconnectedness of Verbal and Nonverbal Communication

Verbal and nonverbal communication are interconnected. We don't speak without embellishing the words with gestures, facial expressions, tone of voice, eye contact, and so forth. This section discusses several ways verbal and nonverbal codes interconnect.

Repetition: Same Message, Different Channels

We say "yes" and then nod our head. We give verbal directions, then point in the appropriate direction. We profess our love for individuals and then hug them. All of these nonverbal cues repeat the verbal message. This repetition diminishes ambiguity and enhances accuracy of message perception. *Consistency of verbal and nonverbal communication increases the clarity and credibility of the message.*

Accentuation: Intensifying Verbal Messages

When we use vocal emphasis, such as *"Please don't touch anything in the store,"* this accents the message. It adds emphasis where it is desired. "Don't you *ever* say that word" accents the unqualified nature of the verbal message. Pounding your fist on a table as you express your anger nonverbally repeats the message but also accents the depth of your emotion. Accentuating enhances the power and seriousness of verbal messages.

Substitution: No Words Necessary

Sometimes nonverbal cues substitute for verbal messages. A yawn can substitute for the verbal "I'm bored" or "I'm tired." A wave can substitute for a verbal "goodbye." Shaking your head "no" doesn't require a verbalized "no." We signal interest in courting another person without actually having to express this message in words. Eye contact, smiles, forward leans, room-encompassing glances, close distance, frequent nodding, and hair smoothing are just some of

This photo illustrates which of the following interconnections between verbal and nonverbal communication?

○ **1.** Regulation

○ **2.** Contradiction

○ **3.** Accentuation

○ **4.** All of the above

Answers at end of chapter

the nonverbal flirting cues (Brown et al., 2009; Muehlenhard et al., 1986). A later stage of courtship, sexual initiation, is usually accepted nonverbally but rejected verbally (Metts et al., 1992).

Regulation: Conversational Traffic Cop

Conversation is regulated by nonverbal cues. Turn taking is signaled by long pauses at the end of sentences and eye contact in the direction of the person expected to speak next, especially if the conversation occurs in a group. Interruptions may be prevented by speeding up the rate of speech, raising one's voice over the attempted interruption, or holding up one's hand to signal unwillingness to relinquish the floor. A teacher can recognize a student's desire to speak by pointing to the person, which means "your turn."

Contradiction: Mixed Messages

"Sure, I love you," when said with eyes cast downward and flat vocal tone, doesn't exactly

inspire belief. Sometimes we contradict verbal messages with nonverbal cues. These are **mixed messages**—inconsistencies between verbal and nonverbal messages. The words say one thing, but the gestures, facial expressions, eye contact, posture, tone of voice, and physical proximity leak contradictory information. Dale Leathers (1979) found that mixed messages had a highly disruptive impact on problem-solving groups. Mixed messages produced tension and anxiety, and group members found it difficult to respond to mixed messages in socially appropriate ways (Leathers, 1986). Young children are especially confused by mixed messages, particularly sarcasm (Morton & Trehub, 2001).

Types of Nonverbal Communication

There are many types of nonverbal communication. This discussion begins with the vast potential of our bodies and their accoutrements to communicate: physical appearance, face, gestures, touch, and voice. At the end, space and environment are addressed. In each instance, note the power of nonverbal communication and the potential for misunderstandings and miscommunication.

Physical Appearance: Looks Matter

How we physically look to others often is the first nonverbal message communicated. In this section, *beauty bias*, *body shape and size*, *body adornments*, *clothing*, and *hair* are explored.

PHYSICAL ATTRACTIVENESS: THE BEAUTY BIAS

There is a popular belief that men place greater emphasis and value on physical attractiveness when choosing a mate than women do. Several reviews involving hundreds of studies, however, showed that physical attractiveness is equally significant for men and women (Eagly et al., 1991; Feingold, 1992; Langlois et al., 2000). Physically attractive people get more dates, and this is of interest to both women and men.

This **beauty bias**—a perceived advantage accorded those who are viewed as attractive—goes beyond simple interpersonal attraction and the advantage that attractive people have in garnering dates, fostering romance, and choosing mates. Beautiful people are thought to be more sociable, poised, independent, happy, sensitive, sexy, and successful than unattractive individuals (Lorenzo et al., 2010, Rhode, 2011). The beauty bias also seems to produce a "beauty premium"—namely, higher wages. Over the course of a working career, employees who are above-average in looks are likely to earn about $230,000 more in wages and salaries than the below-average workers. Even the gap between the attractive individuals and the average-looking workers is about $140,000 over a lifetime of employment (Hamermesh, 2013). Two other economists determined that a self-fulfilling prophecy may be partially responsible for this beauty premium/penalty. Physically attractive employees tend to be more self-confident, and consequently, they are perceived by employers to be more able workers (Mobius & Rosenblat,

2006). Knowing that others find you attractive, and being treated favorably because of your good looks, can bolster self-confidence, and this in turn can be communicated in positive ways in the workplace.

Supermodel Linda Evangelista once remarked, "It was God who made me so beautiful. If I weren't, then I would be a teacher." (If you're not attractive, become a teacher? Really?) Actually, her beauty would likely help her be a successful teacher in the eyes of students. A study of 94 faculty members in 463 courses at the University of Texas, Austin, found that professors rated as very attractive (on a 10-point scale) by students received teaching evaluations (on a 5-point scale) that averaged 4.5, but those rated at the bottom on attractiveness received an average evaluation of 3.5 (Hamermesh & Parker, 2005). RateMyProfessors.com has a chili pepper option to indicate "hotness," apparently in recognition that looks matter. Teachers are not immune to the beauty bias, either. Teachers perceive attractive students as more intelligent, popular, and friendly than less attractive students, and they consequently have higher expectations for them. This may in turn be why attractive students tend to achieve higher grades and academic success (Gordon et al., 2014).

There are some downsides to physical attractiveness as well. Sometimes there is a "pretty penalty." Studies show that good-looking applicants for jobs receive lower ratings from same-sex evaluators. Apparently, beautiful women threaten less attractive female employers, and handsome men threaten more average-looking male employers. Similar results were found for assessments of videotaped college admissions interviews (Agthe et al., 2011).

In one of the more bizarre twists on the pretty penalty, the Iowa Supreme Court ruled 7-0 that bosses can fire employees for being "irresistibly attractive," even when attractive employees have been exemplary in the performance of their jobs and have made no flirtatious gestures toward their bosses (Foley, 2012). The case involved Melissa Nelson, who worked for James Knight, a dentist. Apparently, Nelson's attractiveness threatened Knight's marriage by her mere presence. Nelson's attorney commented on the all-male court's unanimous decision: "These judges sent a message to Iowa women that they don't think men can be held responsible for their sexual desires, and that Iowa women are the ones who have to monitor and control their bosses' sexual desires" (p. A4). In the face of blistering criticism from several quarters, the Court reconsidered its decision, but on July 13, 2013, it reaffirmed its original opinion (Corbett, 2013).

Aside from a few notable negative effects of being physically attractive, the beauty bias is real. This bias, however, is likely to occur during initial attraction to a person, and it may not be enduring "with the weight of additional information about the person" (Berscheid & Walster, 1974, p. 205). The attraction may be fleeting indeed if good-looking individuals' egos swell like pufferfish the moment they open their mouths.

Plastic surgery and vigorous physical exercise can improve a person's looks, but attractiveness can be enhanced in ways other than engaging in an "extreme makeover." Kindness is perceived as a mate preference for both men and women (Brooks, 2011; Li et al., 2002). Kindness also enhances the perception of physical attractiveness (Zhang et al., 2014). Women also rated men as more physically and sexually attractive if they were considerate of others (Jensen-Campbell et al., 1995). Warmth is highly valued by both men and women, and those who display it are perceived as more facially attractive (Little et al., 2006). Offering compliments, expressing affection, and purchasing gifts for your partner can make you appear more physically attractive (the "bling-beauty bonus"?) (Albada et al., 2002). Less attractive individuals, if given a chance, may exhibit a very attractive personality and consequently increase their perceived physical attractiveness (Newman et al., 2000; Zhang et al., 2014). As we get to know others over time and grow to like them, they become more physically attractive in our eyes (Bazil, 1999). This reverses the "beauty is good" stereotype to "good is beautiful" (Little et al., 2006). It thus behooves you to put more focus on attempting to be nice to others and communicating competently.

BODY SHAPE AND SIZE: UNIVERSAL STANDARDS OF ATTRACTIVENESS

You've heard the adage "Beauty is in the eye of the beholder." Is beauty entirely a matter of individual, subjective preferences? Some women find the male bodybuilder physique extremely attractive, but other women think it is repellent (Pope et al., 2000). Individual preferences do play a part in our judgment of physical attractiveness.

Cultural differences also exist, making beauty appear highly subjective. Ubangi women insert wooden disks into their mouths to stretch their lips up to 10 inches in diameter to enhance their attractiveness. Some cultures prefer plump over skinny. One study of 54 cultures discovered that heavy women are preferred to slender women in cultures where food is often limited (Anderson et al., 1992). In Niger and other countries in West Africa, fat is the female beauty ideal (Onishi, 2001). At one festival in Niger called *Hangandi*, women compete for a prize given to the heaviest contestant. Women train for this beauty contest by gorging themselves and drinking lots of water on the day of the festival. Women also take steroids to bulk up, and some even ingest animal feed advertised as a means to increase body weight. In Nigeria, the Warirke people have "fattening rooms" established to help young women pile on the pounds; for four weeks, young women gorge themselves to improve their marriage prospects (McGirk, 1998).

One study found consistency across cultures in perceptions of unattractive individuals, but also some variation in what constituted physical attractiveness (Sorokowski et al., 2013). Yet despite cultural and individual differences that are learned, there are some universal standards of physical attractiveness. First, **bilateral symmetry**—the right and left sides match each other—seems to be a universal attractiveness characteristic (Floyd, 2006; Rhodes et al., 2001). Lopsided features of the face (e.g., one eye slightly lower than the other, a crooked mouth or nose, or uneven ears) are perceived to be less attractive than more symmetrical features (Wade, 2010).

Second, the size of the female body seems to be less important than the body shape (Singh & Singh, 2011). The lower the **waist-to-hip ratio**—the smaller the waist is compared to the hips

Florence Colgate was voted "Britain's most beautiful face" from a group of 8,000 entrants. Her face is almost perfectly symmetrical.

(an hourglass shape)—the greater the perception of attractiveness. This ratio in women was found to be a more important characteristic than facial features, height, body weight, and other physical attributes (Singh, 1993). This was true whether those judging the female shape were 8 years old or 80 and regardless of culture or background (Furnham et al., 2003). The "ideal" shape was a 0.70 waist-to-hip ratio (the waist is 70% the size of the hips) (Dixson, et al., 2010). This same preference was also reported for lesbians and bisexual women, although a heavier body with the 0.70 ratio was considered the "ideal" (Cohen & Tannenbaum, 2001). Despite the "ideal" shape, perceived attractiveness in general varies rather broadly from a 0.60 to a 0.80 ratio (Springen, 1997).

Although research on the male body shape is limited, an attractive physique for men appears to be relatively broad shoulders and narrow waist and hips—in other words, a **wedge shape** (Hughes & Gallup, 2003; Singh, 1995). Thus far, however, no ratio similar to the waist-to-hip ratio in women has been well supported for male attractiveness across cultures.

BODY ADORNMENTS: TATTOOS AND TABOOS

He got his first tattoo—a rosary with a cross, etched on the back of his right hand—when he was 11 years old. At 13, he had Chinese characters

that translate to "trust no man" tattooed on his left shoulder. At 16, an ornate cross that memorialized his dead older brother was added to his right hand. All of these tattoos were rites of passage into gang life in Watsonville, California, for Mando. After his brother's death, however, he began questioning his way of life and looking for alternatives. When he searched for a job, he found that potential employers would eye his gang tattoos and say that no jobs were available.

Tattoos and piercings can be taboo with a large portion of the population. A Harris Interactive survey showed that more than two-fifths of adults who do not have tattoos find tattooed individuals less attractive, less sexy, less intelligent, less healthy, or less spiritual than adults without tattoos ("One in Five U.S. Adults," 2012). A Vault survey also found that 60% of employers admitted they were less likely to hire an applicant with tattoos and piercings (Icon, 2011). Corporate dress codes, however, are beginning to relax a bit in regard to tattoos and piercings (Kell, 2014).

Despite the stereotyping, tattoos and body piercings are more popular than ever. The Harris Interactive survey revealed that 21% of American adults have a tattoo, compared to 14% a decade earlier. Twenty-two percent of adults aged 18 to 24, and 25% of those aged 25 to 29, have tattoos. Half of adult Americans have pierced ears, although only 7% have piercings elsewhere on their bodies.

The increasing popularity and acceptance of tattoos isn't necessarily shared cross-culturally. In Japan, for instance, tattoos are generally viewed negatively. In fact, they are commonly associated with criminal organizations. Disapproving looks and negative comments are not uncommon. Prominently displayed tattoos, such as on the face or neck, may result in being asked to leave restaurants or stores. Even tiny tattoos that are barely visible can get you barred from many public places, such as spas and gyms. (Westlake, 2012).

CLOTHING: NOT JUST FOR WARMTH

Physical appearance can be enhanced or diminished in a variety of ways. Clothing expresses a person's identity. "It is impossible to wear clothes without transmitting social signals. Every costume tells a story, often a very subtle one, about its wearer" (Morris, 1977, p. 213).

Michelle Obama's fashion sense has been a subject of repeated conversation in the media. *Harper's Bazaar* described her as "the First Lady of Fashion. The gorgeous, statuesque Obama is a mix-and-match master ... well on her way to leaving a stylish legacy" ("Michelle Obama Power Fashion," 2015). Here she is dressed in a formal gown for a state dinner. Initially, the Associated Press described the elegant gown as "flesh colored." OOPS! It was quickly changed to "champagne" when an editor pointed out the obvious.

Clothing matters. The traditional burqa worn by Muslim women in many countries, which covers women from head to toe, making them unrecognizable, has become a symbol of women's subjugation in the eyes of many people and nations. France outlawed the burqa, provoking tumultuous protests and controversies. The European Court of Human Rights upheld the ban in 2014 (Raja, 2014).

Dress communicates social position, economic status, level of sophistication, social background, educational level, personal identity, credibility, even moral character and religious affiliation. Appropriate dress is a serious issue for teachers as well. One study found that formal professional attire receives the highest instructor competence ratings from students, with casual professional dress a close second. Casual dress, however, produced the highest sociability ratings (e.g., sociable, cheerful, or good-natured) from students. Interesting presentation of material was also associated with casual instructor dress. Casual professional dress seems to make instructors more approachable for discussions and more interesting from the student vantage point (Morris & Gorham, 1996; see also "Study Indicates," 2015). Again, there are rules for every communication context. What is appropriate in one workplace may be inappropriate in another.

HAIR: STYLING

Another significant element of physical appearance is hair. In the late 1800s, American Indians were forced to attend federal boarding schools. Upon their arrival, their long hair, a tie to their spiritual heritage, was shorn to "civilize" them. It was a traumatic introduction to white society (Arrillaga, 2001).

Hair has enormous communicative potential. The issue of wearing a beard, for example, has even made it to the U.S. Supreme Court. In a 9-0 decision, the Court struck down an Arkansas prison ban on inmates wearing beards. Inmate Abdul Maalik Muhammad challenged the prison policy, claiming that it violated his religious rights. Prison lawyers argued that a ban on even half-inch beards would make it more difficult to stop the flow of contraband and facilitate prisoner identification. The court didn't buy it (Doyle, 2015).

Hair is big business. In the United States, there are approximately 80,000 hair care salons and barbershops, generating about $20 billion of business annually, and about $160 billion globally ("Hair Care Services," 2015). Hairstyles create an image and follow normative trends (long hair in the 1960s was popular with men; short hair is more popular now).

Baldness is a continuing issue for millions of men and women (about 40% of hair loss sufferers are women). Annually, about $3.5 billion are spent in the United States on stopping hair loss or regenerating lost hair, with meager effectiveness (Bergeson, 2014). Hair loss can be traumatic. Spencer Kobren, author of *The Bald Truth*, notes: "A lot of men are suicidal (because of balding). And it is very traumatic for women. It affects their social life and their life with their spouse or partner" (quoted by Bergeson, 2014).

Facial Communication: Your Personal Billboard

"Faces express emotions, thoughts, and character. Brows knit, mouths gape, lips grin, cheeks blush, jaws clench, eyes weep, and pupils dilate with libidinal enthusiasm" (Garland-Thomson, 2009, p. 97.). The subjective judgment of an "untrustworthy face" can result in extreme sentences from jurors, even greater likelihood of a death sentence in cases of murder (Wilson & Rule, 2015). Your eyes and face are the most immediate cues people use to form first impressions. Speed dating preferences are heavily influenced by facial appearance (Olivola & Todorov, 2010). Happy looking faces are perceived to be trustworthy, and angry looking faces create the opposite impression (Said et al., 2009). This section explores how your eyes and face influence communication with others; a discussion of gestures follows. The study of both facial communication and gestures is referred to as **kinesics** by social scientists.

EYES: YOUR PERSONAL WINDOWS

"Eyes wink, gleam, glitter, twinkle, glaze over, cut, make contact, pierce, penetrate, and assist the mouth in fashioning a frown or smile" (Garland-Thomson, 2009, p. 98). They also blink. Boston College neuropsychology professor Joe Tecce (2012) claims that stress can be measured by how often someone blinks and that perceptions of self-confidence and being in control can be subtly affected by blinking rates. He goes further by concluding that presidential candidates with the lower blink rate win elections (Tecce, 2004). Tecce's hypothesis that blinking rates are strongly correlated with presidential victory has been correct in six presidential elections examined. The 2000 election between George W. Bush and Al Gore, however, deviated from the norm. Gore averaged 36 blinks per minute to Bush's 48, but Gore did win the popular vote.

The Tecce blink-rate-equals-stress-level hypothesis is interesting, and it may have some validity. Generalizing from a single-channel nonverbal cue requires caution, however, especially when predicting presidential elections—a dubious undertaking. Nonverbal communication is multichanneled. Thus, one nonverbal cue may suggest relaxed demeanor (e.g., casual posture) while other nonverbal cues (e.g., perspiring, stammering, or a quavering voice) may contradict this observation. Eye-blink rates may also be affected by factors other than anxiety, such as the glare of TV lights on sensitive eyes, mild allergic reactions, wearing contact lenses, lack of sleep, and so forth.

Besides blinking, eye contact is also important, as noted earlier. Its study is called **oculesics**. Eye contact regulates conversational turn taking, communicates involvement and interest, manifests warmth, and establishes connection with others. It can also command attention, be flirtatious, or look cold and intimidating (Andersen, 1999).

Interpersonal communication is quite dependent on eye contact, especially in the United States. Eye contact invites conversation. Lack of eye contact is usually perceived to be indifference or even anger ("I can't even look at you I'm so angry"). Too much eye contact in the form of staring, however, can be viewed as rude and intrusive (Garland-Thomson, 2009). Targets of the staring may wonder whether they have spinach in their teeth or if perhaps the person staring is weird or dangerous.

Cultures differ regarding the appropriateness of direct eye contact (Samovar et al., 2010). Indonesians, Chinese, Japanese, and many Latin Americans will show deference to others by lowering their eyes. This is a sign of respect. It is also easy for "look-you-in-the-eye" Americans to misread this nonverbal cue and assume that Asians and Latin Americans lack self-confidence and can be easily manipulated. In Egypt, men and women who are strangers to each other avoid eye contact to communicate modesty and to act in accordance with religious rules widely practiced in the culture (Meleis & Meleis, 1998). In India, individuals from differing socioeconomic classes avoid eye contact with each other (Luckmann, 1999).

FACIAL EXPRESSIONS: THE LOOK OF EMOTIONS

Imagine what it would be like to be unable to exhibit facial expressions. When someone smiles at you, you cannot smile in return. Your face appears frozen and expressionless. Are you indifferent, irritated, unfriendly, or bored? What do you feel? Imagine how others would respond if you always seemed to be frowning and had no way of changing the sour expression on your face. Think of what that would do to your self-esteem and your ability to communicate with others. Smiling is a primary cue that exhibits friendliness and warmth. A smile makes a person approachable. "We know that genuine smiles may indeed reflect a 'sweet soul.' The intensity of a true grin can predict marital happiness, personal well-being, and even longevity" (Jaffe, 2010, p 23). A person who doesn't smile at us can seem distant, even mean. Teachers who rarely, if ever, smile during class lectures and activities make it difficult for students to ask questions, disagree, or participate in discussions.

Kathleen Bogart, a psychologist at Oregon State University, has a rare congenital disorder called Moebius syndrome that causes facial paralysis. She is unable to smile or express her emotions facially. Those with Moebius syndrome like Bogart are frequently stigmatized as intellectually disabled and odd (Bogart et al., 2012). Adolescents with the condition are also bullied at school and have attractiveness issues. Social interaction is challenging because their condition is immediately noticeable by others and can be easily misunderstood. This may cause disengagement from social contact (Bogart, 2014). Bogart and others with the condition compensate by being vocally expressive and using lively gestures and eye contact to communicate emotions and appear friendly.

There has been extensive research on facial expressions. Research in 20 Western cultures and 11 nonliterate and isolated cultures showed that members of all these cultures recognized the same basic emotions from photographs of specific facial expressions. *These universal emotions identified by all cultures from specific facial expressions are fear, anger, surprise, contempt, disgust, happiness, and sadness* (Ekman & Keltner, 2014; Schubert, 2006). Yet while members of diverse cultures recognize the same emotions from specific facial expressions, they don't necessarily perceive the same intensity of emotion (e.g., from annoyance to rage). (Ekman & Friesen, 1987). Not surprisingly, accurately interpreting emotions from facial expressions is improved when a person views another member from an in-group (e.g., the same ethnicity, nationality, or regional location) (Elfenbein & Ambady, 2002).

There are also differences in **display rules**—culture-specific prescriptions that dictate the appropriateness of behaviors—for facial expressions (Ekman, 1993). The Japanese would be more likely than Americans to suppress negative emotions (e.g., anger or contempt) if the emotion occurred during a private conversation and the target of the emotion were an in-group member (Jaffe, 2010). If, however, the target of the negative emotion were a rival group or individual, the Japanese would be more likely than Americans to display the emotion. Showing contempt or anger toward one of your own group members creates disharmony and may hurt the group; showing anger or contempt to a competitive rival, however, may create in-group cohesion (Matsumoto, 1990).

Gestural Communication: Bodies in Motion

Gestures are everywhere. When we communicate with others, gestures accompany our verbal messages even when we aren't aware that we're using them. People who talk on the telephone usually gesture while they are talking even though the person on the other end cannot see the gestures. When we communicate with others, we often are a wiggling, fidgeting, finger-tapping, hand-waving, toe-tapping, arm-flailing body in motion.

There are three main categories of gestures: *manipulators, illustrators,* and *emblems* (Ekman, 1992). **Manipulators** are gestures made by one part of the body, usually the hands, that rub, pick, squeeze, clean, or groom another part of the body. They have no specific meaning, although people observing such manipulators may perceive nervousness, discomfort, or deceit. Manipulators, however, also occur when a person is

Universal facial expressions of emotions are exhibited naturally by infants. They don't have to be taught expressions for (from top left and clockwise) happiness, sadness, disgust, fear, anger, and surprise. Recently, contempt has been added to the list.

relaxed and feeling energized and when no deceit is occurring. Nevertheless, studies show that people will mistakenly judge deceitfulness when a person exhibits many manipulators (Ekman, 1992). The important point is not to jump to conclusions concerning what manipulators mean.

Illustrators are gestures that help explain what a person says to another person. They usually occur simultaneously with the verbal message, but sometimes they begin while the speaker is still formulating the words. Activating the brain's motor function is simpler than constructing grammatically appropriate sentences. If the words don't come fast enough, the gesture will stop in midstream (Wachsmuth, 2006). Telling a person to go to the left, then pointing in the appropriate direction, is an example of an illustrator. Describing how to "zigzag" while drawing the movement in the air is another example. Many of the unconscious gestures we make that emphasize what we are saying are illustrators. Public speakers, for example, punctuate their points with hand and arm movements (e.g., a stabbing motion with the index finger and hand to illustrate intensity of commitment, or arms spread widely to illustrate a desire to include everyone in the audience). These are rarely planned, however, and when they are, they often come across as stilted and artificial.

Emblems are gestures that have precise meanings separate from verbal communication. The hand wave, for example, communicates "goodbye" in the United States. Fewer than 60 emblems are used in the United States, but Israel uses more than 250 (Ekman, 1992). No emblems are unique to the United States. The French, however, have a unique gesture for "He's drunk"—a fist placed around the nose and twisted. Germans have a unique "good luck" emblem that consists of two fists with the thumbs inside pounding an imaginary table (Ekman et al., 1984).

Many common emblems, especially obscene or vulgar ones, have spread to other cultures around the world (Tibit, 2011). The extended middle finger is used widely beyond the borders of the United States and is recognized almost everywhere as an obscene gesture. Some Latin American cultures add to the gesture by extending the middle finger while raising the arm abruptly and grabbing the arm with the other hand.

The competent communicator needs to be mindful of the vast potential for misunderstanding inherent in the gestural code. Consider one example. A young photographer was flown to a remote area of Alaska one summer. When the weather turned bad, the photographer's father became concerned and sent a plane to look for his son. The pilot spotted the young man's camp and soon saw him waving a red jacket liner, which to a pilot is a signal to leave. The young photographer then showed a thumbs-up gesture as the plane flew over. The pilot kept on flying, concluding that the red

jacket liner and the thumbs-up gesture meant everything was fine. Weeks later, the frozen body of the young man was found. He left a diary. In it, he wrote that he was ecstatic to see the plane and waved the red jacket liner to flag down the pilot. He showed the thumbs-up gesture to communicate his happiness at being rescued. He was dumbfounded to see the plane fly away. When he finally ran out of firewood, he used the last bullet in his gun to end his misery (Burgoon et al., 1996).

Very few gestures are emblems with precise meanings in all contexts. Most gestures are far more ambiguous and require sophisticated interpretation tied specifically to the transactions and contexts in which they occur. Folding your arms across your chest, for example, may mean that you are closing yourself off to others in a defensive gesture, or it may simply be a comfortable way for you to rest your arms. In Fiji, it is a sign of respect when talking to others (Mancini, 2003). Be cautious when interpreting the meaning of gestures. Match them with other nonverbal cues, and look for consistency of meaning.

As cultures increasingly mix and countries become multicultural, misunderstanding can occur when a specific emblem has different meanings in two cultures. The thumb inserted between the index and middle fingers is an old American gesture commonly used playfully with children to mean "I've got your nose!" In Germany, Holland, and Denmark, however, this same gesture is a nonverbal invitation to have sex, and in Portugal and Brazil, it wishes a person good luck or protection. The extended middle finger is obscene in most cultures, but in Uruguay, it means "I don't believe you." Pointing to objects with the index finger in parts of Central Africa is deemed vulgar and crude. A large study of 40 different cultures isolated 20 common hand gestures, all of which had different meanings in each culture (Morris et al., 1979).

Touch Communication: Hands-On Experience

There are approximately 5 million touch receptors in our skin, about 3,000 in a single fingertip, all sending messages to our brain. In fact, skin is the largest organ in the human body, covering about 19 square feet on the average-sized human (Colt, 1997), and touching skin is an enormously powerful and important communication code. Anger, fear, disgust, love, gratitude, sympathy, happiness, compassion, and sadness all can be decoded fairly accurately by those receiving touch, even while blindfolded (Hertenstein et al., 2009). Social psychologist Dacher Keltner notes that touch is "our richest means of emotional expression" (quoted by Carey, 2010). Social scientists call the study of touch **haptics**.

SIGNIFICANCE OF TOUCH: LIFE CHANGING

American playwright Tennessee Williams testified to the power of touch when he wrote, "Devils can be driven out of the heart by the touch of a hand on a hand, or a mouth on a mouth" (quoted in Colt, 1997). Touch is essential to the physical and psychological development of babies (Feldman, 2014). Compared to standard incubator care (sometimes dubbed "Kangaroo Care"), premature infants showed significant cognitive, physical, and psychological benefits from one hour of skin-to-skin contact with their mothers for the first 14 days of their lives. The benefits were evident even 10 years later (Feldman, 2014).

Voluminous research on infant and child development reveals that touch is not only beneficial but even critical for life itself (Hertenstein, 2002; Loots & Devise, 2003). Infants in orphanages who do not receive much, if any, touch from other humans are usually maladjusted and quiet; they show difficulty learning and maturing normally (Andersen, 1999). During Romania's strife in the early 1990s, thousands of infants were warehoused in orphanages, virtually alone in their cribs for two years. They were found to be severely impaired by the lack of physical contact, and some even died (Marshall, 2014).

Touch is essential to the expression of love, affection, warmth, comfort, intimacy, and concern for others (Andersen et al., 2006; Chillot, 2013). It can promote trust and cooperation (Denworth, 2015; Kraus et al., 2010). Fist bumps, high-fives, and half-hugs reflect sports teams' united spirit and social bonding and may even improve performance (Denworth, 2015). Misuse of touch, however, can repel, frighten, or anger others. Touch communicates power. Sexual harassment is often an issue of inappropriate, unwanted touch communication (see Chapter 7).

TYPES OF TOUCH: FUNCTION, USAGE, AND INTENSITY

There are several types of touching. Knowing which type of touch is appropriate for which context is a vital concern to the competent communicator. Richard Heslin (1974) identified five types of touching based on their function, usage, and intensity.

The **functional-professional touch** is the least intense form. The touch is instrumental communication that takes place between doctors and patients, coaches and athletes, and the like. Lately, teacher-student touch communication is limited to this type, if engaged in at all. Functional-professional touching is businesslike and limited to the requirements of the situation. A nurse helping a patient sit up in bed or a football coach demonstrating a blocking technique are examples.

The **social-polite touch** occurs during initial introductions, business relationships, and formal occasions. The handshake is the standard form of social-polite touch in American culture. Many European cultures greet strangers with a hug and a perfunctory kiss on each cheek.

The **friendship-warmth touch** is the most ambiguous type of touch and leads to the most misunderstandings between people. The amount of touch has to be negotiated when showing friendship and warmth toward others. Too little touch may communicate unfriendliness, indifference, and coldness. Too much touch that seems too intimate communicates sexual interest when such interest may not be wanted. Friendly touches, especially those taking place in private, can be mistakenly perceived as sexual, especially by males (Andersen, 1999).

The **love and intimacy touch** is reserved only for a very few special individuals—close friends, family members, spouses, and lovers. This is not sexual touch, although it may blend with it. Tenderly holding a friend's hand, softly touching the cheek of a spouse, or hugging are examples of this type of touch. Hugging can help others cope with stress and its consequences (Cohen et al., 2015), and couples that touch frequently have more satisfying relationships (Oveis, 2010). Even more important than quantity, however, is reciprocation. Is the touch mutual, or does one person mostly initiate the touch (Chillot, 2013)?

The **sexual touch** is the most personal, intimate touch—and also the most restricted. Mutual consent is the most important consideration. Engaging in this type of touch when it is unwanted will produce serious repercussions.

Appropriateness of touch largely depends on understanding which type of touch is acceptable and desirable in which situation. *Types of touch help define relationships between people.* If one person initiates a friendship touch but the other person recoils because no real friendship has been established, clearly this type of touch is inappropriate. Both parties must define their relationship similarly or problems will occur. Ignoring the social-polite touch during introductions can provoke a negative response from the party shown such indifference and disrespect. Choosing to engage in too much or too little touch communication in a particular situation can send a powerful message.

TOUCH TABOOS: KEEPING YOUR HANDS TO YOURSELF

At the Group of 8 Summit in St. Petersburg, Russia, in July 2006, George W. Bush approached German Chancellor Angela Merkel, the only female leader present, and proceeded to give her an unexpected, and apparently unwelcome, neck and shoulder massage. Her reaction became international news. She responded to the Bush touch as though he had stun gunned her. Her shoulders hunched, then she threw up her arms wildly, and her face showed a look of utter dismay. One German tabloid paper headlined the event, "Bush: Love Attack on Merkel." Political scientist and oft-quoted political pundit Larry Sabato of the University of Virginia noted that "almost any male alive today knows that you don't offer uninvited massages to any female, much less the chancellor of Germany" (Vennochi, 2006). Apparently, Vice President Joe Biden never got the message because he is notorious for being "handsy" with women in public settings (Mack, 2015).

There are many touch taboos both within our own culture and in other cultures. According to research conducted in the United States (Jones, 1994), about 15% of all touches on a daily basis are unwanted and rejected. A manual published by the University of California, San Francisco, instructs nurses not to touch Cambodians on the head. That is where they believe their soul resides. Although not always enforced, couples break the law in Dubai if they hold hands, hug, or kiss in public (Surk, 2008). In Korea, young people are forbidden to touch the shoulders of their elders. Min-Sun Kim (1992) notes: "Southeast Asians do not ordinarily touch during a conversation, especially one between opposite sexes, because many Asian cultures adhere to norms that forbid displays of affection and intimacy" (p. 321).

There are several forms of taboo touching in the United States. The competent communicator manifests sensitivity by recognizing these

Touch is taboo in many situations and can be tricky when cultures collide. Richard Gere's overly familiar embrace and kiss of Bollywood star Shilpa Shetty produced an enormous outcry in India.

forbidden forms of touch and adopting more appropriate communication behavior (Jones, 1994). These touch taboos are:

1. *Strangers are the "untouchables."* Nonfunctional touch is usually perceived as too intimate and personal. Inevitably, however, jostling and bumping take place in crowded elevators, buses, stores, and the like. The American norm is to apologize when we bump or otherwise touch a stranger. Sexual touch by a stranger is highly inappropriate, even cause for arrest.

2. *Harmful touches should be avoided.* The initial handshake of a job applicant predicts who is likely to be offered the job after a pool of applicants has been interviewed (Ambady et al., 2000). A crushing handshake that inflicts pain on the interviewer is not likely to create a favorable impression (nor is the limp handshake that seems perfunctory). A handshake that matches the firmness applied by the interviewer tends to be received more favorably.

3. *Avoid startling touches.* Sneaking up on a person and tapping them on the shoulder when they think they are alone will likely startle them and produce a strong negative response. There is no equivalent immediate countermove a person can use; you can't startle the person who tapped you on the shoulder. Even though the startling touch is sometimes done playfully, most people resent it.

4. *Avoid the interruption touch.* Touches should not interfere with principal activities. Throwing your arms around and hugging your partner tightly while he or she desperately tries to mix ingredients for dinner interrupts the primary activity and will likely produce rejection of the touch. Trying to kiss your partner on the lips while he or she is watching an engrossing movie will also likely produce rejection.

5. *Don't move others.* This is especially important advice when dealing with strangers. Ushering people from one place to another without warning or permission is usually seen as an aggressive act. Warning people that they need to move and offering a quick explanation, however, can nullify the negative reaction to being moved by someone. "Excuse me, I need to get through" or "Watch out, this coffee is very hot," followed by a touch gently moving a person out of the way, usually will not produce the response that touch alone will.

6. *Avoid "rub-it-in" touches.* Don't intensify a negative remark with a touch. A husband pinching the thigh of his wife and remarking "That's pretty fattening" as she orders dessert inappropriately rubs in the nasty dig. A woman who tells her male partner to "walk your mother to her car" while slapping his arm intensifies the rebuke.

Dealing with those who violate touch taboos is fairly straightforward (Jones, 1994). Determining how accidental or purposeful the violation is will guide you in your response. Unintentional lapses of touch protocol are easily forgiven. Intentional violations usually require a stronger response.

COMPETENCE AND TOUCH: SOME SUGGESTIONS

Here are some suggestions for dealing competently with touch violations:

1. *Begin by assuming the violation is accidental.* Your nonverbal rejection—pulling away, frowning, and so forth—may be all that's required to convey the message that the touch is unwanted and inappropriate.

2. Use *descriptive statements to identify your reaction and the behavior that ignited it.* "I don't like to be moved out of the way like that. It seems aggressive, so please don't do it" is an example.

3. Use *intense nonverbal cues when faced with a purposeful violator.* Hard-core touch violators are fond of putting the person who is upset on the defensive with statements such as "Don't be so touchy" or "Lighten up, I didn't mean anything by it." There's no need to engage in a tit-for-tat verbal competition. A prolonged glower, a disgusted look held for a bit longer than usual, or a penetrating stare without comment can make

the violator very uncomfortable and communicate the appropriate message.

4. *Repeat offenders require strong nonverbal signs of rejection plus a direct, firm command.* "Don't ever touch me that way again" or "Don't ever grab my shoulder" are examples.

5. A *brief apology should follow your own touch violation.* If you inadvertently violate a touch taboo, simply apologize. For example, "Oh, I'm sorry. I didn't mean to bump you."

Voice Communication: How You Sound

Our voice is second only to our face in communicating our emotions (Simon-Thomas et al., 2009). As is true of the universal facial expressions of emotion already discussed, preliminary evidence suggests universal recognition of emotions from language-free voice samples (Scherer, 2003).

Our voice communicates information about our age, sex, socioeconomic status, ethnicity, and regional background. Vocal cues, or **paralanguage**, are usually divided into three classifications (Samovar & Porter, 2004): *vocal characterizers* (e.g., laughing, yelling, moaning, crying, whining, belching, and yawning), *vocal qualifiers* (e.g., volume, tone, pitch, resonance, rhythm, and rate), and *vocal segregates* (e.g., "uh-hum," "uh," "mm hmm," "oooh," and "shh"). A whispering, soft voice may indicate speech anxiety when it is heard in front of a large audience. A flat, monotone voice can induce sleep in listeners. Speaking at hyperspeed may communicate nervousness and excitement. Typically, listeners prefer a speaking rate that approximates their own speech pattern (Buller & Aune, 1992).

There are cultural differences regarding vocal communication. Arabs speak very loudly because it connotes strength and sincerity. Israelis view high volume as a sign of strong beliefs on an issue. Germans assume a "commanding tone that projects authority and self-confidence" (Ruch, 1989, p. 191). People from Thailand, Japan, and the Philippines tend to speak very softly, almost in a whisper. This communicates good manners and education. In Japan, laughing signals joy, but it also often camouflages displeasure, anger, embarrassment, and sorrow (McDaniel, 2000).

Space Communication: Distance and Territoriality

Space communicates in very powerful and significant ways. Much of human history has been a narration about wars fought over who controls what space. This section is about the influence that distance and territoriality have on our communication, the study of which is called **proxemics**.

DISTANCE: DEFINING RELATIONSHIPS

Anthropologist Edward Hall (1969) identified four types of spatial relationships based on distances between individuals communicating. *These four types are intimate, personal, social, and public distances.* The distance zones identified by Hall are averages. The actual distances in each category vary according to culture, and individual preferences vary within a culture. The distances, their usages, and overlapping nonverbal cues for the mainstream culture of the United States appear in Table 5-1.

Typically, strangers stepping into an intimate zone will produce great discomfort, even hostility. This is usually perceived as an aggressive act.

TABLE 5-1 Four Types of Spatial Relationships and Their Characteristics in Mainstream U.S. Culture

TYPE	DISTANCE	USAGE OF NONVERBAL CUES	OVERLAPPING NONVERBAL CUES
Intimate	0–18 in.	Loving; showing tenderness	Limited eye contact; touch; smell
Personal	18 in.–4 ft.	Conversing with intimates, friends	Eye contact; some touching; gestures
Social	4 ft.–12 ft.	Business talk; social conversing	Formal vocal tone; gestures; eye contact
Public	12 ft. or more	Lectures; speeches	Eye contact; gestures; vocal tones

An intimate partner, however, who avoids the intimate zone signals a distancing in the relationship. Counselors look for such cues to signal trouble or disagreement between relationship partners even when couples verbally insist that a problem doesn't exist. One study found that distressed romantic partners stay 25% farther apart from each other than happy romantic partners (Crane, 1987). We signal that we are "far apart" in negotiations by literally moving away from our adversaries in the bargaining process.

Sometimes we are forced into intimate zones with strangers. A crowded elevator is an example. Being forced to rub elbows with individuals we've never met before is uncomfortable. When the intimacy zone is violated through nobody's fault, we usually try to establish a psychic distance from others. That is why occupants of crowded elevators often stare at the numbers indicating what floor is coming up next. This act distances us mentally from strangers and allows us to cope with an uncomfortable situation.

The personal space of short people is more often violated than that of tall people (Caplan & Goldman, 1981). Males also claim a larger personal spatial bubble around themselves than women, sometimes referred to as *manspreading*—splaying legs and denying space to others (Lang, 2015). Observe males sitting on a couch, for example, and notice how much space they often take by spreading out their arms and legs.

In a multicultural country such as the United States, opportunities for misunderstanding associated with spatial zones are plentiful (Martin & Nakayama, 2010). Comfortable social distance for an Arab may violate personal or even intimate zones of Americans. Arabs typically move very close when conversing. Part of the reason is that Arabs perceive a person's smell to be an extension of the person and, thus, important (Hall, 1969). Not recognizing the cultural differences associated with distance can make an individual seem pushy and aggressive or distant and standoffish.

TERRITORIALITY: DEFENDING YOUR SPACE

"To have a territory is one of the essential components of life; to lack one is one of the most precarious of all conditions" (Hall, 1969, p. 45).

Territoriality is a predisposition to defend a fixed geographic area, or territory, as one's exclusive domain (Burgoon et al., 1996).

We stake out our territory in a variety of ways (Burgoon et al., 1996). We use *markers*, such as hedges, small fences, and signs saying "Keep Out." A coat left on the back of a chair marks temporary possession of that specific seat. Resting a lunch tray on a table in a cafeteria signals "That's my eating area." We also claim a territory by erecting *barriers to entry*, such as walls, locked doors, security guards, and snarling dogs (see Box 5-2). When office space is limited, we erect partitions that make our environment look like a rabbit warren. A third way that we stake out our territory is by *occupancy*. Students who sit in the same chair every class period quickly assume the chair is their recognized place. Homeless people often establish their spot on the street by consistently occupying that small territory.

Invasions of territories (e.g., homes or offices) by others are usually met with physical and verbal aggression. One notable form of such territorial invasion is loud, obnoxious noise from neighbors. Walls prevent outsiders from physically intruding into one's home. Loud noise from megadecibel sound systems, however, penetrates those walls. You can't move your home like you can your automobile to escape the intrusion.

Commuter train cars everywhere from Seattle to Washington, D.C., are being refitted with only rows of paired seats, no three-seat rows, because passengers often refuse to sit in the middle seat even if it means standing for an hour when riding the train. Armrests between seats, as in airplanes, is one way to encourage three-seater occupancies (Marantz, 2005).

Environment: Creating Atmosphere

Winston Churchill once said, "We shape our buildings,, and afterwards our buildings shape us." The design of our environment shapes communication. Airports and fast-food restaurants design brightly lit buildings with uncomfortable plastic furniture to hurry people along and limit communication transactions. Such spaces are not meant for loitering, intimate communication, or relaxation. The environment communicates

BOX 5-2 FOCUS ON CONTROVERSY

Gated Communities: Fortress America?

Millions of families in the United States live in gated communities, which have become a worldwide phenomenon as well. They are popular in China, Argentina, Australia, Brazil, Mexico, Great Britain, and many other countries. Gated communities come in many varieties. Some are housing projects that require using a keypad code to open a metal gate blocking access to the community. Others have erected much more elaborate barriers to entrance. Gates may be accompanied by fences surrounding the community, armed guards, security patrols, and tire-piercing devices that are triggered by improper entrance.

Protection of personal property and security against violent crimes are the primary motivators for gating a community (Nonnemaker, 2009). Proponents claim they feel safer and that gated neighborhoods promote a sense of community where everybody knows everybody else. Opponents see it differently. Edward Blakely (2012), a professor of urban policy, warns, "Not only do the gates breed fear, they also shrink the notion of civic engagement and allow residents to retreat from civic responsibility . . . How can we have a social contract when we can reduce or eliminate social contact?"

The desire to be safe in person and property cannot be taken lightly, however. Do gated communities afford real security or merely the illusion of safety? Studies show no difference in crime rates between gated and ungated communities (Benfield, 2010; "Risk of Crime in Gated Communities," 2013). In Atlanta, burglars targeted gated communities in a crime spree that netted the robbers a million dollars in jewelry, cash, and silver from more than 90 homes (El Nasser, 2002). The gated community acted like a flashing neon sign: "Great Stuff; Come Steal."

Gated communities segregate in-groups from out-groups (Vesselinov, 2008). Dividing America into thousands of enclaves homogenizes neighborhoods and very likely promotes divisiveness and conflict between groups. We see ourselves as adversaries competing for space. Out-group members resent the restraint on their freedom of travel. Social groups insulate themselves from unwanted encounters with outsiders.

When we wall ourselves in against those who look and act differently from us, it is probably more difficult to find common ground between ethnic groups and socioeconomic classes, develop opportunities for cooperation, and work together as teams to make decisions and solve personal and societal problems. As Blakely puts it, "The nation's dream was equality and mutual assistance and the melting pot . . . Take that away and we're just people who live on a piece of territory" (quoted in D. Diamond, 1997, p. 5).

Questions for Thought

1. Do you like the idea of gated communities? Would you like to live in a gated community? Is it ethical to create these enclaves that keep out mostly minorities and the poor?

2. Can you think of alternatives to gated communities that might produce the benefits proponents claim without closing off communication with groups who can't afford to live in such neighborhoods?

"Do your business and leave." Living in dilapidated public housing can produce aggressiveness, violence, and mental fatigue (Kuo & Sullivan, 2001). Students perceive professors as more credible when their offices are attractively decorated and organized than when their offices look like mine does (Teven & Comadena, 1996). Simply removing the desk in a physician's office makes patients feel five times more at ease during office visits than having the desk as a barrier separating doctor and patient (Sommer, 1969).

Some jails and prisons have been designed with communication in mind, primarily because of the dismal failure of traditional prisons to control violence and reduce recidivism (repeat offenders) (Gilligan & Lee, 2004). The traditional prison environment provides little privacy and personal space, separates prisoners from guards, and restricts inmates' mingling. This led the Federal Bureau of Prisons to begin building with a different design to encourage direct supervision of inmates (Wener, 2006, 2015). Prisons now have open areas for inmate interactions. Guards mingle directly with prisoners, developing ongoing relationships with the inmates and spotting trouble before it explodes. There are no enclosed booths for officers. Inmates have small rooms, not cells with bars, and they control the lights in their rooms. There are more televisions available to reduce conflicts over which programs to watch. Furniture is "soft" (cushy and comfortable), not institutional "hard" (plastic and resistant), and floors are carpeted. These new prisons, despite their innovativeness, also cost less to build than traditional jails (Wener, 2006, 2015).

Violent incidents have been reduced 30% to 90% in the prisons with the new design compared to traditional prisons. Inmate rape is virtually nonexistent, and vandalism and graffiti have dropped precipitously. Guards, hesitant at first, now feel safer, and tension between inmates is reduced (Wener, 2006; Wener et al., 1987). The inmates still perceive these direct-supervision jails to be prisons, but the communication outcomes are dramatically different from those in traditional jails.

Communicating Competently with Nonverbal Codes

Knowledge of the myriad ways nonverbal codes influence our communication with others is the first step toward competent nonverbal communication. As indicated repeatedly throughout this chapter, appropriateness and effectiveness of nonverbal communication are key parts of the competence equation. Suggestions have been offered already on how you might improve your understanding and skill in nonverbal communication. This section will tie together common threads linking various nonverbal codes to communication competence.

Monitor Nonverbal Communication

Use your knowledge of nonverbal codes to monitor your own communication and the communication of others. Observe nonverbal communication in action. Become sensitive to the subtleties of these codes. Try experimenting. Maintain eye contact during interviews or in conversations with others. Observe how this affects the outcome of the communication. Try appropriate touching to see if it produces

The world's largest McDonald's restaurant was built for the London Olympics in 2012. Notice that the interior is brightly lit and that the furniture is designed to be uncomfortable. Fast food means not just quick delivery but "move along" and don't get too comfortable and stay. The restaurant was dismantled after the 2012 Olympics ended.

greater closeness and more positive responses from others. If you tend toward a monotone voice, enliven it on purpose. If your facial expressions tend to be constrained, try to communicate your emotions with more dramatic ones.

Resist Jumping to Conclusions

By now, you should be aware that nonverbal communication can be highly ambiguous. Don't make the mistake that others have made. Don't assume that you can "read a person like a book," especially if you don't know that person well (knowing the person well reduces the ambiguity of nonverbal cues). Nonverbal cues suggest certain messages, but you must consider them in their appropriate context. The easiest way to determine if you have interpreted nonverbal cues correctly is to ask. Check your perceptions with others. "I noticed you tapping your fingers and tugging at your ear. Are you nervous or upset about something?" is a quick way to determine if your nonverbal read is accurate.

Observe Multiple Nonverbal Cues

Relying on a single nonverbal cue will often produce a false perception. A slow blinking rate may suggest a relaxed demeanor, but observe other nonverbal cues as well (e.g., posture and gestures). Silence may indicate disagreement, but do other nonverbal cues contradict this assessment? Be careful not to make a broad generalization based on a single nonverbal cue. Look for nonverbal clusters to determine more accurately what is being communicated.

Recognize Cultural Differences

The vast differences in cultural use of nonverbal codes have been stressed repeatedly. When you communicate with individuals from another culture or co-culture in the United States, recognize the nonverbal communication differences. If you come across a nonverbal cue that puzzles you, don't assume anything. Observe members of other cultures to determine what is appropriate behavior. If you still feel doubtful about your interpretation, check your perception by asking someone who would know.

Strive for Consistency

Try to match verbal and nonverbal communication. Mixed messages confuse those who communicate with us. Exhibiting nonverbal behavior that contradicts what we are saying will produce a negative reaction from others.

 ## Summary

Nonverbal communication affects our communication with others in powerful ways, yet it is often ambiguous and difficult to read. Much of the advice offered in the popular media regarding nonverbal communication is incorrect or overstated, with too much emphasis given to a single nonverbal cue. Specific advice on communicating competently has been offered for each type of nonverbal communication (physical appearance, facial communication, gestures, touch, voice, space, and environment), but general, overlapping advice also has been offered: monitor your nonverbal communication, resist jumping to conclusions based on a single nonverbal cue, observe multiple nonverbal cues before drawing conclusions about others, recognize vast cultural differences in nonverbal communication, and strive for consistency in your verbal and nonverbal communication to avoid mixed messages.

Answers for Self-Assessment Test, Box 5-1

1. TRUE: older adults have more experience.

2. FALSE: there is no single nonverbal cue indicating lying.

3. FALSE: in many cultures, direct eye contact would be perceived as rude or disrespectful.

4. FALSE: can just as easily be perceived as suspicious or untrustworthy.

5. **FALSE:** too many other interpretations are possible; may just be comfortable.

6. **FALSE:** smiles can show contempt, sarcasm, fear, misery; different types of smiles.

7. **FALSE:** at least two research studies supported universal standards of beauty.

8. **FALSE:** cultures can vary widely on touch taboos. Unmarried couples holding hands in public is strictly forbidden in some cultures but certainly not in the United States.

9. **FALSE:** there are at least seven universal facial expressions of specific emotions.

10. **FALSE:** female friendly smiles are often misinterpreted by males as a sexual invitation.

Answer for Critical Thinking caption:

MAN PUTS FIST THROUGH COMPUTER (P. 120): #3

Quizzes Without Consequences

Test your knowledge before your exam! Go to the companion website at www.oup.com/us/rothwell, click on the Student Resources for each chapter, and take the Quizzes Without Consequences.

Film School Case Studies

The Birdcage (1996). Comedy; R
A very amusing remake of *La Cage aux Folles* about a gay couple "acting straight" to fool a conservative U.S. senator. Analyze the main characters' nonverbal behavior, especially when Robin Williams attempts to teach Nathan Lane to act like a straight male. Are these merely stereotypic male behaviors, or is there truth in the depiction?

Crazy, Stupid, Love (2011). Romance/Comedy. PG-13
A middle-aged man (Steve Carell) sees his life go into a tailspin when his wife asks him for a divorce. With the help of a "friend" (Ryan Gosling) he meets in a bar, he is schooled in the art of picking up women. Analyze the clothing, hairstyle, and general appearance changes made by the Carell character on the advice of the Gosling character. Do these changes make a difference? Good or bad?

Enchanted (2007). Fantasy/Romance; PG
Fantasy about the idyllic life of Princess Giselle (Amy Adams) in the kingdom of Andalasia until she is exiled by evil Queen Narissa (Susan Sarandon) to New York City, where she meets her Prince Charming (Patrick Dempsey). Examine the many nonverbal cues that produce misunderstandings and comic results.

Hitch (2005). Romantic Comedy; PG-13
A date doctor (Will Smith) teaches his latest pupil (Kevin James) the intricacies of nonverbal communication to romance a woman. Analyze whether Smith's depiction of nonverbal "masculine" behaviors is accurate, and why does his romancing of his own dream woman go badly at first?

Spy (2015). Action/Comedy; R
Melissa McCarthy plays a desk-bound CIA analyst who goes undercover to infiltrate the world of lethal arms dealers. Very funny! Analyze all of McCarthy's clothing and wig changes, gestures, and facial expressions that are part of the storyline and a major part of the humorous effects.

BY THE END OF THIS CHAPTER, YOU SHOULD BE ABLE TO:

1. Recognize the significance of listening to the human communication process.

2. Define and explain the listening process.

3. Describe and avert several listening problems that you may experience.

Listening to Others

CABRILLO COLLEGE HIRED A CONSULTANT to address faculty and staff. The speaker opened with a personal story. When driving home from the cemetery, through tears of unimaginable sadness after visiting the grave of her five-year-old son, who had died the week before her visit, she inadvertently ran a stop sign, pulling in front of another driver who had to brake hard to avoid a collision. The driver who screeched to a halt was a highway patrolman. The grieving mother pulled over to the curb. The officer got out of his patrol car and walked up to the passenger side of her vehicle. He tapped, indicating for her to roll down her window. When she did, he leaned over and asked, "May I get in?" She nodded her head, continuing to sob. The officer sat in the passenger seat for a brief time without saying a word, then he asked, pointing to the cemetery, "Do you have someone in there?" Her eyes welled with tears, but she found comfort in telling him about her little boy. When she finished, the officer asked

4. Distinguish different kinds of listening, and prevent problems unique to each kind.

5. Identify specific ways that you can become a competent listener.

her how far away she lived, and then offered to follow her home to be sure she got there safely. He never mentioned the traffic violation.

The speaker made several points with this poignant story, but an unstated point that struck me the most was the officer's compassionate willingness to listen silently and empathically to a grieving mother. He didn't interject any comments. He didn't offer advice. He didn't warn her about her driving or admonish her for the traffic violation. He just listened quietly to her story, then made certain that she got home safely. "Just sitting with someone and giving him or her permission to cry in your presence can be a lot more meaningful and helpful than platitudes or prosaic statements . . . Sometimes silence can be extremely comforting . . ." (Brustein, 2014).

Listening is a fundamental, essential part of human communication, of connecting with others, but it is often too little appreciated. *The principal purpose of this chapter is for you to learn how to listen competently.*

Significance of Listening

We have speech contests but no listening contests. We give awards to great speakers but not to great listeners. ("And first prize goes to Alexis Van der Houven for listening to a dozen speakers for 24 hours straight without interrupting once.") A list of the hundred greatest speakers of all time doesn't seem ludicrous, but a list of the hundred greatest listeners of all time seems odd at best. Speaking, not listening, earns us power and status. It turns out, however, that being both a good speaker *and* a good listener makes you far more influential with others than simply being an impressive speaker (Ames et al., 2012).

Abundant research indicates the importance of listening. On average, college students spend 11% of their total time communicating by writing, 16% speaking, 17% reading, but a whopping 55% listening (Emanuel et al., 2008). Poor listening in college produces poor academic performance. If you sleep or daydream your way through classes, you had better get used to saying, "Do you want to supersize that drink?"

Business leaders spend more time listening than engaging in any other type of communication. In fact, general managers ranked listening as the most important communication behavior (Brown, 2009), and a survey of corporate recruiters ranked listening skills second only to oral communication skills (speaking) for new hires (Estrada, 2014). "Listening is central to competence" and is a "key management skill" (Dodd, 2012).

Interpersonally, listening is extremely important (Gottman & Gottman, 2006; Whitbourne, 2012). Research shows that "[g]ood listening skills can help you to feel easy in all sorts of social situations, and to build the kind of rapport that leads to solid emotional bonds" (Gottman & DeClaire, 2001, p. 198). We want to be listened to, and we feel rejected when others exhibit indifference when we speak. We affirm the importance of our interpersonal relationships when we make an effort to listen carefully to others.

Despite the impressive rewards available from competent listening, however, most people don't listen very well. Most individuals receive scant instruction regarding how to improve their listening despite the fact that instruction and training can produce significant improvement (Lane et al., 2000; McGee & Cegala, 1998). We all have extensive experience listening to others, but experience alone may simply reinforce bad habits. Some individuals have had "nonlistening habits for so long that they are almost incapable of listening—if they had a listening gland, it would be atrophied from disuse"

DOONESBURY   **BY GARRY TRUDEAU**

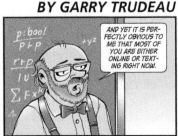

Students' use of electronic devices during college courses is a major distraction and impediment to learning.

(Elgin, 1989, p. 90). Judi Brownell (2013) refers to one study that revealed 60% of errors in business result from poor listening. Poor listening may even have contributed to the *Columbia* space shuttle disaster in 2003. According to the Columbia Accident Investigation Board (2003), "Managers' claims that they didn't hear the engineers' concerns were due in part to their not asking or listening. (p. 170)"

With the rise of social media and the ease of electronic communication, college students are easily distracted listeners while in class. One study of 269 college students showed that 90% of respondents admitted to text messaging during lectures. Another study revealed that the typical college student uses a digital device an average of 11 times a day while in class, and 80% admit that use of these electronic devices can interfere with learning (Clayson & Haley, 2013; Reed, 2013). Texting in particular diverts students' attention and negatively affects learning (Wei et al., 2012).

Doctor-patient communication is a particularly important context for effective listening, but again, competent listening often doesn't occur. "Not listening is at the top of the list of complaints patients have about their physicians" (Goleman, 2013, p. 109). Doctors often fail to understand the complaints and concerns of patients because they aren't listening carefully (Christensen, 2004; Scholz, 2005). Improving physicians' listening skills can reduce physician errors (Kertesz, 2010; Weiner et al., 2010). It can also result in fewer malpractice lawsuits from patients (Lenckus, 2005).

Until recently, listening has been an underappreciated part of communication in our society. The necessity to train people to be effective listeners is a relatively new revelation. Unfortunately, few colleges and universities offer a stand-alone listening course, and even substantial units on listening within communication courses are far from universal (Kehoe et al. 2015).

The Listening Process

With slight modification, the International Listening Association officially defines **listening** as "the process of receiving, constructing [and reconstructing] meaning from, and responding to spoken and/or nonverbal messages" (Brownell, 2013, p. 48). This definition implicitly highlights listening as a dynamic, active process, not a passive one. In the next several sections, the listening process is explored by looking at its three essential elements: *comprehending*, *retaining*, and *responding*.

Comprehending: Discriminating for Understanding

An airline pilot, beginning the takeoff down the runway, glances at his copilot, who looks glum. The pilot encourages the copilot to "cheer up." The copilot, set to hear "gear up," promptly raises the plane's wheels—before they've left the ground (Reason & Mycielska, 1982). The copilot didn't comprehend the message from the pilot, and the plane skidded down the runway. **Comprehension** is shared meaning between or among parties in a transaction. The listening process begins with comprehension.

COMPREHENDING PHONEMES: DISCRIMINATING SPEECH SOUNDS

"Before we are native speakers, we are native listeners. In the first year of life, experience with the native language begins to shape how we perceive speech" (Lim & Holt, 2011, p. 1390). The first challenge facing the listener operates at the most basic level of comprehension—accurately discriminating speech sounds (phonemes) and understanding these sounds as words (see Chapter 4). Making sense out of phonemes, however, is a complex mental process. When speaking, the average adult produces about 15 phonemes *per second* (Kuhl, 1994). This means that a listener must process 900 sounds each minute. More rapid speakers, such as those annoying hucksters speeding through disclaimers and exclusions at the tail end of ads for bank loans or credit cards, can double these numbers and still communicate intelligibly.

Adults have difficulty distinguishing phoneme differences that do not appear in their native language. Japanese, for example, exhibit difficulty distinguishing between the *r* and *l* sounds because no such distinction is meaningful in the Japanese language (Gopnik et al., 2001; Raizada et al., 2010). Thus, *flied lice* and *fried rice* sound identical, provoking dubious mimicry

Comprehending phonemes is the most basic aspect of understanding messages. It's not always so easy to do.

from some smug English speakers. When the word *rake* is repeated and then followed by the repetition of the word *lake*, Japanese speakers do not hear the shift despite straining to recognize the change (Gopnik et al., 2001). Native English speakers, however, struggle to distinguish the *b* and *p* phonemes in Spanish. *Besar*, meaning "to kiss," and *pesar*, meaning "to weigh," get confused, which could translate the sentence "I want to kiss you" to "I want to weigh you." That could certainly kill the romance!

Infants universally have no difficulty recognizing phoneme distinctions in any of the world's languages (Kuhl, 2004). Babies master the phonemes of their native language first, and this phoneme mastery facilitates learning words (Gopnik et al., 2001). Phoneme mastery is easier if infants begin to ignore phonemes that do not exist in their native language. Gradually, the child loses the ability to hear phoneme distinctions not common to the native language, usually at around six or seven months of age (Kuhl et al., 2005). At six months, for example, Japanese and American infants easily distinguish the *r* from the *l* phoneme, but at 10 months, Japanese infants are no longer able to while American infants become even better at making the distinction (Gopnik et al., 2001).

COMPREHENDING WORDS: SOME CHALLENGES

Comprehending meaning from phonemes combined into words is more challenging than you might expect, even if you are familiar with the language. In numerous classes, I have played an audiotape that was created by Dr. John Lilly. The tape repeats a single English word hundreds of times with no variation. In every class, within a 10-minute period, students report hearing 50 to 75 different words or phrases, often in several languages. Most insist that there is more than one word on the tape, and most cannot give the correct word. Unfamiliarity with the correct word and its meaning ("That's a word?") is part of the problem.

Determining the context (e.g., noun or verb placement and companion words that clarify the meaning) is essential to comprehending words in a sentence. One study isolated individual words taken from a recording of ordinary conversation. When the words were played back to listeners one at a time, only 47% were correctly identified. When these same words were replayed in the context of the original conversation, however, almost 100% of the words were correctly identified (Pollack & Pickett, 1964). Note the importance of context for determining the meaning of this sentence: "She had to *crane* her neck to see the *crane* fly onto the tower *crane*."

Comprehending a single word separate from context is more challenging than you might suppose because *hearing and listening are different processes*. Hearing is the physiological process of registering sound waves as they hit the eardrum. The particular sounds have no meaning until we construct meaning for them. Listening is the active effort to construct meaning from verbal and nonverbal messages. Constructing meaning from the messages of others is, in reality, more a process of reconstruction. The speaker constructs the original message; a listener reconstructs that message to match the original intended message as closely as possible. This involves a significant amount of interpretation, and with interpretation comes potential misunderstanding. One study showed a lot of misunderstanding by listeners, but speakers were convinced that listeners understood their utterances even when their statements were clearly ambiguous. For example, consider "The daughter of the man and the woman arrived" and "When you learn gradually you worry more." Can you discern the two different meanings for each sentence (Keysar & Henly, 2002)?

Compounding the challenge to comprehend messages, listeners must be able to discern breaks between recognizable words. This is called speech segmentation. Speakers often make no apparent pauses to segment speech. The childhood chant "I scream, you scream, we all scream for ice cream" makes no apparent distinction between "I scream" and "ice cream" based on sound alone. You have to determine the meaning of the entire sentence before the correct segmentation emerges. When you hear an unfamiliar language, the words seem to blend into one continuous auditory cluster. For instance, say aloud the following sentence:

Kamaunawezakusomamanenohayawewenimtu-
wamaanasana.

Can you segment the sentence? Not likely. If you speak Swahili, however, the sentence divides easily into this: *Kama unaweza kusoma maneno haya, wewe ni mtu wa maana sana.* It means "If you can read these words, you are a remarkable person" (Wade & Tavris, 2008, p. 81).

Finally, ordinary conversational speech is typically full of sloppy pronunciations, hesitations, and mumbled words, making comprehension difficult. Do you ever mumble when speaking to others? Men tend to mumble far more than women (Weinrich & Simpson, 2014). The reasons for the gender difference are still being studied (Wienrich et al., 2014). **Articulation**—speaking words clearly and distinctly—is important for listeners to comprehend speakers' messages. Mumbling becomes just noise.

Comprehension is an important first element of listening, but you have to make an effort to understand the messages of others. In one study, only 5 of 200 college students exhibited any interest in comprehending the messages of others. They were mostly interested in persuading others of the correctness of their own viewpoints (Trosser, 1998).

Retaining: Memories

Memory is essential to the listening process. This may seem obvious once you ponder what you do when you listen to a lecture in a college course. If you retain none of the information, of what value was the lecture to you? You can't construct meaning from nothing. The information we retain when engaged in the listening process is the raw material from which meaning is constructed.

FALLIBILITY OF MEMORY: YOU CAN'T RETAIN EVERYTHING

Naturally, our minds do not retain every morsel of information as we listen to someone. One study found that married couples remembered only 35% of what they discussed in the past hour (Sillars et al., 1990). Ever had the experience of asking your partner "So what were we discussing before we were interrupted by that phone call?" and neither of you can remember? The **forgetting curve**—the rate at which we no longer retain information in our memory—drops rapidly. How rapidly, though, is a

debatable issue. The University of Waterloo publishes a forgetting curve that shows the loss of between 50% and 80% of the information presented in a classroom lecture only two days later if no effort to retain that information is made. After a month, only 2% to 3% of the original information is retained (https://uwaterloo.ca/counselling-services/curve-forgetting). Will Thalheimer (2010), however, compares 14 memory studies with 69 conditions and concludes that "forgetting varies widely." Retaining information depends on numerous conditions, such as the complexity of the information, one's interest in the subject matter, the motivation to learn, the effectiveness of the methods used to present the information, and whether the information is crammed overnight or learned along the way over weeks or months.

Taking effective notes, reviewing them for just 10 minutes within 24 hours of learning the information, and then reviewing your notes for 5 minutes a week later will vastly improve retention (Hoffman, 2014). Using information immediately also enhances retention. "Use it or lose it," as they say in the memory business. If you immediately apply what you have learned in college to your life's profession or your relationships, your retention will improve markedly and last longer. Try explaining to your roommate, partner, or friend the main ideas presented in class soon afterward. Presenting the information to others greatly helps a person to retain that information.

BENEFITS OF FORGETTING: CURSE OF THE INFALLIBLE MEMORY

Retention is important, but remembering everything you hear would be a curse. Imagine what it would be like to forget nothing. Every telephone number, email address, text message, advertising jingle, slogan, song lyric, irritating noise, angry moment, embarrassing episode, and painful event would be available to clutter up your ability to think clearly and analytically. Imagine how this would affect your relationships with others. Wouldn't reliving every hurtful memory and humiliating moment make it difficult for you to be optimistic and constructive in your relationships? Forgetting sometimes has a very constructive effect.

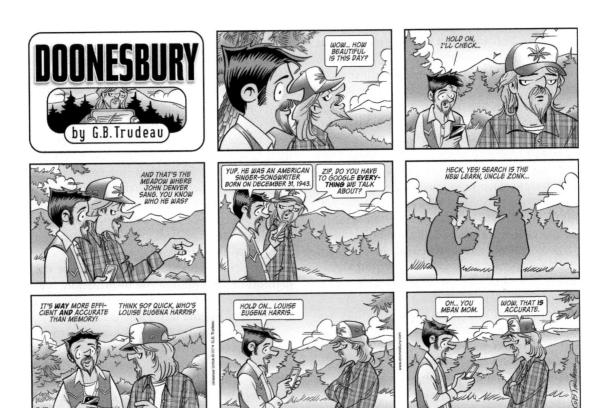

The "Google effect" impedes listening and learning. Looking things up on the Internet does not permit memory to serve the learning process. If our memory becomes atrophied from disuse, then our learning also atrophies. You can't look up everything on the Internet, either (e.g., "What did she tell me I needed to do to earn an 'A' in this class?").

Jill Price, a woman who seems to remember virtually every detail of her life experiences, wrote a book, *The Woman Who Can't Forget*, to publicize her amazing memory of autobiographical facts. James McGaugh, a renowned memory researcher at the University of California, Irvine, and his colleagues extensively tested Price's memory (see Parker et al., 2006; Leport et al., 2012). If given a specific date, she can remember instantly what she was doing and what day of the week it was. The recalled personal facts of her life were checked against more than 50,000 pages of journal entries Price wrote over a period of several decades. Is her memory a blessing or a curse? Price writes in her book that she became a "prisoner" of her own memory. She explains: "The emotional intensity of my memories, combined with the random nature in which they're always flashing through my mind, has, on and off through the course of my life, nearly driven me mad" (Price & Davis, 2008, p. 236).

The inability to forget any detail of a past argument or the feelings you experienced when engaged in past conflicts, for example, presents challenges that we don't normally face when entering into relationships with others. Sometimes it is better to forget past slights and painful events so that we can move on to better moments.

WHY YOU FORGET: INATTENTION, MEANINGLESSNESS, AND DEMOTIVATION

You forget information for a variety of reasons. Sometimes you just don't pay attention. You are introduced to strangers, and you are concerned with what kind of impression you are making on them. Their names glance off the edges of your memory and promptly skip irretrievably into space. You are forced to say, "I'm sorry, but I've forgotten your name."

You may also forget because you don't properly organize the information you hear. You don't attach the information to any meaningful concept, idea, event, or phenomenon. The numbers 1865, 1945, and 1953 don't mean much unless you realize that they are the ending dates of three significant American wars. You can remember the dates more easily knowing that.

Forgetting also results from lack of motivation to listen carefully and remember. Imagine if, at the start of a lecture, your professor stated, "You don't need to know this for the test." Would you pack up your notebook or close your laptop and hunker down in your seat with no concern about your attention drifting or your eyelids slamming shut? Would you listen to the lecture?

Finally, an amnesia dubbed the "Google effect" has been supported by four separate studies. Researchers found that the ready accessibility of the Internet and Google searches primes our memory for where to find information but lowers our ability to recall the information itself (Sparrow et al., 2011). The information is stored on the Internet, so why bother to store it in our brains?

Whenever you listen, you depend on your memories to fill in the blanks. Speakers presume a knowledge of their audiences. If you had no common experiences with others, and no common language to communicate those experiences, you couldn't communicate even rudimentary messages effectively. Retention of information is an integral part of the listening process.

Responding: Providing Feedback

Responding is a third essential element of listening (Barker & Watson, 2000; Brownell, 2013). Listening is a transactional process between speaker and audience. Effective listening depends on both participants in the transaction. Speakers look for responses from listeners to determine whether a message is being processed or ignored. Without a clear response from the listener, you have no way of knowing whether listening actually occurs.

These responses can be both verbal and nonverbal. As listeners, we indicate confusion by frowning or by asking a question for clarification. If listeners are staring out a window, doing a face plant onto the desktop, doodling, talking to the person next to them, or texting when you are talking, then listening to you probably isn't a top priority.

As a listener, helpful nonverbal responses include head nodding, strong eye contact, smiling, and leaning forward during conversation. Helpful verbal behaviors include asking questions, paraphrasing, and perception checking, all discussed later in this chapter (Bodie et al., 2015). In the process of providing helpful responses while listening to a speaker, you are likely to create what is called **immediacy—the perception of closeness and involvement with others.** In other words, a connection between speaker and listener develops.

In summary, the essential elements of listening are comprehending, retaining, and responding. In the next three sections of this chapter, informational, critical, and empathic listening are discussed. Each type, in its own way, incorporates these three elements.

Competent Informational Listening

Informational listening attempts to comprehend the message of a speaker. Your goal is to understand what the speaker has said. When listening to others, it is usually better to be sure that you comprehend the speaker's message before you critically evaluate it. Too often we are prone to judge another person's ideas without fully understanding what the person actually said and believes. Here we consider several problems that thwart competent informational listening and steps a competent communicator should take to correct them.

Information Overload: Too Much of a Good Thing

A study by LexisNexis on international workplace productivity asked workers to respond to the following statement: "It is difficult to maintain my focus on the task at hand when I get distracted by the constant flow of emails and other information." Workers in five countries—the United States, Great Britain, China, South Africa, and Australia—responded. Agreement with this statement varied from a low of 57% in China to a high of 85% in Australia. Respondents from the United States registered 60% agreement (Walsh & Vivona, 2010). Workers also responded to this statement: "Being constantly accessible through mobile phone, email and other means, makes it harder for me to get my job done." Affirmative responses to this statement were 58% in the United States, 45% in Great Britain, 63% in China, 50% in South Africa, and 71% in Australia.

We live in a world of information overload aided and abetted by communication technologies barely conceived of two decades ago. When do we have time to listen to others? We so easily become swamped in the tsunami of information that listening to others speak becomes noise—interference.

Information overload can be addressed in a number of ways. You can begin by occasionally shutting off the technological marvels that inundate us with information that is both useful and useless. Find times to listen and converse with others without the intrusive interruptions of cell phones ringing, vibrating, or otherwise demanding your attention. During meetings at work, shutting off smartphones, laptops, and other electronic devices is important. It permits focused attention on the meeting's agenda without outside distractions. Screen information whenever possible. Spam filters on your email can reduce the trivia and provide more time for you to engage others in conversation instead of sorting information.

Shift Response: Conversational Narcissism

Narcissus was a Greek mythological character who fell in love with his own image reflected in a spring. **Conversational narcissism** is the tendency of listeners "to turn the topics of ordinary conversations to themselves without showing sustained interest in others' topics" (Derber, 1979, p. 5; see also Leit et al., 2008). "Well I've been talking long enough about me, so what do you think of me" typifies the conversational narcissist (Aune et al., 2000). J. B. Priestley, commenting on the reputed good listening abilities of the wife of famous playwright and egotist George Bernard Shaw, remarked, "God knows she had plenty of practice." Conversational narcissists are perceived by others to be socially unattractive and inept communicators (Vangelisti et al., 1990).

Charles Derber (1979) conducted an extensive study of conversational narcissism. Derber recorded and transcribed 100 dinner conversations among 320 friends and acquaintances conducted in restaurants, dining halls, and homes. The predominant pattern found in these conversations was the strong inclination to employ the attention-*getting* initiative, called the *shift response*, as opposed to the attention-*giving* initiative, called the *support response* (see also Vangelisti et al., 1990). The **shift response** is a competitive vying for attention and focus on self by shifting topics. It is Me-oriented. The **support response** is a cooperative effort to focus attention on the other person. It is We-oriented. You can see the difference between the two responses in these exchanges:

Brit: I'm feeling pretty depressed.

Nate: Oh, I felt really depressed last week when I flunked a math exam. (*Shift response; provides information about self that shifts focus*)

Brit: I'm feeling really depressed.

Nate: Why are you feeling depressed? (*Support response; seeks information for understanding*)

As you can see from these examples, the shift response sets the stage for a competitive battle for attention; the support response does not. Conversational narcissism can be exhibited by a single person, or it can be a pattern of interaction by both parties in a conversation, neither of whom may be prone to shift responses. One person's shift response, however, will likely be countered with the other person's shift response, and a narcissistic transaction may ensue, as in this example:

Davon: I love listening to jazz.

Marcella: I hate jazz, but I love country. Don't you think country is more truly native to the U.S.? (*Shift response; no interest exhibited in discussing jazz*)

Davon: I think country is weird. All those silly lyrics like "My baby left me high and dry and now I have altitude sickness and skin like a lizard" are for Gomers. Have you ever listened to jazz, I mean really listened to it? (*Shift response; trying to shift the attention back to jazz*)

Marcella: No, and I don't plan to. It's just a bunch of noise. Sounds like kids first learning to play instruments. Let me play some country tunes for you. You'll like them if you put aside your prejudice. (*Shift response; this is "Let's focus on what interests me, not on what interests you." The conversational transaction began with a comment about loving jazz but shifted to "just try listening to country music."*)

In this conversation, the two individuals each attempt to make their topic the focus of the conversation, first by paying lip service to the other person's conversational focus with a derogatory comment and then by swiftly making a shift response. Neither party exhibits "sustained interest" in understanding the other person's point of view by actually listening and exploring the issues raised. The conversation keeps shifting swiftly back and forth to what interests each speaker.

Support responses encourage elaboration of the topic initially introduced. Three types of support responses encourage the speaker to explore the topic initiated: the *background acknowledgment* (e.g., "Uh huh," "really," or "yeah"), the *supportive assertion* (e.g., "That's great," "I didn't think of that," or "You must have considered this carefully"), and the *supportive question* (e.g., "How is jazz different from blues?" or "Why do you hate math?").

Conversational narcissism is a pattern of overusing the shift response and underusing the support response. The shift response may be necessary in some conversations when individuals drift from the main task. When it becomes a pattern, however, the shift response is an informational listening problem. *The competent communicator primarily uses the support response, not the shift response.* As one study found,

conversational narcissism is pervasive in marital relationships and strongly relates to divorce (Leit et al., 2008).

Competitive Interrupting: Dominating Conversations

Interrupting is closely related to the shift response. Interrupting can be used to shift attention to oneself and away from the other person talking. One study found that interrupting was the second most frequent indicator of conversational narcissism behind the shift response (Vangelisti et al., 1990). The difference between interrupting and the shift response, however, is that *the shift response usually observes the "one-speaker-at-a-time" rule.* **Interrupting** occurs when one person stops speaking when another person starts speaking (Tannen, 1994). Those who interrupt don't wait their turn. They step into the conversation when so moved. Another difference is that the shift response changes topics. An interrupter may break into the conversation and make a point directly relevant to display expertise on the topic.

Interrupting can be competitive, just like the shift response. **Competitive interrupting** occurs when we dominate the conversation by seizing the floor from others who are speaking. Competitive interrupting can create reciprocal interrupting, where both parties battle each other for conversational control.

Competitive interrupting is more of a challenge for women than for men (Hancock & Rubin, 2015). Women are interrupted far more often than men, by both men and women. This means that women have to fight for the floor (and to be taken seriously) in male-dominated jobs, such as the technology sector, but when they refuse to be interrupted until they have completed their thought, they are often described as *bossy, unpleasant,* or *bitchy* (Snyder, 2014).

Interrupting also can be used for a variety of reasons that are noncompetitive. Expressing support ("She's right"), showing enthusiasm for the speaker's point ("Great idea"), stopping the speaker to ask for clarification of a point ("Hold on! I'm lost. Could you give me an example to clarify that point?"), warning of danger ("Stop!

Interpersonal arguments often produce competitive interrupting.

You're going to tip over the computer"), or giving a group a break from a talkaholic's non-stop monologue all are noncompetitive forms of interrupting. Most interruptions are noncompetitive (see James & Clarke, 1993, for a review of 56 studies).

Informational listening problems occur with competitive interrupting but only rarely with noncompetitive interrupting. In competitive interrupting, the focus is Me-oriented narcissism. Interrupters are not concerned with listening to the speaker for understanding or learning. The agenda of interrupters is to break into the conversation and make their own point—to "inform" others. Competitive interrupting creates winners and losers in ordinary conversation. Fighting for the floor, trying to dominate the conversation, and hogging the stage by cutting off other speakers in midsentence create rivalry, hostility, and in some instances, reticence to continue with the conversation. *Typically, competent communicators refrain from competitive interrupting.* When others attempt to interrupt competitively, you need to ask them calmly and politely to allow you or others to continue ("Please let me finish.").

Glazing Over: The Wandering Mind

A prominent informational listening problem is what researchers call *glazing over* (Vangelisti et al., 1990). **Glazing over** occurs when listeners' attention wanders and daydreaming occurs. You have that "screen-saver face." You know the look, "that blank stare in which the eyes are dull . . . and the face has absolutely no expression on it at all" (Whitbourne, 2012).

The average listener can think at a rate of about 500 words per minute (wpm), but a normal conversational speaking pace ranges between 140 and 180 wpm (McCoy et al., 2005). This leaves plenty of opportunity for daydreaming and glazing over. An audience may benefit from a faster speaking rate; listeners' comprehension of speech doesn't decline markedly until the speaker's rate exceeds 250 wpm (Foulke, 2006). A lethargic speaking rate, however, may put listeners to sleep. Linguist Deborah Tannen (2003) also notes that a very slow speaking rate (fewer than 100 wpm) is stereotyped as slow-witted and unintelligent in every culture studied. If the pace is slow, *the competent communicator should try to put the differential between the rate of speaking and thinking to good use*. Think about the speaker's message. Apply the message to your life experience.

Pseudolistening: Faking It

When Franklin Roosevelt was president, he once decided to test whether people that he greeted in a receiving line actually listened to him. As he received each person, Roosevelt remarked, "I murdered my grandmother this morning." Listeners typically responded, "Thank you," "How kind of you," and the like. Many people passed in the receiving line pretending to listen to the president before someone actually did and retorted, "I'm sure she had it coming to her" (Fadiman, 1985).

This pretend listening is called **pseudolistening**, and it is slightly different from glazing over. When listeners glaze over, they are not even pretending to listen. Staring blankly while another person is speaking shows no effort to disguise inattention to the message. Pseudolisteners, however, attempt to disguise inattention to the message. Responding with "Mmm-hmm," "really," and "uh-huh"

as someone speaks fakes attention if one's mind is not focused on the speaker's message. Pseudolistening typically is easier to enact over the phone, where visual cues are unavailable.

People pretend to listen for many reasons. Often we engage in pseudolistening to keep from making a romantic partner upset with us. We don't really want to put any energy into listening because we're not really intending to understand our partner's point or issue, but we don't want to be accused of not listening because that could start a quarrel. So we nod our heads to indicate listening when our minds are actually out in the Andromeda galaxy, floating far away from the topic of conversation.

Students can be skillful pseudolisteners. Pretending to listen to a boring lecture, nodding your head when the professor asks if everyone understood what he or she just explained, and focusing eye contact on the professor can fake listening.

Focusing attention is the responsibility of both speakers and listeners. For informational

ZITS   BY JERRY SCOTT AND JIM BORGMAN

This cartoon illustrates which of the following?

○ **1.** Glazing over
○ **2.** Competitive interrupting
Answers at end of chapter

○ **3.** Shift response
○ **4.** Pseudolistening

listening to be proficient, *speakers should make their points meaningful to listeners*. That which is meaningless, mere trivia, rarely is remembered. As a speaker, answer this question for listeners: "Why should they care?" *Listeners should focus their attention on what is being said by speakers*. This means coming prepared to listen by bringing a notepad or laptop computer to take notes or by mentally reviewing key points made by the speaker.

Ambushing: Biased Listening

We don't necessarily listen openly and without bias. Sometimes we ambush a speaker. **Ambushing** occurs when we listen for weaknesses and ignore the strengths of a speaker's message. An ambusher's bias is to attack what the speaker says. This is focused attention with prejudice. Ambushers may even distort what a speaker says to gain an advantage. Ambushing is competitive and Me-oriented.

Some of the most obvious examples of ambushing occur in the political arena. Candidates for political office are coached to ambush, to tear down, their opponents. It's called "going negative." Journalists also can be ambushers. They're drawn to the mistakes made by public officials and celebrities (Tannen, 1998). They're listening to frame a story as a scandal, a blooper, or an egregious error. If you're always ready to pounce on a speaker who may send messages that oppose your viewpoint, then you may miss important qualifying statements, put words in the speaker's mouth, and reject what was not said or meant in the first place. Don't ambush. It's poor informational listening.

Active Listening: Focused Attention

The listening process is effortful, not effortless. It is an active, not a passive, process. **Active listening** is mindful, not mindless. It requires focused attention (see Box 6-1). This is especially critical for developing competent informational listening, although it also relates to critical and empathic listening, still to be discussed.

The need for focused attention is why listening to a cell phone call, even hands-free mobile calls, while driving can be dangerously distracting (Strayer et al., 2013). As noted in Chapter 2, multitasking splits attention between two competing stimuli and compromises our ability to do either task well. Neuroscientist Marcel Just of Carnegie Mellon University and his colleagues studied subjects who used a driving simulator while conducting a cell phone conversation. Listening to someone speak led to significant deterioration of driving proficiency. In some cases, drivers hit simulated guardrails and veered out of their lanes (Just et al., 2008). A study by the *American Journal of Public Health* showed that cell phone and texting while driving kills about 6,000 individuals per year (Richards, 2010). Nevertheless, while 98% of surveyed drivers realize the dangers, two-thirds do it anyway (Ortutay, 2014).

The airline industry recognizes the need for focused attention. In an effort to get passengers to listen carefully to safety instructions at the beginning of flights (critical information if an emergency were to occur), flight attendants for Southwest Airlines often use humor, such as "In the event of a sudden loss of cabin pressure, oxygen masks will descend from the ceiling. Stop screaming, grab the mask, and pull it over your face" or "Your seat cushion can be used for flotation, and in the event of an emergency water landing, please take them with our compliments." One flight attendant's presentation to passengers on routine safety procedures landed on YouTube and went viral in 2014 (see it at https://youtu.be/07LFBydGjaM). For three minutes, she entertained the passengers with such lines as "As you know, it's a no smoking, no whining, no complaining flight," "Basically, just do what we say and nobody gets hurt," and "To activate the flow of oxygen [to the mask], simply insert 75 cents for the first minute."

Active listening is not always appropriate. You can't focus on everything at once. It's impossible to listen actively to every message you receive daily. Every conversation is not deep and meaningful; some are pointless or peripheral. Active listening can occur because we focus on meaningful conversations, speeches, and learning opportunities while ignoring the trivial. Be an active, focused informational listener when it counts.

BOX 6-1 DEVELOPING COMMUNICATION COMPETENCE

Focused Attention

To make the point that you do not retain information unless you focus your attention, answer the following questions:

1. On which side of the icon for Apple computers is the bite located, left or right?

2. How many sides on a stop sign?

3. In which hand does the Statue of Liberty hold her torch?

4. On which side of their uniforms (to them, not to you) do police officers wear their badges?

5. When you look at a dime, which way does Franklin Roosevelt face, left or right?

6. How many geometric shapes are in the CBS "eye" logo?

7. Is the top stripe on an American flag red or white?

8. What is in the center of the backside of a $1 bill?

9. Every number key on the main portion of a standard computer keyboard has a symbol on it as well. What symbol is on the #5 key?

10. Which of the following can be found on all current U.S. coins?
    a. "United States of America"
    b. "E Pluribus Unum"
    c. "In God We Trust"
    d. "Liberty"

The correct answers (don't sneak a peek until you've finished) for these 10 questions are: 1. *right side*, 2. *eight sides*, 3. *right hand*, 4. *left*, 5. *faces left*, 6. *two geometric shapes: a circle twice and a football shape*, 7. *red*, 8. *ONE*, 9. *%*, and 10. *all of them.*

How did you do? It is not unusual to answer many of these questions incorrectly. *What you don't pay attention to because it isn't meaningful to you isn't remembered.* A coin collector would answer the Franklin Roosevelt question correctly because these collectors spend a great deal of time examining coins for minute details. Such an examination is part of their business. Most of us, however, pay little attention to the details on coins aside from recognizing its worth. If you don't focus your attention during conversations, those conversations will be little more than a blur. If your conversational partner asks, "What did I just say?" you'll look very foolish having to admit you heard next to nothing. Such indifference to others can threaten the quality, even the continuation, of relationships.

Competent Critical Listening

Listening involves more than accurately understanding the messages of others. We're not simply sponges absorbing information. Once we understand the message, we often need to evaluate it. All opinions are not created equal. People used to think that the earth was flat, pus healed wounds, and bloodletting cured diseases. A book published in 1902 entitled *The Cottage Physician*, written by a group of "the best physicians and surgeons of modern practice," claimed that cataracts could be cured by generous doses of laxatives, tetanus could be treated effectively by "pouring cold water on the head from a considerable height," and difficulty urinating could be relieved by marshmallow enemas (cited in Weingarten, 1994).

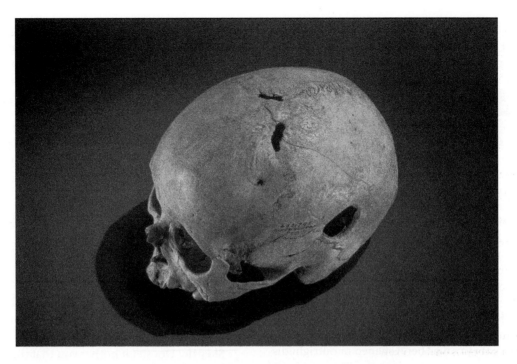

Trephining was a primitive procedure that involved cutting a hole in a person's skull while alive to release evil spirits or "mad thoughts." Clearly, some ideas are better than others, and it is the critical listener's responsibility to make such determinations. Our knowledge can build only if we act as skeptics who critically evaluate claims and reject those that aren't supported by quality evidence.

We hear a dizzying variety of claims every day. As critical listeners, you need to know the difference between prime rib and baloney, between fact and fantasy. One of my favorites is the oft-stated "fact" that the average human uses only 10% of his or her brain, leaving huge potential for personal growth. More than two-thirds of respondents to one survey believed this to be true (Chabris & Simons, 2010). Try getting along after 90% of your brain is surgically removed, however. Dark areas of the brain shown in brain-imaging scans are not inactive; they are simply less active than those colorful areas shown on the images. "There is no reason to suspect evolution—or even an intelligent designer—would give us an organ that is 90% inefficient" (Chabris & Simons, 2010, p. 199).

Measles, one of the most contagious and serious diseases, was virtually eradicated from the United States for years, but it has emerged again because many Americans refused to vaccinate their children and themselves. Before widespread U.S. vaccination programs, 3 to 4 million people contracted the disease annually. Of these, 400 to 500 died, about 48,000 were hospitalized, and 4,000 suffered encephalitis (brain swelling). According to the Centers for Disease Control and Prevention, fears of serious and rampant side effects from the vaccine are simply unfounded ("Measles," 2015).

Separating fact from fantasy is important. You separate the likely facts from the almost certain fantasies and nonsense by listening critically. **Critical listening** is the process of evaluating the merits of claims as they are heard. A **claim** is a generalization that remains to be proven.

Skepticism, True Belief, and Cynicism: Differences

Skepticism—a process of listening to claims, evaluating evidence and reasoning supporting those claims, and drawing conclusions based on probabilities—is the essence of critical listening. Skeptics may seem to be annoying nags, always asking for evidence and challenging people's beliefs. The term *skeptic*, however, is derived from the Greek *skeptikos*, which means thoughtful or inquiring, not doubtful and dismissive.

Conversely, **true belief** is a willingness to accept claims without solid reasoning or valid evidence and to hold these beliefs tenaciously even if a googol of contradictory evidence disputes them. As Winston Churchill put it, a true believer is "one who can't change his mind and won't change the subject." Columnist Leonard Pitts (2011) puts it aptly when commenting on the state of journalism, political discourse, and the rise of blogging sites on the Internet: "If we are all journalists, we all ought to be governed by journalism's most sacred directive. Meaning accuracy. Get the facts straight." He continues, "One encounters little fealty to that directive in surveying the landscape of new media, overrun as it is by *true believers* for whom accuracy is subordinate to ideology and facts useful only to the degree they can be bent, shaped or outright disregarded in service to ideology." This true belief results in "increasing incoherence and intellectual incontinence, an empty shouting match better suited to a fifth-grade schoolyard than to adults analyzing the great issues of the day" (p. A13). Nowhere is critical listening a part of true belief.

Cynicism is nay-saying, fault finding, and ridiculing. H. L. Mencken once described a **cynic** as someone who "smells flowers and looks around for a coffin." Cynics have "a feeling that things will pan out for the worse" (Mole, 2002, p. 45). They are quick to pounce on human frailties and imperfections. Cynicism is mentioned here because skepticism is often confused with cynicism (Mole, 2002). In some instances, skeptics have exhibited condescension and arrogance when commenting on questionable beliefs, justly deserving the criticism leveled at them. True skeptics, however, are hard on the claim but soft on the people making the claim (Sagan, 1996). Skepticism requires humility because no one's ideas and beliefs are immune to challenge. Nobody can honestly claim to be entirely free of foolishness. Skepticism operates as a third choice in between the extremes of true belief and cynicism.

True belief, as used here, does not simply mean strong belief. Skepticism also does not mean no belief. Vincent Ruggeiro (1988) notes,

"It is not the embracing of an idea that causes problems—it is the refusal to relax that embrace when good sense dictates doing so." *The key distinction between a true believer and a skeptic is not the strength of the belief but the process used to arrive at and maintain a belief.*

So how should a skeptic critically listen to a true believer and respond without belittling or showing contempt? Consider this dialogue:

True Believer: You should join my group. We show our true commitment to the group by freeing ourselves of individual material ties.

Skeptic: Does this involve selling all of my possessions and giving the proceeds to the group?

True Believer: Yes, we believe that living frugally in service to the leader is a path of enlightenment and a better life.

Skeptic: Doesn't it bother you that the leader of your group uses those proceeds to buy expensive cars and live a lavish lifestyle, while group members are required to wear inexpensive robes and live frugally?

True Believer: We believe our leader is the exalted one and should have, as you put it, "a lavish lifestyle." We are merely his servants.

Skeptic: It seems contradictory to me to teach commitment and to attack materialism but expect only you to make sacrifices while your leader lives very comfortably without visible sacrifice.

True Believer: That simply shows how little you understand us and our leader.

Skeptic: Perhaps, but I'm trying to understand. Are you ever allowed to doubt the teachings of your leader?

True Believer: No! Doubt leads to confusion and weak commitment.

Skeptic: Well, this is where we really disagree, because I have serious reservations about a group that requires me to accept without question what a group leader teaches.

Throughout this dialogue, respect is shown to the true believer even though differences in belief are obvious and strong. You can disagree, even strongly, with a true believer without being disagreeable. There can be reasonable disagreement even among skeptics. Show others respect when discussing beliefs because few people take their beliefs lightly. Listen carefully and respectfully, but also listen critically.

The Process of True Believing: Uncritical Listening

True beliefs vary widely, and in some instances, they can be contradictory. Nevertheless, despite the differences in the details, true believers all operate in essentially the same way. They exhibit *confirmation bias, rationalization of disconfirmation,* and *shifting the burden of proof.*

CONFIRMATION BIAS: SEARCHING FOR SUPPORT

One of the hallmarks of true belief is **confirmation bias**—the tendency to seek information that supports one's beliefs and to ignore information that contradicts those beliefs (Lilienfield et al., 2009). Once your belief has been confirmed, you are not inclined to listen to disconfirming evidence. *True believers are belief driven, not evidence driven.* Their beliefs are formed first, and then they look for confirming evidence. Research shows that confirmation bias is pervasive (Jonas et al., 2001; Stanovich et al., 2013).

People generally do not give themselves a chance to spot faulty claims while listening because they listen only for information that supports their beliefs and ignore contrary information (Schittekatte & Van Hiel, 1996). Competent critical listeners must be prepared to say to themselves, consistently, "So why would some people disagree with this speaker?" You're listening with an ear for both sides on an issue, not just one side.

RATIONALIZATION OF DISCONFIRMATION: CLINGING TO FALSEHOODS

There is a story of a client with an odd problem who came to see a therapist. The client believed that he was dead. The therapist made several attempts to convince the client that he was not, but nothing worked. Finally, the therapist asked her client, "Do dead men bleed?" The man said no. The therapist then took a pin out of the

drawer in her desk, grabbed the man's hand, and stabbed it. Blood spurted. The man looked at his bleeding hand and responded, "Well, I'll be damned; dead men do bleed."

Even when true believers are confronted with strong, disconfirming evidence, they usually hold tenaciously to their beliefs. True believers use **rationalization of disconfirmation**—inventing superficial, even lame, alternative explanations for contradictory evidence. Christian preacher Harold Camping adamantly predicted that the Rapture—Judgment Day—would occur on May 21, 2011 (after originally predicting that 1994 would see the Rapture). He even posted 1,200 billboards around the country to advertise his prediction. For reasons beyond strange, the popular media gave Camping's prediction wide coverage. As you know, his prediction did not come true. Did he admit his prediction was a fantasy based on no credible evidence? Nope! He "revised" the date to October 21, 2011, claiming that May 21st was the "spiritual" Rapture and October 21st would be the physical Rapture (Maher, 2011). You already know that he was wrong again. Like the man who believed he was dead, true believers' view of reality is invulnerable to challenge because some rationalization can always be concocted.

SHIFTING THE BURDEN OF PROOF: WHOSE OBLIGATION IS IT?

The **burden of proof** is the obligation of the person making the claim to present compelling evidence and reasoning to support it (Fisher, 2003). As a speaker, whenever you make a claim to an audience (e.g., "texting can become addictive"), you assume the burden to prove that claim. As a critical listener, you should be looking to see whether a speaker meets the burden of proof when making claims.

When those making a claim challenge a skeptic to "prove us wrong" before they have offered compelling evidence to support their claim, they are **shifting the burden of proof**—inappropriately assuming the validity of a claim unless it is proven false by another person who never made the original claim (Verlinden, 2005). No one should have to prove that another person's claim is false when that person has failed to present credible reasoning and evidence to show the original claim might be true. If it were otherwise, skeptics would have to disprove all manner of absurd, unsupported claims, such as humans can suddenly burst into flames for no apparent reason (spontaneous human combustion), or humans can train themselves to live without food and on air alone (breatharianism). Remember, _whoever makes the claim has the burden of proof_. When you're sitting at the dinner table celebrating a holiday and a relative offers his latest conspiracy theory, remember that it is his or her claim to prove, not yours to disprove. If you're a member of the student senate and another student claims that the senate has been "completely ineffective" in addressing the poor quality of cafeteria food on campus, remember that proving the claim is that student's burden, not yours. Begin with the question "What evidence leads you to believe this?" You can choose to refute the claim later if it is not true, but you're not obliged to listen to or refute wild, unsupported claims. (See Chapter 13 for a detailed discussion of reasoning and evidence as proof).

The Skepticism Process: Exercising Competent Critical Listening

This section explains the process of becoming a skeptical, critical listener. This same process is also relevant to being a competent speaker (see later chapters on public speaking).

Claims people make assert varying degrees of likelihood (Adler, 1998). Note the differences in the following claims:

Possibility: You could receive an "A" in your communication class even though you flunked all the tests, skipped all the assignments, and rarely came to class.

Plausibility: There is at least one other galaxy besides our own with intelligent life.

Probability: Leaping out of an airplane from 2,500 feet without a parachute will result in death.

Certainty: Everybody dies.

In this section, differences in claims of possibility, plausibility, probability, and certainty to clarify the critical listening process that separates skeptics from true believers are discussed. Self-correction is also discussed.

POSSIBILITY: COULD HAPPEN, BUT DON'T BET ON IT

True belief often rests on the "anything is possible" rationale, but this allows for no distinctions to be drawn between sense and nonsense, fact and fiction. That a student could receive an "A" in a communication class without passing any tests, completing any assignments, or attending class is possible—a student could receive an "A" because of a clerical error by the instructor or a computer glitch—yet highly unlikely.

Suppose, for example, a stranger asks you to walk blindfolded across a busy highway. Would you do it? What if you saw someone else do it without getting hit by a car? One success proves that it is possible to cross a busy highway blindfolded and not get catapulted into the next county by a speeding automobile, but it is not likely. "Anything is possible" is insufficient justification for gambling with your life or accepting an unsupported claim.

PLAUSIBILITY: MAKING A LOGICAL CASE

The next step up from possibility is plausibility. The claim that at least one other galaxy has incubated intelligent life forms can be supported by a rational argument that rests on related knowledge. Astronomers report that there are approximately 100 billion galaxies, each composed of about 100 billion stars. With numbers that large, it does not defy logic to think that life exists elsewhere besides this flyspeck in the universe called Earth (Tarter, 2006). Conditions necessary to sustain life could have developed elsewhere. Scientists at SETI (Search for Extraterrestrial Intelligence) scan the inky darkness of space for signals from any intelligent species that might be out there. SETI bases this search on plausibility alone. There is no proof extraterrestrial life exists, and members of SETI only claim that there is reason to believe that it _might_ exist. They are searching, and at least initially, the search for knowledge may have no better rationale than plausibility.

The assertion that Earth has already been visited by extraterrestrial life, however, is implausible. Consider three reasons. First, other galaxies are thousands of light years away. Thus, only travel far faster than the speed of light, which is contrary to known laws of physics, would make the arrival of alien tourists feasible. "The next nearest star to Earth's sun (Alpha Centauri) is about four light-years away . . . Even traveling at one million miles an hour [25 times faster than our fastest spaceship], it would take more than 2,500 years to get there" (Carroll, 2014). Second, most people's accounts of alien abduction consistently describe extraterrestrials as having humanoid form (heads, eyes, mouths, arms, and legs). Since these beings would have had a separate evolutionary history, it is implausible that they should look so similar to us (Sagan, 1996). Third, two surveys conducted in the 1990s, one by Roper and the other by Gallup, found that approximately 3 million Americans believed they had been abducted by aliens. Assuming aliens do not discriminate by picking only on Americans, this suggests that more than 60 million people worldwide have been abducted. "It's surprising more of the neighbors haven't noticed" (Sagan, 1996, p. 64).

A claim must be at least plausible to be worthy of serious consideration and further exploration. Alien visitation does not even pass this minimal test. *Plausibility is a basis for inquiry, but it is an insufficient basis for acceptance of a claim.* Research that you might conduct during your academic life often is motivated by a plausible hypothesis, but once the research has been conducted, a hypothesis must rest on probability to be deemed credible.

PROBABILITY: LIKELIHOOD OF EVENTS

The claim that falling from an airplane from 2,500 feet without a parachute will result in death is not only plausible, it's probable. People usually injure themselves just falling from an eight-foot ladder. A 2,500-foot free fall does not bode well for the person hurtling toward the earth. Death is highly likely, but it is not certain. On September 25, 1999, Joan Murray, a 47-year-old bank executive and skydiving enthusiast, struggled to open her parachute during a jump. Finally, a reserve parachute opened at 700 feet but became tangled and deflated. Murray slammed into the ground at an estimated 80 miles per hour. She suffered multiple serious injuries, but she survived. Two years later, she resumed skydiving ("Beating the Odds," 2002).

Probability is a concept not well understood by most people (Paulos, 1988). There's a difference in probabilities between making a general claim and making a specific claim. The **Law of Very Large Numbers** notes that with large enough numbers, almost anything is likely to happen to *somebody*. On August 14, 1992, a small meteorite hit a boy in Uganda (Krieger, 1999). The odds of this particular little boy being hit by a meteorite are astronomical (specific claim). Given the more than 7 billion people on our planet and the great regularity of meteorites hitting Earth, however, it is highly probable that someone, somewhere, sometime will be hit (general claim). If some event happens to only one person in a million each day, then with 321 million people in the United States ("U.S. and World Population Clock," 2015), you can expect 321 such events daily.

CERTAINTY: WITHOUT EXCEPTION

Claims of true believers are frequently stated as absolute certainties. A true believer by definition exhibits no doubt. *Skepticism, however, can aspire to no stronger claim than very high probability.* Skepticism does not allow the assertion that any phenomenon is "impossible," although some skeptics have intemperately made such a claim. Consider doubts about homeopathy, an "alternative" medical treatment widely used in the United States. Homeopathy is based on the so-called law of infinitesimals. This means "less is better." Homeopathic solutions are composed of extracts of herbs, minerals, or animal organs diluted many times in water. At the standard dilution of 30 times, patients would have to drink 7,874 gallons of the solution to consume a *single molecule* of the medicine (Park, 2000). Carrying the less-is-better belief to even greater extremes, some homeopathic remedies, such as the standard flu remedy Oscillococcinum, are diluted 200 times or more. It is virtually certain that homeopathic remedies, the "no-medicine medicine," could not have any beneficial effects on patients (De Dora, 2015; Ernst, 2010). In fact, the Australian National Health and Medical Research Council conducted a careful analysis of hundreds of studies on homeopathy and concluded: "There are no health conditions for which there is reliable evidence that homeopathy is effective" ("NHMRC Releases Statement," 2015).

Nevertheless, skepticism allows for no greater claim than that it is "virtually" certain homeopathic remedies are bogus. Nothing is deemed "impossible." This does not, however, open the door to the everything-is-possible, "open-mindedness" justification for true belief (see Box 6-2).

SELF-CORRECTION: PROGRESSING BY MISTAKE

In 1983, Barry Marshall, a resident at the Royal Perth Hospital, Australia, startled the medical world. He argued that most stomach ulcers are not caused by a stressful lifestyle. Instead, he claimed that they are caused by a simple bacterium. Martin Blaser of the Vanderbilt School of Medicine reflected the initial response of the medical community to Marshall's claim when he called it "the most preposterous thing I'd ever heard" (quoted in Monmaney, 1993). Marshall's claim seemed outlandish because it contradicted what the medical community thought it knew about ulcers. Marshall, however, was soon proven correct when the bacterium, now called *Helicobacter pylori*, was discovered and shown to be the cause of most stomach ulcers. This meant that antibiotics, not psychotherapy or antacids and a bland diet, were the effective cure. Despite initial doubt, the medical community now accepts the bacterial cause of most ulcers (Ratini, 2014).

Skepticism goes where the evidence leads, and if the evidence compels change, then change must occur. *Skepticism and self-correction are inseparable.* If, while listening to a speech, strong evidence is presented that clearly contradicts one of your cherished beliefs, defending that erroneous belief is ethically questionable. Honesty demands self-correction. Skepticism mandates tough choices and the courage to correct errors.

Competent Empathic Listening

Informational listening and critical listening achieve important goals for the competent communicator. Informational listening expands our knowledge and understanding of our world. Critical listening helps us sort through bad ideas to discover good ideas that will solve problems and help us make quality decisions that improve our lives.

There are times, however, when the point of conversation is to establish a relationship with or help another person through an emotional event. The police officer in the opening story to this chapter illustrated **empathic listening**, which requires us to take the perspective of the other person, to listen for what that person needs and wants (Goleman, 2013). Research shows that more personal and impersonal information alike is disclosed when listeners exhibit perspective-taking behaviors (e.g., paraphrasing or perception checking). Perspective taking also improves comprehension and retention of another person's viewpoint in conflict situations (Johnson, 1971; Johnson & Johnson, 2000). Failure to perceive another person's perspective is a frequent communication problem for couples (Vangelisti, 1994).

Response Styles: Initial Response Patterns

Response styles are the types of initial verbal reactions we make when another person comes to us with a problem, reveals a frustrating event, or is experiencing an emotional crisis. This next section covers seven styles, some that are non-empathic and others that are empathic (Rogers & Roethlisberger, 1952; see also Kotzman & Kotzman, 2008).

EVALUATIVE RESPONSE: MAKING JUDGMENTS

A friend comes to you, obviously upset, and says, "I hate my job. I've got to find something different to do." You respond, "You haven't given the job much of a try. Perhaps you'd like it better if you put more effort into it." This is an **evaluative response**. It makes a judgment about the person's conduct, and it assumes a standard of evaluation has, or has not, been met. As you read the evaluative response, perhaps you said to yourself, "I wouldn't respond that way." Perhaps not, but the most frequent response people make in situations like the one just presented is to evaluate (Rogers & Roethlisberger, 1952).

BOX 6-2 FOCUS ON CONTROVERSY

Skepticism and Open-Mindedness: Inquiring Minds, Not Empty Minds

Although skeptics avoid claims of certainty, this does not open the door to the everything-is-possible, "open-mindedness" justification for true belief. Years ago, for example, I explored a variety of alternative medical treatments and New Age therapies, partly from curiosity and partly from a need to help a sick friend. I investigated herbal remedies, homeopathy, psychic healing, polarity therapy, crystal healing, iridology, pyramid power, radiesthesia, dowsing, marathon fasts, megavitamin therapy, therapeutic touch, and faith healing. Whenever I expressed doubt concerning the validity of these alternative approaches to health and disease, I was denounced as "closed-minded." It seemed that open-mindedness was equated with never discounting any claim, no matter how poorly supported or implausible.

Open-mindedness does not require us to listen to obviously false claims or to give them a forum for expression (Hare, 2009). Do you really want to listen to a speaker argue that the world is flat or that gravity does not exist? As the bumper sticker says: "Gravity: Not just a good idea; it's the law!" An open mind should not equate with an empty mind. "What truly marks an open-minded person is the willingness to follow where evidence leads" (Adler, 1998, p. 44; see also Petrovic, 2013).

We don't always follow where the evidence leads, however. A Zogby survey of 1,200 Americans reported on NBC's *Today* show revealed that 7% of respondents don't believe that the Apollo astronauts ever landed and walked on the Moon, and an additional 4% were not sure. Since there are about 235 million adult Americans ("U.S. and World

Population Clock," 2015), these results suggest that more than 16 million of them think the Moon landing—one of the most thoroughly documented events in human history—was a hoax, and that an additional 9 million think it might have been faked. Attempting to capitalize on this apparent doubt, the Fox TV network aired *Conspiracy Theory: Did We Land on the Moon?* Striving for the sensational and achieving the nonsensical, the program clearly intimated that the U.S. government faked the Moon landing. The Internet is replete with sites alleging the Moon landing was a hoax.

The Moon landing was documented by scientists from around the world. There is no legitimate "other side" or reasonable debate on this topic. A Moon hoax conspiracy is completely implausible because it would have to involve thousands of NASA collaborators. If any credible evidence of fakery were discovered by Soviet scientists who were monitoring the Apollo Moon flights, they surely would have announced it to the world. The Soviet Union was our Cold War nemesis, after all, and was racing us to the Moon. If you engage in a debate with those who deny the Moon landings or other equally discredited claims, such as Holocaust denial, that is your choice, and you may just be exercising your intellectual muscles. Remember, though, that all claims are not created equal, and being open-minded doesn't mean having to listen to speakers espousing false claims that have already been demolished by careful reasoning and abundant evidence. Be open-minded by following where the evidence leads you.

Questions for Thought

1. Can you have too much skepticism and become closed-minded? Explain.

2. Should we listen "open-mindedly" to claims that women are the inferior sex and men make poor parents?

3. Is it ethical to steadfastly maintain a belief that you know is wrong but makes you feel comfortable nevertheless? Explain.

A hypercompetitive, individualistic culture such as ours promotes the evaluative response. Competition focuses us on discerning weaknesses in our adversaries. Even when we are conversing with a friend, there is a tendency to focus on weaknesses. Competitors don't try to bolster their opponents. Adversaries try to diminish each other to win. Evaluating a friend who comes to you with a problem is nonempathic.

Evaluation is the least effective response when we need to be empathic. Harold Kushner (1981), author of *When Bad Things Happen to Good People*, makes this point:

> It is hard to know what to say to a person who has been struck by tragedy, but it is easier to know what not to say. Anything critical of the mourner ("don't take it so hard," "try to hold back your tears, you're upsetting people") is wrong. Anything which tries to minimize the mourner's pain ("it's probably for the best," "it could be a lot worse," "she's better off now") is likely to be misguided and unappreciated. (p. 89)

When you're suffering, the last things you need are criticism and judgment.

ADVISING RESPONSE: TELLING OTHERS HOW TO ACT

"My roommate drives me crazy. She has so many odd quirks." How would you respond to this? If you would respond with "Why don't you change roommates?" you are offering advice. The **advising response** tells people how they should act. It is a common initial reaction to those who make a complaint or reveal a problem. Despite its frequency, however, advice is as likely to be unhelpful as helpful to others in distress (Brustein, 2014; Goldsmith & MacGeorge, 2000). The distressed person may resent being offered unrequested advice, and the advice may be disastrously incorrect (e.g., telling a violently abused partner to "stand up and fight back").

Men more than women tend to offer advice when others come to them with a problem or complaint (Bernstein, 2013; Eisenchias, 2013). Giving advice under these circumstances does two things (Wood, 1994). First, it fails to acknowledge the other person's feelings. Second,

it communicates superiority of the person giving the advice. Giving advice presumes that the person with the problem hasn't figured out the solution. A common reaction from recipients of fix-it advice is to feel condescension or devaluation of their capabilities from those offering the advice. Researchers at the University of Iowa conducted a series of six studies involving 100 couples during the first seven years of their marriages, and the results were conclusive: both husbands and wives experience lower marital satisfaction when spouses offer too much advice (Bernstein, 2013).

Take the perspective of the other person before giving advice. Does the person seem interested in receiving advice from you? Is that really what he or she is seeking? Have you considered your advice carefully, or is it merely a glib response made without thoughtful examination? Do you have expertise that can provide helpful advice? Here's a novel suggestion: just ask the person directly if they want advice before offering it!

INTERPRETING RESPONSE: EXPLAINING MEANING

A friend says to you, "I don't understand why he says such embarrassing things to me in front of my family." You respond, "Perhaps he is just uncomfortable around your parents and doesn't really know quite what to say, so he says silly things that embarrass you because he's socially clumsy." This is an **interpreting response**. You are expressing what you think is the underlying meaning of a situation presented to you and explaining that meaning for the other person. Interpreting responses are what we pay counselors, psychiatrists, and therapists to do for us when we can't make sense of our relationships, feelings, conflicts, and traumas. The interpreting response is useful in some situations, but like advising, it tends to place the listener (the person doing the interpreting) in a superior position. One can "play guru" too often if the interpreting response becomes frequent.

CONTENT-ONLY RESPONSE: IGNORING FEELINGS

A **content-only response** comprehends the literal meaning of messages from others but doesn't recognize the feelings involved. Consider this example:

> **Bettina:** I can't believe we're so far in debt. Those student loans are killing us.
>
> **Jeremy:** I've been in worse trouble.
>
> **Bettina:** Look at these Visa bills, and the MasterCard is maxed out, too.
>
> **Jeremy:** Actually, we haven't hit the limit on the MasterCard yet. We have another $800 to go.
>
> **Bettina:** That's small comfort. What if we lose our house because we can't pay the mortgage?
>
> **Jeremy:** We could use the MasterCard to buy food and pay some bills up to the $800 that's still short of the limit. Then we could use our paychecks to cover the mortgage next month.

Nowhere does Jeremy, the content-only responder, ever acknowledge Bettina's fears and concerns by perspective taking. ("I understand your fear. I'm feeling very anxious, too, about our pile of debt.") Every response only increases her fears that they are in debt up to their eyebrows and that they may lose their home.

Content-only responding ignores feelings and is nonempathic. Natural disaster communication expert Peter Sandman notes that public officials need to acknowledge people's fears immediately in a crisis situation before presenting clear, concise information regarding how to deal with a disaster (see Tallmadge, 2007). Failure to exhibit empathy will likely diminish fearful individuals' ability to listen to critical emergency information.

PROBING RESPONSE: ASKING QUESTIONS

The **probing response** seeks more information from others by asking questions. As a listener, you're showing interest in the other person's distress by inquiring further about the problem. Several types of questions qualify as a probing response (Purdy & Borisoff, 1997):

Clarifying Question: "Can you give me an example of what you mean when you say that she is insensitive?" Clarifying questions seek understanding.

Exploratory Question: "Can you think of some ways to defuse her anger?" "Can you think of any alternative besides resigning from your position?" Exploratory questions urge the speaker to examine possibilities posed by a problem or situation.

Encouraging Question: "You didn't have any other choice, did you? Who could blame you for sticking to your principles?" Encouraging questions inquire about choices made and imply agreement at the same time.

Probing responses show interest in the speaker by seeking more information from and being attentive to the plight of the other person. Probing questions do not, however, make a person feel like someone being grilled on a witness stand by a prosecutor. "Why did you ever agree to go out with him in the first place?" or "Didn't you realize

Sometimes we are asking for support, not advice.

she couldn't be trusted with money?" smacks of evaluation, not sincere inquiry. These questions seem intended to make a point, not to help you grasp the nature of the other person's distress.

SUPPORTING RESPONSE: BOLSTERING OTHERS

A **supporting response** includes "expressions of care, concern, affection, and interest, especially during times of stress or upset" (Burleson, 2003, p. 552). There are several types of supporting responses:

> *Reassurance:* "First day on the job can be a little nerve-racking, but you have the skills to do the job really well."
>
> *Agreement:* "You're right! Your boss is completely out of line."
>
> *Praise:* "You did a fantastic job even if she doesn't recognize it."
>
> *Assistance:* "I can help you move out if you need me."
>
> *Validating Feelings:* "You should be angry; I know I would be!" (Burleson, 2003)

A person suffering the loss of a loved one needs empathy. In our struggle to help someone shoulder a burden, however, we may choose the wrong response. One survey found that bereaved individuals considered 80% of the responses made to them during mourning to be unhelpful (Davidowitz & Myricm, 1984). Almost half of the responses were advice ("You need to get out more"; "You have to accept this and move on with your life"), but they were hardly ever perceived as helpful to the bereaved. Acknowledging and validating the feelings of the bereaved were the most helpful responses ("I can see how much you miss her"; "He was a warm and sensitive person").

Don't provide "cold comfort" responses (Hample, 2006). These include *denying the right to feel a particular way* ("Stop worrying about it" or "Don't take it so hard; he wasn't worth your tears"), *minimizing the significance of the situation* ("It was only your first real job; there will be others" or "It was just a silly party; so what if you didn't get invited"), or *focusing on the future* ("You'll feel better tomorrow" or "You'll find another girlfriend soon"). When a person is

distressed, such responses are unlikely to seem helpful. Have you ever stopped worrying just because someone told you to?

Compared to men, women generally are more likely to provide emotional support to others in need, are more skillful in providing comfort, and are more prone to seek supporting responses from others (Burleson et al., 2005). This is why, as noted in Chapter 3, both men and women usually seek and prefer support and comfort from women.

UNDERSTANDING RESPONSE: PARAPHRASING AND PERCEPTION CHECKING

The **understanding response** requires a listener to check his or her perceptions for comprehension of the speaker's message or to paraphrase the message to check accuracy. **Perception checking** was discussed in Chapter 2. Briefly, you begin with a behavior description, follow with an interpretation of the behavior, and finish with a request for verification of your interpretation. **Paraphrasing** "is a concise response to the speaker which states the essence of the other's content in the listener's words" (Bolton, 1979, p. 51).

Paraphrasing is not a parroting of a person's message ("I'm Arturo"—"I hear you saying that your name is Arturo"). Paraphrasing is concise and to the point. For example:

Francine: My roommate hums to himself while he studies. He hums stupid, irritating little tunes that stick in my head like annoying ads on TV. I'm trying to study, and I can't concentrate with his humming. I have a major exam in chemistry class tomorrow, and old hum-till-we're-all-dumb never grows tired of the sound of his own noise. I've got a lot riding on this exam.

Teresa: Sounds to me like you're really worried that your roommate's annoying humming will make you flunk your chemistry exam.

Francine: Yeah, and I've never flunked an exam! Got any suggestions for what I should do about him, or to him?

Paraphrasing helps a listener understand the essence of a speaker's message. However, it should be used only occasionally during a conversation. Look for the significant points in a conversation, and then paraphrase. Details and elaborations of unimportant points usually don't require paraphrasing.

Now that you have read about these response styles, test yourself by identifying the listening response in Box 6-3.

Response Styles: Empathic and Nonempathic Listening

Different responses produce different results. Some of these response styles are empathic, and some are nonempathic.

EMPATHIC RESPONSE STYLES: PROBING, SUPPORTING, AND UNDERSTANDING

Empathic listening is composed of probing, supporting, and understanding responses. All three put the focus on the speaker and are therefore **confirming responses**—they enhance the person's self-esteem and confidence. Don Hamachek (1982) explains:

> An understanding response is a way of letting a person know that you're listening to both the content of what's being said and the feeling accompanying it; a probing response lets a person know that you want to know more and, on a deeper level, that he or she is worth knowing more about; a supportive response is a way of saying that you care and that you hope things will get better. (p. 214)

When building a relationship and connecting with a person are the principal goals of your communication, probing, supporting, and understanding responses establish trust, deepen the connections between you and another person, and keep communication open.

NONEMPATHIC RESPONSES: EVALUATING, ADVISING, INTERPRETING, AND CONTENT-ONLY

Disconfirming responses diminish the person, reduce confidence, and are nonempathic. These responses include evaluating, advising, interpreting, and content-only responses (Hamachek, 1982). Should you therefore avoid such responses? *Empathy is not always the type of listening*

that is most appropriate in a given situation, so the answer is "no." Interpreting is an important listening response when someone is confused and wants clarity. Advising others can be constructive and helpful, especially if a person seeks our advice. Evaluating a person's self-destructive behavior may save that person's life.

CHOOSING COMPETENT RESPONSE STYLES: FREQUENCY, TIMING, AND SOLICITATION

Three variables influence the appropriateness and effectiveness of evaluating, advising,

---

BOX 6-3 DEVELOPING COMMUNICATION COMPETENCE

Distinguishing Listening Responses

Read the following situation, then identify which type of response it is. Mark A for advising, E for evaluation, I for interpreting, P for probing, S for supporting, U for understanding, and C for content-only.

My boss is a total jerk. She's always giving me these huge projects to do, then yelling at me for not getting my other work done. She never has anything nice to say to anyone, and she actually times us when we take breaks to make sure we don't take longer than we're allowed. I feel like quitting.

_____ Aren't you being a little unfair? She can't be that bad.

_____ What have you tried so far to deal with your boss?

_____ Your situation is a classic power struggle.

_____ I think you should quit and find a job more to your liking.

_____ You feel overworked and underappreciated.

_____ I know you'll make the right decision because you usually know what is right to do.

_____ Your boss could be worse.

Which response do you think would be the best? Second best? Explain.

ANSWERS: **E, P, I, A, U, S, C.**

interpreting, and content-only responses. The first variable is *frequency*, which refers to how often you use disconfirming responses. Occasional evaluation, interpretation, advice, or content-only responses, especially in a strong relationship, will rarely cause more than a ripple of disturbance. The frequent use of such disconfirming responses, however, can swamp even resilient relationships.

The second variable is *timing*, which refers to when you use nonempathic responses. Consider the following statement: "This is politics, pure and simple. You've handled them wrong. Stand up to these thugs." This statement begins with interpreting, follows with evaluating, and closes with advising—the triple crown of disconfirmation. Such a statement early in a relationship, when the two parties hardly know each other, would likely be received negatively. The same statement much later in a relationship, when the two parties are familiar with each other's style and trust each other, might be received in a more neutral, or even positive, way. Additionally, evaluating, interpreting, advising, or content-only responses that are used when a person is feeling fragile and in need of support will likely disconnect speaker and listener. Such responses can make a person feel inferior and diminished.

Finally, evaluating, advising, interpreting, and content-only responses are more appropriate, and likely to be more effective, when the speaker solicits them (Goldsmith, 2000). *Solicitation* refers to whether you are asked to evaluate, interpret, advise, or concentrate on the content, not the feelings, of the speaker. A person may simply want to be heard by you, not told what to do. He or she may reject unsolicited advice, even resent it. "I already thought of that, and it won't work" is a typical rejoinder to unsolicited advice. Several studies reveal that frequent unsolicited advice from a partner can damage relationships (Bernstein, 2013).

If individuals request such advice, however, they will more likely perceive it to be helpful. People who seek help from a therapist implicitly request an interpreting response. People rarely request evaluation, but if they do, it is more likely to be accepted than if a critique is unsolicited.

 ## Summary

Listening is the most frequent type of communication any of us do on a daily basis. Listening is first and foremost an active process. You cannot comprehend information, retain it, or respond appropriately to what you hear from others without focused attention. Listening is effortful, not effortless. You need to be an active listener.

The competent communicator recognizes when informational, critical, and empathic types of listening are appropriate and effective. Be an informational listener when the principal focus of the communication is learning or retaining information. Be a critical listener when you need to find solutions to problems or make decisions that will have consequences for yourself and others. Be an empathic listener when you are trying to build or maintain a relationship with another person and that person comes to you with a problem or crisis.

Answer for Critical Thinking caption:

ZITS (P. 150): #4

Quizzes Without Consequences

Test your knowledge before your exam! Go to the companion website at www.oup.com/us/ rothwell, click on the Student Resources for each chapter, and take the Quizzes Without Consequences.

Film School Case Studies

He's Just Not That Into You (2009). Romance; PG-13

A relationships-in-trouble film. Both couples and singles seem incapable of listening. Gigi (Ginnifer Goodwin) in particular exhibits many listening problems. What are some of her principal difficulties? How about the Janine (Jennifer Connelly) and Ben (Bradley Cooper) characters?

Inherit the Wind (1960). Drama; Not Rated

Outstanding adaptation of the stage play depicting the Scopes Monkey Trial and its challenge to the Tennessee law forbidding the teaching of evolution in schools. Who are the true believers, cynics, and skeptics in the movie? Explain.

Ordinary People (1980). Drama; R

Robert Redford's Oscar-winning directorial debut presents a family in crisis. Look for examples of listening problems, especially shift response, competitive interrupting, pseudolistening, ambushing, and content-only responses. Also notice response styles, especially evaluative, interpretive, and advising responses.

The Devil Wears Prada (2006). Comedy; PG-13

Anne Hathaway plays Andrea "Andy" Sachs, a beleaguered assistant to a tyrannical, cold, impersonal magazine editor (Meryl Streep). See if you can identify all of the listening problems exemplified, especially by the Streep character.

The Help (2011). Drama; PG-13

A young, aspiring writer during the civil rights movement of the 1960s embarks on a project to write a book from the perspective of African American maids who work for white families. Analyze communication response styles as the African American housekeepers share their stories.

1. Define power, and explain the differences between types of power.

2. Describe the principal verbal and nonverbal indicators and five main sources of power.

3. Recognize the communication of power imbalances and their consequences.

CHAPTER 7

Power

A CAPTAIN SPOTS A LIGHT in the distance, directly in the path of his ship. He orders his signalman to send the following message: "Turn 10 degrees south." A message is transmitted back to the ship: "*You* need to turn 10 degrees north." Irritated, the captain orders a second message transmitted: "I am this ship's captain, and I order you to turn 10 degrees south." An immediate reply is received, "I am a seaman second class, and I am telling you to turn 10 degrees north." Outraged that his authority to issue a clear order is being ignored by a lowly seaman second class, the captain responds: "This is a battleship coming right at you; turn 10 degrees south." This prompts a quick reply: "This is a lighthouse; turn 10 degrees north."

Power is inescapable in human transactions. Relationships between ship captains and seamen, parents and children, doctors and nurses, teachers and students, judges and lawyers, supervisors and employees, or coaches and athletes are

CHAPTER OUTLINE

- Definition of Power
- Communication Indicators of Power
- Power Resources
- Problems of Power Imbalance
- Competent Communication and Balancing Power

4. Contrast competitive with cooperative communication of power.

5. Develop competent communication strategies to balance power in your transactions with others.

hierarchical and fundamentally power oriented. "There is power in a word or a gesture. There is power when women and men live together, work together, talk together, or are simply in each other's company. There is power in a smile, a caress, and there is power in sex." There is also "power in how we choose to resolve our conflicts, and how we negotiate the most intimate aspects of our lives" (Kalbfleisch & Cody, 1995, p. xiii). There is power when a person speaks as an expert to a large group or organization.

Organizations and institutions are typically structured as hierarchies, with the powerful at the top and the more abundant workers experiencing diminishing levels of power below. Access to electronic communication media within organizations can involve issues of power. Monitoring employees' private versus work-related emails and use of social media indicates degrees of difference in power among workers and supervisors. These are but a few examples illustrating the centrality of power in our lives. "To be human is to be immersed in power dynamics" (Keltner, 2007).

Power, however, may connote negative communication transactions (e.g., "power plays," "power struggles," or "power politics"). "Power tends to corrupt, and absolute power corrupts absolutely," Lord Acton reputedly observed. This is a popular perspective. In a low power-distance culture such as the United States (see Chapter 3), exercising power can seem questionable (Carl et al., 2004). We are inclined to think of power as illegitimate or even evil, unless, of course, we are the individual with the power. Then, as former Secretary of the Navy John Lehman once quipped, "Power corrupts. Absolute power is kind of neat."

Research on the communication behavior of high-power individuals doesn't help diminish the generally negative view of power. There is a "wealth of evidence that having power makes people more likely to act like sociopaths. High-power individuals are more likely to interrupt others, to speak out of turn, and to fail to look at others who are speaking." More unsettling, "[t]hey are also more likely to tease friends and colleagues in hostile, humiliating fashion. Surveys of organizations find that most rude behaviors— shouting, profanities, bald critiques—emanate from the offices and cubicles of individuals in positions of power" (Keltner, 2007).

Exercising power, however, can be corrupting or altruistic. Some may use power to bulldoze, bully, and intimidate others for personal gain. Others may use power to build schools and feed starving children in Africa. *You achieve your individual goals, resolve conflicts, and sustain relationships by communicating competently when you exercise power.*

There is no virtue in exercising little power. Feeling powerless creates apathy, shrivels our desire to perform at work, and strains personal relationships (Wilmot & Hocker, 2014). It creates interpersonal disconnection and erodes self-esteem (Lee, 1997). Feeling powerless inhibits the direct expression of ideas and produces withdrawal from interactions with others. The powerful typically feel a sense of well-being, the "good life," that the relatively powerless do not experience (Kifer et al., 2013). Feeling powerless can strangle your spirit and stifle your motivation to improve your life and the lives of those you love. It can also lead to self-destructive behavior or aggression toward others (Keltner et al., 2003).

Your choice is not between using or not using power. "We only have options about whether to use power destructively or productively for ourselves and relationships" (Wilmot & Hocker, 2014). *The primary purpose of this chapter is to learn ways to exercise power by communicating competently.*

Definition of Power

Power is the ability to influence the attainment of goals sought by you or others. This is a general definition. More specifically, this section explores the nature and forms of power.

Above all, <u>power is transactional</u>. This means that power is constantly being negotiated during conversations with others. Consider this dialogue and the comments interjected in parentheses that indicate the power dynamics communicated during the conversation:

> Jennifer is washing the dishes. Geoff seems not to notice.
>
> "I'm tired of dealing with my mother's demands on me," begins Jennifer (*control is an issue*).
>
> Geoff responds, "Don't let her make you feel guilty for not spending every holiday with her and your father" (*advising as a parent to a child*).
>
> Jennifer says, "I'm not letting her make me feel guilty (*asserting control*). I just get emotionally exhausted having to explain over and over again why we aren't coming to her house on Christmas."
>
> Geoff picks up a towel and begins to dry some dishes. "Tell her just once why we won't be coming for the holidays; then refuse to talk about it any further. Stand up to her" (*encouraging assertion of power*).
>
> Jennifer scrubs a plate a bit more vigorously than necessary (*exhibiting tension when implicitly accused of being weak*). "It isn't a question of standing up to my mother (*rejecting Geoff's characterization of weakness*). You make it sound like I'm putty in her hands."
>
> "Well, maybe not putty; more like sculpting clay," Geoff says with a chuckle (*reasserting weakness by Jennifer*).
>
> "You're one to talk," says Jennifer. "You haven't stood up to your father in years. Why don't you practice what you preach?" (*takes the offensive in battle to win the argument; asserts weakness by Geoff*).
>
> Geoff moves next to Jennifer, looking down at her with an unpleasant expression on his face (*dominance posture*). He responds in a stern voice (*power in tone of voice*), "That's hitting below the belt."
>
> "Now you know how it feels to receive such flip advice," Jennifer retorts (*continues with powerful offensive*).

Power, who has it and how it is being exercised, is central to this conversation. Jennifer and Geoff are struggling to define the main issue of contentiousness in an interpersonal tug-of-war for dominance. Both are quick to reject characterizations of weakness by the other. Offering advice becomes a source of dispute because accepting advice is perceived as an acknowledgment of subordination to the person doing the advising. There is friction regarding who should be able to tell whom to do what. Power is the main topic of conversation as well as the subtext, the meaning beyond the words.

The Nature of Power: No Powerless People

Power is relational (Wilmot & Hocker, 2014). The power you exercise is dependent on the relationships you have with others. For example, teachers normally are granted more power than students in the classroom, but this power is quickly taken away when students refuse to pay attention to the teacher's requests or dictates (e.g., substitute teachers). Power is not a characteristic of any individual. Power is determined by our transactions with others (Van Dijke & Poppe, 2004).

No one, however, is all-powerful or completely powerless. Ever see a child pitch a fit in a grocery store, demanding some desired sweet from a parent, and observe the parent cave to the demand just to stop the obnoxious din? Who's running the show in this case, the parent or the child? Even an infant can exercise some power, as many weary parents can attest when they have tried to attend to their crying baby's needs in the middle of the night. If each person has some degree of power in a relationship, the appropriate question is not the false dichotomy "Is Person A powerful or powerless?" The apt question is "How much power does Person A have compared to Person B?"

Forms of Power: Dominance, Prevention, and Empowerment

There are three forms of power: *dominance, prevention,* and *empowerment* (Hollander & Offerman, 1990). **Dominance** is the exercise of power over others. It is a competitive, win-lose transaction. This form of power results from dichotomous, either-or thinking. You're perceived to be either a winner or a loser in a power struggle.

Prevention is power used to thwart the influence of others. It is the flip side of dominance. When someone tries to dominate you, you may try to prevent the dominance. The willingness to say "no" can be formidable, even in the face of dominating attempts. Prevention power is competitive. Dominators and preventers engage in power struggles to become winners and to avoid becoming losers.

Empowerment is power derived from enhancing the capabilities, choices, and influence of individuals and groups. It is power used positively and constructively. It also is a cooperative form of power. You do not have to defeat anyone to achieve personal or group goals. Empowered individuals feel capable, effective, and useful because they performed well, not because they beat someone.

Power Struggles and Power Sharing: A Comparison

The three forms of power—dominance, prevention, and empowerment—are considerably different from each other. Those who try to dominate see power as an active effort to advance personal goals at the expense of others. Power becomes a zero-sum contest. This means that for every increment of power I gain, you lose an equivalent amount of power. From this perspective, the power pie can't be enlarged, so the battle is for the biggest possible slice.

Those who seek to prevent domination by others see power as reactive and competitive. Individuals who attempt to prevent domination react to the power initiatives of others by fighting back. Preventive power is self-protective. You're trying to keep the slice of the power pie

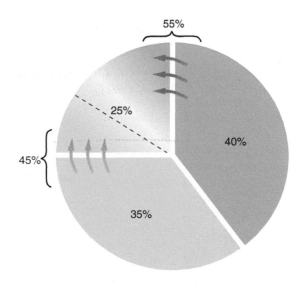

FIGURE 7-1. Power Struggle Dynamic; Competing for a Bigger Slice of the power pie by Preying on the Weak.

that you have, or even enlarge your portion, if possible, by decreasing the portion of those trying to dominate (see Figure 7-1).

The dominance-prevention power struggle can be seen in commonplace transactions. Access to bathrooms on the job rarely poses a problem for white-collar workers. Lawyers, business executives, and college professors don't need to ask for permission to relieve themselves, nor do they have their bathroom activities monitored. Workers in factories, telephone-calling centers, food-processing plants, and construction sites, however, can be refused permission when they request a bathroom break. They also can be timed with stopwatches while they are in the restroom, can be disciplined for frequent restroom visits, and can even be hunted like quarry by supervisors if they remain in the stalls too long (Linder & Nygaard, 1998). One manufacturing company polices potty practices of workers and disciplines employees who exceed a six-minutes-per-day bathroom break rule. Workers, but not supervisors, have to swipe an ID card on entering and exiting bathrooms (Clawson, 2014).

The courts have ruled that these common practices by supervisors are not necessarily illegal (Green, 2011; Clawson, 2014). As a consequence, workers have in some instances taken to wearing adult diapers while working on assembly lines because bathroom breaks are not permitted often enough. Increasingly, workers have fought back in whatever way is available. Train operators on the Norfolk Southern Railway, for example, protested the lack of flush toilets by taking the waste-filled plastic bags they were forced to use and flinging them off their moving trains. Norfolk Southern responded by printing employee numbers on the bags and monitoring which employees brought back the full bags (Walsh, 2000). A dominance-prevention power struggle can quickly deteriorate into outlandish and humiliating power tactics.

In contrast, *those who seek to empower themselves and others see the power pie as expandable* (see Figure 7-2). When the power pie is expanded, there is more for everyone. Thus, no zero-sum competitive game needs to take place. "Empowerment takes an abundance mentality—an attitude that there is plenty for everybody and some to spare, and the more you share the more you receive. People who are threatened by the successes of others see everyone as competitors. They have a scarcity mentality. Emotionally they find it very hard to share power, profit, and recognition" (Covey, 1991, p. 257).

Empowerment is proactive. Individuals take positive actions to assist themselves and others in attaining goals cooperatively (see Table 7-1). For example, working in a study group to

TABLE 7-1 The Three Forms of Power

TYPE	DEFINITION	DESCRIPTION
Dominance	Competitive	Active: zero sum
	Power struggle	(I win; you lose)
Prevention	Competitive	Reactive: zero sum
	Power struggle	(You win; I lose)
Empowerment	Cooperative	Proactive: multiple sum
	Power sharing	(We all win)

enhance performance on an exam potentially benefits everyone at the expense of no one. The goal is for everyone to succeed.

Empowerment can occur even in a competitive arena, such as sports. You can have intragroup (within the group) empowerment for the purpose of intergroup (between groups) competitive success. Different forms of power sometimes operate at the same time.

Dominance and prevention are the primary forms of power in our hypercompetitive society, and this will likely remain so. Establishing a better balance between competition and cooperation, however, requires greater emphasis on empowerment.

Communication Indicators of Power

To understand the role of power in all of your transactions with others, you have to recognize its inherent presence. This recognition can occur by understanding three types of power indicators: *general*, *verbal*, and *nonverbal*.

General Indicators: Defining, Following, Opposing, and Inhibiting

There are several general indicators of power. First, *those who can define others exercise power*. Teachers define students (e.g., smart, slow learner), physicians define patients (e.g., healthy, hypochondriac, or addict), psychiatrists define clients (e.g., paranoid, schizophrenic, or psychotic), parents define children (e.g., incorrigible or obedient),

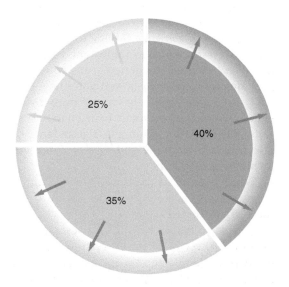

FIGURE 7-2. Empowerment: Expanding the Power Pie.

and bosses define employees (e.g., hard worker or sluggard).

This kind of *definitional prerogative* as an indicator of power can be seen from our attitudes about rape and sexual abuse in prisons. A study by the U.S. Department of Justice in August 2010 estimated that 88,500 adults in prisons and jail in this country are raped or sexually abused annually (Froomkin, 2010; see also Beck, 2010). Despite some recent efforts to implement laws aimed at curbing prison rape, the problem continues (Chammah, 2015). Rape and sexual abuse in prisons are largely ignored by the general population, and when male inmates' victimization is depicted in television sitcoms and movies, it is often a subject of humor (Meslow, 2015). Prisoners are dependent on judges, prosecutors, and lawmakers to label prisoner rape as a criminal act worthy of sanction. We recognize those who can define the actions of others as more powerful than those who cannot.

A second general indicator of power is *who cares less about maintaining a relationship*. The **principle of least interest** indicates that the dominant partner is the one who cares less about terminating the relationship. The only person controlled by a threat to end a relationship is a partner who cares about maintaining it (Sprecher et al., 2006).

A third general indicator of power is *whose decisions are followed*. Employees follow the directives of supervisors, not vice versa. Children obey parents. Wouldn't it be odd to see parents obeying children? ("Dad! Be home by 10 o'clock, and gas up the BMW before you return!") We recognize those whose decisions are followed as having power.

Finally, *behavioral inhibition* is a general indicator of power (Keltner et al., 2003). The more powerful are usually more vocal in groups, more expressive of opinions and ideas, and more assertive or aggressive in pushing those ideas and opinions. The less powerful are more inhibited. They are more passive and withdrawn in groups and more likely to be quiet and not express ideas, especially if those ideas might be unpopular or challenge more powerful individuals.

Verbal Indicators: Language Choices

Power is indicated by the way we speak and by how listeners evaluate these speech patterns. The speech of a less powerful person is often flooded with self-doubt, approval seeking, overqualification, hesitancy, personal diminishment, and deference to authority.

POWERFUL AND POWERLESS LANGUAGE: COMMUNICATING STATUS

Examples of speech patterns commonly viewed as relatively powerless in U.S. culture include the following (Leaper & Robnett, 2011; Mulac & Bradac, 1995):

Hedges: "*Perhaps* the best way to decide is . . ." "I'm a *little* worried that this *might* not work."

Hesitations: "Well, *um*, the central point is . . ." "Gosh, *uh*, shouldn't we, *um*, act now?"

Tag Question: "Dinner will be served at 6 o'clock, *okay?*" "This section of the report seems irrelevant, *doesn't it?*"

Disclaimers: "You may *disagree* with me, but . . ." "This idea is probably very *silly*, but . . ."

Excessive Politeness: "I'm *extremely sorry* to interrupt, but . . ."

Powerless language advertises a person's subordinate status. Exaggerating to make the point, consider how you would perceive this statement from someone talking to you: "This is probably, um, not very important, because I haven't, uh, thought it out much, and you probably already considered it, and you know best anyway, so I am extremely sorry to bother you, but . . ." Would you even care to listen to the ensuing message after hearing this abundance of disclaimers, hesitations, and overly polite comment that screams "I'm not worthy"?

What usually is perceived as powerless forms of speech, however, may not be so in some circumstances. For example, a tag question, usually perceived as powerless speech, can sometimes be used powerfully. If your boss says, "You'll see that this is done, won't you?" this may be more a directive than a request. If so, the tag question is authoritative, not weak.

Powerful language generally is character-ized by the absence of powerless features. Pow-erful speech is also direct, fluent, declarative, commanding, and prone to interrupt or overlap the speech of others. It advertises superior status, dynamism, and credibility (Haleta, 1996; Hosman, 2002).

Powerful forms of speech are not always ap-propriate (Fragale, 2006). Sometimes deferential language is more appropriate as a sign of respect. This is particularly true when cultural differ-ences emerge, as explained in the next section.

GENDER AND CULTURAL INFLUENCES: POWERFUL LANGUAGE DIFFERENCES

The issue of powerless versus powerful speech takes on more complexity when culture is added to the mix (Den Hartog, 2004). When negotiating teams from Japan and the United States meet, for example, misunderstandings triggered by different perceptions of what con-stitutes powerful or relatively powerless speech easily arise (Hellweg et al., 1994). The language of Japanese negotiators is rife with indirect phrases typical of a high-context communica-tion style (see Chapter 3). Japanese negotiators use expressions such as "I think," "perhaps," "probably," and "maybe" with great frequency because they strive to preserve harmony and cause no offense that would result in loss of face for anyone (Kameda, 2003, 2007). This in-direct language, however, is viewed as power-less by American negotiators more accustomed to the direct, explicit, "powerful" language of a low-context communication style.

In the United States, verbal indicators of power show several clear gender differences, the likely product of culturally induced gender ste-reotypes (see Chapter 3). Men are typically more verbose; more inclined to give long-winded verbal presentations; and more talkative in mixed-sex groups than women (Crawford & Kaufman, 2006; Leaper & Ayres, 2007). Men in general also are more verbally aggressive, direct, opinionated, and judgmental than women (Brownlow, 2003; Mehl & Pennebaker, 2002). In online discussions, men "post longer messages, begin and close discussions in mixed-sex groups, assert opinions strongly as 'facts,' use crude lan-guage (including insults and profanity), and in general, manifest an adversarial orientation." Women, however, "tend to post relatively short messages, and are more likely to qualify and jus-tify assertions, apologize, [and] express support of others" (Herring, 2003, p. 207.). Women also tend to use tag questions, hedges, and disclaim-ers more than men (Brownlow, 2003), but this may reflect greater interpersonal sensitivity, not lack of assertiveness (Leaper & Robnett, 2011).

Nonverbal Indicators: Silent Exercise of Power

Anyone who has experienced the "silent treat-ment" from an intimate partner recognizes the power dimension of nonverbal communica-tion. You become a nonperson; your connec-tion to your partner is separated. This experience can be enormously frustrating, even depressing (Burgoon & Dunbar, 2006).

There are numerous nonverbal indicators of power in relationships (see Burgoon & Dunbar, 2006; Hall et al., 2005; Riggio, 2012). *Clothing*, for example, is a strong indicator of power. Most people typically associate uniforms with power and authority and suits with status in-volving financial success and position within an organization. Tattered clothing scrounged from the trash, on the other hand, communi-cates powerlessness associated with poverty.

Touch is another important nonverbal power indicator. The more powerful person can usu-ally touch the less powerful person more fre-quently, and with fewer restrictions, than vice versa (Henley, 1995). Sexual harassment laws recognize this difference and try to protect sub-ordinates from tactile abuse.

Eye contact also indicates a power difference. Staring is done more freely by the more power-ful person (Garland-Thomson, 2009). Less powerful individuals must monitor their eye contact more carefully. A boss can show lack of attentiveness or interest by looking away from a subordinate, but a subordinate doing the same to a boss may invite a reprimand. Imagine how your boss would react to you text messaging

Space communicates power.

and looking mostly at your smartphone while conversing. That might be your last day at work.

Space is a clear nonverbal indicator of power—the more powerful usually have more of it. The master bedroom in a house is reserved for the more powerful parents, for example, and the children often share smaller bedrooms, sometimes sleeping stacked vertically in bunk beds. The higher up in the corporate hierarchy you travel, the bigger is your office space. Reserved faculty parking spaces often are closer to classroom and office buildings. Student parking spaces often are located somewhere in the next time zone.

Much more could be added here, but the point seems clear. You can ascertain the relative distribution of power between individuals by observing general communication patterns and specific verbal and nonverbal communication.

Power Resources

Thus far, power has been defined, types of power have been described, and indicators of power have been explained to sensitize you to the pervasive, unavoidable role that power plays in your transactions with others. But how does power influence our transactions with others in an ongoing basis? To begin this discussion, you first need to understand what power resources are available and how they might be used.

A **power resource** is anything that enables individuals to achieve their goals, assists others to achieve their goals, or interferes with the goal attainment of others (Folger et al., 1993).

The range of power resources is broad. This section lays out the primary resources from which power is most extensively derived.

Information: Scarce and Restricted

Information is power, but *only when it is not easily or readily available* (Sell et al., 2004). In the Age of the Internet, that has become increasingly rare, yet information can still be a positive power resource. Teachers, for example, are accorded stature because they have information that is valuable for students to learn. Sharing this information can empower students. Ministers, priests, and religious leaders have information that brings them respect and prestige, and this information, when shared, is spiritually empowering for laypersons. The information teachers and ministers share is a power resource both because it is restricted to students and laypersons by their limited background and experience and because they don't typically have the background necessary to separate information from the mountain of *mis*information on the Internet. Teachers and ministers can translate the information so that it is understandable and accurate.

Expertise: Information Plus Know-How

Information and expertise are closely related, but a person can have critical information without being an expert. You might possess a valuable technical report without being able to decipher any of the information. You might also know the law but not be capable of practicing it skillfully in the courtroom. Expertise is more than just having information. *An expert understands the information and knows how to use it wisely and skillfully.*

No individual or group could ever hope to function effectively without at some time requiring the services of experts. Families require financial advisers, roofers, carpenters, exterminators, counselors, physicians, hairstylists, mechanics, and those who repair our appliances, phones, computers, broken pipes, and broken hearts. Expertise can be a very positive power resource, but under two conditions. First, the person is *perceived to have the requisite skills, abilities, knowledge, and background* to function as a real expert. Normally, real expertise includes appropriate education and training, intelligence, experience, and demonstrated mastery of relevant information. Second, the person is *considered to be trustworthy.* People everywhere are more influenced by experts who stand to gain nothing personally than by those who would gain personally through lying or distorting information (McGuinnies & Ward, 1980).

Legitimate Authority: You Will Obey

In the famous Milgram studies, participants were told to deliver increasingly painful electric shocks to an innocent victim for every wrong answer on a word-association test. Two-thirds of the participants in some of the studies obeyed the experimenter and delivered the maximum shock to the victim, who in some cases screamed in agony. No shocks were actually delivered. The experiments were made to seem real, however, and none of the participants suspected trickery.

In all, 19 variations of these obedience-to-authority studies were conducted (Milgram, 1974). One replication by Sheridan and King (1972) actually ordered college students to shock a cute, fluffy puppy. All of the female subjects and slightly more than half of the male subjects went to the maximum shock level. Many of the female students wept. All subjects showed signs of discomfort. Others have replicated and updated results of obedience studies with similar findings (Blass, 2009; Burger, 2009; Slater et al., 2006). The more recent studies suggest that nothing much has changed since Stanley Milgram conducted his original experiments.

Participants in the Milgram studies followed orders not because they were evil or sadistic but because they couldn't resist *legitimate authority* (Milgram, 1974). The experimenter was the legitimate authority. He insisted that participants continue to deliver increasing levels of electric shock to the victims. A **legitimate authority** is someone who is perceived to have a right to direct others' behavior because of his or her position, title, role, experience, or knowledge.

The strength of legitimate authority can be seen outside the experimental laboratory as well. David Cline, a driver education instructor at Northern High School in Durham, North Carolina, ordered a teenage student driver to chase a car that cut them off. When they caught up to the offender, Cline jumped out and punched the other drive, Jon David Macklin, in the nose. Macklin took off, and Cline ordered the student driver to chase after him again, which the student did. A police officer finally pulled them over for speeding. In this case, the student broke traffic laws and endangered several people on the orders of a legitimate authority—her driver education instructor. They ultimately obeyed a higher authority, the police officer. Cline resigned from his teaching post.

No individual possesses legitimate authority. It is conferred by others, which sometimes creates a predicament. Parents put babysitters in charge of their children, for example, but the children's perception that the sitter is not a "real parent" can undermine this power resource. Parents, on the other hand, exercise legitimate authority over their children by virtue of their caregiver role and typically use their legitimate authority to guide, protect, and teach their children. Even then, however, a parent's authority is minimized once children become adults and, in some instances, it is perceived as illegitimate. ("I'm not your little boy anymore. You can't tell me what to do.")

The competent communicator must adopt the skeptical view and distinguish between appropriate and inappropriate use of authority. Blindly refusing to obey police officers, teachers, parents, judges, and bosses is as dangerous as blindly obeying. Ethical criteria—respect, honesty, fairness, choice, and responsibility—provide the means for determining when we should defy and when we should comply with dictates from authority.

Rewards and Punishments: Pleasure and Pain

Distributing rewards and punishments can be an important source of power. Salaries, bonuses, work schedules, perks, hirings, and firings are typical job-related rewards and punishments. Money, freedom, privacy, and car keys are a few of the rewards and punishments found in family situations.

The power potential of punishment depends on the degree of certainty that the punishment will be administered. Idle threats have little influence on behavior. Parents who threaten spankings or denial of privileges—but never follow through—soon realize their children have learned to ignore such impotent bluster. Punishment is a source of power if it can, and likely will, be exercised.

Punishing as a power source, however, is delicate business. It can be used positively to change behavior from antisocial to prosocial, but it also is coercive and reinforces dominance. Consequently, it easily triggers backlash (Kohn, 1993). A sign found in some workplaces—"The beatings will continue until morale improves"—expresses ironically the challenge of using punishment to produce positive outcomes. Individuals on the receiving end of punishment typically rebel. Those who punish create interpersonal distance between themselves and those who are punished. We don't normally like our tormenters.

A reward can be an effective power resource, but *intrinsic rewards* generally work better than *extrinsic rewards*. An **intrinsic reward** is enjoying what you do for its own sake and because it gives you pleasure, such as playing a musical instrument just because it is fun. An **extrinsic reward** is an external inducement, such as money, grades, recognition, awards, or prestige (Kohn, 1993). A survey of 500 professionals reported that 95% considered trusting relationships with upper management (intrinsic reward) as

better motivation to remain at their jobs than either pay or benefits (extrinsic rewards) (Shilling, 2000). "Work sucks, but I need the bucks" captures the essence of the difference. When you work diligently on a class project because it is enjoyable and meaningful, not just "busy work," you are motivated by intrinsic rewards. Completing the project for an "A" is being motivated by an extrinsic reward. Both rewards can be motivating, but the former usually is far more powerful than the latter.

Personal Qualities: A Powerful Persona

Mother Teresa, the Pope, several U.S. presidents, some sports and political figures, and some student protest leaders, teachers, and parents exhibit personal qualities that draw people to them and make them positive role models. This constellation of personal attributes that people find attractive is often referred to as **charisma**.

Good looks, an attractive personality, dynamism, persuasive skills, warmth, and charm are some of the personal qualities that make an individual charismatic. There is no precise formula for determining charisma, however. What is attractive to you may be unattractive to others (Haslam & Reicher, 2012).

Before leaving this section on power resources, one final point should be emphasized. *A person does not possess power; a person is granted*

Personal qualities can be a power resource. Which personal qualities account for Katy Perry's power and celebrity?

power by others. Charisma means little in a job interview if a hiring committee prefers diligence, expertise, and efficiency. In this case, charisma might look like flash without follow-through. A reward that nobody wants will influence no one. Information that is irrelevant to the needs of individuals or groups has no power potential. Your relationship partner, a group, an audience, or an organization must endorse the power resource for it to be influential.

Problems of Power Imbalance

Power, regardless of resources, isn't always transacted wisely. When power is unequal, not shared, the potential for mischief or mayhem increases. In this section, five effects of power imbalances are discussed: *relationship failure, aggression, verbal and nonverbal abuse, sexual harassment*, and *commonplace difficulties*. The first four effects are part of what some researchers have called the "dark side" of communicating with others (Cupach & Spitzberg, 2011).

The desire to present communication transactions in a sunny, "positive" framework is understandable. Ignoring the dark side because it is unpleasant, however, would make this text seem sadly unrelated to the all-too-frequent experiences of readers. As communication experts William Cupatch and Brian Spitzberg (2011) observe, "To fully understand how people effectively function requires us to consider how individuals cope with social interaction that is difficult, problematic, challenging, distressing, and disruptive" (p. vii). Few problems in life, especially significant difficulties, are solved by ignoring them. If relationship failures, verbal and physical violence, abuse, and harassment were infrequent, insignificant occurrences, ignoring them here would be appropriate and welcome. These problems, however, occur frequently in our communication transactions, and they are significant. We ignore them at our own peril.

Ultimately, this examination of the more unpleasant side of communicating with others has a very positive goal: to help you recognize the often subtle encroachment of the dark side into your communication transactions. Such recognition is the first step toward preventing the dark side from intruding into your life and strengthening your relationships with others.

Power Sharing: Key to Relationship Success or Failure

Sharing power with your intimate partner is critical to relationship satisfaction and success for most couples (Sanford & Wolfe, 2013). "There's only one path to intimacy. It runs straight through shared power in relationships" (Marano, 2014). *When men refused to share power with their wives, there was an 81% chance that the marriage would fail* (Gottman & Silver, 1999). When power is unequally distributed and dominance becomes the focus, power struggles often ensue (Wilmot & Hocker, 2014). This is not only significant for heterosexual couples; several studies of gay and lesbian couples reveal that sharing relatively equal power leads to higher satisfaction and greater commitment (Eldridge & Gilbert, 1990; Garcia-Navarro, 2014).

Power is shared when partners accept each other's influence (Gottman & Gottman, 2006). When partners disagree, they search for common ground. They solve problems; they discuss issues without insisting that one viewpoint is accepted outright. Everything— careers, cooking and housework responsibilities, paying bills, and child rearing— is open to negotiation. Decisions are not made on the basis of gender role stereotypes (the man is the breadwinner; the woman is the child rearer) (Marano, 2014). Responsibilities are viewed as shared, not the sole obligation of one partner or the other. Raising children, for example, is a co-parenting process, not the principal responsibility of the mother. Attempting to drown out a partner's expressed viewpoint, exhibiting contempt for a partner's feelings, heaping criticism or trying to bully a partner into capitulating during an argument is the opposite of power sharing.

Equal-partner relationships have the greatest potential for success in most instances, and according to a Pew Research Center study, they are becoming more common (George, 2008). They are especially common in gay relationships (Garcia-Navarro, 2014; Gottman et al., 2003). Even across cultures, the wisdom of equal-partner relationships has wide appeal. A cross-cultural Pew research study found that "[i]n 19 of 22 countries, majorities say that a marriage where both husband and wife have jobs and take care of the house and children is a more satisfying way of life than having the husband provide financially while the wife cares for the household" ("Gender Equality," 2010). Equal-partner relationships are not the only avenue to success, but they sure improve the odds (Gottman & Gottman, 2006).

Relationship Aggression: Battle for Dominance

Comedian Elayne Boosler once remarked, "When women are depressed, they either eat or go shopping. Men invade another country." The stereotype is that men are far more aggressive than women. There is truth to the stereotype. Although cultures vary widely in their frequency of homicides, *men commit 95% of all homicides worldwide* ("Global Study on Homicide," 2013), and close to 90% of all homicides in the United States are committed by men (Lilienfeld & Arkowitz, 2010). Men are arrested for 80% of the violent crimes committed each year in the United States ("Crime in the United States," 2013). Research also reveals that male-initiated violence against women is a serious problem worldwide ("Violence Against Women," 2014). Many of these acts of aggression besides homicides qualify as catastrophic events that ignite significant stress for the victims (being held up at gunpoint can be a shattering experience).

AGGRESSION TYPES: DIRECT AND INDIRECT

The substantial gender difference in the tendency to commit aggressive acts, however, is not as clear-cut as quoting crime statistics suggests. **Aggression** is any physical or verbal communication that is intended to inflict harm. **Direct aggression** is hostile communication that targets the victim openly, such as pushing, shoving, physically assaulting, or shouting insults. **Indirect aggression** is hostile communication that intends to harm a targeted person while avoiding identification as

an aggressor, such as gossiping, spreading malicious rumors, or sabotaging behind the victim's back (Bjorkqvist et al., 1994; Willer & Cupach, 2011). Men engage in direct aggression far more than women, accounting for their disproportionate representation in crime statistics. Women engage in indirect aggression far more than men (Card et al., 2008; Willer & Cupach, 2011).

Although men initiate direct aggression outside intimate relationships far more often than women, there is about equal direct aggression initiated by women and by women against their opposite-sex partners within intimate relationships (Archer, 2000b; Spitzberg, 2011; Straus, 2008, 2010). The Partner Abuse State of Knowledge Project, "the most comprehensive review of the scholarly domestic violence research literature ever conducted," supports this claim (Hamel, 2012). Even so, this conclusion, though strongly supported by voluminous research, has not gone unchallenged (see Box 7-1; *read it now*).

SOLUTIONS: THE COMMUNICATION LINK

Ultimately, solutions to problems of relationship aggression require concerted and systematic efforts by individuals and entire cultures. This is particularly true regarding intimate terrorism (have you read Box 7-1 yet?), for which there is no easy or quick-fix communication solution. Treatment programs for batterers, unfortunately, have not proved to be very effective in reducing this serious problem. Nevertheless, some studies that teach batterers new communication skills show promise (Babcock et al., 2011). Focusing on women's safety and the male perpetrator's criminality is the most appropriate approach, at this point, to minimize the effects of intimate terrorism.

Addressing situational couple violence is more promising, however. Our society is not noted for its adept conflict-management skills (see Chapter 9). "The 'ordinary' violence that occurs in so many families is likely traceable to inadequate relationship skills, such as nonviolent methods of resolving conflicts with a partner and poor anger management" (Straus, 2010, p. 351). When conflict arises, small arguments can easily explode into major episodes of aggression if competent communication is absent. Incompetent

BOX 7-1 FOCUS ON CONTROVERSY

Gender and Relationship Aggression: A White-Hot Debate

Research showing about equal amounts of gender violence in intimate relationships startles many, and it has provoked passionate debate among partisan groups (Straus, 2010). Women's groups often point to crime reports to support the claim that men are more directly aggressive than women. Males, however, are reluctant to label a physical attack by a female partner as a criminal assault, so it is underreported (Archer, 2000b). On the other hand, survey data probably vastly underreport male battering of women because batterers are reluctant to fill out surveys requiring them to admit their criminal acts (Johnson, 2006a).

Michael Johnson (2006a, 2006b, 2008) reviewed a vast number of studies and concluded that the gender violence debate is muddied by the mixture of differing and conflicting sets of data. There are two main types of relationship violence. **Intimate terrorism**, the most extreme form, involves "a violent attempt to take complete control of, or at least to generally dominate, a relationship." According to Johnson, 97% *of intimate terrorism is committed by men against women*. It is most likely to increase in frequency and escalate to severe acts of aggression, including murder. More than 2 million women each year are victims of this abuse. **Situational couple violence**, however, "is a product of particular conflicts or tensions within relationships" (Johnson, 2006b). Individuals quarrel with their partners, anger and frustration erupt, and an assault occurs. Here *both partners commit roughly equal amounts of direct aggression* (Johnson, 2006a).

Situational couple violence afflicts a much broader range of couples than the less-common intimate terrorism (Johnson, 2008; Straus,

2008), *occurring among about half of the heterosexual couples in the United States* at some point in their relationship (Johnson, 1995; Klein & Johnson, 1997). Dating couples experience more violence than married couples (Straus, 2001), and newlyweds experience greater violence than more seasoned married couples (Frye & Karney, 2006). Gay and lesbian couples experience about the same frequency and level of violence as heterosexual couples (Spitzberg, 2011). Situational violence is typically less severe, less frequent, and less likely to escalate than what occurs during intimate terrorism (Johnson, 2006a).

Do women typically use violence in self-defense? Women are not likely to use "violent resistance" to prevent intimate terrorism (Johnson, 2008). It is too dangerous, and it isn't likely to be successful in most instances. Female violence is not primarily used in self-defense during situational couple violence, either (Straus, 2010). Self-defense is pegged by Murray Straus (2008) at a mere 7% of female violent acts. Patricia Pearson (1997) found that of the

This is the image most people have when partner abuse is an issue. Hundreds of studies, however, reveal that substantial violence is also initiated by women against their partners (Hamel, 2012).

(continued)

BOX 7-1 FOCUS ON CONTROVERSY

Gender and Relationship Aggression:
A White-Hot Debate (continued)

women she studied, 90% reported they assaulted their male partners because they were furious, frustrated, or jealous, not because they needed to defend themselves. More than 200 studies with both male and female respondents report that women initiate violence against their male partners as often or *more often* than vice versa (Straus, 2010). Women are more likely to initiate physical aggression against men if they believe that their male partners are unlikely to retaliate or may simply try to physically restrain the attack (Archer, 2000b).

By far, the most frequent acts of severe violence by women—kicking, slapping, biting, punching, hitting with an object (Archer, 2002)—may rarely produce severe injuries. Men's far more likely choices against their partners—strangling, choking, beating up—are severe violence of a different magnitude (Straus, 2010). Even seemingly identical acts of aggression ("hit with fist") also can produce markedly different physical injuries (Christopher & Lloyd, 2000). Female severe violence, however, is not inconsequential. A kick to the male groin may not require a trip to the emergency room or even show bruising, but as every male knows, it can reduce a man to a whimpering, writhing blob on the ground. And while this is sometimes played for laughs in the media, the humiliation that men may feel from being kicked or slapped in the face by their female partner, even though no obvious severe physical injury has been suffered, should not be trivialized (Straus, 2010). Initiating physical aggression, even if it doesn't result in blood loss or broken bones, leaves its mark emotionally on the victims, be they male or female (Spitzberg, 2011).

Thus, the evidence supports several conclusions. First, men are almost exclusively responsible for intimate terrorism, making women feel more menaced because they typically are physically weaker and almost always the victims. Second, the more frequent form of direct aggression in intimate relationships is situational couple violence, which is initiated about equally by men and women (Johnson, 2006a; Straus, 2010). Third, the significant level of female aggression deserves greater attention than it usually receives. Some have argued this could become a strategy to obscure men's more serious violence (Berns, 2001), but this certainly is not my intention. The fact that women violently attack men, usually not in self-defense, should make us no less concerned about males battering women. We should, however, be more concerned about female-initiated violence than perhaps we are currently because it is far more frequent and severe than is often supposed. Relationship violence should not be framed as a competition to determine who is the bigger victim, women or men. Our aim should be to stop the aggression. We can't do that well if we look at only male abusers and female victims.

Questions for Thought

1. Are you surprised by the research results showing substantial female-initiated violence in intimate relationships? What should be done to help male victims of female-initiated violence?

2. Do you think men fear violence from their female partners as much as women fear violence from male partners?

3. How can college students address violence in dating relationships? Would this differ from approaches used by married couples with children?

communication during conflicts can lead to "efforts to coerce the partner" either to do or not do something that provokes anger (Straus, 2010).

An imbalance of power, whether actual, perceived, or desired, is not the sole cause of relationship violence, but it certainly is a very significant one (Johnson, 2008; Straus, 2010). *Violence is far more prevalent in relationships where power is unequally distributed than in relationships where the power distribution is relatively equal.* As Straus (2008) concludes, "Whenever there is dominance of one partner, there is an increased risk of violence by the dominant partner to maintain the dominant position or by the subordinate partner to achieve something blocked by the dominant partner, or to change the power structure."

Working to establish a more equitable distribution of power is an essential key to nonviolent relationships. Learning to share power through competent communication, as previously discussed, is an important step toward reducing situational couple violence.

Verbal and Nonverbal Abuse: Expressing Contempt

Power struggles in relationships that take on a dominance-prevention quality do not always end in violence. In fact, more likely than not, no fists will fly, nor will any pots and pans. Partners will simply abuse each other verbally and nonverbally by tearing apart each other's self-esteem and self-worth to gain the upper hand in a power struggle (Spitzberg, 2011). Communicating *contempt* for one's partner has a corrosive effect on a relationship (Gottman & Gottman, 2006).

Contempt is intended to insult and emotionally abuse a person. When couples argue as adversaries trying to win a verbal exchange, contempt can easily become a verbal weapon, both for the dominant partner trying to exert control and for the weaker partner trying to equalize the power distribution. *There are four ways to communicate contempt* (Gottman, 1994a, 1994b).

First, contempt can be communicated by verbal insults and name calling. *Bastard, bitch, moron, jerk, imbecile, fathead,* and even cruder, more vicious insults are targeted at tearing apart the self-esteem of one's partner.

Second, hostile "humor" communicates contempt. Camouflaged as "only a joke," hostile humor, if you're the target, aims to make others laugh at your expense. "Is your clothing style trying to imitate gypsies or clowns? It's hard to tell" ridicules the person shown contempt. Respect, a key ingredient of competent communication, is nowhere to be seen.

Third, mockery communicates contempt. You mock others by imitating them derisively. A man says to his partner, "I really do love you," and his partner responds with a contorted facial expression and in a fake, exaggerated voice, "You really do love me." Mockery is meant to make fun of a person. It assaults that person's sincerity.

Fourth, certain body movements communicate contempt. Sneering, rolling your eyes, curling your upper lip, and using obscene gestures are all signs of contempt for your partner. When a person leaves the room while a partner or coworker is speaking, this nonverbally communicates contempt.

Sexual Harassment: When "Flirting" Is Hurting

Sexual harassment is generally defined as verbal or nonverbal communication of a sexual nature that is unwelcome by the recipient and is likely to interfere with the victim's employment or ability to work (Maass et al., 2003). The U.S. Supreme Court ruled that sexual harassment, although most often applied to the workplace, can also be applied to teachers, professors, and individuals with authority in school systems, including colleges. The law defines two principal types of sexual harassment: *quid pro quo* (you give something to get something) and *hostile environment* ("Sexual Harassment: What Is It?" 2015). **Quid pro quo harassment** occurs when the more powerful person requires sexual favors from the less powerful person in exchange for keeping a job, getting a high grade in a class, landing an employment promotion, and the like. **Hostile environment harassment** is discrimination based on sex that creates a hostile or abusive work environment characterized by insult, ridicule, or intimidation ("Enforcement Guidance," 2010).

Sexual harassment is often more nonverbal than verbal, and it usually involves a power imbalance.

Quid pro quo sexual harassment is blatant, unethical communication behavior. It is disrespectful to victims, often covered by lies, and unfair because preferential treatment is given for sex. Choice is removed when threats of job loss are involved. It is irresponsible Me-oriented behavior.

The hostile environment form of sexual harassment, can also be crude and unethical communication in the extreme. A District of Columbia court awarded Elizabeth Reese $250,000 for damages incurred while she worked for the architectural design firm Swanke Hayden Connell. Reese's male supervisor had repeatedly made lewd comments to her, incessantly asked about her sex life, encouraged her to prostitute herself for the firm, and then told fellow workers that she had.

Sexual harassment is a difficult issue to address because what is perceived as sexual harassment shows a significant gender difference. Women are less tolerant of a variety of objectionable communication behaviors than men (Bitton & Shaul, 2013). Although only a minor gender difference exists regarding agreement with what the courts define as quid pro quo sexual harassment (sexual coercion), larger differences emerge between men's and women's views of hostile environment sexual harassment—for example, sex-stereotyped jokes or repeated requests for dates after a refusal (Rotundo et al., 2001). What is flirtation to men may be harassment to women (Goodboy & Brann, 2010).

Most instances of sexual harassment victimize women. On average, 58% of women have experienced sexual harassment on the job (Berdahl & Moore, 2006). *Sexual harassment against males, however, is not an insignificant problem.* The U.S. Equal Employment Opportunity Commission (2015) reports that men file almost 18% of all sexual harassment complaints. In some states, such as California and Michigan, about a quarter of all complaints come from men (Mattioli, 2010). The consequences to the victims of sexual harassment, both male and female, have been well documented: psychological distress, depression, shame, embarrassment, and diminished job performance (Kelly, 2005; Rettner, 2011).

Sexual harassment is fundamentally an abuse that stems from power imbalances (Uggen & Blackstone, 2004). Quid pro quo harassment is a clear instance of dominance by perpetrators against less powerful victims. Dealing with this kind of sexual harassment is extremely difficult because the harasser has legitimate authority and can punish the victim for openly complaining. Laws forbidding such behavior, policies that explicitly punish such harassment, and enforcement of laws and policies are all helpful in combating quid pro quo harassment. Firm, unequivocal rejection of such harassment by the target of an unwanted sexual advance is also an important communication approach: "Do not ever make sexual remarks to me."

Hostile environment sexual harassment is also promoted by power imbalances and is particularly prevalent where women try to compete in traditionally male occupations (Parker & Griffin, 2002). Smith Barney, a Wall Street brokerage firm with 400 offices nationwide, established a pattern of hostile environment sexual harassment that led to a class action lawsuit by 25 female stockbrokers. Male employees gawked at the women's breasts and made lewd and suggestive remarks. Senior male managers in the Garden City, New York office maintained a basement room dubbed the "Boom-Boom Room," where female employees were confronted with unwanted sexual advances, groping, and kissing on the lips. Women at work were sent condoms and food shaped in the form of penises. Plaintiffs claimed that their complaints to superiors were ignored, and in some cases, women were punished with menial tasks and public humiliations for complaining. Even though the harassment often came from fellow brokers of equal position and power, most of the Smith Barney brokers were men. This put female brokers in a decidedly weaker position when trying to combat the hostile "men's club" environment. Individual women were fighting against a group of men. Smith Barney finally settled the case in October 2010 ("Today in Labor History," 2010).

Hostile environment sexual harassment has spilled over to the Internet video gaming environment. One study reported that 63% of female gamers have experienced sexual harassment while gaming online (Matthew, 2012). The 2015 documentary *GTFO* (a reference to an obscene acronym used to harass gamers) shows widespread sexual harassment of especially female gamers. Jenny Haniver, an experienced gamer, has endured myriad abuse from male players online who felt women were encroaching on their "male-dominated" arena. She has been called fat, ugly, a slut, and threatened with rape. "One guy said he was going to impregnate me with triplets and then force me to have a late-term abortion" (quoted by Ito, 2015). More than a third of female gamers admit to quitting gaming at least temporarily because of sexual harassment. More than two-thirds do not divulge that they are female to avoid the abuse. Almost 16% of male gamers also report sexual harassment, mostly questioning their masculinity.

Unlike work-related sexual harassment, legal remedies are not available for video game victims because of free speech issues and the entertainment nature of video games (Matthew, 2012). Gamers, however, can monitor harassment and combat it verbally by setting rules (e.g., "Everyone is welcome to play. Harassment is out of bounds"). If harassment becomes persistent, ostracizing the offenders is a stronger action that could be employed (e.g., "Leave until you can stop the harassment").

Sometimes the hostile environment is the product of misperceptions and misreading signals, not ugly intentions (Bingham, 1991). For example, men often misread women's communication. A friendly smile is often interpreted as sexual interest, and nonverbal signals from women indicating actual sexual interest are frequently misinterpreted as mere friendliness (Farris et al., 2008). In one study, men were shown silent videos of women's uncomfortable, fake smiles while being harassed. Men often misinterpreted these smiles as flirtatious (Woodzicka & LaFrance, 2005).

Combating hostile environment sexual harassment at work is difficult. A firm, clearly defined policy staunchly supported by those in power positions goes a long way toward diminishing sexual harassment. With such a policy, those who are harassed can more safely and confidently reject poor treatment. Communication strategies of assertiveness, threat of formal complaint, or deflection of sexual remarks by diverting discussion to neutral topics can be successful when hostile environment harassment is clearly not tolerated in the workplace or educational environment (Bingham, 1991).

Commonplace Difficulties: Lighter Side

Power imbalances don't always lead to violence, verbal or physical abuse, and harassment. Many, perhaps most, instances of power imbalance never graduate to the dark side of interpersonal relationships. They remain part of the lighter side of personal difficulties experienced with others.

Power imbalances are apparent in a wide variety of daily occurrences. At work, the shift from work to personal talk is usually initiated by the most powerful person (Tannen, 1994). If the office manager takes a break and begins telling stories and chatting, everyone else in the office sees fit to follow suit. Taking breaks and chatting, however, can be perceived as goofing off unless sanctioned by a more powerful person. Such power imbalance can make employees wary, even resentful, of the "double standard."

Doctor-patient relationships are rarely equal. Patients wait for doctors, sometimes for unreasonably long periods of time, not vice versa. Doctors usually wear white coats as symbols of their authority. Patients wear casual clothes, humiliating hospital gowns with a breezy backside, and sometimes no clothes at all. Patients refer to the physician as "Dr. Schmidt" or "Dr. Martinez," not "Harry" or "Maria." The physician often addresses patients by their first names. This pattern is not always displayed, however, when the doctor is female. Some male patients may inappropriately try to upset the power imbalance by referring to female physicians informally (e.g., "Hi, Kate") or even by making lewd or suggestive remarks (Tannen, 1994). Such references are insulting, and they make the doctor's task of caring for the patient exceedingly difficult.

Apologies for mishaps or misdeeds are expected from the less powerful, reminding them of their subservient position. Children are expected to apologize to parents for cracking up the car, but parents do not normally apologize to their kids for a similar mishap even though the children may be seriously inconvenienced by the car being out of commission. Nevertheless, apologizing can cement relationships between unequal individuals.

Competent Communication and Balancing Power

The quick answer to relationship problems caused by power imbalances is to balance the power. This is glib advice, especially when some individuals would rather maintain their dominance in relationships and groups. There are many ways to balance unequally distributed power. Some involve competent communication, and others are clearly incompetent communication. Both are discussed in the following two sections.

Dominance-Prevention: Competitive Power Balancing

Dominance-prevention power struggles produce several methods of balancing power. These methods are *coalition formation*, *defiance*, and *resistance*. Although none of these methods inherently produces incompetent communication, each, as you will see, is prone to produce negative outcomes.

COALITION FORMATION: POOLING POWER

Individuals form temporary alliances, called **coalitions**, to increase their power relative to others (Simpson & Macy, 2001). Coalitions occur in group situations when there are disputes and group members jointly use their combined power to control a decision and to take action. One study found that arguments and disagreements in families lead to coalitions about 30% of the time (Grusky et al., 1995). Coalitions can balance the power in a group when the relatively powerless form a coalition and increase their strength, but coalitions can create power imbalances when the more powerful move to consolidate their strength by banding together against the weaker members.

In most families, the father is considered the most powerful person, followed by the mother, then the oldest child, and then the younger siblings (Grusky et al., 1995). Parental coalitions predominate in a four-person family, and they are virtually unopposable. Such coalitions maintain the family structure and support the status differences between parents and children. The next most frequent coalition is a parent and an older child. Children-only coalitions are the least frequent and least successful (Grusky et al., 1995).

Coalitions may be useful in the political arena, but they can be destructive in family situations (Rosenthal, 1997). Coalitions create a "them-versus-us" competitive mentality. Parental coalitions are sometimes necessary to present a united front when a dispute with children arises. Parent-child coalitions, however, can disrupt the family structure. Asking children to choose sides in a dispute between parents can rip a family apart, especially if the issue is significant and the dispute is recurrent. It is usually more constructive and effective when parents work out their differences without seeking allies among their children.

DEFIANCE: DIGGING IN YOUR HEELS

Low-power persons sometimes overtly defy higher-power persons. **Defiance** is unambiguous, purposeful noncompliance. It is a refusal to give in to those with greater power. Defiance is the prevention form of power where one stands against those who attempt to dominate.

Defiance can be contagious. Unless parents take effective action, one defiant child can embolden siblings to defy parents, unless the parents take effective action. A single worker who defiantly walks off the job may encourage a wildcat strike. Those in authority are anxious to halt defiance before it spreads, especially with the ready availability of social media to stoke the fires of defiance.

Defiance is a highly competitive communication behavior, and it will make a person a loser far more often than a winner. This is because the very nature of defiance is disagreeable to those who want compliance, and they usually are the most powerful. In general, defiance should be considered an option of last resort.

Defiance is an overt act of noncompliance. This lone unarmed man stands against tanks in the 1989 Tiananmen Square uprising in China. Most defiance is the product of a power imbalance, vividly evident here. (The man's identity has never been discovered.)

Threatened with a potential $500,000 fine from the NFL, Marshawn Lynch attended the Super Bowl media day before the 2015 championship game. He informed everyone that he attended only to avoid the fine, then proceeded to give the same "I'm just here so I don't get fined" answer to every question. Was Lynch being defiant or resistant (passive aggressive)?

RESISTANCE: DRAGGING YOUR FEET

Although defiance is chosen in some instances, resistance is more often the choice of the less powerful to prevent dominance from others (Wilmot & Hocker, 2014). While defiance is overt, unambiguous noncompliance, **resistance** is covert, ambiguous noncompliance. It is often duplicitous and manipulative. Resisters are subtle saboteurs. Truly successful resistance leaves people wondering if resistance even occurred.

Resistance has an advantage over defiance. When faced with a more powerful person or group, it is often safer to use indirect means of noncompliance than direct confrontation. Those who are defiant dig in their heels and openly cause trouble, but those who resist merely drag their feet.

Resistance strategies are sometimes referred to as *passive aggression* (Wilmot & Hocker, 2014). Several common strategies are discussed here.

Strategic Stupidity: Smart People Acting Dumb This is the "playing stupid" strategy. When children don't want to do what their parents tell them, they sometimes act stupid when they know better. "But Mom, I don't know how to fold the laundry" may simply be an effort to frustrate the parent, who might just give up in disgust and fold the laundry rather than show the child for the "bazillionth" time what should be plainly obvious.

Strategic stupidity works exceedingly well when the low-power person claims stupidity, is forced to attempt the task anyway, and then performs it ineptly. In one study, 30% of the men admitted purposely botching household chores to get out of doing them again (Christie, 2014). The poor performance becomes "proof" that the stupidity was real. The passive aggressor can assert, "I told you I didn't know how to do laundry."

Loss of Motor Function: Conscious Carelessness This resistance strategy is an effective companion to strategic stupidity. The resister doesn't act stupid, just incredibly clumsy, often resulting in costly damage. There is a mixed message here of resistance on the one hand but apparent effort on the other. "I tried really hard not to let dishes slip out of my hands; I'm sorry I broke two plates" may be an honest apology from your housemate for accidental behavior. If it becomes repetitive, however, it may be an effort to avoid doing dishes.

The Misunderstanding Mirage: Confusion Illusion This is the "I thought you meant" or the "I could have sworn you said" strategy. The resistance is expressed "behind a cloak of great sincerity" (Bach & Goldberg, 1972, p. 110). Students sometimes excuse late assignments by using this strategy. "You said it was due Wednesday, not today, didn't you?" The implied message is that since this is a simple misunderstanding, penalizing the student for a late paper would be unfair.

Selective Amnesia: Fake Forgetfulness Have you ever noticed that some people are particularly forgetful about those things that they clearly do not want to do? This temporary amnesia is highly selective when used as a resistance strategy because selective amnesiacs rarely forget what is most important to them. No outward signs of resistance are manifested. Resisters agree to perform the task—but conveniently let it slip their minds.

In a sophisticated version of this strategy, the individual remembers all but one or two important items. A person shops for groceries and purchases all but two key items. Hey, no one's perfect. He or she remembered almost everything. The dinner menu, however, will have to be altered because the main course wasn't purchased.

Tactical Tardiness: Late by Design When you really don't want to attend a meeting, a class, a lecture, or a party, you can show contempt by arriving late. Tactical tardiness irritates and frustrates those who value the event. It can hold an entire group hostage while everyone waits for the late person to arrive. Consistently arriving late for class is disruptive as well, especially if the resister requests an update on material missed.

Tactical tardiness may be used on occasion by high-power persons to reinforce their dominance and self-importance. Celebrities often arrive late to functions, possibly hoping to underscore their prestige by making fans wait for them.

Purposeful Procrastination: Deliberate Delays Most people put off doing what they dislike, but there is nothing "purposeful" about this. Purposeful procrastinators, however, pretend that they will pursue a task "soon." While promising imminent results, they deliberately refuse to commit to a specific time or date for task completion. They delay the completion of tasks on purpose. Trying to pin down a purposeful procrastinator is like trying to nail Jell-O to a wall—it won't stick. If those waiting for the task to be completed express exasperation, they appear to be nagging or fussing. Parents who try to get their kids to clean their rooms are often faced with this maddening strategy. When parents grow weary of monitoring their children's room-cleaning progress, they may give up in disgust and either perform the task themselves or leave the room chaotic. This makes the resistance successful.

All six of these resistance strategies result from power imbalances. It is difficult to know for sure when any of these strategies are being used. A single occurrence of forgetfulness or tardiness, for example, doesn't necessarily indicate resistance, even though resistance may be occurring. If the behavior becomes repetitive, however, it is safe to conclude that resistance strategies are being used.

Resistance strategies are dishonest. In extreme cases, they may be the only feasible option available to prevent evil. In most instances, however, there are better ways to prevent dominance, as you will see later in this text. There are two principal ways for competent communicators to discourage resistance strategies:

1. *Confront the strategy directly.* Use first-person singular language to describe the resistance strategy (see Chapter 8). Discuss why the strategy has been used, and work cooperatively with the resister to find an equitable solution so that resistance strategies are not employed.

2. *Produce consequences for resistance.* We become enablers when we allow ourselves to be ensnared in the resister's net of duplicity. When we continue to wait for the tactically tardy, we encourage the behavior. If we perform the tasks for those who use loss of motor function or strategic stupidity, we reward their resistance and guarantee that such strategies will persist.

You thwart the enabling process by making sure consequences result from resistance. If staff members "forget" important items when shopping for office supplies, send them back for the items. Encourage them to make a list and check off items as they shop. If people are persistently late for meetings, continue without them, and do not interrupt the meeting to fill them in on missed information. Encourage them to be punctual. Continued tardiness may necessitate punishment or expulsion from the group. Refrain from rescuing those who use strategic stupidity or loss of motor function. Compensation for damage caused by such resistance strategies should be the responsibility of the resister.

Despite the negative aspects of resistance strategies, the primary focus should not be on how to combat resistance. Instead, focus on how to reduce power imbalances and dominance-submissiveness transactions that foster a desire to resist.

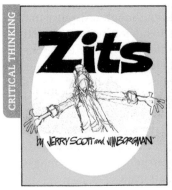

This cartoon illustrates which of the following?

○ **1.** Defiance

○ **2.** Resistance

Answers at end of chapter.

○ **3.** Purposeful procrastination

○ **4.** Selective amnesia

Empowerment: Exercising Positive Power

Empowerment is a constructive form of power. Individuals become empowered by learning to communicate competently. Acquiring communication knowledge and developing a broad range of communication skills can give us the confidence to adapt our communication appropriately whatever the context. In this section, several ways to empower people are explained.

DEVELOPING ASSERTIVENESS: NEITHER DOORMAT NOR BOOT WIPER

The terms *assertive* and *aggressive* are often confused. **Assertiveness** is "the ability to communicate the full range of your thoughts and emotions with confidence and skill" (Adler, 1977, p. 6). Those who confuse assertiveness with aggressiveness tend to ignore the last part of this definition. Assertiveness isn't merely imposing your thoughts and emotions on others. It requires confident and especially skillful expression of thoughts and emotions.

Assertiveness falls between the extremes of aggressiveness and passivity, and it is distinctly different from both (see Box 7-2). Aggressiveness puts your own needs first; you wipe your shoes on other people. Passivity underemphasizes your needs; you're a doormat in a world of muddy shoes. *Assertiveness considers both your needs and the needs of others.*

Although assertiveness can be used to defy others, it is primarily an empowering skill. Assertive individuals try to enhance their significance in the eyes of others, not alienate anyone. When passive, reticent individuals learn assertiveness, they become more productive contributors in groups. When aggressive individuals learn to be assertive, they are more likely to receive a fair hearing.

Lack of assertiveness in relationships can lead to dissatisfaction and conflict. One study of both same- and different-sex couples found that those respondents most dissatisfied with the "chore wars"—the division of labor regarding household duties and responsibility for child care—occurred among those who didn't talk about their dissatisfaction with the current arrangements of duties and responsibilities (Matos, 2014).

Assertiveness requires practice, and it involves five key communication steps (Bower & Bower, 1976):

1. *Describe your needs, rights, and desires or the basis of your conflict with others.* Use first-person singular language, such as "I need us to work more energetically on this presentation."

2. *Express how you feel.* "It upsets me when my ideas are ignored

3. *Specify the behavior or objective you are seeking.* "I want to be included in future decision making" specifies the objective.

BOX 7-2 DEVELOPING COMMUNICATION COMPETENCE

Assertiveness Self-Assessment Questionnaire

Fill out the following Assertiveness Self-Assessment Questionnaire. Be as honest as you can. This is not an assessment of your "ideal self." This should be your "real self." For each situation, indicate how likely you would be to take the action indicated by using the following scale:

⑤ **Very likely**   ④ **Likely**   ③ **Maybe**   ② **Unlikely**   ① **Very unlikely**

1. You have been invited to a party but you don't know anyone except the friend who invited you, who is not present when you enter the room. You see dozens of strangers. You walk up to a group of people, introduce yourself, and begin a conversation.   ◯

2. There is a definite undercurrent of tension and conflict in your group. You are feeling that tension as your group begins discussing its project for class. You stop the discussion, indicate that there is unresolved conflict in the group, and request that the group address this issue.   ◯

3. You strongly disagree with your group's choice for a symposium project. Nevertheless, you say nothing and go along with the majority decision.   ◯

4. During class, your instructor makes a point that angers you greatly. You raise your hand, are recognized by the instructor, and vehemently challenge your instructor's position, raising your voice to almost a shout.   ◯

5. You're sitting in the back of the class. Two students sitting beside you engage in an audible conversation that is distracting. You can't concentrate on the instructor's lecture. You lean over and calmly ask them to stop talking so that you can listen to your instructor.   ◯

6. At a family holiday dinner gathering, your uncle makes a blatantly racist remark, then tells a sexist joke. You sit silently.   ◯

7. While on vacation, you sign up to receive a group lesson in rock climbing. After the instructor has explained the basics, everyone in the group appears to understand perfectly. You, however, are unclear about a couple of instructions. You raise your hand and ask the instructor to repeat the instructions and explain them more fully.   ◯

8. Three individuals representing a religious group knock on your door. When you answer, they begin to proselytize, trying to sell you on their theological point of view. You stand there waiting patiently for them to finish, wishing they would go away.   ◯

9. A small group of teenagers talk loudly during a movie you are attending at a local theater. You become increasingly annoyed but say nothing to them.   ◯

10. You live in a dorm room with two roommates. Next door, loud music is playing, making it impossible for you to study. Your roommates seem not to care, but you are becoming increasingly annoyed. You walk next door, pound on the door, and when it opens, you demand that the music be turned way down immediately.   ◯

11. A member of your group couldn't afford to buy the textbook for the class. He asks you if he can borrow your book for "a couple of days." You agree. He has had the book for more than a week now and shows no sign of returning it to you. You wait for him to return the book or to explain why he hasn't mentioned it.   ◯

12. You are a member of a project team at work. Every member of the team makes considerably more money than you do, yet your jobs are equivalent. You believe that you deserve a hefty raise. You make an appointment with your boss to ask for one.   ◯

(continued)

BOX 7-2 DEVELOPING COMMUNICATION COMPETENCE

Assertiveness Self-Assessment Questionnaire (continued)

13. You receive an email from a team member that has a condescending tone. It angers you that this team member, whom you view as a bit of a screw-up, lectures you on the "right way" to approach your part of the group task. You write back a sarcastic, biting reply. ○

14. Your coach berates players at a team meeting for "lackluster play" and "lackadaisical attitudes." The coach is shouting and abusive. You believe the criticism is mostly unfair and doesn't apply to most of the players. You remain silent, wishing the coach would wind down. ○

15. A group member pulls you aside and begins accusing you of "unethical behavior." She is shouting at you, her face is flush red, and she is gesturing wildly. People are noticing. You shout back at her. ○

16. The family that lives next door has a dog that barks all hours of the night. It is disturbing to you and your family members. You meet one of the dog's owners during a walk through the neighborhood. You stop, begin to talk, and calmly bring up the barking-dog problem. ○

17. While taking an exam, you notice that several students are cheating. You're upset because this gives these students an undeserved advantage and may lower your own grade because the instructor grades on a curve. The instructor doesn't notice the cheating. You report the cheating to the instructor after class. ○

18. During a group discussion, your point of view clashes with that of another group member. You want very much to convince the group that your viewpoint should be accepted. You interrupt when the member who disagrees with you tries to voice her opinion, keep talking when she tries to disagree with a point you make, and insist that she is wrong and you are right. ○

19. A member of your project team "steals" your idea and takes credit for work you have done. You angrily denounce him in front of the entire team and insist that he own up to his deception. ○

20. One of your team members has extremely bad breath. This is a common problem when you meet. His bad breath bothers you a great deal. Nevertheless, you say nothing and try sitting as far away from him as possible during meetings. ○

21. You are waiting in line to be served at a local store. Just as you are about to be waited on, a group of three individuals steps in front of you. You demand that they step aside, insisting that you were in line ahead of them. ○

SCORING DIRECTIONS: Total your scores for numbers 4, 10, 13, 15, 18, 19, and 21 (aggressiveness). Next, total your scores for numbers 1, 2, 5, 7, 12, 16, and 17 (assertiveness). Finally, total your scores for numbers 3, 6, 8, 9, 11, 14, and 20 (passivity). Enter these raw totals in the appropriate blank below:

_____ Aggressiveness (   )   _____ Assertiveness (   )   _____ Passivity (   )

Now, average each raw score by dividing by 7 (e.g., 21 on aggressiveness divided by 7 equals 3.0 average). Put averages in parentheses above.

NOTE: Generally speaking, you want to average between 4.0 and 5.0 on assertiveness and 2.0 or less on aggressiveness and passivity. This reflects the general desirability of assertiveness and the general undesirability of aggressiveness and passivity. A low score on a specific assertiveness scenario or a high score on a specific aggressiveness or passivity scenario may also indicate a need for improvement in these particular situations.

4. *Identify consequences.* The emphasis should be on the positive, not the negative, consequences. "I like working here, and I will continue for as long as I'm treated fairly" is better than "If you continue to treat me unfairly, I'll be forced to quit." The latter is threatening and aggressive.

5. *Remain respectful.* You can remain firm and direct and still be unwaveringly polite and respectful. Tone of voice is especially important. A weak, quavering voice communicates passivity, and a loud voice can seem aggressive. Find the balance in between the two. You can ask for feedback from others to find that balance.

Being assertive when using social media is particularly challenging. Tone without companion nonverbal cues (e.g., facial expressions, tone of voice, gestures, and eye contact) can easily be perceived as aggressiveness. "I need this document to be changed immediately" can seem aggressive and pushy when intended to be merely direct and firm. Using **emoticons** or **emojis**—graphic notations that indicate emotional information—can sometimes convey a softer tone.

The appropriateness of assertiveness, aggressiveness, or passivity is situational. Assertiveness, although generally a desirable skill, is not always appropriate, especially if harm may come to you or others by being assertive. Conversely, aggressiveness, although generally an undesirable communication pattern, is sometimes appropriate (e.g., harassers who won't back off). Occasionally, passivity is the appropriate choice if it avoids danger or harm. The competent communicator analyzes the context to determine the appropriate use of assertiveness.

INCREASING PERSONAL POWER RESOURCES: EXPANDING CHOICES

Individuals can empower themselves in numerous ways by developing their power resources. Women who have been homemakers may significantly empower themselves by returning to college, earning a degree, and finding a job. Self-esteem may be bolstered by her sense of independence resulting from a college education and employment in her field of study, and the additional income benefits the entire family.

Husbands who assume a greater portion of the domestic chores and child rearing may increase their value in the family. They do not have to depend on the expertise of their partners to perform domestic activities competently. The stereotype of the bungling husband and father burning the dinner and falling prey to the antics of his children when his wife is away doesn't have to be the reality. Men can empower themselves to handle domestic responsibilities and tasks with dexterity. They don't have to become the passive victims of their own self-imposed ineptitude.

Developing expertise can be empowering. Learning computer skills can make you a valuable asset in a group or organization. Developing public speaking and interpersonal skills also is empowering. Such skills open up new horizons, new capabilities, and options. Becoming informed on topics, especially if the information is specialized, can make you a valuable group member. The more we develop our personal power resources, the more empowered and significant we can become.

EMPLOYING COOPERATIVE ARGUMENTATION: DELIBERATIONS, NOT COMBAT

Cooperative argumentation is engaging in a process of deliberation with understanding and problem solving as the ultimate goals (Makau & Marty, 2001). Cooperative argumentation focuses on the problem or issue, not on the people deciding. Participants disagree without being disagreeable. Civility is the overarching principle that guides discussions (Makau & Marty, 2013). Critical listening is emphasized, not fighting for the floor to dominate the conversation.

In typical arguments, there is a dominance-prevention power struggle with winners and losers. Cooperative argumentation balances the power by providing a supportive atmosphere where all participants can feel free to join the discussion. Those who are hesitant to disagree are encouraged to participate. Having an opportunity to be heard can be profoundly empowering, especially to those unaccustomed to being taken seriously.

Participants in cooperative argumentation describe objections they have to particular ideas instead of criticizing "rivals" to achieve a personal advantage. Participants solve problems instead of attempting to force others to agree. They assert their points of view instead of aggressively attacking those who disagree. They treat everyone as equals by eschewing arrogance. They are careful to avoid absolute statements that shut off discussion, and they let the force of their arguments change minds instead of employing manipulative strategies of influence, such as ridiculing a rival's idea or being deceptive about the weakness of a proposal.

Summary

Power is the ability to influence the attainment of goals sought by you or by others. It is inherent in all human relationships. There are three forms of power: dominance, prevention, and empowerment. Power imbalances are not inherently harmful, but they increase the likelihood of negative consequences. Some of these negative consequences include: relationship failure, aggression, verbal and nonverbal abuse, sexual harassment, and commonplace difficulties. Power imbalances also produce anger, frustration, wariness, and resentment in common everyday situations.

Information, expertise, legitimate authority, rewards, punishments, and personal qualities are the primary power resources. Coalition formation, defiance, and resistance strategies are the chief power-balancing approaches employed in dominance-prevention power struggles. Although the dominance and prevention forms of power can produce the "dark side" of interpersonal relationships, empowerment is a very positive form of power. Becoming empowered is an important step in becoming a competent communicator. Empowerment is a win-win, cooperative approach to power balancing.

Answers for Critical Thinking caption:

ZITS (P. 188): #2 and #3

Quizzes Without Consequences

Test your knowledge before your exam! Go to the companion website at www.oup.com/us/rothwell, click on the Student Resources for each chapter, and take the Quizzes Without Consequences.

Film School Case Studies

Cool Hand Luke (1967). Drama; PG
Paul Newman wowed audiences with his portrayal of Luke, an irrepressible, spirited man imprisoned and forced to endure a repressive Southern chain gang. Analyze the instances of passive aggression and defiance that exemplify how no one is completely powerless.

Disclosure (1994). Drama; R
An intriguing plot twist propels this film. Michael Douglas plays a business executive who files sexual harassment charges against his female superior (Demi Moore). Analyze the issue of power imbalance and sexual harassment. Does it seem like a stretch to portray a man as the victim of sexual harassment?

Insurgent (2015). Drama/Sci-Fi; PG-13

Beatrice Prior (Shailene Woodley) must fight against an alliance that threatens to rip apart society in this dystopian film. Identify the power resources available to both sides in the struggle. Is there coalition formation? Defiance? Resistance? Empowerment? Be specific.

The Lincoln Lawyer (2011). Drama; R

Matthew McConaughey plays a sketchy defense lawyer who operates from the backseat of his Lincoln town car. While representing a high-profile client (Ryan Phillippe), he becomes immersed in some nasty, tricky business. Examine the power resources employed by the various characters, concentrating on McConaughey's character. Apply the three types of power and the results of power imbalances.

Reign Over Me (2007). Drama; PG-13

Don Cheadle is a dentist in New York City who one day stumbles upon his former college roommate (Adam Sandler). The Sandler character is suffering mental illness following the loss of his entire family (wife and two daughters) in the 9/11 terrorist attacks. Examine the power dynamics, especially the verbal and nonverbal indicators of power, the imbalances in power, the consequences these produce, and the instances of resistance and defiance. Does empowerment emerge anyplace in the movie?

BY THE END OF THIS CHAPTER, YOU SHOULD BE ABLE TO:

1. Explain the main reasons that we form relationships.

2. Identify the 10 phases of intimate relationships.

3. Recognize communication strategies that work or fail during each stage.

Making Relationships Work

JESSICA TANDY AND HUME CRONYN were married for 52 years, and the marriage ended only when Tandy died. The longevity of their relationship was more remarkable because they stayed happily married even though they were both successful, acclaimed actors. Hollywood is legendary for chewing up marriages. Yet Tandy and Cronyn remained steadfast partners for five decades despite great notoriety and professional success, each of them winning numerous stage and screen awards. They starred, sometimes separately and sometimes together, in a variety of successful movies. Given a choice among models of romance that included several famous relationships, respondents to one survey picked Tandy and Cronyn's relationship as the ideal (Kanner, 1995). Contrary to the enduring success of their relationship, both had been married previously. Why does one marriage last until death and another survive for what seems like the blink of an eye? What makes interpersonal relationships of various

CHAPTER OUTLINE

- **Main Reasons for Forming Relationships**
- **Forming Close Relationships**
- **Sustaining Relationships: Lovers, Friends, Relatives, and Coworkers**
- **Technology and Competent Interpersonal Relationships**
- **Intercultural Relationships and Communication Competence**

4. Use competent communication strategies to sustain relationships that are important to you.

5. Recognize and adjust for the significant influence technology has on interpersonal relationships.

6. Address the many challenges posed by intimate intercultural relationships.

kinds succeed or fail? *The purpose of this chapter is to discuss why interpersonal relationships at home, at work, at school, and at play succeed, struggle, or sink and what you can do to make them more durable and rewarding.*

An **interpersonal relationship** is a connection two people have to each other because of kinship (e.g., brother-sister), attraction (e.g., lovers and friends), or power distribution (e.g., boss-employee). An **intimate relationship** is a type of interpersonal relationship that is characterized by strong emotional bonding, closeness, and interdependence in which individuals meaningfully influence each other.

Although intimacy is sometimes associated with sex ("We were intimate last night"), sex is only one way of expressing intimacy (Lenbuck, 2013). A couple can cuddle on a couch and watch a great, or a crummy, movie. Romantic partners can express intimacy by self-disclosing their most personal thoughts and feelings. Some expression of physical affection (e.g., hugging, hand holding, or kissing) is viewed as important in romantic relationships to express intimacy, but physical affection doesn't necessarily mean sexual intercourse (Patrick & Beckenbach, 2009).

You also can have sex without intimacy. Couples can "hook up" and have uncommitted sex that frequently leads to regrets and negative feelings after the fact. One study of males' perception of intimacy showed that sex and

Intimacy is an emotional connection and can be expressed in many ways besides sex. Just sitting together and watching TV can be intimate.

intimacy are not viewed as synonymous (Garcia et al., 2013). Intimacy also occurs in different types of relationships, some of which are nonsexual and nonromantic ("just friends"). This chapter addresses interpersonal relationships, with special emphasis on intimate relationships.

Main Reasons for Forming Relationships

You don't always get to choose your interpersonal relationships with others. Children don't choose their parents, students in elementary and secondary schools rarely get any say in selecting their teachers, and even in college, choices of professors are often limited. Employees usually have little or no say in who their bosses are, and colleagues at work are often the luck of the draw. As relationships become more intimate, however, choices become more plentiful. Consider the main reasons we form interpersonal relationships when we do have choices.

Need to Belong: Like Food and Water

As noted in Chapter 1, humans have a deep-seated need to belong, to make social connections with other humans. Our need for human connection is an imperative, as necessary to our well-being and development as food and water (Lieberman, 2013). "We humans are social animals down to our very cells. Nature did not make us noble loners" (Parks, 2007, p. 1). Then again, loners at least get to decide how the toilet paper roll gets placed on the dispenser (over or under).

Nature has provided each of us with an "affiliative neuropeptide" called *oxytocin*. "The levels of this chemical rise when couples watch romantic movies, hug, or hold hands . . . Oxytocin is also related to the feelings of closeness and being 'in love' when you have regular sex . . ." (Amen, 2007, p. 65). This "love hormone" also seems to increase feelings of trust. "Oxytocin is nature's way of weaving people together" (Brooks, 2011, p. 64).

These human attachments we make, especially in the early, formative stages of our development, are particularly meaningful (Sroufe et al., 2005). **Attachment theory** argues, "Children born into a web of attuned relationships know how to join in conversations with new people and read social signals. They see the world as a welcoming place. Children born into a web of threatening relationships can be fearful, withdrawn, or overaggressive" (Brooks, 2011, p. 62). Communication forms attachments with others, and the quality of these attachments influences the competence of our communication.

Interpersonal Attraction: What Draws Us Together

There are basic factors that attract us to other people and make the idea of developing a relationship with them desirable. These include *physical attractiveness* and *similarities*.

PHYSICAL ATTRACTIVENESS: LOOKING GOOD

In Chapter 2, the beauty bias was discussed. Physically attractive individuals have advantages those with more average looks often do not. Hundreds of studies show that physical attractiveness is equally significant for men and women (Eastwick et al., 2014; Langlois et al., 2000). One study of online dating preferences found that both men and women had a strong preference for "very good looks" in their online prospects (Hitsch et al., 2010). Physical attractiveness, however, may initiate a date, but it takes much more than good looks to grow and develop a long-lasting relationship.

SIMILARITY: BIRDS OF A FEATHER

There's a well-known adage: "Birds of a feather flock together." Is it true that we are drawn to those who are similar to us, or do "opposites attract"? Research strongly supports **similarity attraction theory** (Byrne, 1997). We are drawn to individuals who seem to share our interests, values, attitudes, and personality (McCrae et al., 2008).

Our level of communication skill also plays a part in attraction, friendship, and relationship satisfaction. Highly skilled communicators are drawn to other highly skilled communicators, and less skilled communicators are drawn to each other (Burleson & Samter, 1996). In addition, a study of online dating found that both men and women prefer a partner with about the same educational level, same ethnicity, and same or similar religion. Divorced online daters also prefer divorced partners (true mostly for women), and those with children prefer dating someone who also has children (Hitsch et al., 2010). Online dating services such as eHarmony and PerfectMatch use algorithms to match couples based on similarities to determine compatibility (Finkel et al., 2012).

Why are we attracted to those who are similar to us? First, similarity of values, attitudes, personality, background, and communication skills makes relationships less stressful and easier to manage. There is less likelihood of frustration, bickering, and strife (Duck & Pittman, 1994). Disagreements about such issues as religion, politics, and parenting can stress relationships. Second, individuals who share our attitudes and values validate the correctness of our perceptions. Their worldviews match. When this matching does not occur, attraction can dissipate. For example, a sense of humor is a highly desirable quality in a date or mate

(Hall, 2013), and those who exhibit similar senses of humor will likely discover interpersonal attraction. This attraction, however, is less likely to occur if senses of humor are mismatched—for example, you're telling gross jokes, but your date finds that kind of humor repulsive (Cooper, 2008).

Rewards: Exchange Theory

Sometimes we seek relationships based on **exchange theory**—an analysis that weighs the benefits of a particular relationship against any costs incurred (Jeffries, 2002). We seek *rewards*, anything that we consider desirable, and these rewards may compensate for any perceived imperfections in our partners and friends. We may not be a perfect fit (some dissimilarities), but certain rewards may compensate. A substantial

This couple seems mismatched if judged by physical appearance alone. Other factors, however, sometimes compensate. Research shows that matching on physical attractiveness is more likely in initial relationships than in relationships that grow intimate after longer-term friendships (Hunt et al., 2015). We don't fall in love just because of physical appearance, and we don't remain in love just because of physical appearance.

income might compensate for short stature in men (Hitsch et al., 2010). We tolerate some irritating quirks or even difficult moodiness from our partners because they offer us rewards that are equal to or greater than the costs. Our romantic partner or close friend may talk too much at parties, laugh too loudly, or tell inappropriate jokes to our boss. Yet this same friend or partner can provide social support for us when we are stressed, so we overlook the inappropriate behavior (Rusbult & Van Lange, 2003).

A partner or friend can also offer kindness, sensitivity, and thoughtfulness as compensation for only average looks or a small income (Epstein, 2010). *Kindness, in fact, is the most important quality desired in an intimate partner by both men and women across many cultures* (Buss, 2003; Grewal, 2012). As psychologist John Gottman advises, "If you want to have a stable, healthy relationship, exercise kindness early and often" (quoted in E. E. Smith, 2014).

Although social exchange theory can seem coldly calculating, we do tend to make a cost-benefits analysis of our relationships. When the costs of a relationship (e.g., conflict, stress, unhappiness, and personal safety) outweigh any benefits (e.g., companionship, friendship, and sex), we usually look for the door to escape.

Forming Close Relationships

Despite the challenges and disappointments we often face when forming relationships, we are driven to find those lasting, happy relationships that prove to be so rewarding and life affirming. In this section, intimacy and love and the developmental stages of relationships are discussed.

Intimacy and Love: Romantic Partners and Friends

The previous chapter included a discussion of the "dark side" of personal relationships, but our personal relationships also have a very "bright side." We have many relationships in our lives. Some are casual, some professional, and others are intimate and loving. Intimacy and love are two of the most fulfilling, satisfying experiences humans can enjoy.

INTIMACY: CLOSE CONNECTION

Intimacy is an elusive term. As noted earlier, intimacy does not necessarily equate to sexual activity. Frank Cox and Kevin Demmitt (2014), in their book *Human Intimacy*, draw distinctions between *dating, hanging out,* and *hooking up* among today's college students. "Asking someone if they will be at a party is hanging out. Asking someone if they would like to go to a party is dating." Sexual activity is not necessarily implied in either. Dating, however, for many college students is synonymous with hooking up—"engaging in sexual activity without commitment." Some studies have found that only about a third of hookups involve sexual intercourse, and most hookups are between friends, not strangers (Eshbaugh & Gute, 2008).

Men and women also do not always express and nurture intimacy in the same ways (Wood, 2015). Women typically draw close to one another through talking about personal matters and discussing experiences. When you equate intimacy with only self-disclosure (sharing personal information), it would appear that women are better at establishing intimacy than men. Wood (2015) calls this mistaken notion the *male deficit model,* and she criticizes it as too narrow in perspective. She notes that while men typically talk less about personal matters and share feelings less with other men, they achieve closeness by sharing meaningful activities and helping each other (Wood & Inman, 1993; see also Radmacher & Azmitia, 2006). Engaging in building or repair work, watching or playing sports, and getting stuck in mud while off-roading and having to dig out together are all ways to achieve intimacy (Coontz, 2009).

If styles of communicating intimacy differ between men and women, then it is important that partners recognize this early in the relationship. Otherwise, misunderstandings will emerge. For example, a man fixes an annoying squeak in a door hinge that has bothered his female partner for some time. He assumes that she will recognize this as an act of affection because he perceives it as such. His partner, however, may see this as simple maintenance and

not recognize it as an expression of intimacy. Thus, she experiences no act of closeness, and he's probably upset that his act of affection went unrecognized. Men also may think that physical proximity (e.g., being in the same room or watching television while sitting on the same couch together) is intimate. Women may see this as the "slouch on the couch." These style differences in communicating intimacy should be discussed.

LOVE: JUST AN OCEAN OF EMOTION?

Poet Richard Barnfield described *love* as "a fire, a heaven, a hell, where pleasure, pain, and sad repentance dwell." (The Shepherd's Content, stanza 38). Germaine Greer called it "a drug." Then there's the story of a four-year-old boy whose neighbor had recently lost his wife. The man was crying in his backyard. The boy came over and sat on the grieving man's lap. Asked later by his mother what he'd said to the man, the little boy replied, "Nothing. I just helped him cry." Love almost defies definition, principally because there is not just one kind of love.

Although we tend to think of love in terms of passion, not all types of love are fever pitched. Robert Sternberg (1986, 1988, 1997) has offered his **triangular theory of love** to explain the different types (see Figure 8-1). The three elements of love, according to this theory, are intimacy, passion, and commitment (Sumter et al., 2013). *Intimacy* has already been defined as feeling emotionally close to and strongly influenced by another person. *Passion* refers to both the physiological drives that produce intense physical attraction and sexual responses and the psychological desires and needs expressed as the idealization of a loved one and constant thinking about that person (Yela, 2006). *Commitment* refers to a decision to continue a relationship long term. Seven types of love are related to these three key elements:

1. *Liking*—intimacy without passion or commitment, such as in some friendships.

2. *Infatuated love*—passion without intimacy or commitment, such as "puppy love."

3. *Empty love*—commitment without passion and intimacy, such as in a stagnating, unsatisfying marriage.

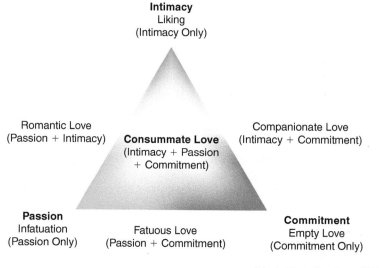

FIGURE 8-1. Triangular Theory of Love.

4. *Romantic love*—passion and intimacy without commitment, such as a romantic affair.

5. *Companionate love*—intimacy and commitment without passion, such as a long-term marriage where partners are more friends than lovers.

6. *Fatuous love*—passion and commitment without intimacy, such as a "love at first sight" relationship.

7. *Consummate love*—intimacy, passion, and commitment; the most satisfying adult relationship.

It is not unusual to mistake passion for consummate love. Passion without intimacy or commitment, however, is more a "one-night stand," and in the absence of intimacy and commitment, passion can flame out quickly, leaving emptiness, disappointment, and regret (Garcia et al., 2013). *Personal relationships that have the greatest longevity and satisfaction are those in which partners are constantly working on sustaining intimacy and reinforcing commitment to each other* (DeWall et al., 2011). This is the companionate love of friendships that plays an integral part in making our lives rewarding.

Passion does not inevitably disappear as a romantic relationship grows long term, but the giddy levels of passion characteristic of the early stages of romance cannot be realistically sustained (Gonzaga et al., 2006; Lyubomirsky, 2012). In fact, such desperate longing, often equated with obsessive passion ("I can't live without you"), is detrimental because it controls you, ultimately making the relationship less satisfying than even a passionless, companionate relationship (Pileggi, 2010).

The giddy passion of blossoming love lasts, on average, about two years (Lyubominrsky, 2012). As romantic relationships mature, passion will be more episodic, appearing sometimes but seeming to disappear at others. When the fires of passion seem to flicker or diminish overall, the warmth of intimacy and the comfort of commitment sustain a long-term relationship (Sprecher & Regan, 1998; Sumter et al, 2013). Engaging in enjoyable activities can cultivate a healthy passion over the long term when passion becomes more episodic. These activities, however, should not be competitive "because the point of the outing should not be winning but enjoying time together" (Pileggi, 2010, p. 39). Expecting romantic relationships to remain as they were when passion first ignited sets expectations that doom those relationships. We form powerful emotional attachments in committed relationships, but these attachments mature and change over time.

CRITICAL THINKING

There are many kinds of love. What are the three elements in Sternberg's theory that determines different types of love?

○ **1.** Intimacy, passion, and commitment

○ **2.** Intimacy, passion, and liking

○ **3.** Passion, liking, and commitment

○ **4.** Infatuation, passion, and commitment

Answers at end of chapter.

Relationship Development: Coming-Together Phases

Mark Knapp and Linda Vangelisti (1992, 2005) examined a large body of research on phases of relationships and communication patterns. They synthesized this research into their **stages of relationships model** that has five "coming-together" and five "coming-apart" phases (see Figure 8-2). This model applies equally well to mixed-sex and same-sex intimate relationships (Haas & Stafford, 1998; Peplau & Spalding, 2000).

Particular patterns of communication occur in each phase. Some advance the development of your relationships, and others lead to deterioration. Recognizing the difference can make or break interpersonal relationships. Movement through the phases may be rapid, especially in the early phases, or it may be slow, such as when one partner wants to move forward or backward but the other partner resists. There may be substantial overlap between phases as you

move in either direction. Movement may not even be sequential because sometimes phases are skipped. Let's look at each of these phases, recognizing that we're describing intimate relationships. Other relationships, such as those with coworkers, follow different patterns.

INITIATING: TAKING THE PLUNGE

During the *initiating phase*, we are surveying the interpersonal terrain. We try to put our best foot forward by appearing friendly, open, and approachable. A study by William Douglas (1987) revealed communication approaches that seem to work effectively during this phase. *Networking* (learning about a person from someone who knows him or her), *offering* (making yourself available for conversation by sitting in an adjacent seat or being in a place the person usually frequents), *approaching* (signally an interest verbally or nonverbally with a smile or a self-introduction), and *sustaining* (keeping the conversation going by asking questions) all work well.

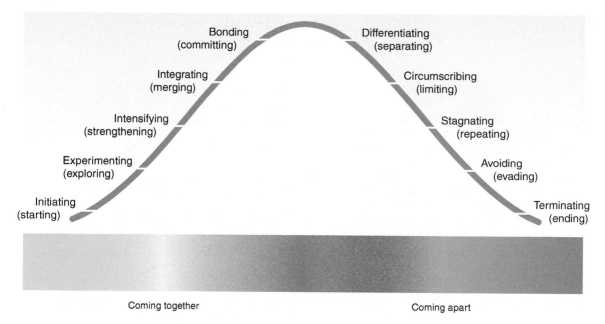

FIGURE 8-2. Stages of Relationship Development.

Communication approaches that don't work effectively during this phase of personal relationship development include *expressing deep feelings* ("I'm afraid to love again"), *keeping silent to create an air of mystery* (there's no mystery in looking doltish), *asking for big favors* ("Will you help me move?"), and *diminishing oneself* (Woody Allen: "My one regret in life is that I am not someone else"). Talking about an "ex" and not making eye contact are additional "don'ts" ("Navigating Today's Complex Dating Scene," 2011). In addition, the mere presence of a cell phone can have a negative effect on a first encounter. You don't have to actually reach for the cell phone to check a score or answer a text. Just having it displayed on the table or bar counter can have a negative effect on social interaction (Przybylski & Weinstein, 2012). Stuff the phone in your pocket or purse.

So what about attempts at clever opening lines? Do they work? "What's on the menu—Menu?" Really? "I'm not really this tall—I'm sitting on my wallet." Impressed? "A man approaches a woman in a bar and says, 'How much does a penguin weigh?' The woman replies, 'How much?' The man responds, 'Enough to break the ice.'" Does this work for you? Then there's this

one: "Is your name WiFi? Cuz I think I feel a connection." (Goldston, 2007; Marie, 2014).

A basic problem with all of these opening lines is that they are not customized for the individual who interests you. Research shows that attempting to find the perfect opening line is wasted effort ("What Social Science Can Tell You About Flirting," 2007). Most openers are awkward, silly, or embarrassingly lame. They may work occasionally, but don't bet that wallet you're sitting on (Munn, 2012). This shouldn't discourage you from ever using humor, but the best openers are simple introductions ("Hi, I'm Glen. What's your name?") or conversation starters ("What do you think of the band?") Just K.I.S.S.—Keep It Simple and Straightforward. (See Box 8-1)

EXPERIMENTING: AUDITIONING FOR THE PART

The *experimenting phase* is when we "audition" for the part of boyfriend or girlfriend. We experiment by engaging in small talk to discover areas of commonality: "What's your major?" or "Do you like ice skating?" We're casually probing, searching for ways to connect with others. All of us have superficial contacts with hundreds

Recognizing Flirting Signals

The majority of young people are terrible at recognizing when a stranger is flirting with them. Detecting when a person is not flirting is far easier and far more accurately deduced (Hall et al., 2014). So how do you tell flirting from nonflirting by strangers, coworkers, or friends? Teasing, joking, and being friendly may be merely nonflirting conversation. Flirting is communication that signals attraction. Misreading a person in this regard can prove embarrassing or even cause you to miss out on a potentially rewarding relationship.

Here are some tips to improve your accuracy based on research:

1. *Look for certain nonverbal cues.* Smiling, leaning forward, touching your hand, and strong eye contact can be indicators of romantic interest (Henningsen et al., 2009). Separate from context, however, all of these can be misleading, so be careful not to assume too much on this alone.

2. *Listen for verbal indicators.* Compliments, overt references to being single, and mild sexual innuendos indicate flirting (DiDonato, 2014).

3. *Analyze the context.* Flirting is more likely to occur in places that encourage sociability (conversation is easily conducted), where alcohol is available (a social lubricant if used in moderation), and when common interests are exhibited (like-minded individuals gather) (McBain et al., 2013).

4. *Look for consistency.* This moves beyond the "bar scene." This may be a coworker or friend who may or may not be flirting with you. Does this person seem to show interest in you other than during work-related tasks (DiDonato, 2014)?

5. *Look for distinctiveness.* Does the coworker or friend show more interest in you than in others (DiDonato, 2014)?

INTENSIFYING: WARMING TO THE RELATIONSHIP

The *intensifying phase* is when relationships deepen. Individuals use a variety of communication approaches to intensify relationships (Taraban et al., 1998). The top-10 approaches identified in one study are these (Tolhuizen, 1989)

1. *Increased contact* (39.2%)—seeing or phoning a partner more often.
2. *Relationship negotiation* (29.1%)—openly discussing feelings about the relationship.
3. *Social support and assistance* (26.1%)—requesting advice from a parent or friend.
4. *Increased rewards* (17.6%)—doing favors, such as taking care of a partner's laundry or fixing a partner's car.
5. *Direct definitional bid* (16.6%)—asking for a commitment from a partner.
6. *Tokens of affection* (16.1%)—giving gifts, sending flowers, giving cards.
7. *Personalized communication* (15.1%)—listening to a partner or friend.
8. *Verbal expressions of affection* (14.1%)—saying "You're really sweet."
9. *Suggestive actions* (13.1%)—flirting.
10. *Nonverbal expressions of affection* (12.1%)—gazing, smiling, touching.

Smiling, gazing, and other nonverbal expressions of affection communicate intensification of a relationship.

of people that never develop to any extent. Most of our transactions do not progress beyond the experimenting phase of development.

Women use relationship negotiation far more often than men; men use direct definitional bid and verbal expressions of affection more often than women (Owen, 1987). *The success of any of these approaches depends on the unique dynamics of a particular relationship.* Which of these approaches do you use most frequently?

Individuals often conduct "secret tests" during this phase to check out the success of their intensification efforts. *Endurance* requires a partner to tolerate unpleasant behavior, such as criticism and inconvenient requests (e.g., taking care of a slobbering, ill-trained dog big enough to saddle and ride). If your partner endures the test, commitment is assumed. *Public presentation* introduces your partner as "my boyfriend/girlfriend" to see if the partner is comfortable with the label. *Separation* keeps the partners away from each other for a period of time to see if the relationship will remain viable. *Third-party questioning* occurs when one partner asks a friend to check out the other person's depth of feeling about the relationship and then report back the results. *Triangle tests* involve asking a friend to make the partner jealous by seeming to express interest in the partner concocting the test (Baxter & Wilmot, 1984). Secret tests generally are "more common in deteriorating [versus stable] relationships" (Goodboy et al., 2010, p. 74).

Endurance, separation, and the triangle tests are the least constructive. They can risk destroying a relationship. Public presentation and third-party questioning, however, are relatively harmless ways to test the depth of a relationship.

INTEGRATING: MOVING BEYOND "JUST FRIENDS"

The *integrating phase* fuses a relationship. Individuals seem to merge into a distinct couple. Social circles of friends mix. Nonverbal markers of intimacy, such as pictures, pins, or clothing belonging to the other person, are displayed. Self-disclosure is more revealing and potentially risky. Life goals and aspirations are shared. A sexual relationship often occurs at this stage (sex on a first date or "hooking up" are not included as examples of this stage). Partners may begin living together, indicating that they have moved beyond the "just friends" phase.

BONDING: STRINGS, RINGS, AND OTHER THINGS

The *bonding phase* involves public rituals that institutionalize the relationship. We are communicating to the world that we have a committed relationship, not just a "no-strings" attachment. An engagement ring may be worn. There may be a public contract, of which marriage is the most obvious example. Gay couples only recently have begun to have this option. Nevertheless, any public announcement, ceremony, gesture, or proclamation that the relationship is considered exclusive and binding moves the couple into the bonding phase.

This phase usually signals a turning point. A **turning point** is "any event or occurrence that is associated with change in a relationship" (Baxter & Bullis, 1986, p. 470). Disclosing a personal secret for the first time or lending your classic car that is in mint condition might be turning points in a relationship. Having sex for the first time, moving in together, or saying "I love you" are typical turning points (Mongeau et al., 2006).

Interestingly, almost half the time partners in heterosexual relationships do not identify the same turning points (Baxter & Bullis, 1986). For example, having sex may be a momentous turning point for a woman that suggests a long-term intimate relationship, even marriage, but it may be merely a pleasant and not very significant event for a man (Mongeau et al., 2006). Realizing for the first time that his female partner enjoys watching sports or backpacking in the wilderness, however, may be a turning point for a man.

As we all know, reaching the bonding phase does not guarantee that partners will remain bonded. Also, *bonding is not an idyllic state.* You may not wish to remain bonded with your partner. Nevertheless, this chapter will offer several key ways to improve your chances of remaining bonded with your romantic partner if that is your desire.

Relationship Deterioration: Coming-Apart Phases

Rita Rudner once joked, "My boyfriend and I broke up. He wanted to get married and I didn't want him to." Romantic relationships often don't move in just one direction—from friendly to intimate to happy to blissful. Relationships can move forward (coming together) or backward (coming apart). Research even shows that more than half of young adults experience *on-again/off-again relationships*, sometimes in recurring fashion until mutual friends may become completely exasperated with the entire pattern of the relationship ("Let me guess—you're back together for, what is it, the 10th or 11th time?") (Dailey et al., 2013).

The direction of a relationship can be upended by significant turning points. A sexual affair can provoke a partner to leapfrog from bonding to termination, skipping four phases in between that are typical of a relationship that is coming apart. A friendship that is just beginning to intensify may suddenly fall apart because of an act of violence or a perceived betrayal of trust. Nevertheless, some relationships do dissolve, not in an instant, but painfully over what may seem a lifetime. *If you want to prevent the demise of a relationship, recognizing the early phases of relationship deterioration can help.* Once you get too far down the path of deterioration, it may be too late to rescue the relationship. Consider the five coming-apart phases (see Figure 8-2).

DIFFERENTIATING: DISINTEGRATING BEGINS

The first phase of disengagement is *differentiating*. What were thought to be similarities are discovered to be differences. The pretense of being alike in most ways begins to erode. Assertions of individuality become more frequent. Conflict occurs, although differentiating can occur without conflict.

Differentiating is an expected phase in romantic relationships. In the beginning of an intimate relationship, partners may be inseparable. Later, giving each other "some space" may be a welcome way to respond. Excessive differentiating, however, can mean trouble ahead.

CIRCUMSCRIBING: DON'T ASK, DON'T TELL

When we establish limits and restrictions on communication with our partner, we are *circumscribing*. Both the breadth and the depth of our communication become constrained. Partners share less. Fewer topics are perceived as safe to discuss for fear of igniting a conflict, and topics that are addressed are discussed superficially. "Let's not talk about that again" becomes a familiar refrain. Communication interactions become less frequent. *You've entered the danger zone in your deteriorating relationship.*

STAGNATING: TREADING WATER

Stagnating relationships aren't growing or progressing. As Woody Allen famously said in the movie *Annie Hall*, "A relationship, I think, is like a shark . . . It has to constantly move forward or it dies." If the feeling is that "nothing changes," communication becomes even more restricted, narrow, hesitant, and awkward than in the circumscribing stage. Even stabs at discussing relationship problems are likely to provoke yet another conflict with an unhappy outcome. Communication begins resembling interactions with strangers. The relationship is barely above water and in danger of sinking.

AVOIDING: THE END IS NEAR

Avoiding is when partners keep a distance from each other, hoping not to interact. Separation, not connection, is desired. Partners stay away from home by working late, or they spend more time with friends. If physical separation is not possible because children need to be parented, partners' communication may be impersonal and infrequent. If you reach this phase, your relationship is nearing its end.

TERMINATING: STICK A FORK IN IT

Terminating is the final pulling-apart phase. The relationship is finished—cooked, ceased, done, dead, kaput! Women more often than men initiate the termination of a relationship, especially a marriage (Sayer et al., 2011). Yet although women typically anticipate the demise of a relationship sooner than men, men take the termination harder. When the Love Boat founders on the rocky shoals, men are more depressed, lonelier, and unhappier than women (McClintock, 2014).

About 60% of ex-partners cut off contact and do not remain friends (Kellas et al., 2008). Couples that break up are more likely to remain friends if they had a friendship before becoming romantically involved (Mattingly, 2012). It is easier for these former partners to transition back to being "just friends." If the breakup was mutual, remaining friends also is more likely if the breakup ended on friendly terms (Mattingly, 2012).

Relationship termination can be traumatic for one or both parties. One study found that individuals who had been rejected by the person they loved spent more than 85% of their waking hours thinking about the one who jilted them. They became love zombies, lurching through life with only one thing on their minds. In addition, they repeatedly exhibited lack of emotional control for weeks or even months. Examples included inappropriate contact by phoning, emailing, texting, pleading for reconciliation, and dramatic entrances and exits from the rejecter's home, workplace, or social space. Uncontrollable weeping for hours and drinking excessively are other examples. This is passion gone awry, and it looks remarkably like withdrawal from addiction (Fisher et al., 2010).

Although there is a tendency to view the coming-together stages of relationships as good and the coming-apart stages as bad, especially given the often dramatic responses to rejection, this is not necessarily true. Some romantic relationships that appear promising initially prove to be less satisfying as we get to know the other person better. Some relationships may even be destructive to one or both parties and should not progress. Terminating an abusive relationship, for example, is constructive. Sometimes relationship participants have to step back before they can step forward. *Stages of relationships merely describe what is, not necessarily what should be.*

Sustaining Relationships: Lovers, Friends, Relatives, and Coworkers

Our relationships with others can seem so fragile. The flavorful wine of a new marriage, for example, may gradually turn into the bitter vinegar of divorce. Actor Tom Cruise went manic on *The Oprah Winfrey Show*, proclaiming that he was wildly in love with actress Katie Holmes. Later, Holmes in turn proclaimed that she had

dreamed about marrying Cruise when she was still a teenager and was marrying the "man of my dreams." The marriage produced one child and lasted fewer than six years. It ended bitterly with the lingering challenges of co-parenting.

Sustaining relationships of all kinds can be an enormous challenge. Competent communication is central to meeting this challenge. Chapter 1 discussed the importance of creating a constructive, cooperative communication climate. This section expands on communication climate with its essential role in sustaining relationships.

Connecting Bids: Keeping Us Together

You enter your living room after a long day at work. Your partner asks, "How was your day?" Do you utter a dismissive "Same stuff, different day"? You're having lunch with your father at a local café. You attempt several times to engage him in conversation, but invariably, his cell phone rings and he conducts business while you both eat.

These exchanges involve what Gottman terms *bids for connection*. A **connecting bid** is any attempt to engage another person in a positive transaction, sometimes at a deep and enduring level and other times at a superficial and fleeting one. It says, "I want to feel connected to you," if only for a brief moment (Gottman & DeClaire, 2001). A bid could be verbal, in the form of a question, statement, or comment whose content includes thoughts, feelings, observations, opinions, or invitations. A bid could also be nonverbal, in the form of a gesture, look, touch, facial expression, or vocalization (e.g., a grunt or a sigh).

MAKING BIDS: REACHING OUT TO OTHERS
Connecting bids vary in importance. There are the hugely significant bids: "Let's move in together" or "Do you want to start a business with me?" Some are seemingly insignificant requests characteristic of day-today communication: "Honey, will you get me a beer?" or "Mommy, will you help me tie my shoe?" or "Did you read the email I sent to you?" Some are subtle attempts to connect: "You look very nice today" or "Good morning," or "How was your vacation?" Others can be very direct: "Do you still love me?" or "Do you think of me as a good friend?" or "May I have your phone number?" A

vague bid may protect our vulnerable self-esteem, whereas a direct bid may be too risky. For example, instead of asking directly "Do you want to see a movie with me on Saturday?" you might ask, "What's your favorite movie?" followed by "Maybe sometime we could check out one of those classic movies you love." The vague bid doesn't risk outright rejection as a more direct bid might.

Everybody makes connecting bids every day because we want to feel as though we are a part of the human experience, not alone and separate. We also want to draw close to those who are most important in our lives. *Not all transactions with others, of course, require us to connect.* When a telemarketer calls in the middle of dinner, you probably want to be disconnected. Obnoxious individuals who harass you for a date are only encouraged by a positive response to their connecting bids. Nevertheless, making bids is a central communication process for establishing and sustaining close relationships (Gottman & DeClaire, 2001). *How you respond to these bids markedly influences the communication climate for relationships to blossom or wilt.*

RESPONSES: TURNING THIS WAY AND THAT

Every bid provokes one of three responses: *turning toward, turning away,* or *turning against* the bid (Gottman & DeClaire, 2001). The **turning-toward response** is a positive reaction to the bid. Your partner tells a joke, and you laugh. A parent asks for help moving furniture, and you agree without complaint. A friend wants to talk, and you engage in conversation. A coworker invites you to lunch, and you accept.

The **turning-away response** occurs when we ignore a bid or act preoccupied when a bid is offered. You ask your partner if she wants her wash put in the dryer, and she waves dismissively as she focuses intently on her computer screen. You ask a friend at work for advice on a project, and without looking up from reading a report, he mutters, "Can't help you now." These turning-away responses are rarely malicious. The turning-away response, however, communicates "You're not very important to me right now," or at least not as important as that person's primary focus of attention (which is something other than you).

A turning-away response can be as destructive to a relationship as a turning-against response. Which is this?

The **turning-against response** is an overtly negative rejection of a connecting bid. You ask your partner, "Do you want to watch some TV?" and your partner responds, "All you ever want to do is watch that lobotomy box. Get a life!" You offer to help your roommate clean up the clutter in your dorm room. Your roommate remarks, "Don't get your tights in a twist. I know how psycho you can get about a little mess." You ask a coworker for assistance figuring out a new software program. The coworker responds, "Can't help now. Try working it out yourself for a change." Unlike the turning-away response, the turning-against response seems harsh, even malicious. In essence, the turning-against response is saying "Get lost" or "I'm angry or irritated with you."

CONSEQUENCES: THE GLAD, THE BAD, AND THE SAD

According to research, husbands heading for divorce turn away from their wives' bids 82% of the time. Wives in similar unhappy circumstances turn away from their husbands' bids 50% of the time. Husbands and wives in strong relationships, however, rarely turn away from their spouse's bids (Gottman & DeClaire, 2001).

When we turn away from the connecting bids of others, we dampen further attempts to connect. The bidder easily loses heart when a bid is ignored. In fact, attempts to **rebid**—to try again after an initial bid has been ignored or rejected—are *near zero*. This is a classic withdrawal reaction typical of a destructive communication climate. *No one can turn toward every connecting bid, but a pattern of turning away can destroy relationships* (Gottman & Levenson, 1999; E. E. Smith, 2014).

Not surprisingly, turning against the bids of others also destroys relationships. Negative responses to connecting bids typically produce hostility or withdrawal. Although turning-against responses may seem to be the worst possible reaction one can make to a bid for connection, research shows that *turning-away and turning-against responses are about equally destructive to relationships* (Gottman & DeClaire, 2001).

Emphasize Supportive Communication: How to Talk to Others

"The principle of openness implies that it is better to talk things over. The principle of supportiveness implies that it makes a great deal of difference *how* you talk things over" (LaFasto & Larson, 2001, p. 17). This section explains "how to talk things over" so that you can prevent a defensive, competitive communication climate and establish a supportive, cooperative one, a subject introduced only generally in Chapter 1 (see also Gibb, 1961) (see Box 8-2).

EVALUATION VERSUS DESCRIPTION

A friend of mine was in his townhouse when the 6.9-magnitude Loma Prieta earthquake hit central California. Objects flew across the rooms, kitchen cabinets emptied onto the counters and floor, and glass shattered throughout his home. When those 15 seconds of tumultuous shaking subsided, the timid voice of my friend's four-year-old daughter came from the back room: "Daddy, it wasn't my fault." We are quick to defend ourselves if we even think an evaluation might be offered.

Evaluations are value judgments made about individuals and about their actions. Statements of praise, recognition, admiration, or flattery are positive evaluations. Research shows that lack of praise for accomplishments produces job dissatisfaction and a desire to quit (Lipman, 2013; Kjerulf, 2012). Praise for significant accomplishments plays an important part in constructing supportive communication climates.

Negative evaluation is the culprit in provoking defensiveness. Interpersonal relationships are strained by even moderate amounts of criticism, contempt, and blame (Gottman & Silver, 1994; Masland et al., 2015). We typically don't respond constructively when we're treated like a defendant being cross-examined on the witness stand. Criticism produces more conflict in the workplace than mistrust, personality clashes, power struggles, or pay (Baron, 1990).

Relationships, even casual associations with coworkers, supervisors, or distant relatives, are strained by negative evaluations. Gottman's research found that *it takes at least five positive communication acts to counterbalance every negative one* (Gottman & Gottman, 2006; Gottman & Silver, 1999). Failure to maintain this five-to-one **magic ratio** leads to relationship failure in almost all cases. Couples headed for divorce communicated fewer than one positive behavior directed toward their partners for every negative one (Gottman & Gottman, 2006). Further research has revealed that even *20 acts of kindness* toward your partner does not usually anesthetize the pain of a single, extremely negative "zinger" (e.g., "I hope you didn't pay for that haircut" or "You're not nearly as good as my previous boyfriend") (Notarius & Markman, 1993). How would you react if someone described you as caring, generous, sensitive, friendly, funny, and DUMB? Would even five glowing descriptors counteract the single zinger? (Remember the negativity bias discussed in Chapter 2.)

The same results hold true for workplace performance. A study conducted by the University of Michigan's Ross School of Business found that the best-performing teams made about six times as many positive comments as negative ones. The worst performing teams, on average, made three negative comments for every positive one

BOX 8-2 DEVELOPING COMMUNICATION COMPETENCE

Reactions to Defensive and Supportive Communication

Project yourself into each situation below, and imagine how you would react. Choose a number for each situation that reflects how much you would like or dislike the statements presented.

1. You live with your roommate in a studio apartment. You forgot to clean your dishes three times this week. Your roommate says to you, "Do your dishes. I'm tired of cleaning up your mess."

   STRONGLY DISLIKE ○5 ○4 ○3 ○2 ○1 STRONGLY LIKE

2. You're working with your partner on a class project. Your partner says to you, "I'm feeling very concerned that we will not finish our project on time. We're barely halfway, and we only have three days before our presentation. What do you think?"

   STRONGLY DISLIKE ○5 ○4 ○3 ○2 ○1 STRONGLY LIKE

3. You are a member of a softball team. Your coach takes you aside and says, "You blew the game last week. Are you prepared to do better this game?"

   STRONGLY DISLIKE ○5 ○4 ○3 ○2 ○1 STRONGLY LIKE

4. You trip and badly bruise your shoulder at work. Later, your boss says to you, "I heard that you injured yourself. That must really hurt. Do you need time off? Can I do anything to make you more comfortable while you work in your office?"

   STRONGLY DISLIKE ○5 ○4 ○3 ○2 ○1 STRONGLY LIKE

5. You want to discuss a nagging issue with your friend. When you approach her to address the issue, she responds, "I haven't got time to hear from you now. I have more important things on my mind."

   STRONGLY DISLIKE ○5 ○4 ○3 ○2 ○1 STRONGLY LIKE

6. You're trying to resolve a dispute with your romantic partner. Your partner says to you, "I have a suggestion that might solve our problem. Perhaps this will move us forward."

   STRONGLY DISLIKE ○5 ○4 ○3 ○2 ○1 STRONGLY LIKE

7. You're having a meeting with your boss to discuss a problem you're having with inappropriate behavior from a co-worker. After some dialogue, your boss finally says, "We obviously don't agree on this issue, but since I'm the boss, I'll make the final decision."

   STRONGLY DISLIKE ○5 ○4 ○3 ○2 ○1 STRONGLY LIKE

(continued)

BOX 8-2 DEVELOPING COMMUNICATION COMPETENCE

Reactions to Defensive and Supportive Communication (continued)

8. During a family meeting, one family member says, "I know we all have strong feelings on this issue, but let's put our heads together and see if we can find a solution everyone can support. Does anyone have ideas they wish to share?"

STRONGLY DISLIKE ○ 5 ○ 4 ○ 3 ○ 2 ○ 1 STRONGLY LIKE

9. During a heated discussion with a fellow classmate, your classmate says, "I know I'm right, and there's no way you will convince me that I'm wrong."

STRONGLY DISLIKE ○ 5 ○ 4 ○ 3 ○ 2 ○ 1 STRONGLY LIKE

10. You propose an idea for a paper that your teacher dislikes. Your teacher says, "I can see that you really like this idea, but it doesn't satisfy the requirements of the project. I suggest that you keep brainstorming."

STRONGLY DISLIKE ○ 5 ○ 4 ○ 3 ○ 2 ○ 1 STRONGLY LIKE

11. You're a member of a hiring panel. During a break from an interviewing session, another member of the panel takes you aside and says, "Look, we've been friends a long time. I want you to support my candidate. This is important to me. Whaddaya say? Can I count on you to back me up?"

STRONGLY DISLIKE ○ 5 ○ 4 ○ 3 ○ 2 ○ 1 STRONGLY LIKE

12. You're part of a committee to solve the parking problem on campus. The chair addresses the committee: "It is my hope that this committee can come to a consensus on solutions to this parking problem. I'll conduct our meetings, but I have only one vote, the same as everyone else."

STRONGLY DISLIKE ○ 5 ○ 4 ○ 3 ○ 2 ○ 1 STRONGLY LIKE

ANSWERS: **Questions 1, 3, 5, 7, 9, and 11 are *defensive communication* (control, evaluation, indifference, superiority, certainty, and manipulation—in that order); questions 2, 4, 6, 8, 10, and 12 are *supportive communication* (description, empathy, provisionalism, problem orientation, assertiveness, and equality—in that order). Find your average score for each set (divide by 6 both the sum of the odd-numbered items and the sum of the even-numbered items). Which do you like best (*lower average score*)—defensive or supportive communication?**

(Ko, 2013). Additionally, research by the Corporate Leadership Council found that employee performance declined 27% when managers focused on workers' weaknesses but improved by 36% when managers focused on employees' strengths (McQuaid, 2015).

The antidote to poisonous negative evaluations is not to ignore the troublesome behavior of others and glide through life uttering the cheery nostrum to "think positive." Enacting the magic ratio of positive to negative communication helps prevent negative evaluations from emerging, but when they do emerge (notice the ratio is five-to-one, not five-to-none), being positive doesn't address the problem. The antidote is to be *descriptive*.

A **description** is a first-person report of how we feel, what we perceive to be true in specific situations, and what behaviors we desire from others. As Elliot Aronson (2012) observes in his book *The Social Animal*, "Feedback expressed in terms of feelings is a lot easier for the recipient to listen to and deal with than feedback expressed in the form of judgments and evaluations (p. 421)." Four primary steps can help you become more descriptive:

1. *Praise first, then describe.* Begin with praise before describing behavior that is problematic: "This is a well-written paper. I do have a few suggestions, however, for improvement." This inclines recipients to accept suggestions for change, and the motives of those giving the suggestions re also more likely to be viewed as constructive (Hornsey et al., 2008). If there is nothing worth praising, however, or if any praise offered would appear lame and superficial, then skip this step.

2. *Use I-statements, not You-statements* (Narcisco & Burkett, 1975; Notarius & Markman, 1993). I-statements begin with an identification of the speaker's feeling followed by a description of behavior connected to the feeling: "I feel ignored when my contributions receive no response." If no significant feelings emerge, simply suggest recommendations for improvement: "I have a few changes I'd like you to consider." Any suggestion that the listener change something carries with it the implication that the listener hasn't "measured up" in some way (criticism), but framing your message as an I-statement can appear less like a disapproving edict ("You need to make these changes").

A You-statement of negative evaluation, on the other hand, makes the listener a target for blame: "You have ignored me, and you make me feel like I don't matter to you." Expect denial from anyone so

accused ("I've never ignored you") or a counterattack ("What do you expect when you act like you're starring in a *Jackass* movie?"). Eschewing You-statements is not always warranted to minimize defensiveness (e.g., "You might find these suggestions useful"), but try getting into the habit of using I-statements instead.

3. *Make your descriptions specific, not vague.* Avoid inexact descriptions: "I feel sort of weird when you act inappropriately around my boss." Words and phrases like "sort of weird" and "inappropriately" require more specific description: "I felt awkward and was embarrassed when you told that joke in front of my boss at this morning's meeting. It ridiculed gays and women."

4. *Eliminate editorial comments.* Use first-person singular, but avoid adding editorial language: "I get annoyed when you waste my time by talking about silly side issues." In this case, "waste my time" and "silly" are editorial asides that spark defensiveness and may lead to a pointless argument. Instead, say, "I get annoyed when you introduce side issues." Then provide specific examples of side issues. If your tone of voice is sarcastic or condescending, your facial expressions contemptuous, or your gestures abusive, however, the editorial is issued nonverbally. The listener will know you disapprove, whether you say so explicitly or not.

CONTROL VERSUS PROBLEM ORIENTATION

"He that complies against his will, is of his own opinion still," observed English poet Samuel Butler. Most people dislike being controlled by others. **Control** is communication that seeks to regulate or direct a person's behavior, such as "Get off the phone" or "Bring me food." Dictatorial, demanding behaviors from teachers are poorly received by students (Schrodt et al., 2008).

Controlling communication can easily lead to a contest of wills brought about by *psychological reactance* (Brehm, 1972). **Psychological reactance** means that the more someone tries to control our behavior and restrict our choices, the more we are inclined to resist such efforts, especially if we feel entitled to choose (Laurin et al., 2012). For example, while returning to your parked car, another car follows you and then waits for your space. Are you inclined to leave faster or slower? What if your parking stalker honked at you to encourage a faster exit? One study found that most people slow their exit, especially if honked (Ruback & Jweng, 1997).

If the pressure to restrict becomes intense, we may be strongly attracted to that which is prohibited. As advice columnist Ann Landers (1995) once observed: "There are three ways to make sure something gets done: Do it yourself, hire someone to do it, or forbid your kids to do it" (p. D5). When parents oppose romantic relationships, such as a teenage daughter dating an older boy, it often intensifies feelings of romantic love (Driscoll et al., 1972). The more strongly parents admonish their children not to take drugs, smoke, or get their tongue pierced, the more likely the kids are to do those very behaviors, if only to restore their sense of personal freedom (Dowd et al., 1988; Graybar et al., 1989). Parents step into the psychological reactance quicksand when they insist that their children obey them. Nevertheless, parents want to protect children from foolish or dangerous behavior. All controlling communication can't be eliminated, but it can be kept to a minimum and used only when other choices are not practical.

We can prevent defensiveness from occurring when we collaborate on a problem and seek solutions cooperatively instead of demanding obedience. Parents and children, for example, can work together, brainstorming possible solutions to troublesome conflicts instead of engaging in power struggles. Consider some examples differentiating controlling and problem-solving communication:

Controlling	Problem Solving
Clean up your room—now!	I've asked you repeatedly to clean your room. You haven't done it. I have a problem with the chores I expect you to perform not getting done. How do you see our situation?
Stop talking on the phone.	I need to make an important call. Please let me know when you're finished.

This cartoon illustrates which of the following?

○ **1.** Criticism
○ **2.** Defensiveness
○ **3.** Psychological reactance
○ **4.** Controlling communication
Answers at end of chapter.

If you don't start pulling your weight, I'll fire you.	We need to talk about how to capitalize on your strengths and improve your performance.

MANIPULATION VERSUS ASSERTIVENESS
Imagine that you have just met an interesting person at a party. This person seems very open, honest, and attentive. You are complimented by the attention this person pays you. Then imagine that you hear later from a friend that this same person was using you to gain favor with your older sibling. You were a pawn in a chess game. How would it feel to be manipulated in such a callous and deceptive way? **Manipulative communication** is an attempt by one person to maneuver another toward the manipulator's goal. Most people resent manipulation, especially if it is based on deception. One study of 6,000 team members in organizations found that playing politics, a particularly cutthroat form of manipulative communication, destroys

interpersonal relationships and team effectiveness (LaFasto & Larson, 2001).

One summer, when such things were done, I sold encyclopedias for a brief time door to door. Working out of Denver, Colorado, I dutifully knocked on doors. The first person to invite me in was a young, friendly woman who had no idea I planned to pitch the benefits of owning encyclopedias. I was trained to camouflage what my actual purpose was for knocking on someone's door. Upon entering the woman's home, I was met by her inebriated husband and his unfriendly German shepherd. "If you're selling something," the unpleasant husband grumbled at me, "I'm sicking my dog on you." I manufactured an excuse and quickly left. I found refuge in the house of an elderly couple from the former Czechoslovakia who served me tea and cake and engaged in friendly conversation about "the old country" for almost three hours. I gave up trying to sell encyclopedias for the evening, having recognized how intensely people resented being disturbed by a stranger attempting to hawk his wares. I've since pondered whether that sweet couple remembered the young man who came to visit them for no apparent reason. I quickly retired from the encyclopedia business.

Assertiveness, a skill discussed at length in Chapter 7, is the antidote to manipulation. Assertiveness requires thought, skill, and concern for others. Assertive communication says, "No games are being played. This is how I feel, and this is what I need from you." It is honest and direct, unlike manipulative communication.

INDIFFERENCE VERSUS EMPATHY

The Fatherhood Project at the Families and Work Institute concluded: "It is presence, not absence, that often lies at the heart of troubled families. It is common for family members to be in the same room and be oblivious to each other's thoughts and feelings" (Coontz, 1997, p. 160). This indifference toward others is a sign of a disintegrating family. It also encourages further family deterioration and conflict.

The lowest self-esteem among teenagers occurs in two-parent families where the father shows little interest in his children (Clark & Barber, 1994). Children often grow resentful of an indifferent or absent father. This resentment can turn into outright hostility, making future reconciliation between parent and child difficult.

You counter indifference with *empathy*. As defined in Chapter 1, **empathy** is "thinking and feeling what you perceive another to be thinking and feeling" (Howell, 1982, p. 108). Strive for understanding, not retaliation. How would you feel if treated with indifference, especially by someone important in your life?

Expressing gratitude for acts of kindness or generosity enacted by your partner ("Thanks for doing those dishes when I know you're really tired") is the antithesis of indifference. It exhibits empathy. *Expressing gratitude is one of the most powerful communication behaviors for sustaining relationships* (Frederickson, 2009b).

SUPERIORITY VERSUS EQUALITY

The line "No matter what this guy does, he thinks that no one can hold a candle to him, although a lot of people would like to" (Perret, 1994, p. 92) expresses the typical feeling most people have to expressed *superiority*. This attitude, which alleges others don't measure up, invites defensiveness. Who likes to be viewed as inferior in anyone's eyes? Research on boastfulness (when we brag about our superiority) reveals that braggarts are generally disliked (Holtgraves & Dulin, 1994). Research in the classroom reveals that teachers who communicate an air of superiority are also generally disliked (Rosenfeld, 1983). Leaders in groups who act superior undermine their credibility and influence with group members (Reicher et al., 2007).

Whatever the differences in our abilities, talents, and intellect, treating people with respect and civility, as equals on a human level, is supportive and encourages harmony and cooperation. Treating people like gum on the bottom of your shoe will invite defensiveness, even retaliation. Note the difference between these examples of expressed superiority and equality:

Superiority	Equality
That's wrong!	Can you think of why that might be incorrect?
When you get to be a parent, you'll know I'm right!	Can you see why I might not agree with you on this?
I'm the boss, and I know what's best.	Let's discuss this and see if we can find agreement.

CERTAINTY VERSUS PROVISIONALISM

Few things in this world are certain. Death, taxes, sock-eating dryers, and computers that always crash at the most inopportune moment are a few that come to mind. Because most things are not certain, however, there is room for discussion and disagreement. When people make absolute, unqualified statements of certainty, they close off discussion and disagreement. Those who communicate certainty easily slip into using terms such as *always, never, impossible, must, can't*, and *won't*, as in "You always ignore me, and you never listen." The result is often that the other party withdraws from the conversation or counterattacks with an attempt to prove the know-it-all wrong (Leathers, 1970).

Provisionalism means qualifying your statements by avoiding absolutes (remember the probability model discussed in Chapter 6), and it is an effective substitute for the attitude of certainty. Provisionalism is communicated by using terms such as *possibly, probably, perhaps, sometimes, occasionally, maybe, might, seems*, and *could be*. Problems and issues are approached as questions to be investigated and discussed.

Defuse Defensiveness: When a Cooperative Climate Isn't Enough

Supportive communication patterns can prevent defensive, hypercompetitive responses from occurring, but what if your partner, relative, friend, or coworker becomes highly defensive despite your best efforts to create a cooperative environment? You're trying to resolve a difference of viewpoint, for example, but the other person becomes defensive the moment the subject is introduced. What do you do? There are several ways to short-circuit the defensiveness of others.

AVOID DEFENSIVE SPIRALS: I DIDN'T DO IT, AND BESIDES, THEY DESERVED IT

Lady Astor, the first female member of the British Parliament, was exasperated by Winston Churchill's opposition to several of the causes she espoused. Frustrated, she acerbically commented, "If I were your wife I would put poison in your coffee." Churchill shot back, "And if I were your husband, I would drink it" (Sherrin, 1996, p. 160).

As Lady Astor and Winston Churchill show, an attack produces a counterattack, and the situation can easily spiral out of control. Refuse to be drawn into a defensive spiral in which you begin sounding like two kids arguing: "You did so."—"I did not."—"Did so!"—"Did not!" This means that you speak and listen nondefensively, even if your partner, friend, relative, or coworker exhibits defensive communication patterns. This takes discipline and patience. You have control over your own communication, however. Try using that control to create a constructive dialogue, not a malignant spiral of defensiveness.

FOCUS ON THE PROBLEM, NOT THE PERSON: KEEP YOUR EYES ON THE PRIZE

Unless the problem is the other person, stick to the agenda for discussion. Do not make turning-against responses even if the connecting bid is provocative. For example, this kind of diverting response is not advisable:

> **Shasha:** We need to go out more. We don't do anything exciting.
>
> **Mike:** Do you have to tap your fingers on the table all the time? It drives me nuts. Maybe we'd go out more if you didn't irritate me so much.

When serious issues get detoured by irrelevant remarks about the person, not the problem, and turning-against responses are made to connecting bids, defensiveness is encouraged (Fisher & Brown, 1988). Mike's response diverts attention from the issue raised and centers the discussion on irritating mannerisms. That shifts the agenda and will likely induce a counterattack. Shasha could respond to the criticism of her finger tapping this way: "We can talk about my finger tapping another time. Let's discuss going out more often, and let's do it without insulting each other." Staying focused on the problem and being constructive can defuse defensiveness.

Address Relationship Deterioration: Beyond Sustaining

As relationships fall apart, the desire to turn things around and rebuild the connection typically is stymied by the negative atmosphere that pervades the deteriorating relationship. It is difficult to short-circuit a failing relationship and recapture the "magic" that once existed between people. It is especially difficult if infidelity is an issue. Depending on the survey, about 25% of married men and women will cheat on their spouses sometime during their life (Tafoya & Spitzberg, 2007). Consider the enormous popularity of the Ashley Madison "cheating" website (Chew, 2015). *Mate poaching*—"trying to woo an individual away from a committed relationship to begin a relationship with them instead" (Tsapelas et al., 2011, p. 543)—is even more prevalent, running at 60% for men and 53% for women (Schmitt & Buss, 2001).

Sometimes we don't recognize threats to our relationships soon enough or see that our relationships are deteriorating. It is critical that you respond quickly to the first signs of deterioration in your relationships. Waiting until you're standing at cliff's edge may be too late to save what once was an important part of your life. All of the suggestions for sustaining relationships supported by extensive research must be applied with extra vigor if you want to salvage a relationship in crisis:

1. *Resist the temptation to reciprocate negative communication.* Fighting fire with fire will make toast of your relationship. Remain unconditionally constructive. Negativity bias is especially problematic for a relationship in crisis, so avoid the negative comments.

2. *Seek opportunities to praise, compliment, and bolster your partner.* Supportive communication is critical when a relationship begins to hit the skids. "You sure have been working hard," "You look nice," and "That place couldn't run without you" are examples of the type of communication that can begin to turn around a negative communication climate.

3. *Avoid turning-away and turning-against responses to connecting bids.* You don't repair relationships by choosing communication responses that tear apart bids to connect. Find every opportunity to make turning-toward responses to bids by your partner. Make this your raison d'être, your vital concern.

4. *Bring in a neutral third party to mediate.* Sometimes you just need a neutral

individual with professional experience (e.g., counselor, psychiatrist, or mediator) to help you sort through the issues and work out your problems.

Cross-Sex Friendships: Sustaining with Complications

Cross-sex friendships are becoming more common and significant (Bleske-Rechhek et al., 2012). They also can be especially fragile and challenging to sustain (Werking, 1997). Part of the reason is that we typically make a stronger effort to sustain same-sex friendships than cross-sex friendships (Afifi et al., 1994). In addition, cross-sex friendships are complicated by ambiguity regarding romantic and sexual potential (Bleske-Rechek et al., 2012). This uncertainty can inhibit maintenance efforts (Dainton, 2003).

There are four types of cross-sex friendships, each requiring different maintenance behaviors to sustain the relationship (Guerrero & Chavez, 2005). These are *mutual romance* (you believe that both of you want the friendship to become romantic), *strictly platonic* (you believe that both of you want the relationship to remain nonsexual and nonromantic), *desires romance* (you want the relationship to become romantic, but you believe your friend does not), and *rejects romance* (you do not want the relationship to become romantic but you believe your friend does).

Behaviors aimed at sustaining cross-sex friendships are many and varied. They include being pleasant and complimentary, self-disclosing private information, sharing activities, being supportive, sharing tasks, incorporating circles of friends, flirting, engaging in humor, talking about the relationship, acting jealous, and trying to change the friend in some way (Guerrero & Chavez, 2005). The more uncertainty in the cross-sex relationship, the less that routine contact and activities, relational talk, self-disclosure, and humor are used. The avoidance of such activities and conversations attempts to maintain the relationship as it is, not as one partner may wish it to be. If one person wants romance but the other does not, for example, the person rejecting the romance may avoid frequent contact and joint activities to discourage any misunderstandings. The person hoping for romance with a partner who seems uninterested also may avoid such contact and activities for fear of rejection or to safeguard the friendship (Messman et al., 2000). Disclosing romantic feelings (expressing a desire to move from platonic to romantic) inevitably complicates a friendship if one party doesn't want romance to flower. Such complication can make cross-sex friendships seem more a burden than a benefit (Bleske-Rechek et al., 2012).

Research on sustaining cross-sex friendships is in its infancy. Clearly, most people sense that cross-sex friendships can be complicated by uncertainty and asymmetry (contradictory desires for the friendship such as one person wanting romance and the other not wanting it). If you are in the situation of wanting romance to develop but are uncertain whether your friend shares this goal, approach carefully. If you offer subtle hints of romantic interest and they are avoided or discouraged by your friend, recognize that continuing along the path of pursuing romance may result in the demise of your friendship. You have to decide whether you can keep the relationship platonic when you desire more.

Technology and Competent Interpersonal Relationships

New technologies have always produced critics. Trains and planes were seen as cacophonous disrupters of pastoral serenity. Telephones interrupted family time and opportunities for quiet contemplation. Radio and television were intrusive and promoted consumerism. Computers made the "need for speed" a fact of life and increased stress. Now it's social media that are under the microscope (Hampton et al., 2015).

Whether the effects of social media are positive or negative is a subject of lively debate. Amanda Lenhart and Maeve Duggan (2014), authors of a Pew Research Center report about the effects of technology on relationships, observe: "Technology is everywhere . . . and for younger adults and those in newer relationships, tools such as cell phones and social media were there at the beginning and play a greater role today for good and for ill."

Social Contact: Pros and Cons

Almost everyone in America uses some type of social media, whether cell phones or myriad social networking sites on the Internet (Sabatini, 2015). Socializing with others is the most popular form of Internet activity globally ("Internet Seen as Positive," 2015). This section discusses the advantages and disadvantages of social media's pervasive influence on our interpersonal relationships.

BENEFITS: EXPANDING SOCIAL NETWORKS
The technological advances provided by the Internet and cell phones offer a number of social benefits (Bargh & McKenna, 2004). Social media such as Facebook, Twitter, LinkedIn, Instagram,

Electronic communication technologies can bring us together or separate us. They can also produce a generational divide regarding appropriate uses of these technologies.

Snapchat, and texting and emailing capabilities, among others, have provided an opportunity for individuals to expand their social networks beyond anything possible in previous historical periods. An early study of Internet and social media use, however, provoked some concern about social isolation spawned by overuse of social networking and Internet sites. More time spent online may lead to less time spent with family and friends engaged in face-to-face social activities (see Kraut et al., 1998). Concern was also raised about online addiction (see Box 8-3).

Despite these initial concerns, *the great bulk of more recent research shows no such negative effects when the Internet is used in moderation* (DiSalvo, 2010; Rainie et al., 2011). A Pew Research Center study concluded: "Although some commentators have expressed fears that technology pulls families apart, this survey finds that couples use their phones to connect and coordinate their lives, especially if they have children at home. American spouses often go their separate ways during the day, but remain connected by cell phones and to some extent by Internet communications" (Kennedy et al., 2008). Another Pew research study found that Facebook users, on average, have more close relationships, receive more social support from others, and are more politically engaged than nonusers ("Social Networking Sites," 2011). Cell phones and the Internet have largely been responsible for less television watching, not less connection with others, and most social media users see the effects as positive on their relationships (Lenhart & Duggan, 2014).

Romantic relationships are also affected by the new technologies. One study found that the greater the use of voice calls by individuals in romantic relationships, "the stronger the love and commitment with their partners" (Jin & Pena, 2010). Mobile voice calls seem to allow couples to experience the feeling of continuous connection. This can be enhanced when video connections are an option (e.g., Skype). Texting, however, does not appear to have a positive effect on romantic couples. Different channels produce different results (see Chapter 1), and texting may be too restrictive or devoid of emotional complexity to function effectively in romantic contexts.

DRAWBACKS: NEGATIVE TRANSACTIONS

Although social media and communication technologies provide significant benefits, there are some drawbacks (see Box 8-3 a discussion of addiction). Young adults ages 18 to 29 are more likely than older adults to complain that their partner has been distracted by cell phone use while both partners were together, and almost a fifth of younger adults have argued with a partner about the amount of time spent online (Lenhart & Duggan, 2014). Younger adults are more immersed in the use of communication technologies than older adults, so these results are not particularly surprising.

Sexting—sending sexually suggestive text messages, or nude, or nearly nude photos and videos via a smartphone—can be a harmless activity between intimate partners, but there is also potential for serious damage if the sexting occurs between a partner and someone outside the relationship, or if the relationship terminates and the sexting is used for revenge by the jilted partner. Almost a tenth of adult cell phone users have sent a "sext" and a fifth have received one (Lenhart & Duggan, 2014), so this practice is not uncommon.

Cell phone use that does not discriminate between a public and a private conversation can also be a source of some concern. One survey by Harris Interactive for Intel found that 63% of respondents were irked by loud talking on cell phones in a restaurant or other public places (S. Johnson, 2009). Personal conversations formerly relegated to one's home, private office, or possibly an enclosed phone booth now regularly take place in crowded restaurants, buses, airport waiting areas, and even public bathrooms. "By engaging in a call, mobile phone users are capable of transforming public space into their own private space, often at the expense of others around them" (Campbell, 2008, p. 70). The Harris survey found that 55% of respondents reported they were bothered by private cell phone discussions in public places (S. Johnson, 2009). One study found that overhearing someone engaged in conversation on a cell phone is more irksome than overhearing two physically present individuals engaged in conversation. Hearing only half the conversation—or a **halfalogue**—is

BOX 8-3 FOCUS ON CONTROVERSY

Addiction to Technology

College students text message while eating (89%), during classes (85%), and while going to the bathroom (83%) (Almendrala, 2015). Almost 20% of young adults ages 18 to 34 use their smartphones during sex (Kleinman, 2013). A Pew Research Center poll reports that 24% of teens admit to going online "almost constantly" (Lenhart, 2015). A Baylor University study reports that 60% of college students admit that they may be addicted to their cell phone, spending between 8 and 10 hours daily on these mobile devices (Wood, 2014).

Whether "addiction" to electronic communication technologies is a real psychological disorder or a mere metaphor for excessive use is open to question. So how much use is too much? There is no firm answer to this question. It's debatable and controversial. If students spend 8 to 10 hours on mobile devices, are they merely surfing websites, playing video games, conducting extensive research for papers and presentations for classes, connecting with family and friends, or all of the above? How these devices are used seems relevant. If a person is sick and alone, is it Internet addiction to spend more than five hours per day communicating with online friends? Is tweeting 100 times a day addiction but talking to friends in person for 2 to 3 hours a day perfectly normal? If a person were to spend hours each day reading books, would we call that an addiction? If smartphone use is primarily focused on playing games for hours each day with family members and friends who live in distant locations, is that also an addiction, or is it a socially constructive activity?

There is no precise formula for determining if or when overuse has been reached. There are some guidelines, however. When our most important relationships suffer from too much use of electronic communication technologies, it is time to cut back. Heavy online video gaming, for example, can negatively affect marital satisfaction, especially if only one of the partners is a gamer. The effects are not necessarily negative, however, if both partners are gamers, unless it causes offline arguments (Sifferlin, 2012). When we fail to meet our responsibilities at home, at work, or at school, it is time to reduce the use. When we find ourselves losing sleep because we can't resist checking our Facebook site or our tweets, texts, or emails, it's probably time either to exercise discipline and refuse to be leashed to our electronic devices or to seek help from a counselor or therapist if such discipline is lacking.

Questions for Thought

1. Do you think Internet addiction is a serious problem? Have you ever spent excessive amounts of time on the Internet at the expense of your interpersonal relationships? Can you be addicted to cell phone use?

2. Is it likely that some Internet addicts spend large amounts of time developing interpersonal relationships online without ignoring important relationships?

3. In India and in many other cultures, close friends spend a great deal of time together most days of every week. That is how a close friendship is defined. Would you classify this as a friendship addiction?

4. Does what kind of communication and with whom you communicate matter in labeling the use of electronic communication technologies an addiction?

actually more distracting because your brain tries to figure out the unheard part of the conversation (Emberson et al., 2010). It's more difficult to tune out the cell phone conversation.

Cell phone conversations in public places such as theaters and classrooms are considered particularly intrusive and inappropriate among individualistic Americans ("You're disturbing *me*"). In collectivist countries, public cell phone use is more tolerated because keeping in contact with members of an in-group (e.g., family or work) is considered more important than preventing strangers who are not in a preferred group from becoming irritated (Campbell, 2008). Etiquette, our set of rules for appropriate public communication, has not kept up with technological change (see Box 8-4).

Finally, lonely people who access the Internet and social networking sites do not assuage their feeling of social isolation; in fact, they may exacerbate it. Psychologist Laura Freberg notes that "chronic loneliness makes people act in ways that push others away. Social networking isn't equipped to handle that and can actually make it worse" (quoted in DiSalvo, 2010, p. 52). Obsessive-compulsive individuals also may use social networking sites in predictably obsessive ways. "A consistent factor across many of the studies in this realm is that social networking is simply a new forum for bad habits" (DiSalvo, 2010, p. 55).

Online Romance: Cyberlove

Online dating has become increasingly popular (Smith & Duggan, 2013). The depth of online relationships certainly can be questioned, however, and since there is no physical proximity, you can hardly separate truth from fiction (Epstein, 2007). Pictures on profiles can be 20 years old, or they may even be photos of other, presumably better-looking people. Research shows that online daters do lie about such things as height and weight, but they also tend to be quite truthful about religion, politics, relationship history, hair, and eye color. Thus, online daters tend to be less honest about personal appearance and more honest about personality (Seidman, 2014).

Cell phone use in movie theaters and other public places is particularly annoying for those who reside in individualist cultures. Why?

Does online dating lead to finding one's "soulmate"? The evidence is mixed. One study of a representative sample of more than 19,000 respondents who married between 2005 and 2012 found that one-third of marriages in the United States began online during this period, and these marriages were slightly less likely to end in separation or divorce than were those that begin with more traditional dating approaches (Cacioppo et al., 2013). These relationships have only met the test of short-term marriages, however, so the jury is still out on whether online dating leads to more true "soulmates" for life.

Eli Finkel and his associates (2012) summarize the pros and cons of online dating from vast research. The advantages of online dating include access to numerous potential partners, the ability to communicate safely with potential partners before choosing to meet face-to-face, the option to screen undesirable prospects before an awkward or even dangerous face-to-face meeting, and the capacity to learn a great deal about someone before committing to a face-to-face meeting. Disadvantages include too many profiles to consider (requiring hours of reviews), no good way of determining whether any chemistry with a potential dating partner exists, difficulty knowing whether a profile is mostly dishonest, profiles based on matching similarities being a relatively crude basis for determining potential compatibility, and similarity profiles not necessarily being predictive of satisfying and long-lasting relationships. Their conclusion?

> Online dating is pervasive, and it has fundamentally altered both the romantic acquaintance process and the process of compatibility matching . . . Online dating offers access to potential partners whom people would be unlikely to meet through other avenues, and this access yields new romantic possibilities. On the other hand, the heavy emphasis on profile browsing at most dating sites has considerable downsides, and there is little reason to believe that current compatibility algorithms are especially effective. (p. 53)

Online dating may not provide a soulmate, but it does open a whole new mode of dating. Where it is headed, however, remains to be seen.

Conflict: Electronic Flame Throwing

Messages communicated by email, texting, or tweeting can be easily misinterpreted. Sarcasm, for instance, or teasing without the

---

BOX 8-4 DEVELOPING COMMUNICATION COMPETENCE

Cell Phone Etiquette for the Competent Communicator

Cell phone use is pervasive and potentially intrusive, making cell phone etiquette essential. Based on the communication competence model, here are some etiquette guidelines:

1. Don't answer a cell phone on a date, during a business meeting, or while conducting a face-to-face conversation unless you know that an emergency has arisen. Most people perceive such behavior as rude and insensitive. It appears that your cell phone conversation takes precedence over your face-to-face conversation. Use the phone's caller ID function to screen calls, and let voice mail handle anything that isn't clearly urgent.

2. Don't text message while conversing with another person face-to-face. Such "multitasking" is cloddish behavior. This is obvious pseudolistening (see Chapter 6).

3. Never use a cell phone (for calls or text messaging) in a restaurant, theater, or during any public performance when such use could disrupt others' enjoyment. If you absolutely must receive a call or need to text message a response in such venues, excuse yourself, and handle the call or text message in a more private location.

4. When using a cell phone in public, *do not raise your voice*. Speak in a normal manner, not a "CELL YELL." Most people do not care to listen to your personal conversations.

5. Don't conduct nonessential business or personal conversations on public transportation, in checkout lines, or in any public place where strangers are a captive audience. Recognize the difference between public and private communication.

6. Avoid using annoying rings. Switch to the vibrating feature when possible.

7. Don't use a cell phone while driving. It's likely to divert your attention from the safe operation of your vehicle. Pull off the road and take a call that seems urgent. Never engage in texting while driving.

8. Use the camera feature with discretion. Most strangers do not welcome being photographed without permission.

Which of these eight guidelines do you adhere to and which do you violate?

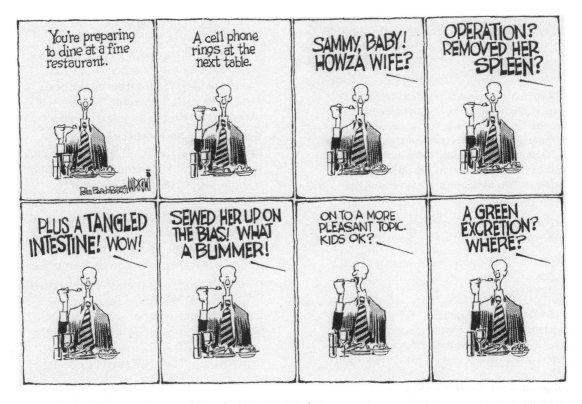

Recognize the difference between public and private conversation.

requisite tone of voice, facial expressions, and physical cues that signal how the message should be interpreted can be mistaken for serious personal attacks. As mentioned in the last chapter, **emoticons** or **emojis**—graphic notations that indicate emotional information—can help in this regard. Men, however, may resist using emoticons or emojis, especially when conducting business by email, because these are more closely associated with female communication patterns and thus may seem unprofessional. Emoticons or emojis also don't produce understanding if receivers are unfamiliar with them.

Email also reduces the natural constraints on incivility and hostility that come from facing a person directly (Thompson & Nadler, 2002; Van Kleef et al., 2004). Conflict can turn destructive more easily when mediated by technology than when conducted face-to-face (Holahan et al. 2008; Zornoza et al., 2002). **Flaming** is a cyberterm for sending an abusive, attacking message (a *flame*) electronically to others. Typical attributes of an electronic flame include profanity, use of all-capital letters, and excessive exclamation points or question marks (Turnage, 2007). A Pew research study revealed that 60% of Internet users have witnessed someone being flamed with offensive names and that 27% were the victims of such flames (May, 2014). The absence of normal constraints on incivility and hostility that come with in-person transactions (e.g., implicit rules against ugly public displays of anger) often couple with the ease and swiftness of email and blogs to the detriment of relationships (Wallace, 1999).

Flaming is competitive, defensive communication. Those given to flaming often experience *sender's regret*—they wish they hadn't sent the angry, emotionally damaging message in the heat of the moment. Once it is sent, however, the damage is done.

So what can you do if using communication technologies increases hostile conflict? Here are four suggestions:

Netiquette

The competent communicator wishes to function within the social norms of a specific community. In this regard, there are certain communication norms that specify appropriate behavior on the Internet. Susan Barnes (2001), author of Online Connections, offers several guidelines for netiquette—etiquette on the Internet:

1. Be *brief*. Lengthy messages can make email management difficult and irksome. Get to the point.

2. *Flame off*. Common courtesy is expected of all netizens. Blogs are notorious for offensive rants. Curb the incivility.

3. *Observe good form*. Grammar, spelling, rules of capitalization, and accepted spacing between words and paragraphs should be observed. It demonstrates respect for the reader. Proofread before sending the message to avoid embarrassing yourself. Beware the autocorrect function!

4. *Avoid spamming*. **Spamming** is sending unsolicited email, especially advertisements for products or activities. Spamming clutters people's email inboxes.

5. *Assume publicity*. When composing emails, assume that anything written could appear on the front page of the local newspaper. If you'd be embarrassed to see what you've written published for all to read, consider carefully whether you should write it at all. Deletion of messages does not wipe out all traces of emails.

Although exceptions can be found to each of these guidelines, most communication should follow them carefully. Which have you followed, and which have you violated?

1. *Use communication technologies selectively.* Plan for times during each day when you will have no access to any of these technologies. Shut off the computer, switch off the cell phone, and turn off the television set. Decompress your stress that can trigger flames. Try simple conversation or social activities with no technological distractions. These devices can be an electronic lasso that binds us to others—or what David Shenk (1997), author of the book *Data Smog*, calls "electronic leashes"— if we can never escape their intrusiveness.

2. *Delay sending any email message that has strong emotional content.* If you want to avoid sender's regret, delay sending any email or text message written in the heat of the moment. Flaming email messages should always be put aside overnight. Never send an angry response to someone else's flame until you have had time to cool down. If an immediate response is required, simply ask for time to reflect on what was said and on the way it was said.

3. *Do not use email to fire or to reprimand an employee, to offer negative work appraisals, or to tender resignations.* These highly personal matters should be conducted face-to-face (Zornoza et al., 2002).

4. *Exercise etiquette on the Net.* See Box 8-5 for details.

Intercultural Relationships and Communication Competence

Different cultures have different perspectives on love and intimacy. When individuals from cultures with different perspectives develop friendships or romantic relationships, difficulties inevitably arise.

Intercultural Friendships: Additional Challenges

The very definition of *friendship* varies among cultures (Martin & Nakayama, 2013). Americans have many types of friendships. Other cultures do not have casual friends and close friends. The "special emotional relationship" that exists in only some close friendships in America is a requirement for *any* designation of friendship in Germany and India, for example.

If you are accorded friendship status, there has to be that special emotional bond.

The initial stages of a developing friendship between individuals from different cultures present three problems (Martin & Nakayama, 2010). First, the differences in values, perceptions, and communication style can be troublesome. These are deep-seated, not superficial, differences (see Chapter 3). Second, anxiety is a common experience in the initial stages of any friendship, but the anxiety within intercultural friendships is likely to be even greater. We experience greater fear of making mistakes and causing offense when we are unfamiliar with the norms and rules of another culture. Third, overcoming stereotypes about a different culture and resisting the impulse to be ethnocentric can be difficult (see Chapter 3).

A study of American and Japanese students who were friends revealed some interesting ways to nurture intercultural friendships (Sudweeks et al., 1990). First, some similarities that transcend the cultural differences, whether they are sports, hobbies, lifestyle, or political attitudes, must be discovered. Bridges must be constructed from common experience. Second, making time for the relationship is critical. It takes more time to develop a friendship with a member of another culture because we are typically drawn to others who are like us, not to those who are unlike us. Third, sharing the same group of friends can be very important. A shared group of friends can lend support to an intercultural relationship. Finally, capitalizing on key turning points (e.g., requesting a favor or revealing a personal secret) is especially vital in developing cross-cultural friendships. Reluctance to respond positively to a turning point may be perceived as an insult and might end the relationship.

Ultimately, cross-cultural friendships require more "care and feeding" (Pogrebin, 1987) than do friendships between similar individuals. More explaining and understanding must take place. "Mutual respect, acceptance, tolerance for the faux pas and the occasional closed door, open discussion and patient mutual education, all this gives crossing friendships—when they work at all—a special kind of depth" (Pogrebin quoted in Gudykunst & Kim, 1992, p. 318).

Intercultural Romance: Tougher Than Friendships

Intercultural romantic relationships can be even stickier than friendships, but also highly rewarding (Ting-Toomey & Chung, 2012). Once the difficulties of developing a friendship have been overcome, additional problems can develop when romance flowers. Families may raise a stink about cross-cultural friendships, and romance may intensify this opposition (Kouri & Lasswell, 1993). Opposition from one's family isn't necessarily based on prejudice, although surely bigotry sometimes plays a part. Concerns about child-rearing styles, religious differences, politics, gender roles, power issues, place of residence, and rituals and ceremonies may also increase opposition.

Dugan Romano (1988), author of the book *Intercultural Marriage*, identifies four strategies

Intercultural relationships present extra challenges for couples. *Consensus*—learning about and adopting aspects of each other's culture—is an effective strategy for meeting intercultural relationship challenges.

that are used in these relationships. *Submission* is the most common strategy. One partner abandons his or her culture and submits to the partner's culture, adopting the religion, value system, politics, and so forth. This is rarely effective, however, because individuals find it enormously difficult to erase their core cultural values and background. A second strategy, *compromise*, means giving up only part of one's cultural beliefs, values, and habits. This is also very difficult in most situations. Asking one partner to forego Christmas decorations and celebration while the other is asked not to observe the Muslim holy month Ramadan isn't likely to be a smooth compromise. A third strategy, *obliteration*, occurs when both partners attempt to erase their respective cultures from the relationship. This is also difficult to accomplish, and it means avoiding basic support groups, such as family and friends. Finally, there is *consensus*, which seems to work best. This strategy is based on negotiation and cooperation. Learning the language, studying the religion, and learning about the cuisine erect bridges between partners. Consensus is built by emphasizing similarities and commonalities in relationships and by de-emphasizing differences (Cools, 2011). Consensus is difficult even among culturally similar individuals, however, and it is doubly difficult between culturally dissimilar individuals who plan to marry.

 ## Summary

Developing relationships with others is a human imperative. Nature inclines us toward such connections. We form relationships because we have a need to belong, because we are attracted interpersonally to those who are physically attractive and similar to us, and because relationships with others can provide benefits that outweigh costs.

Relationships are more challenging than ever. Every relationship travels through specific stages. Recognizing what communication behaviors work best at each stage is important to the development of intimate romantic relationships and close friendships. Keeping a relationship from moving into the coming-apart stages is a principal concern. We sustain relationships in a variety of ways; the most important are by understanding the value of connecting bids and our responses to them, avoiding defensive communication patterns, and encouraging supportive communication.

Advances in technology influence our relationships with others in powerful ways. Technology can help sustain relationships, or it can become an electronic leash that adds stress to our lives and threatens the health of our relationships. Intercultural relationships are probably the most challenging of all. Individuals from collectivist cultures have a We-emphasis, but persons from individualist cultures have a Me-emphasis. This fundamental distinction in cultural values can put a strain on an intercultural relationship.

Answers for Critical Thinking captions:

AFRICAN AMERICAN COUPLE PHOTO (P. 201): #1

URGE TO JUGGLE MACHETES (P. 212): #2, #3 & #4

Quizzes Without Consequences

Test your knowledge before your exam! Go to the companion website at www.oup.com/us/rothwell, click on the Student Resources for each chapter, and take the Quizzes Without Consequences.

Film School Case Studies

The Break-Up (2006). Romantic Comedy (sort of); PG-13

Vince Vaughn and Jennifer Aniston play a couple struggling to make their relationship work. (Actually the Aniston character struggles, and the Vaughn character mostly acts clueless and belligerent.) Examine the coming-apart stages of this relationship. Look for connecting bids and responses to those bids. Examine defensive and supportive communication patterns.

Fifty First Dates (2004). Romantic Comedy; PG-13

Adam Sandler woos Drew Barrymore, who suffers from short-term memory loss. Analyze this repetitive courtship from a stages-of-relationship-development perspective.

(500) Days of Summer (2009). Romantic Comedy; PG-13

Offbeat story about a young woman (Zooey Deschanel), who doesn't believe in true love and a young man (Joseph Gordon-Levitt) who falls hard for her. Examine the coming-together and coming-apart stages of their relationship.

Knocked Up (2007). Romantic Comedy; R

Highly popular, if unrealistic, pairing of Seth Rogen and Katherine Heigl, who play characters that meet at a bar, get drunk, and have sex (really?) that gets the Heigl character pregnant. Apply the similarity attraction theory to this film.

Martian Child (2007). Drama; PG

John Cusack plays a widower who decides to adopt a troubled little boy who thinks he's a Martian. Examine defensive and supportive communication patterns in Cusack's relationship with his new son in this very tender, sweet story.

My First Mister (2001). Comedy/Drama; R

An unusual relationship develops between a 49-year-old man (Albert Brooks) and a 17-year-old girl (Leelee Sobieski). Analyze their relationship using the triangular theory of love.

Notting Hill (1999). Romantic Comedy; PG-13

The charming and extraordinarily entertaining story of a London bookstore owner (High Grant) whose chance encounter with an internationally acclaimed American actress (Julia Roberts) begins an on-again, off-again romance. Analyze the complex, fitful development of their relationship in terms of the stages of relationships. Do the several reversals of direction in their relationship characters coincide with the stages-of-relationships material presented in this chapter? Are there any turning points? Explain.

Second Skin (2008). Documentary; Not Rated

This documentary follows three sets of online gamers, exploring ways that social media influence interpersonal connections. What are the pros and cons depicted in this film of mediated relationships and life in cyberspace?

1. Define conflict in both its constructive and destructive forms.

2. Explain the inevitable contradictions in relationships that provoke conflict.

3. Understand the five principal communication styles available for managing conflict.

Interpersonal Conflict Management

CONFLICT IS AN UNAVOIDABLE FACT OF LIFE, and in college, conflicts are especially pervasive and significant (Erb et al., 2014). A national survey of 31,500 college students reported that 50% of women and 44% of men had "frequent" or "occasional" conflicts with roommates or housemates (Liu et al., 2008). Another study revealed that roommate conflicts hindered academic performance more than use of alcohol (American College Health Association, 2012).

Because most incoming first-year students have never shared a room with a stranger, the potential for conflict as new roommates adjust to each other is high (Yadegaran, 2013). How roommates handle conflict in the world of social media has become increasingly problematic. Students often "lack the will, and skill, to address ordinary conflicts," as Moore (2010) reports. For example, roommates fuming about some small transgression will text each other while present together in their dorm room instead of discussing the matter

4. Manage conflict competently through appropriate communication styles of conflict management, anger management, forgiveness, and intercultural understanding.

openly. Complaints about roommates get posted on Facebook ("My roommate is so irritating"). In some cases, a parent will call and yell at the offending person, avoiding a face-to-face confrontation between roommates but escalating the conflict ("You had your mommy call me? This is college, not kindergarten"). As Norbert Dunkel, the director of housing and residence education at the University of Florida, notes: "Roommate conflicts have intensified. The students don't have the person-to-person discussions and they don't know how to handle them" (quoted by Moore, 2010).

Conflict is a pervasive human experience that extends far beyond roommate disagreements. Families, for example, experience conflict, often exhibited as **serial arguments**—clashes that reoccur and never get resolved. Such repetitive conflicts can be stressful and can adversely affect relational quality and physical and psychological well-being of all involved (Johnson et al., 2014).

Most married couples experience conflict ("Gottman Couples and Marital Therapy," 2015).

Even in the often blissful first year of marriage, about three-quarters of couples admit to experiencing conflict in their relationship (Birditt et al., 2010). *The problem is not that couples have conflict; the problem lies in how couples address conflict when it arises.*

In the workplace, conflict is also a frequent occurrence. In a study of 5,000 full-time employees in nine countries, 85% of respondents reported having to deal with conflict in the workplace, and 29% (36% in the United States) revealed having to address conflict "always" or "frequently." U.S. employees, on average, spend almost 3 hours per week addressing conflict, costing approximately $360 billion in lost productivity and 385 million aggregate workdays spent on conflict management on the job (Hayes, 2008).

Interpersonal conflict is an inevitable part of human transactions. *The main purpose of this chapter is to discuss ways to manage interpersonal conflict in a competent manner.*

Definition of Conflict

In this section, conflict is defined generally. Then differences between destructive conflict and constructive conflict are explained.

General Definition: Essential Elements

Janice Lightner is a student in Professor Winthrop's intensive, six-week Human Communication summer course that meets four times per week. Professor Winthrop has a strict policy on attendance. Four absences result in an automatic "F" for the course. Janice has earned an "A" on all tests and assignments through the fourth week of the class, and she has perfect attendance. The sudden death of her grandfather, however, requires Janice to fly from Eugene, Oregon, to Toronto, Canada, to attend his funeral. She must be absent from class for an entire week. She asks Professor Winthrop for an exemption from the attendance policy, revealing the news of her grandfather's sudden death. She promises to make up the work and miss no other classes. Professor Winthrop expresses regret but tells Janice that she will not pass the course if she misses a week of class. Janice becomes upset and tells Professor Winthrop that the attendance policy is unreasonable and unfair. "What do you expect me to do, miss his funeral?" Professor Winthrop defends the policy as essential for students to learn difficult class material. Professor Winthrop and Janice part feeling angry.

Conflict is the expressed struggle of interconnected parties who perceive incompatible goals and interference from one or more parties in attaining those goals (Wilmot & Hocker,

2014). Janice's situation with Professor Winthrop illustrates each element of this definition.

First, conflict is an *expressed struggle* between two or more parties. If Janice had accepted the attendance policy without confronting Professor Winthrop about it, no conflict would have existed. Even if Janice had been angry about the policy, she would have had to indicate her unhappiness to Professor Winthrop in some fashion for a conflict to exist. The expression of the struggle could be obvious, such as Janice talking directly to Professor Winthrop. The expression could also be very subtle, even exclusively nonverbal, such as cold stares or slouching posture by Janice during class.

Second, conflict involves *interconnected parties.* The behavior of one party must have consequences for the other. Professor Winthrop and Janice are interconnected. Janice faces a dilemma because of Professor Winthrop's attendance policy. Professor Winthrop affects the choice Janice must make. Does she miss her grandfather's funeral so that she can pass the class, or does she attend her grandfather's funeral and flunk? Janice affects Professor Winthrop because she is a disgruntled student challenging the Professor's attendance policy. Professor Winthrop may wonder whether the policy is too harsh or unfair.

Third, *perceived incompatible goals* must be present for conflict to occur. The goals of Professor Winthrop and Janice seem incompatible. Professor Winthrop's goal is to have students attend class regularly so they can learn difficult material. Janice's goal is to attend the funeral without failing the class. Professor Winthrop's attendance policy and Janice's desire to attend her grandfather's funeral clash directly.

Finally, *perceived interference from parties* who pursue incompatible goals is necessary for conflict to occur. For two people to have a conflict, either one or both must actually interfere with the other's goal attainment or be perceived as interfering. Professor Winthrop is clearly interfering with Janice's goal to attend her grandfather's funeral without affecting her class grade. If Janice attends the funeral, she thwarts Professor Winthrop's goal because Janice will fall seriously behind in the class.

Types of Conflict: It's Not All Bad

To most people, conflict always seems destructive. Couples who do not fight, however, are more likely to divorce than couples who do ("Gottman Couples and Marital Therapy," 2015), so the absence of conflict is not the desirable goal even though conflict can be disruptive. Conflict can make us angry, fearful, and frustrated, and it can trigger verbal, and even physical, aggression. Nevertheless, there are two general types of conflict: destructive and constructive (see Figure 9-1) (Holahan et al., 2008). *Our communication determines the difference.*

DESTRUCTIVE CONFLICT: TAKING NO PRISONERS

Destructive conflict is characterized by escalation, retaliation, domination, competition, defensiveness, and inflexibility (Lulofs, 1994; Wilmot & Hocker, 2014). Typical communication tactics employed during destructive conflict include threats, intimidation, condescension, dishonesty, and personal assaults (verbal or physical). In the nine-country study of workplace conflict mentioned earlier, 89% of respondents reported experiencing a disagreement that escalated in duration and intensity into destructive conflict while on the job (Hayes, 2008).

A conflict between two coworkers at the Fresh Vegetable Package Company in Denver, Colorado, illustrates the sometimes ludicrous nature of destructive conflict. The victim accused her assailant of throwing fruit at her because she "laughed at her." The conflict escalated to vegetables, at which point the assailant "for no reason" hurled a four-inch-diameter carrot at the victim. The victim, who was five months pregnant, complained about stomach pains and was rushed to Denver General Hospital. A detective investigating the altercation reported, "All she [the victim] wants is that the suspect leave her alone. I'm going to call up and talk to the supervisor and have the assailant moved from the dangerous weapon section—back from vegetables to fruit." (quoted in Isenhart & Spangle, 2000, p.3). No charges were filed against the assailant, presumably because it would have been difficult to prosecute

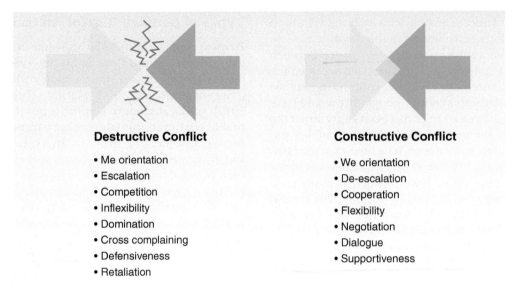

Destructive Conflict

- Me orientation
- Escalation
- Competition
- Inflexibility
- Domination
- Cross complaining
- Defensiveness
- Retaliation

Constructive Conflict

- We orientation
- De-escalation
- Cooperation
- Flexibility
- Negotiation
- Dialogue
- Supportiveness

FIGURE 9-1. Destructive Versus Constructive Conflict.

the attacker for "assault with a deadly vegetable" (Isenhart & Spangle, 2000).

Donohue and Kolt (1992) argue that the key to recognition of destructive conflict is the ability to say to oneself, in the middle of a conflict, "Gee, I'm getting stupid" (p. 24). When you begin to lose sight of why you're battling with someone and you become petty, even infantile, in your tactics to win a conflict (e.g., throwing vegetables), you're getting stupid. When hurting your adversary becomes your principal goal, not problem solving, you're getting stupid. When divorced parents, for example, express contempt for each other in front of their children, insist children choose sides in a conflict, use children as leverage in a power struggle, or ridicule their ex-spouse's new partner, they are engaged in destructive conflict.

When you can no longer think clearly because conflict triggers emotional reactions that clog the brain's ability to reason, you are moving into destructive conflict territory. John Gottman calls this **flooding**, which he operationally defines this way: "The body of someone who feels flooded is a confused jumble of signals. It may be hard to breathe. People who are flooded inadvertently hold their breath. Muscles tense up and stay tensed. The heart beats faster and it may seem to beat harder" (Gottman & Silver, 1994, p. 112). *Men are far more likely than women to experience flooding.* According to Gottman, "the male cardiovascular system remains more reactive than the female and slower to recover from stress" (Gottman & Silver, 1999, p. 37).

CONSTRUCTIVE CONFLICT: WORKING IT OUT

Despite its negative potential, conflict can be constructive (Dovidio et al., 2009). Conflict can signal that change needs to occur for a relationship to remain vital. Women, far more than men, may use conflict to provoke attention to a relationship problem and trigger discussion of a possible solution (Haefner et al., 1991). Conflict can also encourage creative problem solving in the workplace by raising tension, which may encourage an energetic search for innovative answers. As the previously referenced nine-country study of workplace conflict reported, 76% of employees (81% in the United States) experienced conflict that led to a positive outcome (Hayes, 2008).

Constructive conflict is characterized by communication that is cooperative, supportive, and flexible (Lulofs, 1994; Wilmot & Hocker, 2014). The focus is on achieving a solution that is mutually satisfactory to all parties. Participants work together flexibly to deal effectively with their conflicts by de-escalating them.

Remaining unconditionally constructive during a conflict can be a huge challenge, but responding to abuse with abuse merely angers both parties and produces destructive conflict. Flooding fogs the brain during shouting matches.

Partners in happy marriages, for example, approach each other in gentle, positive ways when conflict arises. They listen respectfully, and they work to find solutions that benefit both partners (Gottman & Gottman, 2006). Reducing the severity of conflict episodes by learning conflict-management techniques is a key to constructive conflict.

Constructive conflict doesn't mean you have to feel all warm and fuzzy as you work out your differences with others. *Constructive conflict can be contentious, frustrating, and difficult*. It is constructive, however, because supportive communication patterns are employed; participants are assertive, not aggressive or passive; and there is an overriding commitment to cooperating, not competing. Thus, certain communication styles of conflict management are emphasized, a subject discussed later in this chapter.

Relationship Dialectics

Relationships are often messy. As we move through the phases of relationships (see

Chapter 8) and become increasingly intimate, relationships will rarely follow the profile for textbook-perfect communication. Many romantic partners talk to each other, on average, for a mere hour a day, rarely self-disclose, are more concerned with task accomplishment than with sharing intimacies, are less polite to each other than they are to strangers, often fight, and even become violent verbally and sometimes physically (Baxter & Montgomery, 1996). We typically don't measure up to the ideal because romantic partnerships, close friendships, family relationships, and even work relationships face difficult contradictions every day. These contradictions are called *dialectics*, the focus of this section.

Interpersonal **dialectics** are the tensions arising from contradictory needs that simultaneously push and pull us in opposite directions in our relationships with others (see Figure 9-2). *Interpersonal dialectics can be a fundamental source of relationship conflict and meltdown when they are not managed competently* (Erbert, 2000). Conflicts can arise when relationships are asymmetrical—when individuals do not share the same needs equally.

Dialectics Within Relationships: Pushing Us/Pulling Us

Dialectics are an intrinsic part of romantic partner-partner, friend-friend, parent-child, roommate-to-roommate, and boss-employee relationships. Individuals have many motives, goals, and needs, and in relationships, these often unavoidably clash. *Dialectics never disappear from these relationships* (Baxter & Montgomery, 1996; West & Turner, 2007). They are managed, not eradicated. Three common dialectics (there are others) that occur within these interpersonal relationships are *connection-autonomy*, *predictability-novelty*, and *openness-closedness* (Baxter, 2011; Baxter & Erbert, 1999; Baxter & Montgomery, 1996).

CONNECTION-AUTONOMY: HUG ME/LEAVE ME ALONE

The desire to come together with another person (connection) yet remain independent and in control of one's own life (autonomy) is called the **connection-autonomy dialectic**. We want to be an "us" without losing the "me." Adult children, for example, want to be connected to their parents in a loving relationship, but they usually rebel when parents interfere in their lives too much or make them feel as though they are still children to be supervised. An inherent tug-of-war exists between parents and nonadult children as well. There appears to be "a universal need for autonomy whose fulfillment may be undermined by controlling environments" (Pomerantz & Wang, 2009, p. 288).

Conversely, excessive emphasis on connection usually leads to feeling smothered by partners, parents, or personal friends, to feeling entrapped and to having no independent life. Excessive emphasis on autonomy, however, leads to complaints of insufficient time spent together, lack of commitment, and loss of affection (Baxter, 1994). Too much emphasis on either connection or autonomy can push a relationship into one of the phases of coming apart.

PREDICTABILITY-NOVELTY: BE STABLE/BE SPONTANEOUS

Relationships require a fair degree of stability and constancy to survive—that is, some predictability. Dating relationships can be quite unpredictable in their early stages. Do both individuals define the relationship similarly? Is one person at the experimenting, "auditioning" stage but the other already at the integrating, "beyond just friends" stage? Such unpredictable dating relationships can lead to tension and conflict.

Predictability can be comforting because you know what to expect. Excessive predictability, however, can induce boredom, possibly leading to the stagnating phase of an intimate, long-term relationship. As relationships become increasingly predictable, a desire for novelty, for excitement and unpredictability, easily surfaces (Tsapelas et al., 2009). Thus, you are faced with the **predictability-novelty dialectic**—a desire for both stability and change in interpersonal relationships.

If one partner has a stronger need for predictability and the other partner has a stronger need for novelty, conflict easily looms. This asymmetry also can emerge between roommates. A roommate can be too novel by never letting you know what strange person or bizarre event awaits. Sometimes you'd just like peace and quiet, not a wild party with strangers galore, and so a conflict develops.

The early phases of relationships—initiating, experimenting, intensifying—are inherently novel. Everything seems new and different, and that can be exciting. Interacting with a new college roommate can be an interesting and challenging enterprise. Dating someone for the first time can be exciting because both individuals are exploring and discovering. At some point, however, dating partners may wish to settle into a long-lasting partnership to provide some predictability because of the comfort and stability it produces.

The push and pull of predictability and novelty needs that clash is particularly challenging for long-distance relationships (Sahlstein, 2006). Almost 4 million married people in the United States are living apart for reasons other than marital discord, and almost 4.5 million college students who are unmarried are trying long-distance relationships (Migdol, 2015). There is built-in unpredictability in relationships in which infrequent face-to-face interactions can occur ("When can I see you again?"). Even making plans that appear to provide predictability may be disrupted more often in long-distance relationships than in more proximate relationships. The complexity involved in planning when two people are not physically present, and the distance that acts as a barrier to smooth organization, can be daunting.

OPENNESS-CLOSEDNESS: TELL ME MORE/ TELL ME LESS

U. S. culture encourages openness and discourages closedness (Klapp, 1978). We view an open mind and an open society with admiration. We usually view a closed mind and a closed society with disdain. Open expression of feelings and self-disclosure are necessary for bonding and intimacy to occur in a relationship. Some privacy, however, is also necessary if a relationship is to survive. Sharing every thought that enters your head, aside from being annoying, can provoke embarrassment, hurt, or conflict. This tension between accessibility and privacy is called the **openness-closedness dialectic**.

Openness versus closedness is an important dilemma that every relationship faces, especially romantic partnerships (Baxter, 2011; Baxter & Erbert, 1999). How much self-disclosure and openness is enough, and how much is too much (see Box 9-1)? Self-disclosure is essential for interpersonal intimacy (Chen & Nakazawa, 2009), but indiscriminate self-disclosure strains most relationships and is incompetent communication (see Chapter 2). Openness is a matter of appropriateness of context. Excessive closedness, however, makes you a silent partner. Friendship and intimacy don't flourish when you share little with another person about who you are.

The three relational dialectics—connection-autonomy, predictability-novelty, and openness-closedness—typically emerge as more intense and challenging at different phases of a personal relationship (Baxter, 1990). During the initial phases of a developing relationship, openness-closedness is of paramount concern. How much should you self-disclose to your friend or romantic partner? Is your self-disclosure reciprocated? As a relationship becomes more established, however, connection-autonomy often predominates. Are you losing your identity and independence? Are you becoming distant from

Life in the same routine can make a relationship overly predictable and boring, creating friction and a need for greater novelty to prevent potential relationship conflict ("We never do anything fun"). Relationships need some excitement.

each other, burdened by the daily concerns of work and earning a living? Are you both still strongly committed to the relationship? Finally, as a relationship settles in for the long term, predictability-novelty often becomes a primary concern. Has the relationship become tediously predictable and boring? One study showed that significant boredom in year 7 of a marriage predicts significant dissatisfaction with the relationship in year 16 (Tsapelas et al., 2009).

Dialectics With Outsiders: Us and Them

Dialectics occur not only within relationships but also with outsiders. Anyone who is not

BOX 9-1 FOCUS ON CONTROVERSY

Ethical Conundrum: Is Honesty Always The Best Policy?

You are gay, and will be celebrating Christmas with your parents and siblings. You want to bring your partner to the festivities. Your father, however, is intensely homophobic. Do you pretend that your partner is just a friend, or do you reveal the true nature of your relationship (revelation-concealment)?

Your spouse asks whether you've ever had an affair. You have, but it ended two years ago. There is little chance that the affair would ever be discovered unless you confess. Your spouse would be devastated to know that you had cheated, even though you have no intention of ever being unfaithful again. It was a "horrible mistake," a moment of "temporary insanity" fueled by mass quantities of alcohol. Would you be honest with your spouse (openness-closedness)?

Your close friend at work has a body-image concern. Your friend is very overweight and poorly groomed. When asked what you think of your friend's appearance ("Am I fat and unattractive?"), would you tell the truth (openness-closedness),

or would you make an excuse, then run like a cheetah?

You feel smothered by your partner. You have little time alone. When you plan outings with friends, your partner wants to come along. Do you tell your partner that you need time alone or with friends, knowing that your partner will feel excluded (connection-autonomy)?

Dialectical forces pose a challenge to the oft-stated claim that honesty is always the best policy in relationships. The issue of lying brings into focus a principal dilemma we all face in relationships. Honesty is an important ethical guideline and the cornerstone of trust, but relationship dialectics complicate the glib, chirpy advice to "just be honest."

Complete honesty can sound very good in the abstract, but total honesty has the potential to destroy relationships. Most people recognize that lying in some circumstances is justified (Gamer, 2009; Knapp, 2006). As psychologist Bella DePaulo explains, "[I]t would be a disaster if everyone tried to

DILBERT   BY SCOTT ADAMS

SO, TELL ME A LITTLE ABOUT YOURSELF, AND BE TOTALLY HONEST.

TOTALLY HONEST? OKAY. . .

I LIKE TECHNOLOGY MORE THAN I LIKE PEOPLE.

I DON'T BELIEVE IN FREE WILL, SOUL-MATES, OR FOLLOWING MY PASSION.

I THINK LIFE IS A BRIEF, MEANINGLESS EVENT IN A RANDOM UNIVERSE THAT DOESN'T CARE.

I ONLY ASSOCIATE WITH OTHER PEOPLE BECAUSE I HAVE BIOLOGICAL AND ECONOMICAL NEEDS.

I THINK ALL HUMAN ACTIONS ARE DRIVEN BY SELFISHNESS.

UM. . . OKAY. DO YOU HAVE ANY QUESTIONS FOR ME?

AM I STILL BEING TOTALLY HONEST OR SHOULD I ACT CURIOUS?

(continued)

(continued)

tell the truth all the time. If you tell the whole truth, you start alienating people. You'd have to go back and apologize because you've made a mess of your interpersonal relationships" (quoted in Chen, 1996).

In the four scenarios presented earlier, would you lie, tell the truth, or equivocate? **Equivocation** occurs when our language permits more than one plausible meaning. For example, when asked "Do you think I look fat in this outfit?" you might respond, "You look fine in whatever you wear." The questioner can interpret this answer as a compliment, damning with faint praise, or avoidance. Perhaps the subtext of the question was a desire for support and affirmation that you still find your partner attractive, not a literal desire by your partner to be told the unequivocal truth. Equivocation can also allow others to draw their own conclusions without you having to be pinned down. For example, an ambiguous job reference for an incompetent worker might be "You will be lucky to get this person to work for you." One for an applicant with no talent could be "I recommend this candidate with no qualifications" (cited in Adler & Proctor, 2007, p. 321).

So when is it appropriate to tell the truth, and when is lying acceptable?

1. *Honesty should be the norm, and lying should be the exception.* Communication with others would be chaotic if we could never trust what others say to us. Relationships must have a foundation of honesty even if an occasional lie for selfless reasons seems warranted.

2. *Try to determine what the questioner is seeking.* This requires sensitivity—picking up signals from the person. If the person is clearly seeking support and encouragement, not absolute honesty, then a small lie may be appropriate.

3. *Weigh the likely consequences of an honest response versus a lie.* Lying to a friend or spouse about his or her weight may encourage the person to continue an unhealthy lifestyle. An honest response may sting initially, but it may also motivate change.

Bok (1978) summarizes the issue this way: "To say that white lies should be kept at a minimum is not to endorse the telling of truths to all comers. Silence and discretion, respect for the privacy and for the feelings of others must naturally govern what is spoken" (p. 76). *Honesty isn't always the best policy, but it usually is.*

Questions for Thought

1. How would you have answered the questions posed in the situations described at the beginning of this box? Explain your answers.

2. Do you agree that honesty is usually the best policy? Why or why not?

3. What would occur in your own relationships if dishonesty were the norm?

directly involved in a specific relationship is considered an outsider. In a parent-child relationship, for instance, everyone who is neither the parent nor the child is an outsider. In a marriage, anyone not in the marriage is an outsider, even a parent of either spouse. Three common dialectics with outsiders are inclusion-seclusion, conventionality-uniqueness, and revelation-concealment (Baxter, 2011; Baxter & Montgomery, 1996).

INCLUSION-SECLUSION:
BE TOGETHER/BE ALONE

In a relationship with another person, you may be pulled in two directions when outsiders enter the picture. You may want you and your partner to spend time with outsiders (inclusion), yet you may also want time alone together to nurture your relationship (seclusion). This is called the **inclusion-seclusion dialectic**. Including a larger network of friends and

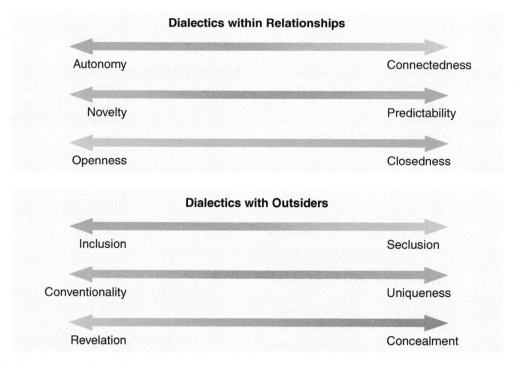

FIGURE 9-2. Relationship Dialectics.

family can provide emotional support and encouragement that bolster the relationship. Too much involvement of outsiders, however, can provide few moments for relationship partners to connect. Thus, you may be torn between larger "family responsibilities," such as spending holidays together, and a desire to be alone with your partner without stress from outsiders. Serial arguments are often a product of this tension.

CONVENTIONALITY-UNIQUENESS:
CONFORM/DON'T CONFORM

When we have relationships with others, we usually want to "fit in" and conform to certain family and societal expectations. Such conventionality just makes life less difficult generally. We're not bumping against how others believe we should act. Yet by conforming to familial and societal expectations, our relationships may begin to look like everyone else's. Considering the high divorce and breakup rates for most relationships, this can be unsettling. If your relationship is "unique," perhaps you have a better chance of sustaining it over the long haul. When we are torn between wanting our

relationships to be the same yet different, we are experiencing the **conventionality-uniqueness dialectic**.

Consider marriage, for example. The conventional institution of marriage has not lost its appeal, although the median age of first marriages has increased to 27 for women and 29 for men (Wang, 2014). Very few adults will live out their entire lives never having been married. More than half of divorced or widowed adults remarry (Livingston, 2014). Among LGBT Americans, 93% favor same-sex marriage ("A Survey of LGBT Americans," 2013), an option legitimized nationally by the Supreme Court on June 26, 2015. At the same time, couples typically want outsiders to view their relationship as unique. Talk of a "soulmate" expresses a desire to have a special relationship with an "irreplaceable" person.

REVELATION-CONCEALMENT:
GO PUBLIC/BE PRIVATE

Both romantic relationships and friendships face the following dilemma: how much do we reveal to outsiders about the relationship, and how much do we keep private? This is the

revelation-concealment dialectic. Revealing too much breaks the confidentiality that intimacy requires, but revealing too little denies the couple an important source of support and legitimation from outsiders. This support and legitimation, however, may not always be there, as interracial couples still experience today (Brummett & Steuber, 2015).

Revelation and concealment is a key dilemma present in office romances. A survey by Vault.com, a career information website, found that 51% of respondents admitted having had an office romance at some time ("Finding Love," 2015). Almost a quarter of office romances end in marriage (Fisher, 2007). Despite their frequency, however, and contrary to most couples' desire to announce their romance to friends and coworkers, office romances are often concealed. Couples fear coworkers' strong disapproval, or they fear being fired. Although attitudes toward workplace romances have softened recently, research still indicates that romantic relationships at work, especially between superiors and subordinates, are viewed negatively (Cowan & Horan, 2014).

The boundaries between what is considered public communication or private communication have blurred considerably with the explosive rise of social media and electronic communication in the workplace (McDonald &

CRITICAL THINKING

The gay marriage conflict for gay couples involved which of the following dialectics?

○ **1.** Revelation-concealment   ○ **3.** Conventionality-uniqueness

○ **2.** Inclusion-seclusion   ○ **4.** Novelty-predictability

Answers at end of chapter.

Thompson, 2015), also raising issues of revelation and concealment. Does an employee have the right to conduct a workplace relationship using technologies provided by the employer to conduct work-related tasks? Does the employer have the right to snoop into email and other media files to determine nonwork communication conducted during work hours?

In the LGBT community, about three-quarters of gay men and lesbians report that most or all of the important people in their lives know about their sexual orientation, but only 28% of bisexuals report the same. Bisexual women are three times as likely as bisexual men to reveal their sexual orientation ("A Survey of LGBT Americans," 2013).

Battered women also are faced with issues of revelation and concealment. Most abused women wrestle with the impulse to conceal their abuse because they fear triggering further violence from a partner angry that others know what occurs. They also want to avoid public embarrassment and perceived shame from the revelation that abuse occurs. Public revelation, however, can be a first step in escaping an abusive relationship (Dieckmann, 2000).

Addressing Dialectics: Not a Balancing Act

It may be tempting to assume that the most effective means of addressing dialectics in relationships is to achieve a balance between the contradictory needs that produce tension and conflict. *There is no balancing of these contradictory impulses, however, because they are always in flux* (Littlejohn & Foss, 2011). This is so because change is the inevitable constant in all relationships. What was important to us yesterday may be relatively unimportant today. Our moods and circumstances change, so we must constantly adapt to the seesaw of competing tensions. There is no ultimate resolution, no single balancing point to maintain, because when that imagined "ideal balance" allegedly occurs, it soon changes and we must adjust.

AMALGAMATING: ADDRESSING BOTH NEEDS

Relationships need openness *and* closedness, connection *and* autonomy, predictability *and* novelty. Addressing both impulses is usually preferable to addressing one need at the expense of the other (Baxter & Montgomery, 1996). Called **amalgamating**, this can be a highly effective approach (Miller, 2005). Relationships can provide an abundance of novelty (exciting new events) *and* plenty of predictability. Both needs can be satiated without compromising or diluting either contradictory need. Taking frequent vacations to locations never visited before or carefully planning a variety of exciting, new events amalgamates the novelty of new experiences and the predictability of careful planning. Novelty can thwart relationship boredom (Tsapelas et al., 2009), but as most people recognize, it is also enjoyable to return to the fond predictability of home and hearth, relaxing with your partner.

SELECTING: CHOOSING ONE NEED ONLY

Giving attention to one contradictory impulse while ignoring the other is called **selecting** (Wood, 2004). It is a weak method because attention to only one of the two contradictory forces inevitably creates a stronger impulse from the other direction (Baxter, 1990). Spending "quality time" together on a rare, pleasurable vacation, for example, may not satisfy the partners' need to connect on a more regular basis. The residual "glow" from a wonderful vacation may not sustain a relationship for 11 months until the next booster shot of connection is administered.

SEGMENTING: CATEGORIZING

When partners divide certain parts of their relationship into domains, or categories, they are **segmenting** (West & Turner, 2007). In dealing with the clashing needs of openness and closedness, for instance, partners may designate certain subjects as "off-limits" to avoid serial arguments. They also may express closeness at home but more distance at work or in public. Previous boyfriends or girlfriends may be segmented as a taboo topic. How each partner spends money from a personal bank account may also be categorized as off-limits. Couples might set aside certain holidays to visit parents and relatives (inclusion) but keep certain special occasions, such as birthdays or New Year's, just for themselves (seclusion). Couples might

also agree that career and work-related matters fall under the category of autonomy (each person decides independently) but that relationship issues and social situations fall under the connected category. Segmenting is usually an effective means of managing relational dialectics (Baxter & Montgomery, 1996).

Communication Styles of Conflict Management

Despite conventional wisdom, research indicates that marital happiness has less to do with whom you marry and more to do with how you both manage conflict (Notarius & Markman, 1993). A **communication style of conflict management** is a typical way a person addresses conflict (DeChurch et al., 2007). There are five communication styles: collaborating, accommodating, compromising, avoiding, and competing (Blake & Mouton, 1964; Kilmann & Thomas, 1977).

Collaborating: Looking for Win-Win Solutions

When we work together to maximize the attainment of goals for all parties in a conflict, we are *collaborating*. The **collaborating style** is a cooperative form of conflict management and is often referred to as a *win-win style*. The collaborating style has three key components: *confrontation, integration,* and *smoothing.*

Confrontation is the overt recognition of conflict and the direct effort to manage disagreements effectively. Although mass media often use the term *confrontation* in a negative sense (e.g., "There was a violent confrontation between police and protesters"), this is not the meaning that applies here. Confrontation should utilize all the elements of supportive communication already discussed in Chapter 8 (describe, problem solve, empathize, be assertive, treat others as equals, and qualify your statements). In fact, the initial effort to address a conflict is usually crucial to the subsequent pattern of the entire conversation. *Gottman (1994a) found that in only 4% of the instances he examined did couples reverse a negative beginning to* *a conflict conversation (attack, demand, criticism, or contempt).* Further research revealed that the outcome of a 15-minute conversation could be predicted within the first 3 minutes with 96% accuracy (Gottman & Gottman, 2006). It's probably all downhill after an opening such as "Is it laziness or just plain stupidity that makes you so insensitive?"

Although confrontation is a critical element of collaboration, sometimes disagreements are too trivial to confront, and incessant confrontation can become annoying and counterproductive. "Can't you just let some things slide?" will be the likely response to excessive use of confrontation.

Someone once quipped that the most terrifying statement in the English language for men is "Let's talk about our relationship." *In more than 80% of the instances of confrontation, women raise the issue, not men* (Gottman & Silver, 1999). This gender difference undoubtedly arises from men's greater difficulty handling conflict and women's greater difficulty tolerating emotional distance in a relationship (Notarius & Markman, 1993). This gender difference in itself is not necessarily a sign of a troubled relationship, however, because how men respond to the confrontation, not who initiates it, is a more important concern.

Integration is a collaborative strategy that meets the goals of all parties in the conflict. Two integrative tactics are expanding the pie and bridging (Pruitt & Rubin, 1986). *Expanding the pie* refers to finding creative ways to increase resources, typically money. Scarce resources often cause conflict (power struggles). As researcher Michael Sion (2011) notes, money isn't what couples fight about most, but intense conflict over finances is a leading source of turning "'Til death do us part" into "'Til debt do us part" (p. A11). If you can garner scholarships or grants to pay for your college education, it would reduce stress on your relationship if a conflict existed about increasing debt.

Bridging considers the goals of all parties in the conflict and offers a new option that satisfies the interests of everyone involved. For example, consider partners who want to take a vacation together, but one wants the full resort experience (goal: comfort) and the other wants to camp and commune with nature (goal: get away from stressful urban life and a demanding job). Initially, this may appear to be mutually exclusive. Taking their vacation at a resort with nearby camping facilities, however, may bridge the supposed gap in partners' vacation goals. The couple could then share certain mutually interesting activities, such as hiking, fishing, swimming in the pool, taking a sauna, and eating at the resort restaurant, but also have the opportunity to either camp or be pampered in a comfortable room. This may not satisfy every couple with a similar problem, but it can't hurt to explore this potential solution.

When tempers flair and anger turns to screaming or tears, no collaborating is possible. You want to postpone problem solving until you've addressed inflamed emotions (Gottman & Gottman, 2006). **Smoothing** is the act of calming the agitated feelings of others during a conflict episode, and it can make integrative solutions possible by defusing emotionally volatile situations. The ultimate smoothing attempt is probably saying "I'm sorry" and meaning it when an apology is deserved. Other useful attempts include: "Can I take that back?" "How can I make things better?" "I see your point." "Let's start over." "I understand." "I didn't say that out loud did I?" Using humor, especially self-deprecation, is also an effective smoothing technique (Gottman et al., 1998). Smoothing isn't always necessary for every conflict situation, but it is an important element of collaborating when anger emerges.

Accommodating: Yielding to Others

When we yield to the needs and desires of others during a conflict, we are *accommodating*. The **accommodating style** of conflict management generally is used by less powerful individuals, such as employees, who are expected to accommodate more often and to a greater degree than more powerful individuals, such as bosses (Lulofs, 1994).

Regardless of relative power, when you are clearly wrong about an issue or point of contention, it makes sense to yield on it. This yielding demonstrates reasonableness and enhances your relationship with the other person.

It shows commitment to the relationship (Wieselquist et al., 1999). Yielding also makes sense if the issue is more important to the other person. This flexibility is an aspect of constructive conflict management. The roles may be reversed in the future, and it may be appropriate for the other party to yield. Accommodating by others is more likely when there is a history of mutual flexibility.

Accommodating can be an appropriate style of conflict management in many contexts (DeChurch et al., 2007). A less powerful person may need to adjust to a more powerful person to keep a job, maintain a relationship, or avoid nasty consequences. Yielding can sometimes maintain harmony in a relationship. Demonstrating a willingness to sacrifice personal benefit to cement a relationship, but not to avoid disagreements, can strengthen the bonds between partners (Impett et al., 2005). This is an especially important consideration in collectivist cultures that typically emphasize harmonious relationships (Ting-Toomey et al., 2000). Nevertheless, being too accommodating and making too many sacrifices, particularly when the sacrifices become lopsided toward one, can make you someone's lackey.

Compromising: Halving the Loaf

When we give up something to get something, we are *compromising*. The **compromising style** of conflict management occurs most often between parties of relatively equal power. More powerful individuals do not usually consider compromising to be necessary. They can dominate, and they do.

Compromising emphasizes workable, but not optimal, decisions and solutions. Some have referred to compromising as a lose-lose style of conflict management because trade-offs and exchanges are required to reach agreement. Despite the limitations and disadvantages of compromising it may be the only feasible goal in some situations. Half a loaf is better than starvation, or so goes the thinking. Compromising can be a useful strategy when an integrative decision is not feasible, issues are not critical, essential values are not undermined,

and such a settlement is to last only until a better solution can be found and negotiated.

Avoiding: Ignoring Conflict

When we sidestep or turn our back on conflict, we are *avoiding*. The **avoiding style** is exhibited in many ways (Wilmot & Hocker, 2014). We avoid conflict when we ignore it or deny it exists, even though it does. When we shift topics so that we don't have to address a conflict, we avoid. We may crack jokes to deflect a focus on disagreeable issues. We may quibble about the meaning of a word used by another who is probing uncomfortably about a subject of some dispute, or we may simply not respond to a question (turning-away response).

Stonewalling is an especially troublesome form of avoiding. **Stonewalling** occurs when one partner refuses to discuss problems or physically withdraws when the other partner is complaining, disagreeing, or attacking. It is "like talking to a stone wall" (Gottman & Gottman, 2006, p. 5). Stonewallers often justify their withdrawal from conflict by claiming that they are merely trying to remain under control and not make the contentiousness worse by responding. Stonewalling can be extremely frustrating to those faced with the withdrawal, and it can jeopardize the relationship itself (Nichols et al., 2015). It can also communicate disapproval, conceit, self-righteousness, and cold indifference—a defensive communication pattern.

Earlier, we noted that women far more than men confront issues in relationships that trigger conflict. Conversely, men are far more prone than women to avoid such issues and to withdraw (Canary et al., 1995). *About 85% of the stonewalling in relationship conflicts comes from men* (Gottman & Silver, 1999). Men are more likely to stonewall because they experience flooding more easily than women, and they may hope to prevent it by clamming up or retreating (Gottman & Carrere, 1994). Avoiding is not always an inappropriate and ineffective style of conflict management. We can avoid trivial issues without damaging our relationships. Avoiding "hot button" issues that trigger intense disagreements and may not be

Men stonewall far more than women. Notice the differences in nonverbal communication between the man and the woman shown here.

resolvable can be appropriate. Reminding a partner of an affair confronted long ago, for instance, dredges up anger and hurt feelings with no likelihood of a constructive outcome. Older couples tend to avoid escalating conflicts much more than younger couples, who tend to approach conflicts more aggressively (Holley et al., 2013). Consequently, "[o]lder adults typically report better marriages, more supportive friendships, less conflict with children and siblings, and closer ties with social-network members than do younger adults" (Fingerman & Charles, 2010, p. 172).

Competing: Power-Forcing

When we approach conflict as a win-lose contest, we are *competing*. The **competing style**, sometimes referred to as power-forcing, is exhibited in a variety of ways that are likely to produce defensiveness: threats, criticism, contempt, hostile remarks and jokes, sarcasm, ridicule, intimidation, fault finding and blaming, and denials of responsibility (Wilmot & Hocker,

2014). The competing style is aggressive, not assertive. It is not confrontation as previously defined; it is an attack. The chief flaw of the competing style is that the focus is on victory for oneself, not on a mutually satisfactory solution for all parties. This is particularly evident in celebrity divorce disputes.

Most couples prefer to share power, not engage in power struggles and adversarial behavior. They realize that "winning an argument" can diminish intimacy and relationship satisfaction (Sanford & Wolfe, 2013). This is especially true for same-sex relationships (Marano, 2014).

Managing Conflict Competently

This section addresses how to transact conflict competently. Topics include appropriate and effective use of communication styles of conflict management, anger management, forgiveness,

Power-forcing is sometimes an unavoidable conflict-management style, but it should be a last resort, used only when other styles have proved ineffective or cannot be used because of an emergency.

workplace bullying, and the communication challenges presented when cultures clash.

Styles in Action: Smooth Sailing to Whitewater Rafting

In my small-group communication classes, at least one group every semester approaches me about problems with a group member. Typically, the group member is unreliable, fails to show for group meetings, and hasn't shared the group workload on class projects. Consistently, their first question to me is "Can we kick [insert name] out of the group?" When I ask if they have confronted this person and expressed the group's concerns and feelings, virtually every time they admit that they have yet to confront their slacker. They avoid the problem because confrontation makes them uncomfortable, but when the problem keeps getting worse, they choose power-forcing. This is not surprising in a hypercompetitive society.

The five communication styles of conflict management have been explained, as have the types of situations in which each is likely to be appropriate and in what contexts the reverse is likely. In general, however, how do these five styles rank in terms of overall probability of effectiveness in conflict situations? They rank generally in the order in which they were discussed (collaborating, accommodating, compromising, avoiding, and competing).

Research shows clearly that *the collaborating style has the greatest likelihood of managing conflicts effectively* (DeChurch et al., 2007; Johnson & Johnson, 2000a). Accommodating is a mixed style of conflict management (Impett et al., 2005). When you sacrifice your own needs out of genuine concern for your partner's well-being, this can be constructive. When you sacrifice your needs to prevent further conflict, however, the results are typically unhappiness, increasing resentment, and a weakened relationship (Neff & Harter, 2002). The compromising style has already been dubbed a lose-lose style because you begin with an expectation of achieving only part of what you hope to achieve. You may end up compromising because an integrative solution is not always possible, but why start with compromising as the end goal? The avoiding style increases the frequency of marital disagreements because unresolved issues keep re-emerging (Cramer, 2002; Gottman & Gottman, 2006). Similar patterns are likely to result when roommate disputes are avoided. The avoiding style is only slightly better than the competing style (Holman & Jarvis, 2003). The competing style is the least effective because of the disadvantages of competition and the drawbacks of the dominance form of power, as previously discussed in Chapters 1 and 7 (DeChurch et al., 2007; Kuhn & Poole, 2000).

Despite the clear advantages of the collaborating style, research shows that *we typically use the least effective and most inappropriate style when trying to manage conflict* (Johnson & Johnson, 2000a). The competing and avoiding styles are the most often used approaches to interpersonal conflict management. The "I'm going to kick your butt" power-forcing approach to conflict management is modeled everywhere—in movies, television dramas, sitcoms, video

games, even advertisements for consumer products. Can you find any examples in "reality" television programs when conflict is handled in a productive way? Mostly, we see profanely abusive individuals "acting stupid" by viciously attacking each other. The avoiding style is used by students in more than half of their conflicts (Warters, 2005). Additional studies report that avoidance is a chief style used by nurses when faced with abuse from doctors (C. Johnson, 2009; Maxfield et al., 2005). The consequences not only to nurses but to patients under their care are serious. "The Silence Kills study found countless examples of caregivers who delayed action, withheld feedback or went along with erroneous diagnoses rather than face potential abuse from a colleague" (Grenny, 2009).

Timing is a relevant concern when employing any of the five conflict-management styles. If you begin by using a competing style, the likely result will be anger, hostility, and retaliation. Realizing that the competing style isn't working well, you may decide to try the collaborating style. Good luck! Once you have competed, it is much more difficult to cooperate. Suspicion and mistrust will permeate your transactions. It is far better to begin with the collaborating style. If collaborating does not work and the issue is not very important, accommodating or avoiding might be an appropriate choice. You could use compromising as an interim style until you find a more integrative solution. *Competing is the style of last resort, but you may have to use it when all other styles fail or are inappropriate.* Employees who are frequently tardy or absent, do not complete required work on time, and manifest a negative attitude may have to be fired if no other style changes their behavior. Divorce may be the last-resort solution to years of bitter conflict and power struggles. It isn't pretty, but it may be necessary in some circumstances.

Culture and Conflict: Different Styles

"Recent research on conflict management strategies indicates that there are no universal resolutions to conflict. In fact, attempts to remedy

CRITICAL THINKING

"Just another of our many disagreements. He wants a no-fault divorce, whereas I would prefer to have the bastard crucified."

This cartoon illustrates which of the following communication styles of conflict management?

○ **1.** Avoiding   ○ **3.** Collaborating
○ **2.** Compromise   ○ **4.** Competing
Answers at end of chapter.

conflict may be culturally inappropriate, yield unfavorable results, and even increase the propensity toward future conflict" (Gibson & McDaniel, 2010, p. 456).

Individualist and collectivist values markedly influence the communication styles of conflict management that are preferred when conflict erupts (Ting-Toomey & Chung, 2012). For example, avoidance of confrontation is "a core element of Thai culture. Expressions of emotion and excitement are seen as impolite, improper, and threatening" (Knutson & Posirisuk, 2006, p. 211). From the Thai viewpoint, a competent communicator is one who avoids conflict; exhibits respect, tactfulness, modesty, and politeness; and controls emotions (Knutson et al., 2002; Sriussadaporn-Charoenngam & Jablin, 1999). For collectivist cultures, expressing anger during conflict-management efforts is likely to evoke negative reactions (Brescoll & Uhlmann, 2008).

Consider also differences between the Chinese and Americans. Chinese culture, far more collectivist than American culture, emphasizes harmony as a goal. "The Chinese consider harmony as the universal path which we all should pursue. Only when harmony is reached and prevails throughout heaven and earth can all things be nourished and flourish" (Chen & Starosta, 1998b, p. 6). A conflict-free interpersonal relationship, therefore, is the ultimate goal (Chen & Starosta, 1998b).

The Chinese philosophy of harmonious relationships translates into a strong desire to avoid a conflict with a friend or member of an in-group (e.g., family). When conflicts are unavoidable, there is a preference for accommodating—not confronting—the dispute so that harmony is maintained (Chen & Starosta, 1998b). Handling a dispute ineptly can bring shame, a loss of face, not just on the individual but also on the individual's entire family. Thus, one must avoid stirring up trouble for fear of bringing shame on the family (Yu, 1997).

Conflicts with individuals from an out-group, however, are often handled quite differently among Chinese than are conflicts within the group. Although not the initial choice, competing is a common way to approach conflict with outsiders, especially if the interests of the opposing parties are highly incompatible. Vicious quarrels, even physical fights, are not uncommon in such circumstances (Chen & Starosta, 1998b; Yu, 1997).

Imagine the difficulty that would occur when an American and a Chinese try to resolve a conflict. Americans favor direct, competing, or compromising styles of conflict management. These styles clash with the avoiding and accommodating styles initially favored by the Chinese. Consider a slightly different intercultural conflict with similar difficulties. Tannen (1998) cites an example of a Japanese woman married to a Frenchman. The French love to argue; in fact, they may change topics at the dinner table until they find one that ignites a disagreement. For the first two years of marriage, this Japanese woman spent a great deal of time in tears. She tried accommodating her husband and avoided arguing with him. This seemed to frustrate him. He would try to find something to start an argument. Finally, she couldn't take it anymore, and she began yelling at him. Her husband was thrilled. To him, starting an argument with his wife showed that he valued her intelligence and that he was interested in her. Enthusiastic debate between partners was considered a sign of a solid relationship.

The key to effective intercultural conflict management is flexibility (Knutson et al., 2003). If you find yourself in a situation or a relationship that calls for intercultural conflict management, try broadening your approach to conflict. Learn to use all communication styles well, not just those you are most comfortable with or are accustomed to using. Change to a different style when one seems to clash with another person's cultural values. If you know that someone comes from a collectivist culture, don't abandon collaborating; one study found this cooperative approach to conflict worked well for Chinese employers with their workers (Chen et al., 2005). Be prepared, however, to seek accommodation wherever possible.

In any case, *recognize that competing is as ineffective and troublesome to use interculturally as it is to use intraculturally*. When you make mistakes, and you will, be prepared to apologize. Seek forgiveness for embarrassing or shaming the other person. Elaborate apologies work best when the insult or embarrassment seems to be great. Above all, try to empathize with people whose cultural values and standards are different from your own. Consider their perspective, and respect their right to disagree. Find ways to build bridges between culturally diverse individuals, not tear them down.

Transforming Competing into Collaborating: Cooperation Revisited

Conflicts are transactional (Wilmot & Hocker, 2014). What one party does affects the other party in a conflict. It takes two to compete, and it takes two to cooperate. Individuals' communication styles of conflict management appear to be largely governed by the **norm of reciprocity**—you give back what you get from others. Individuals are likely to choose a conflict style that is used by the other party or parties in a conflict (Park & Antonioni, 2007). The big question is: *"What do I do when I want to cooperate but the other person wants to compete?"*

Here are some suggestions for how you might transform a competitor into a collaborator:

1. *Always be "unconditionally constructive"* (Fisher & Brown, 1988). Refuse to be abused, but also refuse to be abusive. Break the norm of reciprocity. Don't return contempt with contempt, or intimidation with intimidation. If others become abusive, remain civil. If they confuse issues to hide their weak position, clarify. If they try to intimidate you, don't bully back. Attempt to persuade them of the merits of your viewpoint. If they lie, neither trust nor deceive them. Remain vigilantly trustworthy at all times. If they don't actively listen to you, encourage them to listen carefully. Always listen actively and empathically to them. Meet defensive communication with supportive communication. This is not a guide to sainthood, although you probably deserve some small award for remaining composed when dealing with certain individuals. Remaining unconditionally constructive serves your own interests. As Fisher and Brown (1988) explain, "If you

are acting in ways that injure your own competence, there is no reason for me to do the same. Two heads are better than one, but one is better than none" (p. 202).

2. *Ask problem-solving questions* (Ury, 1993). Your goal is to move the other party from a power-forcing, controlling communication pattern to a problem-solving, collaborative pattern. One way to do this is to engage the other person in joint problem solving (encouraging a cooperative norm of reciprocity). Encourage joint effort to find an integrative solution. Ask "Why?" "Why not?" and "What if?" questions. "Why is it a problem that I don't talk much when I come home from work?" "Why not do it this way? Can you see some problems?" "What if you let me do extra credit? What would happen?" (You should not ask these questions, of course, as if you are cross-examining a terrorist on the witness stand.)

3. *Confront the process* (Ury, 1993). Confronting the process can encourage collaborating. Don't attack; be assertive. Simply make an observation about the process. "Have you noticed that every time I try to explain my point of view, I am interrupted before I can finish my thought? Perhaps we can both agree to listen to each other without comment for one minute. What do you think?" If the other party gets nasty and belligerent, don't return fire. Address the process. "Do we really want to get nasty with each other? I don't see any good coming of it, do you?" This forces the other party to justify the nastiness, which is not an easy thing to do. Notice that the phrasing uses *we* to express inclusiveness. This removes the appearance of accusation. Sitting next to instead of across from each other to discuss a family budget or credit card debt also nonverbally shows inclusiveness, not exclusiveness.

4. *Ask for advice* (Ury, 1993). "What would you do if you were in my position?" This requires some empathy—taking the perspective of the other person. "What do you suggest we do to satisfy both of our needs?" Again, the focus is on mutually solving

problems and moving away from power-forcing strategies. To paraphrase Ury (1993), you're trying to bring others to their senses, not bring them to their knees.

Remaining unconditionally constructive is the most crucial of these four suggestions. Don't try to learn all four steps at once. Concentrate on remaining unconditionally constructive first until it becomes second nature to you. Then gradually use and refine the other three suggestions, one at a time.

Styles and Partner Abuse: Addressing Aggression

Physical abuse is directly relevant to students. Murray Straus (2001) studied university students in 31 countries (including the United States) and determined that, on average, 29% admitted to physically assaulting a dating partner in the previous 12-month period. The lowest rate for any university was 17%, and the highest was 45%.

The problem of partner abuse was addressed at length in Chapter 7. The relationship between partner/date abuse and communication styles of conflict management, however, has not been discussed. *A person's style of handling conflict can be an important indicator of potential abuse early in a relationship.* The competing (power-forcing) style is the most common style used in abusive relationships (Sabourin, 1995). If a partner's chief style of resolving conflict is competing, you should take this as a warning sign of possible future abuse. In particular, controlling behaviors, such as wanting to know whom you were with when you weren't with your partner, trying to specify which friends you should associate with, and attempting to dictate with whom you can socialize, are troublesome power-forcing behaviors. Even if your partner presents these controlling behaviors as requests rather than demands at first, be concerned. Accommodating such requests or demands won't end disagreement, and it may feed the abuser's desire to control you.

Psychologically abusive communication, such as contemptuous remarks, ridicule, and humiliating comments, are dominance strategies aimed at keeping a partner "in line."

Verbal threats of physical violence when resistance is offered, of course, are even more serious power-forcing behaviors. Verbal aggression in relationships either precedes or accompanies physical violence in 99% of abuse cases (Straus & Sweet, 1992). Psychological abuse as an intimidating power-forcing conflict strategy is dangerous and cause for alarm (Hartwell-Walker, 2013).

Accommodating is normally an ineffective conflict style to use when signals of possible abuse first appear. Yielding to power-forcing demands, however, may be necessary in the immediate situation if one's partner is showing signs of losing self-control. Nevertheless, accommodating the demands of a partner out of fear for one's safety places the potential abuser in charge of his or her partner's life.

Compromising usually doesn't satisfy a potential abuser. Abusers, especially outright batterers, want total control and obedience (Jacobson & Gottman, 1998). There should be no compromise on the goal of eradicating verbal and physical aggression. Do not try to defend or rationalize "a little bit of abuse."

Avoiding is the most common style used by women to deal with physical abuse from their partners, especially in cases of intimate terrorism, as previously discussed in Chapter 7 (Gelles & Straus, 1988). It reduces the frequency of physical violence in relationships by avoiding "hot buttons" that trigger violence in a partner. This style, however, is difficult to recommend except in the most dire situations, where avoiding might be a temporary expedient necessary for self-protection. As a long-term style, it is woefully deficient. It reinforces power imbalances and perpetuates intimate terrorism.

Confrontation is most effective for dealing with potential or actual abuse in relationships. As Gelles and Straus (1988) explain, "Delaying until the violence escalates is too late. A firm, emphatic, and rational approach appears to be the most effective personal strategy a woman can use to prevent future violence" (p. 159). They suggest *confronting the very first incident of even minor violence* and stating, without equivocation, that such behavior will not be tolerated and must never occur again ("If you hit me, I will leave you").

In a study of college students, almost a third of college women admitted slapping their partners, and almost a fifth admitted slapping a partner in the face (Vitanza & Marshall, 1993). During my first year in college, I dated a woman who, when angry at me, would slap me in the face. The first time it happened, I avoided discussing it, mostly because I was embarrassed. When it happened a second time, months later, I still did not confront her. Finally, when it happened a third time, I confronted her. I described how it made me feel when she slapped me. I explained to her that when she slapped me my first reaction was to slap her back, but that might injure her physically. I further explained that I hated the feeling of wanting to strike her in retaliation. Finally, I said to her, "I cannot and will not hit you when you slap me, but you put me in an embarrassing and unfair position. You can hit me, but I can't hit back. What am I supposed to do?" She responded by saying that she had never considered her actions from my perspective. She promised never to slap me again, and during a long relationship, she never did. It is vital that even relatively minor acts of aggression be confronted before they escalate into tragic abuse. I should have confronted my partner sooner than I did.

If physical or psychological abuse continues after you confront it, you should seriously consider ending the relationship. Abuse that is excused, rationalized, or ignored almost always recurs and grows worse (Jacobson & Gottman, 1998). *The best way to handle abuse is assertively, directly, and unequivocally at the outset.* Partners can stop their abuse, but it is infinitely more difficult—and more dangerous—once it has become standard practice. If there is a threat of imminent serious injury from your partner, avoid, don't confront, and put distance between yourself and your abuser at the first safe opportunity.

Anger Management: Controlling the Beast Within

Anger is a frequent companion of interpersonal conflicts. Workplace anger often increases during trying economic times and spills into verbal and physical aggression (Szivos, 2010).

The most common communication behaviors associated with workplace anger include yelling, swearing, flinging insults, criticizing, using sarcasm, crying, giving dirty looks, making angry gestures, throwing things, and physical assault (Glomb, 2002; C. Johnson, 2009).

Learning to manage anger is an important step in managing conflicts competently. Constance Ahrons (1994), author of *The Good Divorce*, notes that the chief difference between divorced parents who were effective co-parents to their children and those who were ineffective "was that the more cooperative group managed their anger better" (p. 145). Also, anger decreases integrative offers proposed by parties in conflict and heightens the likelihood of competitive, not cooperative, behavior (Liu, 2009).

CONSTRUCTIVE AND DESTRUCTIVE ANGER: INTENSITY AND DURATION

Twenty-nine-year-old Rene Andrews pulled onto I-71 near Cincinnati, Ohio. Apparently upset by the way Andrews pulled into her lane, 24-year-old Tracie Alfieri attempted to pass Andrews on the right shoulder of the freeway, then passed on the left, cut in front of Andrews, and slammed on the brakes. Andrews swerved and crashed into a stopped tractor-trailer rig. Andrews suffered multiple injuries, and her 6-month-old fetus died. Alfieri was convicted of aggravated vehicular homicide and was sentenced to 18 months in prison (Horn, 1999). Clearly, road rage is an example of destructive anger. Unfortunately, it is quite common. One survey found that 90% of drivers "in the past year" were either victims of road rage or had witnessed such an event (Arkowitz & Lilienfeld, 2009).

Two conditions determine how destructive or constructive anger is (Adler & Proctor, 2007). The first condition is the *intensity*, or relative strength, of the anger. Anger can vary in intensity from mild irritation to rage. Mild, or even moderate, anger can be constructive. It can signal the existence of a problem, and it can motivate necessary change. Rage, however, is destructive (Glomb, 2002). Temper tantrums and screaming fits are never endearing. In intimate relationships, rage frightens partners and children. In the workplace, rage is

Road rage produced four wrecked cars and three dead people in this horrific Washington, D.C., crash.

never appropriate because it "shows you've lost control—not to mention that it's tough to be articulate if you're having a conniption" (Black, 1990a, 1990b). Ranting and raving make you look like a lunatic. When used to get your way on an issue, rage is a power-forcing style of conflict management that will likely produce an equivalent response. *Rage times rage equals rage squared.*

Duration, or how long something lasts, is the second condition that determines to what degree anger is constructive or destructive. The length of an anger episode can vary from short to prolonged. Quick flashes of temper may hardly be noticed by others. Even fairly intense expressions of anger, if short-lived, can make the point powerfully that you are upset. Protracted anger episodes, however, can make conflict management extremely difficult. When expressions of anger are highly intense and long-lasting, the combination can be extremely combustible.

There is a popular notion that venting one's anger is constructive and that suppressing one's anger is unhealthy. This popular notion is wrong. *Venting anger, or "blowing off steam," usually increases one's anger* (Bushman, 2013; Lohr et al. 2007). Replaying our anger about past events, especially if the anger is unresolved, simply rehearses it. When we tell friends of past "injustices," blood pressure rises, heartbeat increases, and the face flushes. We are

experiencing the anger all over again. This doesn't put the anger to rest. It awakens it, pops it out of bed, and starts it doing jumping jacks.

ANGER AND ATTRIBUTION: IS IT INTENTIONAL?

Anger and the desire to lash out at others are choices. Imagine, for instance, that you are stopped at an intersection in your car. Another car "steals" your right of way by moving into the intersection before you do. Do you get angry? Do you make an obscene gesture? Do you shout at the driver? Now imagine what your reaction would be if you saw that it was your best friend or your mother driving the car. Would your reaction be the same? Probably not. We can be righteously indignant, or we can choose to be calm, even amused, by the same stimulus.

Anger can be a thoughtful choice unless it reaches the level of rage (Zillmann, 1993). Rage floods our thought process: we can't think straight, and we "get stupid." Attributing meanings, causes, or outcomes to conflict events shapes the way we think about and respond to disagreements and perceived poor treatment. Attribution can influence enormously whether we get stupid or we get smart on potentially volatile issues (Baron, 1990).

Intent and blame are two common forms of attribution that ignite anger (McKay et al., 1989). Trying to ascertain the intention of another person is mind reading, or "intention invention" (Stone et al., 1999). Unless a person tells us, we must guess about motivation, and unfortunately, we often assume the worst. Negative behaviors from others that we perceive to be intentional, not accidental, easily trigger our anger. Deliberately shoving someone, for example, is perceived to be more worthy of anger and hostility than accidentally tripping and shoving a person while trying to regain your own balance.

Blaming someone for negative behavior is the companion of intent. If the behavior of others is intentional and negative, it "deserves" reproach. We can justifiably blame them for unfortunate outcomes. If their behavior is not intentional, we can still blame them for the outcome, but we don't seem as justified to be angry with them. How we frame potential conflict-producing events influences our emotional response.

Consider an example. A patient named Margaret had her hip replaced by a prominent surgeon, a man she perceived to be gruff and difficult to confront. When Margaret appeared for her first office visit following the surgery, she was informed that the doctor had unexpectedly extended his vacation. Margaret was furious. She imagined her doctor soaking up the sun on some Caribbean island, probably with his wife or girlfriend. When Margaret returned for her postponed appointment, she asked her doctor curtly how his vacation had turned out. He replied that it had been wonderful. "I'll bet," Margaret responded in a sarcastic tone. Before she had a chance to express her anger about being so cavalierly inconvenienced, however, her doctor continued, "It was a working vacation. I was helping set up a hospital in Bosnia. The conditions there are just horrendous" (Stone et al. 1999, p. 47). Understandably, Margaret's anger subsided with this news.

MANAGING YOUR OWN ANGER: SEIZING CONTROL

There are several ways to defuse and de-escalate anger, both your own and others' (Gottman & Gottman, 2006). Try these suggestions for managing your own anger:

1. *Reframe self-talk.* Thoughts trigger anger. Reframing the way we think about events

can deflate our anger before it has a chance to escalate (Baron, 1990; Gottman & Gottman, 2006). Very often we have no way to know whether the act of another person was intentional or not. Instead of assuming that it was intentional, assume that it was not. "He probably didn't see me." "She looked stressed out." This kind of self-talk reframes events as unintentional, even haphazard, not intentional.

2. *Speak and listen nondefensively.* Criticism, contempt, and cross-complaining ignite angry passions (Baron, 1990). Refuse to become defensive. Insulting your partner or hurting his or her feelings dooms the possibility of constructive conversation (Gottman & Gottman, 2006). Reframe criticism as a problem or a challenge. Use supportive communication.

3. *Deliberately calm yourself.* Exercise some discipline, and refuse to vent your anger. Be prepared to take steps to calm yourself (Fisher & Shapiro, 2005). When you feel the adrenaline surge, take slow, deep breaths, and concentrate on reducing your heartbeat. Count to 10 before responding. A cooling-off period works well to calm one's anger and may be necessary in serious cases. (Gottman & Gottman, 2006). Typically, it takes 20 minutes to recover from an adrenaline surge. Take those 20 minutes, and stay away from the person or situation that triggered your anger. Go for a walk, shoot a basketball, or do whatever diverts your attention and moves you out of the situation. Return to discuss your anger with others only when you are certain that flooding has subsided. Then express your anger to others in a calm, descriptive manner (first-person singular language).

4. *Change your focus.* Don't rehearse your anger. Revisiting past injustices won't change your history. You can't get beyond old issues if you keep replaying them in your mind (Gottman & Gottman, 2006). Change your focus when old hurts resurface. Play a video game, update your Facebook page, or call a friend. Just get

your mind off your anger for a little while (Rusting & Nolen-Hoeksema, 1998).

Don't attempt to learn all four of these suggestions at once. Pick one, and work on learning it until it becomes virtually automatic. Then you can attempt a second suggestion and so forth.

MANAGING THE ANGER OF OTHERS: COMMUNICATION JIU JITSU

A person can feel angry for excellent reasons. Anger acts as a signal that changes need to occur. Anger should not, however, be used as a weapon to abuse others. We need to learn ways to cope with and express anger constructively, not be devoured by it.

You can defuse and de-escalate the anger of others so you can confront issues constructively. It is usually best to address the person's anger first, then deal with the substance of the dispute that triggered the anger (Donohue & Kolt, 1992). Dialogue cannot take place when tempers are white hot. Try these suggestions to defuse another person's anger and restore a climate conducive to dialogue:

1. *Be asymmetrical.* When a person is exhibiting anger, particularly if it turns to rage, it is critical that you do not strike back in kind. Resist reacting signally to words of criticism. Be asymmetrical; that is, do the opposite. Counteract rage with absolute calm. Stay composed (Black, 1990a, 1990b). Hostage negotiators are trained to defuse highly volatile individuals by remaining absolutely calm throughout the negotiations and employing the smoothing technique to quiet the enraged person. Matching a person's rage with rage can produce ugly, violent outcomes.

2. *Validate the other person.* Validation is a form of the smoothing technique of collaborating. Let the person know that his or her point of view and anger have some validity, even though you may not agree. You can validate another person in several ways. You can take responsibility for the other person's anger. "I upset you, didn't I?" acknowledges your role in provoking anger. You can apologize. "I'm sorry. You're right to be angry" can be a very powerful validation of the other person. Don't apologize, of course, unless you really bear some responsibility. Sometimes a compliment can defuse another person's anger. "I actually think you handled my abrasiveness rather well." Finally, actively listening to the other person and acknowledging what the person has said can be very validating. "I know it upsets you when I play my music too loudly while you're trying to study" makes the other person feel heard, even if conflict still exists.

3. *Probe.* Seek more information from the other person so you can understand his or her anger (Gottman & Gottman, 2006). When you ask a question of the angry person, it forces the person to shift from emotional outburst to rational response. Simply asking, "Can we sit down and discuss this calmly so I can understand your point of view?" can momentarily defuse another person's anger. If your partner angrily criticizes you, listen and then probe. "Wow! Any chance you might give me some examples so I can understand why you think I'm such a jerk?" probes for specific information necessary to resolve the conflict.

4. *Distract.* When someone is really out of control, distracting that person by introducing a topic that shifts the focus can sometimes divert attention away from the source of the rage (Rusting & Nolen-Hoeksema, 1998). A humorous quip, an odd question, pointing to some event unrelated to the anger, and requesting help on a thorny problem not associated with triggering the rage are ways to distract and short-circuit the tirade.

5. *Assume a problem orientation.* This is a supportive communication pattern. This step should occur once you have calmed the angry person by the previous steps. Approach the emotional display as a problem to be solved, not as a reason to retaliate. The question "What would you like to see occur?" invites problem solving.

6. *Refuse to be abused.* Even if you are wrong, feel guilty, or deserve another person's

anger, do not permit yourself to be verbally battered (McKay et al., 1989). Abusive assaults are unproductive no matter who is at fault in a conflict. "I don't engage in conversations in which I am called names" sets a ground rule on how anger can be expressed.

7. *Disengage*. This is the final step when all else fails to calm a person's anger. Disengaging is particularly important if the person continues to be abusive and enraged. Simply and firmly state, "This meeting is over. I'm leaving. We'll discuss this another time."

Keeping track of all seven of these steps, especially when faced with an enraged person, is too much to expect. Concentrate on one or two steps until you have learned them so well that they become a habit. *Being asymmetrical is the crucial step, with validation a close second.* The remaining steps can be learned gradually.

Workplace Bullying: Conflict and Anger Meet

Workplace bullying is "persistent verbal and nonverbal aggression at work" that "includes public humiliation, constant criticism, ridicule, gossip, insults, and social ostracism—communication that makes work tasks difficult or impossible, and socially isolates, stigmatizes, and discredits those targeted" (Lutgen-Sandvik, 2006, pp. 406, 408). It is also unethical behavior, egregiously disrespectful, and irresponsible action against others. "Adult bullying at work is shockingly common and enormously destructive" (Lutgen-Sandvik & Sypher., 2009, p. 41).

Workplace bullying is an especially challenging problem because conflict, anger, and power are melded. Psychologist Gary Namie, co-founder of the Workplace Bullying Institute, notes that damage from workplace bullying can be worse than harm from sexual harassment (cited by Tulshyan, 2013). In a survey by the Workplace Bullying Institute and Zogby International, 27% of U.S. employees reported having suffered abusive conduct in the workplace, and an additional 21% witnessed

bullying (Namie et al., 2014). Descriptions offered in one study of workplace victims indicate the intensity of these bullying events. As one victim described such an event: "[She was] intimidating—right in your face—less than an inch away from your face, where her spit would hit you in the face. She would scream at us, her face getting all red and her eyes watering. It was almost like she wanted to reach out and choke you." Another victim described it this way: "He'd scream and yell every day. Veins would pop out of his head; he'd spit, he'd point, he'd threaten daily, all day long to anyone in his way, every day that I was there. *Every single day . . .* He'd swear profusely" (quoted in Lutgen-Sandvik, 2006, p. 411). Rage (and apparently flying spit) appear to be common manifestations of workplace bullying.

Workplace bullying is fundamentally a dominance-prevention power struggle (Young, 2015). Between 60% and 80% of bullies at work are supervisors and upper management (Einarsen et al., 2003; Lutgen-Sandvik et al., 2007). Bullying is allowed to persist primarily because transgressors (legitimate authority) are in more powerful positions than victims. Even higher-ups who could address the problem constructively often implicitly or explicitly approve of the aggressive behavior, or the problem is simply ignored. In many cases, those who complain are reprimanded for making complaints, or they are fired from their jobs. Most bullies suffer no negative consequences; some are even promoted (Lutgen-Sandvik & Sypher, 2009).

How victims should address bullies is a complicated challenge. What works well in other conflict situations may not work well with more powerful bullies. Confrontation may get you fired, or more abuse may be heaped on you until you quit. Some victims use resistance strategies. They choose to drag their feet, a frequent choice of the relatively powerless. For example, they might use the *work-to-rule* resistance strategy, where they perform the absolute minimum amount of work necessary to keep their job according to work rules in place. This is emotionally satisfying because it likely results in lowered productivity for the organization. It doesn't really end the abuse, however. Some victims try avoidance,

Workplace bullying has become a serious problem. A boss screaming at employees is "acting stupid."

by keeping as much distance as possible between themselves and the bully at work. You can't become invisible, however, so this is only a temporary fix at best. Other workers withdraw completely and quit their jobs. but in tough economic times, this may not be a feasible option. Finally, victims of workplace bullying individually, or collectively in the form of coalitions with other abused workers, may adopt the power-forcing conflict style by filing formal grievances with external authorities (e.g., unions, courts, or governmental agencies) (Lutgen-Sandvik, 2006; Lutgen-Sandvik & Sypher, 2009). This usually takes years, and it doesn't guarantee a satisfactory outcome for abused workers.

Ultimately, prevention is far more effective than any of the preceding strategies. A zero-tolerance policy in organizations for any acts of bullying is the place to start. This would, of course, need to be backed up with confrontation and integration strategies, such as addressing directly the first signs of bullying behavior and providing training for bullies to change their ways. If the bullying persisted, this would be followed by power-forcing, firing the offender. Developing a constructive

communication climate is also essential. A supportive communication climate at work can significantly diminish workplace bullying if the constructive climate is modeled by those in positions of legitimate authority.

Forgiveness: Healing Conflict's Wounds

Forgiveness plays an important role in resolving conflict and dealing with anger (Exline & Baumeister, 2000; Fincham et al., 2008). Studies show that forgiveness seems to promote marital adjustment and satisfaction (Sheldon et al., 2014) and to reduce hostile anger (Williams & Williams, 1993). "Forgiveness is the final stage of conflict and is the one thing that is most likely to prevent repetitive, destructive cycles of conflict" (Lulofs, 1994, p. 288).

FORGIVENESS DEFINED: HEALING, NOT HURTING

In Neil Simon's play *California Suite*, a woman catches her husband committing adultery and says to him, "I forgive you. And now I'm going to go out and spend all your money." Good line, but this isn't forgiveness. **Forgiveness** is "letting go of feelings of revenge and desires to retaliate" (Lulofs, 1994, p. 276; see also Philpot, 2008). The focus of forgiveness is on healing wounds, not inflicting them on others.

Forgiveness is not simply forgetting what happened. When we forgive, we remove the desire to mimic the behavior we hate. Forgiveness is also not tolerating reprehensible behavior ("Oh, that's okay."). Forgiveness "still allows for holding the offender responsible for the transgression, and does not involve denying, ignoring, minimizing, tolerating, condoning, excusing or forgetting the offense" (Witvliet et al, 2001, p. 118). The best indicator that you have forgiven someone is honestly wishing that person well when you think of him or her (Smedes, 1984). Forgiveness, therefore, is the opposite of the bumper sticker "Don't get mad—get even."

Forgiveness is particularly difficult when the offense is severe, intentional, repeated, and the transgressor is unrepentant (Bachman & Guerrero, 2006; Exline & Baumeister, 2000). When a friend ridicules your style of dress or taste in music in front of others, it can hurt and make you angry, but you can usually forgive the insult easily. In fact, as Smedes (1984) explains, "It is wise not to turn all hurts into crises of forgiving . . . We put everyone we love on guard when we turn personal misdemeanors into major felonies" (p. 15). Stealing your boyfriend or girlfriend from you on purpose (mate poaching) with no apparent guilt, however, makes forgiving a bit more difficult.

Revenge may be our first impulse in response to transgressions, but seeking revenge doesn't resolve conflict. It stimulates anger and perpetuates and escalates conflict. Revenge fantasies and blaming can lead to psychopathology, criminality, poor recovery from bereavement, and health problems (Exline & Baumeister, 2000).

THE PROCESS OF FORGIVENESS: FOUR STAGES

Forgiveness is a process that occurs in stages. Smedes (1984) offers a *four-stage model*: we hurt, we hate, we heal, and we come together. Hurting and hating are natural results of the painful actions of others. Dwelling on the hating stage, however, paralyzes us. Hate is like a parasite drawing our life's energy from us, making us too weak to move forward. The only way to break free from the grip of hatred is to forgive, which starts the healing process.

Perhaps you're thinking "Easy for you to say, but there are just some things that can't be forgiven." Remember that forgiveness doesn't mean acceptance or tolerance of bad behavior by others. It doesn't mean you shouldn't get angry when you are mistreated. It also doesn't mean you necessarily return to a relationship (Morse & Metts, 2011; Wade & Worthington, 2005). Think, though, about the alternative. Holding on to hatred and seeking revenge do nothing constructive to enhance your life. Hatred and desire for revenge are physically and psychologically damaging (Lulofs, 1994). Moving away from a desire for vengeance is crucial to the forgiveness process (Burnette et al., 2013).

Mary Nell Verrett is the sister of James Byrd Jr., a 49-year-old African American who was beaten and dragged to death behind a pickup truck in Jasper, Texas, on June 7, 1998. Despite her terrible loss, Verrett eloquently testifies to the futility and danger of hating: "Our family has no use for destructive hate . . . it tears away at you. You become sick. You become a victim all over again. It can keep you from sleeping, eating, and thinking straight. It can keep you from going forward" (quoted in "Message of Hope," 1998, pp. 9–10). If Mary Nell Verrett can forgive what racist white men did to her beloved brother, surely we can forgive those who hurt us.

Forgiveness is a transactional process. Although some people can readily forgive others, it is extremely difficult for others to forgive. In such cases, what the transgressor does to encourage forgiveness can help. Individuals who have inflicted pain on us can take two steps to initiate the forgiveness process. First, they can openly and sincerely accept responsibility for what they have done. "What I did to you was wrong and totally unprovoked" accepts responsibility. Second, transgressors can apologize: "I'm very sorry for hurting you." An apology is a particularly important step that encourages forgiveness (McCullough et al., 1997). *Elaborate, sincere apologies work best when the transgression is serious* (Morse & Metts, 2011; Weiner et al., 1991). As one study showed, "the perception that one received a sincere apology was a fairly good predictor of forgiveness" (Bachman & Guerrero, 2006, p. 54).

Others can start the forgiveness process, but ultimately, we have to forgive in our hearts. *As victims, we can forgive by reframing the event.* We recast the behavior that hurt us into an uncharacteristic departure from the norm. The hurtful act doesn't have to become a defining moment in our relationship with the other person. A friend can hurt us and still remain a friend. We can also reframe the event by attributing situational causes for the act. "He stole my money because he lives in desperate circumstances, not because he is evil" reframes the event for forgiveness.

The final stage of the forgiveness process is the coming-together part. There are three forms of communicating our forgiveness of others (Merolla, 2008). First, *direct forgiveness* is explicit and unambiguous ("I forgive you"). Second, *indirect forgiveness* is "just understood." There is no direct acknowledgment of the forgiveness. Third, *conditional forgiveness* attaches stipulations that make it clear any further transgression will not be tolerated ("Stay off the booze, or I'm leaving you"). *Coming together occurs most completely with direct forgiveness when the victim openly communicates forgiveness to the transgressor.* A hug or some expression of affection, if possible, is helpful in bringing parties together (Sheldon et al., 2014). In cases of serious transgressions, indirect forgiveness or conditional forgiveness is likely, and this tends to delay actual coming together until trust is rekindled (Merolla, 2008). The transgressor may have to demonstrate his or her commitment to make amends (Tavris, 1989). If the transgressor, for instance, stays off alcohol for three months as promised, this might serve as an outward sign that regaining trust is important. It indicates that commitment to the relationship is firm.

Personal injury inflicted on us by others becomes a part of who we are, but it need not be the whole of who we are (Lulofs, 1994). Expressing forgiveness and acting in ways that show forgiveness can heal.

Summary

Most people view conflict with some dread. Conflict, however, can be constructive as well as destructive. Our communication determines the difference. Destructive conflict is typified by escalating spirals of conflict that can easily turn ugly. Constructive conflict is characterized by controlling or de-escalating conflict by using a We-orientation, cooperation, and flexibility in applying communication styles of conflict management.

There are five communication styles of conflict management: collaborating, accommodating, compromising, avoiding, and competing. Collaborating has the greatest potential for appropriately and effectively managing conflict; competing has the least potential. Learning to control our anger and to manage the anger of others is an important part of dealing with conflict effectively. Intercultural conflicts can be extremely difficult to manage because members of individualist and collectivist cultures differ dramatically in how they view conflict and how best to manage it. The final stage of conflict management is forgiveness, letting go of the desire for revenge and retaliation.

Answers for Critical Thinking captions:

GAY MARRIAGE PHOTO (P. 237) #1 & #3

NEW YORKER CARTOON (P. 243): #4

Quizzes Without Consequences

Test your knowledge before your exam! Go to the companion website at www.oup.com/us/rothwell, click on the Student Resources for each chapter, and take the Quizzes Without Consequences.

Film School Case Studies

An Unfinished Life (2005). Drama; PG-13
Morgan Freeman, Robert Redford, and Jennifer Lopez star in this story about grief and healing. Examine this film for conflict-management styles and elements of forgiveness.

August: Osage County (2013). Drama; R
Dysfunctional family conflict is everywhere in this depiction of the Westons, who gather because of a family crisis. Analyze the conflict-management styles used.

Changing Lanes (2002). Drama; R
Gavin Banek (Ben Affleck) and Doyle Gipson (Samuel L. Jackson) are strangers who collide as a result of a traffic accident. Examine the elements of destructive conflict depicted in this film.

The Holiday (2006). Romantic Comedy; PG-13
Fairly predictable but somewhat charming piece of fluff. Analyze the many dialectics portrayed in the relationships. Is it possible that the Kate Winslet character could really be attracted to the Jack Black character? (That's just a personal aside.)

Juno (2007). Romantic Comedy; PG-13
Juno, a pregnant teenager played by Ellen Page, must deal with finding the perfect couple to raise her child in this offbeat, coming-of-age comedy. Examine the dialectics depicted throughout the film.

The Invention of Lying (2009). Comedy; PG-13
Ricky Gervais plays an average guy in an alternate reality where lying does not exist; there isn't even a word for it. One day, however, he realizes that lying can be beneficial to him and to others, but there is a downside. Analyze the conditions in which lying may or may not be appropriate. Apply the five criteria for ethical communication: respect, honesty, fairness, choice, and responsibility.

The Upside of Anger (2005). Drama; R
This movie has an interesting perspective on anger. Does it depict anger in ways that coincide with this chapter's material? Does it deviate from what has been presented from a research standpoint?

What's Cooking? (2000). Comedy/Drama; PG-13
Diversity is not lacking in this portrayal of four inter-related families trying to celebrate Thanksgiving. Look for the many dialectical sources of conflict. Is honesty always the best policy? Identify the communication styles of conflict management depicted in the film.

BY THE END OF THIS CHAPTER, YOU SHOULD BE ABLE TO:

1. Define groups, and recognize their strengths and pitfalls.

2. Understand the structure of small groups.

3. Recognize evolving theories of leadership as well as their strengths and weaknesses.

The Anatomy of Small Groups

WE LIVE IN A WORLD of groups, and we reap significant rewards from our group experiences, some quite profound (Rains & Young, 2009). The rewards include feelings of belonging and affection from *primary groups* (e.g., family and friends) and *social networks* (e.g., Facebook, Twitter, Snapchat, and Instagram), social support from *self-help* and *support groups* (e.g., Parents Without Partners, Alcoholics Anonymous, and Cancer Survivors Network), satisfaction from solving challenging problems in *project groups* (e.g., ad hoc groups and self-managing work teams), achieving social justice from *advocacy* and *judicial groups* (e.g., civil rights groups and the U.S. Supreme Court), increased knowledge from *learning groups* (e.g., study groups and mock trial teams), thrills and entertainment from *activities groups* (e.g., athletic teams and bridge clubs), sense of community from *neighborhood groups* (e.g., homeowners associations and the PTA), identity and pleasure from helping others through *social* and *service groups*

4. Understand how competent leadership occurs in small groups.

(e.g., fraternities, sororities, and Rotary, Lions, and Kiwanis clubs), and a creative outlet in *music* and *artistic groups* (e.g., bands, choirs, and quilting circles). These rewards provide the main reasons we join groups: desire to belong, attraction to group activities, desire to achieve group goals, excitement, personal growth, and a boost in self-esteem and development of self-identity.

Group experiences, however, don't always prove to be rewarding. Winston Churchill once described a committee as "the organized result of a group of the incompetent who have been appointed by the uninformed to accomplish the unnecessary." On my own campus, committees metastasize like cancer, devouring the time and energy of faculty, staff, students, and administrators alike and threatening to suck the lifeblood from the institution. At last count, there were 63 committees on my campus, with more being contemplated. Students serve on many of these committees, enduring long meetings. In the misguided hope to rein in the proliferation of campus work groups, a serious proposal was once offered to establish a committee on committees. The proposal was, of course, sent to a committee, where it died.

Often groups seem to be an impediment, not an aid, to decision making and problem solving. Groups can be time consuming, sometimes indecisive, conflict provoking, and slow to react to urgent needs. Group members may not all exhibit the same level of motivation and attention to task accomplishment. Frequent group meetings at work can make employees feel fatigued, and this can put everyone in a surly frame of mind (Luong & Rogelberg, 2005). Susan Sorensen (1981) coined the term **grouphate** to describe how troublesome the group experience is for many people. Surveys of students reflect prevalent grouphate (Karau & Elsaid, 2009). One such survey reported that 58% of respondents did not like working in groups (Gurrie, 2013).

Why are some group experiences pleasurable and rewarding whereas others are about as enjoyable as eating raw Brussel sprouts? Sorenson

(1981) provides one key answer. *There is a direct relationship between communication competence and attitudes regarding group work.* Two studies, for example, show that negative attitudes about group meetings disappear when meetings are conducted competently (Rogelberg et al., 2006). In fact, "When meetings are well facilitated, employees tend to want more of them (Rogelberg et al., 2012, p. 244). Groups are much more likely to be successful, rewarding experiences when group members are competent communicators.

No matter what your attitude about working in groups, there is no escaping the group experience. The American Association for the Advancement of Science, the National Council of Teachers of English, the National Council of Teachers of Mathematics, and the National Communication Association all promote frequent group activity in college courses. A massive study of 355,000 college students revealed that 92% of first-year students worked in groups composed of diverse members (57% did so "often" or "very often") and that 94% of seniors did likewise (65% did so "often" or "very often") (National Survey of Student Engagement, 2014). Four-fifths of both Fortune 1000 companies and manufacturing organizations employ **self-managing work teams**—teams that regulate their own performance free from outside interference while completing an entire task (MacDonald, 2014). **Virtual teams**—groups whose members are connected by electronic communication technologies— have become a worldwide phenomenon. A major study of multinational corporations reported that 80% of employees work at least some of the time in virtual groups and that "virtual teams are an ever-growing component of global business" (Solomon, 2010). The "virtual classroom" is an increasingly popular distance learning choice at colleges and universities globally. The National Center for Education Statistics reports that 5.5 million college students in the United States in 2014, almost 26% of all students, enrolled in online degree programs or in some distance education courses ("Enrollment in Distance Education Courses," 2014). Most of these courses require online group discussions and team activities and projects.

Because working and participating in groups is an inevitable human experience, it is important to learn how to make that experience a

positive one, and communication competence holds the key to that success. Thus, *the primary purpose of this chapter is to learn how to improve your communication in groups by first understanding the nature of small groups.*

The Structure of Small Groups

Every group has a discernible **structure**—a form or shape characterized by an interrelationship among its parts. In this section, key terms are defined, and then group structure is explored.

Definitions: Setting the Scope

A **group** is composed of three or more individuals, interacting for the achievement of some common purpose(s), who influence and are influenced by one another. Two people qualify as a couple, or **dyad**, not a group (Moreland, 2010). They engage in *interpersonal* communication. Typically, and for good reason, we don't refer to a couple by saying "Aren't they a cute group?" There are qualitative differences between a dyad and a group.

One study revealed that two individuals working together to solve complex problems performed no better than two individuals working alone. Three individuals working together, however, proved to be the "tipping point" for significant improvement in problem solving compared to individuals working alone (Laughlin et al., 2006). Also, coalition formation and majority-minority communication processes when making decisions and solving problems can only occur in units of three or more members. Two individuals in agreement cannot logically form a coalition or argue against a "minority" of no one else. A group dynamic, therefore, begins with no fewer than three individuals.

Also, a group is not merely any aggregation of people, such as 10 strangers waiting in line to buy tickets to a rock concert. These strangers are not standing in line to achieve a common purpose, such as helping each other buy tickets. The same is true for a crowd in a shopping mall or a collection of people waiting to board a plane. In both cases, the presence of other individuals is irrelevant to the achievement of a common purpose, which is buying tickets or clothes or traveling from point A to point B. *To qualify as a group, three or more people must succeed or fail as a unit in a quest to achieve a common purpose.* The essence of a group, therefore, is a We-orientation, not a Me-orientation. Any of these examples, of course, could qualify as a group if circumstances required united action to achieve a mutual goal (e.g., flash mob in a shopping mall).

Group Size: Influencing Structure

Trying to draw a meaningful line between small and large groups is problematic. Communication theorists typically set the upper limit on small groups at about 12 (the size of most juries). There is no absolute number, however, that clearly demarcates small from large groups. It seems more appropriate to define group size in terms of process, not number of individuals. *Groups are small as long as each individual in the group can recognize and interact with every other group member.* Recognition means knowing who is in the group and remembering something about their specific behavior when the group met.

Group size largely determines group structure and, consequently, how we communicate. All small groups are not created equal. A group of three members doesn't function the way a group of eight does. As the size of the group increases, the complexity of group transactions and decision making increases enormously, affecting the group's structure. The possible number of interpersonal relationships between group members grows exponentially as group size increases. Bostrom (1970) provides these calculations:

Group Size	Possible Relationships
3	9
4	28
5	75
6	186
7	441
8	1,056

A triad, or three-member group, has nine possible interpersonal relationships, a four-person group has 28 and so forth, as shown in Figure 10-1.

The relationship that Member A has with Member B may not be the same as the relationship that Member B has with Member A. Member A may see the relationship with Member B as close; Member B may see it as just a work relationship and nothing more. Different perceptions of relationships increase the complexity of transactions between group members. Individual members also can have very different relationships with two or more other members (see relationships 7, 8, and 9 in Figure 10-1). Adding even one member to a group is not an inconsequential event. As newscaster Jane Pauley once observed, "Somehow three children are many more than two."

INCREASING GROUP SIZE: SEVERAL CHALLENGES

Several challenges emerge as groups increase in size and complexity (Lowry et al., 2006). First, *the number of nonparticipants in group discussions increases when groups grow much beyond seven members.* Reticent members may be intimidated by the prospect of speaking to a group, especially a large one. Second, *larger groups easily become factionalized—members of like mind may splinter into smaller, competing subgroups—to withstand pressure from other members to conform to the majority opinion on an issue. Discussion and decision making can become fragmented.* Third, *larger groups may take much more time to make decisions than smaller groups.* With more members, there are potentially more voices to be heard on the issues discussed. Some of these voices may be difficult to silence, holding the group hostage to talkaholics' time-consuming monologues. Fourth, *even scheduling a meeting when all members are available can be a daunting task when groups grow large.* Schedule

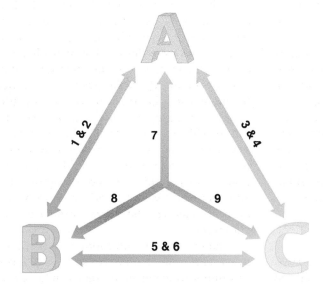

1. A to B   2. B to A

3. A to C   4. C to A

5. B to C   6. C to B

7. A to B and C   8. B to A and C

9. C to A and B

FIGURE 10-1. Nine Possible Relationships in a Group of Three.

conflicts are almost inevitable with groups of more than seven. Finally, group productivity typically decreases as groups grow larger. Too many group members can create decision paralysis. Research shows that each member added to a decision-making group that starts with seven members reduces decision effectiveness by 10%. If you take this *rule of seven* to its logical conclusion, a group of 17 members or more "rarely makes any decisions" (Blenko et al., 2010, p. 88). Another study of 2,623 members in 329 work groups shows that groups composed of three to eight members are significantly more productive than groups composed of nine or more members. Groups of three to six members proved to be the most productive (Wheelan, 2009).

So what is the ideal group size? Amazon CEO Jeff Bezos uses the "two-pizza rule"—A group is too large if it can't be fed by two pizzas (Yang, 2006). That's obviously not a very precise rule (small, medium, or large pizzas? deep dish or thin crust?). *There is no single ideal-sized group for all situations.* Each group experience is unique. For example, complex, politically charged issues may require much larger groups (10 or more) just to give a voice to all interested factions. Groups may be faced with a trade-off between *speed* and *quality* of decision making. Smaller groups of three or four members are faster, but somewhat larger groups often produce higher-quality decisions because their knowledge base is greater. Groups of about five members are a nice compromise when speed and quality are equally important (Pavitt & Curtis, 1994). Offering a precise number, however, is arbitrary and debatable. Instead, *the smallest size capable of fulfilling the purposes of the group should be considered optimum* (Sawyer, 2007). The key point is to keep groups relatively small to reap the greatest advantages. As groups grow in size, complexity increases, and formal structure becomes necessary. Some small groups even evolve into large organizations.

GROUPS VERSUS ORGANIZATIONS: STRUCTURAL DIFFERENCES

What began as a very small business in 1940 with a half-dozen employees grew into 36,000 establishments worldwide employing almost 2 million workers ("Getting to Know Us," 2015). One of every eight workers in America has at some time been employed by this organization (Schlosser, 2002). Can you guess what it is? If you guessed McDonald's, you are correct.

Small groups sometimes grow into large organizations. The transition produces changes in structure and attendant communication processes. Small groups typically operate with an informal structure. Communication is usually conducted as conversation rather than as formal public presentations. Procedures for managing conflict also remain informal. There is little need for formal grievance procedures; differences among three group members can usually be handled through discussion and a meeting. A meeting of a three-person group also certainly doesn't require formal communication rules of parliamentary procedure, such as Robert's Rules of Order, although larger groups may require such procedures. Smaller groups would appear silly using such formal rules. "Point of order," "Call the question," "I move to table the motion," and "I rise to a point of privilege" sound goofy when communicating in a group of three or four friends or colleagues. "Dude, relax! This isn't Congress."

As groups increase in size, complexity increases. Thus, when small groups become large groups and, eventually, organizations, structure typically becomes more formal to cope with the increased complexity. Individuals receive formal titles with written job descriptions. Power is distributed unevenly. Those with the most prestigious title typically are accorded the most status and decision-making power (and salary). The larger the organization, the more likely the structure will become **hierarchical**, meaning that members of the organization will be rank ordered. This pyramid of power has those at the top—the CEOs, presidents, and vice presidents—wielding the most power, with middle managers coming next, and then the "worker bees" or low-level employees having the least influence and autonomy.

Changes in communication follow changes in structure (Adler & Elmhorst, 2008). Formal communication networks emerge in large organizations. In most organizations, low-level employees' communication with those at the top of the power pyramid is restricted. If everyone in the McDonald's organization—all 2 million workers—felt free to email or text message those at the top, information overload would overwhelm decision makers. Formal lines of communication, or networks, are established to control information flow. These chains of command can make **upward communication**—messages that flow from subordinates to superordinates in an organization—very difficult. Typically, there are risks for low-level employees who communicate with bosses, especially if the information is negative. Criticism and complaints can get you fired, ostracized, or perceived as a troublemaker.

Downward communication—messages that flow from superordinates to subordinates in an organization—also can be problematic. Communicating policy changes, giving rationales for assignments, explaining proper procedures and practices for the smooth running of the organization, motivating workers, and offering sufficient feedback to subordinates so that they know when they have performed well and when improvement is needed are vital messages. What you don't want in an organization is what former United Airlines president Ed Carlson called NETMA—Nobody Ever Tells Me Anything.

Horizontal communication—messages between individuals with equal power, such as office workers in the same department—is another common communication pattern in organizations. Horizontal communication coordinates tasks, aids problem solving, shares

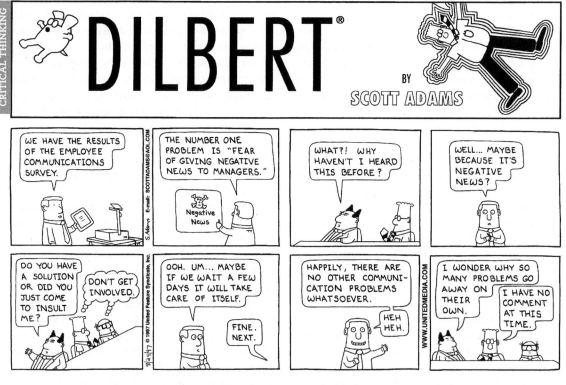

This cartoon illustrates which of the following?

○ **1.** Hierarchical structure of organizations

○ **2.** Upward communication is difficult in organizations

○ **3.** As groups increase in size complexity increases

○ **4.** Communicating negative information to higher-ups within organizations is risky

Answers at end of chapter.

information, enhances conflict management, and builds rapport (Adler & Elmhorst, 2008). It is predominately informal, even casual.

Task and Social Dimensions: Productivity and Cohesiveness

Every group has two primary interconnected dimensions: *task* and *social*. The **task dimension** is the work performed by the group and its impact on the group. The **social dimension** consists of relationships between group members and the impact of these relationships on the group.

Although technical, task-oriented skills are important, a study by the U.S. Department of Labor Employment and Training Administration showed that the critical skills are all socially oriented—oral communication, interpersonal communication, and teamwork abilities (Carnevale, 1996; see also "Top 10 Skills," 2013). Gifted athletes who haven't mastered how to work cooperatively with team members, for example, can create havoc. Walter V. Clarke Associates, a consulting firm, conducted a study of more than 700 professional athletes, NFL draft choices, and college players. The study found that skill at performing tasks is not enough to be successful (cited in Goleman, 1998). Athletes who listened poorly, wouldn't take directions, and came late to meetings were rated by their coaches as less motivated, harder to coach, less talented, and less likely to be leaders.

Productivity is the goal of the task dimension. The extent of a group's productivity is determined by the degree to which it accomplishes its work efficiently and effectively. Five workers performing the same amount of work with the same proficiency as ten workers doubles the group productivity.

Cohesiveness is the goal of the social dimension. The extent of a group's cohesiveness depends on the degree to which members identify with the group and wish to remain in it. Cohesiveness is developed primarily by encouraging compatible membership when possible, developing shared goals that members find challenging and exciting to achieve, accomplishing important tasks that meet these shared goals, creating a positive group history of cooperation, and promoting acceptance of all group members by making each feel valued and welcome.

Cohesiveness and productivity (performance) are interconnected; one affects the other (Cohen & Bailey, 1997). High cohesiveness alone doesn't guarantee group success, but it seems to be a necessary condition for successful task accomplishment. When groups lack cohesiveness, their productivity typically suffers (Beal et al., 2003). Small groups of exceedingly talented individuals will not accomplish tasks well if interpersonal relations among members are immersed in disharmony, anger, resentment, hostility, and rivalries. Low cohesiveness almost always dooms a group to poor performance and low productivity. Members who do not like each other and wish they weren't a part of the group typically exhibit feeble effort and poor performance. Competitiveness among group members, especially when combined with time pressure to accomplish tasks, diminishes cohesiveness (Klein, 1996).

Group members can be so cohesive, however, that they become too concerned with maintaining harmony, and productivity can suffer because of this (Evans & Dion, 2012). When disagreement is avoided because members fear disrupting group cohesiveness, error correction may be sacrificed. This is one aspect of *groupthink*, a problem discussed in Chapter 11.

Finding the proper relationship between productivity and cohesiveness is a persistent dialectical struggle in all groups. Too much focus on productivity can strain interpersonal relationships within a group ("Work, work, work—that's all we ever do"). Too much focus on cohesiveness can lead to anemic effort on the task ("It's party time") (Hardy et al., 2005). Strong cohesiveness combined with a strong group work ethic is an effective combination (Langfred, 1998). The more interconnected group members must be to accomplish important tasks (e.g., performing surgery, flying a passenger jet, or studying for and taking a group exam), the stronger is the cohesiveness-productivity connection (Gully et al., 2012). Both task and social dimensions should be addressed, not one at the expense of the other.

Norms: Rules Governing Group Behavior

Every group, large or small, has *norms* that guide behavior. **Norms** are rules that indicate what group members have to do (obligation), should do (preference), or may not do (prohibition) if they want to accomplish specific goals. This section discusses types of small-group norms, their purpose and source, and conformity to norms.

TYPES OF NORMS: EXPLICIT AND IMPLICIT

There are two types of norms: *explicit* and *implicit*. **Explicit norms** specifically and overtly identify acceptable and unacceptable behavior.

Imagine if the people on the top photo were at a rock concert and those on the bottom photo were attending a symphony. It doesn't work, does it? Every social situation has norms for appropriate attire and conduct.

Explicit norms are typical of a low-context communication style. You want group members to know unambiguously what behavior is expected, preferred, and prohibited, so you tell members explicitly. "No Smoking" signs posted around campus and in public buildings indicate an explicit norm. Laws of society and bylaws of a group are explicit norms. When your instructor tells the class not to interrupt a student during discussions or to attend regularly and be on time, he or she is providing an explicit norm.

In small groups, however, most norms are implicit. **Implicit norms** are observable patterns of behavior exhibited by group members that identify acceptable and unacceptable conduct. Examples might include the following: all group members sit in the same seats for every meeting, no one eats or drinks during meetings, all members dress neatly, everyone is polite, humor is never sarcastic or offensive, and no one says anything derogatory about any other member. These patterns indicate implicit norms. There is no book of rules on how to behave during such meetings, yet members all act as though there were.

Implicit norms may become explicit on occasion, especially when there is a norm violation. Instructors rarely feel compelled to tell students at the beginning of a school term that loud talking during lectures is unacceptable. This is an implicit norm that is taken for granted. It is unlikely that you would find such a rule in the college catalogue, on the schedule of classes, or on a syllabus. If students have ignored this implicit rule, however, instructors may make the implicit norm explicit by pointedly telling the class that talking while a lecture is in progress should cease. It should also be apparent that listening to an iPod, checking or sending text messages, answering cell phones, perusing websites from a laptop, or blogging during class violates implicit norms of appropriate student behavior, but probably every instructor has had to note the norm violation to some students.

CONFORMING TO NORMS: BEING LIKED AND BEING RIGHT

Group members tend to *conform* to group norms. **Conformity** is the inclination of group members to think and behave in ways that are consistent with group norms. Conformity creates a sense of belonging, helps groups accomplish important goals, and can be a positive force. Groups couldn't exist without some conformity. Group discussion would be tumultuous if there were no rules governing such interactions (e.g., taking turns speaking).

Conformity can also be negative. Consider how drinking to excess is encouraged by group norms (Kinard & Webster, 2010; Wechsler & Nelson, 2008). The social norm at many college sporting events, fraternity and sorority parties, and initiation practices to gain membership into various college groups, for example, is to drink to excess. **Binge drinking**—consuming five or more drinks for men and four or more for women in a two-hour period—illustrates not just the power of social norms to promote conformity but also the sometimes negative consequences of such conformity. A major study of binge drinking reported that 37% of college students in the United States binge drink and 14% of college students had consumed 10 or more drinks in a row at least once in the two weeks prior to the survey. Also, 5% reported consuming 15 or more drinks in a row (Johnston et al., 2014).

The consequences of binge drinking are severe. An estimated 1,825 college students die every year from binge drinking, another 600,000 are injured as a direct result, an estimated 700,000 students are physically assaulted by an intoxicated student, and almost 100,000 college students are sexually assaulted or raped as a result of such drinking (Hingson et al., 2009). Conformity to dangerous norms can be serious.

Members conform to group norms for two principal reasons: to be right and to be liked (Cialdini & Trost, 1998). We typically do not want to suffer the embarrassment of being wrong in front of our group, so we look to the group for information on correct behavior. Conformity can keep lines of communication open. Sources of information are likely to be shared when we conform to group norms. Failure to conform, however, can lead to the severing of informational sources that may be critical to meeting personal goals within the group. We also are inclined to strive for acceptance from our group. We "go along to get along." Social acceptance, support, and friendship are often the rewards for conformity; nonconformity typically triggers a negative response from the group, such as social ostracism, personal attack, or expulsion from the group.

Binge drinking is encouraged by group norms. More than a third of all college students binge drink, often with calamitous consequences.

Group conformity is strongest when cohesiveness is high, when members expect to be in the group for a long time, and when members perceive that they have somewhat lower status in the group. Groups have little leverage against members who are not committed to the group, don't plan on remaining in the group for long, or have high status that gives them "the right" to occasional nonconformity.

Roles: Expected Patterns of Behavior

Small-group **roles** are patterns of expected behavior associated with parts that you play in groups. Roles and norms are interconnected. Norms are broad rules that stipulate expected behavior for *every* group member, whereas roles stipulate specific behaviors expected of *individual* group members, not the entire group.

There are two general types of roles: *formal* and *informal*. **Formal roles** assign a position. They are a standard part of the structure of organizations. Titles such as "president," "chair," or "secretary" usually accompany formal roles. Formal roles do not emerge naturally from group transactions; they are assigned. Normally, an explicit description of expected behaviors corresponds to each formal role.

In small groups, roles are mostly informal. **Informal roles** identify functions, not positions. They usually emerge naturally from group transactions. The informal roles a group member plays are identified by observing patterns of communication. If a member often initiates group discussions, the member is playing the role of initiator-contributor. The group does not explicitly tell a member to play an informal role. Groups do, however, indicate degrees of approval or disapproval when a member assumes an informal role.

Informal roles are generally divided into three types: task, maintenance, and disruptive roles. **Task roles** advance the attainment of group goals. The central communicative function of task roles is to extract the optimum productivity from the group. **Maintenance roles** address the social dimension of small groups. The central communicative function of maintenance roles is to gain and maintain group cohesiveness. **Disruptive roles** are Me-oriented. The central communicative function of disruptive roles is

to focus attention on the individual at the expense of group needs and goals. Group members who play these roles often deserve the label "difficult group member."

Because competent communicators recognize the interconnectedness of the task and social dimensions of groups, they look for the optimum balance between task and maintenance roles to achieve group success. They also avoid disruptive roles. Table 10-1 identifies some common task, maintenance, and disruptive roles found in small groups (Benne & Sheats, 1948; Mudrack & Farrell, 1995).

The list in Table 10-1 is not exhaustive. It is also a static list and description, while informal roles unfold transactionally, during discussion, debate, and disagreement. Consider the following transaction:

> **Darise:** I think we should choose the original game option for our group presentation. (*initiator-contributor*)
>
> **Chanelle:** Does anyone have any ideas for an original game? (*information seeker*)
>
> **Daniel:** I'm a video gamer, so I might have some ideas . . . (*information giver*)
>
> **Patrick:** This gaming project just sounds boring. (*blocker*)
>
> **Darise:** I don't see you offering anything more interesting, so why don't you stifle yourself? (*fighter-controller*).
>
> **Patrick:** Really? You just love this project? Stifle your own self! And who uses words like *stifle* anyway? (*fighter-controller*)
>
> **Chanelle:** Come on, you guys; this won't get us anywhere. This isn't bare-knuckle cage fighting. (*harmonizer-tension reliever*) We're a great team, so let's start acting like it. (*supporter-encourager*) Let's get back to Darise's idea of an original game. (*coordinator-director*). What do the rest of you think? José and Brittany, we haven't heard from you. Any thoughts? (*information seeker*).

In this brief transaction, group members assume roles in response to members' communication. Some members play more than one role in rapid-fire succession, while others play only a single role, depending on reactions from participants.

TABLE 10-1 Sample of Informal Roles in Small Groups

Task Roles

1. *Information giver*—provides facts and opinions; offers relevant and significant information based on research, expertise, or personal experience. "I have this report I found on this very subject . . ."

2. *Information seeker*—asks for facts, opinions, suggestions, and ideas from group members. "So, does anyone know why textbooks are so expensive?"

3. *Initiator-contributor*—provides ideas; suggests actions and solutions to problems; offers direction for the group. "Maybe we should consider our first idea again, but from a different angle."

4. *Clarifier*—explains ideas; defines the group position on issues; summarizes proceedings of group meetings; raises questions about the direction of group discussion. "I don't think we're as far apart as it might seem. Consider everything we already agree should occur . . ."

5. *Elaborator*—expands the ideas of other group members; helps the group visualize how an idea or solution would work if the group implemented it. "I think your suggestion would work in the following ways . . ."

6. *Coordinator-director*—pulls together the ideas of others; promotes teamwork and cooperation; guides group discussion; breaks the group into subgroups to work effectively on tasks; regulates group activity. "Let me get everyone's work schedule so that we can find a time to meet."

7. *Energizer*—tries to motivate the group to be productive; acts as a task cheerleader. "Let's keep going; we're making real progress."

8. *Procedural technician*—performs routine tasks, such as taking notes, photocopying, passing out relevant materials for discussion, finding a room to meet, and signaling when allotted time for discussion of an agenda item has expired. "Our time allotment for this issue has expired. Does the group want to add more time for discussion or end it here?"

9. *Devil's advocate*—gently challenges prevailing viewpoints in the group to test and evaluate the strength of ideas, solutions, and decisions. "So, what happens if our plan doesn't play out as we hope it will? Do we have a backup strategy?"

Maintenance Roles

1. *Supporter-encourager*—offers praise; bolsters the spirits and goodwill of the group; provides warmth and acceptance of others. "Great job everyone."

2. *Harmonizer-tension reliever*—maintains the peace; reduces tension with gentle humor; reconciles differences between group members. "Let's try not to make this personal, and perhaps we need to take a break. I think we are growing weary."

3. *Gatekeeper*—controls the channels of communication, keeping the flow of information open or closed depending on the social climate of the group; encourages participation from all group members and open discussion. "We haven't heard from many of you. Any suggestions that you'd like to make?"

Disruptive Roles

1. *Stagehog*—seeks recognition; monopolizes discussion and prevents others from expressing their points of view; wants the spotlight. "Listen to me! I'm not done yet."

2. *Isolate*—withdraws from group; acts indifferent, aloof, and uninvolved; resists inclusion in group discussion.

3. *Fighter-controller*—tries to dominate group; competes mindlessly with group members; abuses those who disagree; picks quarrels, interrupts, and generally attempts to control group proceedings. "You're kind of slow to catch on, aren't you? Try keeping up if you can."

4. *Blocker*—expresses negative attitude; looks to tear down other members' ideas without substituting constructive alternatives; incessantly reintroduces dead issues. "This will never work. Let's stop wasting time on such dumb ideas."

5. *Zealot*—attempts to convert group members to a pet cause or viewpoint; delivers sermons on the state of the world; exhibits fanaticism; won't drop an idea that has been rejected or ignored by the group. "I know I keep saying this and you don't like it, but if you would just listen to me again . . ."

6. *Clown*—interjects inappropriate humor during discussions and meetings; engages in horseplay; diverts attention from the group task with comic routines.

Assuming appropriate task and maintenance roles during group discussion is a matter of timing. A *devil's advocate* (check Table 10-1) is not needed during initial discussion. You do not want to kill potentially creative ideas by immediately challenging them. A *harmonizer-tension reliever* is needed when conflict emerges and threatens to derail the group discussion. This role is irrelevant if there is no tension or disharmony.

Disruptive roles embody incompetent communication. Deal with those who act out disruptive roles the way you would approach difficult group members (discussed in Chapter 11).

Role playing is a fluid process. During a single meeting, a group member may play several informal roles. Groups usually function better when members exhibit flexibility by playing several roles depending on what is required to make the group effective. **Role fixation**—when a member plays a role rigidly with little or no inclination to try other roles—will decrease group effectiveness. The chosen role will be appropriate only some of the time but irrelevant or inappropriate most of the time. Every group needs an *energizer*, but no group needs an energizer bunny all of the time. Constant cheerleading grows tiresome. If that is the only role a member chooses to play, the member will be mostly an annoyance for the group. See Box 10-1 to examine your own role playing behaviors.

BOX 10-1 DEVELOPING COMMUNICATION COMPETENCE

Playing by the Roles: A Self-Assessment

Fill out the self-assessment on roles for any important group that you choose: family, study group, project group, and so on. Optional: Have members of your chosen group fill out this same form about you. *Compare the results.*

1. What was your degree of participation in group activities?   LOW ○1 ○2 ○3 ○4 ○5 HIGH

2. How task oriented (showed interest in meeting group goals) were you?   LOW ○1 ○2 ○3 ○4 ○5 HIGH

3. How socially oriented (concerned about the relationships among group members) were you?   LOW ○1 ○2 ○3 ○4 ○5 HIGH

4. How much influence did you have on the group's decisions?   LOW ○1 ○2 ○3 ○4 ○5 HIGH

Using the scale above, indicate the degree to which you played the following roles by writing the appropriate number:

TASK
_____ **Information giver**   _____ **Information seeker**
_____ **Initiator-contributor**   _____ **Clarifier**
_____ **Elaborator**   _____ **Coordinator-director**
_____ **Energizer**   _____ **Procedural technician**
_____ **Devil's advocate**

MAINTENANCE
_____ **Supporter-encourager**   _____ **Harmonizer–tension reliever**
_____ **Gatekeeper**

DISRUPTIVE
_____ **Stagehog**   _____ **Isolate**
_____ **Fighter-controller**   _____ **Blocker**
_____ **Zealot**   _____ **Clown**

Leadership

The *leader* is often thought to be the most important group role, and learning how to be an effective leader is a fascination for many people. Scholars, philosophers, social scientists, and even novelists have written and spoken extensively about effective leadership. If you type *leadership* in the Google search window, you'll get millions of hits. Business executives and management consultants regularly author books on leadership, mainly offering an abundance of anecdotes that purport to provide sage advice gained from years of corporate experience or management training. Matthew Stewart (2009), a former management consultant turned disapproving critic of the field, offers this assessment: "Upon putting the gurus' books down, however, I find that I get the same feeling I get after reaching the bottom of a supersized bag of tortilla chips. They taste great while they last, but in the end, what am I left with?" (p. 8). He later answers, "platitudes," "bundles of nonfalsifiable truisms," and "transparently unsubstantiated pseudotheories."

Reflecting Stewart's criticism, what I see most of these "business experts" often offering is ego gratification for the authors, who tout their self-proclaimed mastery of leadership based on experience only as CEOs—and sometimes not even that. Untroubled by the paucity of social scientific research to bolster their advice, they share it anyway with those who must adapt to very different situations and circumstances than a corporate CEO might face (Vroom & Jago, 2007). Stewart (2009) notes that these leadership gurus "write with complete indifference to or even against the academics" (p. 249). This assessment highlights the abundant, insightful academic research on leadership effectiveness that is largely ignored while these flashy, quick-fix books are lionized by the press, the public, and the popular culture. With few exceptions, these superficial best-sellers have minimal merit.

Fortunately, you don't have to rely on the self-promotional, peppy platitudes of these personal testimonials on leadership. Thousands of research studies have been published on leadership effectiveness (Vroom & Jago, 2007). One highly acclaimed, bulky reference work fills more than 1,500 pages reviewing the abundant research and theory on leadership (Bass & Bass, 2008).

This reservoir of research serves as the basis for a useful discussion of leadership effectiveness in small groups. In far fewer than 1,500 pages—much to your relief I'm sure—three topics are discussed in this section: *defining leadership, leader emergence,* and *competent leadership.*

Defining Leadership: A Process of Influence

Despite myriad definitions, most agree that *leadership* is primarily a social influence process (Northouse, 2013; Vroom & Jago, 2007). Leaders influence followers, but followers also influence leaders by making demands on leaders to meet expectations and by evaluating their performance in light of those expectations (Avolio, 2007). A person may have an authoritative title, a position that comes with an expectation of leadership, but if no one follows the designated leader, this person is the drum major in a phantom marching band. Longtime leadership researcher Warren Bennis (2007) observes that "the only person who practices leadership alone in a room is the psychotic" (p. 3). He further notes that leadership requires the willingness of followers to be led, so leadership is grounded in the relationship that leaders and followers establish.

The term *follower* evokes negative connotations, such as passive, sheeplike, and even unintelligent. Henry Ford, who pioneered the mass production assembly line, once remarked: "Why is it that when I ask for a pair of hands, a brain comes attached?" (Ford, 2003). This vision of followers parking their brains at the door and mindlessly following orders from leaders, however, has been relegated to the trash heap of archaic thinking. Modern researchers and theorists see leadership as a partnership. Leaders and followers act like contestants on *Dancing with the Stars.* One dancer leads, the other follows, but both influence each other and must operate in tandem to be effective. "Leadership, in short, is very much a 'we thing'" (Haslam et al., 2011, p. xxi).

Thus, "*Leadership is a process and not a person*" (Hollander, 1985, p. 487; see also Vroom & Jago, 2007). When you look at leadership from this perspective, focusing only on leaders without analyzing the complex communication transactions that occur between leaders and followers is largely irrelevant. For example, one study addressed whether angry leaders (e.g., chef Gordon Ramsay on *Hell's Kitchen*) motivate followers better than leaders who are generally positive (e.g., Barack Obama). The answer depends on the degree of agreeableness among followers. *Agreeableness* is an inclination to be pleasant and accommodating with others. Groups composed of members with higher average levels of agreeableness performed more effectively when their leader was supportive and generally positive, whereas groups composed of members with low levels of agreeableness performed more effectively when their leader expressed anger, even though they may have disliked the emotional outbursts (Van Klee et al., 2010). There is no one-size-fits-all leader-follower relationship.

To further clarify what constitutes leadership, a distinction between what Pulitzer Prize-winning historian James MacGregor Burns (1978) originally called *transactional leadership* and *transformational leadership* needs explanation. Transformational leadership inherently involves change. Transactional leadership does not. Transactional leadership, therefore, should be equated with being a manager, not a leader, because *all leadership is transformational* (Rost, 1991). "People expect leaders to bring change about, to get things done, to make things happen, to inspire, to motivate" (Husband, 1992, p. 494). Managers instead maintain the status quo: they implement and enforce policy, but they don't try to change it (Hackman & Johnson, 2013). The primary goal of managers is efficiency (getting the job done).

If someone functioning in a management position is an agent of change, then that person is operating not as a manager but as a transformational leader. Managers can exercise leadership, and leaders can exhibit good management practices (e.g., balance budgets and implement policies efficiently). Some argue that this is the ideal (Kotter, 1990). Again, it's the process (working to produce change), not the person (someone in a position with the title "leader"), that typifies leadership.

Leaders who are perceived to be *extremely* transformational, capable of producing great change, are sometimes called *charismatic leaders* (Judge & Piccolo, 2004). Hackman and Johnson (2013) refer to these leaders as the "superstars of leadership" (e.g., Mahatma Gandhi, Mother Teresa, Martin Luther King, or Pope Francis). Charismatic leaders are visionary thinkers, highly inspirational, decisive, and self-sacrificing (House & Javidan, 2004). They exhibit strong listening skills, self-confidence, empathy, and speaking ability (Levine et al., 2010).

Given this brief theoretical foundation, **leadership** is defined as a leader-follower influence process with the goal of producing positive change that reflects mutual purposes of group members and is largely accomplished through competent communication (Hackman & Johnson, 2013; Rost, 1991). Defining leadership, however, neither informs you regarding how leaders emerge nor, more importantly, indicates what constitutes *effective* leadership.

Leader Emergence: A Process of Elimination

In formal groups and organizations, the role of leader is often assigned; in certain cases, it is a formally elected position. In some small groups, the leader role is designated (chair of a committee), but in most small groups, a leader emerges from group transactions.

Leader emergence is a process of elimination (Bormann, 1990). Small groups typically know what they don't want in a leader but are less certain what they do want. The first to be eliminated from consideration for the leader role are quiet, uninformed, seemingly unintelligent, and unskilled members (Riggio et al., 2003). Group members who express strong, unqualified assertions and those perceived to be poor listeners are also quickly eliminated as candidates (Bechler & Johnson, 1995). A second phase of this process of elimination rejects bossy, dictatorial members and individuals with irritating or disturbing communication styles.

If a leader hasn't emerged after these two phases, the group typically looks for a member who provides a solution to a serious problem or helps the group manage a crisis. Members who are perceived to be effective listeners also frequently emerge as leaders during this stage (Johnson & Bechler, 1998). In addition, members who display high levels of **emotional intelligence**—"the ability to perceive, glean information from, and manage one's own and others' emotions"—emerge as group leaders more readily than those who show a lack of emotional intelligence (Lopez-Zafra et al., 2008; see also Goleman, 2013). Finally, a member may acquire a *lieutenant*, an advocate who promotes him or her for the leader role. This "promoted" member will likely become

the leader unless another member acquires a lieutenant. If there are competing lieutenants, a stalemate may ensue, and no clear leader will emerge.

Groups expect more from leaders who emerge naturally from group transactions than they do from assigned leaders (Hackman & Johnson, 2013). Emergent leaders are held to a higher standard, and failure is less tolerated because the group has more invested in its chosen leader. How the leader performs reflects well, or badly, on the group.

When an outsider (i.e., supervisor or executive) assigns a leader to a group, gaining credibility with group members may be the biggest hurdle for that leader. Gaining credibility to become leaders and to function effectively as leaders in groups is especially difficult for women and ethnic minorities (see Box 10-2).

BOX 10-2 FOCUS ON CONTROVERSY

Gender and Ethnicity: Glass Ceiling or Glass Cliff?

Group bias against women and ethnic minorities is still an issue in leader emergence and leader effectiveness. How much bias still exists, however, remains a controversy.

Groups tend to favor white men when selecting and evaluating leaders (Eagly, 2007). When most people think "leader," they typically think "male" (Koenig et al., 2011). This bias in choosing group leaders occurs despite impressive evidence that women exhibit leadership effectiveness equivalent to or greater than that of men (Eagly, 2007; Eagly et al., 2003). One study of 7,289 leaders showed that women outranked male leaders on 15 of 16 leadership competencies (Zenger & Folkman, 2012). Regarding ethnicity and leadership, research showed that African Americans (male and female) were perceived to have more leadership ability than whites (Craig & Rand, 1998).

Nevertheless, the **glass ceiling**, an invisible barrier of subtle discrimination that excludes

Fortune magazine's "Most Powerful Women Summit" featured Facebook Chief Operating Officer Sheryl Sandberg, whose best-selling book *Lean In* explains the challenges women confront when rising to the highest levels of leadership in business and industry. Sandberg also offers approaches that can be used to improve gender equality.

(continued)

BOX 10-2 FOCUS ON CONTROVERSY

Gender and Ethnicity: Glass Ceiling or Glass Cliff? (continued)

women and ethnic minorities from top leadership positions in corporate and professional America, appears almost bulletproof. In 2015, only 23 women (4.6%) were CEOs of the S & P 500 companies in the United States ("Women CEOs," 2015). Less than 20% of the S & P 500 board members are women (Glinski, 2015). In politics, the situation is only marginally better. In 2015, women held only 20 of the 100 U.S. Senate seats, just 84 of the 435 House seats, and a mere quarter of state legislative seats ("Current Numbers," 2015).

The situation for ethnic minorities gaining important leadership positions is not very encouraging, either. In 2015, only one African American woman and only four African American men were CEOs of a Fortune 500 company (Berman, 2015). Only 24 CEOs (4.8%) of Fortune 500 companies were minorities, a classification that includes African Americans, Asians, and Latinos (Zillman, 2014). Corporate boards of directors are also very white. Almost 87% of total board seats are occupied by white people, African Americans have 7.4%, and Hispanic/Latinos and Asian/Pacific Islanders have 3.3% and 2.6%, respectively (Zillman, 2014).

All of these positions, admittedly, are in organizations, not small groups. Nevertheless, they provide a snapshot of societal leadership opportunities for women and minorities, and all of these top positions offer plentiful chances for leading small groups within organizations (e.g., budget committees, planning councils, and cabinet groups) and for promoting change (transformational leadership), not merely enforcing current policies (managing).

Gaining access to the halls of power, of course, does not automatically ensure leadership effectiveness. Women and minorities often have less power and authority than men who occupy comparable leader positions. When women exercise leadership by being assertive, reactions from followers are often negative, but if women act in stereotypic ways, such as by showing a kind, gentle

approach, they are often viewed as ineffectual and poor leaders (Eagly, 2007; Eagly & Carli, 2007). Women and minorities also can be victimized by what professors Christy Glass and Alison Cook have dubbed the "glass cliff"—the precarious position when a crisis looms and a woman or minority is brought in to solve the problem. As Glass explains, "After they're promoted, if the firm suffers in both the short-, medium- and long-term, they're at very high risk of being replaced by a white CEO." She continues, "White men CEOs lead failing firms all the time. Women and minorities aren't given the benefit of the doubt. When they slip up—even if it's not their fault—it's really easy to blame them because we already have these biases that they may not be as competent as other leaders" (quote by Berman, 2015).

Women and ethnic minorities can improve their chances of emerging as group leaders in several ways:

1. *Increase the proportion of women and ethnic minorities in groups* (Carli, 2001; Shimanoff & Jenkins, 1996). Flying solo is the most difficult position for women and minorities (Taps & Martin, 1990; Yoder, 2002). Being the only woman or minority in a group can brand a person as a "token," thus diminishing his or her chance of emerging as leader. Admittedly, increasing their own representation is a difficult challenge for those in underrepresented groups, so the task falls mostly on those in positions to determine the composition of groups. Consider the **Twenty Percent Rule** (Pettigrew & Martin, 1987), which holds that discrimination decreases when at least 20% of group membership is composed of women or minorities.

2. *Encourage mingling and interaction among members before a leader is chosen.* Getting to know group members while working on a project puts the emphasis on individual

(continued)

(continued)

performance instead of gender and ethnicity (Haslett, 1992).

3. *Emphasize task-relevant communication during group discussions*. Play task roles. This can be empowering. Task-oriented female group members are as likely to become small group leaders as are task-oriented male group members (Hawkins, 1995). This suggestion applies primarily to work groups. Support groups may prefer a more social-oriented leader, which can favor women (Eagly & Carli, 2007).

4. *Be among the first to speak in the group, and speak often* (Shimanoff & Jenkins, 1996). One study of all-male groups found that "token" white males (one white male, three Chinese males) were judged to be leaders in every instance, whereas token Chinese males (one Chinese male, three white males) were never seen as leaders (Kelsey, 1998). The key factor was not ethnicity, however, but degree of participation. In every instance, token white males spoke much more often and longer than the majority Chinese males. Speaking first and often marks a person as leadership material in U.S. culture.

5. *Hone communication skills, and become a competent communicator* (Hackman & Johnson, 2013). Communication is the core of leadership, and communication skills are empowering. The best communicators have the best chance of emerging as group leaders. Those who combine high quantity and high quality of contributions during group discussions have the best chance of being perceived by group members as effective leaders (Jones & Kelly, 2007).

Questions for Thought

1. Have you experienced discrimination in small groups that prevented you from emerging as leader? Discuss the ethics of this discrimination.

2. Will men easily accept greater representation of women and ethnic minorities in groups? What about historically male-dominated occupations and professions, such as firefighters, coal miners, and airline pilots?

Competent Leadership: Evolving Perspectives

Emerging as the leader of a group doesn't automatically evolve into exercising effective leadership. In this section, several perspectives on leadership effectiveness are discussed.

TRAITS PERSPECTIVE: BORN LEADERS

Do you have the "right stuff" to be an effective leader in small groups? That is the core question of the *traits* approach to leadership. This is the "leaders are born, not made" perspective, sometimes referred to as the "heroic model" of leadership (Vroom & Jago, 2007). Thus, we search for heroic, exceptionally talented individuals to idolize as model specimens of leadership. This journey has taken us to odd places. You can buy books on the leadership secrets of Jesus, Colin Powell, Meg Whitman, Donald Trump, Attila the Hun, and Osama bin Laden. One poll found that 80% of Americans viewed Russian President Vladimir Putin as untrustworthy and dishonest, and a third doubted his mental stability, yet 57% of these same respondents saw Putin as possessing "strong leadership qualities" ("Obama Approval," 2014). One survey of CEOs in 60 countries asked which leaders respondents most admired. The top-10 list included Winston Churchill, Mahatma Gandhi, Nelson Mandela, and Napoleon Bonaparte. A notable 96% of male respondents and 83% of female respondents did not include a single female leader in the top 10 ("Leaders CEOs Most Admire," 2014). Clearly, such vastly different, male-dominated lists of model leaders suggest a perspective with significant limitations.

"Our mental representation of what a leader looks like is at odds with what actually makes for a successful leader" (Lieberman, 2013, p. 271). As psychologist Tomas Chamorro-Premuzic (2013) explains, "We commonly misinterpret displays of confidence as signs of competence" and leadership potential, but it is often no more than hubris that results in poor leadership. One disturbing study of 200 business executives (Babiak & Hare, 2006) found that nearly 4% qualified as *psychopaths*—"someone who has no conscience and feels no remorse or empathy" (Perman,

2011). Qualities often associated in the popular mind with effective leadership, such as charm, confidence, aggressiveness, and decisiveness, are often present in abundance in these same psychopathic "horrible bosses." We often don't see the darker side of repellant traits of such manipulative, antisocial bullies until after the charm offensive gets them the job or promotion (Babiak and Hare, 2006). Focusing on stereotypic traits of supposed "leaders" can be misleading.

Traits are relatively enduring characteristics of a person that highlight differences between people and that are displayed in most situations. There are physical traits, such as height, weight, physical shape, physique, and beauty or attractiveness. There are personality traits, such

The trait perspective on leadership explains very little. What do Barack Obama; Facebook CEO Mark Zuckerberg; members of Congress (past and present) Steve King, Louie Gohmert, Michelle Bachmann, and Ted Cruz; president of STX Entertainment Sophie Watts; and Supreme Court Justices Elena Kagan, Sonia Sotomayor, and Ruth Bader Ginsburg have in common that would explain their leadership? Certainly not looks, personality, gender, ethnicity, age, intelligence, physical size, or a host of other traits.

as being outgoing or sociable. There are traits associated with inherent capabilities, such as intelligence and quick-wittedness. There are traits associated with consistent behaviors, such as integrity, trustworthiness, and confidence.

Hundreds of studies have generated separate lists of traits that identify leaders. The traits often differ, and are even contradictory in some cases, when these lists are compared (see Northouse, 2013). Despite some disillusionment with the trait approach after decades of research and contradictory results, however, there do seem to be some universal traits associated with effective leadership, such as persistence, tolerance for ambiguity, honesty, drive, achievement motivation, and self-confidence, to name a few (Avolio, 2007). The trait approach to leadership, however, is no more than a starting point, not an end in itself, for determining competent leadership. This is because, in addition to inconsistent lists of leadership traits, other problems exist.

First, *certain negative traits (e.g., arrogance, dishonesty, and laziness) can predict who will not become leader and be effective, but positive traits can also be neutralized by negative traits.* Intolerance may cancel verbal skills. Arrogance may cancel intelligence or self-confidence. How does one predict which traits, positive or negative, will be most important with which group?

Second, *certain sets of traits may be necessary but not sufficient to become an effective leader.* Fiedler and House (1988) claim that "effective leaders tend to have a high need to influence others, achieve, and they tend to be bright, competent, and socially adept, rather than stupid, incompetent, and social disasters" (p. 87). Intelligence, social and verbal skills, integrity, sense of humor, confidence, or other traits may influence a group. Such traits, however, are not sufficient to be an effective leader. Why? *The trait approach assumes that leadership is a person, not a process.* Such a view is too narrow to be very useful (Hollander, 1985; Vroom & Jago, 2007). The trait approach provides an incomplete explanation of competent leadership.

STYLES PERSPECTIVE: THE AUTOCRAT AND THE DEMOCRAT

There are two general leadership styles (see Box 10-3). The **directive style**, originally called *autocratic*, puts heavy emphasis on the task

dimension with slight attention to the social dimension of groups. Member participation is not encouraged. Directive leaders assume that they have greater power than other group members. Such leaders tell members what to do, and they expect obedience. The **participative style**, originally called *democratic*, places emphasis on both the task and social dimensions of groups. Task accomplishment is important, but social relationships must also be maintained. Unlike the directive style, which uses the dominance form of power, the participative style is empowering. Group members are encouraged to participate meaningfully in discussions and decision making. Participative leaders work to improve the skills and abilities of all group members.

Originally offered by psychologist Kurt Lewin (see Lewin et al., 1939), the **laissez-faire style** is a sit-on-your-derriere approach to leadership, which is to say no leadership at all is exercised (Kozlowski & Ilgen, 2006). There is theoretical consensus that leadership is a social influence process. By definition, however, the laissez-faire style makes no attempt to influence anyone. Thus, it provides no insight regarding effective leadership in groups. "Without influence, leadership does not exist" (Northouse, 2013, p. 5).

Initially, researchers thought the participative style would prove to be superior. Study results, however, have been mixed (Gastil, 1994). Both directive and participative leadership styles can be productive, it seems. Although the participative style fosters more member satisfaction than the directive style (Van Oostrum & Rabbie, 1995), the difference is neither large nor uniform (Gastil, 1994). Some groups don't want their leaders to be participative. The military, for example, wouldn't function effectively if every soldier got to vote on the wisdom of a military action: "All those in favor of attacking the heavily armed enemy on the ridge signal by saying aye; those opposed, nay. Okay, the nays have it. We'll stay put and live another day."

Again, as you might expect from the discussion in Chapter 3, high power-distance cultures tend to expect and prefer the directive leadership style (Brislin, 1993). In such cultures, the participative style may not work as well as the directive style. The directive style also tends to be more effective when groups face stressful circumstances or time constraints (e.g., a cardiac

BOX 10-3 DEVELOPING COMMUNICATION COMPETENCE

What is Your Leadership Style Preference?

Fill out the self-assessment on leadership styles. *Note:* **The rating scale ALTERNATES.**

1. I like it when my supervisor at work admits openly that he/she made a mistake.
   STRONGLY AGREE ○1 ○2 ○3 ○4 ○5 STRONGLY DISAGREE

2. I want to be told what to do on the job, not have to figure it out for myself
   STRONGLY AGREE ○5 ○4 ○3 ○2 ○1 STRONGLY DISAGREE

3. If my team were hiring a new applicant, I prefer that the entire team interview the candidate and make the final decision, not the team leader only.
   STRONGLY AGREE ○1 ○2 ○3 ○4 ○5 STRONGLY DISAGREE

4. I don't want my boss to be my friend; I prefer that my boss remain aloof from the group so he/she can be objective when decisions need to be made.
   STRONGLY AGREE ○5 ○4 ○3 ○2 ○1 STRONGLY DISAGREE

5. I do not think that my boss should reverse the decision of his/her team except in extraordinary circumstances (dangerous mistake).
   STRONGLY AGREE ○1 ○2 ○3 ○4 ○5 STRONGLY DISAGREE

6. I prefer to be told what decisions have been made then informed what I should do to implement these decisions, not engage in time-consuming debate.
   STRONGLY AGREE ○5 ○4 ○3 ○2 ○1 STRONGLY DISAGREE

7. I prefer having many opportunities to provide input before my team leader makes a final decision.
   STRONGLY AGREE ○1 ○2 ○3 ○4 ○5 STRONGLY DISAGREE

8. I want my boss to make the important decisions, not get me and others on our team involved; that's why he/she gets paid the big bucks.
   STRONGLY AGREE ○1 ○2 ○3 ○4 ○5 STRONGLY DISAGREE

9. I want my boss to encourage robust debate and differences of opinion before any decisions are made.
   STRONGLY AGREE ○1 ○2 ○3 ○4 ○5 STRONGLY DISAGREE

10. I want my boss to be decisive, to make decisions confidently, and model a person who is totally in charge.
    STRONGLY AGREE ○1 ○2 ○3 ○4 ○5 STRONGLY DISAGREE

Tally your total score, and divide by 10. The *lower* your average score, the more you prefer *participative* leadership from supervisors/bosses/team leaders. The *higher* your average score, the more you prefer the *directive* leadership style.

Source: Taken from Rothwell (2016).

surgical team performing a heart transplant), whereas the participative style is usually more effective in unstressful situations (e.g., that same cardiac team discussing ways to improve surgical procedures and improve patient survival) (Rosenbaum & Rosenbaum, 1985). These research results indicate that the effectiveness of leadership styles depends on the situation.

SITUATIONAL PERSPECTIVE: LEADERSHIP DEVELOPMENT

Leader traits and styles must operate within a context. The *context* is the situation a leader confronts. No set of traits will provide effective leadership in every group, and no single style of leadership will be suitable for all situations. In fact, it is probably more accurate to speak of directive (autocratic) *situations* and participative (democratic) *situations* faced by a leader than of separate styles isolated from context (Vroom & Jago, 2007).

The Hersey and Blanchard Situational Leadership Model is one of the most widely recognized approaches to leadership effectiveness (Hersey et al., 2007). It highlights the process nature of leadership and the importance of adapting to changing contexts. The model subdivides the directive and participative leadership styles into four types: the *telling style* emphasizes task, not relationships; the *selling style* emphasizes both task and relationships; the *participating style* emphasizes relationships, not task; and the *delegating style* has little focus on either the task or the social dimension of groups. The key situational variable that every leader must consider to determine which style is appropriate is the development level of followers (see Figure 10-2). **Development** (sometimes called *readiness*) is composed of the ability of group members, their motivation, and their experience with relevant tasks. Lots of experience and strong motivation to accomplish a task aren't enough if a member's ability is poor. Likewise, substantial ability and experience don't compensate for weak motivation.

When the development level of followers is low, the telling and selling styles are most appropriate. As development level increases, effective leaders choose the participative and delegating styles. When someone is hired for a job, for example, effective leaders begin diagnosing the development level of the employee. Development levels vary from D1 (low task competence, high motivation to tackle the task) to D4 (high competence, high commitment). Normally, a person at the D1 level would not be hired. Who would want someone of this caliber? Thus, the telling style would mostly be used with an employee whose development level falters because of stress, personal trauma, or technological advances beyond the employee's abilities. Using the telling style with an able worker would seem like micromanaging. The selling style requires interaction between leader and follower. This style would normally be used with a new employee, as the supervisor and the employee begin to establish a relationship. With greater development comes a further shift in

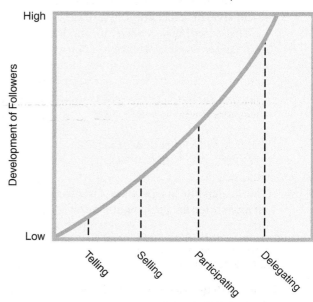

FIGURE 10-2. Situational Leadership Model: The Telling (D1), Selling (D2), Participating (D3), and Delegating (D4) Leadership Styles Related to Development of Followers.

leadership style. The participating style is appropriate for the worker who now knows the ropes and has sufficient readiness to offer suggestions and engage in decision making. Finally, when the development level is high, an effective leader steps out of the way and delegates responsibility and decision making to the worker.

The situational leadership perspective makes intuitive sense, although the research to support this perspective is somewhat skimpy, even contradictory (Northouse, 2007; Vecchio et al., 2006; Yukl, 2006). One leadership style does not fit all situations. An effective leader matches the style with the development level of followers and the group as a whole. Newly formed groups require greater supervision and direction than experienced groups. Experienced, capable groups work best when leaders are "guides on the side." They offer relational support and encouragement but allow the group to perform its task without much interference. As mentioned, leaders can become more directive (telling or selling) if groups or individual members slip in their development levels because of stressful events or personal difficulties. This means that leaders should be sensitive to signals from group members that development levels have diminished and a different style of leadership is required.

The situational leadership model rightly emphasizes the importance of context to leadership effectiveness. A drawback of this particular model, however, is that the role of follower influence on leaders is viewed as indirect. What the leader does gets center stage.

COMMUNICATION COMPETENCE PERSPECTIVE: THE OVERRIDING PERSPECTIVE

The leadership perspectives discussed in this chapter offer useful insights about leadership effectiveness. Effective leadership, however, is ultimately a matter of communication competence. No set of traits, particular styles, or matching of styles with situational development will be effective without competent communicators. The most effective leaders are the most proficient communicators. As Hackman and Johnson (2013) conclude, "Extraordinary leadership is a product of extraordinary communication" (p. 98).

The We-orientation of the communication competence model is crucial for leadership effectiveness. Carl Larson and Frank LaFasto (1989) studied 75 highly diverse teams (e.g., mountain climbing, cardiac surgery, and professional football teams), and their conclusion was unequivocal: "The most effective leaders . . . were those who subjugated their ego needs in favor of the team's goal" (p. 128). Effective leaders try to empower group members, not stand out as dominant and deserving of adoration or blind obedience. Charles Garfield (1986) interviewed more than 500 top leaders and concluded that they use three primary skills: delegating, stretching the abilities of group members, and encouraging thoughtful risk-taking. All three skills empower group members. As Larson and LaFasto (1989) concluded, "[L]eaders create leaders" (p. 128).

Competent communication is critical to effective leadership because a leader sets the emotional tone of the group. Top executives who fail as leaders exhibit insensitivity to others, are brutally critical, and are too demanding (Goleman, 1998). *They lack emotional intelligence* (Goleman, 2013). They are either blind to the impact their negative communication patterns have on followers, or they just don't care. When a leader expresses rage, shows disrespect for group members, berates those who make mistakes, humiliates members in front of the group, and exhibits arrogance and pettiness, the entire group is tarnished by this incompetent communication. Such "emotional incontinence," as Birgitta Wistrand calls it, ripples throughout the group (quoted by Goleman, 1998). When leaders fail to control themselves emotionally, members become hesitant, anxious, fearful, angry, and depressed.

These behaviors also raise ethical issues. Disrespecting followers violates a key ethical standard discussed in Chapter 1: competent leadership is to "serve others" not issue edicts and threats. Ethical leaders are **servant leaders** who "place the good of followers over their own self-interests and . . . demonstrate strong moral behavior toward followers" (Northouse, 2013, p. 220).

Finally, effective leaders create a supportive climate, encourage open communication, stimulate cooperation and a collaborative spirit, show empathy, and express optimism and a positive attitude (Goleman, 2013). Effective leaders adapt to changing circumstances and a variety of personalities.

Summary

Many benefits can be derived from working effectively in groups, and communication competence is central to our attitude about groups. Those who have little communication training typically find the group experience daunting and frustrating. Those who learn to communicate competently typically find the group experience far more beneficial.

The structure of small groups is largely shaped by group size and is composed primarily of norms and roles. Norms are rules that govern the behavior of group members. Roles are patterns of behavior that group members are expected to exhibit. The leader role is central to group structure. Playing the role of leader, however, does not equate to effective leadership. Effective leadership is not a person; it is a transformational process. Effective leadership requires competent communication. Leaders should be sensitive to the changing needs and situations within the group, assume the appropriate style for a given situation, and resist displays of competitive, defensive communication when dealing with group members.

Answer for Critical Thinking caption:

DILBERT (P. 262): #1, #2, #3, and #4

Quizzes Without Consequences

Test your knowledge before your exam! Go to the companion website at www.oup.com/us/rothwell, click on the Student Resources for each chapter, and take the Quizzes Without Consequences.

Film School Case Studies

A League of Their Own (1992). Comedy/Drama; PG

Director Penny Marshall's amusing and entertaining treatment of the first women's professional baseball league. Analyze leadership styles, especially those used by the Tom Hanks character. Does Hanks change leadership styles as the movie progresses?

Crimson Tide (1995). Drama; R

Taut drama about a nuclear submarine given an order (or so it seems) to launch a pre-emptive strike against a dissident rebel group in Russia. Examine the leadership style of the two main characters, played by Gene Hackman and Denzel Washington.

Further analyze the leader-follower relationship and the ethics of leadership.

Horrible Bosses (2011). Dark Comedy; R

Three friends set out to murder their psychopathic bosses. Beware the vulgarity and the dark humor. Examine horrible bosses from the traits perspective and research on psychopathic leaders.

Steve Jobs: The Man in the Machine (2015). Documentary; R

The iconic Steve Jobs is revealed to be a "leader" with deeply disturbing traits in this hard-hitting documentary by Academy Award winner Alex Gibney. Analyze Jobs as a leader, applying the various perspectives on effective leadership.

Pleasantville (1998). Comedy/Drama; PG-13

David (Tobey Maguire) and Jennifer (Reese Witherspoon) are two modern teenagers zapped into the black-and-white world of a 1950s sitcom. This is a trippy little movie with a nice message. Analyze the impact of norms on behavior and the reactions to nonconformity.

Star Trek (2009) and Star Trek Into Darkness (2013). Action/Adventure; PG-13

Terrific reboot of the *Star Trek* movie series. Analyze Captain Kirk's (Chris Pine) leadership style. Does he adapt to the changing situations? Contrast Kirk's leadership style with Spock's.

The Jane Austen Book Club (2007). Romance; PG-13

Several women and one man form a book club to read and discuss all six books by Jane Austen. Examine the roles that develop in the group. Identify who plays task, maintenance, and disruptive roles. Analyze leadership emergence and leadership effectiveness.

The Wolf of Wall Street (2013). Biography/Comedy; R

Jordon Belfort (Leonardo DiCaprio) is a ruthless stockbroker and business executive. Beware graphic sex and vulgarity. Is Belfort a psychopathic leader? Compare his positive and negative traits, analyze his leadership effectiveness, and consider his ethics.

1. Recognize and combat problems of disruptive group members and social loafers.

2. Implement the Standard Agenda for competent group decision making and problem solving.

3. Identify constructive ways to build the structure of teams.

Creating Effective Groups

THE UNITED STATES FIELDED an imposing lineup for the 2006 World Baseball Classic, which included superstars Derek Jeter and Ken Griffey Jr. This was the first year that teams from around the world, comprised of professional players, competed for the world title in baseball; some viewed it as the real World Series. The U.S. team was embarrassed, however, when it lost to Mexico, Canada, and South Korea and failed to make even the semifinal round. In the second World Baseball Classic in 2009, the U.S. team did better, but even though they fielded a team whose aggregate annual professional salaries amounted to $160 million, they lost to Japan 9-4 in the semi-finals. The 2013 results for the United States marked a step backward. The U.S. team ranked sixth. In the three tournaments, the U.S. win-loss record is 10-10, which ranks seventh overall ("World Baseball Classic," 2015).

In stark contrast, the 1980 U.S. Olympic ice hockey team was a group of college players who had never played together

4. Develop teamwork in small groups.

until six months before the Olympic Games. At the time, the Soviet Union had the most powerful hockey team in the world (maybe ever), with a 44-0 win-loss record in international competition. The Soviet team was capable of defeating a professional group of NHL all-stars, which it did before the Olympics (the score was 6-0). In one of the most stunning upsets in modern sports history, however, the U.S. team defeated the Soviet team 4-3 in the "Miracle on Ice." The Americans went on to win the gold medal.

Why do some groups and teams succeed and others fail? Why doesn't assembling a group of the most highly skilled individuals assure success? Shouldn't the best produce the best? *The primary purpose of this chapter is to examine why groups succeed and fail and how to make groups effective.*

Why Groups Succeed and Fail

James Surowiecki (2005), author of *The Wisdom of Crowds*, claims that groups can often outsmart individuals working alone. Psychologist Keith Sawyer (2007) refers to this collective wisdom as "group genius."

Synergy: Creating Group Genius

Groups often outperform individuals, and sometimes they outperform individuals spectacularly. In academic circles, this group genius effect is called *synergy*. **Synergy** (*syn* = together; *ergon* = work) occurs when the work of group members yields a greater total effect than the sum of the individual members' efforts could have produced. When this joint action of group members produces performance that exceeds expectations based on the perceived abilities and skills of individual members, synergy has occurred (Salazar, 1995). Thus, the whole is not equal to the mere sum of its parts but is greater than the sum of its parts. Synergy is like combining cancer-fighting drugs to produce far greater effects than taking the drugs separately could produce. This is the basis of chemotherapy.

The 1980 U.S. hockey team is a stunning example of group synergy. Comparing the individual abilities of players on the U.S. and Soviet teams, it should have been no contest. The Soviet team, on paper, was the far superior team. In fact, a couple of weeks before the Olympics, the U.S. team played a practice match against the Soviet team and lost badly (the score was 10-3). Sometimes, however, less capable individuals working smoothly as a team pull off a synergistic miracle.

A June 23, 1998, *NBC News at Sunrise* report provides another apt example of synergy. A Little League team in Tucson, Arizona, called the Diamondbacks, was composed of players no other teams wanted because they were considered misfits who were not good enough to play. These misfits compiled a perfect record (18-0) to win the league championship. The group effort far exceeded expectations of success based on the individual abilities of the players.

How does synergy happen? Synergy is typically the product of cooperation within a group (Sawyer, 2007). It occurs primarily by group members working together, unselfishly, in a coordinated effort to achieve a common goal, not by individual, independent effort (Carey & Laughlin, 2012). The 1980 U.S. Olympic hockey team achieved synergy because the team's coach, Herb Brooks, was unrelenting in his emphasis on players working together in a coordinated effort that strongly discouraged individual glory to accomplish the group's mission (winning a gold medal). As Brooks put it, "You're looking for players whose name on the front of the sweater is more important than the one on the back" (quoted in "Coach Known Best," 2003).

In addition to cooperation, groups composed of members with **deep diversity**—substantial variation among members in task-relevant skills, knowledge, abilities, beliefs, values, perspectives, and problem-solving strategies—have greater potential to produce synergy than groups with little diversity (Harrison et al., 2002). "Group genius can happen only if the brains in the team don't contain all the same stuff" (Sawyer, 2007, p. 72). In one simulation study comparing groups with deep diversity and those without, the deeply diverse groups produced a synergistic effect, outperformed even their best individual member, and cooperative interaction among members during problem solving benefited their performance. Groups without deep diversity didn't perform nearly as well (Larson, 2007).

Finally, synergy is the product of group members who are highly motivated to achieve a strongly desired common goal, such as when grades, jobs, or lives are at stake (Forsyth, 2014). If you are working on a group presentation for class and all members are strongly motivated to achieve an "A" grade, then there is strong potential for synergy to occur, especially if the previous two conditions for synergy (cooperation and deep diversity) are also present.

Groups don't always produce the group genius of synergy, however. Synergy won't occur simply because individuals form a group. A single expert on a technical topic, for example, can provide better advice than a group of uninformed members. If you have a legal question, go see a good lawyer. Seeking legal advice from your roommates who know next to nothing about the law is inviting serious consequences, such as prison (criminal charges) or poverty (civil suit).

Nevertheless, groups often produce exceptional results because they can share the labor required to research even technical or complex subjects, can pool knowledge and share information, and can correct errors more readily because there are more heads devoted to spotting mistakes and misjudgments. As the Japanese proverb says, "None of us is as smart as all of us."

Challenges That Can Impede Group Genius

Groups often face significant challenges that can prevent synergy from occurring. In this section, the challenges you face from *difficult group members*, *social loafers*, and *diverse membership* are discussed.

DIFFICULT GROUP MEMBERS: ADDRESSING DISRUPTION

In one of my small-group classes, a group of six women was formed to work on a project. Their communication was warm, friendly, and harmonious. They appeared enthusiastic about working together. They brainstormed a long list of ideas for their project and settled on one option within a short period of time. The following period, however, a male student needed to join a group because he had missed the previous class and the other groups were already somewhat larger. This new group member single-handedly transformed a harmonious, task-effective group into a frustrating group experience for everyone. This particular individual enjoyed telling sexist jokes, making derogatory remarks to the other members, and fighting any suggestions that were not his own. He also told his astonished group members that he "hoped PMS wouldn't be a problem" when they worked on their project.

The women were stunned. After class, they all approached me, told me what he had said to them and how he had acted, and requested that this disruptive individual be assigned to another group. I turned down their request, not wanting to pass the problem to another group. I did confront the disruptive student, however, about his behavior. This improved the situation somewhat, but he was never a productive group member.

Difficult group members exhibit a wide variety of troublesome behaviors. *The disruptive roles identified in Chapter 10 provide a common list of such behaviors.* The male student who disrupted the previously all-female group adopted the fighter-controller and clown roles. Disrupters are not team players but Me-oriented individualists. They diminish the group performance by disrupting social relationships. Difficult group members can destroy group cohesiveness

(Wellen & Neale, 2006). (See Box 11-1 to assess your own group communication in this regard)

Research on **bad apples**—disruptive members who poison the group ("One bad apple spoils the barrel")—demonstrates just how disturbing even one such group member can be (Felps et al., 2006; "Ruining It for the Rest of Us," 2008). In one study, a skilled student actor portrayed three versions of "bad apple" behavior in several groups ("Ruining It," 2008). He played a *jerk* who made insulting comments to other group members, such as "Do you know anything?" and "That's a stupid idea." He played a *slacker* who refused to contribute during a 45-minute difficult group task but text messaged a friend and responded with "Whatever" or "I really don't care" to other group members' ideas. Finally, he played a *depressive pessimist* who called the task boring, predicted group failure, and placed his head on the table.

The results were stunning. Regardless of team talent and capabilities, those groups that had a single bad apple scored between 30% and 40% lower on a challenging task compared to teams with no bad apple. The bad apple's disruptive behavior was also contagious. When playing the jerk, the bad apple's insults triggered counter-insults from group members. When playing the slacker, his indifferent behavior encouraged indifferent behavior from

Bad apple research shows which of the following?

○ **1.** One bad member can reduce the productivity of the group between 20% and 25%

○ **2.** Bad apple behavior by a single member can be highly contagious, infecting other group members and causing them to be disruptive

Answers at end of chapter.

○ **3.** A single bad apple can be easily controlled because he or she is badly outnumbered

○ **4.** You need more than one bad apple to poison a group and negatively affect its productivity.

BOX 11-1 DEVELOPING COMMUNICATION COMPETENCE

Are You a Difficult Group Member?

Rate honestly your likely behavior in each of the scenarios that follow. This should reveal whether you are a difficult group member. Optional Alternative: After answering this questionnaire, ask fellow class or team members to complete this same assessment about you, but only if you feel comfortable making such a request. If team members are hesitant, encourage them to complete the assessment without identifying themselves in the questionnaire (ideally, all team members should complete the assessment to preserve anonymity). Compare the results by following the scoring system at the end of this assessment.

1. When a topic of great interest to me is discussed in my group, I tend to talk much longer and more forcefully than I know I should.   FREQUENTLY ○ 5 ○ 4 ○ 3 ○ 2 ○ 1 RARELY

2. During group discussions, I typically remain silent, exhibiting lack of interest in the proceedings.   FREQUENTLY ○ 5 ○ 4 ○ 3 ○ 2 ○ 1 RARELY

3. When my group attempts to work on a task, especially one of little interest to me, I prefer to joke around and be comical instead of focusing on the task.   FREQUENTLY ○ 5 ○ 4 ○ 3 ○ 2 ○ 1 RARELY

4. When I oppose what my group decides, I am inclined to reintroduce the issue already decided, even though I know there is little chance the group will change its decision.   FREQUENTLY ○ 5 ○ 4 ○ 3 ○ 2 ○ 1 RARELY

5. I often quarrel openly with group members by raising my voice, interrupting to interject forcefully my own opinion, and criticizing those who disagree with me.   FREQUENTLY ○ 5 ○ 4 ○ 3 ○ 2 ○ 1 RARELY

6. I have strong opinions that often color my participation during group discussions, and I attempt to convert group members to my way of thinking even if they are unresponsive.   FREQUENTLY ○ 5 ○ 4 ○ 3 ○ 2 ○ 1 RARELY

7. I'm inclined to predict failure of the group, especially if a risk is involved, and I tend to focus on what will go wrong with my group's decisions, not on what will go right.   FREQUENTLY ○ 5 ○ 4 ○ 3 ○ 2 ○ 1 RARELY

Total your responses for all seven of your answers (maximum score = 35; minimum score = 7). Determine your average score (divide total score by 7). If your average score is 3.0 or higher, you tend toward being a difficult group member. Any single answer that is 3, 4, or 5 indicates trouble for your group on that particular behavior. These seven scenarios correspond to the disruptive informal roles discussed in Chapter 10.

other group members, who said things such as "Let's just get this over with. Put down anything." When playing the depressive pessimist, other group members became disengaged.

Another study showed that a disruptive member of a work team who exhibited rude behavior toward coworkers had prompted half of those who were interviewed to contemplate leaving their jobs, and 12% actually quit (Pearson et al., 2000). The best employees are the most likely to leave a job to escape a disruptive coworker because they have a better chance of finding a new job (Mitchell & Lee, 2001). This leaves less capable coworkers and leads to a further deterioration in group performance (Felps et al., 2006). Even more disturbing are several studies of disruptive behavior among health care teams in hospitals. The results? "The impact of disruptive behaviors threatens not only patient safety, but also the wellbeing of health care workers and their ability to perform competently in their job" (Longo, 2010; see also Martin & Hemphill, 2013).

You can take several steps to deal with difficult group members:

1. *Make certain a cooperative climate has been created by the group.* Are communication patterns supportive or defensive (see Chapter 8)? Is meaningful participation encouraged? Are all group members treated with respect?

2. *Don't encourage disruptive behavior.* Laughing nervously at a disrupter's offensive "jokes" encourages the antisocial behavior. Don't allow the disrupter to dominate conversations, interrupt other members, or in any way intimidate the group. Giving the trouble maker a soapbox only encourages the bad behavior. Difficult as it may be, simply ask the disrupter to wait his or her turn, respect the other members, and listen. The six women who endured their bad apple admitted later that this had been a problem for them.

3. *Confront the difficult person directly* (see Chapter 9). If the entire group is upset with the disrupter, the group should confront the trouble maker. Follow the guidelines for supportive communication when confronting a difficult member (see Chapter 8).

4. *If all else fails, remove the disrupter from the group* (LaFasto & Larson, 2001; Longo, 2010). One clothing retailer, for instance, fired a top salesman for constant disruptive behavior. Store sales jumped nearly 30% once the bad apple was dismissed (Sutton, 2011). If the troublesome group member cannot be removed for some reason, keep interactions with this person to a minimum.

5. *Be unconditionally constructive.* Imitating the disrupter's troublesome behavior produces

a conflict spiral. Only one group in the "bad apple" study resisted the disrupter's negative influence and performed effectively. This group had a strong member who didn't return insults with insults, didn't get angry, but instead listened intently to everyone and asked lots of questions. He set a constructive tone and refused to be sidetracked. His father was a diplomat, so perhaps he learned to be diplomatic from him.

In most situations, these steps will work well. If you lose your temper when using these steps, don't fret. It may be no more than a temporary setback, but at the very least, the trouble maker is put on notice that "bad apple" behavior will not be suffered in silence.

SOCIAL LOAFERS: DEALING WITH LACKLUSTER EFFORT

Social loafing is one of the most common complaints about working in groups, especially among students working on class projects (Aggarwal & O'Brien, 2008). This is a particularly challenging bad apple behavior worthy of additional focus. **Social loafing** is the tendency of individuals to reduce their work effort when they join groups (Piezon & Ferree, 2008). Social loafers "goof off" when tasks need to be accomplished. They miss some meetings and show up late to others. They fail to complete tasks important to overall group performance. Social loafers exhibit scant effort because of weak motivation, disinterest in the group, or poor attitude (see Box 11-2).

Social loafing is not the same as shyness. Shy individuals may be strongly committed to the group but reluctant to participate in discussions because of communication anxiety or fear of disapproval (McCroskey & Richmond, 1992). Shy members may attend all meetings and never be tardy.

Social loafing increases with group size (Chidambaram & Tung, 2005). It is easier to reduce effort expended in a larger group than in a smaller group and not be noticed. Social loafing also occurs because individual group members often do not see the connection between their personal effort and the outcomes desired by the group (Karau & Williams, 1993).

BOX 11-2 DEVELOPING COMMUNICATION COMPETENCE

Social Loafing: A Self-Assessment

Make honest assessments of your participation in small-group decision making and problem solving.

1. I am on time for small-group meetings.　　RARELY ○1 ○2 ○3 ○4 ○5 ALMOST ALWAYS

2. I leave small-group meetings early.　　RARELY ○1 ○2 ○3 ○4 ○5 ALMOST ALWAYS

3. I am quiet during small-group discussions.　　RARELY ○1 ○2 ○3 ○4 ○5 ALMOST ALWAYS

4. My attention during small-group discussions is focused on the task.　　RARELY ○1 ○2 ○3 ○4 ○5 ALMOST ALWAYS

5. I am strongly motivated to perform well in small groups.　　RARELY ○1 ○2 ○3 ○4 ○5 ALMOST ALWAYS

6. When other group members show little interest in accomplishing a task successfully, I lose interest in achieving success.　　RARELY ○1 ○2 ○3 ○4 ○5 ALMOST ALWAYS

7. When other group members seem uninvolved in participating on the group task, I also reduce my participation.　　RARELY ○1 ○2 ○3 ○4 ○5 ALMOST ALWAYS

Determine your average score on statements 1, 4, and 5 (add the scores, and divide by 3), then determine your average score on items 2, 3, 6, and 7 (add the scores, and divide by 4). Your average score on statements 1, 4, and 5 should be high (4–5), and your average score on statements 2, 3, 6, and 7 ideally should be quite low (1–2), indicating little social loafing.

Groups that achieve success and receive rewards for such success typically have little problem with loafers. This is especially so when each group member perceives that his or her individual effort is necessary for the group to succeed on a valued task (Hart et al., 2001).

There are several ways to address the problem of social loafers (Forsyth, 2014):

1. *Choose meaningful tasks* (Dean, 2009; Karau & Williams, 2001). Few group members will be motivated to work on tasks that hold no interest or meaning for them. Granted, not all tasks can be motivating. Some tasks must be performed even though they are dreary, mind-numbing jobs. Nevertheless, busy work should be kept to a minimum so that the totality of a group's work is viewed as involving and interesting. Try letting group members choose which part of a project they would most like to tackle. Some members may enjoy doing Internet research, others interviewing experts on a topic, and still others constructing a PowerPoint demonstration.

2. *Establish a group responsibility norm* (Hoigaard et al., 2006; Longo, 2010). Make clear that every group member is expected to pull his or her weight and live up to a code of conduct.

3. *Hold members accountable* (Aggarwal & O'Brien, 2008). Face-to-face peer appraisal that concentrates on developing each member's abilities, not on criticizing weak effort, reduces social loafing.

4. *Confront the loafer.* Use supportive communication patterns and assertiveness when

Social loafing:

○ **1.** is the same as shyness exhibited by a group member

○ **2.** decreases as the size of the group increases

○ **3.** occurs because individual group members often do not see the connection between personal effort and group outcomes

○ **4.** is, at root, a lack of group member motivation

Answers at end of chapter.

confronting the lackluster effort of the loafer.

5. *Expel the loafer* (Felps, 2006; Longo, 2010). This should be your last resort, if all else fails.

DIVERSE MEMBERSHIP: THE CHALLENGE OF DIFFERENCE

Chapter 3 documented the increasing diversity of our population. The likelihood that you will participate in groups composed entirely of individuals very much like yourself is becoming ever more remote. This is an opportunity and a challenge. Research shows that gender diversity in small groups enhances team performance (Curseu & Schruijer, 2010). Also, groups that include a mix of genders and ethnicities combat biases more effectively than more homogeneous groups (Marcus-Newhall et al., 1993).

Member diversity, however, poses significant challenges to groups and individuals alike (Chao & Moon, 2005; Mannix & Neale, 2005). Older students in a group of mostly teenagers

may have a challenge identifying with younger members, and vice versa. Individuals fresh out of college and thrown into the corporate world of much older and more experienced individuals may find it intimidating to work with more mature, experienced members. With diversity may come greater difficulty finding agreement in the group. This is especially true with deep diversity, in which members have a wide variety of opinions, beliefs, and values (Harvey, 2013). Cohesiveness and group satisfaction may be more difficult to develop and maintain. There can even be a perceived competition for power and resources between majority and minority members that could result in hostile communication and discrimination (Mannix & Neale, 2005).

Competent communication provides a promising approach to meeting these challenges posed by group member diversity. If small groups are to succeed, using communication to develop perceptions of commonality among diverse members to create a sense of strong group identity that transcends stereotypes and issues of gender, race, socioeconomic status, values, and power differences is particularly essential.

Avoid Groupthink: Preventing Decisions Beyond Bad

How could the United States have been caught sleeping when the Japanese executed a sneak attack on Pearl Harbor, resulting in the worst naval disaster in U.S. history? Why did John Kennedy and his cabinet advisers ever launch the Bay of Pigs invasion? After all, 1,400 poorly trained Cuban exiles were facing a 200,000-strong Cuban army in a fruitless attempt to overthrow Fidel Castro. Kennedy lamented afterward, "How could I have been so stupid to let them go ahead?" (quoted in Janis, 1982, p. 16). Add to these disasters the space shuttle *Challenger* explosion, the ill-advised U.S. entry into the Iraq War, and more recently, the implosion of the energy colossus Enron and the Pennsylvania State University sex abuse scandal that forever tarnished the legacy of football coach Joe Paterno. Each of these events is an instance of *groupthink* (Janis, 1982; Mansfield,

1990; Cohen & DeBenedet, 2012; Senate Select Committee on Intelligence, 2004).

Groupthink is "a mode of thinking that people engage in when they are deeply involved in a cohesive in-group, when the members strivings for unanimity override their motivation to realistically appraise alternative courses of action" (Janis, 1982, p. 9). The group places excessive emphasis on cohesiveness (getting along) and concurrence-seeking (presenting a unanimous front to outsiders). Consensus seeking, cooperation, and cohesiveness are all part of competent group decision making, but these normally vital and constructive elements can produce terrible consequences when taken to an extreme. The more cohesive a group is, the greater is the danger of groupthink (Rovio et al., 2009).

Groupthink has several specific characteristics (Janis, 1982; Mohamed & Wiebe, 1996; Street, 1997). First, disagreement is discouraged during group discussions because it is viewed as disruptive to group cohesiveness. Second, there is strong pressure to conform, so there is at least the appearance of group unity. Dissenters are pressured to be "team players." Third, the group lacks a structured decision-making process that encourages consideration of divergent options and opinions. Fourth, there is an in-group/out-group competitive mentality. Everyone who is not a group member is considered part of the out-group. This in-group/out-group mentality gives rise to feelings that the in-group is morally superior to out-groups; outsiders are often negatively stereotyped or branded as evil. An offshoot of this in-group/out-group view of the world is a strong group identity that gives members a feeling of pride and prestige from belonging to the group. Those who knew about the sex abuse at Penn State feared damaging the reputation of the institution with which they closely identified, so they kept quiet and permitted the abuse to continue (Cohen & DeBenedet, 2012).

Janis (1989) offers four suggestions to prevent groupthink:

1. *The group could consult an impartial outsider with expertise on the problem discussed.* This would reduce the danger from excessive cohesiveness leading to poor group decisions. This is sometimes why consultants are hired from outside an organization or group to give advice and counsel.

2. *Reduce pressure on group members to conform.* The group leader could withhold his or her point of view during early discussions. In this way, the appearance of dominance in power relationships between a more powerful group leader and less powerful members can be avoided, and members will be more inclined to express honest opinions.

3. *The group could assign the devil's advocate role* (see Chapter 10) to a specific member. This role, in which an individual "for the sake of argument" challenges a prevailing group viewpoint, combats the excessive concurrence seeking typical of groups that slide into groupthink. The devil's advocate tests the strength and validity of group ideas to prevent poor decision making.

4. *The team could set up a "second chance" meeting where members reconsider a preliminary decision.* This allows teams to reflect on any proposal and avoid making impulsive decisions.

Ultimately, what is required to combat groupthink is a group climate that encourages robust discussion of opposing viewpoints.

Developing Competent Group Decision Making and Problem Solving

Small groups succeed or fail for many reasons, such as disruption from difficult group members and social loafers, challenges posed by group diversity, and groupthink. Addressing each of these challenges as already advised is important, but that still does not assure group success. In this section, additional approaches to achieve group success are presented.

Structure Decision Making: Using the Standard Agenda

Without a structure for decision making, groups often leap to consideration of solutions before adequately discussing and exploring the causes of problems. Free-floating discussions usually result in poor time management, aimless conversation, high-status members' domination of discussions, squelching of minority viewpoints, and escalation of conflict spirals (Sunwolf & Frey, 2005). This leads to ineffective decision making. Thus, successful groups typically have a systematic, structured method of decision making and problem solving; unsuccessful teams typically do not (LaFasto & Larson, 2001).

The **Standard Agenda** provides one such highly effective structured method of decision making and problem solving. It is based on the **reflective thinking model** of John Dewey (1910)—a sequence of logical steps that incorporates the scientific method of defining, analyzing, and solving problems. These are the six steps in the Standard Agenda:

1. *Identify the goal(s)*. Establish a clear, specific goal or set of goals. Let's say that your group has a project assigned in class. Your instructor says that each group must choose a project from a list of five options. Your group's overall specific goal might be to choose an option that will earn the team an "A" grade. A secondary goal might be to work on a project that interests all group members.

2. *Analyze the problem*. When we analyze a problem, we break it down into its constituent parts. We examine the nature of the problem. The group project assigned in class might produce an analysis of the pros and cons for the five options available. Group members might consider how much research will be required and what information is readily available for each option, how much time the group has to do the necessary research, how much background knowledge is necessary to do the project well, and how interested members are in each option.

3. *Establish criteria*. *Criteria* are standards for judgment, guidelines for determining effective decision making and problem solving. Criteria should answer the question "What standards should be met for the decision/ solution to be a good one?" You use criteria to choose which college to attend (e.g.,

cost, prestige, and quality of program in your chosen major) and which movie to see (e.g., body count, buckets of blood, or—hopefully—quality of acting and storyline). Without establishing criteria in advance of final decisions, it is very difficult to gauge whether group choices will likely prove effective. In the case of a class project, the instructor normally provides the specific criteria for the groups. In other circumstances, the group should discuss criteria and choose three to five before proceeding with the next step. Some possible criteria for a group project in a class might be the following:

a. Stay within the prescribed time limits for the class presentations.

b. Exhibit clear organization.

c. Use at least one clear attention strategy, and cite at least three credible sources of information during each group member's presentation.

d. Employ one visual aid per member's speech.

The extent to which the group meets these criteria will determine whether members all earn an "A" on their project.

4. *Generate solutions*. Brainstorming possibilities is an effective method of generating solutions to problems (and will be discussed in detail later). When weighing the merits and demerits of each project option, don't assume that the objections to each option can't be solved. Suppose, for example, that your group is torn between two options: exploring a campus problem (e.g., parking) or researching an international problem (e.g., climate change). Initially, the parking problem might seem a less satisfactory choice. Finding credible sources and information of sufficient quality in the limited time available might seem like insurmountable impediments. If the group has a greater interest in the parking problem than in climate change, however, group members might brainstorm possible solutions to these impediments. Perhaps the

group could conduct a campus survey to generate credible information where a lack of such information might be a problem. School officials and members of campus security could be interviewed as well.

5. *Evaluate solutions, and make the final decision.* Before deciding on the project, the group should consider each option in terms of the criteria. For example, will exploring a campus problem such as parking or an international problem such as climate change best permit the group to reach its goal of an "A" grade? Which option is most interesting to group members? The likelihood of satisfying the criteria will allow group members to make a reasonable decision.

It is particularly important during this step that group members consider both the positive and the negative aspects of each choice. Groups often become enamored of a solution without considering **Murphy's Law**—anything that can go wrong likely will go wrong. When the Boeing Company builds an airplane, designers account for Murphy's Law in the plans. An airplane with four engines is designed to fly temporarily with a single engine. Boeing doesn't expect three engines to malfunction during the same flight, but just in case, it is better to err on the side of safety. Boeing commercial jets have even lost all four engines and still glided safely to airports. Expect the unexpected, and build it into your group decision.

6. *Implement the decision.* Group decisions don't amount to much if they aren't implemented, and implementation takes planning, which is something groups often fail to do. To implement the group's decision, divide labor among the members in a coordinated fashion. Each member must be given a clear role to perform that contributes to the eventual implementation of the group decision. One or two members might do interviews, another write a survey, and still others research the parking problem. All of these tasks are interdependent. Leave any out, however, and successful implementation may be jeopardized. Deadlines for completing each stage of the project should also be set so that all members know what is expected of them and when the product of their labor is due. Members should then discuss the results, condense the material into usable form, and organize the presentation of results to outsiders.

Some groups don't stick rigidly to the Standard Agenda. They may jump around from step to step. Two points are critical, however. First, the problem should be explored thoroughly before any solutions or options are considered. Second, establish criteria before making any important decisions.

Groups should consider what might go wrong before making a final decision. Once a bad decision is implemented, it is too late.

Employ Decision-Making Rules Competently: Making Choices

Choices must be made at every step of the Standard Agenda. How those decisions will be made depends on rules of decision making. There are three chief decision-making rules for small groups: *consensus rule*, *majority rule*, and *minority rule*. Each has its benefits and drawbacks. Groups may choose to use more than one decision-making rule depending on developing circumstances.

CONSENSUS RULE: IT'S UNANIMOUS

Some groups operate under the *unanimity rule*, which is usually referred to as *consensus decision making*. **Consensus** is "a state of mutual agreement among members of a group where all legitimate concerns of individuals have been addressed to the satisfaction of the group" (Saint & Lawson, 1997, p. 21). Juries are one example of consensus decision making. Criminal trials in most instances require all jurors to agree. Thus, all legitimate concerns of jurors must be addressed to achieve a consensus. If jurors ignore a legitimate concern, even a single dissenter can hang the jury and force a retrial or dismissal of charges.

Consensus requires unanimity, but it doesn't mean that every group member's preferred choice will be selected. Consensus is reached when all group members can support and live with the decision that is made. This means that group members interact cooperatively (see Box 11-3). Some group members may have to modify a preferred choice. *There are several advantages to using the unanimity rule to structure decision making.* First, consensus requires full discussion of issues, which improves the chances that quality decisions will be made. Minority opinions will need to be heard. Second, team members will likely be committed to the final decision and will defend the decision when challenged by outsiders. Dissenters may undermine a group decision that is less than unanimous. Third, members typically are satisfied with the decision-making process and the outcome (Miller, 1989).

The unanimity rule has two chief drawbacks. First, consensus is very difficult to achieve; the process is time consuming and sometimes

How to Achieve a Consensus

Achieving a consensus is a major challenge for any group. Here are several suggestions that can guide a team toward consensus (Hall & Watson, 1970; Saint & Lawson, 1997).

1. *Follow the Standard Agenda, and use suggestions for running productive meetings.* Consensus requires structured deliberations, not aimless, brain-killing conversation.

2. *Encourage supportive patterns of communication throughout discussions, and discourage defensive patterns that creep into discussions.* A cooperative group climate is essential.

3. *Identify the pros and cons of a decision under consideration.* Write these for all to see.

4. *Discuss all concerns, and try to resolve those concerns to everyone's satisfaction.* Look for alternatives if concerns remain.

5. *Avoid arguing stubbornly for a position.* Be prepared to give in when possible. Look for ways to break an impasse.

6. *Ask for a stand-aside.* Standing aside means a group member still has a reservation about the decision but does not feel that continued opposition is warranted.

7. *Avoid conflict-suppressing methods.* These include coin flipping and swapping ("I'll vote for your proposal this time if you vote for mine next"). A straw vote to ascertain the general level of acceptance for a decision or proposal is useful, but the goal should be unanimity.

8. *If consensus cannot be reached, seek a supermajority (minimum two-thirds agreement).* This at least captures the thrust of consensus decision making by requiring substantial, if not total, agreement.

contentious. Members can become frustrated by the length of deliberations and perturbed with holdouts who resist siding with the majority. Second, consensus becomes increasingly unlikely as groups grow larger. Teams of 15 or 20 will find it difficult to achieve consensus on anything (even a time to meet).

Consensus decision making is useful when policy, priorities, and goals are being considered (Romig, 1996). Consensus is most relevant for important group decisions. *Many choices made by group members, however, do not require consensus.* If you've ever tried to reach a family consensus when choosing a restaurant for dinner or a movie to watch, then you know consensus cannot always be reached. If consensus cannot be reached, other decision-making rules can be used to break a deadlock.

MAJORITY RULE: EFFECTIVE BUT NOT ALWAYS APPROPRIATE

The most popular method of decision making in the United States is *majority rule*. The U.S. political system depends on it. It has determined winners on *American Idol, Dancing with the Stars, Survivor,* and other media-created contests. Majority rule has important benefits. It is efficient and can provide rapid closure on relatively unimportant issues. In large groups, majority rule may be the only reasonable way to make a decision. Unlike consensus, majority rule can usually break a deadlock. Once a majority emerges, a decision can be made.

Majority rule also has significant disadvantages. First, majorities sometimes support preposterous, unethical positions. Majorities have supported racism, sexism, and homophobia at various times in the history of the United States. Second, groups using majority rule may encourage a dominance power dynamic within the group. Those with the most power (the majority) can impose their will on the less powerful minority. This could easily lead to a competitive power struggle within the group. Third, majorities may be tempted to decide too quickly, before proper discussion and debate have taken place, squelching the chance of creating synergy. Groups can make reckless, ill-conceived decisions. Minority opinion can be ignored.

Typically, *effective groups use majority rule when consensus is impossible or quick decisions about commonplace issues must be made.* A consensus decision regarding where, when, and for how long the group should meet is useful, but getting bogged down from lengthy discussions about such "housekeeping" tasks will quickly grow annoying. A simple majority vote may prove satisfactory to move the group along.

MINORITY RULE: DECISION BY EXPERT OR AUTHORITY

Occasionally, a group will designate an expert to make the decision for the group (e.g., chief surgeon on cardiac surgical team). Sometimes a group merely advises a person in authority but doesn't actually make decisions. The authority can choose to listen to the advice or ignore it because he or she has the power of the position granted by the larger organization. On rare occasions, a forceful faction, a small but powerful subgroup, can intimidate a group and assert its will on the majority.

Minority rule has serious disadvantages. First, a designated expert can ignore group input or simply not request it. Second, members may engage in power plays to seek favor with the authority figure who makes the decision. Third, group members will likely have weak commitment to the final decision because they had little participation in the outcome.

Manage Meetings Effectively: Stop Wasting Time

Columnist George Will once noted: "Football combines two of the worst things about American life. It is violence punctuated by committee meetings" (quoted in Fitzhenry, 1993, p. 426). Having to attend meetings is perceived by many to be a serious disadvantage of group work. Meetings, however, are an indispensable means of making group decisions and solving problems (Blenko et al., 2010; Luong & Rogelberg, 2005).

Group meetings can actually increase the productivity of groups (Kauffeld & Lehmann-Willenbrock, 2012). Cecilia Sharpe, head of an auditing team of six accountants, decided to calculate the effects of eliminating the team's weekly meeting while encouraging team members to maintain direct communication with each other to coordinate task accomplishment. When a single proposal to revise work schedules for her auditing team arose, she found that eliminating the team's weekly meeting to discuss this proposal resulted in a net loss of

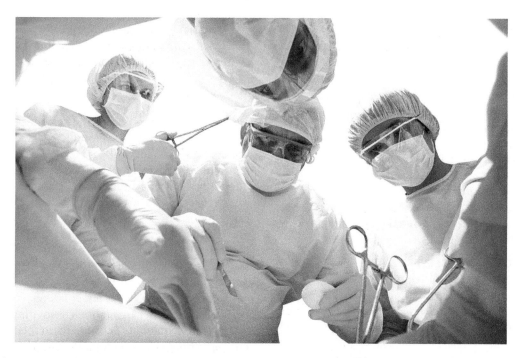

Both consensus and majority vote would be inappropriate for a surgical team performing an operation. "All those in favor of cutting here raise your hand"—it wouldn't work! Split-second decisions must be made, so minority rule (chief surgeon makes the decisions) applies.

18 person-hours in productivity, 102 disruptions of team members because of phone calls to discuss proposals (compared to seven disruptions of any kind during regular team meetings), a decision that was two days late, and significant team member dissatisfaction with the final decision (Shaffner, 1999).

Group meetings don't have to be time wasters, but they often are (Lehmann-Willenbrock et al., 2013). Business consultant Mitchell Nash (see Dressler, 1995) identifies six common complaints made about group meetings: (1) the meeting has an unclear purpose, (2) participants are unprepared, (3) key individuals are absent or tardy, (4) discussion drifts into irrelevant conversation, (5) some group members dominate the discussion, and (6) decisions made at meetings often are not implemented.

Whoever chairs a meeting can take procedural steps that will make the meeting productive and efficient (Lehmann-Willenbrock et al., 2013). Here are some suggestions:

1. *Don't call a meeting unless no good alternative exists.* Hold a meeting if immediate action is required, group participation is essential, group members are prepared to discuss relevant issues, and main players can be present. If objectives can be met without a meeting, don't meet. One of life's small pleasures is the unexpected notification "Meeting has been canceled."

2. *Identify the specific purpose of the meeting* (Kauffeld & Lehmann-Willenbrock, 2012). Notify each group member of where, when, and how long the meeting will be held. Let participants know if they should bring certain materials or resources. Encourage each member to be prepared to discuss important issues.

3. *Prepare a clear agenda.* An **agenda** is a list of topics to be discussed in a group meeting presented in the order in which they will be addressed. An agenda typically includes a time allotment for discussion of each issue (see Box 11-4). Provide any necessary information, along with the agenda, that may help members understand the topics to be discussed.

A Sample Agenda for Group Meetings

Meeting of the Student Senate
November 15
Boardroom
2:00–4:00 P.M.

Purpose: Biweekly meeting
 I. Call meeting to order
 II. Approval of the minutes of last meeting
    (5 minutes)
 III. Additions to the agenda (2 minutes)
 IV. Committee reports
    a. Student clubs committee (5 minutes)
    b. Student transportation committee
       (5 minutes)
    c. Student activities committee
       (5 minutes)
 V. Officers' reports
    a. Treasurer's report (3 minutes)
    b. President's report (10 minutes)
 VI. Old business (previously discussed but
    unresolved)
    a. Campus security problems (15 minutes)
    b. Cost of textbooks (10 minutes)
    c. Parking garage proposal (10 minutes)
    d. Student credit card proposal
       (5 minutes)
 VII. New business
    a. Hate speech on campus (15 minutes)
    b. Expanding the bookstore (10 minutes)
    c. Open access computer use (10 minutes)
    d. Student elections (5 minutes)
 VIII. Agenda building for next meeting
    (5 minutes)
 IX. Adjournment

4. *Keep the discussion on track.* Above all, don't allow drifting. Aimless discussion sucks the life out of meetings and causes eyelids to droop. As Ronald Reagan once quipped, "I have left orders to be awakened at any time in case of national emergency, even if I'm in a cabinet meeting" (Kurtzman, 2015). Also, squelch stagehogs. No one should be permitted to dominate the

discussion. A simple "Let's hear from some other individuals" is usually sufficient to short-circuit the stagehog. Encourage participation from all members.

5. *Start the meeting on time, and be guided by the "what's done is done" rule.* Do not interrupt the flow of the meeting by bringing latecomers up to speed, except to indicate which item on the agenda is under discussion. Latecomers can be filled in briefly after the meeting or during a break, if necessary. Instructors don't restart classes each time a student comes in late. Rock concerts aren't stopped in midstream to accommodate those who are tardy.

6. *Don't discuss an issue longer than the time allotted unless the group decides to extend the time.* This prevents talkaholics from pointlessly extending the meeting well beyond expectations. Meetings that end ahead of time are cause for celebration; those that end late are cause for exasperation.

7. *Take a few minutes at the end of the meeting to determine if all the objectives were accomplished.* Schedule time in the next meeting to consider any unresolved issues.

8. *Distribute minutes of the meeting to all participants as soon as possible.* The minutes should indicate what was discussed, what action was taken, and what remains to be discussed and decided.

Meetings do not have to be a form of torture if these simple steps are followed to keep them efficient and productive. Well-run meetings can be a satisfying experience for all.

Enhance Creative Problem Solving: Becoming Unstuck

Four deer hunters hire the same floatplane every hunting season, fly into northern Maine, and "bag" a deer apiece. This season is no different. As they prepare to return home, the pilot of the plane looks at the four deer carcasses and informs the hunters that he can't fly all the men and deer in one trip. The hunters complain, the pilot resists; the hunters complain more strenuously, the pilot wavers; finally, they load the plane. The pilot taxis across the lake, guns the engine, picks up speed, and lifts off. A few minutes into the flight, the plane crashes. The men crawl from the wreckage, and one hunter asks, "Where are we?" The pilot looks around and answers, "Looks like we're about 100 yards from where we crashed last year."

Groups can get into ruts. Creative problem solving requires breaking free from thinking that is repetitive, ritualistic, and rigid. The rigid thinking that characterizes the hunters' problem solving is an impediment. They continue to repeat the same mistake because their thinking is stuck.

This section explains ways to unstick a group's thinking so creative, original, and effective solutions to problems can be devised. Creative problem solving is a vital aspect of competent small groups (Miura & Hida, 2004). As Peter Carnevale and Tahira Probst (1998) note, "Successful conflict resolution often requires that disputants develop novel alternatives, new perspectives, and a fresh outlook on the issues. Creative problem solving is often required in negotiation" (p. 1308). Solving problems is a primary purpose of small groups working on a task, and doing it effectively requires creativity.

PROMOTING GROUP CREATIVITY: NECESSARY CONDITIONS

Several conditions can promote creative problem solving in groups. First, *establish a cooperative communication climate*. Competitive expectations can freeze thinking. When group members anticipate an adversarial exchange, thinking often becomes rigid, and counterproductive power struggles can distract the team. "An individual who anticipates competition may use precious cognitive resources . . . to plan, strategize, and coerce rather than to problem solve and collaborate" (Carnevale & Probst, 1998, p. 1308). A cooperative communication environment can unfreeze thinking. Group members have little reason to be combative, and the focus is on solving a problem together to everyone's satisfaction.

Second, *creativity is promoted by challenges*. As the adage says, "Necessity is the mother of invention." Trying to discover a solution to a previously insoluble problem can stir the creative juices. Attempting to do what others have not been able to accomplish can be a powerful motivator.

Third, *creativity flourishes when there is a moratorium on judging ideas*. Create an atmosphere where any idea, no matter how zany, can be offered without fear of ridicule. Ideas must be evaluated for their practicality and effectiveness, but instant assessments are creativity killers (Goleman, 2013).

Fourth, *relaxing deadlines as much as possible can free team members' thinking*. Creativity can flourish under pressure, but relentless and unreasonable deadlines can panic a group. Panic doesn't usually spur creativity, but it can lead to a mental meltdown.

Fifth, *a fun, friendly atmosphere usually promotes creativity best* (Goleman, 2013). Fun relaxes group members and reduces concerns about power, status, and esteem. Having fun is the great equalizer among diverse individuals. Having fun also means modifying some nonessential rules. Casual dress instead of more formal work attire may help signal a looser, friendlier, less power-conscious atmosphere.

BRAINSTORMING: GENERATING IDEAS

"Encourage Wild Ideas" reads the sign on the wall of each brainstorming room at IDEO Product Development in Silicon Valley, California. Brainstorming rooms are sanctuaries for creativity where product design teams composed of engineers, industrial designers, and behavioral psychologists hurl ideas back and forth in a frenzy of mental activity (O'Brien, 1995). IDEO brainstormed designs for Levolor blinds, virtual reality headgear, AT&T's telephones and answering machines, medical devices, and a host of other diverse products. IDEO has even brainstormed functional spatial designs for entire hospitals and worked with some of the largest corporations in the world (Hyatt, 2010). One of its most notable and early accomplishments was the design for the Apple computer's original point-and-click mouse.

Team creativity is enhanced by structured methods of problem solving (Romig, 1996). Edward DeBono (1992), author of several books on creativity, argues that unstructured creativity "is a dead end. It appears to be attractive at first, but you really can't go far" (p. 37). The first and most popular structured approach is **brainstorming**—a creative problem-solving method characterized by encouragement of even wild ideas, freedom from *initial* evaluation of potential solutions, and energetic participation from all group members. Team members produce the best results when several rules (a structure) are followed (Kelley & Littman, 2001; Nussbaum, 2004). These rules include:

Brainstorming is one effective method of generating creative ideas.

1. *All members should come prepared with initial ideas.* Most research that shows disappointing results from group brainstorming excludes this vital first step (Feeney, 2013). Team members must be adequately prepared to brainstorm in the group. Provide necessary background information to all team members. Make certain the problem is clearly defined and the goals are specific and apparent (e.g., design a spill-proof coffee cup for bicycle commuters that doesn't distract the rider). Each member generates ideas prior to team interaction.

2. *Don't criticize any idea during the initial brainstorming process.* Idea slayers, such as "You can't be serious," "What a silly idea," "That'll never work," or "We don't do it that way," will quickly defeat the purpose of brainstorming. This is especially true if the more powerful members criticize ideas offered by less powerful, hesitant members. An air of equality is important for productive brainstorming. If less powerful members concentrate on what more powerful members will think of them, they will be overly cautious about contributing ideas. Prohibiting instant evaluations of ideas can reduce initial reluctance to participate fully in brainstorming because all ideas are treated as equal during the session.

3. *Encourage freewheeling idea generation* (Goleman, 2013). Even crazy ideas may provoke a truly terrific solution to a problem by causing team members to think "outside the box." You want team members to expand their thinking and to think in new ways. This is where the fun atmosphere is important. A loose, relaxed, enjoyable brainstorming session encourages freewheeling idea generation, and it can minimize power distinctions between members. When team leaders are as zany and relaxed as other members, it momentarily equalizes power in the group. Team members see the leader as "one of them," which can be empowering for the more hesitant, cautious members.

4. *Don't clarify or discuss ideas during the idea-generation phase.* That will slow down the brainstorming process (Dugosh et al., 2000). Clarification can come later.

5. *Stay focused on the topic* (Goleman, 2013). You want all suggestions to be related to

the topic. Wild ideas that are not on topic are not helpful. Idea generation is significantly diminished when conversation is permitted during brainstorming sessions (Dugosh et al., 2000). With conversation often comes irrelevant chatter. A brainstorming facilitator should invoke this rule whenever talking interrupts idea generation.

6. *Piggyback on the ideas of others.* Build on the suggestions of team members by modifying or slightly altering an idea.

7. *Record all ideas for future reference.* Don't edit any ideas during the initial phase of the brainstorming session.

8. *Wait to evaluate ideas generated until the brainstorming session is completed*, but do evaluate ideas afterward to garner the best suggestions (Sawyer, 2007). The group must decide which of the ideas generated are best to implement. New ideas may even emerge during the evaluation process (Lehrer, 2012).

The proper brainstorming technique is exhibited by IDEO. Presented with the challenge to design a commuter coffee cup that allows pedaling a bicycle without spilling the drink, becoming distracted, and keeping the drink hot, the brainstormers rapidly fire questions at the customer who requests the product. "Do you want to sip or suck the coffee as you ride?" "Sip" is the response. The brainstormers quickly draw designs of 15 contraptions; among them are a "camelback" that puts a container with a plastic hose in a backpack, a coffee cup (with temperature gauge) attached to a helmet, and a "Sip-o-matic" with a suction valve. The brainstorming atmosphere is kept lighthearted and fun. No idea is too goofy during the idea-generation phase of the brainstorming session, and all are written on "writable walls." Brainstormers repeatedly piggyback on the ideas of other team members, and all members are totally engrossed, enjoying the challenge. The final prototype is determined by an assessment process (voting with Post-It notes or asking the customer for a preference). The Sip-o-matic is a hit with the customer. Brainstorming, if conducted properly, can be a highly effective creative group problem-solving technique (Goldenberg et al., 2013).

NOMINAL GROUP TECHNIQUE: AVERAGING INDIVIDUAL BRAINSTORMING

A second structured method of creative problem solving—the **nominal group technique**—involves these steps:

1. Team members work alone to generate ideas.

2. The team is convened, and ideas are shared in round-robin fashion. All ideas are written on a chalkboard, tablet, or easel. Clarification of ideas is permitted, but evaluation is prohibited.

3. Each team member selects five favorite ideas from the list generated and ranks them from most to least favorite.

4. Team members' rankings are averaged, and the ideas with the highest averages are selected.

Research shows that brainstorming is as effective—or slightly more effective—than the nominal group technique in generating a high number of ideas and high-quality ideas when a trained facilitator guides group brainstorming and when a video of effective versus ineffective brainstorming is shown to group members prior to idea generation (Baruah & Paulus, 2008; Kramer et al., 2001). The nominal group technique also is more impersonal than brainstorming, tends to be less fun and involving, and does not capitalize on the benefits of working in groups. Nominal groups also show no advantage over brainstorming groups in the final evaluation of ideas once brainstorming has concluded (Rietzschel et al., 2006)

Nominal group technique may be a relevant option, however, when teams experience substantial unresolved interpersonal friction and tension, but need to make creative choices "now." Brainstorming, because of its emphasis on high participation, may prove to be ineffective in such an atmosphere.

REFRAMING: BREAKING RIGID THINKING

Another method of creative problem solving is **reframing**—the creative process of breaking rigid thinking by placing a problem in a different frame of reference (see Chapter 4). A service station proprietor put an "Out of Order" sign on a soda machine. Customers repeatedly paid no attention to the sign, lost their money, then complained to the station owner. Frustrated and annoyed, the owner changed the sign. It now read "$5" for a soda. No one made the mistake of putting money in the soda machine after that. The problem was reframed. Instead of wondering how to get customers to recognize that the machine was out of order, the owner changed the frame of reference to what would make customers not want to put money in the dispenser.

Reframing opens up possible solutions hidden from our awareness by rigid thinking. Reframing a team dispute from a competitive, adversarial contest of wills to a cooperative problem to be solved by mutual effort and goodwill can prevent conflict from becoming destructive. Winning a contest and solving a problem are distinctly different frames of reference. When teams become stumped by narrow or rigid frames of reference, asking certain open-ended questions can help reframe the problem so new solutions might emerge. "What if . . . ?" is a very useful question. "What if we don't accept the inevitability of worker layoffs and downsizing?" "What if we tried working together instead of against each other?" "What if management is telling the truth about the budget?" All these questions encourage a different frame of reference and a different line of thinking. Additional reframing questions include:

Why must we accept what we've been told?

Why are these the only choices?

Can the problem be described in any other way?

Is there any way to make this disadvantage an advantage?

To summarize, brainstorming, nominal group technique, and reframing are three useful methods of creative problem solving. In some instances, methods can be combined, such as brainstorming ways to reframe a problem before brainstorming ideas to solve the problem.

Teambuilding and Teamwork

A disturbing study revealed the alarming statistic that more than 400,000 patients die each year from medical errors in hospitals (James, 2013). This should concern everyone. Although the causes of this unsettling situation are varied, poor teamwork is emerging as a principal source (Catchpole et al, 2008; Nurok et al. 2011). Teamwork and patient safety are so interconnected, that the American Heart Association issued a "scientific statement" on teamwork and patient safety in the cardiac operating room. It reads in part: "Nontechnical skills such as communication, cooperation, coordination, and leadership are critical components of teamwork, but limited interpersonal skills underlie adverse events and errors" (Wahr et al., 2013, p. 1). Others have noted the same problem: "Health care must have as much improvement in teamwork skills as there has been in technical skills" (Pronovost & Freischlag, 2010, p. 1721).

Developing effective teams is an important concern for all of us, not just those who need medical care in hospitals. Discussing teamwork and teambuilding marks the culmination of research on competent small group communication. Teams are not merely another type of small group. They have the potential to be small groups capable of extraordinary accomplishment. Effective teams have launched humankind successfully into space, produced the personal computer, invented and developed the Internet, solved many of the world's most vexing problems, and provided enthusiastic sports fans with endless hours of exciting entertainment and pride in their accomplishments.

Most of us have our first exposure to teams during our early participation in sports. Theater productions in high school and college also require team effort, as do fundraising activities to support college clubs and service groups. In addition, group projects in college classes are most successful when approached from a team perspective. Perhaps our most important and long-term exposure to teams, however, occurs in the workplace. The annual survey of employers from across the nation conducted by the

National Association of Colleges and Employers ranks teamwork skills second among its most important qualities for successful job applicants ("Top 10 Skills," 2013). Ability to work in teams has become a critical skill for employment.

Defining a Team: Not Just a Small Group

Every team is a group, but not every group is a team (Hackman & Johnson, 2013). There are three primary distinctions between small groups and teams. First, teams commonly exhibit a higher level of cooperation and cohesiveness than standard groups. Teams are inherently We-oriented. Each member develops skills "for the good of the team." A forward may have to switch to playing center to help his or her basketball team, for example, even though this may mean scoring fewer individual points. Teams may function within a competitive, *intergroup* (between groups) environment, but to be successful, they depend on *intragroup* (within group) cooperation. Second, teams normally consist of individuals with more diverse skills. Not everyone can be a goalie in soccer or a pitcher in baseball. A team requires complementary, not identical, skills. Third, teams usually have a stronger group identity. Teams see themselves as an identifiable unit with a common mission. Thus, a **team** is a small number of people with complementary skills who act as an interdependent unit, are equally committed to a common mission, subscribe to a cooperative approach to accomplish that mission, and hold themselves accountable for team performance (Katzenbach & Smith, 1993b).

Boards of directors, standing committees, student and faculty senates, and similar groups are not usually teams. These groups often lack cohesiveness and cooperation, and group members may have similar, rather than diverse, skills. Members are asked to attend periodic meetings where discussion occurs and an occasional vote is taken, but they do not have to work together. Members may factionalize and even work against each other. Contact with fellow members may never take place except indirectly and formally during meetings.

Although some groups are not and never will become teams, *most groups can profit from acting more teamlike. Teams embody a central theme of this text*—that cooperation in human communication arenas has distinct advantages. These benefits of cooperation should be exploited far more than occurs at present.

Establishing Team Goals: An Important First Step

Teambuilding begins with goal setting (LaFasto & Larson, 2001). A team needs a purpose, and goals provide that focus. In addition, team goals improve task performance (Crown, 2007). Goals should be clear, challenging, and cooperative, and team members must be committed to achieving them.

CLEAR GOALS: KNOWING WHERE YOU'RE HEADED

An ancient Chinese proverb states, "If you don't know where you are going, then any road will take you there." Groups that have no particular focus drift aimlessly. They achieve little because little is planned. In a study of 600 teams and 6,000 team members, the authors concluded "Goal clarity is critical for team members to have confidence in their direction and to be committed to making it happen" (LaFasto & Larson, 2001, p. 101). Vague goals such as "Do your best" or "Make improvements" provide no clear direction. "Complete the study of traffic congestion on campus by the end of the term" or "Raise $100,000 in donations for a campus child care center within one year" are clear, specific goals. For a group to become a team, clearly focused goals are essential.

Romig (1996) found one department in an organization had developed 60 goals to achieve in a single year. This department accomplished none of its goals but threatened the future of the entire organization by losing huge sums of money flailing in all directions. Too many goals can diffuse effort and scatter group members. A few clear goals are preferable. Each member should be able to recite from memory the primary goals of the team. This allows all team members to have a shared mission and a common vision. *Goals for a team work best when they are clearly stated and limited in number.*

CHALLENGING GOALS: PUTTING A DENT IN THE UNIVERSE

Accomplishing the trivial motivates no one. Groups need challenging goals to spur interest among members. Such goals can stretch the limits of group members' physical or mental abilities. Groups are elevated to teams when they see their mission as important, meaningful, and beyond the ordinary.

The team that developed the original Macintosh computer had this elevated sense of purpose. Randy Wigginton, a team member, put it this way: "We believed we were on a mission from God" (quoted in Bennis & Biederman, 1997, p. 83). Steve Jobs, the team leader, promised team members that they were going to build a computer that would "put a dent in the universe" (p. 80). They may not have put a dent in the universe, but subsequent creations from Apple teams certainly became cultural icons and shaped an entire consumer market.

COOPERATIVE GOALS: REQUIRING TEAM EFFORT AND INTERDEPENDENCE

In individualist cultures, such as the United States, the cooperative aspects of teambuilding are a bit more challenging than in collectivist cultures, such as Singapore, China, and Malaysia (Hofstede & Hofstede, 2010). Competitive goal structures abound in the United States. Thus, developing cooperative goal structures can seem perplexing initially.

There are two primary elements that compose cooperative goals. First, cooperative goals require interdependent effort from group members. This is achieved by all members working together in a coordinated fashion. *Collaborative interdependence is essential to teamwork* (Johnson & Johnson, 2003b).

Second, cooperative goals necessitate a We-orientation. A study at Cambridge University of 120 teams found that assembling highly intelligent (high-IQ) team members didn't produce stellar results (Belbin, 1996). High-IQ members were intensely competitive. Instead of working together, they sought to impress each other with their brilliance. Each member's individual status became more important than any group goal. Teams composed of members with more ordinary intellectual abilities outperformed the high-IQ teams. They exhibited a We-orientation by putting personal agendas aside for the sake of team goals. The result was synergy.

COMMITMENT TO GOALS: STIMULATING THE PASSION WITHIN MEMBERS

Teams need unified commitment from all members to be effective (Aube & Rousseau, 2005). "The essence of a team is common commitment. Without it, groups perform as individuals; with it they become a powerful unit of collective performance" (Katzenbach & Smith, 1993a). For those members who do not demonstrate sufficient commitment and effort, use the suggestions given for dealing with social loafers and difficult group members.

Goals established by team members, not imposed by outsiders or a team leader, usually gain greater commitment (Romig, 1996). Cooperative goals are the product of member participation. It is very difficult for members to get excited about goals that have been foisted on them.

The 1996 U.S. Olympic women's basketball team illustrates the importance and value of team goals. This team soundly defeated its longtime nemesis, Brazil, for the gold medal. A powerful team that had humbled previous U.S. teams in the 1991 Pan American Games, the 1992 Olympics, and the 1994 world championships, Brazil was no match for the smooth teamwork of the U.S. women. The final score was 111-87. The success of the U.S. women's team was achieved primarily by establishing cooperative goals from the outset. Interdependence and a We-orientation were critical to the team's success. Sportswriter Ann Killion (1996) summed it up when she attributed the U.S. women's success to "setting [their] sights on a goal and working for it, [and] sacrificing one's self for the team" (p. D1).

Contrast this example of flawless teamwork with the 2004 U.S. Olympic men's basketball team. Composed of top NBA players, such as Allen Iverson and Tim Duncan, this new version of the "Dream Team" was embarrassed in a

The Blue Angels illustrate which of the following?

○ **1.** Clear goals

○ **2.** Challenging goals

Answers at end of chapter.

○ **3.** Cooperative goals

○ **4.** Commitment to goal achievement

preliminary round by Puerto Rico 92-73. The U.S. team went on to lose three games—equal to the team's total losses in all previous Olympic Games. Collaborative interdependence was missing. Players operated as individuals, not as teammates. Initially, most players seemed to view the entire Olympic event as not very challenging. After the embarrassing loss to Puerto Rico, however, coach Larry Brown remarked, "We have to become a team in a short period of time. Throw your egos out the window" (quoted in Killion, 2004, p. 3D). The U.S. team improved (but still lost to Lithuania) and earned the bronze medal. There's much more to building a team and establishing teamwork than choosing the best players.

The 2008 U.S. Olympic men's basketball team learned from its previous disappointing showings by concentrating on developing teamwork and foregoing individual stardom. In its eight games, all victories, the U.S. team had more assists than its opponents each time, exhibiting the players' willingness to pass and engage in team play. In the final game against Spain, all five starters scored in double figures, showing a willingness to spread the scoring around and not seek personal glory ("Olympic Basketball," 2008). This "Redeem Team" won the gold medal with teamwork. Using a similar teamwork formula, the U.S. repeated its gold medal performance in the 2012 Olympics, defeating eight opponents by an average of 32 points per game.

Developing a Team Identity: Who Are You?

James Carville, chief strategist for Bill Clinton's 1992 presidential campaign, knew how to create a team identity. Self-described as the "Ragin' Cajun" from Louisiana, Carville ran the "War Room" team. The team name was Hillary

Clinton's idea, and it gave the team an instant identification.

The War Room was the political nerve center of the Clinton campaign. Located in Little Rock, Arkansas, the team responded to every perceived threat, every attack from the George H. W. Bush campaign, and every stumble or miscue by Clinton himself with lightning speed. As Carville put it, "You create a campaign culture, and ours was based on speed" (quoted in Bennis & Biederman, 1997, p. 93).

The War Room team's identity also combined speed with informality. The T-shirt was part of the War Roomers' uniform. Carville liked wearing one that read "Speed kills . . . Bush." He also wore ragged jeans with holes. There was a constant air of immediacy and high drama. Team members ran to copy machines; they didn't walk. Carville promoted a 24-hour-a-day sense of urgency. Like him or

hate him—and he does have vociferous detractors—Carville unquestionably built a remarkably effective team.

Hillary Clinton's run for the presidency in 2007–2008 tried to mirror the original War Room approach. Barack Obama, who eventually bested Hillary Clinton and ultimately John McCain for the presidency, chose a less intense team identity: "No Drama Obama." Stay cool under fire! The formula worked again in the 2012 presidential campaign when Obama defeated Mitt Romney.

Group identity is an important part of building a team. There isn't a single way to do this. Often team identity is fostered by a uniform or style of dress common to team members. At IDEO the dress is casual on purpose. A team name is not essential, but it helps. An identifiable style of behaving, such as the War Room's focus on speed, also creates an

Every team is a group, but not every group is a team. What stands out immediately as a means of showing team identity?

identity, especially if the style is different from other groups. Offering awards and prizes for team accomplishments, creating rituals and ceremonies unique to the group, establishing a clearly identifiable space that belongs to the team, and sometimes creating an air of secrecy all contribute to team identity. Every team will create its own identity in its own way. Part of being an effective team, however, is building that identity early in the group's life.

Designating Clear Team Roles: Avoid Duplication

Roles emerge informally in most small groups, but teams require greater structure than groups in general. You don't want role ambiguity (Klein et al., 2009). Group members won't function as a team if they are uncertain of the roles they are supposed to play or if too many team members want to play the same role and other roles are left unfilled. You don't want 10 quarterbacks and a dozen wide receivers but no punter or cornerback on a football team. A team of lawyers will divide the responsibilities among members. One lawyer may be the chief researcher (information giver). Another may write the legal briefs (clarifier-elaborator). A third may challenge the briefs to find flaws in the arguments (devil's advocate), and a fourth may direct the entire team (leader). In each case, team members are given specific responsibilities befitting their talents, experience, and expertise. The team leader often makes this assignment of roles, but in some cases, team members volunteer to play specific roles.

The leader role (e.g., coach, project director, or task force chair) is usually designated in advance. Although there are exceptions, the general pattern of leadership for most teams should be participative. Team leaders should encourage participation from team members. "The guide on the side, not the sage on the stage" is the typical model of team leadership. Competent leaders emphasize development and maintenance of constructive communication climates (see Chapter 8). Conflict management focuses on collaboration and avoids power-forcing (see Chapter 9).

Virtual Groups and Teams

Virtual groups, whose members are connected by electronic technology and rarely, if ever, meet face-to-face—have three characteristics that distinguish them from conventional face-to-face groups (Fisher, 2000; Schiller & Mandviwalla, 2007). First, members of virtual groups are spread across multiple locations, even across multiple time zones (Rutkowski et al., 2007). Second, members often come from more diverse backgrounds and cultures in which multiple languages are spoken and organizational allegiances may be varied (Ebrahim et al., 2009). Third, membership tends to be less stable, with members dropping out more frequently. In short, virtual-group members are "working together apart" (Fisher, 2000).

Although distinctions between *virtual groups* and *virtual teams* are rarely offered by researchers and theorists, differences do exist. Both have electronic technologies and remote communication in common, but they differ in the same ways that conventional face-to-face groups and standard teams differ: degree of cooperation, diversity of skills, level of group identity, and commitment of members. For example, online class discussion groups are virtual groups but not virtual teams. Class members join online discussions to fulfill class requirements and share opinions. Little cooperation is required, class members are not chosen because of skill diversity, no real group identity is necessary, and commitment to the online discussion may be lackluster and sporadic.

The worldwide opportunities for collaboration are enormous with the development of the Internet and complementary technologies (Sunstein, 2006; Tapscott & Williams, 2006). Virtual groups are a natural result of this global electronic network that has emerged. Virtual teams are becoming the norm for businesses and government globally (Solomon, 2010).

With the emergence of virtual teams come new and varied communication challenges (Poole & Zhang, 2005). First, language choice may be an issue if group membership spans diverse cultures with widely varying languages. Switching from one language to another may result in serious misunderstandings and give rise to ethnocentrism (e.g., "Why wouldn't we use English?").

Second, virtual-group members may have difficulty determining the meaning of long silences. When a group member fails to answer emails, for example, the tendency is to assume that the member lacks commitment and is a social loafer instead of assuming another possibility—namely, that a technical difficulty has prevented a timely response (Cramton, 2001).

Third, virtual-group members are more likely than members of conventional groups to make negative dispositional attributions (e.g., lazy or unskilled) for behavior that perturbs the group (e.g., failure to meet deadlines or long silences) than they are to make situational attributions (e.g., family or work difficulties intruding on virtual-group time). Such attributional bias can lead to greater conflict than occurs in conventional groups (Cramton, 2002). Managing conflict in virtual groups is especially tricky because of the lack of face-to-face contact to resolve issues (Solomon, 2010).

Fourth, in the absence of video- or audio conferencing, lack of nonverbal cues limits the ability of members to accurately discern emotional states of those emailing or blogging (Solomon, 2010). This presents problems for students taking online courses (Klaas, 2015).

Fifth, social loafing is a potentially greater problem in virtual groups than in conventional groups (Driskell et al., 2003; Piezon & Ferree, 2008). A survey of 600 employees of multinational corporations who actively participate in virtual groups found that 75% saw social loafing as a serious challenge (Solomon, 2010). Confronting a loafer is problematic in text-only formats, however. If the loafer refuses to read the messages, deletes them, or does not respond to the confrontation, group members have few options. Members can try working around the loafer by ignoring lackluster participation, but this merely increases the workload of more motivated members. Online classes that require team projects are especially subject to this problem.

Sixth, developing cohesiveness may be a bigger challenge because virtual-group members may never meet each other face to face (Solomon, 2010). This can be a particularly serious problem for online classes that require team projects.

Finally, if virtual-group members are spread across several time zones, the timing of virtual meetings can be a stumbling block. Nine P.M. on the West Coast is five A.M. in London, after all.

These challenges can be addressed (Ebrahim et al., 2009; Klaas, 2015). First, there are "degrees of virtuality" (Poole & Zhang, 2005). Occasional face-to-face meetings of virtual-group members can help build social relationships and enhance cohesiveness (Kirkman et al., 2002; Maznevski & Chudoba, 2000). If some face-to-face contact is impossible, videoconferencing may suffice as an alternative (Lipnack & Stamps, 1997). Videoconferencing has developed to the point that the quality of the video can allow members to forget they are in completely different locations, sometimes thousands of miles away. Members have even been known to offer each other refreshments during videoconferences, forgetting that they are communicating in a virtual world ("Who wants a chocolate? OOPS! I forgot that two of you are in England. Oh well, more for us!"). Second, it is helpful to set agendas, draft timelines and deadlines for projects, and schedule regular communication among group members (Connaughton & Daly, 2005; Yoo & Alavi, 2004). Also, agreeing to specific times for meetings so all can attend is important (Poole & Zhang, 2005). Third, decide on which language will be used for all meetings and communication. Switching back and forth between different languages leads to difficulties and less effective virtual groups (Knoll & Jarvenpaa, 1998). Fourth, members of virtual groups should agree to explicit norms regarding responsiveness and punctuality, etiquette (no flaming), and so forth. Finally, confronting any conflicts immediately so they don't fester and grow is essential (Ebrahim et al., 2009).

Virtual groups present new challenges for group members. These challenges, however, are likely to diminish with time as we become more accustomed to working in these groups (Van der Kleij et al., 2009).

Summary

The advantages of working in groups are many. Groups can pool knowledge and information, correct errors often missed by an individual working alone, accomplish broad-range tasks by sharing the load among members, and above all, produce synergy. The main disadvantages of groups—factionalism, disruptive members, scheduling conflicts, social loafing, groupthink, and wasting time in meetings—are correctable. The group experience can be unpleasant, but it need not be that way.

Teams are cooperative groups. Teambuilding provides the structure for teams: clear, challenging, and cooperative goals and commitment to these goals; clear roles; use of the Standard Agenda; and consensus decision making whenever possible. Teamwork often requires creative problem solving. The three structured methods of creative problem solving are brainstorming, nominal group technique, and reframing. Finally, virtual groups present additional challenges, but with experience, these challenges should diminish significantly.

Answers for Critical Thinking captions

BAD APPLE (P. 284): #2

SOCIAL LOAFING (P. 288): #3 and #4

BLUE ANGELS (P. 302): #1, #2, #3, #4

Quizzes Without Consequences

Test your knowledge before your exam! Go to the companion website at www.oup.com/us/rothwell, click on the Student Resources for each chapter, and take the Quizzes Without Consequences.

Film School Case Studies

The Flight of the Phoenix (1965 and 2004). Drama; Not Rated (1965) and PG-13 (2004)

Taut drama about a plane crash and efforts of survivors to rebuild their damaged aircraft into a smaller flying machine to escape their plight in the desert. The original, 1965 version is probably better than the remake. In either case, examine the creative group problem solving required. What methods were used to fashion the final product? What decision-making rules (unanimity, majority, or minority) were used?

Glory Road (2006). Drama; PG

Dramatic depiction of coach Don Haskins's effort to mold a winning team at Texas Western University in the early 1960s, eventually making it to the finals of the NCAA basketball tournament and fielding an all-black starting five against an all-white Kentucky team when racial tensions were heightened nationally. Examine the major elements of teambuilding and teamwork.

Miracle (2004). Drama; PG-13

Faithful re-creation of the 1980 U.S. Olympic hockey team defeating a far more talented Soviet team and proceeding to win the gold medal. Explain group synergy and the process that produced the "Miracle on Ice." Also, analyze teamwork and teambuilding.

Remember the Titans (2000). Drama; PG

In this film based on a true story, a high school football coach (Denzel Washington) must integrate his team in the face of racism and ignorance. Analyze how the Denzel Washington character accomplishes the feat of molding a championship team from warring factions. Focus especially on types of team goals and team identity.

The Avengers (2012) and Avengers: Age of Ultron (2015). Action/Adventure/ Sci-Fi; PG-13

Earth's mightiest heroes become a team to defend against evil adversaries. Analyze teambuilding and teamwork elements of this group, which forms awkwardly in the first film but flows more cohesively in the second film. Also, examine deep diversity issues.

The Cove (2009). Documentary; PG-13

A team of environmental activists exposes the mass slaughter of dolphins in this Oscar-winning documentary. It's a tough film to watch but an important one. Examine how the team handles decision-making and problem-solving challenges.

The War Room (1993). Documentary; PG

Oscar-nominated documentary on the 1992 Clinton presidential campaign. Whatever your political leanings, this is a fascinating inside look at politics in action. Analyze how Clinton's campaign team capitalized on the elements of teambuilding and teamwork to forge a winning combination.

BY THE END OF THIS CHAPTER, YOU SHOULD BE ABLE TO:

1. Reduce your speech anxiety.

2. Identify and distinguish the five types of audiences.

3. Choose and narrow your speech topic appropriately for different audiences.

Preparing and Presenting Your First Speech

ELOQUENCE CAN INFLUENCE THE COURSE OF HISTORY.
The oratory of Martin Luther King and others was a powerful instrument of the civil rights movement. More recently, both the Tea Party and the Occupy movement, which emerged from the original Occupy Wall Street protests, have relied heavily on public speeches to marshal support. The entire history of student protest in this country exhibits the centrality of public speaking to evoke change, and even a single student gifted in public speaking can produce important change. For example, a student in my public speaking class gave a terrific persuasive speech that argued for a smoking ban on campus. I encouraged her to present this speech to various decision-making bodies, which she did, provoking a campuswide debate and, in the end, producing her desired result.

There are many other important reasons to become a competent public speaker. College courses in diverse disciplines increasingly assign oral presentations. One survey of

CHAPTER OUTLINE

- **Addressing Speech Anxiety**
- **Audience Analysis**
- **Topic Choice and Analysis**
- **Researching the Topic**
- **Competent Outlining and Organizing**
- **Competent Delivery of Speeches**

4. Research your topic effectively.

5. Accurately outline and organize speeches.

6. Use extemporaneous delivery effectively.

students at hundreds of U.S. colleges and universities revealed that 90% of first-year college students and 95% of seniors gave formal class presentations. Among first-year students, more than two-fifths gave oral class presentations "often" or "very often," and two-thirds of seniors did likewise ("National Survey," 2012). The more you progress in college, the more you need public speaking knowledge and skills. Those of you who do acquire such knowledge and skills early in your studies enjoy an enormous advantage when giving class presentations. Whether viewing oral presentations with reluctance or relish, you will undoubtedly be required to give them in your classes, so why not learn to do them well? Yet in one massive study of first-year college students, only 38% rated their public speaking ability even "above average" (Eagan et al., 2014). Clearly, there's work to be done!

Competent public speaking is also essential to career building. One Prezi/Harris survey reported that 70% of employed Americans found public speaking skills to be critical to their career success (Gallo, 2014). Employers, however, do not believe most job applicants possess such skill ("Bridge That Gap," 2013). Teaching, law, religion, politics, public relations, business, and marketing, among other careers, all require substantial public speaking knowledge and skill.

Competent public speaking is also quite useful in other circumstances. Average citizens are frequently called upon to give speeches of support or dissent at public meetings on utility rate increases, school board issues, and city or county disputes. Toasts at weddings or banquets, tributes at awards ceremonies, and eulogies at funerals for loved ones are additional common public speaking situations (see Appendix B).

Competent public speakers know how to present complex ideas clearly and fluently, keep an audience's attention, critically analyze important issues, conduct effective research, make reasonable arguments, and support claims with valid proof. They entertain but also move people to listen, to contemplate, and to change their minds. This is an impressive array of practical knowledge and skills, and its application is virtually boundless.

The communication competence model serves as a guide throughout this discussion of public speaking. Public speakers must make choices regarding the appropriateness and likely effectiveness of topics, attention strategies, style and delivery, evidence, and persuasive strategies. When you are giving a speech, you must be sensitive to the signals from an audience that indicate lack of interest, disagreement, confusion, enjoyment, support, and a host of additional reactions. This allows you to make adjustments during the speech if necessary. The effectiveness of a speech must also be tempered by ethical concerns. What works may not always be honest, respectful, responsible, noncoercive, or fair.

Thus, *the principal purpose of this chapter is to explain how to prepare and present your first speech*. This chapter seeks to get you up and running at a basic level. Ensuing chapters build on this discussion and provide more advanced ways to develop and present speeches in a variety of situations.

Addressing Speech Anxiety

Ricky Henderson, longtime baseball star for the Oakland Athletics, fretted before giving a speech at the ceremony inducting him into the National Baseball Hall of Fame at Cooperstown, New York, on July 26, 2009. As he described it, giving a speech, especially of this magnitude, is like "putting a tie too tight around your neck . . . I've sweated to death about it and then wondered why" (quoted in Steward, 2009a, pp. C1, C5). Henderson wisely sought help from speech instructor Earl Robinson at Laney College. He also received critiques from Robinson's students, who were taking a summer public speaking class and heard Henderson's speech. Henderson practiced his speech for two weeks. One journalist who listened to Henderson's 14-minute presentation at the Hall of Fame ceremony offered this assessment: "He seized the stage in Cooperstown, N.Y., and commanded it as he did as a player . . . He wasn't perfect, but he was pretty close. Moreover, he was gracious, highly effective and suitably entertaining" (Poole, 2009, pp. 1A, 6A). Another journalist remarked that his speech "was stunning for its clarity, poignancy, humor and humility" (Steward, 2009b, p. 1A).

Ricky Henderson's experience says two things. First, speech anxiety is a significant problem for many people about to present a speech. Second, with proper knowledge and training, speech anxiety can be addressed successfully.

Speech anxiety is an immediate concern of most students who anticipate giving a speech (Behnke & Sawyer, 1999a), so it is the immediate concern addressed here. **Speech anxiety** is fear of public speaking and the nervousness that accompanies that fear. In this section, the pervasiveness and symptoms of speech anxiety, its typical causes, and several strategies for managing it are discussed.

Pervasiveness: You're Not Alone

Mark Twain once remarked, "There are two types of speakers: those who are nervous and those who are liars." Overstated, perhaps, but according to a 2014 survey by the National Institute of Mental Health, 74% of respondents reported fear of public speaking ("Fear," 2015). Another study put the fear factor at 62% ("The Chapman University Survey," 2015). That same study also showed fear of public speaking as the top phobia in America, greater than fear of heights (61%), flying (39%), drowning (47%), or zombies (18%). Some surveys even show that many people fear public speaking more than they fear death (Bruskin & Goldring, 1993; Thomson, 2008), prompting Jerry Seinfeld to quip that if you attend a funeral, you would prefer being in the casket to delivering the eulogy.

These "death before public speaking" preferences are dubious at best (Davies, 2011). Can you imagine anyone choosing the firing squad to the firing line of a speech delivered before even the most hostile audience? These preference surveys do, however, reflect some individuals' intense speech anxiety. Public speaking is a challenge, not a fate worse than death, and it should not be avoided at all costs.

Symptoms: Fight-or-Flight Response

Howard Goshorn observed, "The human brain is a wonderful thing. It operates from the moment you are born until you stand up to make a speech." "Going blank" is one of the most common concerns of novice speakers. Learning to manage your speech anxiety, especially for your first speech, begins with identifying its common symptoms and explaining why these symptoms occur.

BASIC SYMPTOMS: RESPONDING TO THREAT

Walter Cannon (1932) labeled the physiological defense-alarm process triggered by stress the **fight-or-flight response**. The myriad physiological changes that are activated by a perceived threat prepare both animals and humans either to fight the foe or flee the fear-inducing threat.

The fight-or-flight response produces a complex constellation of physiological symptoms. Some of the more notable include an accelerated heartbeat and increased blood pressure (increases oxygen), increased perspiration (enhances cooling), increased respiration (supplies oxygen), increased glucose supply (increases energy), inhibited digestion (shuts

The "death before public speaking" poll results undoubtedly are more figurative than literal. Who would actually choose death? Nevertheless, irrational fear of public speaking can make it seem like a fate worse than death. This makes speech anxiety an issue worth addressing right away.

down unnecessary energy drain), stimulated adrenal glands (improves alertness and strength), release of red blood corpuscles (aids in clotting wounds), and increased white corpuscle production (fights possible infection) (Zimbardo, 1992). Some of the more prominent corresponding verbal and nonverbal symptoms are quivering, tense voice, and weak projection (constricted throat muscles); frequent dysfluencies, such as ums and uhs and going blank (increased blood flow to major muscle groups but simultaneous restricted blood flow to the brain); and dry mouth that makes speaking difficult (digestive system shutdown) (Lewin et al., 1996).

APPROPRIATENESS OF SYMPTOMS: RELEVANCE

The physiological symptoms of the fight-or-flight response make sense if you are about to grapple with a crazed grizzly bear or run with the bulls at Pamplona. There is little likelihood, however, that you will be doing any grappling or sprinting in your speech class. Granted, if the speech is lengthy, the room hot and stuffy, and the occasion momentous, the increased glucose, respiration, perspiration, and adrenaline will help sustain you through your presentation. Adrenaline can also assist you in performing at a peak level, very similar to athletes "psyching up" for an important contest. Clothes saturated with perspiration, increased red and white corpuscles, nausea, pounding heart, quivering voice, and dry mouth, however, are unnecessary and unwelcome distractions. Nevertheless, your sympathetic nervous system, which controls the fight-or-flight response, doesn't pick and choose relevant symptoms (Kuchinska, 2008). When the response is triggered, you get the whole package. Thus, *the useful approach to speech anxiety is to moderate the fight-or-flight response, not hope to activate only selective symptoms.*

Causes: Dysfunctional Anxiety

Dysfunctional speech anxiety occurs when the intensity of the fight-or-flight response prevents an individual from giving a speech effectively. **Functional speech anxiety** occurs when the fight-or-flight response is managed and stimulates an optimum presentation. *The degree of anxiety and your ability to manage it, not the anxiety itself, determine the difference.* Individuals who experience low to moderate anxiety that is under control typically give better speeches than those who experience little or no anxiety (Motley, 1995). If you care very little about the outcome, you'll experience little anxiety, but your presentation will likely be lackluster.

Causes of dysfunctional speech anxiety fall primarily into two categories: *self-defeating thoughts* and *situational factors*. Understanding these causes of dysfunctional anxiety is the first step in learning to maintain your anxiety at a level that is functional.

SELF-DEFEATING THOUGHTS: SABOTAGE

Some individuals see giving a speech as a challenging and exciting opportunity, whereas others see it as an experience equivalent to being swallowed by a python. How you think about speaking to an audience will largely determine your level of speech anxiety (Bodie, 2010). Self-defeating thoughts that can sabotage your speech are grounded in the excessive concern that your audience will judge and reject you (Cunningham et al., 2006).

Catastrophic Thinking: Fear of Failure Wildly exaggerating the magnitude of potential failure is a common source of stress and anxiety (Ackrill, 2012). Novice speakers often fear that they will embarrass themselves and be viewed by audiences as irredeemable fools (Kuchinskas, 2008). Predictions of public speaking catastrophes are unrealistic, however, because they are highly unlikely to occur (Peterson, 2000; Seligman, 1991).

Catastrophic thinking, or *catastrophizing* as it is often called (Boyes, 2013b), sees only failure, not an opportunity for exhilarating success produced by embracing challenges. Such catastrophic thinking can create a self-fulfilling prophecy whereby you create a mental condition that can produce the failure you fear (Grohol,

The degree of anxiety + your ability to manage it, not the anxiety itself.

Don't paralyze yourself w/ catastrophic, unrealistic thinking

The fight-or-flight response is quite appropriate if you are running from the bulls at Pamplona, Spain. It would be a strange response, however, to having to give a speech in class.

2013). Thomas Edison made more than 2,000 attempts to invent the electric light bulb. When asked how it felt to fail so many times, Edison responded, "I never failed. It just happened to be a 2,000-step process." Don't paralyze yourself with catastrophic, unrealistic thinking. •

Perfectionist Thinking: No Mistakes Permitted Perfectionists anguish over every perceived flaw, and they magnify the significance of even minor defects. Examples include "I feel so stupid. I kept mispronouncing the name of an expert I quoted" and "My knees were shaking. The audience must have thought I contracted rabies." Flawless public speaking is a desirable goal, but why beat yourself up when it doesn't happen? Even the most talented and experienced public speakers make occasional errors in otherwise riveting and eloquent speeches.

The Illusion of Transparency: Being Nervous about Looking Nervous Substantial research shows that those who fear public speaking are often overly worried about appearing nervous to their audience. This **illusion of transparency**—the overestimation of the extent to which audience members detect a speaker's nervousness—is usually just that: an illusion (MacInnis et al., 2010). Zach Wahls, while a student at the University of Iowa, gave a powerful three-minute speech to the Iowa State Legislature about being raised by "two moms." The speech went viral on the Internet and received almost 19 million hits (Grim, 2014). Wahls confessed afterward on *The Ellen DeGeneres Show* that he was shaking while he gave the speech, but you cannot tell this from looking at his speech on YouTube (see *TED Talks and YouTube Links* at end of this chapter). He appears very composed and confident. Telling a person not to be nervous, of course, is unhelpful advice, but informing a speaker about the illusion of transparency, that their anxiety isn't obvious, can free individuals from the cycle of anxiety and help them present better speeches (Savitsky & Gilovich, 2003).

SITUATIONAL FACTORS: CONTEXT
Several anxiety-provoking situations are relevant to public speaking. The three principal ones are *novelty*, *conspicuousness*, and *types of speeches*.

Novelty of the Speaking Situation: Uncertainty We often fear what is unpredictable or unfamiliar (Witt & Behnke, 2006). For inexperienced speakers, the mere novelty of the speaking situation may trigger speech anxiety (Kelly & Keaten, 2000). What if your listeners seem bored? Is the audience likely to be supportive or hostile? Based on uncertainty reduction theory, as you gain experience speaking in front of groups, even just a well-prepared first speech, the novelty begins to wear off, and anxiety diminishes (Roby, 2009).

Conspicuousness: In the Spotlight I have polled more than 1,000 students in public speaking classes. When asked what causes their speech anxiety, most identify being "on stage" or "in the spotlight." Being conspicuous, or the center of attention, can increase your anxiety. You feel as if you are under a microscope being meticulously examined. As the size of an audience grows, conspicuousness increases in most individuals' minds. Gaining confidence from speaking often to a variety of audiences, large and small, is a strong antidote for alleviating speech anxiety provoked by conspicuousness.

Types of Speeches: Varying Responses Types of speeches combined with situational challenges affect whether you experience anxiety. Suddenly being asked to "say a few words" with no warning typically stirs greater anxiety than giving a more prepared speech (Witt & Behnke, 2006). Giving a speech to an audience hostile to your expressed point of view may also engender high levels of anxiety (Pertaub et al., 2002).

These causes of speech anxiety, both self-defeating thoughts and anxiety-provoking situations, can produce a spiraling effect that feeds on itself. *A key to managing your speech anxiety is to prevent the spiral of fear from ever occurring*, the subject of the next section.

Strategies: Managing Anxiety

Many individuals, from famous actors and celebrities to self-anointed consultants, have suggested strategies for managing speech anxiety. These include swearing at your audience backstage, sticking a pin in your backside (pain as diversion), and imagining members of your audience clothed only in their underwear or in diapers. If these dubious suggestions work for you, that's fine, but there is no good evidence that they have widespread application. They are unquestionably limited, however, because they are diversionary tactics rather than strategies that directly address the primary causes of speech anxiety. In this section, several ways to manage your speech anxiety that are supported by research are presented.

PREPARE AND PRACTICE: NOVELTY TO FAMILIARITY
As in most social situations, you fear making a fool of yourself when you don't know what you're doing. First and foremost, this means

don't delay preparing and practicing your speech until the night before you give it. *Procrastination increases anxiety* (Boyes, 2013a).

Being adequately prepared removes most of the novelty and uncertainty from the speaking situation. Begin the necessary research well in advance, organize and outline your speech carefully, and practice your presentation. Give it in your car on your way to class. Give it to your dog; they're eager listeners (cats not so much). *Practice, practice, practice!* Do a dress rehearsal for friends or family members, or record your performance on video and play it back so that you can study parts to improve (Svoboda, 2009). Giving speeches to a variety of audiences, even just for practice, will gradually build your confidence and reduce your anxiety (Finn et al., 2009).

Poor physiological preparation, however, will sabotage even the most carefully prepared and practiced speech. You require appropriate nutrition to manage the stress of public speaking. Do not deliver a speech on an empty stomach. Complex carbohydrates (e.g., whole grains, pastas, and legumes) work well to stoke your energy, but eat lightly. You want blood traveling to your brain (for thinking clearly), not to your stomach (for digestion). Avoid empty-calorie foods (e.g., doughnuts and Twinkies). A high intake of caffeine, simple sugars, and nicotine can stoke the physiological symptoms of fight or flight (e.g., increased heart rate and sweating). Alcohol and tranquilizers are also counterproductive solutions. Alcohol restricts oxygen to your brain and dulls mental acuity, and tranquilizers can send you on a "Valium vacation" in which you feel pleasantly numb but mentally dumb. The same goes for marijuana. Lastly, never take even a mild amphetamine. Speed kills a speech. It will increase your heart rate beyond what anxiety already induces.

There is no substitute for preparation and practice. If you do both, most of your anxiety will melt away, and your confidence will soar.

GAIN PERSPECTIVE: RATIONAL THINKING

Understanding the progression of your speech anxiety can give you a realistic perspective on what is a reasonable amount to expect. It will improve naturally (see Figure 12-1). There are four phases to speech anxiety symptoms (Witt et al., 2006). The *anticipation phase* occurs when your symptoms elevate just before giving your speech. The *confrontation phase* occurs when you face the audience and begin to speak. Adrenaline surges; heart rate soars, sometimes to 180 beats per minute; and perspiration and other symptoms increase. Then the *adaptation phase* kicks in, usually about 60 seconds into the speech. Adaptation takes place even more swiftly for low-anxiety speakers, however, usually 15 to 30 seconds into the speech. During this phase, symptoms steadily diminish, reaching a more comfortable level within a minute or

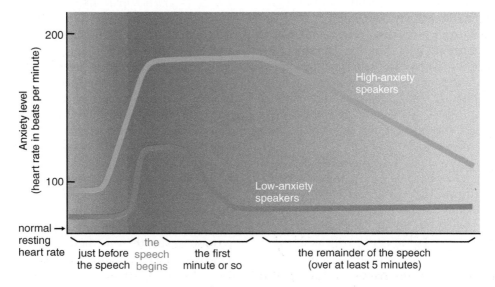

FIGURE 12-1. Heart-Rate Patterns of Typical High- and Low-Anxiety Speakers (Source: Motley, 1995).

two. Finally, there is the *release stage*—the 60 seconds immediately following the speech. Recognizing that your anxiety will diminish dramatically and quickly as you speak should provide some comfort.

Another aspect of gaining a realistic perspective is learning to recognize the difference between rational and irrational speech anxiety (Allen et al., 2009). A colleague of mine, Darrell Beck, concocted a simple formula for determining the difference: *the **severity** of the feared occurrence times the **probability** of the feared occurrence.* This formula gives a rough approximation of how much anxiety is rational and when you have stepped over the line into the irrational.

Severity is approximated by imagining what would happen if catastrophic failure did occur: your knees and hands shake violently, and you go blank, perspire profusely, babble incoherently, feel nauseous, and eventually faint. Imagine all of this occurring, the entire mess. Would you renew your passport and make plans to leave the country? Would you hide from friends and family, afraid to show your face? Would you drop out of college? None of these choices seems likely. You might drop the class, but even this choice is uncertain. Even a disastrous speech does not warrant significant life changes. A few moments of disappointment, mild embarrassment, or discouragement because you received a low grade on one speech among several is about as severe as the consequences get.

Next, consider the probability of this nightmare scenario actually happening. It is highly improbable that all of these feared occurrences would transpire. When you consider the probability of the "worst-case scenario," you should realize there is not much to concern you. Stop catastrophizing and predicting utter failure (Boyes, 2013b). *Concentrate on the probable (low-severity occurrences), not the improbable (high-severity occurrences).*

Even individuals for whom English is a second language benefit from gaining a realistic perspective on their speech anxiety. Giving a speech in a second language can easily increase anxiety (Woodrow, 2006). Normally, however, students admire a speaker who tries hard to give a good speech in a relatively unfamiliar language. They usually listen more intently as well.

COMMUNICATION ORIENTATION: REFRAMING

Desiring complete approval, engaging in perfectionist thinking, and fretting over your conspicuousness onstage all occur when you view public speaking from a **performance orientation**—an attempt to satisfy an audience of critics whose members are focused on evaluating your presentation (Motley, 1997). Giving a speech is not an Olympic event; you're usually not competing to score more points than someone else or to earn a gold medal and get your face on a cereal box. Your audience won't hold up cards indicating your score immediately after you sit down. Granted, your speech instructor will likely give you a grade on your speech, but even here, the performance orientation is counterproductive. You're *expected* to make mistakes, especially during your first presentation. Speech classes are learning laboratories, not speech tournaments.

Reframe the performance orientation with a **communication orientation**—a focus on making your message clear and interesting to your listeners. *You will perform more effectively as a speaker if you move from the competitive performance orientation to the communication orientation* (Motley, 1995, 2009). Scrutinizing your performance while speaking is counterproductive (Svoboda, 2009). Simply concentrate on communicating your message clearly to your audience, and if you have prepared and practiced well, the rest will follow.

One way to develop the communication orientation is to practice your speech conversationally. Choose a friend or loved one with whom you feel comfortable. Find a private location, and sit in chairs or on a couch. Using a conversational style, begin describing the speech that you have prepared. Do not give the speech. Merely talk about it—what the speech covers and how you plan to develop it. Use notes if you need to, but refer to them infrequently. In subsequent practice sessions with your listener, gradually begin to introduce elements of the actual speech, such as an introduction. Eventually, deliver the entire speech while sitting down. Finally, present the entire speech standing, using only an outline of the speech for reference.

In summary, these methods for reducing and controlling your speech anxiety work so well that little else needs to be said. Nevertheless, there are additional methods for reducing speech anxiety that may provide optimal assistance if needed.

COPING STATEMENTS: RATIONAL REAPPRAISAL

Negative self-talk leads to catastrophic thinking (Bodie, 2010). You stumble at the outset of your speech and say to yourself, "I knew I couldn't do this well" or "I've already ruined the introduction." You're immediately scrutinizing your performance. A rational reappraisal can help you cope effectively with your anxiety (Ellis, 1995, 1996). Try making coping statements when problems arise. "I'm past the tough part," "I'll do better once I get rolling," and "The best part is still ahead" are examples of rational reappraisal engendered by positive coping statements. Coping statements shift the thought process from negative and irrational to positive and rational self-talk (O'Donohue & Fisher, 2008). Make self-talk constructive, not destructive.

POSITIVE IMAGING: VISUALIZING SUCCESS

Prepare for a speech presentation by countering negative thoughts of catastrophe with positive images of success. Sometimes called **visualization**, this can be a very effective strategy for addressing your speech anxiety (Ayres, 2005). Picture yourself giving a fluent, clear, and interesting speech. Imagine your audience responding in positive ways as you give your speech. Exercise mental discipline, and refuse to allow negative thoughts to creep into your consciousness. Keep imagining speaking success, not failure.

RELAXATION TECHNIQUES: REDUCING FIGHT OR FLIGHT

A number of simple relaxation techniques can reduce physiological symptoms of the fight-or-flight response (O'Donohue & Fisher, 2008). Deep, slow, controlled breathing is very helpful. Five to seven such breaths per minute are optimal (Horowitz, 2002). Relaxing your muscles through a series of tense-and-relax exercises also can be beneficial, especially right before giving a speech (if you can be unobtrusive about it—perhaps backstage or outside). Slowly lifting your shoulders slowly up and down and then rotating them is relaxing.

Wiggling your facial muscles by moving your cheeks, jaw, mouth, nose, and eyebrows and by smiling broadly may seem silly, but it loosens tight muscles. Even big, exaggerated yawns can help. Another muscle relaxation exercise is tensing and then relaxing sets of muscles (e.g., diaphragm, stomach, legs, and arms).

SYSTEMATIC DESENSITIZATION: STEP BY STEP

Systematic desensitization involves incremental exposure to increasingly threatening stimuli coupled with relaxation techniques. This method of managing anxiety is very effective (Bodie, 2010). It is time consuming, however, so you must be committed to this technique.

Applied to giving speeches, systematic desensitization involves making a list of perhaps 10 progressive steps in the speaking process, each likely to arouse increased anxiety. Find yourself a comfortable, quiet place to sit. Read the first item on your list (e.g., your speech topic). When you experience anxiety, put the list aside, and begin a relaxation exercise. Tense the muscles in your face and neck. Hold the tensed position for 10 seconds, then release. Then do the same with your hands, and then your feet, and so on, until you've tensed and relaxed all the muscle groups in your body. Now, breathe slowly and deeply as you say the word "relax" to yourself. Repeat this for one minute. Pick up the list, and read the first item again. If your anxiety remains pronounced, repeat the process. If your anxiety is minimal, move on to the second item (e.g., gathering your speech material), and repeat the tense-and-relax procedure. Work through your entire list of 10 items. Use systematic desensitization several days in a row before your speech presentation.

The more severe your speech anxiety, the more you need to try several of the anxiety-reducing techniques discussed. Don't try to employ all of these techniques at once. Begin with preparation, practice, and the communication orientation, and work from there.

Audience Analysis

Edmund Muskie, a former Governor of Maine and U.S. senator, once remarked, "In Maine we have a saying that there's no point in speaking unless you can improve on silence." Improving on silence requires careful audience analysis. Almost 2,500 years ago, Aristotle wrote: "Of the three elements in speechmaking—speaker, subject, and person addressed—it is the last one, the hearer, that determines the speech's end and object" (cited in Cooper, 1960, p. 136). Meeting audience expectations is a key element in competent public speaking.

Think of audience analysis as the process of discovering ways to build bridges between yourself and listeners, to identify with their needs, hopes, dreams, interests, and concerns. In general, *you construct your speech with the audience always in mind*. In this section, types of audiences and audience composition are discussed.

Types of Audiences: The Five Cs

Begin analyzing your audience by considering what type of audience will hear your speech. There are five general types of audiences: *captive, committed, contrary, concerned,* and *casual*. Each type presents its own challenge to a speaker and has its own expectations that a speaker must address to be successful

CAPTIVE AUDIENCE: DISENGAGED LISTENERS

A *captive* audience assembles to hear you speak because it is compelled to, not because listeners expect entertainment or intellectual stimulation. A required speech class is an example of a captive audience. Formal ceremonies, luncheon gatherings of clubs and organizations, and most meetings conducted in places of business are other examples. Power, especially in its dominance form, can be an issue with captive audiences. Listeners may attend a speech only because those with greater power (e.g., supervisors or teachers) insist.

Gaining and maintaining the interest of a captive audience are primary considerations. When listeners prefer to be elsewhere, snaring their attention and keeping them listening to you are not small accomplishments. (Chapter 13 discusses many attention strategies necessary to meet these challenges.)

COMMITTED AUDIENCE: AGREEABLE LISTENERS

A *committed* audience voluntarily assembles because members want to invest their time and energy listening to and being inspired by a speaker. A committed audience usually agrees with the speaker's position already and, because it consists of people who voluntarily appeared to hear the speech, is presumably interested. Listeners who gather for Sunday sermons, political rallies, and social protest demonstrations are all examples of committed audiences. Inspiring action, persuading, and empowering listeners to act decisively are primary considerations for a speaker addressing a committed audience.

CONTRARY AUDIENCE: HOSTILE LISTENERS

You don't usually get to choose your audience, so sometimes the audience that forms is initially hostile to your position on issues. School board meetings, public meetings of the county board of supervisors, meetings on public utility rates, and political gatherings often attract hostile listeners ready to do battle. It is vitally important in such circumstances that you have researched your topic and are well prepared. Your demeanor when addressing a hostile audience must remain unconditionally constructive. You want to defuse audience anger, not ignite it against you. Be prepared for personal attacks, but resist personal counterattacks. Ask audience members who get rowdy to disagree without becoming disagreeable.

CONCERNED AUDIENCE: EAGER LISTENERS

A *concerned* audience is one that gathers voluntarily to hear a speaker because listeners care about issues and ideas. A concerned audience is a motivated audience. Unlike a committed audience, however, listeners haven't attended the speech to show commitment to a particular cause or idea. Concerned listeners want to gather information and learn. Listeners who gather for book and poetry readings or lecture series are examples of concerned audiences. Your main consideration is to be informative by presenting new ideas and new information in a stimulating and attention-getting fashion. Concerned listeners may eventually become committed listeners.

CASUAL AUDIENCE: UNEXPECTED LISTENERS

A *casual* audience is composed of individuals who become listeners because they hear a speaker, stop out of curiosity or casual interest, and remain until bored or sated. When I was in Bath, England, I happened upon a street performer. He gathered an audience mostly with clever banter, corny jokes, audience interaction, and whimsical tricks. Curious about the gathering crowd, I joined the audience. Within minutes, I was picked out of the crowd to "assist" him in performing one of his "daring" tricks. My job was to tie his hands tightly behind his back with a chain, put a bag over his head, and count to 30 as the performer "escaped" from his confinement while on his knees with his head submerged in a one-gallon bucket of water. Not surprisingly, he performed this "underwater escape" successfully and garnered great laughter and applause from his casual audience.

Your primary consideration when addressing a casual audience is to connect with listeners immediately and create curiosity and interest. The street performer did this well. Unlike a captive audience, members of a casual audience are free to leave at a moment's whim.

Audience Composition: Making Inferences

Students sometimes poll classmates about issues and problems before composing their speeches. Often, however, you must make educated guesses (inferences; see Chapter 4) about an audience based on **demographics**—characteristics such as age, gender, culture, ethnicity, and group affiliations. Even then, audiences often are composed of diverse members, so there are competing attitudes, beliefs, and values among listeners, making audience adaptation especially challenging. Recognize that few audiences are entirely of one mind.

AGE: GENERATION GAP

The average age of an audience can provide valuable information for a speaker. College instructors, for instance, must speak to the experience of college students, and most of you weren't even born until 1990 or later. You

With a casual audience, people are free to leave at any moment, so keeping their attention is paramount.

haven't experienced a time when space travel was not possible, color television didn't exist, computers wouldn't fit on a desktop or in your hand, the Internet or cell phones weren't available, and remote controls didn't operate all your electronic entertainment systems.

Generalizations based on age define what we consider to be a generation gap in cultural beliefs and practices. Assumptions about age-based cultural divides should be embraced cautiously, but the Pew Research Center (2009) reported the largest generation gap in the United States in four decades. A more recent Pew study found that 64% of older Americans believe that the United States is the greatest country in the world, but only 32% of younger Americans share this opinion (Reilly, 2013).

As a speaker, develop the content of your speech so it relates to the experience of your listeners. References to insider trading, mutual funds, problems of leadership in corporations, and retirement accounts don't speak directly to the experience of a young audience. Older audiences, however, may relate to detailed explanations of such topics. Conversely, don't assume older audiences are necessarily technologically proficient or embrace technology, its advantages, and its necessity as readily as younger generations.

GENDER: FINDING COMMON GROUND

Gender differences in perception and behavior do exist, as discussed in Chapter 3. Competent audience analysis, however, means going beyond simplistic stereotypes. Develop your speech from different perspectives to include all listeners. A speech on sexual harassment, for instance, could be linked to both men and women by discussing that while victims are typically women, they are also increasingly men (see Chapter 7). In addition, men can relate to the indignity and powerless feelings associated with sexual harassment indirectly by seeing what wives, girlfriends, or daughters experience when victimized. Men don't want to see the women they love or care about subjected to indignity and injustice. With more and more women now holding positions of power, offering ways to avoid charges of sexual harassment should concern them as well as men.

ETHNICITY AND CULTURE: SENSITIVITY TO DIVERSITY

Students who fail to analyze the multicultural makeup of college audiences can create embarrassing speaking situations. A Jewish student referring to Palestinians as "terrorists and warmongers" while giving a speech on peace agreements in the Middle East would not sit well with Arab students, and neither would the reverse sit well with Jewish students. Despite my efforts to encourage sensitivity to individuals from diverse cultures, I have witnessed several student speeches that ignited awkward, even hostile, moments in class. Policies and issues can be questioned and debated without resorting to insults and sweeping generalizations. Avoid ethnocentrism (see Chapter 3).

GROUP AFFILIATIONS: POINTS OF VIEW

The groups we belong to tell others a great deal about our values, beliefs, and attitudes. Membership in Save Our Shores indicates a strong belief in protecting our ocean environment. Working with Habitat for Humanity indicates an interest in charitable work and a concern for poor people with inadequate housing. Membership in clubs, sororities, fraternities, national honorary societies, or educational groups provides information about your listeners that can be helpful in shaping your speeches, especially informative and persuasive presentations (see Chapters 14 and 15).

Be cautious, however, and don't assume too much. Group affiliations suggest possible aspects

to consider about your audience, but religious affiliations, for example, can be tricky. A huge majority of Catholics (82%) disagree with the Vatican ban on contraception (Newport, 2012). In May 2015, Ireland, a strongly Catholic country, held a referendum in which that country's ban on gay marriage was voted down overwhelmingly (62% to 38%). Ireland became the first nation to eliminate the ban on gay marriage by popular vote (McDonald, 2015). Who would have guessed this, if judging only by religious affiliation?

Additional audience affiliation factors, such as sexual orientation, income, and education level, also can affect your audience analysis. With some exceptions, however, these may not be so apparent. Some people purposely hide their sexual orientation or consider it nobody else's business, and others consider it rude to ask about or discuss income level. Nevertheless, be sensitive to these elements of audience composition.

Topic Choice and Analysis

A frequent concern of students is what topic to choose for a speech. In some instances, you may be asked to give a speech on a particular subject because of your expertise (e.g., a nurse asked to give a speech on flu shots or a student volunteer for Food Not Bombs asked to speak about homelessness). In a speech class, however, the choice, within broad limits, will likely be up to you. This section covers how to choose a topic that is appropriate for you, your audience, and the occasion. How to narrow your topic to a specific purpose statement is also explained.

Potential Topics: Important Choice

There are four primary ways to explore potential speech topics systematically: *personal inventory, brainstorming, crowdsourcing,* and *scanning.*

PERSONAL INVENTORY: YOU AS TOPIC SOURCE

Begin your exploration of appropriate topics by looking at your own personal experiences and interests. Make a list. What are your hobbies?

What sports do you play? Have any unusual events occurred in your life (e.g., caught in a tornado or observed a bank robbery)? Have you done any volunteer work? What forms of entertainment interest you? Do you have any special skills? Have you traveled to any interesting places (e.g., Ayers Rock or Machu Picchu)? Have you met any exciting people? What's the worst thing that's ever happened to you? What's the best? This list will contain many possible choices for a speech topic.

BRAINSTORM: NEW POSSIBILITIES

Take your list of interests, and choose five topics that seem most promising. Write down each topic on a separate list, and with each topic, brainstorm new possibilities. For example, brainstorm "trip to London" by letting your mind free-associate with any related topics, such as double-decker buses, driving on the left, British accent, Parliament, Buckingham Palace, royalty, Hyde Park, Soho, British money, and British rock groups. Consider each one, and try to brainstorm a more specific topic. British money, for example, might lead to a comparison of British money with American currency. Driving on the left could lead to an interesting presentation on why the British drive on that side yet we drive on the right. Parliament could trigger a comparison between the U.S. Congress and the British legislature. If this approach does not generate excitement, try other methods.

CROWDSOURCING FOR TOPICS

If you are struggling to find a suitable topic, you might solicit ideas from fellow classmates and have suggestions posted on a shared Google doc or on your Facebook page. California Lt. Governor Gavin Newsom used just this technique, known as *crowdsourcing*, to generate ideas for his commencement address at San Francisco State University in May 2015. "Don't want to give a speech that will bore the graduates and their families," Newsom wrote on his own Facebook page (Garofoli, 2015).

SCANNING FOR TOPICS: QUICK IDEAS

Scanning books can help generate ideas for speech topics. Log on to Amazon.com, and scan the latest nonfiction best sellers. This process can produce some real surprises. My own casual search for interesting books to read led me to one by Dennis DiClaudio (2006) entitled *The Hypochondriac's Pocket Guide to Horrible Diseases You Probably Already Have*. In it, the author identifies 45 terrible diseases, among them alien hand syndrome, "in which your own hand may attempt to choke you to death," (p. 74), and candiru infestation, "in which you don't even want to know what happens." (p. 130) This book could prove to be a useful resource for developing an interesting informative speech on hypochondria, on serious diseases and prevention, or on a history of human disease epidemics.

Scan magazines, such as *Time, Consumer Reports, Ebony, O Magazine, Sports Illustrated, People, Psychology Today, Men's Health*, or *Scientific American Mind*. Look at the table of contents, and leaf through the articles. If you see a promising topic, write it down, and note the magazine, the article, and the date. Do the same with newspapers. Your library will have local, national, and international newspapers and magazines that are filled with hundreds of potential topics for speeches.

Finally, scan blogging sites. *The Huffington Post*, for example, has a potpourri of articles and opinion columns on politics, sports, news items, gossip, comedy, business, entertainment, and fashion. If you can't find a topic of appropriate interest after scanning this site, you aren't looking hard enough.

Appropriateness of Topic: Blending Topic and Audience

Appropriateness is one of the two variables that define communication competence. There are three central elements to consider when analyzing the appropriateness of your topic choice: *speaker, audience*, and *occasion*.

SPEAKER APPROPRIATENESS: SUITABLE FOR YOU?

If a topic is chosen merely to fulfill an assignment but you find it uninteresting, then it is not appropriate for you, the speaker. Choose a topic that interests or excites you. It is a rare individual who can take a topic that he or she finds as dull as watching slugs race and then successfully fake interest in front of an audience. If you think the subject is dull, what must your audience think?

Some topics are inappropriate because they are trivial and offensive.

You and the topic may be a poor fit. A white person speaking about "the black experience in America" is an awkward fit. Similarly, young people talking about "what it's like being old" sounds goofy. Men speaking about female menopause or women discussing the care and feeding of a prostate gland are also awkward. No matter how gifted you are as a speaker, some topics will sink your chances of presenting an effective speech.

AUDIENCE APPROPRIATENESS: SUITABLE FOR LISTENERS?

Over the years, my colleagues have shared many horror stories about student speeches that were startlingly inappropriate, such as "how to assassinate someone you hate," "proper methods to induce vomiting after a big meal" (accompanied by demonstrations), "spitting for distance," "harassing the homeless," "constructing a bong," and "shoplifting techniques that work." These topics are inappropriate because they are offensive, trivial, demeaning, or encourage illegal, unethical behavior. Most of them are pointless, adolescent silliness.

There are other reasons a topic might be inappropriate. An audience may find a topic difficult to relate to or appreciate. Giving a speech on how to surf to people living in Kansas, for example, is a bit weird. A topic can also be too technical or complex. Explaining string theory is a hopeless task for a short student speech, after all, because it requires an understanding of physics and is deeply complex.

The increasingly multicultural makeup of audiences provides an additional risk for inappropriate topic choice. Even without intending to, a speaker's topic can insult individuals from other cultures or co-cultures. Giving a speech on religion or politics should be approached cautiously lest insult be given to those with different cultural or political perspectives.

OCCASION APPROPRIATENESS: SUITABLE FOR THE EVENT?

When you're speaking at a particular event, topic choice must be appropriate to the occasion. A graduation ceremony invites topics such as "employment possibilities for the future," "skills for success," and "thinking in the future tense." A sermon at a Sunday religious service warrants a topic related to ethical or moral behavior. Don't choose a topic unrelated to the occasion. It won't fulfill audience expectations. Soliciting support for a political cause at a graduation ceremony or an awards banquet, for example, may even get you booed off the stage.

Narrowing the Topic: Recognizing Constraints

Sometimes you are given a very broad topic on which to speak. Other times you find an interesting topic, but it is too broad and general for the time available to speak. Narrowing your topic to fit the audience and the occasion is a significant task for the competent speaker.

TIME CONSTRAINTS: STAYING IN BOUNDS

Woodrow Wilson, a former college professor and the only U.S. president to earn a PhD, took his public speaking very seriously. A reporter interviewed him once regarding his speech preparation. "How long do you spend preparing a 10-minute speech?" Wilson was asked. He replied, "About two weeks." "How long do you spend preparing an hour-long speech?" the reporter queried. "About a week," answered Wilson. Surprised, the reporter then asked Wilson how long he prepared for a two-hour speech. Wilson replied, "I could do that now." Giving a long-winded speech takes less effort than narrowing the speech to fit neatly into a shorter time allotment.

Once you have settled on a general topic that is appropriate for the speaker (you), the audience, and the occasion, begin narrowing the topic to fit your time limit. Don't choose a topic that is so broad and complex that you couldn't possibly do it justice in the time allotted. *Staying within your time limit is critical*. If you are asked to address a luncheon meeting of a civic organization and are scheduled for a 15-minute presentation, you'll be addressing a roomful of empty chairs if you go much beyond the time limit. People attending luncheon meetings often have only an hour, of which your speech is but a small part.

Abraham Lincoln's "Gettysburg Address," which is considered one of the great American speeches, lasted about *two minutes*. Famed orator Edward Everett, who preceded Lincoln, gave a two-hour-plus speech. He later wrote Lincoln, "I shall be glad if I could flatter myself that I came as near to the central idea of the occasion in two hours as you did in two minutes" (cited in Noonan, 1998, p. 65). Stay within your time limit. That requires preparation.

PURPOSE STATEMENTS: INTENT

Once you have narrowed a general topic into more specific subtopics, identify a *general purpose*, decide on a *thesis*, and compose a *specific purpose statement*. A **general purpose** identifies the overall goal of your speech and tells the audience why you are giving it (to inform, describe, explain, demonstrate, persuade, celebrate, memorialize, entertain, or eulogize). If your speech is a classroom assignment, the general purpose will be given to you (e.g., "give a demonstration speech"). If you have no direction from others, you must decide what general purpose is appropriate for the audience and the occasion.

Once you have determined the general purpose, decide what will be your thesis. The **thesis** identifies the central idea that you want the audience to understand, believe, or feel. The thesis becomes the one concise thought, separate from all the details provided in the speech, that audience members are likely to remember.

We compose a specific purpose statement when we have a clear thesis in mind. A **specific purpose statement** is a concise, precise infinitive phrase composed of simple, clear language that encompasses both the general purpose and the central idea and that indicates what the speaker hopes to accomplish with the speech. For example:

Topic: Cost of a college education.

Narrowed Topic: The high cost of textbooks.

General Purpose: To inform.

Thesis: Complaining about the high cost of textbooks is not as helpful as knowing why textbooks are so expensive.

Specific Purpose Statement: To explain the three primary reasons textbooks are expensive.

Once you have constructed your specific purpose statement, test its appropriateness and likely effectiveness. Ask the following questions:

1. Is *your purpose statement concise and precise?* You should be able to phrase an effective purpose statement in 15 words or fewer.

2. Is *your purpose statement phrased as a declarative statement?* Phrasing a purpose statement as a question asks your listeners to provide the answers (e.g., "Why are textbooks so expensive?"). Make your purpose statement declarative (declare the direction of your speech), and begin with an infinitive phrase (e.g., "to inform," "to persuade," or "to eulogize").

3. Is *your purpose statement free of figurative language?* Keep your purpose statement plain and direct. Figurative language is fine for the body of your speech, but it can be confusing in a purpose statement. For example, "To tell you why textbooks are the golden fleece of education" will likely leave your listeners mystified.

4. Is *your purpose statement more than simply a topic?* "To inform my audience about the cost of textbooks" is a topic statement, not a specific purpose statement. What about the cost of textbooks? Tell your listeners specifically what you seek to accomplish. "To discuss the feasibility of a private college bookstore lowering textbook prices" provides direction.

5. Is *your purpose statement practical?* Can your listeners accomplish what you ask them to do? "I want to teach you to be a top-notch computer programmer" will not happen in a single speech, or even in a lengthy one. Make your specific purpose statement practical, such as "I want to convince you that taking a computer programming course is worthwhile."

Now you know how to choose a topic, determine its appropriateness for the speaker (you), the audience, and the occasion. You also know how to construct a specific purpose statement that appropriately narrows your topic for the time allotted. The next step is to research your topic so that you have something useful to say.

Researching the Topic

Researching your topic should be a focused undertaking. Wandering aimlessly through a library or searching randomly on the Internet will waste time and accomplish little. The advent of electronic technologies such as the Internet has ushered in the Information Age, or more accurately, the Age of Information Overload. The amount of information available digitally by 2020 is estimated to be *50 times greater* than what was available in 2010, an already prodigious amount (Gantz & Reinsel, 2012). As Nate Silver (2012) observes, however, most of this abundance of information is useless noise. Your challenge is to mine the nuggets of credible information that are buried in the cavernous refuse of misinformation and trivialities. This section explains how to conduct data mining and research on a speech topic systematically.

The Internet: First Stop

The Internet has quickly become a primary source for research. A University of California, Los Angeles (UCLA) survey of more than 153,000 first-year college students revealed that 82% frequently used the Internet for research (Eagan et al., 2014). Using the Internet efficiently and effectively for researching your speech, however, requires some basic knowledge.

SEARCH TOOLS: FINDING WHAT YOU NEED
Often your research effort will begin with an Internet search engine. Google, Bing, and Yahoo! are among the most popular ("Top 15," 2015). A **directory** is an Internet tool in which a person trained in library or information sciences chooses prospective sites based on the quality of the site. Two popular directories are AcademicInfo (www.academicinfo.net) and Look Smart (www.looksmart.com). A **metasearch engine** will send your keyword request to several search engines at once. *Metasearch engines work best when your request is a relatively obscure one,* not a general interest topic. Popular examples include WebCrawler.com, Dogpile.com, and Infospace.com. Finally, a **virtual library** is a search tool usually associated with colleges, universities, or organizations with

strong reputations in information dissemination. One popular example is WWW Virtual Library (http://vlib.org).

EVALUATING WEBSITES: USING BASIC CRITERIA

The UCLA survey of first-year college students found that only 44% of those who use the Internet for research evaluate the quality or reliability of the information (Eagan et al., 2014). This is a problem because the Internet can be a prime source of loopy conspiracy theories and misinformation. For example, I received the following attachment in an email from a friend:

> These are actual comments made on students' report cards by teachers in the New York City public school system.
>
> 1. Since my last report, your child has reached rock bottom and has started to dig.
> 2. I would not allow this student to breed.
> 3. Your child has delusions of adequacy.
> 4. Your son is depriving a village somewhere of an idiot.
> 5. Your son sets low personal standards and then consistently fails to achieve them.
> 6. The student has a "full six-pack" but lacks the plastic thing to hold it all together.
> 7. This child has been working with too much glue.
> 8. When your daughter's IQ reaches 50, she should sell.
> 9. The gates are down, the lights are flashing, but the train isn't coming.
> 10. If this student were any more stupid, he'd have to be watered twice a week.
> 11. It's impossible to believe that the sperm that created this child beat out 1,000,000 others.
> 12. The wheel is turning, but the hamster is definitely dead.

When any of these "actual" comments are typed verbatim into the Google search window, hundreds of websites emerge that print the same comments but claim that the list was garnered from, among others, British military officer fitness reports, employee performance evaluations, military performance appraisals, and appraisals of federal employees. The list is almost certainly fabricated. What teacher would risk legal action or job loss by making such comments on a report card sent home to parents? Who has access to student report cards to compile such a list?

The Internet is a rich source of rumor, gossip, and hoaxes (check the validity of Internet rumors at Snopes.com). So how do you separate the high-quality information from the hokum? Follow these three easy steps:

1. *Consider the source.* Are you looking at medical information from the Mayo Clinic or from Fred Smith with no accompanying credentials? In some instances, no source is identified for an article. In that case, be doubly cautious. Check to see if sources are cited in the article, and make a quick check of some of them to see if they exist and are from credible sources (see Chapter 13 for tests of credible sources).

2. *Try to determine if the source is biased.* No matter what the source, if the website uses a hard sell to peddle products, therapies, or ideas, be wary. Look for sites that have no vested interest, no products to peddle, and no ax to grind. Look at the website address. If it is a *.gov* or a *.edu*, this means that the website is sponsored and maintained by a governmental or educational institution with a reputation to protect. If the address is a *.com* site, it is commercial and therefore more likely to be biased. Websites with *.org* in their address are sponsored by organizations with varying credibility.

3. *Determine whether the document is current.* Websites sometimes indicate when the site was last updated. Many documents indicate the date at the beginning or at the end. You can also make a rough estimate for the currency of the document from the recency of the information in the article. Be as current as possible.

As humorist Will Rogers reportedly said, what gets us into real trouble is "what we know that ain't so." Consult Snopes.com to correct urban myths and misinformation on the Internet, such as the spiders and sex statistics that "ain't so."

Libraries: Bricks-and-Mortar Research

The Internet is a wonderful virtual resource, but brick-and-mortar library buildings still house books, documents, and reference works that can't be found on the Internet. College libraries also are computerized, and most allow students to access the Internet on library computers. Thus, college libraries provide "one-stop shopping" for information on speech topics.

THE LIBRARIAN: EXPERT NAVIGATOR

If you do not know quite where to begin, ask the librarian; there is no better single source of information on researching a speech topic. They are the experts on information location. Use them. Do not expect the librarian to do your research for you, but he or she will guide you on your journey through the maze of information if you get stuck.

LIBRARY CATALOGUES: COMPUTER VERSIONS

The computer catalogue, like its predecessor the card catalogue, lists books according to author, title, and subject. An important characteristic of the computer catalogue is that you can do a keyword search. Type in "mountain climbing," and a list of titles related to this subject will appear. You can also keyword search by author names. Computer catalogues also indicate if the book is available or checked out, saving you time.

PERIODICALS AND NEWSPAPERS: POPULAR INFORMATION SOURCES

There are many periodical indexes, including *Psychological Abstracts*. Check with your librarian to discover which are available at your college library. Newspapers are also one of the richest available sources of information on current topics. Your college library undoubtedly subscribes to the local newspaper. *The New York Times Index* is also a valuable resource.

REFERENCE WORKS: BEYOND WIKIPEDIA

Encyclopedias are standard references used for researching a wide variety of topics. The most widely known encyclopedias are the *Encyclopaedia Britannica, Collier's Encyclopedia, World Book Encyclopedia*, and *Encyclopedia Americana*. Many encyclopedias can be accessed by computer. *Wikipedia* is probably the most controversial (see Box 12-1). Other useful general reference works besides encyclopedias are *Statistical Abstracts of the United States, World Almanac, Monthly Labor Review*, the FBI's *Uniform Crime Reports, Vital Statistics of the United States*, and *Facts on File*.

DATABASES: COMPUTERIZED COLLECTIONS OF CREDIBLE INFORMATION

Libraries are your best bet for accessing computerized databases because you can avoid substantial subscription fees. LexisNexis, which accesses millions of articles from books, magazines, academic journals, and additional

---

Wikipedia: Credible Scholarship or Mob Rule?

Wikipedia is the most widely used general reference source on the Internet. In 2015, there were 35 million articles, in multiple languages, available on *Wikipedia* ("Wikipedia Stats," 2015). As Association for Psychological Science President Mahzarin Banaji (2011) notes, "It is the largest collaboratively produced knowledge repository that has ever existed."

One serious problem with *Wikipedia* is that the information it contains can be unreliable, even wrong. An assessment by the Project on Psychology of 935 articles on *Wikipedia* found only 2% were above "B level" in quality, and many were woefully inadequate, even inaccurate (Banaji, 2011). Authors of articles contributed are omitted. Even though *Wikipedia* articles often include links to valid and credible sources and some articles are first-rate scholarly works, you may nevertheless be quoting merely an interested party with no expertise and a decidedly biased view. *Wikipedia* has also been characterized as offering "middling quality and poor representation of the world's diversity" (Simonite, 2013), and one study notes the decline in quality of articles because of several structural reasons (Halfaker et al., 2013).

The criticisms are harsh, but are they entirely fair? Duke University interdisciplinary studies and English professor Cathy Davidson (2007), thinks not. She views *Wikipedia* as "the single most impressive collaborative intellectual tool produced at least since the *Oxford English Dictionary*" (p. B20). She notes that studies have shown *Wikipedia* is no more error-prone than some standard encyclopedias, and it has the added advantage that errors can be corrected sometimes within hours of discovery. As a starting point for research, *Wikipedia* can be "a quick and easy reference before heading into more scholarly depths" (p. B20).

Davidson's points have merit. Nevertheless, be cautious using *Wikipedia*. It is probably best to use it as Davidson suggests—as one possible starting point for your research, but not as a primary, reliable reference.

Questions for Thought

1. Do you see any ethical concerns with using *Wikipedia* as a primary source?

2. Can you think of ways to improve the accuracy and integrity of *Wikipedia*?

sources, is a highly useful database. Other credible options include Academic Search Premier (EBSCOhost), ProQuest, and Factiva.

Interviewing: Questioning Experts

Research interviews are sometimes a very productive resource for your speeches. Interviewing local artists about standards for determining the difference in quality between a Picasso painting and a three-year-old's crayon drawing could be quite useful. Interviewing an expert on self-driving car technology might be a great place to begin your research on this topic and its implications for the future. Experts can often guide your search by telling you where to search and what to avoid.

Student speakers often assume that no expert would want to be interviewed by just a student. That is usually untrue, especially when you consider how many experts are college professors on your campus. If your topic is a campus issue, such as parking problems or theft of car stereos, interviews with the campus chief of security could provide valuable information for your speech.

INTERVIEW PLAN: BE PREPARED

No research interview should be conducted without a specific plan of action. Your plan should include what you hope to find, who you will interview and why, a specific meeting time and place arranged with the interviewee, and prepared questions that will likely elicit helpful information. Avoid leading questions, such as "You couldn't possibly believe that this campus has no parking problem, could you?" Also avoid hostile or belligerent questions, such as "When you screwed up the arrest of that student accused of stealing car stereos on campus, did you make the arrest because you are biased against Middle Eastern people?" Ask difficult questions if you need to, but be respectful to the interviewee.

Open-ended questions are usually a good way to begin a research interview. Consider a few examples:

Do you believe we have a parking problem on campus?

What actions have been taken to address the parking problem on campus?

What more should be done about campus parking?

INTERVIEW CONDUCT: ACT PROFESSIONALLY

The manner in which you conduct yourself during the interview will usually determine whether the interview will be a success and provide useful information. Dress appropriately. Sloppy or bizarre dress will likely insult the interviewee. Always be on time for your meeting. If you are late, the interview may be canceled. Never record your interview without the expressed permission of the interviewee. Stay focused, and don't meander into unfruitful side discussions. Take careful notes. Stay within the allotted time for the interview. Thank the interviewee for answering your questions. Review your notes after the interview, and write down any additional clarifying notations that will help you remember what transpired.

INTERVIEWING BY EMAIL: SURPRISE YOURSELF

Not all interviews need to be in person. You might be surprised by how readily experts from around the world are happy to answer a few short questions posed to them by inquiring, eager students. Many experts have home pages with an email address. Make a short, initial inquiry about being interviewed. Lengthy emails may go unread. If the expert agrees to answer questions, be brief and concise. Ask only a few well-phrased, precise questions. Proofread every email for proper spelling and grammar. Fewer questions are more likely to get answers than a lengthy survey.

Plagiarism and Ethics: Cutting Corners on Research

In 1987, while still a U.S. senator from Delaware, Joe Biden ran for president of the United States. A gifted orator, Biden was given a decent chance of securing the Democratic nomination. His candidacy went into the dumpster, however, when news accounts revealed that Biden had plagiarized the conclusion to a speech he gave at the Iowa State Fair. He lifted his conclusion almost verbatim from a speech by British Labour Party leader Neil Kinnock (Jamieson, 1988). Biden's presidential campaign came to a screeching halt, and he didn't attempt another presidential bid until the 2008 campaign, ultimately receiving the consolation prize—vice president.

The issue of plagiarism emerged again in the political realm in 2013, when Rand Paul was found to have lifted whole passages from various sources for his speeches and book without citing the original sources, or making only vague reference after pilfering long passages from original sources with only minor word changes. Jonathon Bailey, founder of the ethics blog *Plagiarism Today*, characterized this behavior as fitting the definition of plagiarism despite Paul's initial response to the charges that he was being attacked by "haters" (Carrier, 2013).

With the explosive growth of the Internet and the easy availability of whole speeches by others, student plagiarism has become an increasing problem (Noguchi, 2008). Studies show that a majority of students plagiarize to some degree (Perez-Pena, 2012). Documented cases of students stealing lines, even entire passages, from the graduation speeches of other students for use in their own graduation speeches have produced lively debate on YouTube, a frequent resource used by students for such plagiarism.

These student speakers were guilty of selective plagiarism, or stealing portions of someone else's speech or writings. That is bad enough, but plagiarism becomes even more serious when entire speeches are stolen and presented as one's own. Some students attempt such blatant theft of another's words usually because the development of a speech has been left until too little time remains to conduct adequate research. Stealing someone's words is pilfering a part of that person's identity. That is never an inconsequential act.

Competent Outlining and Organizing

The quality of speech organization directly influences how well your listeners understand your key points (Titsworth, 2004). A speaker who doesn't seem able to connect two thoughts doesn't inspire confidence (Chesebro, 2003). A disorganized speech creates confusion. Actress Jodie Foster gave a rambling speech at the 2013 Golden Globes awards ceremony, prompting the *Vanity Fair* headline "Ten Wildly Varying Interpretations of Jodie Foster's Golden Globes Speech" (Miller, 2013). Christy Lemure of the Associated Press gave this assessment: "Jodie Foster came out without really coming out, and suggested she was retiring from acting without exactly saying so, in a long, breathless and rambling speech" (quoted by Miller, 2013). Foster's *Wikipedia* page was "updated" soon afterward to announce her retirement, but when reporter Amy Kaufman asked Foster whether she had, in fact, announced her retirement as an actress in her speech, Foster replied, "Oh, no, I could never stop acting." (quoted in "Jodie Foster Speech," 2013).

The organizational process begins with an understanding of the rudiments of outlining your thoughts so they are clear to an audience. Common organizational patterns are then discussed.

Effective Outlining: Making Sense

Microsoft Word offers many outlining formats. The bulleted format is one of the most popular, especially for PowerPoint slides. This format can easily become PowerPoint*less*, however, when every point has a bullet in front of it, making nothing very noteworthy. Thus, the standard outlining form required in most speech classes uses a specific set of symbols that more obviously demarcates main points from subpoints. This standard outlining form is clear, precise, logical, and follows a few basic criteria.

SYMBOLS: STANDARD FORMATTING

Standard outlining form uses a specific set of symbols, shown in brief here:

    I. Roman numerals for main points
      A. Capital letters for primary subpoints
        1. Standard numbers for secondary subpoints
          a. Lowercase letters for tertiary subpoints

Note that *each successive set of subpoints is indented to separate the main points visually from the primary, secondary, and tertiary subpoints.* Thus, you would not format an outline as follows:

I. Student debt has reached staggering levels.
A. The average student debt upon graduation from college is $30,000.
1. 70% of students meet or exceed this average debt.
a. Such crushing debt has serious consequences.

You can readily see that lack of indentation merges all of your points into a list that doesn't clearly differentiate main points from subpoints.

COHERENCE: LOGICAL CONSISTENCY AND CLARITY

Logical consistency and clarity are qualities of an effective outline. Begin with your topic, narrow the topic to your specific purpose statement, and from that, develop main points that break down further into subpoints. Work from the most general to the most specific. For example:

I. [TOPIC] The aging U.S. population.
II. [THESIS] Longer life spans pose new challenges.
III. [PURPOSE STATEMENT] To explain in what ways longer life spans stress fragile support systems for elderly Americans.
IV. [MAIN POINT] Americans are living longer than ever before.
V. [MAIN POINT] Longer life spans stress fragile support systems for the elderly in three significant ways.

Coherence requires that main points flow directly from the purpose statement. Subpoints, however, should also flow from main points. For example, look at the development of Main Point I:

I. [MAIN POINT] Americans are living longer than ever before.
A. [PRIMARY SUBPOINT] Average life span of an American is at its highest level in history.
B. [PRIMARY SUBPOINT] Americans are increasingly living to 100 years old and beyond.

Each primary subpoint flows from the main point on "living longer."

Each primary subpoint can be further divided into secondary subpoints. For example:

A. [PRIMARY SUBPOINT] Average life span of an American is at its highest level in history.
1. [SECONDARY SUBPOINT] Average life span of an American is now a record 77 years old.
2. [SECONDARY SUBPOINT] Average life span of an American has increased from 69 years old just two decades ago.
B. [PRIMARY SUBPOINT] Americans are increasingly living to 100 years old and beyond.
1. [SECONDARY SUBPOINT] A record 30,000 Americans are 100 years old or older.
2. [SECONDARY SUBPOINT] There will be an estimated 800,000 Americans at least 100 years old by the year 2050.

Following this pattern of working from the most general to the increasingly specific will assure coherence.

If primary subpoints relate directly to a main point, secondary subpoints relate to primary subpoints, and tertiary subpoints relate directly to secondary subpoints, then every point will flow logically from the purpose statement.

COMPLETENESS: USING FULL SENTENCES

Your first attempt to outline your speech will prove to be more successful if you use complete sentences. Complete sentences communicate complete thoughts. A word or phrase may suggest a thought without communicating it completely or clearly. For example:

PURPOSE STATEMENT: To explain hazing (initiation rituals).

I. Hazing
A. Campus hazing
B. Military hazing
C. Corporate hazing
II. Solutions
A. Laws
B. Policies
C. Penalties
D. Education

This word-and-phrase outline creates informational gaps and questions that can't be answered merely by referring to the outline. The purpose statement provides no direction. Will you explain how hazing is done? Why it is a problem? How it can be controlled?

The main points and subpoints are no clearer. Main Point I is about hazing, and the subpoints indicate three types: campus, military, and corporate. Still, no direction or complete thought is communicated. Are these three types of hazing serious problems? Should they be prevented? Should we find them amusing? Should we encourage hazing on campus, in the military, and in the corporate world? Main Point II suffers from the same problem. Solutions are suggested, but solutions imply a problem has been described yet no problem is indicated in the previous main point or in the purpose statement. If a problem exists, what type of legal, policy, and educational solutions are offered? This remains unclear.

Consider how much more complete a full-sentence outline is when compared to the incomplete and confusing word-and-phrase outline:

PURPOSE STATEMENT: To explain specific ways to prevent the problem of hazing.

I. Hazing is a growing problem in the United States.
   A. More than 50 deaths and numerous injuries have occurred from hazing in just the last decade.
   B. The number of hazing incidents requiring intervention by authorities has doubled in the last decade.
II. There are several ways to prevent hazing.
   A. Hazing could be outlawed in all states.
   B. College, corporate, and military policies could specifically ban hazing rituals.
   C. Penalties for violations of laws and policies could be increased.
   D. Students, employees, and soldiers could receive instruction on the dangers of hazing and the consequences of violating laws and policies banning the practice.

BALANCE: NO LOPSIDED TIME ALLOTMENT

Each main point deserves substantial development. This does not mean that you have to allot an equal amount of time to each. Nevertheless, you want a relatively balanced presentation. If you have three main points in the body of your speech, don't devote four minutes to the first main point and only one minute or less to your two remaining main points. Such a lopsided time allotment means either that your second and third main points aren't really main points at all or that you haven't developed your last two main points sufficiently. Increase the development of main points given insufficient treatment, combine insufficiently developed points into a single point to give the point some beef, or drop the two underdeveloped points and replace them with more substantial points.

DIVISION: MINIMUM OF TWO SUBPOINTS

Main points divide into subpoints. Note the plural on subpoints. Logically, you don't divide something into one. *You divide main points into two or more subpoints.* If you can't divide a point into at least two subpoints, your point probably doesn't need division or isn't substantial enough. It's time to rethink the development of your speech (see Box 12-2).

Even when you have only a single example or two to illustrate a point, the principle of division still applies. For example:

I. Professional baseball players' salaries are astronomical.
   A. Average player salaries are almost $4 million per year.
   B. Jon Lester and Clayton Kershaw make $30 million a year.

You can't generalize from a single example or two, so don't let it dangle as a subpoint all its own. Group them together, as shown above.

In summary, competent outlining requires the proper use of symbols, coherence, completeness, balance, and appropriate division of points. An outline maps the flow of a speaker's ideas.

Effective Organization: Creating Patterns

Organization requires a pattern for your thoughts, unlike what Jodie Foster provided in

A disorganized speech can be as confusing and pointless as this mess of road signs. Strive for clarity by using appropriate patterns of organization to make sense, not a mess.

her Golden Globes speech. There are several patterns for organizing a speech: topical, chronological, spatial, causal, problem-solution, problem-cause-solution, and Monroe's

Motivated Sequence. Signposts, transitions, and internal summaries also help to create effective organization.

TOPICAL PATTERN: BY THE SUBJECTS

A *topical* pattern shapes information according to types, classifications, or parts of a whole. For example:

> PURPOSE STATEMENT: To explain the three types of prisons in the United States.
>
> I. The first type is minimum security.
> II. The second type is medium security.
> III. The third type is maximum security.

A topical pattern doesn't suggest a particular order of presentation for each main point. You could begin with maximum and work to minimum security prisons just as easily as the reverse.

BOX 12-2 DEVELOPING COMMUNICATION COMPETENCE

A Student Outline: Rough Draft and Revision

Constructing a competent outline can be a struggle, especially if appropriate outlining form and criteria are not well understood. Initial attempts to outline a speech may prove challenging, and first attempts especially may produce seriously flawed results. Don't despair. Outlining is a process that trains our minds to think in an orderly fashion. It takes time to learn such a sophisticated skill.

Compare this rough draft of a student outline to the revised outline constructed by the same student (my comments appear in *italics*).

ROUGH DRAFT OUTLINE
PURPOSE STATEMENT: To eliminate the drug problem by making drug testing mandatory. (*Where's your central idea? You overstate the potential outcomes of mandatory drug testing. Try "significantly reduce drug use," not "eliminate the drug problem." General purpose is only implied—will you try to convince us?*)

I. The drugs among society. (*No clear direction is provided. What do you want to say about "the drugs among society"? This is also not a complete sentence.*)
  A. The effects of drugs. (*Are you concerned with only negative effects? Unclear! This is not a complete sentence.*)
    1. The immediate effects of drugs.
    2. The permanent effects of drugs. (*1 and 2 are not complete sentences.*)
  B. The effects of using drugs. (*This seems to repeat "A" above. Do you have a different idea in mind? Unclear! This is not a complete sentence.*)
    1. Memory loss.
    2. Addicted babies.
    3. Brain damage.
    4. Physical harm. (*1–4 are not complete sentences.*)

(continued)

(continued)

II. Ways to solve drug abuse. (*Your purpose statement indicates only one solution—mandatory drug testing. Stay focused on your purpose statement.*)
    A. The first step is to be aware of the problem. (*"Awareness" doesn't seem related to mandatory drug testing. Let your purpose statement guide your entire outline.*)
        1. Establish drug testing in all companies.
        2. Establish stricter laws against drug users.
        3. Start more drug clinics. (*Good use of complete sentences. Subpoints 1–3 do not relate directly to "A"—they are not kinds of awareness. Subpoints 2 and 3 also seem unrelated to mandatory drug testing. These are coherence problems.*)

(In Main Point II, you have an "A" point without a "B" point—problem of division. Also, Main Point II is less developed than Main Point I—problem of balance.)

REVISED VERSION
CENTRAL IDEA: Drug use in the workplace is a serious problem requiring a new approach to solving this problem.

PURPOSE STATEMENT: To convince my audience that every place of employment should start a mandatory drug-testing program. (*This is a much-improved purpose statement. "Every place of employment," however, seems a bit drastic. Try narrowing the application of your proposal to workers who might jeopardize the health and safety of others if drugs were used—airline pilots, bus drivers, etc.*)

I. Drug use in the workplace is a serious problem. (*Good, clear main point.*)
    A. Drug use in the workplace is widespread.
        1. Many employees in large companies use drugs.
        2. Many employees in factories use drugs.
    B. Drug use in the workplace is dangerous.
        1. Workers injure and even kill themselves.
        2. Customers have been injured and killed. (*Doesn't the risk go far beyond customers? If a plane crashes on a neighborhood because the pilot was loaded on drugs, the dead and injured include far more than customers.*)

(This entire main point with its subpoints is much improved. One question—are you focusing only on drugs used on the job, or do you include drug use that occurs hours before starting work?)

II. Mandatory drug testing in the workplace will reduce drug abuse. (*This is a solid second main point that flows nicely from your purpose statement.*)
    A. Drug testing will catch drug users.
        1. Testing is very accurate.
        2. Drug testing will provide absolute proof of drug use by workers. (*"Absolute proof" seems overstated. Try "solid proof."*)
    B. Drug testing will prevent drug use in the workplace.
        1. Workers will worry about getting caught using drugs.
        2. Drug testing can prevent drug users from being hired. (*Second main point is coherent, balanced, divided appropriately, and complete sentences are used throughout. One final question: What do you propose should happen to employees who use drugs? Rehabilitation? Immediate job termination?*)

CHRONOLOGICAL PATTERN: ACCORDING TO TIME

A *chronological* pattern suggests a specific sequence of events. When speeches provide a biographical sketch, explain a step-by-step process, or recount a historical event, chronological order is an appropriate pattern of organization. For example:

> PURPOSE STATEMENT: To explain the renovation plan for our local downtown city center.
>
> I. The old Cooper House and Del Rio Theatre will be demolished.
> II. Main Street will be widened.
> III. A Cinemax theater complex will replace the Del Rio Theatre.
> IV. A new, twice-as-large Cooper House will replace the old Cooper House.

Each main point follows a logical sequence. You don't replace buildings on the same sites until the old buildings are demolished. There is a sequence that must be followed.

SPATIAL PATTERN: ACCORDING TO SPACE

Some speeches provide information based on a *spatial* pattern. Explaining directions to a particular place requires a spatial order—a visualization of where things are spatially. Explaining how the Brooklyn Bridge was built would necessitate starting the explanation at the base of the bridge and working up spatially. Or consider this example of a backpack:

> PURPOSE STATEMENT: To explain how to load up a backpack for camping.
>
> I. Certain items must go on the bottom of the pack.
> II. Some items are best packed in the middle.
> III. There are several items that pack well on top.
> IV. A few items fit well lashed to the outside of the pack.

The outline focuses on segments of space. Actually loading a backpack while you explain your four points is an essential visual aid.

CAUSAL PATTERN: WHO OR WHAT IS RESPONSIBLE

There are two *causal* patterns of organization. The *causes-effects* pattern looks for why things happen and then discusses the consequences. For example:

> PURPOSE STATEMENT: To explain the causes and effects of staggering tuition increases at U.S. colleges.
>
> I. There are several causes of annual tuition increases.
> II. Tuition increases that are far greater than yearly inflation produce serious consequences.

The *effects-causes* pattern begins with the effects of an event and then moves to what caused the event. For example:

> PURPOSE STATEMENT: To show that grading systems create learning deficiencies.
>
> I. There are serious deficiencies in student learning.
> II. Grading systems promote these learning deficiencies.

PROBLEM-SOLUTION PATTERN: MEETING NEEDS

The *problem-solution* pattern explores the nature of a problem and proposes a solution or possible solutions. For example:

> PURPOSE STATEMENT: To argue for a flat income tax to replace the current graduated income tax.
>
> I. The present income tax system has several serious problems.
> II. A flat income tax will solve these problems.

PROBLEM-CAUSE-SOLUTION PATTERN: KNOWING WHY AND HOW

The *problem-cause-solution* pattern expands on the problem-solution pattern by exploring causes of the problem and addressing these causes in the solution. For example:

> PURPOSE STATEMENT: To advocate a government-sponsored program to prevent hearing loss among teenagers and young adults.

I. Teenagers and young adults are suffering serious hearing loss.
II. There are several causes of this hearing loss.
III. A government-sponsored program to prevent hearing loss is critical.

MONROE'S MOTIVATED SEQUENCE: FIVE-STEP PATTERN

Monroe's Motivated Sequence was first designed for sales presentations. It is an organizational pattern with five steps (Gronbeck et al., 1998). The five steps are:

I. *Attention:* Create interest; use attention strategies ("I have cancer"; see also Chapter 13).
II. *Need:* Present a problem to be solved and relate it to your audience ("College students are not immune to the ravages of cancer").
III. *Satisfaction:* Provide a solution to the problem that will satisfy your audience ("Research is providing real cures, but more is needed").
IV. *Visualization:* Provide an image for your audience of what the world will look like if your solution is implemented ("Imagine a world without cancer").
V. *Action:* Make a call to action; get the audience involved and committed ("Donate what you can to the American Cancer Society").

A lengthy example of this organizational pattern is presented in Chapter 15 in a sample speech.

SIGNPOSTS AND TRANSITIONS: CONNECTING THE DOTS

Listeners need assistance during your speech to follow your organizational pattern. *Signposts* and *transitions* are valuable tools for helping listeners understand the key points of your speech.

Signposts are organizational markers that indicate the structure of a speech and notify listeners a particular point is about to be addressed. Student Joseph Jones (2011) provides an example: "*The first cause* is that for-profit universities are willing to mislead students to persuade them to enroll," and "*A second cause* . . . is that

---

BOX 12-3 DEVELOPING COMMUNICATION COMPETENCE

Examples of Signposts and Transitions

SIGNPOSTS

My first point is	The key points are
My second point is	There are two ways
There are three points to explore	My final point is

TRANSITIONS

So what does this mean?	However
For example	Why should we care?
Nevertheless	Along the same lines
In summary	Therefore
Consequently	Granted
Conversely	But

---

innocent people are intrigued by false advertising" (p. 74). **Transitions** connect what was said with what will be said with a word, phrase, or sentence. They are bridges between points. Student Angela Wnek (2012) illustrates both transition and signposting: "*Why isn't our government doing more to stop honey laundering* [tainted/illegal honey imports]? Two forces are driving the laundering: First, money, and second, the FDA's lax policies" (p. 144). (Box 12-3 offers additional examples of typical signposts and transitions.)

CLARIFYING AS YOU GO: INTERNAL SUMMARIES

When you say "summary," most people think of a final wrap-up to a speech or essay. There is another type, however. An **internal summary** restates a key point in a speech. It occurs in the body of the speech, not in the conclusion. Internal summaries help listeners follow the sequence of ideas. "As you can now see, protecting homes from wildfires begins with clearing a defensible space around each home" is an example of an internal summary. It signals that a main point has concluded, and it suggests a new point is about to be addressed. "Closely related to this, a second way to protect homes from wildfires . . ." is a transitional statement and a signpost that both follow the internal summary.

Competent Delivery of Speeches

Cornell University psychology professor Stephen Ceci had been receiving average student evaluations of his teaching. Unsatisfied with this, he decided to change his delivery of class lectures. He spoke more loudly than usual, varied the pitch of his voice more dramatically, and gestured more emphatically than normal. The student ratings for his class and his instruction went up noticeably from an average of between 2 and 3 on a 5-point scale to a 4-plus (Murray, 1997). Ceci was perceived by students to be more effective, knowledgeable, and organized because of the change in delivery. Students also believed they had learned more material even though their test scores were identical to those of previous classes. Does delivery make a difference? Unquestionably, it does.

Methods of Delivery: The Big Four

There are four primary methods of delivery, each with its own pros and cons. They are manuscript, memorized, impromptu, and extemporaneous speaking.

MANUSCRIPT SPEAKING: IT'S ALL THERE IN BLACK AND WHITE

Speakers often refer to "writing their speeches." It is very difficult to write a speech for oral presentation that won't sound like an essay read to an audience. Effective speeches are not merely spoken essays. An essay read to an audience can sound stilted and overly formal. A *manuscript speech* may be an appropriate method of delivery in certain situations. If you must be scrupulously precise in your phrasing for fear of being legally encumbered or causing offense, then a manuscript may be necessary. Political candidates spend millions of dollars for television and radio ads. They cannot tolerate mistakes in phrasing or wordy speeches.

It takes extensive practice to present a manuscript speech effectively. A chief drawback of manuscript speaking is that the speaker will appear too scripted, too stilted, and overly formal, and that ownership of his or her ideas becomes suspect. Another drawback is that the speaker usually gets buried in the manuscript and fails to establish eye contact with an audience. Reading to an audience can disconnect the speaker from listeners. Yet another drawback is that digressions from the prepared manuscript are difficult to make smoothly, yet such changes may be critical if the audience does not respond well to a portion of the speech. Generally, manuscript speaking should be left to professional speakers who have substantial experience using this delivery method.

MEMORIZED SPEAKING: MEMORY, DON'T FAIL ME NOW

Some speakers attempt to *memorize their speech*es. A short toast at a wedding, a brief acceptance speech at an awards ceremony, or a few key lines in a lengthy speech may benefit from memorization, especially if what you memorize is emotionally touching or humorous (no one wants the punch line of a joke to be read). Memorizing a speech, however, runs the risk of forgetting portions of it. Have you ever grown frustrated or felt uncomfortable when someone tries to remember a joke or a funny story, keeps forgetting important details, and then following an agonizing oral search for the correct version ("Oh, wait, that's not the way it goes . . . "), finally flubs the punch line? Forgetting can be painful for listeners and speaker alike. Awkward silences while you desperately attempt to remember the next sentence in your speech can be embarrassing. Also, making a memorized speech sound natural, not artificial and robotic, requires considerable experience. Those who have acted on stage know this well.

IMPROMPTU SPEAKING: OFF-THE-CUFF PRESENTATIONS

An **impromptu speech** is one delivered without preparation, or so it seems. You are asked to respond to a previous speaker without warning or to say a few words on a subject without advance notice. Although impromptu speeches can be challenging, a few simple guidelines can help.

1. *Anticipate impromptu speaking.* If you have any inkling that you might be called on to give a short speech on a subject, begin preparing your remarks. Don't wait until you are put on the spot.

2. *Draw on your life experience and knowledge for the substance of your remarks.* F. E. Smith once remarked, "Winston Churchill has devoted the best years of his life to preparing his impromptu speeches." Churchill had clarified his ideas and points of view in his mind. Thus, when called on to speak in an impromptu fashion, he was already prepared. Life experience is preparation for impromptu speaking. Draw from that experience.

3. *Formulate a simple outline for an impromptu speech.* Begin with a short opening attention strategy—a relevant story, a humorous quip you've used successfully on other occasions, or a clever quotation you've memorized. State your point of view or the theme for your remarks, then quickly identify two or three short points that you will address. Finally, summarize briefly what you said. You are not expected to provide substantial supporting material for your points during an impromptu speech, but if you have some facts and figures memorized, you will impress your audience with this ready knowledge. Impromptu speaking is usually less formal than a standard speech, so be conversational in tone and presentation.

EXTEMPORANEOUS SPEAKING: THE VIRTUES OF AN OUTLINE

An **extemporaneous speech**, often shortened to *extemp*, is delivered from a prepared outline or notes. There are several advantages to extemp speaking:

1. *An extemp speech sounds spontaneous.* Even though fully prepared in advance, it is not read from a manuscript. Instead, the speaker glances at an outline or notes, then puts his or her thoughts into words on the spot.

2. *Extemp speaking permits greater eye contact with the audience.* You are not buried, head down, in a manuscript. Of course, an outline can take on the form of a manuscript if it is too detailed. Typically, a speaker prepares an extemp speech by constructing an outline composed of full sentences (preparation outline). The speaker delivers the speech, however, from an abbreviated outline (presentation outline) composed of simple words or phrases that trigger complete thoughts. Here is a brief example comparing the two:

Preparation Outline	Presentation Outline

I. Texting while driving is dangerous
  A. Texting is distracting
  B. Severe accidents, injuries, even death result
	I. Texting dangerous
	  A. Distracting
	  B. Accidents, injuries, deaths

3. *Extemp speaking allows the speaker to respond to audience feedback as it occurs.* You can adjust to the moment-by-moment changes in audience reactions much more so than with manuscript or memorized speeches.

The one drawback of extemp speaking is that learning to speak from notes or an outline takes practice. There is no substitute for practicing extemp speaking. Once you learn how to do it, however, you may never want to use any other method of delivery.

Developing Competent Delivery

Inexperienced public speakers often fail to notice problems of delivery that interfere with the effectiveness of their message. Most are commonplace problems that are easily corrected: *eye contact, tone of voice, fluency, speaking rate, body movements,* and *distracting behaviors.*

EYE CONTACT: CONNECTING WITH YOUR LISTENERS

Eye contact is an important element of a speaker's credibility (Neal & Brodsky, 2008). Weak eye contact is a common delivery problem. This is often the case when speakers make Power-Point presentations. They look at the slides, not the audience.

There are simple ways to improve your eye contact when delivering a speech. First, be very familiar with your speech so that you won't get pinned to your notes or read from a manuscript. Second, practice looking at your entire audience, beginning with the middle of your audience, then looking left, then right, then to the middle again, and so forth. With practice

Direct eye contact is a critical part of effective delivery. You cannot connect with your audience if you are buried in a manuscript and always looking down. Here North Carolina state senator Don Davis exhibits direct eye contact and is not chained to a manuscript, which permits animated facial expressions.

(an imaginary audience will do fine), your eye contact will become automatic.

TONE OF VOICE: DEVELOPING VOCAL VARIETY

Your *tone of voice* can influence the mood of your audience. One study showed that people listening to a speaker deliver a message in either a happy tone or a sad tone experienced **emotional contagion**—they felt happy or sad depending on the speaker's tone of voice (Neumann & Strack, 2000). Some individuals have very little range in their voices when giving a speech (a monotone). Their voices sound flat and uninteresting. Strive for vocal variety. You can avoid attention-killing monotony by raising and lowering the pitch of your voice. The singing voice has a range of pitch from soprano to bass. Similarly, you can vary your speaking voice by moving up and down the vocal range, from high sounds to lower sounds and then back.

Monotony can also be avoided by varying the loudness or softness of your voice. A raised voice signals intense, passionate feelings. It will punctuate portions of your presentation much as an exclamation point punctuates a written sentence. Using vocal volume to gain attention,

however, can be excessive. As Mark Twain noted, "Noise proves nothing. Often a hen who has merely laid an egg cackles as if she laid an asteroid." Incessant, unrelenting, bombastic delivery of a message can irritate and alienate your audience. Speak loudly only when you have an especially important point to make. All points in your speech do not deserve equal attention.

Speaking softly can also induce interest. When you lower the pitch and loudness of your voice, the audience must strain to hear. This can be a nice, dramatic twist in a speech—if used infrequently. Vocal variety signals shifts in mood and does not permit an audience to drift into the hypnotic, trancelike state produced by the white noise of the monotone voice.

Practice vocal variety on your friends during casual conversations. Experiment with different voice inflections, volume, and pitch.

FLUENCY: AVOIDING EXCESSIVE VOCAL FILLERS

The *fluency* of your delivery suffers mightily when **vocal fillers**—the insertion of *um, ah, like, you know, know what I mean, whatever,* and other variants that substitute for pauses and often draw attention to themselves—are used more than occasionally. Almost all speakers use vocal fillers once in a while, and an audience will not notice infrequent use. When these "vocal hiccups" become frequent, however, it can diminish your credibility (Croucher, 2004). Don't be concerned about filling in a few pauses in your delivery. Recent brain research shows that a one- to two-second pause powerfully combats wandering attention. Brief silence can awaken the brain (Swaminathan, 2007).

Practice not using vocal fillers during casual conversation with friends and family. Focus on noticing how often other people use vocal fillers during conversation. Practice your speech in front of a friend, or video record it. Have your friend tap a pencil on a table every time you use a vocal filler during your speech. When you review the video recorded practice speech, count the number of vocal fillers. With time, you will eliminate the habit.

SPEAKING RATE: PACING YOURSELF

Sean Shannon, a Canadian residing in Oxford, England, recited the famous soliloquy "To be or not to be..." from Shakespeare's *Hamlet* at a 650-words-per-minute clip. Normal conversation has a *speaking rate* of between 140 and 180 words per minute (wpm; McCoy et al., 2005). This pace can allow an audience to scrutinize complex messages. Faster speaking rates (180 to 210 wpm), however, increase the audience's perception of you as intelligent, confident, and effective compared to slower paced speakers (Smith & Shaffer, 1995). Speaking fast shows that you are quick on your feet and can handle ideas swiftly. Listeners' comprehension of speech, however, declines rapidly once the speaking rate exceeds 250 wpm (Foulke, 2006). Conversely, a very slow speaking pace (about 100 wpm) can induce a stupor in an audience.

Speaking pace should be lively enough to keep attention, but not so fast that you appear to have consumed three hyper-caffeinated energy drinks. A speaking pace of 175 to 200 wpm is usually appropriate. Without actually measuring your speaking pace, *you can get a rough idea of the appropriate pace by enunciating your words carefully and pausing to take breaths without gasping for air.*

BODY MOVEMENTS: FINDING THE EFFECTIVE BALANCE

Too little *body movement* when speaking can anesthetize an audience. A speaker stands before an audience, grabs the podium in a viselike grip (white knuckles clearly visible to everyone), assumes an expressionless face reminiscent of a marble statue in a museum, and appears to have feet welded to the floor. This is an example of too little body movement. Excessive body movement, however, can be a distraction. Aimlessly pacing like a caged panther, wildly gesticulating with arms flailing in all directions, or awkwardly wrapping legs and arms around the podium diverts attention away from the speech's message.

Strive for a balance between excessive and insufficient body movement. An animated, lively delivery can excite an audience, but you don't want to appear to have insects in your underwear. Posture should be erect without looking like a soldier standing at attention. Slumping your shoulders, crossing and uncrossing your legs, and lurching to one side with one leg higher than the other call attention to awkward movements. Practice speaking in front of a mirror, or record your practice speech to determine whether you have any of these awkward movements.

Proper gesturing can be a concern for the inexperienced public speaker. Don't let it overly concern you. Unless you have adopted some really odd or distracting gestures while speaking, they will rarely, if ever, torpedo your speech. Let gestures emerge naturally. You don't need to plan gestures. As Motley (1995) explains, gestures "are supposed to be nonconscious. That is to say, in natural conversation we use gestures every day without thinking about them. And when we do consciously think about gestures, they become uncomfortable and inhibited" (p. 99). Focus on your messages and your audience, and gestures will follow.

DISTRACTING BEHAVIORS: STOP CLICKING THE PEN

She crawled on her hands and knees across the courtroom floor while the jury watched transfixed. She kicked the jury box, cried, flailed her arms, and screamed. One journalist said she "behaved like she needed a rabies shot during the trial" (Hutchinson, 2002, p. 9A). Defense attorney Nedra Ruiz's delivery during the emotion-charged trial of Marjorie Knoller and Robert Noel, in the highly publicized 2002 dog

Lawyer Nedra Ruiz's delivery was vivid and memorable during her animated defense in a California dog mauling trial. Nevertheless, it was so extreme, including crawling like a dog, that she was more distracting than effective.

mauling murder case in Los Angeles, became a subject of considerable comment. Laurie Levenson, a law professor at Loyola University in Los Angeles, remarked, "Most people I talk to just shook their heads . . . It's borderline bizarre" (Curtis, 2002, p. A4). As Levenson explained, "There's a pretty decent defense here, but it's getting lost in her [Ruiz's] mannerisms and her theatrics. She's not smooth. She's not polished. She crosses the line from what I think is effective advocacy to cheap theatrics" (Curtis, 2002, p. A4).

The Ruiz example is an extreme case of delivery subverting substance, but there are dozens of quirky behaviors that speakers can exhibit, often without realizing they are distracting an audience's attention from the message. Playing with change in your pocket while speaking is one example. Playing with a pen or a pencil is another. Sometimes a speaker will unconsciously click a ballpoint pen or tap the podium while speaking. Distracting behaviors can easily be eliminated,. Don't hold a pen in your hand, and you won't play with it while speaking. Take change out of your pocket before speaking if you have a tendency to jiggle coins. Distracting behaviors won't destroy a quality speech unless the behavior is beyond weird (like Ruiz's). Nevertheless, eliminating them helps create the impression of a polished performance.

One final note: *delivery should match the context for your speech*. A eulogy calls for a dignified, formal delivery. The speaker usually limits body movements and keeps his or her voice toned down as a sign of respect. A motivational speech, however, requires a lively, enthusiastic delivery. Your voice may be loud, body movements dramatic, eye contact intense, and facial movements expressive. During a motivational speech, the podium is usually moved aside or ignored, and the speaker moves back and forth across a stage or even into the audience. An after-dinner speech or "roast" calls for a lively, comic delivery. Facial expressions consist mostly of smiles, gestures may be gross or exaggerated, and a speaker's voice may be loud, even abrasive, for effect. Match your delivery to the speech context.

Summary

Speech anxiety can significantly interfere with competent speech presentations. Addressing this potential problem is critical. All speeches begin with audience analysis. Determining which of the five types of audiences—captive, committed, contrary, concerned, or casual—you're speaking to is the first step. Demographic features also help you make inferences about the attitudes, beliefs, and values of that audience. Choosing a topic is a matter of appropriateness and effectiveness. Tailor your choice to your audience. Researching your speech is a lengthy process. There are many valuable sources of information available. Organizing and outlining your ideas in a logical, understandable pattern are essential. Delivery should incorporate strong eye contact, vocal variety, moderate body movements, and be free of distracting mannerisms. Extemporaneous speaking is the type of delivery to master for most occasions.

Quizzes Without Consequences

Test your knowledge before your exam! Go to the companion website at www.oup.com/us/rothwell, click on the Student Resources for each chapter, and take the Quizzes Without Consequences.

Film School Case Studies

Selma (2014). Biography/Drama; PG-13

Powerful recreation of Martin Luther King's leadership to secure civil rights and the intended epic march from Selma to Montgomery, Alabama, in 1965 that shocked the country when police ruthlessly attacked marchers. Examine David Oyelowo's portrayal of King's speeches. Concentrate on the delivery of the speeches and the organizational patterns chosen.

Speechless (1994). Romantic Comedy; PG-13

Imperfect comedy about two competing speech-writers who fall in love. Analyze the speechwriters' attention to audience analysis and careful construction of political speeches.

The King's Speech (2010). Drama; R

The story of King George VI of Great Britain, played by Oscar-winning actor Colin Firth. King George suffered terribly from a pronounced stutter. Forced to give numerous speeches, especially upon his ascension to the throne, he was helped by a speech therapist, played by Geoffrey Rush. Examine the depiction of the king's speech anxiety for symptoms of fight-or-flight, and analyze the methods of treatment offered by the therapist.

TED Talks and YouTube Links

These speeches are offered for you to analyze and perhaps discuss in class. Some are very good examples, and some are problematic. Apply text material in this chapter to each sample speech.

1. Extemporaneous delivery: Zach Wahls' "Two Moms" Speech
   https://www.youtube.com/watch?v=FSQQK2Vuf9Q

2. *Speech Anxiety:* Zach Wahls on *The Ellen DeGeneres Show*
   https://www.youtube.com/watch?v=gu8RkskFi78

3. *Social Anxiety:* Celebrities with Social Anxiety Disorder
   https://www.youtube.com/watch?v=7ZgnTNDliPs

4. *Delivery:* Sean Shannon, World's Fastest Talker (One-Minute Demonstration)
   https://www.youtube.com/watch?v=JEiFl8O5lV4

5. *Delivery:* Barack Obama's Eulogy of Clementa Pinckney
   https://www.youtube.com/watch?v=RK7tYOVd0Hs

6. *Delivery:* Jim Key, Toastmasters' Speech
   https://www.youtube.com/watch?v=kBdWyzjrjK0

7. *Delivery and Organization:* Tony Robbins, TED Talk, Why We Do What We Do
   https://www.ted.com/talks/tony_robbins_asks_why_we_do_what_we_do

8. *Organizational Pattern:* Kelly Cornell, Toastmasters' Speech
   http://www.youtube.com/watch?v=m7rrWMRyS7A

BY THE END OF THIS CHAPTER, YOU SHOULD BE ABLE TO:

1. Recognize and use specific strategies to gain and maintain audience attention.

2. Build and present competent introductions and conclusions.

3. Develop and present credible supporting materials.

CHAPTER

Building Better Speeches

**IN FEBRUARY 2015, FORMER ATLANTA BRAVES BASE-
BALL PLAYER CHIPPER JONES** claimed on Twitter that the
2012 massacre of twenty children and six staff members at
Sandy Hook Elementary School in Newtown, Connecticut,
never occurred. He said that the FBI had confirmed this but
was pounded on social media for his inane assertion. Cristina
Hassinger, daughter of slain Sandy Hook principal Dawn
Hochsprung, offered this tweet in reply: "Come for dinner. You
can meet my grandmother-less children and I'll show you my
mom's clothes riddled with bullet holes." Jones apologized with
this tweet: "My apologies for my Sandy Hook tweet yest. I had
heard something from someone which I thought to be credible
and tweeted w/out researching" (quoted by Dicker, 2015).

This incident exemplifies key topics discussed in this chapter. First, the startling nature of Jones' tweet drew immediate
attention from the Twitterverse. It was deservedly negative
attention, however. Second, Jones' admission that he "had

CHAPTER OUTLINE

- **Gaining and Maintaining
  Attention**
- **Effective Introductions and
  Conclusions**
- **Developing Supporting
  Materials**
- **Competent Style of
  Presentation: A Signature
  Event**

4. Build and present credible
arguments.

5. Recognize and
demonstrate effective methods
of oral style.

heard something from someone" without researching to determine its truth underlines the importance of using credible supporting materials to bolster your claims, especially startling claims. No one should blow off their "big bazoo," to use the words of Kurt Vonnegut, without being informed. Third, the style of the response from a victim's daughter is vivid and memorable. It has credibility and commands attention.

The purpose of this chapter is to explain important ways to develop and present better public speeches than just a standard presentation. This chapter builds on the previous discussion of basic speech concepts and processes. It delves into more substantial material to move you beyond the basics by discussing in depth attention strategies (good and bad), effective introductions and conclusions, credible supporting materials, how to build an argument, and effective oral style.

Gaining and Maintaining Attention: Strategies

An enormously popular British ad that featured a sexy model acting seductively as she climbed inside a sleek automobile drew attention to the wrong stimulus. A study of this ad showed that the gorgeous model commanded attention while the automobile being advertised was virtually invisible to almost everyone watching (Clay, 2002). As a speaker, being seen in our kaleidoscopic world of flashing images, and heard above the clamoring din, is your great challenge. How do you induce an audience to attend to your message and ignore all distractions? Minds easily wander (Kane et al., 2007; McVay & Kane, 2009). Attention is unavoidably selective (see Chapter 2).

One national survey of individuals from a wide variety of professions revealed that the top-ranked skill for preparing and delivering a speech was keeping an audience's attention (Engleberg, 2002). Corporate media consultant Steve Crescenzo (2005) observes, "In today's short-attention-span, sound-byte society, the one thing people cannot afford to be is boring" (p. 12). Why prepare and present a speech that induces a nap? You want your listeners excited, engaged, touched, and anxious to hear what comes next. You don't want them yearning for those signal words "in conclusion." It's a lesson every teacher

learns when lecturing to students for an entire class period and every religious leader comprehends when delivering a sermon or homily to a congregation. Most speeches are not meant to be purely entertainment, but if listeners are bored when you speak to them about significant issues, then your substantial ideas fall on deaf ears.

It is important to note here that your task is not merely to grab your listeners' immediate attention but to maintain that attention throughout your entire speech. Whether for five minutes or fifty, keeping your listeners' rapt attention throughout your presentation is a supremely difficult task, making it a topic worthy of considerable discussion and illustration that goes well beyond mere attention-grabbing introductions.

Gaining and maintaining the attention of your listeners require a fairly sophisticated understanding of key stimulus triggers that can be exploited to ignite listeners' attention involuntarily throughout your entire speech. Specific types of stimuli trigger attention involuntarily (see Chapter 2). These include appeals to that which is *novel, startling, vital, humorous,* or *intense* (Passer & Smith, 2011). When a direct effort is made to exploit such triggers, they become strategies for galvanizing audience attention.

Novelty: The Allure of the New

Novelty attracts attention (Escera et al., 1998). Audiences are naturally drawn to the new and different. The commonplace can produce a comalike stupor. Recognizing this means never beginning your speech with a snoozer, such as "My topic is . . ." or "Today I'd like to talk to you about . . ." Stimulate interest in your subject before giving your purpose statement. There are several ways to make novel appeals.

UNUSUAL TOPICS: CHOOSING CREATIVELY

In this age of high-tech weapons systems and sophisticated counterterrorism tactics, sometimes it's the low-tech solutions that save lives. American troops in the Iraq and Afghanistan wars were constantly faced with potential booby-trapped dwellings. A solution? Shoot Silly String across a room before entering to locate possible tripwires attached to bombs. This is an unusual topic for a great speech: low-tech creative solutions to significant problems. For instructors who may have heard far too many speeches on legalization of marijuana or the abortion controversy, unusual topics presented by students can be refreshing.

UNUSUAL EXAMPLES: THE ANTISEDATIVE

Sprinkle your speech with unusual examples that illustrate important points. For instance, consider using real examples, such as these pulled from a newspaper story:

> "The check is in the mail" used to be the standard ploy to ward off bill collectors. Not so anymore. Delinquent customers have adopted more original stalling tactics. One woman claimed that she had run over her husband with a car, breaking both of his arms, thereby making it impossible for him to write checks or pay by computer. A flower-shop owner insisted that she couldn't pay her bills until someone died and had a funeral. "Business should pick up soon," she said hopefully. These are silly excuses for failing to pay one's bills, but mounting personal debt is no laughing matter.

Compare the opening above to the more commonplace "I want to talk to you about how to handle personal debt." The more novel opening with unusual examples invites attention. The commonplace opener does not.

UNUSUAL STORIES: THE NOVEL NARRATIVE

We all love a good story, especially one we haven't heard. Newspapers are filled with novel

Gaining audience attention is a good start, but maintaining that attention throughout your speech is a huge challenge.

stories, some uplifting and some distressing. For example:

> Doctors estimated that Hall of Fame Pittsburgh Steelers' center Mike Webster suffered the equivalent of 25,000 car crashes without a seatbelt in the 25 years he played football from high school through the NFL. After retiring, he experienced amnesia, dementia, and depression from his football-induced head trauma. Webster's experiences reflect a serious problem, one that led to the stunning retirement at age 24 of Chris Borland, San Francisco Forty-Niners' star linebacker, who quit in March 2015 after his rookie season because of safety concerns about repetitive brain trauma. Football at all levels, from high school to the NFL, is hazardous to your brain. Stronger regulation of football injuries must be implemented.

Stories such as these invite attention because they are not trivial, commonplace episodes we've heard many times. They make us sit up and take notice.

UNUSUAL PHRASING: IT'S IN THE WORDING

Colorful phrasing or unusual wording can transform an ordinary statement into a novel, memorable one:

> **Ordinary:** Most books are carried less than 60 days by bookstores unless they become best sellers.

Novel: The shelf life of the average book is somewhere between milk and yogurt. (Calvin Trillin)

Ordinary: Choosing the right word is important.

Novel: The difference between the right word and the almost right word is the difference between lightning and the lightning bug. (Mark Twain)

Ordinary: She really said nothing of importance.

Novel: She plunged into a sea of platitudes, and with the powerful breast stroke of a channel swimmer made her confident way towards the white cliffs of the obvious. (W. Somerset Maugham)

Ordinary: Our office was way too small.

Novel: He and I had an office so tiny that an inch smaller and it would have been adultery (Dorothy Parker)

Startling Appeal: Shake Up the Audience

Daniel Hale, a pediatric diabetes specialist, commenting on a study documenting pervasive childhood obesity, notes: "These kids will have strokes and heart attacks in their 20s and 30s. The diseases we thought of as being problems in their grandparents are on their way to being diseases in their grandchildren" ("The Week," 2006, p. 2P). Hale's startling appeal tries to shake his audience out of its complacency.

STARTLING STATEMENTS, FACTS, OR STATISTICS

A startling statement, fact, or statistic can rouse audience attention. Kathy Levine (2001), when a student at Oregon State University, offered this startling revelation in her speech on dental hygiene:

> As the previously cited *20/20* investigation uncovered, the water used in approximately 90% of dental offices is dirtier than the water found in public toilets. This means 9 out of 10 dental offices are using dirty water on their patients. Moreover, the independent research of Dr. George Merijohn, a periodontist who specialized in dental waterlines, found that out of 60 randomly selected

offices from around the nation, two-thirds of all samples taken contained oral bacteria from the saliva of previous patients. (p. 77)

Wondering if you're rinsing your mouth with someone else's saliva should be disturbing. That which is startling alarms, shocks, and astonishes an audience into listening intently to what you have to say.

Consider other startling statistics. The average CEO of an American business made *373 times* as much as the average worker in 2015. CEOs were paid an average of $13.5 million a year, while average American workers were paid $36,134 (Belser, 2015). Liberal firebrand Michael Moore, in a March 5, 2011, speech in Madison, Wisconsin, asserted that the 400 richest Americans have a combined wealth that exceeds the bottom 50% of American households' aggregate wealth. Turns out that this startling statistic is an underestimation, as verified by the fact-checking organization PolitiFact. The more accurate statistic is that the top 400 richest Americans' combined wealth is equal to the bottom *60%* of Americans' combined wealth (Kertscher, 2011; see also Bell & Ashwood, 2016). Income inequality in the United States has never been greater (DiGangl, 2015). These and similar startling statistics fanned the flames of the Occupy movement that emerged in 2011-12, gave rise to the populist rhetoric and prominence of Senator Elizabeth Warren, and fueled the campaigns of several candidates for president (especially Bernie Sanders) in the 2016 election.

INAPPROPRIATE USE: BEWARE BIZARRE BEHAVIOR

Every speech instructor remembers notable examples of student miscalculations when using a startling appeal to gain an audience's attention. My colleagues have shared some with me. For instance, one student punched himself so hard in the face that he was momentarily staggered and produced a large bruise under his eye (the speech was on violence in America). Another student shrieked obscenities to his stunned audience (the speech was on FCC legislation banning verbal obscenity and profanity on the media airwaves).

The competent public speaker exercises solid judgment when choosing to startle listeners. *The speaker's goal should not be to gain attention by being outrageous, irresponsible, or by exercising poor judgment.* The competent public speaker considers the implied or stated rules of a speech context when choosing appropriate attention strategies. An audience can turn on a speaker when angered or offended. Startle an audience, but be appropriate.

The Vital Appeal: Meaningfulness

We attend to stimuli that are meaningful to us, and we ignore stimuli that are relatively meaningless (Ruiter et al., 2006). Problems and issues that vitally affect our lives are meaningful. In this sense, audiences tend to be Me-oriented. Listeners heed warnings when a societal problem affects them personally.

When attempting to grab the attention of your listeners, don't just make a general appeal, citing the seriousness of the problem for nameless, faceless citizens. Personalize the appeal to your listeners. Student Jake Gruber (2001) did exactly this when, in his speech on heart disease in women, he stated: "Whereas one in 28 women will die of breast cancer, one in five will die of heart disease. And guys, before you take the next nine minutes to decide what you'll eat for lunch, ask yourself one question: what would my life be like if the women who make it meaningful are not there? Clearly, this is an issue that concerns us all" (p. 16). Vital concerns that affect us personally focus our attention.

Humorous Appeal: Keep 'Em Laughing

"We've childproofed our house, but they keep finding a way in." This ironic, anonymous quip has been circulating on the Internet for years. Its humor gives it staying power. Humor is a superior attention strategy if used adroitly. Using humor effectively, however, can be very tricky. It requires far more than glib advice such as "be funny." Issues of appropriateness and effectiveness are always present. There are several guidelines for using humor competently as an attention strategy.

DON'T FORCE HUMOR: WE'RE NOT ALL FUNNY

If you've never told a joke without flubbing the punch line, avoid humiliating yourself. Listening to a speaker stubbornly try to be funny without

You can bring an audience to its feet with a stunt, such as giving a speech naked, but is this ever appropriate for a public speech? Explain.

success can be an excruciatingly uncomfortable experience for all involved. Nevertheless, you can still use humor. Use humorous quotations; tell funny stories or amusing occurrences to amplify or clarify points. Don't telegraph stories as intentionally humorous, however, by using a risky lead-in, such as "Let me tell you a really funny joke." Such a lead-in invites embarrassment if your listeners do not laugh.

USE ONLY RELEVANT HUMOR: STAY FOCUSED

Humor should amuse listeners while making a point. Tie the humor directly to a main point or principal theme. For example, "Someone once said, 'I want to die peacefully in my sleep like my grandfather, not screaming in terror like his passengers.' You've all experienced it—the nerve-racking anxiety every time you see an old person driving a car. I want to convince you that greater restrictions on elderly drivers should be instituted." The humor is simple, and it leads to the specific purpose of the speech.

BE SENSITIVE TO CONTEXT: HUMOR CAN BACKFIRE

Glib one-liners and slapstick do not mesh well with funeral services. Sexist, racist, and homophobic "jokes" exhibit poor taste and a lack of ethics. Coarse vulgarities, obscenities, and sick jokes invite comparisons to the *Jackass* movies—not everyone's idea of amusement. Humor that rests on stereotypes and putdowns may alienate vast sections of an audience (unless it is an official "roast"). I once heard a speaker crack this "joke" to his mixed-sex audience: "What's the difference between a terrorist and a woman with PMS? You can negotiate with the terrorist." Watching the audience's reaction was instructive. Some laughed. Some started to laugh, then thought better of it. Others not only didn't laugh, they booed. The speaker seemed surprised by the mixed response and searched for a graceful recovery. He never found one.

USE SELF-DEPRECATING HUMOR: "I'M NOT WORTHY"

Humor that makes gentle fun of one's own failings and limitations, called **self-deprecation**, can be quite appealing. Abraham Lincoln was a master of self-deprecation. During the famous Lincoln-Douglas debates, U.S. Senator Stephen Douglas called Lincoln "two-faced," whereupon Lincoln calmly replied, "I leave it to my audience. If I had another face, do you think I would wear this one?" (quoted by Lamb, 2008). Bob Uecker, a Major League Baseball player of no consequence but a Hall of Fame announcer for the Milwaukee Brewers, made this comment at a Brewers' winter banquet: "Look, people have differing opinions on many issues. Take my career. Half the people thought I was the worst player they've ever seen, and the other half thought I was a disgrace to the uniform" (quoted in "Chatter Box," 2007, p. 2C).

Self-deprecating humor can disarm a hostile audience. On May 21, 2001, George W. Bush was the commencement speaker at the Yale University graduation. An alumnus who had partied hard and earned mediocre grades, Bush faced his most hostile audience. More than 170 faculty members boycotted the graduation ceremony, and scores of graduates greeted Bush with protest signs. Many thought he had "stolen" the 2000 election from Al Gore. Bush encouraged mediocre students, "You, too, can be president of the United States." Referring to his party animal reputation while at Yale, Bush remarked, "If you're like me, you won't remember everything you did here. That can be a good thing." Making fun of his penchant for using tortured syntax, Bush remarked, "As I recall, one of my academic advisers . . . said I should focus on English. I still hear that quite often" ("President George W. Bush," 2001). Bush likely did not change many minds, but he defused the overt hostility, and his audience listened to his speech because it is tough to be angry when the person you dislike is making you laugh.

Making fun of yourself instead of other people can work well with an audience, but again, the advice is more complicated than simply "be self-deprecating." Higher status individuals may benefit more from self-deprecation than lower status individuals because self-deprecation exhibits lack of arrogance and ego without jeopardizing credibility and esteem (Greengross & Miller, 2008). As President of the United States, George W. Bush could make fun of himself without jeopardizing his role as the most powerful leader in the world, but if you are self-deprecating during a job interview and teaching demonstration, you may handicap yourself compared to other applicants who present a more capable image. Nevertheless, gentle self-deprecation can be attractive, if not overdone.

Intensity: Concentrated Stimuli

We attend to the intense (Pashler, 1998). **Intensity** is concentrated stimuli. It is an extreme degree of emotion, thought, or activity. Relating a tragic event, a moving human-interest story, or a specific instance of courage and determination plays on the intense feelings of your audience. For example, a youth minister, Melvyn Nurse, at the Livingway Christian Fellowship Church International in Jacksonville, Florida, wanted to make his point emphatically that sin is like Russian roulette. His congregation of 200 parents and youngsters saw him place a .357-caliber pistol to his temple and pull the trigger. Nurse apparently expected that the blank cartridge in the pistol's chamber would cause him no harm. Unfortunately, in front of his wife and four daughters, the blank cartridge shattered Nurse's skull. He died instantly. His attempt to capture attention was successful but with a horrifying result (Schoettler, 1998).

This is an intense example because it provokes a sense of profound tragedy. Who could be callous or indifferent to such painful human drama? The example, however, is also unpleasant, and this raises an issue: should speakers use unpleasant examples to capture attention? Might your listeners be repelled by such stark, negative examples? *There is often a potential risk when you employ intensity as an attention strategy.* Any time deep human emotion is aroused, your listeners may respond in a variety of ways, both positive and negative. Nevertheless, research shows that highly unpleasant stimuli can be highly interesting and attention grabbing, whereas highly pleasant stimuli can be so uninteresting that attention is easily diverted (Turner & Silvia, 2006). Whether to use an unpleasant-yet-intense example, such as the Melvyn Nurse story, is a judgment. Unpleasant examples are likely to work most effectively when they are used occasionally. The extremely difficult challenge you face as a speaker to gain and maintain the attention of your audience, however, may require moving beyond just happy stories and uplifting examples, as pleasant and comforting as these can be. Human interest runs the gamut, from pleasant to unpleasant, so don't restrict yourself to only one or the other.

Intensity can also be created in ways other than by powerful stories and examples. Direct, penetrating eye contact can be riveting. If you doubt this, try staring at someone for a prolonged period of time. The intensity can be quite powerful. When you don't look directly at your audience, listeners' minds can easily wander.

To recap, gaining and maintaining the attention of your audience is a critical challenge for any speaker. Attention does not just happen; you have to plan it carefully. Although voluntarily making an effort as a listener to attend to a speaker's message is important, responsibility for attention resides mostly with the speaker. Involuntary stimulus triggers, such as appealing to what is novel, startling, vital, humorous, and intense can provoke audience interest and keep listeners paying attention to your speech.

Effective Introductions and Conclusions

The beginning and ending can be as important as the body of your speech. Getting off to a good start presenting your speech alerts your audience to expect a quality presentation. Ending with a bang leaves a lasting impression on your listeners.

Objectives for Competent Introductions

A competent introduction to a speech achieves four principal objectives: (1) gain attention, (2) make a clear purpose statement, (3) establish your topic's significance, and (4) preview your main points. Developing your credibility is sometimes considered a fifth objective. Before explaining each, however, it should be noted that these goals in some cases might overlap. Your attention strategy may establish the significance of your topic and purpose statement, making additional focus on significance redundant. Some gatherings for speeches make a direct reference to significance during the introduction unnecessary because the audience has assembled in recognition of the importance of the topic (e.g., ceremonies commemorating the victims of the 9/11 terrorist attack). Nevertheless, if no such exceptions exist, make certain that all four objectives are addressed directly.

GAIN ATTENTION: FOCUSING YOUR AUDIENCE

The previous section covered general attention strategies you can use throughout your entire speech. For the introduction to your speech, however, more specific suggestions apply. Getting your speech off to a good start sets the stage for the rest of your presentation.

Begin With a Clever Quotation: Let Others Grab Attention Opening with a clever quotation can capitalize on the wit and wisdom of others. For example:

> President John F. Kennedy, in a speech at a White House dinner honoring several Nobel Prize winners, said, "I think this is the most extraordinary collection of talent, of human knowledge, that has ever been gathered together at the White House with the possible exception of when Thomas Jefferson dined alone." President Kennedy deftly complimented his esteemed honorees without becoming effusive in his

praise. He demonstrated skill in giving compliments. Complimenting others is an important but often overlooked way to cement interpersonal relationships, build teamwork, and promote goodwill among coworkers and friends. Giving compliments unskillfully, however, can provoke embarrassment and awkwardness between people. Today I will discuss three effective techniques for giving compliments.

Note that the quotation not only grabs attention with ironic humor, it relates specifically to the purpose statement.

Use Questions: Engage Your Audience Asking questions of your audience can be an effective technique for gaining listeners' attention immediately. A question asked by a speaker not intended to be answered out loud is a **rhetorical question**. Consider this example:

When you walk downtown and are approached by street people begging for change, do you oblige them? When members of the Salvation Army stand in front of stores during Christmas shopping season ringing their bells and asking for donations, do you drop change into their pots? Have you ever wondered what happens to the money donated to the poor? Well, I plan to inform you where that money goes and on what it is spent.

Rhetorical questions can involve the audience and invite interest in the subject. Rhetorical questions can also be quite powerful triggers of thought and emotion. "Who will be last to die for a mistake?" is a biting rhetorical question that challenges the very purpose served by continuing a perceived-to-be-flawed war policy that needlessly sacrifices human lives. Make sure, however, that your rhetorical questions are meaningful and not merely a commonplace device to open a speech. "Have you ever wondered why our college doesn't have a chess team?" is likely to produce a "not really" mental or even verbal response from the audience. The question doesn't spark interest if interest is already lacking.

Is this a rhetorical question or a direct question? Although questions can engage listeners, they also may invite smart-aleck listeners to make abusive remarks. If you are uncomfortable with unexpected responses from an audience, use a different attention strategy.

You may want to ask **direct questions** that seek overt responses from listeners. "Raise your hands, please—how many of you have attended a rock concert?" or "Let's see a quick show of hands—have you tried an exercise program in the last year and quit?" are examples. Polling an audience can be engaging and even amusing. "How many in this audience have used a dangerous, illegal drug in the past six months? Whoa, two of you actually raised your hands; that's a first. You might want to check the Fifth Amendment protections against self-incrimination. Americans revere the Bill of Rights, but how many of you can even identify the first 10 amendments to the U.S. Constitution?"

Expecting listeners to respond overtly to a question can be tricky business. Asking an audience to cop to illegal behavior is questionable in its own right even if it offers an opportunity for humor and playfulness with the audience. It could also easily produce an awkward silence with no hands raised. Conversely, you may expect (and hope) no hands are raised. One student began his speech this way: "How many of you have ever played Frisbee golf?" Almost every student raised a hand. "Wow, I didn't expect that response," blurted the speaker. Some listeners may even see your question as an opportunity to heckle or ridicule you. "How many of you have difficulty losing weight?" might trigger "Not as much trouble as you seem to have." Only certain audiences would likely be so boorish (high school comes to mind), but skip polling your audience unless you feel comfortable ad-libbing responses.

Begin With a Simple Visual Aid: Show and Tell Student Lauren Holstein (2012) began her speech with a simple visual aid apparent from her introductory remark: "I know I'm taking a chance here offering tomatoes to an audience at the beginning of a speech, but the difference between these two is the difference between a fair market and slavery" (p. 34). Another example might be holding a smartphone for your audience to see while noting:

> This tiny, wafer-thin device has more computing power than the super computers of only 40 years ago that filled a large portion of a room. So why hasn't there been an equivalent downsizing of solar cells and enhancement of solar power in the same time period? Shouldn't we be able to replace huge, bulky solar panels with smartphone-size solar cells with the capacity to power an entire house? I'm going to explain why this hasn't occurred and what can be done to make greater progress.

Beginning with a simple visual aid can draw in your audience and also make a point.

Tell a Relevant Story: Use Narrative Power Juan Roberto Melendez-Colon languished on Florida's death row for "17 years, 8 months, and 1 day." He became the 99th death-row inmate in the United States to be exonerated and freed since 1973. He told his story at the 2007 Los Angeles Religious Education Congress. I was there. The room was packed to hear his tragic story of dehumanization, of wrongful imprisonment that nearly led him to commit suicide.

A short, entertaining story is usually called an **anecdote**. Research shows that introductions that begin with an anecdote motivate your audience to listen and promote understanding and retention of your message (Andeweg et al., 1998). Anecdotes that have a personal relevance can be particularly captivating. Student Buey Ruet (2006) gave this novel, intense introduction at the Interstate Oratorical Association competition:

> On October 15, 1994, a woman by the name of Workinsh Admasu opened a letter, which required her 8- and 13-year-old boys to immediately report to military training camp. Three weeks after basic training, the boys, along with another 300,000 8- to 14-year-olds, strapped on AK-47s that were half their body weight and headed off to fight in Sudan's civil war . . . If you are wondering why I care about this topic so much, that 8-year-old boy was me. My 13-year-old brother and I were forced to experience things that no other child should ever have to experience. (p. 49)

The Sudan War can seem extremely remote for most Americans until a victim is standing in front of them telling his personal story of tragedy and outrage.

Refer to Remarks of Introduction: Acknowledge Your Audience In some cases, your planned introduction may need to be altered slightly following remarks made about you by the person introducing you to the audience. A simple, clean reference to those remarks is sufficient before launching into your prepared speech. Walter Mondale, former U.S. senator from Minnesota and vice president, had a standard response when he was extravagantly introduced to an audience: "I don't deserve those kind words. But then I have arthritis and I don't deserve that either." Former President Lyndon Johnson also had a standard line prepared if his introduction to an audience was effusive in its praise: "That was the kind of very generous introduction that my father would have appreciated, and my mother would have believed." (quoted by Noonan, 1998)

MAKE A CLEAR PURPOSE STATEMENT: PROVIDING INTENT

Purpose statements were discussed in some detail in Chapter 12. The purpose statement provides the intent for your entire speech. Consider this example that flows from an opening narrative:

> Matthew Shepard, a gay 21-year-old University of Wyoming student, was lured away from a bar in October 1998 by two young males pretending to be gay. Shepard was then robbed, beaten senseless, and tied to a fence outside of Laramie, Wyoming, and left for dead. He was found in a coma, and five days after his horrific assault, Shepard died. During his funeral, a dozen protesters stood across the street from the church chanting and holding signs that read, "No Tears for Queers" and "Get Back in Your Damn Closet." A prominent conservative Christian church created a web photo of Matthew Shepard burning, with a link allowing visitors to hear him "scream in hell." More recently, the Westboro Baptist Church regularly holds small protests at funerals for dead soldiers holding signs and shouting "God Hates Fags" and "Thank God for Dead Soldiers."

> The vileness of hate speech may incline us to support laws that ban it, and that's

understandable. Hate speech is repellant. I hope to convince you, however, that outlawing hate speech, no matter how venomous, produces significant disadvantages.

This introduction accomplishes two critical objectives of an introduction: gaining attention and providing a clear purpose statement.

ESTABLISH YOUR TOPIC'S SIGNIFICANCE: MAKING YOUR AUDIENCE CARE

Listeners typically want to know "How does this affect me?" when you address a topic. If you are an avid golfer, surfer, poker player, quilter, scrapbooker, or woodworker, your audience will see your enthusiasm for your topic. Why should listeners be enthusiastic, though, if they haven't ever tried such activities or if they proved to be inept when they did? Suppose your listeners, for example, never considered playing golf because it seemed uninteresting. You could make the topic relevant and significant to your listeners this way:

> Mark Twain once said that golf was a good walk spoiled. For many of you, that may seem true. Most members of my family tell me that watching golf on television is as exciting as watching mold form on rotting food. I beg to differ with these assessments. Golf is a good walk, but it is only spoiled if you lack knowledge of the strategy behind the game and your skill level is deficient. Understanding the strategy, and learning to play golf well, can make for an extremely enjoyable few hours of recreation in the bright sun and fresh air. Also, millions of dollars' worth of business are negotiated on the golf links every day. Even if you don't foresee a business deal on the horizon, it's never too early to begin learning the game in case your big chance comes unexpectedly. To put it succinctly, golf can be entertaining, and it can enhance your life physically, psychologically, economically, and occupationally.

> I can't teach you to play golf well in a five-minute speech. You'll want to find a qualified golf instructor to help you do that. I can, however, briefly explain four qualities to consider when choosing a golf instructor.

Some topics are more challenging to make relevant to an audience's interests than others. Nevertheless, every topic needs to be made relevant to an audience, or listeners will quickly tune out and let their minds wander freely.

PREVIEW YOUR MAIN POINTS: THE COMING ATTRACTIONS

A preview presents the coming attractions of your speech, the (normally) two to four main points that flow directly from the purpose statement. For example, "I want to explain how you can save money when purchasing a new car. There are three ways: comparison shopping, lowering your interest payments, and purchasing at the end of the year."

Although the purpose statement and the significance can be reversed in order, attention is always the first requirement. The preview is the final requirement of an introduction.

Some speech experts suggest that there is a fifth objective for a good introduction: *establishing the credibility of the speaker*. If you have expertise relevant to your purpose statement that is unknown to your audience, don't hesitate to mention it. That you have surfed for 10 years, worked as an auto mechanic for three years, or have a degree or certificate in computer science would likely induce your listeners to grant you credibility on those subjects. If asked to make a presentation because you are viewed as a credible expert or authority on a subject, however, no effort to establish credibility is necessary, especially if your credentials are listed when you're introduced to the audience.

Student speakers and laypersons, however, often cannot establish their credibility in this way during the introduction to their speech. They may have no particular experience or expertise on a subject that would produce initial credibility with an audience. Even informing an audience that you have conducted extensive research on the subject could sound self-serving. Why not let your evidence and command of the facts make that point obvious and leave it at that?

Credibility is created primarily by developing your purpose with logic and supporting materials throughout the body of your speech. If you sound as though you know what you are talking about,

listeners will be inclined to perceive you as credible. Establishing credibility in this way, however, takes an entire speech, not merely a few statements during the introduction. Credibility as a persuasive strategy will be discussed in greater detail in Chapter 15. At this point, *establishing credibility may be one element of an introduction, but it is not always a requirement.*

Objectives for Competent Conclusions

Conclusions should do what introductions do, except in reverse. Your conclusion should create a sense of unity, like completing a circle. You want your introduction to begin strongly, and you want your conclusion to end strongly.

SUMMARIZE THE MAIN POINTS: A REMINDER OF WHAT'S IMPORTANT

In your introduction, you preview your main points as a final step. In your conclusion, you summarize those main points, usually as a first step. For example, "In brief review, we learned a little history of the martial arts, I explained how to choose a qualified martial arts school, and I demonstrated some common martial arts defense techniques." Summarizing during your conclusion reminds the audience of the main points in your speech.

REFER TO THE INTRODUCTION: BOOKENDING THE SPEECH

If you used a dramatic story or example to begin your speech, referring to that story or example in your conclusion, known as *bookending*, provides closure. After using the tragic example of Justin Pearson to grab the audience's attention in her opening, student Amanda Brossart (2009) concluded her speech on pharmaceutical drug poisoning by referring to Pearson again:

> Justin Pearson was 24, close to the average age of many of us in this room. He was from Saint Cloud, Minnesota, less than 200 miles away from my hometown. Today, we looked at the dangers of counterfeit medications within the online pharmacy network, why they are used, and embraced solutions that can help stop the use of dangerous online pharmacies. Whitney Pearson, Justin's 18-year-old sister,

says the life-threatening consequence of an online pharmacy is "just a click away." It is imperative that we tell others about the dangers of online pharmacies. (p. 63)

Bookending your speech by referring to an opening story or dramatic example is not always an objective of an effective conclusion, especially if you did not use either in your introduction. If you have the opportunity to bookend, however, it can prove to be a very strong finish to your speech.

MAKE A MEMORABLE FINISH: SIZZLE, DON'T FIZZLE

Surely one of the most powerful conclusions came in Martin Luther King's "I Have a Dream" speech in 1963:

> When we allow freedom to ring, when we let it ring from every city and every hamlet, from every state and every city, we will be able to speed up that day when all of God's children, black men and white men, Jews and Gentiles, Protestants and Catholics, will be able to join hands and sing in the words of the old Negro spiritual, 'Free at last! Free at last! Thank God almighty, We are free at last!' (King, 1963)

You begin your speech with an attention strategy, and you should end your speech in similar fashion. A strong quotation, a moving rhetorical question, an intense statement, a moving example or story, or a humorous statement makes an effective attention grabber for introductions. They serve the same purpose for effective conclusions. Student Jenna Surprenant (2012) finished her speech on the dangers of the lobbying group called the American Legislative Exchange Council with an expert reference and a quotation:

> Supreme Court Justice Louis Brandeis referred to states as the laboratories of democracy, speaking to the notion that every state is different and should have different approaches. As *The Nation* reports on July 12, 2011, we "rely on our elected representatives' efforts to restore what's left of the American Dream. But through ALEC, billionaire industrialists are purchasing a version that seems like a real nightmare for most Americans" (p. 55).

Martin Luther King's "I Have a Dream" speech had a powerful finish.

One final note about conclusions: *do not end abruptly, apologize for running short on time, or ramble until you fizzle like a balloon deflating.* Be concise and to the point when finishing your speech. Your conclusion should be no more than about 5% to 10% of your total speech. Don't diminish the effect of a great speech with a bloated, aimless conclusion. Student Tunette Powell (2012), winner of the 2012 Interstate Oratorical Association contest, effectively concluded her oration this way:

> Now is the time to separate the war on drugs from the war on addiction. Today you've heard the problems, impacts, and solutions of criminalizing addictions. Bruce Callis is 50 years old now. And he is still struggling with his addiction. While you all are sitting out there listening to this, I'm living it. Bruce Callis is my father and for my entire life, I have watched our misguided system destroy him. The irony here is that we live in a society where we are told to recycle. We recycle paper, aluminum, and old electronics. But why don't we ever consider recycling the most precious thing on earth—the human life?

Powell summarizes her main points, makes reference to her opening anecdote about Bruce Callis, and closes with a memorable revelation and poignant rhetorical question. Her conclusion was a forceful finish.

Developing Supporting Materials

Supporting materials are the examples, statistics, and testimony used to bolster a speaker's theme or viewpoint. Supporting materials accomplish four specific goals: (1) to clarify points, (2) amplify ideas, (3) support claims (assertions), and (4) gain interest. *This is an audience-centered process.* For example, some audiences require greater clarification of points than others; a group of lawyers won't require examples to clarify legal procedures nearly as often as a lay audience assuredly would. This section covers the types of supporting materials and ways to present them effectively to accomplish the four specific goals.

Examples: Various Types and Effectiveness

A well-chosen example is often memorable for audiences and may have a great impact on listeners. There are four types of examples: *hypothetical, real, brief,* and *extended.*

HYPOTHETICAL EXAMPLES: IT COULD HAPPEN

Hypothetical examples describe imaginary situations concocted to make a point, illustrate an idea, or identify a general principle. Hypothetical examples help listeners envision what a situation might be like, or they call up similar experiences listeners have had without citing a historically factual illustration that may not be readily available. *As long as the hypothetical example is consistent with known facts, it will be believable.*

Imagine what it would be like to experience a hurricane, tornado, or tsunami. In what ways would your life be changed if you suddenly lost your job, were laid up in a hospital for three months, or became permanently disabled? Hypothetical examples like these help listeners picture what might happen and motivate them to take action that might prevent or prepare them for such occurrences.

REAL EXAMPLES: IT DID HAPPEN

During the tumultuous protests in Iran following the disputed presidential election in June 2009,

26-year-old Neda Agha-Soltan stepped from her car to get fresh air while caught for an hour in traffic clogged by mass protests. Within seconds, she was shot in the chest from a suspected government sniper ("Who Was Neda?" 2009). Caught on a video cell phone by a bystander, her agonizing death almost instantly became a rallying cry for the antigovernment protesters in the streets. The video was posted on YouTube and seen by millions around the world. Protesters brandished copies of a picture showing her last moment of life. Neda Agha-Soltan became a symbol of the Iranian uprising. Mehdi Karroubi, an opposition leader and presidential candidate, called Neda a martyr: "A young girl, who did not have a weapon in her soft hands, or a grenade in her pocket, became a victim of thugs who are supported by a horrifying intelligence apparatus" (quoted in Fathi, 2009).

Actual occurrences are **real examples**. Because real examples are factual, they are more difficult to discount than hypothetical examples. A real example can personalize a problem. Hypothetical examples can be discounted as simply "made up." Unlike hypothetical examples, real examples can sometimes profoundly move an audience.

BRIEF AND EXTENDED EXAMPLES: TIMING AND IMPACT

Often a brief example or two makes a point well. The examples are clear, and no explanation or elaboration is required. An **extended example** is a detailed story or illustration. The Neda Agha-Soltan story is an extended example. A story's length must fit the confines of the time permitted for your speech, but for full impact, a story sometimes must have at least minimal elaboration.

MAKING EXAMPLES EFFECTIVE

Using examples effectively requires skill. Well-chosen examples can make a speech come alive. Here are some basic tips.

Use Relevant Examples: Stay on Point Examples should be relevant to the point you make. A young Abraham Lincoln, acting as a defense attorney in a courtroom trial, explained what "self-defense" meant by using a relevant story to clarify his point. He told the jury a story about

The killing of Neda Agha-Soltan sparked a huge outcry and massive demonstrations in Iran. Real examples can be far more powerful than hypothetical examples. Picture the difference between saying, "Someone could get killed" and "My mother was killed."

a man who, while walking down a country road with a pitchfork in hand, was attacked by a vicious dog. The man was forced to kill the dog with his pitchfork. A local farmer who owned the dog asked the man why he had to kill his dog. The man replied, "What made him try to bite me?" The farmer persisted, "But why didn't you go at him with the other end of the pitchfork?" The man responded, "Why didn't he come at me with the other end of the dog?" (cited in Larson, 1992, p. 181). Lincoln made his point that the degree of allowable force depends on the degree of force used by the attacker.

Choose Vivid Examples: Create Strong Images Examples usually work best when they are vivid. A vivid example triggers feelings and provokes strong images (Pratkanis & Aronson, 2001). Student Kittie Grace (2000) uses a vivid example to evoke a powerful image on her main theme that hotels in America are unsanitary:

> According to the August 8, 1999, *Hotel and Motel Management Journal* or *HMMJ*, in Atlantic City, New Jersey, two unsuspecting German tourists shared a motel room which had been cleaned that morning, but a foul smell permeated through the room. After the third complaint, housekeeping cleaned under the bed, finding the body of

a dead man decomposing, all because housekeeping failed to clean under the bed in the first place. (p. 86)

This example is so vivid that it quite likely will stick in many of your memories the next time you stay at a motel or hotel.

Stack Examples: When One Is Not Enough Sometimes a single example does not suffice to make a point clear, memorable, interesting, or adequately supported. Note the value of using plentiful examples stacked one on top of another in the following:

> Male residents of Boonville, California, who obviously had lots of time on their hands, created a lingo of their own in the late 1800s, mostly to talk around women without them understanding what was being said. The rules for Boontling are those of English. The lexicon (total vocabulary) of more than 1,300 words, however, is mostly unintelligible to speakers of standard English. Those individuals who *harp Boont* (speak Boontling) concocted some colorful words. Examples include *burlapping* (having sexual intercourse), *fence-jumpy* (given to adultery), *grey-matter kimmie* (college professor), *mink* (a female of easy morals), *wheeler* (lie), *shoveltooth* (medical doctor), and *high-split* (very tall, slender man). Knowing just these few Boont words gives you the ability to translate this sentence: "The high-split, fence-jumpy, grey-matter kimmie told a wheeler to cover up his burlapping with a mink, daughter of the local shoveltooth." There are still a few speakers of Boontling, but most have *piked to the dusties* (died).

In this instance, using only one or two examples of Boontling wouldn't clarify the main point well, create much impact, support claims well, or spark much interest

Statistics: Quantifying Your Points

Statistics are measures of what is true or factual expressed in numbers. They can provide magnitude and allow comparisons. For example, the first Internet website was *info.cern.ch*, created by Tim Berners-Lee in December 1990 ("How We

Got," 2008). The number of websites (not webpages) worldwide jumped to 24 million by 2000, and by 2010, it had exploded to more than 200 million sites ("March 2010 Web Server Survey," 2010). In 2015, the number of websites had rocketed to 1 billion ("Total Number of Websites," 2015). The magnitude of the Internet today and its astronomical growth in just 25 years (comparison) are exhibited by these statistics.

Statistics, however, can be manipulated to distort truth. Later in this chapter, several fallacious uses of statistics are discussed. Nevertheless, when statistics are used validly, they can add real substance to your speech. A well-chosen statistic can support claims, show trends, correct false assumptions, validate hypotheses, and contradict myths, perhaps not as dramatically and memorably as a vivid example but often more validly and effectively (Lindsey & Yun, 2003). There are three ways to use statistics effectively and not degenerate into a boring recitation of figures and numbers: make statistics concrete, make statistical comparisons, and stack statistics.

MAKE STATISTICS CONCRETE: CLARIFY MEANING

Large statistics don't always communicate meaning to listeners. For example, the difficulty in sending a spaceship to even the closest star to Earth is hard to grasp. Alpha Centauri, the nearest star, is 4.4 light years from the Sun; that's equivalent to about 26 trillion miles (Angier, 2002). These statistics are so large that they have little meaning beyond "really big." Dr. Geoffrey Landis of the NASA John Glenn Research Center, however, provides a concrete referent for us. Referring to the *Voyager* interplanetary probes, the fastest objects humans have ever launched into space, he explains: "If a caveman had launched one of those during the last ice age, 11,000 years ago, it would now be only a fifth of the way toward the nearest star" (quoted in Angier, 2002). Landis doesn't merely present the statistics. He presents them effectively by providing a clear, concrete example.

MAKE STATISTICAL COMPARISONS: GAIN PERSPECTIVE

An effective way to make a statistic have meaning for listeners and provide perspective is to use statistical comparisons. For example, student Davis Vaughn (2013) makes this comparison: "The *American Journal of Public Health*'s May 2012 issue details, while LGBT youth only make up 3.5% of the total adolescent population, they disproportionately represent almost 40% of homeless youth across the country" (p. 11). Student Sarah Werner (2005), in a speech on federal mandatory minimum prison sentences, notes that Weldon Angelos, convicted of selling marijuana on a first-time offense, was sentenced to a maximum of *63 years* in prison "despite the fact that a jury of his peers—the jury that convicted him—favored a sentence of 15–18 years." She further notes that "the federal maximum sentencing for hijacking an airplane is 24 years, for detonating a bomb in a public place, 19 years" (p. 60). The comparison greatly enhances the impact of her central claim that mandatory minimum sentences are unjust.

STACK STATISTICS: CREATE IMPACT

Student Caleb Rawson (2013) effectively stacks statistics to make the point that few Americans are financially ready for retirement:

> Retirement savings woes are affecting every American. According to a report published by the Employee Benefit Research Institute this March, since 2007 the percentage of Americans "not at all confident" that they will have enough money for retirement has increased from 10% to 28%. The percent of those who are confident has decreased from 27% to 13%, and with good reason. Only 66% of American workers have anything set aside for retirement and 57% of workers have less than $25,000 set aside for retirement. (p. 29)

Stacked statistics, however, should be used sparingly and only to create an impact on the central points in a speech. Audience members will tune out if they become weary hearing you stack a mountain of statistics.

Testimony: Expert and Otherwise

Testimony is a first-hand account of events by witnesses or the conclusions offered publicly by experts on a topic. In this section, several kinds of testimony that you can use to support your points are discussed, and ways to use testimony competently are explored.

TYPES OF TESTIMONY: RELYING ON OTHERS

There are three principal types of testimony you can use as a supporting material. Testimony of *experts* is probably the most commonly used, but there is also testimony of *eyewitnesses* and testimony of *nonexperts*.

Testimony of Experts: Relying on Those in the Know

We live in an often baffling world of mind-boggling complexity. None of us can be expected to know enough to make rational, informed decisions without the help of experts. Is climate change real, and is it primarily caused by human activity? Ask the experts. Does raising the minimum wage bolster the economy? Ask the experts. Combined with statistical evidence (data), expert testimony can be powerfully informative and persuasive.

Eyewitness Testimony: You Had to Be There

Using the testimony and accounts of those who have observed some event or activity is a staple of criminal and civil trials. Eyewitnesses support factual claims for both sides in the courtroom, and their testimony is often critical to the outcome of a case. Eyewitnesses can also be a source for news events. In the June 2009 disputed presidential election in Iran, hundreds of thousands of protesters hit the streets of Tehran in defiance of the ruling regime. In an attempt to control global perceptions of these exploding events, the Iranian government expelled foreign journalists. Major news networks and cable shows scrambled for any bits of news that they could garner. Twitter became an important source of eyewitness messages from protesters clashing with the police and the government (May, 2009). Although the service was scheduled to be shut down for maintenance, the U.S. State Department made the highly unusual request that Twitter remain online to keep the limited information from Iran flowing (Hannah, 2009). Protesters sent tweets continually as events were occurring to counter the spin coming from official news sources within the Iranian government.

Testimony of Nonexperts: Ordinary Folks Adding Color to Events

You do not have to be an expert or an eyewitness to world events to add compelling testimony to your speech. Follow the example of newspapers, television news media, and documentary films. They all use interviews with "common folks" to spice up a story and personalize coverage of events.

USING TESTIMONY EFFECTIVELY

When you cite testimony to support your speech, you have to decide whether to quote exactly or merely paraphrase. Typically, you use a direct quotation when the statement is short, well phrased, and communicates your point more eloquently or cleverly than you can. Paraphrasing is appropriate when a direct quotation is not worded in an interesting way, such as in most government documents, or when a quotation is very lengthy and needs to be shortened. Whether directly quoting or merely paraphrasing, however, there are a couple of ways to present testimony appropriately and effectively during your speech.

Quote or Paraphrase Accurately: Consider Context

It is imperative that you not misquote or inaccurately paraphrase either an expert or an eyewitness supporting your claims or an opponent in a debate or discussion. When quoting someone's testimony, do not crop the quotation so it takes on a different meaning than communicated in context. Do not delete important qualifiers from any statement. During the 2012 Republican presidential campaign, Mitt Romney claimed in a speech a day before the New Hampshire primary, "I like being able to fire people who provide services to me." Despite the clumsiness of the statement, taken in context Romney clearly meant that he liked firing health insurance companies that provide bad service to consumers. Nevertheless, his Republican opponents jumped on the statement, clearly distorting it. John Huntsman retorted, "Governor Romney enjoys firing people; I enjoy creating jobs." Rick Perry offered his supporters a downloadable ring tone for their cell phones that repeatedly played Romney's edited comment as "I like to fire people" (Madison & Boxer, 2012).

During the same campaign, Romney distorted a speech made by Barack Obama. In one of his attack ads, he quoted Obama saying, "If we keep talking about the economy, we're going to lose." The quote, however, was taken from the 2008 presidential campaign speech but made to seem current, and it omitted a key statement. The entire quote states: *"Senator McCain's campaign actually said, and I quote, 'If we keep talking about the economy, we're going to lose'"* (Huffington, 2011). Obama clearly wanted to talk about the economy in 2008 because it favored his election. Editing Obama's statement made him seem to be saying the exact opposite of what his claim actually was. Editing quotations to change the meaning of the speaker's intended message is unethical. It is dishonest, and as explained in Chapter 1, honesty is an essential criterion for ethical public speaking.

Use Qualified Sources: Accuracy Matters Abundant research shows the unreliability of eyewitness testimony (Wells et al., 1999; Wright et al., 2009). The Twitter tweets from Iranian "eyewitnesses" on the 2009 uprising could not be verified. News organizations often took these accounts as factual, yet some of these tweets could have been government plants trying to confuse the issue and create seeds of doubt for outsiders. Others may only be reporting gossip or hearsay, not direct observations of events. As Mark Glaser, host of PBS's online show *MediaShift*, observed about the Twitter phenomenon in Iran, "I feel like I'm not getting what I get at the BBC's site with confirmed sources" (quoted in May, 2009).

Evaluating Supporting Materials: Criteria

The three main types of supporting materials have been explained, and basic ways to use them effectively in your speeches have been discussed. Competent use of supporting materials, however, goes deeper than the basic advice offered so far. For example, you can stack statistics effectively for maximum impact on your listeners, but what if the statistics are made up or inaccurate? After Donald Trump announced his candidacy for the 2016 Republican presidential nomination, FactCheck.org, a multiaward-winning fact-checking site, found several statistical claims made by him to be false (Jackson et al., 2015). Trump claimed, for example, that economic growth has "never" been below zero for a quarter (a three-month period), but since 1946, the U.S. economy has actually fallen below zero economic growth

42 times. He claimed the "real" unemployment rate was "anywhere from 18 to 20 percent" and "maybe even 21 percent," but he made up the statistics. Trump also asserted that "there are no jobs to be had," but according to the Bureau of Labor Statistics (BLS), there were 5.4 million job openings at the time of his announcement, a record number since the BLS started keeping such statistics (McBride, 2015).

You want to use high-quality supporting materials, and this requires a careful assessment based on specific criteria. There are three primary criteria, or standards, to evaluate supporting materials: *credibility, relevance,* and *sufficiency.* This section discusses these criteria and explores the errors that occur, called **fallacies**, when using supporting materials. Evaluating supporting materials is applicable to both informative and persuasive speeches, and even to inspirational and special occasion speeches (see Appendix B). You don't want to use fallacious supporting materials in any speech that you present.

CREDIBILITY: IS IT RELIABLE AND VALID?

A key criterion for evaluating supporting materials that provide the underpinnings of claims made by speakers is credibility. **Credibility** is determined by reliability and validity. **Reliability** means consistency, and **validity** means accuracy. A source of information should be consistent when citing facts and interpreting data. The facts and the data should also be accurate. Quoting the Centers for Disease Control and Prevention (CDC) on the likelihood of a serious outbreak of the West Nile virus or the swine flu is credible because the CDC is an internationally recognized authority often called upon to investigate outbreaks of disease all over the world. It is consistently objective, relying on scientific studies to support claims about diseases, and has a track record of providing accurate information based on the best data currently available.

Evidence used to support claims is often not credible, however. Several common fallacies significantly diminish the credibility of supporting materials.

Questionable Statistic: Does It Make Sense? Question every statistic you plan to use in your speeches, be they an informative, persuasive, or even a tribute speech (you don't want to claim that the person being honored wrote 15 books when they actually wrote only 4). Ask yourself whether the statistic seems sensible and accurate. In January 2011, for example, websites began trumpeting that in the United States *"200 trillion text messages are received in America every single day"* (e.g., http://www.psfk.com/2011/02/two-hundred-trillion-text-messages-infographic.html). Simple arithmetic shows that for this to be true, every person (including infants) in the United States (320 million) would receive, on average, *625,000* text messages *each day*. The statistic is wildly implausible. Note, however, that another website in May 2015 stated the more plausible statistic that *worldwide*, more than 350 *billion* text messages are exchanged *each month* (http://www.grabstats.com/statmain.aspx?StatID=402).

Consider another commonly asserted implausible statistic. Both the Academy of Motion Picture Arts and Science (the hosts of the Oscars) and the award winners during acceptance speeches assert repeatedly that a billion people worldwide watch the Academy Awards (Sinha-Roy, 2013). It is highly likely, however, that this statistic is pure nonsense (Lynch, 2014). Consider just a few facts: According to a Nielsen ratings survey only 36.6 million Americans saw the Oscars presented in February 2015 (Kissell, 2015). The Academy Awards also are probably of greater interest to Americans than to other countries because most movies nominated for Oscars are American. The program is aired in English, which is not the language of most other countries, and it is broadcast abroad on satellite or cable feeds that have very few subscribers. Typically, there are only about 7 million viewers of the Oscars tracked in China—which has one-sixth of the world's total population (Radosh, 2005). "There is no evidence that a Hollywood-hosted self-aggrandizing English-language event would manage to pick up the roughly 960 million viewers it would need from outside of the U.S. to reach the one-billion figure" (Young, 2013). The billion viewers claim is almost certainly a preposterously inflated statistic.

Biased Source: Grinding an Ax Special-interest groups or individuals who stand to gain money,

prestige, power, or influence if they advocate a certain position on an issue are biased sources of information. You should consider their claims as dubious. Look for a source that has no personal stake in the outcome of a dispute or disagreement—a source that seeks the truth, not personal glory or benefit.

Consider several examples of biased sources: There is currently a huge debate taking place on the safety of e-cigarettes and "vaping." The potential long-term harms of vaping are unknown, but dependence on nicotine, among other health risks, is a serious concern. In any case, big tobacco companies have invested heavily in the marketing of e-cigarettes. You don't want to listen to tobacco or any other companies selling e-cigarettes regarding safety (Senthilingam, 2015). These companies are inherently biased by a profit motive, and the track record of tobacco companies regarding honesty about their products has not exactly been stellar.

Websites are often biased. For example, any website providing nutritional information while pushing vitamins, minerals, and other "health" products (e.g., GNC, Vitacost, or Vitamin World) is biased. In contrast, WebMD and MayoClinic.com are more neutral sites that do not push products, and they provide useful medical and health-related information.

Incomplete Source Citation: Something to Hide? A complete citation of the source of your information adds credibility to your claim, if your source is qualified. A complete citation includes, as a minimum, (1) the name of the source, (2) the specific title or expertise of the source (if not obvious) to build credibility, and (3) the specific publication in which the evidence can be found with the relevant date of the publication. Student Hailey Simmons (2014) illustrates a complete citation: "Reggie Wilkerson, former director of the Ohio Department of Rehabilitation and Correction, states in a ProPublica article published June 6, 2013, that . . ." (p. 42)

It is easy and common to cite sources incompletely, leaving out one or more of the minimum requirements, but the skeptic holds speakers to a higher standard. Citations with references only to a vague title, such as "Dr. Smith" or "Professor Jones," are incomplete. What type of doctor or

Even usually credible newspapers have repeated this bogus, implausible statistic. Check Snopes.com for an explanation.

professor is being cited? What are his or her specific credentials to speak as an expert on a particular topic? Even references to qualified experts leave us wondering how current they are if the publication source and date are missing. When you cite your sources completely, you signal to your audience that you have nothing to hide, and your transparency likely increases your credibility. (See Box 13-1 for additional examples of credible citation of various sources.)

Expert Quoted Out of Field: No Generic Experts Iben Browning, the chief scientist for Summa Medical Corporation, had a doctorate in physiology and a bachelor's degree in physics and math. He predicted a major earthquake for December 3 and 4, 1990, along the New Madrid Fault in the American Midwest. Schools in several states dismissed students for these two days as a result of Browning's prediction. Browning had some scientific expertise, but not in the area of earthquake prediction (Fowler, 1991). In fact,

earthquake experts around the country denounced Browning's predictions because even those who study earthquakes cannot accurately predict them ("Earthquake Facts," 2015). No earthquake, large or small, occurred on the dates Browning predicted. There wasn't even a sizable earthquake on the New Madrid Fault until April 17, 2008, and it was considered "moderate" by quake experts, causing little damage. As this example shows, quoting experts outside their field of expertise runs the substantial risk of promoting inaccurate claims supported by invalid and unreliable supporting materials.

RELEVANCE: DOES IT FOLLOW?

Supporting materials must have **relevance**; they must relate directly to claims made. Consider two fallacies that fail the relevance test: *ad hominem* and *ad populum.*

Ad Hominem Fallacy: Diversionary Tactic In December 2006, Rosie O'Donnell, apparently irked that business tycoon and beauty pageant

Oral Citation of Sources

Here are some examples from student speeches presented at the annual Interstate Oratorical Association contest on how to cite a variety of sources concisely and effectively during your speeches:

Expert Source: "Susan Dooha, Executive Director of the New York Center for Independence of the Disabled, told NPR on November 9, 2013..." (Lauren Galloway, 2014, p. 39)

Website: "The Centers for Disease Control and Prevention website [cdc.gov], last accessed April 4, 2012, reports..." (Stephanie Stovall, 2012, p. 136)

Academic Journal: "[Law] Professor Robin Feldman explains in the *Stanford Technology Law Review* on January 23, 2012, that..." (Katie Lese, 2012, p. 161)

Television Program: "CBS News of June 25, 2013, points out that..." (Jordan Carrillo, 2014, p. 60).

Magazine: "*Time* magazine on June 24th, 2014 explains..." (Goldfarb, 2015).

Personal Interview: "Margot Saunders, a legal expert affiliated with the National Consumer Law Center, stressed to me in an April 11th, 2014, personal interview..." (Neil Decenteceo, 2014, p. 25)

Newspaper: "Nationally, the *Washington Post* of April 14th, 2014 reports..." (Nordin, 2015, p. 58)

Organization: "According to a 2011 Public Safety Performance Project conducted by the Pew Research Center..." (Tunette Powell, 2012, p. 101)

Book: "As author John Nichols describes in his 2011 book *The Death and Life of American Journalism*..." (Jenna Surprenant, 2012, p. 54)

the moral compass for 20-year-olds in America" ("Donald and Rosie," 2007; "Donald Trump Tells FNC," 2007). Later, she called Trump a "snake-oil salesman," "a hot bag of wind with bad hair," and a "pimp," and she made fun of his "comb-over" hairdo. Trump fired back by calling O'Donnell "a loser," "despicable," "a degenerate," "a fat slob," "ugly," a "mental midget," and "a stumbling buffoon" ("Trump Versus Rosie," 2006). The verbal war continued over the years. As recently as July 11, 2014, Trump commented on Twitter: "Rosie is crude, rude, obnoxious, and dumb" (quoted by Taibi, 2014). During Trump's presidential campaign, true to form, he called NBC "Meet the Press" host Chuck Todd a "moron" and a "dummy"; conservative columnist and Pulitzer Prize winner George Will "a political moron," "stupid," and "a dummy"; Republican strategist Karl Rove "a total loser"; characterized *National Review* writer Jonah Goldberg as "truly dumb as a rock"; and former "Daily Show" host Jon Stewart was deemed a "dummy" (quoted by Moody, 2015). These are ad hominem (Latin meaning "to the person") attacks, personal character assaults, but are they ad hominem fallacies?

The **ad hominem fallacy** is a personal attack on the messenger to avoid the message. *It is a diversionary tactic.* Trump's litany of abusive name-calling is a distraction from any issues raised or questions asked by reporters or adversaries. These are ad hominem fallacies. In the Rosie-versus-Donald verbal food fight, Trump never responded directly to the challenge to his moral authority but instead assaulted O'Donnell's character and physical attractiveness. This was diversionary character assassination, not a reasonable or relevant response to her initial claim. In effect, Trump was making the irrelevant argument "Your allegation is weak because you're a fat, ugly slob." O'Donnell, on the other hand, minimized the force of her main claim that Trump has no credibility as a "moral compass" by mixing in irrelevant and distracting personal attacks on Trump's physical attractiveness. Both, then, are guilty of the ad hominem fallacy.

Not all personal attacks are ad hominem fallacies. If a claim raises the issue of a person's credibility, character, or trustworthiness, the attack is not irrelevant to the claim made. Examples of alleged corruption and malfeasance that led to Richard Nixon's resignation and Bill Clinton's

sponsor Donald Trump gave Miss USA Tara Conner "a second chance" to redeem herself and not lose her beauty crown after revelations of underage drinking and drug use, attacked Trump. "Left his first wife, had an affair, left the second wife, had an affair. Had kids both times, but he's impeachment involved legitimate questions about their character and credibility.

Ad Populum Fallacy: Arguing from Public Opinion Typically, in annual surveys, about two-thirds or more of the American people favor capital punishment (Newport, 2010). A Pew Research Center survey in 2015, however, showed that support for the death penalty had slipped significantly, to 56% ("Less Support for Death Penalty," 2015). Should we decide whether to maintain the death penalty or abandon it based on popular opinion? The answer is no. Claims should be weighed on the basis of valid reasoning and high-quality supporting materials that bolster that reasoning, not on the whim of the majority, which could change in a flash.

SUFFICIENCY: GOT ENOUGH?

The person who makes a claim has the burden to prove that claim (see Chapter 6). This means that sufficient supporting materials must be used to support a claim you make. *Sufficiency* is a judgment. There is no precise formula for determining it. Generally, high-quality supporting materials and solid reasoning meet the sufficiency criterion. Several fallacies, however, clearly exhibit insufficiency.

Self-Selected Sample: Partisan Power A **random sample** is a portion of the population chosen in such a manner that every member of the entire population has an equal chance of being selected. A **self-selected sample** attracts the most committed, aroused, or motivated individuals to fill out surveys on their own and answer polling questions. Printing a survey in a magazine and collecting those that have been returned is an example of a self-selected sample. Calling an 800-number to answer questions about politics or social issues is another example. Any statistics from a poll or survey that depends on respondents selecting themselves to participate provides results that are insufficient to generalize beyond the sample.

During the George W. Bush administration, a continuing MSNBC online "live poll" asked whether President Bush should be impeached. When accessed on July 26, 2007, the results from 487,217 self-selected respondents showed 88% for impeachment and the rest opposed or unsure ("Politics," 2007). All surveys taken during July 2007 using a random sample showed a country deeply divided on the impeachment question, but *none* showed majority support (e.g., *USA Today*/Gallup showed 36% favored impeachment; see "Public Support for Impeaching," 2014). The Daily Kos, a liberal blogging site, posted results of an online survey it conducted for the 2012 presidential election showing that 4,268 respondents (94%) supported Barack Obama for president and a mere 99 (2%) respondents supported Mitt Romney ("Poll," 2012). In the actual election, Obama received 51% to Romney's 47% of the total popular vote (Wasserman, 2013).

Online surveys attract partisan respondents. Thus, they produce unrepresentative results. Note that the problem is not an insufficient sample. Self-selected samples often involve huge numbers of respondents. Increasing the number of respondents does not improve the results (unless you survey everyone in the population) because the sample is unrepresentative.

Inadequate Sample: Large Margin of Error So what is an adequate sample size? In general, the **margin of error**—a measure of the degree of sampling error accounted for by imperfections in sample selection—goes up as the number of people surveyed goes down. *Margin of error applies only to random samples*, not self-selected samples. An adequate sample size will have a margin of error no greater than plus or minus 3% to 4%. A poll of 1,000 people randomly selected typically has a margin of error of about plus or minus 3%. This means that if the poll reports 65% of respondents approve of the job the president is doing, then the actual result, if every adult American were surveyed, would be between 62% and 68%. No poll is without some margin of error because it is usually impractically expensive and time consuming to survey every person in a population, but increasing the sample size improves the chances that the poll is accurate if the sample is random, not self-selected.

Hasty Generalization: Arguing from Example Television producer Gary David Goldberg once sardonically observed, "Left to their own devices, the networks would televise live executions. Except Fox—they'd televise live naked executions" ("TV or Not TV," 1993, p. 5E). The graphic, gruesome, and grand event can galvanize our

The vividness effect is illustrated by the dramatic crash of Asiana Airlines Flight 214 in San Francisco.

attention. When the outrageous, shocking, controversial, and dramatic event distorts our perceptions of the facts, this is called the **vividness effect** (Glassner, 1999). The vividness effect can fallaciously distort your perception of events because the shocking example can negate a mountain of contradictory evidence (Sunstein & Zeckhauser, 2009). For example, a single airline disaster can provoke fear of boarding a jetliner and induce many people to choose driving their automobile instead. Yet the odds of perishing in a plane crash are 1 in *11 million*, whereas the odds of dying in a car crash in the United States are 1 in *5,000* (Barrabi, 2015).

When individuals jump to a conclusion based on one or only a handful of examples, especially vivid ones, they have made a **hasty generalization** (Govier, 2010). The mass media tend to sensationalize each new scientific study that gets published, for example. *A single study, however, is insufficient to draw any general conclusion.* In science, studies are replicated before results are given credence because mistakes can be made. No scientist wants to fall victim to a hasty generalization that may prove inaccurate upon further study.

Correlation as Causation: How Related? We humans are intensely interested in discovering causes of events that remain unexplained. Here we try to connect factual examples to their causes. Why do some people live to be 100 years old, for instance, and others die at a much younger age? Scientists, journalists, and health seekers have visited the people of Vilcabamba, Ecuador, for a half-century to discover the causes of their unusual longevity. Manuel Picoita, 102 years old, thinks getting along with his neighbors is the cause of his reaching centenarian status. Josefa Ocampa, 104, believes the secret to her long life is that each morning she drinks a glass of goat's milk with a bit of her own urine added (Kraul, 2006, p. 16A).

We all are prone to draw causation (*x* causes *y*) from mere correlation. A **correlation** is a consistent relationship between two variables. A **variable** is anything that can change. Finding a strong correlation between two variables doesn't necessarily have significance. One large research team, for example, explored variables that might determine causes of contraceptive use in Taiwan (Li, 1975). The number of electric appliances (e.g., ovens, irons, and toasters) found in the home correlated most strongly with birth control use. As the number of appliances increased, the use of contraceptives also increased. So, based on this study, do you think distributing free blenders and microwave ovens would likely reduce teen pregnancies? More probably, this correlation merely reflects socioeconomic status, which is also strongly correlated with contraceptive use and is a better candidate for causation.

Correlations suggest possible causation, but correlations alone are an insufficient reason to claim probable causation. Kids with big feet are better readers than those with small feet. Why? Do big feet cause reading proficiency? Not likely. Children with big feet are usually older, and older children have had more experience reading. Increases in U.S. spending on science, space, and technology correlate almost perfectly with increases in the number of suicides by hanging, strangulation, and suffocation. Likewise, the divorce rate in Maine correlates with the per capita consumption of margarine in the United States (Vigen, 2015). Do these correlations prove causation? Hardly! The statistics or examples don't necessarily connect logically as a cause-effect relationship.

False Analogy: Mixing Apples and Oranges A claim based on an analogy alleges that two things closely resemble each other. Thus, both things should be viewed in similar ways. Historically, marriage recognized by the state exempted husbands from any criminal charge of rape against their wives even if sex was obtained by force. These laws began to change in the United States in 1975, however, primarily based on analogical reasoning. Is there any essential difference between rape by a stranger and rape by a spouse argued those who supported marital rape laws? Both acts involve nonconsensual sexual penetration achieved by force and violence. This should be viewed as rape in either instance. The analogy was a good one, and marital rape laws have been passed in all 50 states.

False analogies occur when a significant point or points of difference exist despite some superficial examples of similarities between the two things being compared (Govier, 2010). In numerous fiery speeches, for example, both George W. Bush and Barack Obama have been characterized by opponents as the new Hitler. Demonstrators have prominently displayed posters showing each with Hitlerian mustaches and swastikas. "If you hate Hitler, you should hate this guy because they are so similar" goes the bizarre analogy. Whether referring to measures taken to fight terrorism (Bush) or the health care legislation passed in 2009 or more recent executive orders on immigration (Obama), analogies to "Gestapo tactics" and "big government" enforced by the "jack-booted Nazis" are false analogies. The comparison in both cases boggles the mind of any reasonable person.

Hitler was a mass murderer of unparalleled infamy, systematically exterminating whole populations and instituting a worldwide reign of terror. He was evil incarnate. In what universe of perverse thinking, regardless of political leanings, do either Bush or Obama compare to this madman? Disagree passionately with their policies, or with the policies of any other person you dislike, or even warn of potential dangers in their ideologies and practices when speaking to audiences, but do not accept or use the analogy to Hitler. Former *Newsweek* editor Jon Meacham (2009) said it well: "We are in danger of turning evil itself into a triviality when we draw on the images of Hitler's Germany to make political points in debates that are in no way comparable to

Comparing either George W. Bush or Barack Obama to Hitler is a false analogy. Avoid making foolish and indefensible comparisons.

the terrors of Nazism" (p. 9). The analogy to Hitler is grossly misapplied in speech after speech, and it is false because the dissimilarities are enormous.

Competent Style of Presentation: A Signature Event

Irish author Oscar Wilde once said, "One's style is one's signature always." Your speaking style reveals an identity. It is part of who you are. A speech is a combination of substance (claims and supporting materials) and style. Your **style** is composed of the words you choose to express your thoughts and the ways you use language to bring your thoughts to life for an audience. No one wants to endure a tedious presentation of bland arguments and a laundry list of supporting materials. You want your speech to come alive! Style can transform a tedious but well-structured and effectively delivered speech into a powerful, vibrant presentation.

A verbose style may tag you as boring or confused, a clear and precise style as interesting or instructive, and a vivid style as exciting or even inspiring. Take your style seriously. With it, you are putting your individual stamp on your speech. In this section, the differences between written and oral style as well as the primary elements of an effective and appropriate style are examined. Developing an effective oral style is a sophisticated skill. This discussion of style was not included in the previous chapter because concerning yourself about style for your first speech or two is probably ill advised. Developing an effective oral style takes time and practice, but an effective style can benefit your speeches enormously.

Oral Versus Written Style: An Essay Is Not a Speech

There are distinct differences between oral style and written style. First, *when we speak, we usually use simpler sentences than when we write.* An audience must catch the speaker's meaning immediately. When you read a sentence, however, you can reread it several times if necessary to discern the correct meaning, even consult a dictionary if you don't know the meaning of unfamiliar words. When you hear a sentence, however, a very complex structure can confuse listeners, who cannot normally rewind the speech to hear it again.

Second, *oral style is highly interactive; written style is not.* When speaking, you can look directly into the faces of your listeners. If you sense that they do not understand your point, you can adjust by rephrasing your point, adding an example, even asking if they are confused. Feedback is immediate from listeners. Even in text messaging, however, feedback from readers is delayed, and it is often nonexistent. The speaker and the audience influence each other directly. If you crack a joke and no one laughs, you may decide to dump other attempts at humor.

Third, *oral style is usually less formal than written style.* Spelling errors only occur in written language. Even highly educated individuals diminish their credibility when they send emails or letters with obvious spelling mistakes. Grammar errors may go unnoticed when words are spoken but jump off the page when words are written. More slang and casual forms of address creep into spoken language than appear in written form. We tend to be more conversational when we speak than when we write.

Standards of Competent Oral Style: The Language of a Speech

Oral style is effective and appropriate when it fulfills certain criteria: *clarity, precision,* and *vividness.* This section presents these criteria and some examples of effective oral style.

CLARITY: SAY WHAT YOU MEAN

Oral style works more effectively when language is clear and understandable. This often means avoiding jargon, euphemisms, and slang (see Chapter 4). *Clarity comes from a simple, concise style.*

A clear style is simple but not simplistic. Lincoln's second inaugural address included this memorable line: "With malice toward none, with charity for all, with firmness in the right as God gives us to see the right." The words are simple, yet the meaning is profound, even moving. Including an occasional complex sentence or more challenging vocabulary, however, can also work well. Although Lincoln used a simple, clear style, his sentence structure and phrasing were not always so. In his "Gettysburg Address," he included several lengthy, complex sentences. He also included this one: "We cannot dedicate, we cannot consecrate, we cannot hallow this ground." He could have said, "We cannot set aside for the special purpose of honoring, we cannot make holy this ground." Sometimes more challenging vocabulary provides an economical use of language. By occasionally using more sophisticated vocabulary, Lincoln spoke more concisely, clearly, and eloquently. If in doubt, however, default to simple sentence structure and vocabulary.

PRECISION: MAKE SENSE

Baseball great Yogi Berra once observed this about the game that made him a household name: "Baseball is 90 percent mental and the other half is physical." Yogi also said, "When you get to a fork in the road, take it," and "Our similarities are different" (Yogi Berra Quotes, 2015). Yogi was not renowned for his precise use of the English language (or his mastery of arithmetic).

Jeb Bush, prior to officially announcing his candidacy for the Republican nomination for president, made this tortured statement while speaking in Nevada: *"I'm running for president* in 2016, and the focus is going to be about how we, *if I run,* how do you create high sustained economic growth" (quoted by Collins, 2015). So which is it? Are you running, or are you still on the fence?

Everyone has misused a word or gotten tangled on syntax occasionally. Nevertheless, strive to be as precise in your use of language as possible. Using words imprecisely or inaccurately diminishes your credibility and can make you appear foolish.

VIVIDNESS: PAINT A PICTURE

Simple, concise, precise use of language doesn't mean using words in a boring fashion. A vivid style paints a picture in the minds of listeners and makes a speaker's ideas memorable. William Gibbs McAdoo, twice an unsuccessful candidate for the Democratic nomination for president, vividly described the speeches of President Warren G. Harding this way: "His speeches left the impression of an army of pompous phrases moving over the landscape in search of an idea." (quoted in "Wingnut History,"2015). The words are simple, and the point is clearly drawn. The style, however, is quite vivid. Student Meaghan Hagensick (2008) referred to those who claim that sitting in the backseat of a car makes wearing a seatbelt unnecessary as "backseat bullets." Sarah Hoppes (2008) noted that a proposal to sell ad space on the Golden Gate Bridge to cover an $80 million deficit would turn a national landmark into "The Google Gate Bridge." Each of these examples leaves a visual impression in the listener's mind.

Consider the difference vivid style makes by comparing the phrasing of famous statements with a plainer version of the same:

Vivid: "Friends, Romans, countrymen, lend me your ears." (Shakespeare's version of a speech by Mark Antony from *Julius Caesar*)

Plain: "Friends, Romans, countrymen, may I please have your attention?"

Vivid: "I have nothing to offer but blood, toil, tears and sweat." (Winston Churchill,

May 13, 1940, first speech as Prime Minister to the House of Commons)

Plain: "I have nothing to offer but a struggle."

How can you make your own style vivid? A few suggestions follow.

Metaphor and Simile: Figures of Speech Two main figures of speech that can add vividness to your speeches are *metaphors* and *similes*. A **metaphor** is an implied comparison of two seemingly dissimilar things. In his State of the Union speech delivered on January 6, 1941, Franklin Roosevelt said that selfish men "would clip the wings of the American eagle in order to feather their own nests." Mark Jackson, former Golden State Warriors basketball coach, commenting on Steve Kerr's rookie success coaching the Warriors after Jackson's departure, commented, "I think while giving him [Kerr] credit, there's no need to take credit away from the past. You cannot disrespect the caterpillar and rave about the butterfly" (quoted by Thompson, 2015).

Be careful not to mix your metaphors; otherwise, your vivid imagery may sound laughable. A **mixed metaphor** is the use of two or more vastly different metaphors in a single expression. Famous movie producer Samuel Goldwyn once remarked, "That's the way with these directors. They're always biting the hand that lays the golden egg." Then there's Alabama Senator Jeff Sessions, who in his opening statement at the Senate Judiciary Committee confirmation hearings for Sonya Sotomayor as Supreme Court justice in July 2009 argued for a "blindfolded justice calling the balls and strikes fairly and objectively" (quoted in Goodman, 2009, p. A13). A blindfolded justice metaphorically symbolizes lack of bias, but a baseball umpire, making inherently subjective perceptual judgment calls, surely doesn't. Even more to the point, would you ever want an umpire of any sort to be blindfolded when they "call the balls and strikes"? Mixing metaphors can just sound goofy.

A **simile** is an explicit comparison of two seemingly dissimilar things using the word *like* or *as*. Curt Simmons used a simile to describe what it was like pitching to Hank Aaron: "Trying to get a fastball past Hank Aaron is like trying to get the sun past a rooster." Bill Clinton, in a speech at Galesburg, Illinois, on January 23,

The use of similes can have a very vivid effect on listeners.

1995, used simile in an amusing way: "Being president is like running a cemetery; you've got a lot of people under you and nobody's listening."

Similes and metaphors can enhance a speech, but not if they become clichés. A **cliché** is a once-vivid expression that has been overused to the point of seeming commonplace. "Dull as dishwater," "dumb as a post," and "smooth as a baby's butt" are a few overused similes. "It's not rocket science," "It's an emotional roller coaster," and "I'm between a rock and a hard place" are metaphors that have become shopworn. A survey by Accountemps found "leverage," "It's above my pay grade," and "crunch time" to be among the most annoying clichés ("The Top 20," 2014).

Alliteration: Several of the Same Sounds The repetition of the same sound, usually a consonant sound, starting each word is called **alliteration**. It can create a very vivid cadence. Classic examples of alliteration were spoken by the Wizard in the movie *The Wizard of Oz*. He called the Tin Man a "clinking, clanking, clattering collection of caliginous junk." He referred to the Scarecrow as a "billowing bale of bovine fodder." In her speech on poor sanitation in hotels, student Kittie Grace (2000) noted that the rooms had become "a biological banquet for bugs and bacteria that cause us physical harm" (p. 87). Use alliteration sparingly lest it become annoyingly repetitious.

Parallelism: Vivid Rhythm A parallel construction has a similar arrangement of words, phrases, or sentences that create a rhythm. Here are two examples:

Yes, we can . . . Yes, we can, to opportunity and prosperity. Yes, we can heal this nation. Yes, we can repair this world. Yes, we can. (Barack Obama, 2008; see "Remarks of Senator Barack Obama," 2008)

Enough is enough. Enough is enough with Wall Street insiders getting key position after key position and the kind of cronyism that we have seen in the executive branch. Enough is enough with Citigroup passing 11th hour deregulatory provisions that nobody takes ownership over but everybody will come to regret. Enough is enough! (Elizabeth Warren, 2014; see "Enough Is Enough," 2014).

As is true of any stylistic device, however, a little goes a long way. *Be careful not to overuse parallel constructions.*

Antithesis: Using Opposites Charles Dickens began his famous novel *A Tale of Two Cities* with one of the most memorable lines in literature: "It was the best of times; it was the worst of times." This is an example of the stylistic device called **antithesis**—the use of opposites to create impact. Former First Lady Barbara Bush offered this example of antithesis: "Your success as a family, our success as a society, depends not on what happens at the White House, but on what happens inside your house." Perhaps the most famous example of antithesis in public speaking is from John F. Kennedy's inaugural address in 1961: "Ask not what your country can do for you, ask what you can do for your country."

Ultimately, your style must be your own. Work on clarity, precision, and vividness by listening to successful speakers, but explore what fits you well. Metaphors and similes may come easily to you, but antithesis may seem artificial and awkward.

Develop your own style by experimenting. Try including metaphors in your conversations with others. Play with language informally before incorporating stylistic devices in your formal speeches. Remember, style is your signature.

 ## Summary

Gaining and maintaining the attention of your audience increase the likelihood that your carefully prepared speech will resonate with listeners. An effective introduction gets your speech off to a good start, and an effective conclusion ends it with a bang. Backing your claims and bolstering your arguments with supporting materials used effectively are critical elements of competent public speaking. Style—the way that you use language to express your ideas—should be clear, precise, and vivid. The next two chapters take both the basic (Chapter 12) and more advanced (Chapter 13) concepts and processes and apply them to informative and persuasive speeches. (Appendix B explores special occasion speeches.)

Quizzes Without Consequences

Test your knowledge before your exam! Go to the companion website at www.oup.com/us/rothwell, click on the Student Resources for each chapter, and take the Quizzes Without Consequences.

Film School Case Studies

. . . And Justice for All (1979). Dark Comedy/Drama; R
Al Pacino delivers a very famous speech ("You're out of order!") in a courtroom. Analyze his style for appropriateness and effectiveness.

Malcolm X (1992). Historical Drama; PG-13
Denzel Washington plays Malcolm X in this Oscar-nominated performance. Analyze the numerous public speeches delivered by Washington for style. Do they match well with his varied audiences?

To Kill a Mockingbird (1962). Drama; Not Rated
Atticus Finch (Gregory Peck) is a small-town lawyer in the South who defends a black man accused of raping a white girl. Peck earned an Oscar for his touching performance. Analyze the lengthy speech delivered to the jury for its style. Contrast this style with that of the Al Pacino character in . . . And Justice for All.

TED Talks and YouTube Links

These speeches are offered for you to analyze and perhaps discuss in class. Some are very good examples, and some are problematic. Apply text material in this chapter to each sample speech.

1. *Introduction, Organization, and Conclusion:* Ashley Mengwasser, Briefing Speech, College Public Speaking Class http://www.youtube.com/watch?v=5WplllrnLcY.

2. *Humor to Gain and Maintain Attention:* Stephen Colbert, Commencement Address, Wake Forest University. https://www.youtube.com/watch?v=VbzrmIqstd8

3. *Humor (Especially Self-Deprecation) and Novelty to Gain and Maintain Attention:* Brad Delson, UCLA Commencement Address https://www.youtube.com/watch?v=esQ7WSzJUxk

1. Distinguish between informative and persuasive speaking.

2. Explain the five different types of informative speeches.

3. Use guidelines and strategies to deliver a competent informative speech.

Informative Speaking

TWO THEORISTS SPEAK METAPHORICALLY of surfing, swimming, and drowning in information to underline the need to manage it effectively (Crawford & Gorman, 1996). Although discussing information in the context of electronic technology, their metaphors seem applicable to informative speaking. An informative speech that presents too little information is unsatisfying to an audience; this is analogous to surfing, merely skimming the top of a subject without delving deeply. Presenting too much information is analogous to drowning, swamping an audience in a tidal wave of information too voluminous to appreciate or comprehend. An informative speech works best when the speaker swims in the information, finding the right balance between too little and too much information for the audience.

Everywhere you look, informative speaking occurs. Infomercials are pervasive on the mass media. YouTube and other Internet sites provide access to all manner of informative

CHAPTER OUTLINE

- Distinguishing Informative From Persuasive Speaking
- Types of Informative Speeches
- Guidelines for Competent Informative Speaking
- Visual Aids

4. Use specific visual aids to enhance your speeches.

speeches from education and industry, some great (see especially www.ted.com) and some not so great. Teachers spend the bulk of their time in the classroom speaking informatively. Managers present information at meetings. Military officers give briefings. Religious leaders speak informatively when interpreting religious doctrines and organizing fund drives, charitable activities, and special events. Students give informative presentations in a wide variety of courses and disciplines. Competent informative speaking is a valuable skill. Thus, *the principal purpose of this chapter is to explain how you construct and present a competent informative speech.*

Distinguishing Informative From Persuasive Speaking

The overriding difference between an informative and persuasive speech is your general purpose. *The general purpose of an informative speech is to teach your audience something new, interesting, and useful.* You want your listeners to learn. *The general purpose of a persuasive speech is to convince your listeners to change their attitude and behavior.* You want your listeners to think and act differently.

Don't think of informative and persuasive speeches as dichotomous. They differ more by degree than in kind. A teacher, for example, is primarily interested in informing students, but controversial issues arise and advocacy of a particular theory or perspective may occur. So teaching isn't purely informative. Persuasive speeches also inform. You often have to teach your audience about the magnitude of a problem that listeners may not have been aware of before advocating solutions. Nevertheless, two specific distinctions between informative and persuasive speeches can help you understand where a speech falls on the informative-persuasive continuum.

Noncontroversial Information: Staying Neutral

Informative speeches do not usually stir disagreement and dissension. It's hard to imagine any audience getting worked into a froth if you offered study tips to improve students' test scores or ways to avoid the common cold as long as the information is accurate. Some information, however, has the potential to ignite disagreement without prompting. For example, noting the billions of dollars spent each year on alternative medical therapies can upset those who view alternative therapies as quackery even though no position is advocated by the speaker.

Nevertheless, presenting all relevant sides of an issue in a neutral fashion, as most journalists report the news, focuses on teaching something new, interesting, or useful, not on advocating a specific point of view. "I've explained three ways that you can build your finances for the future. Whichever one you choose, know that there is a strong financial future awaiting you" doesn't advocate; it informs. You aren't being told which choice to make. If, however, you draw a conclusion regarding which side is correct after weighing the evidence and advocate a specific choice, then you are trying to persuade.

Precursor to Persuasion: No Call to Action

An informative speech may arouse your listeners' concern on a subject. This concern may trigger a desire to correct a problem. Thus, your informative speech may act as a precursor, or steppingstone, to a subsequent persuasive speech advocating strong action. If you hear a speech informing you of the pros and cons of electric cars, you might be encouraged without any prompting from the speaker to investigate such cars further or even to buy one. If a speaker relates a personal story about the rewards he or she experiences teaching young children, you might begin to consider teaching as a profession, even though the speaker never makes such an appeal.

In some cases, you may be presenting interesting information to your audience without connecting it to any particular issue, but someone in the audience might. For example, do you know who Otis Blackwell was? He died May 6, 2002, at the age of 71. He was credited with writing more than 1,000 songs that were recorded by such international stars as Elvis Presley, Ray Charles, Billy Joel, The Who, Otis Redding, James Taylor, Peggy Lee, and Jerry Lee Lewis (Edwards, 2002). His songs sold more than 185 million copies. Providing further details about the life of this remarkable African American talent would be an interesting informative speech. Someone listening to such a speech, however, might wonder why

Otis Blackwell wrote songs for Elvis and numerous other famous singers but is largely unknown to most Americans. His story could trigger an interesting informative speech.

mainstream America is mostly oblivious that Blackwell ever lived. A persuasive speech that advocates teaching more African American history to American college students might be triggered by an informative speech on Otis Blackwell.

If you are given an assignment by your teacher to present an informative speech to the class, are told by your boss to make a report to a committee or group, or are asked to explain a new software package to novice computer users, remember that your focus will be on teaching, not convincing, your listeners. The more neutral and even-handed your presentation, the more essentially informative it is. When you take a firm stand, present only one side without critique, or advocate a change in behavior from your listeners, you have moved into persuasive territory.

The competent public speaker recognizes when persuasion is appropriate and when the specific context calls for a presentation more informative in nature. When teachers use the classroom as a platform for personal advocacy, they may step over the not-always-clear line between informative and persuasive speaking. Advocacy on issues directly relevant to the teaching role—such as advocating the scientific method as a means of critical thinking—is appropriate. Advocacy of "correct" political points of view, however, can run dangerously close to proselytizing, or converting the "unbelievers," not teaching. Again, *it can be a blurry line that separates informative from persuasive speeches.*

Types of Informative Speeches

The issue of what constitutes an informative speech becomes clearer by looking at the different types: *reports*, *explanations*, *demonstrations*, *narratives*, and *comparisons*. There is some overlap between the types, but each one has its own unique qualities.

Reports: Facts in Brief

A *report* is usually a brief, informative presentation that fulfills a class assignment, updates a committee about work performed by a subcommittee, reveals the results of a study, provides

Astrophysicist Neil DeGrasse Tyson is the great explainer of cosmic complexities.

recent findings, or identifies the latest developments in a current situation of interest. Students give reports in classes and during meetings of student government. Scientists give reports on research results. Press secretaries give reports, or *briefings*, to members of the mass media. Military officers give briefings to fellow officers and to the press.

Reports need to be clearly presented. Make sure you have your facts straight and that all the information presented is accurate. Complex, detailed information should be summarized succinctly. Present the main points and the most significant specifics. Don't get lost in minutiae.

Explanations: Deeper Understanding

Unlike a simple report stating facts to an audience often already familiar with the topic (e.g., reporters at a presidential press conference), speeches that seek to *explain* are concerned with advancing deep understanding of complex concepts, processes, events, objects, and issues for listeners who are typically unfamiliar with the material presented. Astrophysicist Neil deGrasse Tyson's 2014 presentations during the television series *Cosmos: A Spacetime Odyssey* are

apt examples of informative speaking that explains complex ideas.

The *lecture* is a common example of an informative speech that explains. Students are most familiar with this type, having heard hundreds from numerous instructors. Unlike reports, which typically run about 15 minutes or less, lectures often last an hour or more. Also unlike most reports, lectures work best when they are highly entertaining. Attention strategies (discussed extensively in Chapter 13) are extremely important to the success of a lecture. Maintaining the attention of a sometimes captive audience for long periods of time is a huge challenge. Celebrities, famous authors, politicians, consultants, and experts of all types use the lecture platform to explain ideas. The wildly popular TED (Technology, Entertainment, and Design) lecture series is a stellar example of mostly informative (but sometimes persuasive) presentations that explain often complex topics in 20-minute lectures.

Demonstrations: Acting Out

A *demonstration* is an informative speech that shows the audience how to use an object or to perform a specific activity. Dance teachers demonstrate dance steps while explaining how best to perform the steps. Cooking and home improvement television programs are essentially demonstration speeches. These speeches require the speaker to show the physical object or to display the activity for the audience; a demonstration is not a mere description of objects or activities. If you are going to give a speech on martial arts, show the audience specific movements and techniques; don't just ask your audience to imagine them. A speech on how card tricks and magic are performed must demonstrate the trick slowly and clearly so that the audience can understand.

Narratives: Storytelling

Consider the narrative of neuroanatomist Jill Bolte Taylor. One morning, when she was 37 years old, a blood vessel burst in Dr. Taylor's brain. As a brain scientist, however, she realized she had a rare opportunity to witness her own stroke and to understand what was happening while it occurred: movement, speech, memory, self-awareness all became impaired. As she observed, "How many brain scientists have been able to study the brain from the inside out? I've gotten as much out of this experience of losing my left mind as I have in my entire academic career" (quoted in "Jill Bolte Taylor," 2008). She spent eight years recovering her ability to walk, talk, and think. She tells her amazing story of what it was like experiencing a stroke, and what it took to recover her ability to walk, talk, and think, in a best-selling book entitled *My Stroke of Insight: A Brain Scientist's Personal Journey*. She also gave an 18-minute narrative presentation at the TED conference in Monterey, California, on February 27, 2008, explaining what her stroke was like and what insights she learned. She shows a real human brain with spinal cord attached (a captivating visual aid) and provides insights about your own brain. Her story is intensely moving. By the conclusion, she is in tears, and so are many in the audience. It became one of the top 10 presentations for the TED organization (see *TED Talks and YouTube Links* at the end of this chapter).

A story well told, such as Dr. Taylor's fascinating journey, can be thoroughly engaging. Why do we watch movies if not to enjoy storytelling? Sophie Watts, president of STX Entertainment, wowed an audience at the Produced By Conference on May 30, 2015, when she enthusiastically spoke these words: "We are building a movie studio from the ground up to provide a custom-made home for the world's best storytellers" (quoted by Robb, 2015). Our brains are wired to enjoy storytelling (Hsu, 2008).

Narratives may be about you or about other people. Instructors may give a short presentation at the beginning of a course informing students about their number of years spent teaching, where teaching occurred, the joys and challenges of teaching, and prospects for teaching in the future. Some also relate really dumb things tried in the classroom that went embarrassingly wrong, which can make a professor seem more human and approachable. Narratives may be historical ("The Struggles of Thurgood Marshall"), personal ("My Life as a Surgeon"), self-disclosing ("I Once Lived a Life of Drug Addiction"), or merely amusing ("What

Neuroanatomist Dr. Jill Bolte Taylor suffered a severe stroke and told her story at a TED lecture entitled "My Stroke of Insight" (also the title of her book).

It's Like Being a Technophobe"). Narratives are most effective when they entertain as well as inform an audience.

Comparisons: Pros and Cons

Some informative speeches explain serious problems that exist and then *compare* a variety of potential solutions without taking a stand on any of the remedies offered. For example, the increasing price of college textbooks is a recognized national problem. There are several possible solutions: increasing the availability of used books, using open-source public domain materials, establishing textbook rental programs, urging professors to adopt only textbooks that have minimal ancillaries (e.g., websites and CDs), discouraging publishers from producing new editions sooner than every three or four years, encouraging customized versions of textbooks, and offering more "stripped down" versions of standard textbooks that can be priced more cheaply than the elaborate versions. Each of these solutions has pros and cons. For instance, expanding the availability of used books means more students can purchase textbooks at three-quarters the cost of a new textbook ($75 used compared to $100 new), but as the availability of used books increases, textbook publishers are pressured to increase the cost of new versions of textbooks to counter losses engendered by used books. Presenting the positives and negatives of various solutions without taking a stand on any of them is structured as an informative speech. You leave it to the audience to make choices based on a balanced presentation of possible remedies for a problem.

Overlapping Types: Using Variety

These five types of informative speeches can overlap. A report may occasionally veer into a demonstration when listeners don't appear to understand what is reported. A teacher may lecture for a majority of a class period but also do demonstrations to add variety and make a point more memorable and meaningful. I have used a fairly lengthy demonstration of a polygraph, or lie detector machine, with student volunteers to drive home several points related to nonverbal communication and connotative meaning related to words. It never fails to engender interest, even fascination, from the class. Years later, students tell me they still remember that particular demonstration and what it showed.

Guidelines for Competent Informative Speaking

In general, informative speeches work best when the information presented is clear, accurate, and interesting instead of opaque, wrong, and boring. Thus, review Chapters 12 and 13 for tips on outlining and organizing, gaining and maintaining attention, employing effective delivery and style, using supporting materials effectively, and avoiding fallacies. In this section, additional tips for presenting effective informative speeches are provided.

Inform: Tell Us What We Don't Know

An informative speech, first and foremost, must tell your audience something it doesn't already know. Your first, and seemingly most obvious, guideline is to provide new information to your listeners. I say *seemingly* obvious because I've sat through far too many "informative" presentations that never told me a thing I didn't know previously, and in some cases, the speaker should have known that the points being made were trivial and lacked any insight. You don't want your listeners saying after your presentation, "I didn't learn a thing." This doesn't mean that everything you present must be new information, but the emphasis should be on providing that which is not widely known.

Adapt: Audience Analysis

How do you know whether your informative speech goes beyond what your listeners already know? That requires an analysis of your audience (see Chapter 12). If the topic choice is at your discretion, choose what will likely interest your listeners and is well suited to their knowledge, concerns, and expectations. If the subject of your speech is too high level, complex, and abstract for the educational level of your audience, then you've chosen poorly. Presenting information on systems theory or thermodynamics, for example, won't resonate with very young audiences because the information is well over their heads. Set theory in mathematics will probably baffle a lot of adult audiences.

If the choice is not up to you and the topic is very high level, complex, and abstract (e.g., a professor teaching quantum physics to students), your challenge is to [explain clearly each facet of your subject using multiple examples, personal stories, visual aids, metaphors, analogies, and demonstrations to clarify difficult material.] Albert Einstein, when faced with explaining his immensely complex theory of relativity to laypeople, offered this as a starting point: "When you sit with a nice girl for two hours you think it's only a minute. But when you sit on a hot stove for a minute you think it's two hours. That's relativity" (quoted in "Famous Quotes," 2009). Remember that oral style requires simpler language than written style. Strive for language simplicity, as discussed in Chapter 13, and avoid highly complex language that may confuse even a well-educated audience.

If your subject is fairly simple and you're addressing an educated audience, be careful not to condescend to your listeners. Acting as though they are third-graders is patronizing and will insult them. If your audience is already knowledgeable about your subject, more difficult material can be included earlier and with less need to elaborate extensively.

Clarify: Define Key Terms

Key terms, especially unfamiliar or technical ones, should be defined clearly and precisely. For example, student Nick Dorman (2014) began his speech: "Methicillin-resistant *Staphylococcus aureus*, more commonly known as flesh-eating bacteria MRSA . . ." (p. 63). This is a nice, understandable definition of a technical term for a lay audience. Similarly, student Tess Drager (2013) defined *Clostridium difficile* this way: "It is a deadly bacterium, which infects the human colon, causing a person to become extremely ill" (p. 79).

Supporting Materials Revisited: Additional Advice

Much has been said already in Chapter 13 about using supporting materials competently. At its most basic, your information should be credible, relevant, and sufficient. This section provides two brief, additional pieces of advice for an effective informative speech.

CHOOSE INTERESTING SUPPORTING MATERIALS: COUNTERACTING BOREDOM

Learning doesn't usually occur when listeners are uninterested in the subject matter. This doesn't mean substituting colorful but weak supporting material for strong but bland ones. Your first consideration when choosing supporting materials should be their credibility and strength. Nevertheless, strong, credible, but interesting supporting material is the best of all choices. Startling statistics, dramatic examples, and clever quotations by experts add interest to a speech that could become tiresome if supporting materials are dull and lifeless (see Box 14-1 for numerous examples).

ABBREVIATE SOURCE CITATIONS: BRIEF REFERENCE REMINDERS

The initial citation of a source should be complete, but subsequent references to the same source can be abbreviated to avoid tedious repetition unless the abbreviation might cause confusion (e.g., two articles from the same magazine). Student Treya Brown (2014) abbreviates this way: "According to the previously cited GAO Reports . . ." (p. 68). After qualifying her source earlier in her speech, student Angela Wnek (2012) makes this secondary reference: "According to Scheider's article . . ." (p. 143). Student Laura Streich (2012) makes this abbreviated reference: "During the previously cited interview with Leah Holmes, she stated . . ." (p. 147). Abbreviating secondary citations makes your speech flow more smoothly.

Avoid Information Overload: Don't Drown in Data

We live in the Age of Information Overload (Silver, 2012). The ready availability of huge quantities of information because of computer technologies can tempt a speaker to provide way too much detail and complexity in a speech. Don't make your speech a tedious "data dump." Know when to quit. Preparation and practice are essential. Prepare a well-organized informative speech, then practice the speech and *time it precisely* before giving it. Timing your speech will immediately indicate whether you have provided too much information for the time allotted. Be careful not to offer needless details. Ask yourself, "Does my audience really need to know this?"

Tell Your Story Well: Narrative Tips

Stories can be short vignettes or lengthy, detailed narratives. Randy Pausch, a 47-year-old Carnegie Mellon University computer science professor who contracted pancreatic cancer in 2007, gave a lecture at his university on September 18, 2007, to a crowd of 500 students, faculty, and friends. In a 75-minute presentation, Pausch told many stories about his life, each relating to his central idea about achieving his childhood dreams. His stories were humorous, poignant, and very entertaining. Although he knew he was dying, he conducted himself as though he were perfectly healthy, at one moment dropping to the floor and doing push-ups both one- and two-handed. When he finished his final lecture, his audience gave him a

BOX 14-1 DEVELOPING COMMUNICATION COMPETENCE

Outline and Text of An Informative Speech

Here is an outline and the text of an informative speech. Each incorporates the suggestions offered for constructing a competent informative speech.

INTRODUCTION
  I. *Attention Strategy:* Use startling examples.
   A. Describe the Spanish flu pandemic of 1918–1919.
   B. Refer to the 1957 Asian flu pandemic and 70,000 deaths.
   C. Mention the 1968 Hong Kong flu pandemic.
   D. Mention the 2009 swine flu pandemic.
  II. *Significance:* We should all be concerned about yearly flu viruses for two reasons.
   A. A serious flu epidemic could strike again.
   B. Everyone is susceptible to deadly flu viruses each year.
  III. *Central Idea:* Flu is a serious problem, but there are effective ways to prevent contracting this yearly disease.
  IV. *Purpose Statement:* To inform my audience about ways to prevent contracting the flu.
  V. *Preview:* Three main points will be discussed.
   A. Flu viruses pose serious health hazards to all of us.
   B. Flu viruses are difficult to combat.
   C. There are several ways to prevent contracting the flu.

BODY
  I. Flu viruses pose serious health hazards to everyone.
   A. Flu viruses are killers.
   B. Flu viruses can make you very sick.
   C. Flu viruses are highly contagious.
  II. Flu viruses are difficult to combat.
   A. "Influenza" was thought to be the "influence" of the stars, making it exceedingly difficult to combat.
   B. There are many strains of flu, even in a single flu season.
   C. Occasionally, a flu virus will mutate, causing a pandemic.
  III. There are three primary ways to prevent contracting the flu.
   A. Stay generally healthy.
    1. Get exercise.
    2. Eat a healthy diet.
    3. Avoid crowds during flu season.
    4. Practice good hygiene.
   B. Get a flu shot.
    1. Flu shots are between 50% and 60% effective.
    2. Flu shots cannot cause the flu.
   C. Take an antiviral prescription drug.

CONCLUSION
  I. Provide summary of main points.
   A. Flu viruses can be hazardous to humans.
   B. Combating flu viruses can be difficult.
   C. Flu viruses can be prevented.
  II. Make reference to the introductory example of Spanish flu.
  III. Give a memorable finish by making a reference to this annual plague.

(continued)

(continued)

BIBLIOGRAPHY

Barry, J. M. (2005). *The great influenza.* New York: Penguin.

Centers for Disease Control and Prevention. (2015, January 8). What you should know about flu antiviral drugs. Retrieved from http://www.cdc.gov/flu/antivirals/whatyoushould.htm

Centers for Disease Control and Prevention. (2015, January 14). Vaccine effectiveness: How well does the flu vaccine work? Retrieved from http://www.cdc.gov/flu/about/qa/vaccineeffect.htm

Centers for Disease Control and Prevention. (2015, February 26). Advisory Committee on Immunization Practices (ACIP) reaffirms recommendation for annual influenza vaccination. Retrieved from http://www.cdc.gov/media/releases/2015/s0226-acip.html

Centers for Disease Control and Prevention. (2015, May 22). Key facts about influenza (flu) & flu vaccines. Retrieved from http://www.cdc.gov/flu/keyfacts.htm

Dawood, F., Luliano, D., Reed, C., et al. (2012). Estimated global mortality associated with the first 12 months of 2009 pandemic influenza A H1N1 virus circulation: A modelling study. *The Lancet, 12,* 687–695.

Garrett, L. (1994). *The coming plague: Newly emerging diseases in a world out of balance.* New York: Penguin Books.

Haney, D. (1998, November 8). Researchers breaking new ground on flu front. *San Jose Mercury News,* p. 10A.

Kolata, G. (1999). *Flu: The story of the Great Influenza Pandemic of 1918 and the search for the virus that caused it.* New York: Farrar, Straus & Giroux.

Murray, C., Lopez, A. D., Chin, B., Feehan, D., & Hill, K. H. (2006). Estimation of potential global pandemic influenza mortality on the basis of vital registry data from the 1918–20 pandemic: A quantitative analysis. *The Lancet, 368,* 2211–2218.

U.S. Department of Health and Human Services. (2015, June 1). Pandemic flu history. Retrieved from http://www.flu.gov/pandemic/history/index.html

THE ANNUAL PLAGUE
(Prepared June 2015; about an 8-minute speech)

It killed an estimated 50 million people worldwide and 675,000 Americans, according to the U.S. Department of Health and Human Services website *flu.gov* accessed on June 1, 2015. [*CREDIBLE SOURCE; USE OF STARTLING STATISTICS GAINS ATTENTION*] City morgues across the United States became overwhelmed with bodies stacked like cords of wood. Undertakers rapidly ran out of coffins, and graves couldn't be dug fast enough to accommodate the rising death toll, so bodies often lay in homes for days or even weeks. According to Gina Kolata, author of the 1999 book *Flu,* victims of this disease suffered agonizing symptoms that included high fever and violent coughing fits that cracked ribs and spewed blood from victims' mouths. Fluid filled their lungs causing many to drown in their own juices. [*VIVID DESCRIPTION KEEPS ATTENTION; DATE IS FINE FOR HISTORICAL FACTS*]

What was this terrifying disease? [*TRANSITION*] The Black Death of the 14th century revisiting the human species? AIDS? Some biological warfare agent? The start of the Zombie Apocalypse? [*RHETORICAL QUESTIONS INVOLVE AUDIENCE, CREATE CURIOSITY*] The global killer was the flu! The Spanish flu of 1918–1919 caused a pandemic, or worldwide epidemic.

The previously cited website *flu.gov* notes more recent flu pandemics in its article "Pandemic Flu History." A 1957 "Asian flu" killed almost 70,000 Americans and 2 million worldwide. In 1968, the "Hong Kong flu" killed almost 34,000 Americans. Finally, according to a September 2012 article published in the medical journal *Lancet* by researchers Fatimah Dawood and associates, as many as 575,000 people worldwide died from the 2009 H1N1 flu strain. Medical researcher Chris Murray of Harvard University and his associates, in a frightening December 23, 2006, issue of *Lancet,* estimates that the H5N1 so-called "avian flu," still circulating mostly among birds, could kill as many as 81 million people globally if it were to mutate. [*MORE REALLY STARTLING STATISTICS*] No one knows if or when this could happen.

Why should we care about flu pandemics of the past? [*RHETORICAL QUESTION INVOLVES AUDIENCE, MAKES TRANSITION*] There are two good reasons: (1) a flu pandemic could strike again, and (2) everyone in this room is a potential

(continued)

BOX 14-1 DEVELOPING COMMUNICATION COMPETENCE

Outline and Text of An Informative Speech (continued)

victim of a deadly flu virus. [*SIGNIFICANCE OF TOPIC TO THE AUDIENCE IS ESTABLISHED*] Consequently, you'll want to listen carefully as I inform you about ways to prevent contracting the flu. [*CLEAR PURPOSE STATEMENT*] My careful and extensive research on this subject [*BRIEF REFERENCE TO CREDIBILITY*] leads me to make three main points: First, even seasonal flu viruses are a serious health hazard; second, flu viruses are difficult to combat; and third, there are several ways to prevent the flu. [*CLEAR, CONCISE PREVIEW OF MAIN POINTS; PROBLEM–CAUSE–SOLUTION ORGANIZATIONAL PATTERN USED*]

Let's begin by [*TRANSITION*] discussing the serious health hazards produced by a normal flu season. [*SIGNPOSTING FIRST MAIN POINT*] Even ordinary flu viruses that hit the United States every year between the months of October and April are killers. A May 22, 2015, report by the Centers for Disease Control and Prevention, usually referred to simply as the CDC, notes in an article entitled "Key Facts About Influenza" that flu-associated deaths in the United States vary from a low of 3,000 to a high of 49,000 annually. [*STARTLING STATISTIC MAINTAINS ATTENTION AND INTEREST; USE OF CREDIBLE, RECENT SOURCE FOR STATISTICS*]

Most of you won't die from a common flu virus, but you may wish you were dead. [*TRANSITION*] According to the CDC "Key Facts" article, typical flu symptoms include high fever, sore throat, intense muscle aches, congestion, cough, and severe fatigue. My friend Terry once described how he feels when he gets the flu: "It's like being suddenly hit by a speeding car, catapulted into a concrete wall, roasted in an oven, then forced to participate in the Ironman Triathlon. Death, by comparison, seems pleasant." [*VIVID USE OF SIMILES; INTENSITY USED TO MAINTAIN ATTENTION*] Symptoms of flu can last from a few days to several weeks. The flu can often lead to severe complications, such as bronchitis and pneumonia, which may require hospitalization.

In addition to the severity of its symptoms, [*TRANSITION*] flu is hazardous to humans because it is highly contagious. According to Daniel Haney, science reporter for the Associated Press, in a November 8, 1998, article in the *San Jose Mercury News,* young children are "flu incubators." [*CREDIBLE SOURCE; DATE IS FINE SINCE PHENOMENON DOES NOT CHANGE*] Haney continues, "In epidemiological terms, children are in the same category as ticks, rats, and mosquitoes: they are vectors of disease." [*COLORFUL, ATTENTION-GETTING QUOTE*] Day care centers and classrooms are flu breeding grounds where sick children spew the virus everywhere by coughing, sneezing, and wiping their runny noses. [*VIVID DESCRIPTION CREATES ATTENTION*] Children also bring the flu home and infect adult parents, who pass it along to coworkers, and so it spreads throughout the population.

Naturally, we're all interested in why flu is an annual event about as welcome as flies, frogs, and the other plagues God visited upon the ancient Egyptians in the biblical story of the Exodus [*VIVID TRANSITION*]. This brings me to my second main point, [*SIGNPOSTING MAIN POINT*] that flu viruses are difficult to combat.

Over the centuries many theories about the causes of the flu emerged. Influenza, flu being the shortened version of this term, reflects the 15th-century astrological belief that the disease was caused by the "influence" of the stars. According to Laurie Garrett, award-winning author of the 1994 book *The Coming Plague,* [*CREDIBLE SOURCE*] prominent American physicians of the time thought the 1918 Spanish flu might have been caused by nakedness, fish contaminated by Germans, dirt, dust, Chinese people, unclean pajamas, open windows, closed windows, old books, or "some cosmic influence." [*HISTORICAL EXAMPLES ARE NOVEL ATTENTION GETTERS*]

Unlike our predecessors and their wrong-headed prejudices and ignorance, we know that a virus causes flu, but a flu virus is difficult to combat. There are many strains, not just a single type. For instance, again according to the CDC "Key Facts" article, there are typically three strains of flu circulating each year. There are many strains of flu because flu viruses continually change over time. Thus, your immune system's antibodies produced to fight a previous flu will not combat the disease as well when exposed to a slightly altered virus. Occasionally, a flu strain will mutate, altering the genetic structure of the virus so greatly that human antibodies from previous exposures to flu will be useless. The pandemics of 1918, 1957, 1968, and 2009 were mutated flu strains according to the CDC article [*REFERENCE TO EARLIER EXAMPLES PROVIDES CONTINUITY TO THE SPEECH; CREDIBLE SOURCE*] The changing structure of flu viruses and their many strains make finding a cure very challenging. [*INTERNAL SUMMARY OF MAIN POINT*]

Now that you realize how hazardous flu can be and understand that its chief cause is a frequently changing virus, [*BRIEF INTERNAL SUMMARY*] what can be done about the flu? [*RHETORICAL QUESTION; TRANSITION*] This brings me to my final main point, [*SIGNPOSTING MAIN POINT*] that there are several ways to prevent catching the flu. First, [*SIGNPOSTING SUBPOINT*] stay generally healthy. Those in a weakened or vulnerable physical state, such as the very young, the

(continued)

(continued)

elderly, those with chronic health conditions, and pregnant women, are most likely to catch the flu. All reputable health care professionals encourage a series of preventive steps, including exercise, healthy diet, sufficient rest, frequent hand washing, and avoiding touching your eyes, nose, and mouth. Also, whenever possible avoid large crowds and confined spaces where flu sufferers can spread the disease. Airplanes, classrooms, and offices are flu factories. [*ALLITERATION FOR VIVIDNESS*]

Second, [*SIGNPOSTING SUBPOINT*] a yearly flu shot is an effective preventive. A January 14, 2015, report by the CDC entitled "Vaccine Effectiveness" concludes that annual flu vaccinations typically reduce the risk of contracting the virus by 50% to 60% overall, with higher effectiveness among younger individuals. [*CREDIBLE SOURCE; CREDIBLE STATISTICS*] Younger, healthier individuals typically receive greater protection than older, less healthy individuals. Those who are vaccinated but still get the flu usually experience less severe symptoms. Despite the common belief, a flu shot cannot give you the flu because, as the CDC article explains, flu shots contain no live virus. [*CREDIBLE SOURCE*] If you contract the flu soon after receiving the shot, it is because you were exposed to the flu, and the vaccine does not provide protection until two weeks after being vaccinated. The most frequent side effect is brief soreness at the site of the shot.

For those who get weak in the knees at the very sight of a syringe, nasal spray flu vaccines are available. These sprays do contain live virus, so there is a small chance of experiencing flu-like symptoms from the spray. Its side effects are minimal, however, especially when compared to some things people shoot up their noses. Pain phobics take note—it doesn't hurt! The Advisory Committee on Immunization Practices of the CDC in a February 26, 2015, statement offered no preference for either the shot or the spray. Researchers are also working on a pain-free skin patch to inoculate against flu and a universal flu vaccine that combats all flu types.

None of these options is guaranteed to prevent the flu, so if you do contract this seasonal sickness, there are antiviral prescription drugs. A January 8, 2015, CDC article on antiviral drugs reports that they are effective in reducing flu symptoms and preventing serious complications if taken soon after the onset of the flu.

In review, [*TRANSITION TO CONCLUSION*] I have shown that flu viruses can be hazardous to humans, that combating flu can be difficult because flu viruses easily change, but that catching the flu can be prevented. [*SUMMARY OF MAIN POINTS*] I began with a reference to the 1918 Spanish flu. [*REFERENCE TO THE SPANISH FLU EXAMPLE IN THE INTRODUCTION GIVES CLOSURE TO THE SPEECH*] Author John Barry called the Spanish flu "the deadliest pandemic in history" in his critically acclaimed 2005 book *The Great Influenza.* [*QUOTATION AS ATTENTION-GETTER*] Nobody knows where the Spanish flu virus went or whether it will surface again. Until we find a lasting cure for the flu, we'll have to be vigilant in our effort to prevent this annual plague. [*REFERENCE TO SPEECH TITLE, "THE ANNUAL PLAGUE," MAKES A MEMORABLE FINISH*]

prolonged, standing ovation. The video of his lecture was seen by millions on YouTube (see link at end of chapter), and in 2008, it became a book entitled *The Last Lecture.*

How do you tell an effective story when giving a public speech? When *The Moth Radio Hour* won the prestigious Peabody Award in 2010, the Peabody judges noted: "Storytelling, likely the oldest art, is revered and reinvigorated by this hour for everyday raconteurs" (quoted by Firestone, 2011). The show's website provides several tips for effective oral presentation of stories ("Storytelling Tips, 2015), as do other experts (see Collins & Cooper, 1997; Hendricks et al., 1996)?

First, *choose a story that fits your audience.* A story about a Jewish rabbi and a Catholic priest told to an audience filled with Muslims

Dr. Randy Pausch delivers his "The Last Lecture" before a packed arena at Carnegie Mellon University. Knowing he was dying from pancreatic cancer, Pausch nevertheless displayed great storytelling ability and injected humor throughout his presentation. He joked that he had experienced a near-deathbed conversion—he bought a Macintosh computer.

probably won't resonate. Second, _make sure the story fits your purpose and illustrates a key point_. Don't tell stories just to entertain if they have no relevance. Third, _keep the stories concise_. Don't get bogged down in details that can become confusing or tedious for your listeners or lose sight of the key theme. If a detail sidetracks rather than advances the story, cut it. Fourth, _practice telling your story_. Tell it to friends, to family members, or to anyone who will listen. Fifth, _do not read your story to your listeners_. This is not an essay. You want to sound natural, not artificial. Sixth, _be animated, even visual, when telling a story_. If you're not interested in telling the story, why should your listeners care? Pausch was very engaging because he was unafraid to do pushups, wear a crazy looking Jabberwocky hat, and walk around with fake arrows in his back while lecturing. Seventh, _have an effective beginning and ending_. Grab attention immediately, and end with a bang.

Terry Hershey, is a Protestant minister who for more than two decades has presented enormously popular lectures at the annual Religious Education Congress in Anaheim, California. He tells this story often at this conference to make the point that we learn very early in life to fear making mistakes:

> There's a terrific story about a first-grade Sunday school class. The children were restless and fussy. The teacher, in an attempt to get their attention, said, "Okay kids, let's play a game. I'll describe something to you. And you tell me what it is."
>
> The kids quieted down. "Listen. It's a furry little animal with a big bushy tail, that climbs up trees and stores nuts in the winter. Who can tell me what it is?" No one said anything. The teacher went on. "You are a good Sunday school class. You know the right answer to this question. It's a furry little animal with a big bushy tail, that climbs up trees and stores nuts in the winter." One little girl raised her hand. "Emily?" "Well, teacher," Emily declared, "it sounds like a squirrel to me, but I'll say Jesus." (Hershey, 2000, pp. 100–101)

Unfailingly, when Hershey tells this story, the audience roars with laughter. The story is brief, humorous, fits the audience perfectly because it has religious overtones and a moral, is delivered in an animated style (you had to be there), and is told fluently, as though Hershey has told this story many times.

Terry Hershey is a great storyteller and has clearly practiced the art of telling a narrative. He also has written many inspirational books, each containing numerous stories he's collected over the years. Each of you have stories to tell as well, whether they be personal experiences, stories told to you by parents or relatives or friends, or perhaps those you've seen and heard presented on television, on the Internet, or at Sunday sermons. When you're researching your topic, don't fail to notice clever, amusing, poignant, and powerful stories told by others. You can retell many of these to make a point. "Let me tell you a story" immediately perks up an audience (see Box 14-1 for a comprehensive informative speech).

Visual Aids

I once had a student who realized five minutes before his speech that a visual aid was required for the speaking assignment. I actually saw him open his lunch bag, pour out the contents, take a black marker pen, and quickly sketch a drawing for his visual aid. When he gave his speech and showed his lunch bag drawing, audience members had to stifle their laughter. When discussing visual aids, it's important that you recognize both words in that term. The _visual_ part is necessary, but so is the _aid_ part. You don't choose just anything visual to show during your speech. You choose something that aids your presentation and doesn't invite ridicule or serve as a distraction.

Visual aids should only be used if they serve a clear purpose, and they can accomplish several:

1. _Visual aids clarify difficult points_ or descriptions of complex objects. Showing an object to an audience helps listeners understand. Many topics are truly difficult to describe without a visual aid. Consider the difficulty of using words alone to explain the human anatomy or an internal combustion engine.

2. *Visual aids gain and maintain audience attention.* A riveting image can capture attention during the opening of a speech, reinforcing your words by engaging the visual perception of the audience.

3. *Visual aids enhance speaker credibility.* Presenting impressive statistics in a graph, chart, or table drives home an important point in your speech and improves your credibility.

4. *Visual aids can improve your delivery.* Novice speakers find it difficult to stray from notes or a manuscript, and a good first step toward an extemporaneous delivery (see Chapter 13) is to make reference to a visual aid. When you are showing a visual aid, you move away from reading your speech, and you assume a more natural delivery when you explain your visual aid to your listeners.

5. *Visual aids can be memorable.* Demonstration speeches rely heavily on visual aids. We can remember a magic trick, a martial arts move, the proper way to arrange flowers, or how to decorate wedding cakes when we have seen them demonstrated.

This section explains how to use visual aids competently. Visual aids can and sometimes are used for persuasive or other types of speeches besides informative presentations, but they are most often used for informative speeches. The types of visual aids available and presentational media for the competent use of visual aids also are discussed.

Types: Benefits and Drawbacks

There are several types of visual aids: objects, models, graphs, maps, tables, and photographs. Each has its own advantages and disadvantages as well as strengths and limitations.

OBJECTS

Sometimes there is no substitute for the actual *object* of your speech. For example, giving a speech on playing different types of recorders really requires a demonstration with the musical instruments themselves. "Bass and tenor recorders have very different sounds" just doesn't work if you merely show a photograph of the instruments. You must actually play the recorders.

There are limitations, however, to the use of objects as visual aids. Some objects are too large to haul into a classroom. One student in my class wanted to show how the size of surfboards has changed over the years, so he brought in four different-sized boards. His immediate problem was that his longboard hit the ceiling when placed on its end, punching a hole in the ceiling tiles. Some objects are also impractical to bring to most speaking venues. A speech on building a bullet train in the United States may benefit from a visual aid, but you surely can't drive a real train into a classroom or auditorium.

Some objects are also illegal, dangerous, or potentially objectionable to at least some audience members. One of my students long ago thought it was a good idea to bring in a live marijuana plant he had been cultivating as a "show-and-tell" object. Firearms, poisons, combustible liquids, or sharp objects are dangerous and should be avoided as well. One student wanted to give a speech on "the dangers of pornography." She asked me in advance—thank goodness—if she could bring in explicit pornographic photographs as a visual aid. I nixed her idea. Offending an audience with a visual aid, as abortion protesters often do with graphic pictures of aborted fetuses and PETA has with several of its more famous animal cruelty ad campaigns, can easily backfire and call into question a speaker's credibility and good taste. Simply exercise responsible judgment. Check for rules or laws that could invite trouble before using any visual aid that seems questionable.

Inanimate objects are usually preferable to living, squirming objects. Puppies are unfailingly cute and great attention grabbers, but they are also very difficult to control. A student of mine brought a puppy to class for her speech. The puppy whined, barked, and howled throughout her presentation. At first, it was cute; after five minutes, the audience was thoroughly annoyed. My student ended her speech as the puppy urinated on the classroom carpet.

Some living objects can frighten audience members. A live snake, especially one not in a cage, will make some audience members extremely uneasy, even agitated. One student brought a live tarantula to class and let the spider walk across a table as she presented her

Consider enlarging visual aids to show detail and inform your audience. Large visual aids, such as this gigantic lottery check, garner attention as well.

informative speech. Audience members were transfixed—not by what she was saying but by the hairy creature moving slowly in front of them.

MODELS

When objects relevant to your speech are too large, too small, expensive, fragile, rare, or unavailable, *models* can often act as effective substitutes. A speech on dental hygiene is an apt example. Speakers usually bring in a larger-than-normal plastic model of a human mouth full of teeth. It isn't practical or effective to ask for a volunteer from the audience to open wide so the speaker can show the volunteer's teeth, after all. The teeth will be too small to see well, especially for audience members in the back row. Such a demonstration will also be extremely awkward. The speaker may have to point out tooth decay, gum disease, and fillings in the volunteer's mouth—not something most people want others to notice, much less have spotlighted.

Demonstration speeches on cardiopulmonary resuscitation (CPR) require a model of a person. You can't ask for an audience member to serve as a victim for the demonstration. Pushing forcefully on a person's chest could be dangerous and potentially embarrassing.

GRAPHS

Graphs are visual representations of statistics in an easily understood format. There are several kinds. Figure 14-1 is a *bar graph*. A bar graph

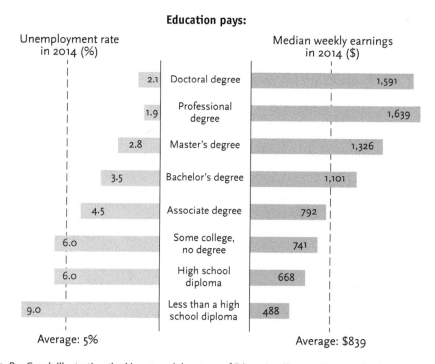

FIGURE 14-1. Bar Graph Illustrating the Monetary Advantage of Education (Source: Bureau of Labor Statistics, 2015).

compares and contrasts two or more items or shows variation over a period of time. Bar graphs can make a dramatic visual impact. Figure 14-2 is a _line graph_. A line graph is useful for showing a trend or change over a period of time. A _pie graph_, as shown in Figure 14-3, depicts a proportion or percentage for each part of a whole.

Graphs are effective if they are uncluttered. Too much information makes a graph difficult for an audience to understand. A graph must be immediately understandable to an audience. More detailed graphs published in print media can be effective because readers can examine the graphs carefully. During a speech, this is neither possible nor desirable

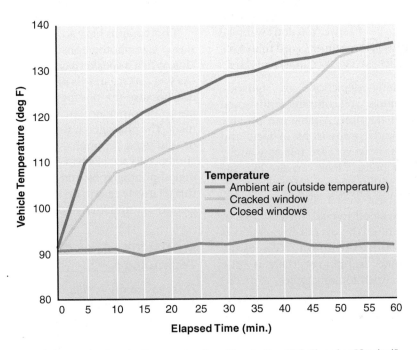

FIGURE 14-2. Line Graph Comparing Interior Temperature Over Time in Cars With Closed or "Cracked" Windows (Source: McLaren et al., 2005).

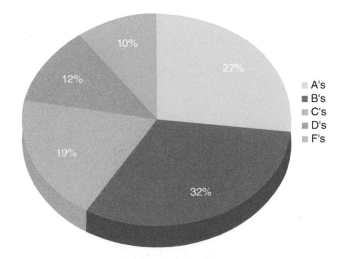

FIGURE 14-3. Pie Graph Depicting the Breakdown of Student Grades in a Public Speaking Class.

MAPS

Maps help audience members see geographic areas, allowing the speaker to make important points. Commercial maps are normally too detailed to be useful as a visual aid for a speech. The most effective maps are large, simple, and directly relevant to the speaker's purpose. Some speakers attempt to draw their own maps, but the proportions and scale of continents, countries, or bodies of water are often badly represented. A map should be exact to be effective. You don't want the United States to look three times bigger than Asia.

TABLES

Tables are orderly depictions of statistics, words, or symbols in columns and rows. Table 14-1 is an example. A table can provide easy-to-understand comparisons of facts and statistics. Tables, however, are not as visually interesting as graphics. Tables can also become easily cluttered with too much information.

Tables will be a visual distraction if the headings are too small to read, the columns or rows are crooked, or the overall impression is that the table was hastily drawn. With readily available computer technology, there is little excuse for amateurish-looking tables.

PHOTOGRAPHS

The many *photographs* included in this textbook underline the effectiveness of this type of visual aid to make a point, clarify a concept, and draw attention. When objects are too big or unwieldy, unavailable, or too fragile to use as visual aids, photographs may serve as effective substitutes. Instead of bringing the wiggling, fussing, barking, and urinating puppy to class, perhaps several photographs of the cute pet will suffice. Instead of violating the law by displaying a real marijuana plant in class, show a (legal) photograph of the plant.

Photographs have some drawbacks. Postage-stamp-size photographs are worthless as visual aids. When a speaker says to his or her audience "As you can see in this photograph," but no one can because the photograph is minuscule, the photo becomes not an aid but an embarrassment. The photograph should be large enough— or enlarged enough—for everyone in the audience to see easily. Fortunately, advances in digital photography and Photoshop have made this relatively easy to do if you have access to the technology and know how to use it.

Media: Simple to Complex Technology

There are many *media*, or means of communicating, with visual aids. Tables or graphs, for example, can appear on chalkboards, posters, PowerPoint slides, Smart Boards, or other

TABLE 14-1   World's Deadliest Earthquakes Last 100 Years

LOCATION	MAGNITUDE	DEATHS
1. Haiti region (2010)	7.0	316,000
2. Tangshan, China (1976)	7.5	255,000
3. Sumatra, Indonesia (2004)	9.1	228,000
4. Haiyuan, China (1920)	7.8	200,000
5. Kanto, Japan (1923)	7.9	143,000
6. Turkmenistan (1948)	7.3	110,000
7. Eastern Sichuan, China (2008)	7.9	88,000
8. Northern Pakistan (2005)	7.6	86,000
9. Chimbote, Peru (1970)	7.9	70,000
10. Western Iran (1990)	7.4	50,000

Source: U.S. Geological Survey (2015).

media. The most frequently used media are discussed here.

CHALKBOARD AND WHITEBOARD: ALL DINOSAURS AREN'T EXTINCT

Every student is familiar with the *chalkboard* or *whiteboard*. Despite their current "dinosaur" reputation, however, chalkboards and whiteboards are a useful visual aid medium when time and resources don't permit more sophisticated media. Every visual aid doesn't have to be delivered electronically. Chalkboards and whiteboards are widely available and allow great flexibility. Tables, drawings, and graphs all can be drawn on them. Lecture material can be outlined. Mistakes can be immediately, and easily, erased.

Chalkboards and whiteboards, however, do have several serious drawbacks. The quality of the table, drawing, or graph is usually inferior. Students are sometimes tempted to draw on a chalkboard or whiteboard during their speech, consuming huge portions of their allotted speaking time creating their visual aid. If a student uses the chalkboard or whiteboard prior to his or her speech, the class waits impatiently while the speaker creates the visual aid. It is too time consuming. Turning to write or draw on the board also breaks eye contact with your audience. Most instructors discourage use of these boards as a visual aid medium for student speakers, but if you become a teacher, the chalkboard and whiteboard, unlike the dinosaurs, likely will have avoided extinction because they are cheap and easy to use.

SMART Boards are advanced, computer-assisted versions of interactive whiteboards with a variety of bells and whistles. They are expensive, and your classroom may not have access to one, but if you do have access, there are a number of tutorials online to help you with using this option (e.g., https://www.youtube.com/watch?v=oGqKNqZf_20).

POSTERS: SIMPLICITY ITSELF

Posters are a very simple medium for visual aids. With technological advancements, however, the simple poster has fallen into relative disuse. Nevertheless, communication, psychology and other academic conferences still include poster presentations.

Making the poster appear professional, however, is a primary challenge. Several guidelines can help. First, *all lettering and numbering should be large enough for anyone in the back of the room to see easily*. Second, *your poster should be neat and symmetrical*. Headings, lettering, and numbering should be even. Letters and numbers should be of the same size or font. Third, *strive for simplicity*. Don't clutter the poster with a collage of pictures that meld into a blob of images unless the assignment requires a collage.

HANDOUTS: AN OLD STANDBY

Handouts are a popular form of visual aid. Tables, maps, drawings, PowerPoint slides, or even photographs can be copied onto a handout. One significant advantage of a handout is that listeners can keep it long after the speech is over, letting it serve as a useful reminder of the information presented.

Handouts have several potential disadvantages, however. Circulating a handout in the middle of your speech wastes time, breaks the flow of the speech, and can be a huge distraction when you try to regain audience attention. If your listeners are busy reading your handout while you're speaking, they will not be attending to your message. You may even be speaking on a different point entirely while audience members are still reading about a previous one on your handout.

If the handout will be an integral part of your presentation, distribute it just prior to giving your speech. Then, if the handout is necessary for explanation of important points throughout your speech, it will not distract but will assist audience members to maintain focus and increase their understanding of your message. A handout can be distributed during a speech if you are lecturing for a long time (an hour or two) and if the handout is vital to a later portion of your presentation. During short speeches (5 to 10 minutes), however, don't distribute a handout in the middle of your presentation. It's too disruptive to the flow of your short speech. A handout with names, email addresses, and phone numbers of organizations or agencies that provide additional information on your subject can be distributed after your speech.

VIDEO EXCERPTS: DVDS, YOUTUBE, AND VISUAL POWER

A video excerpt from a movie, YouTube clip, or a video segment you shot yourself can be a valuable visual aid. Videos can be dramatic, informative, and moving. They often are great attention grabbers. Videos used during a speech, however, have several limitations. First, *the sound on a video will compete with the speaker for attention*. Shut off the sound when you are trying to explain a point while the video is playing unless the video excerpt is very short (30 seconds or less) and sound is essential. (Longer video excerpts with sound may be effective in lengthy presentations.) Second, with its dramatic action, *a video can make your speech seem tame, even dull, by comparison*. It is tough to compete with a Hollywood production. Third, *a video isn't a speech*. There is a real temptation to show a video as a major portion of a speech without any narration or direct reference to it while it is playing.

If you use a video excerpt during your speech, cue it properly ahead of time so that you won't have to interrupt the flow of your presentation looking for the right place to start. Downloading several short excerpts onto a blank DVD is preferable to loading several separate DVDs. Also, downloading any YouTube excerpts onto a blank DVD or thumb drive is less cumbersome and time consuming to set up and use than accessing the YouTube site itself. Most laptops can be connected directly to flat-screen TVs by an HDMI cable, so links to YouTube or other video excerpts can be placed in a file or directory in advance and accessed easily from your computer. YouTube video excerpts should also be embedded into any PowerPoint presentation to avoid interrupting the flow of your speech (go to YouTube and search for "Embed YouTube video"). Typically, use only very short video excerpts (30 seconds) when your speech is relatively short (10 minutes).

Tim Berners-Lee, credited with inventing the World Wide Web, delivered a TED lecture entitled "The Year Open Data Went Worldwide." During his 20-minute lecture, he used slides and brief video excerpts effectively. Since the video excerpts required no sound, he narrated the excerpts, always talking directly to his audience and not to the large video screen behind him. (see *TED Talks and YouTube Links* at end of this chapter)

PROJECTION EQUIPMENT: BLOWING IT UP

There are several options for projecting images onto a large screen. Slide projectors were very common, but they have neared extinction as a visual aid medium, mostly replaced by Power-Point slide presentations. Kodak stopped manufacturing slide projectors in 2004.

Overhead projectors are another type of projector that, despite being an aging technology, continues to be used in some circumstances to display enlarged images. They are still around because they are easy to use, relatively problem free, and a flexible piece of equipment. Transparencies are placed on the overhead projector, enlarging a table, map, picture, graph, or drawing. Transparencies are very simple to prepare. Whatever can be photocopied can be made into a transparency. The relative ease with which this equipment can be used, however, tempts speakers to overdo the number of transparencies shown during a speech. Be careful not to substitute transparencies for an actual speech.

Document cameras, such as the ELMO series, offer advantages similar to those of overhead projectors, but they do not require creating transparencies. Almost any image from a magazine, book, pamphlet, or even a simple object can be projected onto a large screen. The ELMOs can also magnify very small images a hundred-fold, and it allows you to zoom in and out on images. Some versions of this technology have wireless remote control, split-screen, masking, and highlighting capabilities. Becoming familiar with this equipment is essential to using it effectively.

COMPUTER-ASSISTED PRESENTATIONS: POWERPOINT

By now, you should be familiar with the many options available for computer-assisted presentations. *PowerPoint* is probably the most widely available and utilized example of this visual aid medium, although other computer-assisted presentational software options, such as Prezi and SlideRocket, are available. Space constraints do not allow a "how-to" explanation for using any of these options. Several excellent sites on the Internet, however, provide step-by-step instructions (see, e.g., http://www .electricteacher.com/tutorial3.htm *or* http:// www.gcflearnfree.org/powerpoint2013/5).

For relatively short presentations (5 to 10 minutes), this technology may be overkill. If you have critically important slides to show (e.g., pictures of a Southeast Asia trip to illustrate cultural differences), then PowerPoint slides are appropriate. For longer speeches (an hour-long lecture), computer-assisted presentations can be wonderful. The biggest drawbacks are the time it takes to prepare the slides, the potential for glitches to occur during the actual speech (Murphy's Law hides in the shadows), and the tendency to become so enamored with the software capability that it detracts from the speech (see Box 14-2). "PowerPoint presentations are often so poorly executed that they actually obstruct the brain's cognition of the material being presented" (Hoffeld, 2015). You might want to check out award-winning comedian Don McMillan's amusing YouTube presentation "Life After Death by PowerPoint" to see what not to do in this regard (see *TED Talks and YouTube Links* at the end of this chapter).

Consultant Cliff Atkinson (2008), author of *Beyond Bullet Points*, offers several research-based suggestions for improving PowerPoint presentations (see also Reynolds, 2012). Unlike some conventional suggestions, such as the "rule of seven" (no more than seven bulleted lines on a slide or seven words per line), Atkinson translates theory and research on communication into solid advice for improving PowerPoint presentations:

1. *Don't overwhelm listeners with complicated slides.* Text-heavy slides with numerous bullet points (what Atkinson calls the "grocery list approach") that require listeners to read for 10 to 15 seconds or more distract from your speech and are not visually interesting (Reynolds, 2012).

2. *Don't read the slides to your audience,* and do not wait for your listeners to read lengthy slides. This interrupts the flow of your presentation. Research also shows that reading a list of bulleted points diminishes learning the information (Mayer, 2005). Attention fades.

3. *Narrate your PowerPoint slides.* You tell the story that focuses listeners on your main points as you advance your slides. (Reynolds, 2012).

4. *Most slides should have a full-sentence headline at the top with a descriptive graphic (picture) underneath.* Use a full-sentence headline for the same reasons full-sentence outlines work better than word or phrase outlines (see Chapter 12): full-sentence headlines explain the main point, but word or phrase headers only suggest what the point might be. Research shows that full-sentence headlines improve listeners' knowledge and comprehension when compared to sentence fragments or phrase headings (Alley, 2005).

BOX 14-2 FOCUS ON CONTROVERSY

Powerpoint: Lots of Power, Little Point?

The year 2007 marked the 20th anniversary of PowerPoint, "one of the most elegant, most influential and most groaned-about pieces of software in the history of computers" ("PowerPoint Turns 20," 2007, p. B1). Edward Tufte (2003), Yale political scientist and specialist in graphic display of information, wrote an editorial in *Wired* magazine entitled "PowerPoint Is Evil: Power Corrupts, PowerPoint Corrupts Absolutely." Tufte claimed that PowerPoint "elevates format over content,

(continued)

BOX 14-2 FOCUS ON CONTROVERSY

Powerpoint: Lots of Power, Little Point? *(continued)*

betraying an attitude of commercialism that turns everything into a sales pitch." Tufte even suggested that PowerPoint might have played a role in the *Columbia* shuttle disaster because vital technical information was swamped in its glitzy slides and endless bullet points. The report by the Columbia Accident Investigation Board (2003) seemed to agree: "It is easy to understand how a senior manager might read this PowerPoint slide and not realize that it addresses a life-threatening situation." The report then went on to criticize "the endemic use of PowerPoint briefing slides" as a substitute for quality technical analysis. Robert Gaskin and Dennis Austin, the inventors of the software, agree with Tufte's criticisms: "All the things Tufte says are absolutely true. People often make very bad use of PowerPoint" (quoted in "PowerPoint Turns 20," 2007, p. B1).

The heavy reliance on PowerPoint during speeches, or what consultant Nancy Stern (2004) calls "slideswiping" and others call "death by PowerPoint" or "hypnotizing chickens" (Bumiller, 2010), should be discouraged. As Brigadier General. H. R. McMaster, who banned PowerPoint presentations when he led forces in Iraq, notes, "Some problems in the world are not bulletizable" (quoted in Bumiller, 2010). Imagine a bullet point presentation of Martin Luther King's inspiring "I Have a Dream" speech.

"I Have a Dream" (several dreams, actually)—M. L. King

- Dream #1: Nation lives true meaning of "all men created equal"

- Dream #2: Sit down at table of brotherhood
- Dream #3: Mississippi: transformed into oasis of freedom/justice
- Dream #4: My 4 children—judged by content of character, not color of skin
- Dream #5: Alabama: black and white boys/girls become sisters/brothers

This PowerPoint slide drains the vitality from a powerful, beautifully composed speech (Witt & Fetherling, 2009). No one is likely to feel moved to march for freedom after reading this lifeless laundry list of longed for "dreams."

Consider carefully whether multimedia presentations are appropriate and really enhance the content of your presentation. PowerPoint can be very powerful and useful, but only if used effectively (Atkinson, 2008). Too often speakers obsess about font size and choices for animation, which frequently distract an audience's attention, instead of concentrating on developing a quality speech.

If you do use PowerPoint, avoid listing every point in your outline. This is tedious and uninteresting. Remember that the power of PowerPoint is in its ability to make presentations far more interesting than your standard chalkboard or whiteboard listing of main points. When PowerPoint becomes little more than a high-tech version of a chalkboard or overhead transparencies, little is gained by using it. PowerPoint slides should meet the same criteria as visual aids in general (see next section).

Questions for Thought

1. Should PowerPoint be banned so it can't be misused?

2. Is there any technology that can't be misused by someone unskilled?

3. What do you think is the best use of PowerPoint—what can't be presented in a speech nearly as well without using PowerPoint?

5. *Remember that PowerPoint is a visual aid*, so the slides should be visually interesting (Reynolds, 2012). Seven bulleted points are a snooze; a simple but interesting graphic for each slide is not. The **Picture Superiority Effect** based on brain research indicates that when text alone is presented, audience members usually remember only about *10%* of the information three days later. If you combine brief text with relevant, interesting images, however, audience members typically remember about *65%* of the information three days later (Medina, 2014).

6. *Don't get graphic crazy.* As Atkinson (2008) notes, "When you finish the presentation, you want the audience to talk about your special ideas, not your special effects" (p. 323). Heavy use of animation and clever graphics can make the razzle-dazzle memorable but the main points of your speech opaque and unmemorable.

Animation to create humor may be appealing, but only if used infrequently.

7. *Use a remote to advance slides.* Having to press a key on the keyboard chains you to the computer. Either you must stay next to the computer keyboard the entire time, which makes your presentation stilted, or you must keep running back to advance the slides, which can look comical and unprofessional.

[*There are exceptions to every rule, so don't treat these PowerPoint guidelines as absolute requirements.*] A list of bulleted points may be necessary in some circumstances, particularly where a list (e.g., budget categories and numbers or assignments and due dates) is the topic of the presentation. Some photographs or cartoons that need no explanation, or slides that convey easy-to-grasp points, would require no full-sentence header. Atkinson's suggestions are excellent guidelines for using PowerPoint effectively as a wonderful *visual* aid.

Although this slide avoids the bullet point "grocery list" problem, it is a collage, not a simple PowerPoint slide. To exaggerate all that can go wrong with PowerPoint slides, this example has no full-sentence header; the different font sizes, colors, and typefaces are confusing; there are too many pictures to be useful; far too much text is provided, and the extensive text bleeds into images; the tight spacing is difficult to read; and the italics and underlining are not useful because too much is highlighted. "Breath" also should be "breathe."

Guidelines: Aids, Not Distractions

Poorly designed and clumsily presented visual aids will detract, not aid, your speech. Here are some guidelines for the competent use of visual aids.

KEEP AIDS SIMPLE

Complex tables, maps, and graphics can work well in print media, such as magazines and newspapers, where readers can closely examine a visual aid. Listeners, however, do not have the same option. Complex visual aids do not work well for speeches, especially short ones, where the information needs to be communicated clearly and quickly. Your audience will be intent on figuring out a complex visual aid, not listening to you speak. Keep visual aids simple.

MAKE AIDS VISIBLE

The general rule for visual aids is that people in the back of the room or auditorium should be able to see your visual aid easily. If they can't, it is not large enough to be effective. Audience members should not have to strain to see words or numbers. Your audience will quickly grow uninterested in your visual aid if it is not large enough to be easily seen. Effective font size depends on the size of the screen and the room. A huge screen in a large auditorium requires a larger font size for PowerPoint presentations—typically 44 points for headlines, 32 points for main points, and 24 points for subpoints—than a regular-sized classroom (Earnest, 2007). Transparencies or typed sheets shown on an ELMO usually work well in standard classrooms when the font size is between 16 and 20 points.

MAKE AIDS NEAT, ATTRACTIVE, AND ACCURATE

Don't embarrass yourself by showing a visual aid of poor quality. Sloppy drawings, posters, tables, and the like won't suffice. Your visual aids should look neat and attractive, which means taking the time to prepare them well. This includes proofreading your aids before showing them. Misspelled words or grammatical mistakes on PowerPoint slides, posters, charts, or tables scream *carelessness!*" Tea Party protesters in particular have been ridiculed for carrying signs reading "No Pubic Option," "Politians Are Like Dipers: They Need to Be Changed Often," "Get a Brain Morans," and "Crisis of Competnce." (Signs, 2015). The impression created by even a few such misspelled signs has been that Tea Party protesters are uneducated (note the vividness effect produced by stark examples). Yet a *New York Times*/CBS survey of April 14, 2010, shows Tea Party supporters are better educated than the general public (Zernike & Thee-Brenan, 2010). Carelessness kills credibility.

DON'T BLOCK THE AUDIENCE'S VIEW

A very common mistake, one made even by professional speakers, is that they block the audience's view of the visual aid. Standing in front of your poster, graph, drawing, table, or Power-Point slide while you talk to the visual aid, not to your audience, is awkward and self-defeating. You want your audience members to see the visual aid. Audience members should not have to stand and move across the room to see a visual aid, crane their necks, or give up in frustration because a speaker's big pumpkin head is blocking their view. Simply stand beside your poster, drawing, graph, or video excerpt while you explain it to the audience. Point the toes of your shoes toward the audience, and imagine that your feet are nailed to the ground. If you don't move your feet, you will continue to stand beside, not in front of, your visual aid. *Talk to your audience, not to your visual aid.*

KEEP AIDS CLOSE TO YOU

Don't place a visual aid across the room from where you speak. This is particularly problematic when using PowerPoint (Atkinson, 2008). You don't want to split the listeners' attention and create the look of a crowd at a tennis match shifting eye contact back and forth from projection screen to you speaking across the room.

PUT THE AID OUT OF SIGHT WHEN NOT IN USE

Cover your poster or drawing, graph, or photo when not referring to it. Leaving it open to view when you are no longer making reference to it, or showing it before you actually use it, distracts an audience. Atkinson (2008) suggests including blank slides between images on Power-Point slides when you are not referring to them for a while (a minute or more). Shut off

Standing in front of a visual aid and talking to it, not to your audience, are two common mistakes. Speakers need to get their planet-size heads out of the way, stand beside their visual aid, and speak directly to their audience.

the overhead projector or video player when you are finished using the visual aid.

PRACTICE WITH AIDS

Using visual aids competently requires practice. At first, using a visual aid may seem awkward, even unnatural. Once you have practiced your speech using a visual aid, however, it will seem more natural and less awkward. Practice will also help you to work out any problems that might occur before giving your speech for real.

DON'T CIRCULATE YOUR AIDS

Don't pass around photos, cartoons, drawings, objects, or anything that can distract your audience from paying attention to you while you're speaking. If audience members want to see your visual aid again, let them approach you after the speech for a second viewing.

DON'T TALK IN THE DARK

I have had to advise student speakers not to turn off the classroom lights when they are showing video clips during their presentations. When the lights are off, the room becomes so dark that the speaker becomes a disembodied voice. The audience can't see the nonverbal elements of the presentation, and it all comes off as just weird. I've seen professional speakers do the same thing as well. With a huge screen and PowerPoint slides flashing one after the other, the speakers could have merely provided a voice-over recording for the slides, making their actual, physical presence unnecessary. They become "little more than well-educated projectionists whose major role is to control the PowerPoint and video displays projected on the screen" (Nevid, 2011, p. 54). If possible, dim the lights so that slides or video excerpts show more effectively without putting everyone in darkness. If there is no dimmer switch to partially lower the lights, try bringing in a lamp with a low-wattage bulb and lighten the room that way with the main lights switched off. If the room is very large and there is no way to merely dim the lights, try focusing a light on you at a podium so that the audience can at least see you as you speak.

ANTICIPATE PROBLEMS

The more complicated your technology, the greater the likelihood that problems will occur before or during your presentation. Projection bulbs burn out unexpectedly; computers crash; programs won't load. Have a backup plan. If the audience is small (30 or fewer), a hard copy of PowerPoint slides, for example, can be prepared just in case your computer fails. Overhead transparencies of slides also can be prepared if the audience is large. Show up early, and do a quick test to see if all systems are GO! If your easel falls over during your presentation, be prepared with a casual remark to lighten the moment ("Just checking to see if everyone is alert; obviously, I wasn't"). Think about what might go wrong, and anticipate ways to respond appropriately.

 ## Summary

A key difference between informative and persuasive speaking is that informative speeches attempt to teach listeners something new and persuasive speeches, although oftentimes informative, move beyond and attempt to change behavior. There are five types of informative speeches that sometimes overlap during the same presentation: those that report, explain, demonstrate, tell a story, or compare the pros and cons of a proposal without taking a position. Competent informative speaking is achieved by considering your audience when choosing a topic, avoiding information overload, keeping your audience interested, using interesting supporting materials, and telling stories well.

Visual aids must be both visually interesting and an actual aid to your speech. Sloppy, poorly prepared, and poorly selected visual aids can bring you ridicule and embarrassment. Always choose and prepare your visual aids carefully. Visual aids can clarify complicated points, gain and maintain audience attention, enhance your credibility, improve your delivery, and make your information memorable. You have many types of visual aids to choose from, but make sure that you don't become enamored with the technologically sophisticated and glitzy aids when you aren't well versed in their use. If you do, your speech could be diminished by too much flash and not enough substance. Follow the guidelines for using visual aids.

Quizzes Without Consequences

Test your knowledge before your exam! Go to the companion website at www.oup.com/us/rothwell, click on the Student Resources for each chapter, and take the Quizzes Without Consequences.

Film School Case Studies

Dangerous Minds (1995). Drama; R
Michelle Pfeiffer (probably miscast) plays a teacher in an inner-city school. Contrast her informative speaking with that of the Robin Williams character in *Dead Poets Society*. Consider especially differences in audience analysis that are required when comparing the two.

Dead Poets Society (1989). Drama; PG
Robin Williams delivers an effective performance as an English teacher in a private New England prep school. Evaluate his use of the lecture format for informative speaking. Does the Williams character remain informative, or does he move into persuasive territory? Is he proselytizing inappropriately? Is his communication always ethical?

Mona Lisa Smile (2003). Drama; PG-13
Julia Roberts plays a free-spirited professor at staid Wellesley College in the 1950s. Examine the Roberts character and the quality of her audience analysis.

Does her informative speaking mesh well with the Wellesley crowd? Compare the Roberts character to the Robin Williams character in *Dead Poets Society* regarding whether she sticks to informative speaking or crosses the blurry line into proselytizing and persuasion.

TED Talks and YouTube Links

These speeches are offered for you to analyze and perhaps discuss in class. Some are very good examples, and some are problematic. Apply text material in this chapter to each sample speech.

1. *Informative Speech on Strokes and the Brain:* Jill Bolte Taylor, TED Talk, "My Stroke of Insight" http://www.ted.com/talks/jill_bolte_taylor_s_powerful_stroke_of_insight

2. *Using Video Excerpts and PowerPoint Slides:* Tim Berners-Lee, TED Talk, "The Year Open Data Went Worldwide" http://www.ted.com/talks/tim_berners_lee_the_year_open_data_went_worldwide.html).

3. *Using PowerPoint effectively:* Garr Reynolds (2012), author of *Presentation Zen*, TED https://www.youtube.com/watch?v=zQpGf1gPY7M).

4. *PowerPoint-Less:* Don McMillan, "Life After Death by PowerPoint" https://www.youtube.com/watch?v=MjcO2ExtHso

5. Randy Pausch, "The Last Lecture" https://www.youtube.com/watch?v=ji5_MqicxSo

BY THE END OF THIS CHAPTER, YOU SHOULD BE ABLE TO:

1. Understand the relationship between attitudes and behavior.

2. Identify the principal goals of persuasion.

3. Distinguish between peripheral and central processing of persuasive messages.

Persuasive Speaking

IT WAS the 60th annual convention of the California Federation of Teachers. Keynote speaker Charles Kernaghan, director of the National Labor Committee, was addressing an audience of California teachers. His central idea (theme) was that extreme poverty of much of the world's workforce accrues from economic globalization and the exploitation of workers. His speech was a rousing anti-sweatshop call to arms. Kernaghan held up garments produced overseas, and he told stories about the exploitation of workers who made these garments, most of whom are between the ages of 6 and 16. Referring to a Nike document from the Dominican Republic, he noted: "There are 22 steps to the production of a T-shirt, which in total take 6.6 minutes, or 11% of an hour's labor. The worker gets 8 cents for that time—0.3% of the retail price. Advertising that same shirt costs them $2.32. They spend 32 times more on branding (brand identification) than they do on the worker" (quoted in "Anti-sweatshop

4. Use competent persuasive speaking strategies.

Activist," 2002, p. 4). He argued that young people "have a right to ask, how do the people live who produce the clothes they wear?" (p. 4). Kernaghan discussed the Students Against Sweatshops movement in the United States and its hundreds of chapters on college campuses. The audience cheered when he thundered, "These kids are on fire!" Kernaghan brought his listeners to their feet when he concluded, "There can never be peace without social justice, or in a world with child labor" (p. 4).

Kernaghan's speech was masterful and an enormous success. "Of all the speakers at the 60th annual convention, none stirred delegates as deeply as Charles Kernaghan" (p. 4). His speech was successful for several reasons. First, *the CFT convention had social justice as one of its prime themes.* Kernaghan's keynote address was well suited to this theme. As members of a powerful teachers union, listeners were receptive to his message that nonunion workers can be—and are—exploited as "cheap labor." Note, however, that this same speech would likely trigger a much less favorable reaction from an audience composed of Chamber of Commerce members or small-business owners who depend on selling inexpensive clothing to stay competitive in a tough business climate. Second, *he evidently researched his topic* very carefully. He had the facts to support his claims. Third, *he used very effective attention strategies.* His speech was not a dry recitation of facts and figures. It was a passionate presentation that was at times intense, startling, and vital in its depiction of the plight of garment workers in countries around the world; it aroused anger at injustice. He told stories about young women he interviewed who worked in deplorable sweatshop conditions for a $1.38 a day after expenses. Fourth, *he ended with a rousing appeal* to stamp out exploitation of workers worldwide.

Possessing the persuasive knowledge and skills demonstrated by Kernaghan has practical significance. Lawyers, counselors, managers, administrators, salespersons, and public relations specialists are required to speak persuasively in our culture. News networks interview individuals every day who engage in persuasive speaking before the cameras. Most talk shows display persuasive speaking from panelists and audience members, although many persuasive attempts are dismal efforts by unskilled and untrained speakers. Several "people's court" television programs show average citizens defending themselves in small claims cases.

Almost 2,500 years ago, Aristotle systematically discussed persuasion in his influential book *Rhetoric.* The scientific study of persuasion, however, began less than a century ago in the United States. Much has been learned from this research on persuasion, with many useful insights gained. Capitalizing on this research and insight, *the primary purpose of this chapter is to explain how you can construct and present a competent persuasive speech.* The foundations of persuasion are discussed first, followed by specific persuasion strategies for public speaking that flow from an understanding of the foundations.

Foundations of Persuasion

Persuasion is a communication process of converting, modifying, or maintaining the attitudes and/or behavior of others. An **attitude** is "a learned predisposition to respond favorably or unfavorably toward some attitude object" (Gass & Seiter, 2011, p. 42). "The iPhone is better than the Droid phone" is an attitude, and so is "Consistency requires you to be as ignorant today as you were a year ago" (Bernard Berenson). An attitude sets our mind to draw certain judgments.

In this section, the relationship between persuasion and coercion, attitude change and behavior change, the goals of persuasion, the elaboration likelihood model that explains how persuasion works generally, and the influence of culture on persuasion are discussed.

Coercion Versus Persuasion: Choice

Although much effort to persuade audiences is aimed at attitude change, the behavior of others can also be altered without a change in attitude. Threats of violence may produce behavioral change without attitude change. Forced compliance from threats of physical harm, damage to one's reputation, financial ruin, and the like, however, are usually seen as coercion, not persuasion.

So what is the difference? *The essential difference between coercion and persuasion is the perception of free choice* (O'Keefe, 2016; Perloff, 2013). Those who coerce seek to eliminate choice by force, threats of force, or intimidation with consequences that are contrary to a person's preference. Those who persuade seek to convince a person by using logical and emotional appeals, not threats, force, and intimidation. Logical and emotional appeals can influence your listeners, but your listeners are still free to choose what to believe and how to behave. *Persuasive speaking is a communication process of convincing through open and honest means.* When your listeners can choose for themselves which attitude to accept or which behavior to perform, they are in charge of their decision making. If your listeners refuse to pay attention to your speech, ignore your persuasion effort, or do not heed your advice or plea, your persuasive speaking simply fails.

Attitude-Behavior Consistency: Variables

Although attitudes often predict behavior, there isn't always a consistent relationship between the two (Perloff, 2013). For example, most Americans think the Ten Commandments should guide our lives (we embrace them as strong attitudes—e.g., killing is wrong, coveting is bad, and stealing is immoral). Yet everyone violates at least some of the commandments as though they were merely the Ten Suggestions. Thus, our behavior doesn't always match our attitudes.

Changing attitudes very often is not sufficient. It is behavior that needs to change. Consider the abstinence-only programs to prevent premarital sex among teenagers. Despite a vigorous campaign to convince teenagers to take a public pledge to abstain from premarital sex, a careful analysis of data reveals that, within a five-year period, those who took the "virginity pledge" were just as likely as nonpledgers to have premarital sex, but they were less likely to use birth control (Rosenbaum, 2009). If a principal purpose of abstinence-only programs is to prevent teen pregnancy and the many problems associated with it, then this study's results are quite disheartening. The pledge (stated attitude) doesn't produce the desired behavior. There are ways to strengthen abstinence-only persuasive efforts (see Jemmott et al., 2010), but inducing teens to make public pledges of abstinence is, by itself, unlikely to produce the desired result.

Several variables affect how consistent our attitudes and behaviors are likely to be. These are *direct experience, social pressure,* and *effort required*.

DIRECT EXPERIENCE: NO SECONDHAND ATTITUDES

Attitudes that are formed from direct experience usually conform more closely to actual behavior than those formed more indirectly (Perloff, 2013). When you have encountered a problem in your life, thought about it, felt its implications, and considered appropriate responses, your relevant

Attitudes and behavior are not always consistent. Thus, changing an attitude will not necessarily change a behavior.

attitude has been formed through direct experience. Have you ever been unemployed, experienced poverty, or had to solicit money from strangers? Have you ever been a small-business owner worried about high taxes jeopardizing your ability to thrive or even just survive? That's direct experience. Your attitudes about food stamps for the poor, unemployment benefits, and business taxation are likely influenced strongly by these directly related experiences. Your behavior toward those similarly disadvantaged is more apt to coincide with these attitudes than if you have only indirect experience of such things.

Those attitudes that are shaped more indirectly by media images, what friends and others have told you, or by your participation in discussions on blogging sites tend to be inconsistently related to behavior. These "secondhand attitudes" (Gass & Seiter, 2011) derived from indirect experience usually serve as weak predictors of behavior because, when faced with actual situations, the attitudes are more borrowed than personal. For example, it's far easier to ignore panhandlers begging for money when you've never had the desperate, frightening experience of joblessness and homelessness. Directly formed attitudes derived from personal experience are also likely to be more strongly held than secondhand attitudes.

[These strong attitudes are more likely to predict behavior than weakly held, borrowed attitudes] (Wallace et al., 2005). For instance, you may steadfastly avoid drinking alcohol because you have experienced firsthand what alcoholism can do to a family. Perhaps a parent was an alcoholic, became abusive, and provoked constant discord that eventually led to divorce. In this case, your attitude about alcohol has been formed directly through personal experience, and your attitude about the dangers of alcoholism is strongly held. If, however, your attitude about alcohol is mostly formed indirectly, such as from watching public service announcements on the dangers of alcohol, and is only weakly held, then when prodded to drink by friends and peers, you may cave under the pressure more easily. The more directly you can make your audience feel that they are affected by the problem you describe (e.g., general state budget cuts threaten your access to higher education), the greater is the chance that their behavior will move in the direction you desire (e.g., support tax increases).

SOCIAL PRESSURE: HEAT FROM OTHERS

Social pressure has been shown to be a very strong influence on human behavior. In 2015, the drought emergency in California prompted Governor Jerry Brown to set a statewide water conservation target of 25%. California consumers, however, surpassed this goal by May of that year, dropping water usage by 29%. A principal reason for the significant drop was social pressure (Krieger & Mattson, 2015). If your lawn is green when your neighbors have let theirs go brown from lack of water, you become a social pariah.

Social pressure is a significant reason that your attitudes and behavior may be inconsistent at times (Wallace at al., 2005). Your attitude may be that a green lawn is beautiful and desirable, but your neighbors' verbal or nonverbal communication may signal that you need to "get down with brown." As a result, you stop watering your lawn to avoid social disapproval. You may want to speak up when someone makes a racist or sexist remark, but you may remain quiet if you fear social disapproval from others for being a "troublemaker." Social pressure and fear of disapproval make standing before an audience and giving a speech that you know will incite a negative reaction very challenging.

EFFORT REQUIRED: MAKE IT EASY

Despite the best intentions, attitudes and behavior will often be inconsistent because consistency may require too great an effort to perform the behavior (Wallace et al., 2005). You will likely see recycling your cans, bottles, and newspapers as too labor intensive if you have to separate each item into separate bins, load them into the trunk of your car, then drive to the nearest recycling center to unload the waste. Increasingly, however, communities around the country are recognizing the benefits of curbside recycling. Participation in recycling programs grows explosively when it is no more difficult than

hauling a trash bin out in front of your home. More than half the U.S. population had access to curbside recycling by 2014 ("2014 National Recycling Survey," 2014), and actual participation rates in available curbside recycling programs are often very high (Catala, 2015; Scheer & Moss, 2012).

When trying to persuade an audience to act on a problem, find the easiest ways for listeners to express their support. Signing a petition or donating a dollar on the spot are two examples. Asking people to canvass neighborhoods, to call strangers on the phone to solicit support for a cause or a candidate, or to raise money for a program. however, is hampered by the effort required to perform the behavior. Far less participation in such activities should be expected as a result.

Consider how Sean McLaughlin (1996), a student at Ohio University, offers simple yet effective solutions for the problem of food poisoning:

> First, wash hands well and wash them often . . . If you prefer to use sponges and dishcloths, be sure to throw them in the dishwasher two or three times a week. Also, try color coding your sponges—the red one for washing dishes and a blue one for wiping up countertops . . . Experts also suggest using both sides of a cutting board—one side for meats and the other side for vegetables. And those who wash dishes by hand, be careful. Scrub dishes vigorously with an antibacterial soap and rinse with hot water. Air drying is preferred to drying with a towel . . . Finally, and perhaps the best advice—don't become lax when it comes to food safety in your home. Don't write your congressperson, write your mom. As we have seen today, re-educating yourself and spreading the word on kitchen safety can significantly reduce chances of food poisoning. (p. 75)

This speaker provides several easy steps that will protect you from food poisoning. One step, air drying dishes, actually reduces labor as well. Towel drying requires effort; air drying requires merely waiting.

Solutions to serious problems cannot always be simple and easy to implement. Nevertheless, try to offer ways that even complex solutions can be implemented in relatively simple, straightforward steps.

Goals of Persuasion

Persuasive speaking can have several goals: *conversion, modification*, and *maintenance*. Choosing the appropriate goal for the situation will largely determine your degree of success or failure.

CONVERSION: RADICAL PERSUASION

Psychologist Muzafer Sherif and his associates (1965) developed the **social judgment theory** of persuasion to explain attitude change (see also Littlejohn & Foss, 2011). This theory states that when listeners hear a persuasive message, they compare it with attitudes they already hold. The preexisting attitude on an issue serves as an **anchor**, or reference point. Surrounding this anchor is a range of possible attitudes an individual may hold. Positions a person finds tolerable form the **latitude of acceptance**. Positions that provoke only a neutral or ambivalent response form the **latitude of noncommitment**. Those positions the person would find objectionable because they are too far from the anchor attitude form the **latitude of rejection**. Figure 15-1 depicts this range of possible opinions on an issue.

Research found that when persuasive messages fall within a person's latitude of rejection, they almost never produce a change in attitude (Sherif et al., 1965). The further away a position is from the anchor attitude, the less likely persuasion will be successful (Littlejohn & Foss, 2011; Sherif et al., 1973). This is especially true when the listener has high ego involvement

with the issue. **Ego involvement** refers to the degree to which an issue is relevant or important to a person. Students who work hard for a political candidate, for example, are highly unlikely to vote for the opponent.

Social judgment theory strongly suggests that setting conversion as your goal for persuasion is usually unrealistic. Conversion asks your listeners to move from their anchor position to a completely contradictory one. This is especially unlikely when conversion is sought during a brief persuasive speech. Students often make the attempt to convert the "unbelievers" in speeches on abortion, religion, and other emotionally charged topics. Such efforts are doomed from the start. If your message seeks conversion from your audience, it will likely meet with quick resistance, especially if these listeners have strongly formed attitudes on the subject.

Unless a *significant emotional event* occurs, conversion almost never happens from a single persuasive attempt. Hearing a 10-minute persuasive speech, no matter how eloquent, rarely converts anyone holding strong views. If, however, you have been a strong advocate of gun control but experience a home invasion in which your life and those of your loved ones were threatened, then you may think seriously about purchasing a gun for future protection. Absent such an emotional event, however, conversion from strong gun control advocate to a defender of relatively unrestricted gun ownership is unlikely. Conversion, then, is an unrealistic goal for most persuasive speeches.

MODIFICATION: DON'T ASK FOR THE MOON

Research suggests that moderate, not extreme, positions relative to a particular audience are

Strongly Agree	Agree	Indifferent	Disagree	Strongly Disagree
Anchor	**Latitude of Acceptance**	**Latitude of Noncommitment**		**Lat. of Rejection**
College should be free	Minimal tuition & fees can be charged.	Public colleges should be supported by taxes		Students should pay entire cost or students should pay at least 75% of cost

FIGURE 15-1. Social Judgment Theory.

most persuasive (Edwards & Smith, 1996; Rhodes, 2015). Positions that lie at the outer fringes of a listener's latitude of acceptance may become the new anchor position as a result of a persuasive speech. For example, very restrictive gun control legislation may be a person's anchor. A strong persuasive speech, however, may realistically modify this person's position to an outright ban on handguns. Once this position is embraced, it may become the new anchor. Subsequent persuasive efforts may move the anchor incrementally until the person eventually accepts a complete ban on ownership of *all* guns. The change in attitude occurs bit by bit; it is rarely a one-shot effort. Modification of attitudes and behavior is an appropriate, realistic goal for a persuasive speech.

MAINTENANCE: KEEP 'EM COMING BACK

When most people think of persuasion, changing attitudes and behavior immediately comes to mind. Much persuasion, however, does not aim to produce change. Charles Kernaghan's speech to the CFT was mostly "preaching to the choir." Few in that audience of active labor organizers and members would have disagreed with much of what Kernaghan said in his rousing oration. Preaching to the choir, however, can inspire the faithful, energize believers, and reinforce preexisting attitudes.

Most advertising of well-established products, such as Coke or the Toyota Camry, for example, aims to *maintain*, not change, the buying habits of the public. The goal is to keep consumers purchasing your products over and over and to prevent purchases of competing products. In political campaigns, initial persuasion is usually aimed at "securing the base." This means motivating Democrats to keep voting for Democratic candidates and Republicans to keep voting for Republican candidates. The message is "do what you've been doing." Sunday sermons usually change few minds because most people who attend a church service require no such change. They already believe the religious dogmas articulated by the minister, priest, or rabbi.

Part of maintaining the current attitudes and behavior of your audience, however, is inducing resistance to **counterpersuasion**, or attacks from an opposing side. There are two principal ways you can induce resistance to counterpersuasion: forewarning and counterarguing (Compton & Ivanov, 2012).

Forewarning your audience members that an attempt to change their attitudes or behavior will occur creates a sense of threat. Prosecution and defense attorneys often use forewarning in their opening statements to juries, such as "The defense will try to appeal to your emotions by presenting her client as a desperate father attempting to save his dying child. Don't be fooled. The defendant is a cold, calculating murderer." Here there is a threat of releasing a dangerous killer. Forewarning gives your listeners time to generate arguments that thwart attempted persuasion and to rehearse their responses (Gass & Seiter, 2011).

Counterarguing means exposing your listeners to a weakened version of opposing arguments and then refuting them. Studies aimed at preventing teenagers from starting to smoke cigarettes found that merely mentioning arguments for smoking (e.g., smoking is cool and peers will like you) and then refuting these weakly presented arguments induced resistance to peer persuasion to start smoking (Pfau & Van Bockern, 1994). In fact, substantial evidence shows that both forewarning and refutation of weakened opposing arguments can effectively induce resistance to counterpersuasion (Compton & Ivanov, 2012; Pfau et al., 2005).

Elaboration Likelihood Model: Mindful or Mindless Persuasion

The **elaboration likelihood model** of persuasion is an overarching explanation for how listeners cope with the bombardment of persuasive messages by sorting them into those that are important, or central, and those that are less relevant, or peripheral (Petty & Cacioppo, 1986a, 1986b). The *central route* requires mindfulness; the content of the message is scrutinized for careful reasoning and substantial, credible evidence. Counterarguments are considered and weighed. Questions come to mind, and a desire for more information (elaboration) emerges. The *peripheral route* is relatively mindless; little attention is given to processing a persuasive message. The listener looks for mental shortcuts to make quick decisions about seemingly peripheral issues. Credibility, likability, and attractiveness of a persuader, how other people react to the message, and the consequences that might result from agreeing or disagreeing with the persuader are some of the shortcuts used in the peripheral route (Shadel et al., 2001).

To illustrate the two routes to persuasion, consider an example offered by Gass and Seiter (2011). Let's say that Michael and Maria are on a date and about to order dinner at a nice restaurant. The waiter suggests several specials, all of them meat or fish. He even volunteers which one is his favorite. Ordering first, Maria is very careful to choose only vegetarian dishes from the menu. She asks the waiter numerous questions. Is an entrée cooked in animal fat? Is there any butter on the pasta? Does the sauce contain any dairy products? After ordering, Maria turns to Michael and says with an animated delivery that he should eat vegetarian because it is healthier and reduces animal deaths. Michael has no strong opinion on the subject, but he is very attracted to Maria. He tells the waiter, "I'll have what she ordered." Maria used the central route to decide her order. She was very mindful of her decision. She considered her decision carefully because it was important to her. Michael, on the other hand, used the peripheral route. The decision was relatively unimportant to him, so he based his order on a cue unrelated to the menu, the waiter's preference, or the arguments offered by his date. He ordered vegetarian because he hoped to gain favor with Maria.

Your listeners use both central and peripheral routes, called **parallel processing**, when presented with persuasive messages (Petty et al., 1987). They tend to use one route more than the other, however. The degree to which a receiver emphasizes the central or peripheral route depends primarily on the person's *motivation* and *ability* to think about and carefully assess the quality of a persuasive message (Petty et al., 2004). We are more motivated to use the central route when the issues affect us personally. We are more likely to use the peripheral route when issues seem tangential to our interests, are largely inconsequential to our lives, our knowledge of a subject is limited, and we are distracted or preoccupied. If you were

Michael in the situation described, you are motivated to please your date, not to learn about vegetarianism. Your knowledge of issues related to vegetarianism is superficial at best, and you are distracted by your attraction to Maria. It's a wonder you can think at all.

Also, some persuasive messages are too complex and require technical knowledge to evaluate. In such cases, our ability to use central processing is limited. Typically, peripheral cues, such as how other audience members respond to the messages, will be used.

Attitude change produced by the central route tends to be more persistent, resistant to change, and predictive of behavior than attitude change produced by the peripheral route (Petty et al., 2004). If Michael never again went on another outing with Maria, he probably would eat dead cow flesh with relish because his flirtation with vegetarianism was arrived at by peripheral influences.

Clearly, *central processing of persuasive messages should be encouraged*. Central processing is what skeptics do primarily when presented with a persuasive message (see Chapter 6). You can increase central processing by making issues relevant to listeners' lives. Complex, technical issues can be simplified for lay audiences. If listeners understand the basic concepts, they can analyze the arguments and evidence presented. Even highly involved listeners, however, will use parallel processing. Because of time constraints and information overload, we sometimes have no choice but to use peripheral processing. Persuasive strategies that typically trigger parallel processing will be discussed later.

Culture and Persuasion: A Question of Values

The scientific investigation of persuasive speaking is a peculiarly Western interest. In Asian countries, for instance, spirited debates to influence decision making have been viewed as relatively pointless. Debates create friction and disharmony, and they usually end inconclusively (Jaffe, 1998). Japan, for example, began implementing a jury-style system in its criminal courts in 2009 (Kawatsu, 2009). This is a momentous change from the long-standing practice of judges making decisions in criminal cases. To acclimate a hesitant populace to the new system, 500 mock trials were held. Nevertheless, 80% of Japanese surveyed about the new jury system expressed dread at the prospect of participating. Japanese reluctance emerges from a deeply rooted cultural revulsion to expressing personal opinions, arguing with others in public, and questioning authority (Onishi, 2007).

Persuasion works best when it is adapted to the cultural context. Persuasive strategies that may successfully change attitudes and behavior in an individualistic country, such as the United States. may not be so successful in collectivist countries (Murray-Johnson et al., 2001). A survey cited in Chapter 3 showed clearly that respondents from the United States highly valued individual rights but not an orderly society; respondents from Asian, collectivist countries expressed opposite preferences (Simons & Zielenziger, 1996). Thus, appeals to order should be more persuasive in collectivist cultures, and appeals to individual rights should be more persuasive in individualist cultures.

One study examined slogans used in magazines for their cultural persuasiveness (Han & Shavitt, 1994. Slogans such as the following were considered:

1. The art of being unique.
2. We have a way of bringing people closer together.
3. She's got a style all her own.
4. The dream of prosperity for all of us.
5. A leader among leaders.
6. Sharing is beautiful.

Which of these slogans do you think would work best in individualist cultures, and which would work best in collectivist cultures? When comparing the United States and Korea, it was found that slogans like the first, third, and fifth were used more in the United States and were more persuasive than the others. These three slogans appeal to individual success, personal benefits, and independence. Slogans like the second, fourth, and sixth were used more in Korea and were more persuasive than the

others. They appeal to group harmony, cooperation, and collective benefit.

Clearly, your choice of persuasive strategies should be influenced by the diversity of your audience. It is only one element of the complex persuasion equation, but it is an important one.

Persuasive Speaking Strategies

Suppose you plan to give a speech convincing your listeners that poor signage is a serious problem warranting a strong solution. You might begin this way:

"Drop Your Pants Here and You Will Receive Prompt Attention" says the sign outside a dry cleaners. "Kids with Gas Eat Here Free" says another. "Hidden Entrance" reads a third sign. They can be funny, but signs are a critical element of our everyday transit from place to place. Signs such as "Soft Shoulder, Blind Curves, Steep Grade, Big Trucks, Good Luck!" warn us of impending dangers with a touch of humor, but poor signage is no laughing matter. An April 2008 study by psychologists Oliver Clark and Simon Davies from the University of Hull presented at the British Psychological Society conference even found that too many signs bunched together can cause accidents. Poor signage shouldn't be life threatening. Therefore, Congress should mandate that all public signs receive advanced governmental approval for clarity, simplicity, and accuracy.

This opening tries to persuade an audience by using humor, appealing to fear, and presenting evidence. These are but three ways that a speaker can attempt to persuade an audience. Their effectiveness is not sure fire, however, because they must be used under the right conditions. Consideration of all possible persuasive speaking strategies would require a lengthy book. In this section, significant, often used persuasion strategies and conditions that make them most likely to be effective are the focus.

Establish Identification: Connecting With Your Audience

Identification is the affiliation and connection between speaker and audience. Finding commonalities that resonate with audience members can move you beyond perceived initial differences in attitudes, beliefs, and values (de Graaf et al., 2012).

LIKABILITY: I CAN RELATE TO YOU

A key element of identification is *likability* of the speaker. Even when your audience is composed of highly diverse members, people are more inclined to listen if they grow to like you. Compliance and assent on controversial positions are more probable if you are liked than if you are not (Perloff, 2013).

How do you enhance likability? Praising and complimenting your audience ("This class did better on the exam than any previous one"), saying you like your audience ("What a great group"), and expressing genuine concern and showing empathy for problems and pain faced by audience members enhance likability (Cialdini, 1993). Using humor that doesn't offend improves likability (Covin, 2011). Telling stories well is also very effective. Substantial research shows that storytelling promotes **social cohesion**—it binds us together in mutual liking (Hogan, 2003). "Storytelling is one of the few human traits that are truly universal across culture and through all of known history" (Hsu, 2008, p. 46). An audience can be highly diverse, but who doesn't love a great story and like the person who tells it well? Both Ann Romney and Michelle Obama used a storytelling, or narrative, style when delivering their speeches to the Republican and Democratic conventions, respectively, in 2012. Both were highly personal narratives about their husbands. Both speeches were generally regarded, especially by less partisan commentators, as effective and well-received presentations.

Likability alone, of course, may not be enough to move audience members to change their attitudes and behavior. Likability is just one of a complex set of variables that influence others, and it may be less influential than the credibility of you, the speaker (O'Keefe, 2016).

STYLISTIC SIMILARITY: LOOKING AND ACTING THE PART

We tend to identify more closely with individuals who appear similar to us. One way to appear similar is to look and act the part, which is called **stylistic similarity**. For example, when you go for a job interview, you should dress, look, and speak as an interviewer would expect from someone worthy of the job. Showing up in baggy pants and a T-shirt emblazoned with an imprint of your favorite rock band when applying for a teaching job, for example, likely won't work in your favor. Throwing in an occasional verbal obscenity during a teaching demonstration also probably won't endear you to an interview panel.

When the situation is formal, such as a valedictory speech at a graduation ceremony, dress and speak formally. Avoid slang and offensive language. When the situation is less formal, such as some classroom speeches, country fair presentations, many protest marches, and public gatherings, however, you need to shift styles and speak, dress, and act more casually so your audience can relate to you.

Finding the appropriate level of formality can be tricky when the situation doesn't call for a clear-cut choice. For example, as a student, how do you respond to your instructor dressing formally, insisting you address him or her as "Professor" or "Doctor" so and so, and being required to always raise your hand to be recognized before speaking? Would you relate better if your instructor were more casual, or do you appreciate the formality? A *formal style* communicates seriousness of intent and significance of the event. An *informal style* communicates less seriousness, perhaps even playfulness, and sets a more casual atmosphere that encourages student participation. Your style needs to match your expectations and goals, just as teachers make choices about formality or informality based on their goals for the class.

In June 2009, comedian Stephen Colbert exhibited the power of stylistic similarity in producing identification with an audience when he took *The Colbert Report* to Iraq and performed four shows for the troops. He dubbed the series of shows *Operation Iraqi Stephen: Going Commando*. To great applause and laughter from the assembled troops, Colbert marched on stage dressed in a camouflage business suit and tie. He also had his head shaved by General Ray Odierno to exhibit solidarity with the soldiers. The crowd roared its approval. One soldier, Ryan McLeod, remarked afterward, "Definitely the highlight was seeing him sacrifice his hair." Later, Colbert declared, "By the power vested in me by basic cable, I officially declare we have won the Iraq War" (quoted in Baram, 2009).

SUBSTANTIVE SIMILARITY: ESTABLISHING COMMON GROUND

Highlighting similarities in positions, values, and attitudes also encourages identification. This **substantive similarity** creates identification by establishing common ground between speaker and audience. If listeners can say, "I like what I'm hearing," they can identify with the speaker. If you're speaking to a contrary audience, it is helpful to build bridges by pointing out common experiences, perceptions, values, and attitudes before launching into more delicate areas of disagreement. Listeners will be more inclined to consider your more controversial viewpoints if they initially identify with you.

Appealing to broadly accepted rights and values also works well to create identification. As Lawrence Harrison (2000) notes, based on a paraphrase of several clauses in the United Nations Universal Declaration of Human Rights: "The vast majority of the planet's people would agree with the following assertions: life is better than death, health is better than sickness, liberty is better than slavery, prosperity is better than poverty, education is better than ignorance, and justice is better than injustice" (p. xxvi). Here is your common ground. As Secretary of State, Hillary Clinton made such appeals in a December 6, 2011, speech in Geneva, Switzerland, to celebrate International Human Rights Day: "It is a violation of human rights when people are beaten or killed because of their sexual orientation." She continued, "Violence toward women isn't cultural; it's criminal. Likewise with slavery, what was once justified as sanctioned by God is now properly reviled as an unconscionable violation of human rights." She also noted, "Combating Islamophobia or anti-Semitism is a task for people of all faiths" (Clinton, 2011).

Stephen Colbert's head shaving and camouflage suit created a strong identification with his audience of American soldiers in Iraq.

All elements of identification interact in complex ways. Being likable alone does not necessarily sway listeners. Exhibiting similarities with audience members can be attractive to listeners, but stylistic similarity may be negated by substantive dissimilarity. Nevertheless, working to identify with your audience is an important part of the persuasive process.

Build Credibility: Can We Believe You?

O'Keefe (2016) defines **credibility** as "judgments made by a perceiver (e.g., a message recipient) concerning the believability of a communicator." In *Rhetoric*, Aristotle identified the ingredients of credibility, or **ethos** in his terminology, as "good sense, good moral character, and good will." Recent research affirms Aristotle's observation and expands the list of dimensions somewhat. The primary dimensions of credibility are *competence, trustworthiness, dynamism, and composure* (Gass & Seiter, 2011; Pornpitakpan, 2004). All four are developed throughout your speech.

NASA astronaut Joan Higginbotham has credibility working for her the moment she begins addressing an audience on her area of expertise—the space program. Higginbotham was the third African American woman in space, and she actively participated in 53 space shuttle launches.

COMPETENCE: KNOWLEDGE AND EXPERIENCE

Competence refers to the audience's perception of the speaker's knowledge and experience on a topic. It addresses the question "Does this speaker know what he or she is talking about?" You can enhance your credibility when you identify your background, experience, and training relevant to a subject. Citing sources of evidence used, speaking fluently, and avoiding vocal fillers (e.g., *uhm, ah, like,* and *you know*) also enhance credibility (O'Keefe, 2016).

TRUSTWORTHINESS: HONESTY MATTERS

Trustworthiness refers to how truthful or honest we perceive the speaker to be. It addresses the question "Can I believe what the speaker says?" We don't feel comfortable hiring a dishonest plumber, electrician, or carpenter. We hesitate to buy anything from a salesperson we perceive to be dishonest. Likewise, we probably won't believe a speaker we don't find trustworthy.

One way to increase your trustworthiness is to argue against your self-interest (Pratkanis & Aronson, 2001). If you take a position on an issue that will cost you money, a job, a promotion, or some reward or benefit, most listeners will see you as presenting an honest opinion. In 2012, billionaire Warren Buffett advocated higher taxes for the wealthy. He received accolades when he noted that his tax rate was lower than his secretary's and argued that this was wrong. Trying to capitalize on Buffett's credibility in this instance, Barack Obama, in his 2012 State of the Union speech, referred to his own proposal to correct this claimed inequity in the tax code as the "Buffett Rule."

DYNAMISM: FEEL THE POWER

Dynamism refers to the enthusiasm, energy, and forcefulness exhibited by a speaker. Sleepy, lackluster presentations lower your credibility. Over-the-top enthusiasm, however, can be equally problematic. Those who pitch products on infomercials are invariably enthusiastic, sometimes bordering on frenzied. Howard Dean killed his presidential campaign in 2004 when, after a disappointing showing in the Iowa caucuses, he gave what political pundits labeled his "I Have a Scream" speech while trying to whip up enthusiasm from his disappointed supporters. As his vocal volume escalated, he seemed almost maniacal.

Former Michigan governor Jennifer Granholm's 2012 speech before the Democratic National Convention reminded some of Dean's speech. Although whipping the partisan crowd into a frenzy, many critics on both sides of the partisan aisle mostly agreed that she was a tad "out of control" and that her delivery was too manic. She rocked her immediate audience, but the remote television audience was likely split on the effectiveness of her speech. Granholm admitted afterward that "I probably shouldn't have gotten so worked up" (quoted in Eggert, 2012). Too little dynamism can diminish your speech, but too much can backfire.

COMPOSURE: KEEPING IT TOGETHER

A final dimension of speaker credibility is **composure**. Audiences tend to be influenced by speakers who are emotionally stable, appear confident and in control of themselves, and remain calm even when problems arise during a speech. Cable news shows are notorious for shouting matches between political adversaries. To some, these episodes are entertaining, but it is doubtful that any listeners are swayed by witnessing two verbal combatants savage each other with cross-talk to the point where unleashing fire hoses to dampen their tempers almost seems appropriate.

Displaying emotion overtly, however, does not always destroy a speaker's credibility. Too much composure may be perceived as hard-heartedness or insensitivity. Shedding tears at a funeral or expressing outrage at an atrocity may enhance your credibility with some listeners. *The appropriateness of displaying composure depends on the context.*

INTERACTING DIMENSIONS

Establishing your credibility with your audience is an important persuasive step, but it does not assure success influencing your listeners. There is a complex interaction among the elements of credibility. A speaker can be high on trustworthiness, for example, but low on dynamism, even dull, so that audience members may not want to listen. A speaker could also be high on competence and dynamism but low on trustworthiness, negating the positive effects of the first two elements. Finally, a speaker could be perceived as competent, dynamic, and trustworthy but lack composure, suggesting the speaker is an emotional wreck and unstable. Which elements of credibility are most desired by listeners can be a matter of individual choice. The best of all worlds, of course, is to exhibit strength in the minds of listeners on all four elements of credibility—to be highly competent, dynamic, trustworthy, and composed.

Build Arguments: Persuasive Logic and Evidence

Aristotle identified **logos** (logic bolstered by supporting materials) as one of the three modes of persuasion. Ethos (credibility), already discussed, and **pathos** (emotional appeals), soon to be discussed, are the other two. In this section, how arguments are structured and the overriding claim for a persuasive speech, the proposition, are addressed. Finally, what makes arguments persuasive beyond strict logic and evidence is explored.

TOULMIN MODEL: ELEMENTS OF AN ARGUMENT

When a speaker wanders into controversial territory (e.g., "College education should be free"

By her own admission, Jennifer Granholm, an accomplished public speaker, probably was overly animated in her delivery when speaking at the Democratic National Convention in 2012.

or "Guns should be allowed on college campuses"), arguments are required to make a case for such claims. An **argument** "implicitly or explicitly presents a claim and provides support for that claim with reasoning and evidence" (Verlinden, 2005, p. 5). **Reasoning** is the thought process of drawing conclusions from supporting materials. **Evidence** consists of supporting materials whose purpose is to bolster claims that are controversial. Examples, statistics, and testimony serve as evidence for controversial claims. A claim without evidence is like a haystack in a hurricane—easily blown apart from lack of supporting materials.

As discussed in Chapter 6, human decision making and problem solving navigate in a sea of relative uncertainty. Probability, not certainty, is the best we can hope to achieve. Thus, informal logic described by British philosopher Stephen Toulmin aptly depicts the nature of an argument based on probabilities. (Rieke et al., 2005; Verlinden, 2005). Toulmin (1958) identified and explained the six elements of an argument (see also Figure 15-2). These are:

1. *Claim*—that which is asserted and requires support.

2. *Grounds* (Reasons/Evidence)—reasons to accept a claim and the evidence used to support those reasons. Reasons justify the

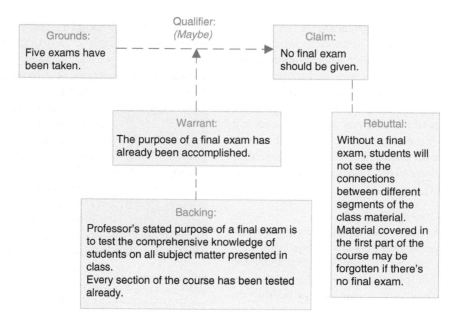

FIGURE 15-2. Toulmin Structure of Argument.

claim, and evidence provides firm ground for these reasons.

3. *Warrant*—the reasoning that links the grounds to the claim. It is usually implied, not stated explicitly.

4. *Backing*—the reasons and relevant evidence that support the warrant.

5. *Rebuttal*—exceptions or refutation that diminishes the force of the claim.

6. *Qualifier*—degree of truth to the claim (e.g., possible, plausible, probable, or highly probable).

Everyday reasoning follows this pattern, known as the **Toulmin structure of argument**. For example, suppose you are a guy who wants to date a supermodel. Your train of reasoning might proceed as follows:

Claim: I can date supermodel Jasmine.

Grounds: I am a brainy (I.Q. of 125; B.A degree from Stanford University), average-looking, very nice, sensitive guy with a moderate income ($65,000 annual salary). *(At this point, the logical question that should occur to a skeptic is "Why would someone so described have any chance of dating a supermodel?" Thus, your warrant must supply that logical connection.)*

Warrant: Jasmine dates brainy, average-looking, very nice, sensitive guys with moderate incomes. *(Next question worth asking is "What evidence supports the warrant?")*

Backing: The last three guys Jasmine dated were brainy. Two of them had college degrees, and one had a PhD. All three were average looking according to five girls I asked at random. All three had very average incomes and drove three- or four-year-old sedans. I've read interviews with Jasmine in which she said that all of these guys were very nice, sensitive, caring human beings, and that was attractive to her.

Rebuttal: Jasmine is a supermodel who could date almost any guy she wanted. I'm a stranger to her. She has a body-guard who could rearrange my internal organs if I tried to approach her. I can't just call her. She might think I'm a stalker. *(Now the pros [grounds, warrant, backing] and cons [rebuttal] must be weighed to judge the strength of the claim, represented by the qualifier.)*

Qualifier: Jasmine *possibly* would accept a pity date with me—when pigs can fly and taxes are abolished.

PROPOSITIONS: FACT, VALUE, AND POLICY CLAIMS

The Toulmin structure of an argument begins with a *claim*. The primary, overriding claim for a persuasive speech is called a **proposition**. The proposition becomes the essence of your persuasive purpose statement. Propositions define and focus the argument, limit issues to what is relevant, and set standards for what should be addressed (Inch & Warnick, 1998). The proposition is "the overall claim that an arguer tries to prove" (Verlinden, 2005, p. 116).

There are three types of propositions: fact, policy, and value. A **proposition of fact** alleges a truth, such as "Open carry gun laws would provide significant protection against criminals." A **proposition of value** calls for a judgment that assesses the worth or merit of an idea, object, or practice, such as "Abortion is immoral." A **proposition of policy** calls for a significant change from how problems are currently handled, such as "Smoking should be banned in all public places." Main reasons (grounds) offered to support the proposition (principal claim) that calls for a ban on smoking in public places, for example, include:

1. Secondhand smoke is dangerous to nonsmokers.
2. Secondhand smoke is annoying to nonsmokers.
3. Employees in bars and restaurants cannot escape the smoke.

Skeptics, those who make a strong effort to analyze and evaluate arguments presented by speakers attempting to persuade, are more likely to be moved by strong, carefully developed arguments (the central route) than by peripheral issues and concerns. Strong arguments, of course, do not persuade everyone.

PERSUASIVE ARGUMENTS: QUALITY AND QUANTITY

The quality and number of arguments advanced for a proposition can be factors in persuasive speaking. One study tested to what degree students could be persuaded that completing comprehensive examinations as a condition for graduating from college is a good proposal. Student groups were told either that the exams would begin in a year (meaning they would have to take the exams) or in a decade (meaning they would not have to take the exams). Presumably, those directly affected by the proposal (must take the exams) would scrutinize the persuasive message, whereas those unaffected by the proposal would see the message as peripheral and see the number of arguments, even if weak, as decisive (Petty & Cacioppo, 1984).

In this study, the quantity and the quality of arguments both made a big difference. Mindful students directly affected by the proposal were not persuaded by nine weak arguments. In fact, the more weak arguments they heard, the more they disliked the proposal. They were persuaded only when strong arguments were used, especially many strong arguments. For students unaffected by the proposal, however, the quality of the arguments was relatively unimportant. They were more persuaded that the proposal was a good idea when nine arguments were presented than when only three were offered, no matter how strong or weak the arguments.

When constructing your persuasive speech, don't be satisfied when you find one or two strong arguments to support your proposition. If several strong arguments emerge when you research your proposition and time permits, present them all. Several strong arguments can be persuasive to listeners who process your message either peripherally (quantity of arguments) or centrally (quality of arguments).

PERSUASIVE EVIDENCE: STATISTICS VERSUS NARRATIVES

"The use of evidence produces more attitude change than the use of no evidence" (Reynolds & Reynolds, 2002, p. 428). To be persuasive, however, your evidence must be attributed to a highly credible source, should be seen by audience members as legitimate (free of fallacies), must gain the attention of your audience and not put listeners to sleep, and should not overwhelm your audience with an excessive abundance (Perloff, 2013).

What about types of evidence? Vivid narratives and examples can be more persuasive than statistics (Glassner, 1999), partly because they typically are more interesting and memorable (Green & Brock, 2000). A strong narrative can be "a potent persuasive tool" (Hsu, 2008, p. 51). Finding vivid stories more interesting and memorable, however, doesn't automatically make them a better choice than statistics. Research is mixed on which is more persuasive (Feeley et al., 2006). So what should you conclude? Use both narratives and statistics as your optimum strategy, thereby capitalizing on the strengths of both forms of evidence (Allen et al., 2000).

Use Emotional Appeals: Beyond Logic

We are not like Spock or Data on *Star Trek*. Although logic and evidence can be enormously persuasive, especially for highly involved listeners, emotional appeals—what Aristotle termed pathos—are also powerful motivators. As social psychologist Drew Westen (2007) observes, "We do not pay attention to arguments unless they engender our interest, enthusiasm, fear, anger, or contempt . . . 'Reasonable' actions almost always require the integration of thought and emotion . . ." (p. 16).

GENERAL EMOTIONAL APPEALS: MOTIVATING CHANGE

Appeals to sadness, pride, honor, hope, joy, guilt, envy, and shame all have their place as persuasion strategies that ignite emotional reactions and change behavior (Gass & Seiter, 2011). Research on the actual persuasiveness of these particular emotional appeals, however, is sparse. Nevertheless, some evidence suggests that these emotional appeals do have persuasive potential (Dillard & Nabi, 2006; Nabi, 2002). Hope, for example, is sometimes a cornerstone of an entire political campaign. Barack Obama's successful run for the presidency revolved around a strong appeal to hope, including this appeal in a victory speech given on the night of the 2008 Iowa presidential caucus:

> We are choosing hope over fear . . . Hope is what led me here today—with a father from Kenya, a mother from Kansas, and a story that could only happen in the United States of America. Hope is the bedrock of this nation, the belief that our destiny will not be written for us, but by us, by all those men and women who are not content to

> settle for the world as it is; who have the courage to remake the world as it should be. ("Remarks," 2008)

Appeals to hope and other emotions can be persuasive. This section, however, concentrates on two frequently used emotional appeals: fear and anger, then discusses the ethics of emotional appeals.

FEAR APPEALS: ARE YOU SCARED YET?

"Don't put that in your mouth. It's full of germs." "You'll poke your eye out if you run with those scissors." "Don't ever talk to strangers. They may hurt you." "Never cross the street before looking both ways. You could be killed."

From childhood, we are all familiar with fear appeals. Our parents give us a heavy dose to keep us safe and out of trouble. Fear appeals are used on adults as well, however. In 2001, Canada began using the most shocking, fear-inducing warnings on cigarette packages ever used anywhere in the world (Bor, 2001). Photos of blackened and bleeding gums, a diseased heart, a lung tumor, or a gangrenous foot appeared on a rotating basis on all cigarette packs along with information about the hazards of smoking. The U.S. Food and Drug Administration followed the Canadian example by requiring tobacco marketers to include extremely graphic antismoking images on all cigarette packs and in 20% of tobacco advertisements, effective as of October 2012. In 2013, however, that effort failed due to court rulings favoring tobacco companies' lawsuits to halt the antismoking images on their product ("FDA's Graphic Cigarette Labels," 2013). You can view the proposed graphic images (if you have the stomach for it) by doing a simple Google search ("graphic images on cigarette packs".)

Do fear appeals work? More research has been conducted on the efficacy of fear appeals than on all other emotions combined. In general, the more fear is aroused in listeners, the more vulnerable they feel, and the more likely they will be convinced (Dillard, 1994; Witte & Allen, 1996). The graphic images on cigarette packs are more persuasive than simple text warnings (Stromberg, 2012). In Montana, a state plagued by methamphetamine use, young people were targeted for a barrage of extremely graphic, terrifying video ads of teens hooked on the drug (Montana Meth Project, 2015). The fear appeals appeared to work (Siebel & Mange, 2009). A dramatic shift occurred in attitudes about meth use according to two reports from Mike McGrath (2007, 2008), Montana's attorney general. Teens' perceptions of great risk from trying meth even one time increased substantially to 93% of respondents, and 87% of young adults believed their friends would give them a hard time for using meth. Behavioral changes also followed attitudinal changes. Teen meth use has declined by 65% in Montana since the beginning of the campaign. Other states have subsequently followed the Montana meth persuasive model with similar results: 63% decrease in meth use in Arizona and 52% in Idaho (Montana Meth Project, 2015).

Fear appeals, however, don't always work with audiences. Regarding the graphic anti-smoking ads and images on packages with a threatening message ("You'll die"), recent research shows a possible "boomerang effect" that creates an aversive, defensive avoidance reaction to look away or ignore the images (Hurst, 2011). _Five conditions determine whether high fear appeals will likely produce constructive action_ (Gass & Seiter, 2011):

1. _Your audience must feel vulnerable._ We don't all fear the same things. Some people fear heights, whereas others relish skydiving. Some individuals fear pit bulls, whereas others see them as wonderful pets. Teens feel more threatened by social rejection than physical harm caused by drug use (Schoenbachler & Whittler, 1996). Recognizing this, the Montana Meth Project (2015) tried to create strong social disapproval for meth use in addition to fear appeals about physical harm. There are also cultural differences in what we fear most. A cross-cultural study showed that audiences from individualist cultures were more persuaded by fear appeals that described personal harm, but that audiences from collectivist cultures were more persuaded by fear appeals that described harm to the family (Witte et al., 2000).

2. A _clear, specific recommendation for avoiding or lessening the fear is important_ (Devos-Comby & Salovey, 2002). To assuage the fear of having to drop out of school and be left with an uncertain future, for example, a vague recommendation (e.g., get financial

Carefully handled fear appeals can be very effective. Montana's graphic anti-Meth ad campaign has been credited with a huge decline in teen use of the drug.

aid) is not as effective as a specific recommendation (e.g., fill out this application for a Pell grant).

3. *The recommendation must be perceived as effective* (Cho & Witte, 2004; Keller, 1999). Getting a vaccination against the flu is an effective recommended behavior. Wearing a mask to avoid infection is not nearly as effective and is often impractical as well. Imagine your professors lecturing through a mask, or you and your classmates working on group activities in class while all are wearing masks.

4. *Listeners must perceive that they can perform the actions recommended.* Again, the effort required to perform the behavior is a key variable. Giving up sugary sodas entirely for the rest of your life to avoid dental and health problems may not be possible for most people. The effort is too great. Cutting soda consumption in half, however, may be realistic.

5. *Fear appeals are more persuasive when combined with high-quality arguments* (Gleicher & Petty, 1992; Rodriguez, 1995). The fear appeal becomes more believable when it is bolstered by credible arguments.

In conclusion, fear appeals can be highly effective motivators of behavior, but only under certain conditions (Witte, 1998). When a threat is perceived by listeners to be low, no action is likely. Thus, the speaker's fear appeal must be strong, and the threat must be shown to have a personal impact on individuals to arouse concern. When the personal threat is perceived to be high but the solution is viewed by listeners as ineffective or too difficult to implement, denial ("We can't do anything anyway, so why worry?") or rationalization ("You've got to die of something") typically neutralizes fear-arousing messages. When the personal threat is perceived by listeners to be high and a solution is viewed as effective and relatively easy to implement, however, fear-arousing messages will likely be successful in producing constructive action.

ANGER APPEALS: MAKE 'EM MAD

Arousing anger in an audience is a common persuasive appeal. Anger can be a strong, effective motivation to act (Kim & Niederdeppe, 2014). Note how student Hope Stallings (2009) intended to trigger anger: "Now that we understand the catastrophic impact of [deferred prosecution agreements] on our economy and personal economic well-being, we should be sufficiently angry to do something about it" (p. 15).

Anger doesn't always provoke constructive behavior, however. People sometimes become verbally and/or physically violent when angry (Guerrero, 1992; Tavris, 1989). The intensity of the anger is key. Intense anger can short-circuit an individual's ability to think clearly and act responsibly (Fein, 1993). Intensely angry individuals may lash out at any perceived source of their anger, real or imagined (Lazarus, 1991; Pfau et al., 2001). Hecklers at town hall meetings across the nation in 2009 convened to discuss the health care law sometimes became so enraged with the speaker or other audience members that security had to drag them screaming from the room. This creates a volatile, even dangerous, situation. Likewise, protests by members of the anti-war group Code Pink have erupted into screaming scenes with security hauling demonstrators from Congressional hearings and other events. As a speaker, you want to keep calm, be unconditionally constructive in your comments even when others are losing their heads, and not taunt a heckler in your audience—especially if your audience is predominantly hostile. You could provoke a physical confrontation or even a riot. Arousing anger in your audience can be persuasive, but it can also backfire.

The target and context of anger arousal largely determine its persuasive implications (Nabi, 2002). The **Anger Activism Model** helps explain the relationship between anger and persuasion (Turner, 2014; Turner at al., 2013). This model posits that anger provokes desired behavior change when (1) the target audience initially agrees with your persuasion message, (2) the anger produced by your message is intense, and (3) your audience members perceive that they can act effectively to address their anger. Studies show that if all three conditions are met, intense anger has the potential to motivate action even if the action required to quell or satiate that anger is very difficult to perform

Expressing anger can be an effective persuasive strategy, but it is tricky to channel the anger percolating among listeners in a positive direction.

(Turner et al., 2013; Turner et al., 2007). Remember that the more difficult a behavior is to perform, the less likely our attitudes and behavior will be consistent. Intense anger, however, can rouse people even if action requires great effort. Intense anger appeared to be the prime motivator for tens of thousands of people to protest "big government" and "taxation" at Tea Party rallies across the country on April 15, 2009. Some traveled long distances to participate. Anger fomented the 2012 "Occupy" movement worldwide. Living in tents with limited access to food and facilities is tough.

How can you use anger in a speech to persuade? Consider this:

Abdullah al-Kidd, a U.S. citizen and former University of Idaho student and running back for the football team, was detained for more than two weeks as a witness in a federal terrorism case in 2003. He was handcuffed, strip-searched, and repeatedly interrogated. There was no evidence of wrongdoing by al-Kidd. He was jailed and then investigated, not the other way around as required by the U.S. system of justice. A three-judge panel from the Ninth Circuit Court ruled in September 2009 that his incarceration was "repugnant to the Constitution and a painful reminder of some of the most ignominious chapters of our national history" (quoted in Boone, 2009, p. A5). As a result of the illegal detention, al-Kidd lost a scholarship to graduate school, lost his security clearance and subsequently a job with a government contractor, lost his passport, and was ordered to live with in-laws in Las Vegas. We should all be furious that our government so blatantly abused one of our citizens.

This story is one way anger can be used as a persuasive appeal.

ETHICS AND EMOTIONAL APPEALS: IS IT WRONG TO BE PERIPHERAL?

Emotional appeals can be very persuasive, but are they ethical? It depends. Shouldn't we be angry about racism, sexism, homophobia, and all manner of injustice? Shouldn't we fear terrorism, drunk drivers, food poisoning, and flu pandemics? Shouldn't we feel guilt about the treatment of Japanese Americans during World War II? Emotional appeals are not inherently unethical just because they aren't a logical appeal. An emotional appeal is considered a peripheral route to persuasion, however, and the central route should be encouraged. Nevertheless, emotion in the service of logic and truth can equal constructive action to do good. Emotional appeals motivate action. They also create attention so that we might listen more intently to a clearly reasoned and supported argument.

Emotional appeals are ethical as long as they complement the central route to persuasion (skepticism). Emotional appeals in the service of fabrications, distortions, and rumors are unethical. During the debate on health-care reform in the summer of 2009, Sarah Palin asserted that a proposal in a congressional bill would require "my parents or my baby with Down syndrome . . . to stand in front of Obama's 'death panel' so his bureaucrats can decide, based on a subjective judgment of their 'level of productivity in society,' whether they are worthy of health care" (quoted in "Report," 2009). The allegation was explosive but utterly false, and it was denounced by more than 40 media outlets. PolitiFact.com, the nonpartisan fact-checking website of the *St. Petersburg Times* and winner of the 2009 Pulitzer Prize, called it a "pants on fire" lie and voted it "Lie of the Year" (Holan, 2009; "Report," 2009). The nonpartisan Factcheck.org. dubbed it "whopper of 2009" (Weiner, 2009). A skeptic must ask why any politician would even suggest euthanizing the elderly (e.g., Palin's parents), the most active voting bloc in America? It is completely implausible. The "death panels" allegation, however, scared a lot of older people who then showed up at town hall meetings understandably outraged by the misinformation. The death panels accusation was a combined appeal to fear and anger in the service of dishonesty. That's unethical persuasion.

Similarly, liberal MSNBC television talk show host Keith Olbermann, on his former *Countdown* show, made this wildly unsupported characterization of Scott Brown, a soon-to-be-elected Republican U.S. senator from Massachusetts: "Scott Brown [is] an irresponsible, homophobic, racist, reactionary, ex-nude model, teabagging supporter of violence against women and against politicians with whom he disagrees" (quoted in Sheppard, 2010). Jon Stewart, on *The Daily Show*, ripped Olbermann for wallowing "in the fetid swamp of baseless name-calling." Stewart noted that Olbermann had in past "commentaries" called Chris Wallace "a monkey posing as a newscaster," Rush Limbaugh a "big bag of mashed up jack-ass," and Fox News contributor Michelle Malkin "a mindless, morally bankrupt, knee-jerk, fascistic . . . mashed-up bag of meat with lipstick on it" (quoted in Sheppard, 2010). Olbermann soon after apologized on his show for his "over-the-top" comments.

Name-calling is unethical if there are no solid facts to support the labels. If a person has clearly lied, then you can call him or her a liar, although this may not be effective persuasion because it can alienate listeners who dislike such abrasive labeling. If a person hasn't lied, then it is wrong to fling the label. Emotional appeals should not be a substitute for logic and evidence. If an emotional appeal contradicts sound logic and solid evidence, then it becomes the tool of the true believer.

Induce Cognitive Dissonance: Creating Tension

When we want to persuade others to change their attitudes or behavior, one of the most common strategies is to point out inconsistencies between two attitudes or between attitudes and behavior. A student asks her professor for more time on an assignment, for example. The professor says "no." The student retorts, "But you gave extra time to Jamie. Why won't you give me the same extension?" The professor sees herself as a very fair-minded person. Faced with this apparent inconsistency in the treatment of two students, the professor feels tense and uncomfortable. Festinger (1957) called this unpleasant feeling produced by apparent inconsistency **cognitive dissonance**, and it can be an effective persuasive strategy (Tavris & Aronson, 2007).

Whenever a person holds two inconsistent ideas, beliefs, or opinions at the same time, or when an attitude and a behavior are inconsistent, dissonance likely occurs (McKimmie et al., 2003; Tavris & Aronson, 2007). Parents often confront this persuasive strategy from their children. "Why can't I stay up past midnight on weekends? You let Tommy when he was my age." "Why do I have a curfew? You never gave a curfew to José or Magdalena."

Generally, we want to be perceived as consistent, not hypocritical or nonsensical, so dissonance emerges when inconsistencies are pointed out to us (McKimmie et al., 2003; Tavris & Aronson, 2007). If we view ourselves as unbiased but laugh at a sexist joke, some dissonance will likely surface. If we consider ourselves honest but use a copy machine at work for personal projects, we will likely experience some dissonance, especially if someone confronts us with the inconsistency. This arousal of cognitive dissonance seems to be a universal phenomenon, appearing in a variety of cultures studied (Hoshino-Browne et al., 2005).

"Cognitive dissonance is a motivating state of affairs. Just as hunger impels a person to eat, so does dissonance impel a person to change . . . opinions or . . . behavior" (Festinger, 1977, p. 111). According to this theory, you have to awaken dissonance in listeners for persuasion to occur. Without dissonance, there is little motivation to change attitudes or behavior. Therefore, *the strategy for the persuader is to induce dissonance in the audience, then remove that dissonance by persuading listeners to change their attitudes and behavior in the direction desired.* More specifically:

> The [persuader] intentionally arouses feelings of dissonance by threatening self-esteem—for example, by making the person feel guilty about something, by arousing feelings of shame or inadequacy, or by making the person look like a hypocrite or someone who does not honor his or her word. Next, the [persuader] offers one solution, one way of reducing this dissonance—by complying with whatever request the [persuader] has in mind. The way to reduce that guilt, eliminate that shame, honor that commitment, and restore your feelings of adequacy is to give to that charity, buy that car, hate that enemy, or vote for that leader. (Pratkanis & Aronson, 2001, p. 44)

Does inducing dissonance change behavior? It certainly can (Aronson et al., 1991; Stone et al., 1997). Important decisions arouse more dissonance than less important ones (Gass & Seiter, 2011). Pointing out to a teacher that he or she was not consistent when grading a test could elicit varying degrees of dissonance. If the inconsistency involves a single point on a 100-point exam, the teacher can easily downplay the inconsistency as minor and inherent to any subjective grading system. If the inconsistency involves an entire grade difference and seems based on gender bias, however, the dissonance could be quite large.

Notice how Gary Allen (1996), a student at Northeastern State University, uses cognitive dissonance on the topic of drug testing in the military:

> The final problem is caused by a double standard, because a program is only as good as the goal it achieves. While alcohol is universally recognized as the most commonly abused drug, the military does not test for alcohol as regularly as for other drugs . . . Soldiers caught drunk on the job are given 45 days extra duty, that is work that must be performed after the regular duty day, they have a letter put into their permanent file, and they are returned to light duty. Yet the soldier who receives a positive [drug] test result is, currently, kicked out of the military with a dishonorable discharge. Let me say that again. Every day soldiers are required to undergo a test of their innocence without suspicion of guilt. The soldier who is found guilty is kicked out and marked for life with a dishonorable discharge, while soldiers drunk on the job, endangering everyone's life, are returned to duty with a slap on the hand. (p. 82)

The speaker points out a glaring inconsistency to induce dissonance in the audience. Supporting such a "double standard" is hypocritical and unjust, so the speaker implies. One could argue that there is a big difference between alcohol and other drugs—namely, legality. Nevertheless, concerning possible dangerous effects of use, an inconsistency does seem apparent.

Use the Contrast Effect: Minimize the Magnitude

You're a salesperson, and a woman comes into the dress store where you work. Most of your pay is based on commission, so you want to sell as much merchandise as you can at the highest prices possible. Do you show the woman the inexpensive dresses first, then gradually show her more expensive ones, or do you begin with very expensive dresses probably outside her price range, then show her less expensive choices? Which will net you the biggest commission? According to research on the *contrast effect*, you'd make a better choice if you began expensive and moved to less expensive (Cialdini, 1993).

The **contrast effect** says listeners are more likely to accept a large second request or offer when contrasted with a much larger initial request or offer. The contrast effect, sometimes referred to as the **door-in-the face strategy**, is used in all types of sales. If shown a really nice dress that costs $250, most shoppers will balk at purchasing it because it is "so expensive." If shown a $475 dress first, however, and then shown the $250 dress, the second dress seems less expensive by contrast with the first. Once the $250 dress is purchased, "accessorizing" it with $30 worth of jewelry, scarves, or whatever will also seem like very little by contrast.

Cialdini (1993) provides a stellar, and amusing, example of the contrast effect in action in parent-child persuasion (p.14). Although this example is a letter, you can easily see how the strategy could apply in a persuasive speech.

Dear Mother and Dad:

Since I left for college I have been remiss in writing and I am sorry for my thoughtlessness in not having written before. I will bring you up to date now, but before you read on, please sit down. You are not to read any further unless you are sitting down, okay?

Well, then, I am getting along pretty well now. The skull fracture and the concussion I got when I jumped out the window of my dormitory when it caught on fire shortly after my arrival here is pretty well healed now. I only spent two weeks in the hospital and now I can see almost normally and only get those sick headaches once a day. Fortunately, the fire in the dormitory, and my jump, was witnessed by an attendant at the gas station near the dorm, and he was the one who called the Fire Department and the ambulance. He also visited me in the hospital and since I had nowhere to live because of the burnt-out dormitory, he was kind enough to invite me to share his apartment with him. It's really a basement room, but it's kind of cute. He is a very fine boy, and we have fallen deeply in love and are planning to get married. We haven't set the date yet, but it will be before my pregnancy begins to show.

Yes, Mother and Dad, I am pregnant. I know how much you are looking forward to being grandparents and I know you will welcome the baby and give it the same love and devotion and tender care you gave me when I was a child. The reason for the delay in our marriage is that my boyfriend has a minor infection which prevents us from passing our premarital blood tests and I carelessly caught it from him. I know that you will welcome him into our family with open arms. He is kind and, although not well educated, he is ambitious.

Now that I have brought you up to date, I want to tell you that there was no dormitory fire, I did not have a concussion or skull fracture, I was not in the hospital. I am not pregnant, I am not engaged, I am not infected, and there is no boyfriend. However, I am getting a "D" in American History and an "F" in Chemistry, and I want you to see those marks in their proper perspective.

Your loving daughter,

SHARON

As a strategy to use in a persuasive speech, *the contrast effect works well when presenting your solution to a problem.* For example, say you have argued that taxpayer dollars don't begin to cover the costs of educating college students. You could begin the solution portion of your speech this way:

Clearly, we cannot expect taxpayers to continue shouldering almost the entire burden of higher education expenses. I think it would be entirely justified if our state legislature immediately doubled tuition for every student in the state. This would provide some relief for already over-burdened taxpayers while still covering less than half the cost of educating each student.

Although doubling student tuition is justified, fair, and beneficial, I can see that such a proposal probably isn't entirely practical for a number of reasons, not the least of which is the suddenness of such a large increase. Having weighed the potential merits and demerits of such a proposal, let me propose instead that the state phase in a much smaller tuition increase over the next decade to ease the burden on students and still provide taxpayer relief in the long run.

Peruse the sample speech in Box 15-1 for another example of the contrast effect.

Although voluminous research shows that the contrast effect changes peoples attitudes, more recent research shows that behavioral change is less likely using this strategy (Feeley et al., 2012). This simply underlines previous discussion of the not-always-consistent relationship between attitudes and behavior.

Use a Two-Sided Strategy: Refutation

Is it better to present arguments in favor of your proposition and ignore opposing arguments (one-sided message), or should you make your case and then refute opposing arguments (two-sided message)? *Two-sided persuasive messages are more effective than one-sided messages in convincing listeners to change attitudes* (Allen, 1998; O'Keefe, 2016).

A *two-sided organizational pattern* begins with a presentation of main arguments supporting your proposition. After you have laid out your case, you then answer common objections, or opposing arguments, against it. This, of course, means that you need to anticipate what an audience might question about your position. Answering opposing arguments is called **refutation**. (The sample speech in Box 15-1 provides a detailed example of two-sided organization with refutation.)

There are four steps to refutation. First, *state the opposing argument.* "A common objection to colleges shifting from a semester to a quarter system is that not as much subject matter will be covered each term" is a statement of an opposing argument. Second, *state your reaction to the opposing argument.* "This isn't true. Courses that meet three hours per week could meet five hours per week under the quarter system" is a statement of response to an opposing argument. Third, *support your response with reasoning and evidence.* Failure to present strong arguments backed by strong reasoning and solid evidence may backfire and promote more entrenched attitudes instead of changing attitudes (Rucker & Petty, 2004). Weak refutation can be worse than no refutation at all because listeners may deduce that poorly supported counterarguments mean currently held attitudes are meritorious. Fourth, *indicate what effect, if any, opposing arguments have had on the strength of your case.* If some disadvantage will occur from your proposal, admit it, but weigh the damage against the claimed advantages. "No quarter system is perfect. Yes, students will be pressured in some instances to work more intensely in a condensed period of time. Overall, however, the advantages of a quarter system—greater number and variety of courses, more diversity of instructors, better vacation schedules, and greater retention and success rates—far outweigh the minor objections to my proposal."

BOX 15-1 DEVELOPING COMMUNICATION COMPETENCE

A Sample Outline and Persuasive Speech

This is a sample outline and the text of an approximately 15-minute persuasive speech. This speech is longer than most in-class presentations but shorter than many public presentations. The length allows a more comprehensive illustration of several persuasive strategies than could be included in a shorter version.

This speech uses the *Monroe's Motivated Sequence* organizational format discussed in Chapter 12. Steps in this sequence are identified in brackets.

INTRODUCTION
I. [*ATTENTION STEP*] Begin with notable examples of big money in college sports.
  A. CBS/Turner will pay NCAA $10 billion for TV rights for "March Madness" basketball championship until 2024.
  B. Athletic department budgets have ballooned to an average of $62 million among 103 Division I-A schools.
  C. Corporate sponsorship of college athletics has never been bigger.

(continued)

BOX 15-1 DEVELOPING COMMUNICATION COMPETENCE

A Sample Outline and Persuasive Speech (continued)

II. Proposition: To convince you that colleges and universities should significantly reduce the scale of their athletic programs.

III. Establish significance to the audience.

    A. All college students partially pay for athletic programs with tuition, fees, and taxes.

    B. Student scholars must compete with student athletes for scholarships.

IV. Preview the main points.

    A. Big-time athletic programs contradict the educational mission of colleges.

    B. A specific plan will be offered to solve this problem.

    C. Common objections to such a plan will be addressed.

BODY

I. [*NEED STEP*] Big-time intercollegiate athletic programs contradict the educational mission of colleges and universities.

    A. Athletic prowess, not academic ability, is often given priority.

        1. Academic admission standards are often waived for athletes.

        2. "Ghost courses," easy classes, and easy majors are encouraged.

    B. Student nonathletes and athletes alike are academically harmed by the emphasis on athletic ability.

        1. Student scholars may be bumped from academic admittance to make space for the student athlete with lower academic qualifications.

        2. Admitting marginal students because of their athletic ability is also harmful to the athlete and the college.

    C. Colleges' primary mission is often diminished by athletic department deficits and out-of-control spending.

        1. Most colleges suffer big athletic department deficits.

        2. Huge deficits threaten academic programs.

II. [*SATISFACTION STEP*] Take the money out of college sports.

    A. Drop all college sports entirely (contrast effect).

    B. The real plan is as follows:

        1. All athletic programs must be self-sufficient.

        2. No athletic scholarships; only academic or financially based scholarships will be awarded

        3. Admission standards must be the same for both athletes and nonathletes. Student athletes must maintain minimum 2.5 GPA.

        4. No corporate sponsorships, logos, names on arenas, and so forth allowed.

        5. No money from TV rights will go to college athletics, only to academic programs.

        6. Plan will be enforced by the NCAA and/or the colleges themselves. Enforcement sanctions include probation, suspension, and/or banishment from league play.

III. Three common objections to this proposal will be addressed.

    A. Objection 1 is that disadvantaged student athletes will lose scholarships and be denied an education.

        1. This is true, but the total number of student scholarships will not decrease.

        2. Student athletes will realize the importance of academics.

    B. Objection 2 is that career training for pros will be lost.

        1. This is also true, but colleges shouldn't be farm teams for sports corporations.

        2. A minuscule percentage of college athletes go on to be professionals.

    C. Objection 3 is that sports fans lose a source of entertainment.

        1. There will still be college sports programs.

        2. There will still be gifted athletes entertaining us.

        3. There just won't be big money distorting academics.

(continued)

(continued)

IV. [*VISUALIZATION STEP*] Imagine what it will be like when money is removed from college sports.
   A. Colleges won't need to reduce or eliminate academic programs because of athletic department deficits.
   B. More scholarship money will be available for students with academic merit.
   C. Colleges will no longer contradict their mission.
   D. Student tuition and fees will not be raised to pay for athletics.
   E. Failure to implement this plan means increased deficits and reductions in academic programs.

CONCLUSION

I. [*ACTION STEP*] Take action now.
   A. Summarize main arguments.
      1. Big money has corrupted college sports, thwarting colleges' academic mission.
      2. The proposed plan takes the money out of college sports.
      3. Common objections are meritless.
   B. Take action.
      1. Contact your student representatives.
      2. Discuss this proposal with the college administration.
   C. Memorable finish.

BIBLIOGRAPHY

Berkowitz, S. (2015, May 19). If athletes ruled employees, Notre Dame will seek new sports model, AD says. *USA Today*. Retrieved from http://www.usatoday.com/story/sports/college/2015/05/19/notre-dame-northwestern-knight-commission-nlrb-labor-unions/27598219/

Drake Group. (2015, April 16). *Position statement*. Retrieved from https://drakegroupblog.files.wordpress.com/2015/04/tdg-position-protecting-athletes-from-acad-exploitation-final.pdf

Editorial Board (2015, January 4). What college bowls cost you: Our view. *USA Today*. Retrieved from http://www.usatoday.com/story/opinion/2014/12/31/harbaugh-michigan-football-salaries-editorials-debates/21114631/

Ganin, S. (2014, January 8). CNN analysis: Some college athletes play like adults, read like 5th-graders. *CNN*. Retrieved from http://www.cnn.com/2014/01/07/us/ncaa-athletes-reading-scores/index.html

Kaufman, T. (2015, March 6). The triumph of big money over college sports. *Delaware Online*. Retrieved from http://www.delawareonline.com/story/opinion/columnists/ted-kaufman/2015/03/06/triumph-big-money-college-sports/24508479/

Knight Commission on Intercollegiate Athletics. (2001). *A call to action*. Retrieved from http://www.knightcommission.org/images/pdfs/2001_knight_report.pdf

Knight Commission on Intercollegiate Athletics. (2010). *Restoring the balance: Dollars, values, and the future of college sports*. Retrieved from http://www.knightcommission.org/images/restoringbalance/KCIA_Report_F.pdf

Knight Commission on Intercollegiate Athletics. (2015, May 19). Knight Commission urges a student-centered approach in college sports. Retrieved from http://knightcommission.org/recent-news/936-may-19-2015-knight-commission-urges-a-student-centered-approach-in-college-sports

Krupnick, M. (2014, November 27). Would your tuition bills go up if college athletes got paid? *Money*. Retrieved from http://time.com/money/3605591/college-athletes-sports-costs-students/

National Collegiate Athletic Association. (2014, April). *NCAA Division I intercollegiate athletics programs report: Revenues & expenses*. Retrieved from https://www.ncaapublications.com/p-4344-division-i-revenues-and-expenses-2004-2013.aspx

New, J. (2015, January 27). A long shot. *Inside Higher Ed*. Retrieved from https://www.insidehighered.com/news/2015/01/27/college-athletes-greatly-overestimate-their-chances-playing-professionally

Raissman, B. (2015, March 20). During March Madness, everyone gets paid but the players. *New York Daily News*. Retrieved from http://www.nydailynews.com/sports/college/raissman-paying-players-march-madness-article-1.2156444

(continued)

BOX 15-1 DEVELOPING COMMUNICATION COMPETENCE

A Sample Outline and Persuasive Speech (continued)

Schoof, R. (2015, May 19). NCAA urges caution on idea of paying college athletes. *McClatchy DC*. Retrieved from http://www.mcclatchydc.com/news/nation-world/national/article24784735.html

Tracy, M., & Rohan, T. (2014, December 30). What made college football more like the pros? $7.3 billion, for a start. *The New York Times*. Retrieved from http://www.nytimes.com/2014/12/31/sports/ncaafootball/what-made-college-ball-more-like-the-pros-73-billion-for-a-start.html

GET BIG MONEY OUT OF COLLEGE SPORTS
(Prepared June 2015; about a 15-minute speech)
[APPLICATION OF TEXT MATERIAL IN BRACKETS]

[*ATTENTION STEP—MONROE'S MOTIVATED SEQUENCE*] "We want to put our materials on the bodies of your athletes, and the best way to do that is buy your school. Or buy your coach." So said Sonny Vaccaro in 2001 before shocked members of the Knight Commission on Intercollegiate Athletics. Vaccaro was a slick athletic shoe salesman, sometimes dubbed the "sneaker pimp" by his detractors, who worked for companies such as Nike, Reebok, and Adidas to establish licensing rights with universities for his products. Asked by Penn State University President Emeritus and Knight Commission member Bryce Jordan "why should a university be an advertising medium for your industry?" Vaccaro responded, "You sold your souls, and you're going to continue selling them. There's no one of you in this room that's going to turn down any of our money. You're going to take it. I can only offer it." What Vaccaro asserted was true then, and it is even truer now.

Intercollegiate athletic programs are being corrupted by massive mountains of money. Intercollegiate sports programs have become a multibillion-dollar enterprise. A December 30, 2014, *New York Times* article by Marc Tracy and Tim Rohan reports that "ESPN is paying $7.3 billion over 12 years to telecast seven games a year—four major bowl games, two semifinal bowl games and the national championship game." CBS/Turner television contracted with the National Collegiate Athletic Association to pay the NCAA $10 billion from 2011 to 2024 to broadcast the men's college "March Madness" basketball tournament, according to a March 20, 2015, article in the *New York Daily News*. Football and basketball at major universities are huge commercial enterprises sponsored by corporations anxious to sell their products to fans of these athletic spectacles.

An April 2014 report by the NCAA itself entitled "Division I Intercollegiate Athletics Programs" shows that the median expenditure by the 103 colleges in NCAA Division I-A is a whopping $62 million. [*STARTLING STATISTIC*] That's more than the total operating budget of many small and medium-sized colleges and universities in the United States.

Let's be honest: college athletics, especially Division I-A big-time football and basketball programs, are a commercial entertainment venture far removed from the educational mission of colleges and universities. Because this is a serious problem, I will try to convince you that colleges and universities should significantly reduce the scale of their athletic programs. [*PROPOSITION OF POLICY*]

Every college student listening to me speak today is affected by this commercialization of college sports. [*PERSONAL IMPACT*] As I intend to prove, it is you who partially pay for big-time athletic programs with increased student fees and tuition. Student scholars are forced to compete against student athletes for resources. Academic programs central to your educational goals and dreams may be jeopardized by huge deficits incurred by athletic programs, especially those with losing records.

I can guess what some of you are thinking. "He wants to reduce college athletic programs because he hates jocks and was a geek who always lost at sports." Not true! Baseball and basketball were my two favorite sports, and I earned my share of trophies and accolades playing both. I am an avid University of Oregon Ducks and San Francisco Forty-Niners football fan. You can question my choice of teams to support, but I do not propose reducing the scale of college athletics because I hate sports. [*IDENTIFICATION*] A college education, however, can open the doors of success for each and every one of you. It is your ticket to a better future. College sports should never serve as a substitute for academic success or impede any student's chance to acquire the best education possible, but the commercialization of college athletics threatens to do just that. [*PERSONAL IMPACT*]

(continued)

(continued)

Let me make several arguments to support my proposal to significantly reduce the scale of college athletic programs. First, I will show how big-time athletic programs contradict the educational mission of colleges. Second, I will offer a specific plan to rectify this serious problem. Finally, I will respond to primary objections you may have to my proposal.

[*NEED STEP*] Returning to my first argument, that big-time athletic programs contradict the educational mission of colleges, let me begin with what I think we all know is true. The principal mission of a college or university is to provide a quality education for all students, including athletes. The NCAA's own Regulation 2.5 states: "Intercollegiate athletics programs shall be maintained as a vital component of the educational program, and student-athletes shall be an integral part of the student body." Excessive emphasis on sports programs, however, contradicts this stated mission in three ways. [*COGNITIVE DISSONANCE*]

First, athletic prowess, not academic ability, is often given priority. Cardale Jones, quarterback for the Ohio State Buckeyes who won the national football championship in 2014 against my Oregon Ducks, tweeted this message in 2012: "Why should we have to go to class if we came here to play FOOTBALL, we ain't come to play SCHOOL, classes are POINTLESS." Jones can hardly be blamed for thinking this way. An April 16, 2015, report on academic integrity in collegiate sport by the Drake Group concludes: "Institutional admissions standards are routinely waived for academically underprepared athletes whose performances can deliver millions in gate and television revenues." The report continues by citing common practices motivated by the need to win athletic competitions that include "ghost courses" for athletes, awarding them unearned grades, disproportionate enrollment of athletes in independent studies, and online courses or less demanding courses and majors. Clearly, athletic prowess, not academic potential, is what counts.

Second, excessive emphasis on athletic programs contradicts the educational mission of colleges because student athletes and nonathletes alike are harmed by the emphasis placed on athletic ability. [*CONTINUATION OF COGNITIVE DISSONANCE*] Admitting less-qualified students because of their athletic abilities prevents other, more academically qualified students from gaining entrance to some of the best colleges and universities. Some of you may have been denied entrance to the college of your choice and had to settle for a second, third, or even fourth choice because athletes with far weaker academic records were granted preferential admittance. Sarah Ganin, in a January 8, 2014, article, "Some College Athletes Play Like Adults, Read Like 5th-Graders," reports a CNN study found that the national average on the reading comprehension portion of the SAT is 500. She also writes, however, that "[m]any student-athletes scored in the 200s and 300s . . . a threshold that experts told us was an elementary reading level and too low for college classes." Does this seem fair to you that your academic future is jeopardized by such admission practices? Dr. Richard Southall, director of the College Sport Research Institute and a professor at University of South Carolina, quoted in the same article, claims: "It is in many ways immoral for the university to even admit that student [with an elementary school reading level]." [*MILD ANGER APPEAL; PERSUASIVE EVIDENCE*]

In addition, admitting marginal students with superior athletic ability does no favors for the student athletes. In response to a request to unionize by Northwestern University football players in 2014, the National Labor Relations Board researched the amount of time football players at major universities devote to their sport each week. Typically, players spend 40 to 60 hours per week on football. As former Senator from Delaware Ted Kaufman concludes in his March 6, 2015, column *Delaware Voice*, "Exactly how can you expect a 'student' to devote even 40 hours a week to his 'extra-curricular activity,' and find any time at all for his supposed full-time pursuit of a degree?" In a word, it's a farce, but an expensive one. The 2014 NCAA report shows that expenditures for aid to student-athletes (tutoring, etc.) amounts to 16% of athletic programs' total budgets. Athletes who are underprepared sop up huge amounts of college resources while they struggle to maintain even passing grades in classes.

Third, the primary mission of colleges and universities—to educate students—is often diminished by athletic department deficits. [*CONTINUATION OF COGNITIVE DISSONANCE*] The 2014 NCAA report documents that 83 of the 103 Division I-A athletic programs are running deficits. The median deficit is a staggering $11.6 million. The same report also notes that combining all three subdivisions of Division I colleges (including smaller colleges and universities), only 20 out of 228 schools were financially self-sustaining. The Knight Commission's report on

(continued)

BOX 15-1 DEVELOPING COMMUNICATION COMPETENCE

A Sample Outline and Persuasive Speech (continued)

college athletic programs concluded in 2010 that "reliance on institutional resources to underwrite athletics programs is reaching the point at which some institutions must choose between funding sections of freshman English and funding the football team." The situation has gotten markedly worse since this report. A 2015 *USA Today* study of college athletic program deficits concludes: "The vast majority of public colleges in Division I subsidize their athletic programs with millions from mandatory student fees or their general funds." You're paying for the deficits with excessive increases in tuition and fees. [*USE OF PERSUASIVE EVIDENCE*]

So what should be done about this problem? Clearly, since football and basketball programs are typically the source of all these problems, we should eliminate them from all colleges and universities. [*CONTRAST EFFECT*] If we were to eliminate football and basketball, less visible and far less costly sports, such as baseball, golf, gymnastics, and field hockey, could provide some athletic opportunities for students. Intramural football and basketball programs could be established for students who prefer those sports at virtually no cost to the college. Let's face facts—getting the money out of college sport is essential if we are going to solve the problems I've outlined.

Total elimination of football and basketball except for intramural programs solves the problems I've underscored. Perhaps, however, we don't need such a radical solution. As a sports fan and former athlete, I would be disappointed if colleges dumped their football and basketball programs entirely. [*IDENTIFICATION*] I do strongly believe, however, that the big money must be taken out of college sports.

[*SATISFACTION STEP*] My plan to do this is simple.

1. All athletic programs (including all sports, male and female combined) must be self-supporting. Ticket sales and sports merchandise will be primary sources of funds. This does not mean that every sport must be self-sufficient. Football receipts, for example, could be used to sustain less popular college sports, such as golf or field hockey.
2. There will be no scholarships for students based on athletic ability. Scholarships and grants must be based on academic potential and financial need. This is a strong recommendation of the National Alliance for College Athletic Reform. It is also the current practice of Division III NCAA schools.
3. Student athletes must be admitted according to the same standards as all other students. They must maintain a minimum 2.5 GPA to participate in athletic programs.
4. Absolutely no corporate money goes to athletic programs. No corporate logos or names should appear on any sports facilities, equipment, or apparel of any kind. Private donations must go entirely to academic programs and facilities only.
5. Any revenue earned from television or other media programming must be used exclusively for academic programs.
6. My plan will be enforced by the NCAA where legally possible and by all member colleges individually or in concert within each league where antitrust laws prohibit NCAA action. Enforcement sanctions will include probation, suspension, and/or banishment from league play.

This plan will substantially reduce college athletic programs without eliminating them. I have merely taken the big money out of college sports. Leagues, championships, and bowl games can continue, but without the huge financial incentives to distort the academic mission of colleges. Academic programs will no longer be threatened by huge athletic department debts. Without the big money, colleges can return to their primary mission—to provide a quality education for all students.

[*SATISFACTION STEP CONTINUED*] In case you're not completely convinced that my plan is a good idea, let me address common objections to my proposal. [*TWO-SIDED PERSUASION*] The first objection might be that disadvantaged student athletes will lose scholarships and be denied a college education. That's true, but eliminating all athletic scholarships could save money for general scholarships and grants at each college. The net effect on students as a group would be zero. The faces would change, but the same number of students, many financially disadvantaged, could receive financial help. In addition, if student athletes realize that they

(continued)

(continued)

cannot play college sports unless they qualify academically, this will provide an incentive for them to take their studies seriously or risk ineligibility.

A second objection might be that, without scholarships, many academically unprepared student athletes will lose a training ground for a career in professional sports. [*TWO-SIDED PERSUASION CONTINUED*] This may be true, but is it relevant? Should a college be a farm team for professional sports corporations? Why should a college create false hope for athletes, most of whom will never make it into professional sports? Official NCAA statistics reported in a January 27, 2015, article by Jake New at InsideHigherEd.com show that a majority of college students who play football and basketball believe that they will make it to the pro ranks. The actual figure is less than 2% for both men and women athletes. Too many student-athletes are attending college to play ball as a way of auditioning for professional teams. Educational success often gets lost in the hoopla and hubbub over athletic accomplishment. Colleges should not be a party to the exploitation of college athletes. [*COGNITIVE DISSONANCE*] Colleges should stop serving as a farm team for professional sports corporations interested only in profit.

Finally, won't sports fans lose a key source of entertainment if my plan is implemented? [*TWO-SIDED PERSUASION CONTINUED*] This is not true. Notre Dame and USC will still remain archrivals on the football field. Bowl games will still exist. Championships will still be contested, simply in scaled-down versions, as they were in the 1950s and 1960s before big money began exerting its corrupting influence. The difference will be that academic programs will not be diminished because of huge deficits from athletic programs, and the academic mission of colleges will not be distorted to pay for a bloated athletic program. The scale of college athletics will be substantially reduced, but the excitement and spectacle can remain.

[*VISUALIZATION STEP*] Imagine what my plan will accomplish. No longer will colleges be tempted or forced to reduce or eliminate an academic program, perhaps a program in your major, to pay for deficits incurred by bloated athletic programs. Millions of dollars in scholarships and grants will be available for academically qualified and needy students. Colleges will no longer serve as mere farm teams for profit-motivated corporations. Colleges will no longer appear hypocritical, espousing an educational mission on one hand while undermining it on the other. Your student fees and tuition will not have to be raised to support a faltering, expensive sports program.

Imagine what will happen if this problem is ignored. Athletic budgets will continue to swell, and deficits will rise. Your tuition and fees will increase, academic programs will be cut, and some programs and majors will be eliminated to cover the athletic department deficits. The quality of your education and your opportunities for academic success will be threatened. There are several pending federal court cases concerning compensation for college athletes that could make college athletic programs even more prohibitively expensive by requiring athletes be paid to play. In a May 19, 2015, article in *USA Today*, Notre Dame's athletic director, Jack Swarbrick, claimed that if college athletes are ruled by the courts to be employees of their respective schools and paid accordingly, then he foresees Notre Dame "withdrawing from the current setup of big-time sports." [*MILD FEAR APPEAL*] As the 2001 Knight Foundation Commission report concluded, "If it proves impossible to create a system of intercollegiate athletics that can live honorably within the American college and university, then responsible citizens must join with academic and public leaders to insist that the nation's colleges and universities get out of the business of big-time sports." I submit to you that we have now reached that point.

[*ACTION STEP*] I ask that you support my proposal to significantly reduce college athletic programs. Stop the erosion of academic values and quality. Speak to your Student Senate officers and representatives. [*EFFORT REQUIRED IS MINIMAL*] Discuss the issues I have raised with the college administration. This college can be a beacon of light signaling the way for other colleges to follow. Change begins with us. Get big money out of college sports!

⊛ Summary

When you attempt to persuade an audience, you try to convert, modify, or maintain your listeners' attitudes and/or behavior. Conversion is the goal least likely to be achievable. Attitudes do not always predict specific behavior. Reasons for possible inconsistency include whether the attitudes are derived from direct or indirect experience, the degree of effort required to perform the behavior, and the amount of social pressure applied to behave differently from your attitudes. The elaboration likelihood model explains persuasion in general by noting that there are two paths to persuasion. The peripheral route includes likability, attractiveness, and emotional appeals of the speaker, and the central route embraces skepticism and its emphasis on reasoning and evidence. Persuasion that works well in American culture may be ineffective in other cultures, especially those that are collectivist.

There are many persuasive strategies a speaker can use. Among these are establishing identification, building credibility, building strong arguments, inducing cognitive dissonance, making emotional appeals, using the contrast effect, and employing a two-sided organizational pattern. Competent public speakers will likely find success if they utilize some or all of these strategies to persuade others. There are conditions that determine the likelihood of success using each strategy, so make sure that you are cognizant of these conditions and adapt your persuasive strategy to meet them.

Quizzes Without Consequences

Test your knowledge before your exam! Go to the companion website at www.oup.com/us/rothwell, click on the Student Resources for each chapter, and take the Quizzes Without Consequences.

Film School Case Studies

American History X (1998). Drama; R
Powerful depiction by Edward Norton of a young man lured into a white supremacy movement in Venice, California. Examine this film for differences between coercion and persuasion. Apply the social judgment theory and elaboration likelihood model to Norton's conversion and attempt to steer his brother from a life of racist violence

Boiler Room (2000). Drama; R
Young sales reps (Giovanni Ribisi, Vin Diesel, and Ben Affleck) for a brokerage house pushing junk stocks adopt questionable persuasive strategies. Analyze the ethics of their persuasion, and apply the five key elements of ethical communication explained in Chapter 1.

My Cousin Vinny (1991). Comedy; R
This is a "must see" comedy if you haven't already had the pleasure of viewing this hilarious account of a bumbling New York lawyer (Joe Pesci) attempting to free his cousin (Ralph Macchio) from a murder charge in a small town in Alabama. Analyze this film for the persuasive, and often not so persuasive, use of identification in the courtroom.

The Great Debaters (2007). Drama; PG-13
Surprisingly entertaining drama about college debaters, with Denzel Washington (who also directed) playing the debate coach. Analyze the different persuasion strategies depicted in the movie.

TED Talk and YouTube Links

These speeches are offered for you to analyze and perhaps discuss in class. Some are very good examples, and some are problematic. Apply text material in this chapter to each sample.

1. *Two-Sided Persuasion:* Jim Jefferies, Gun Control Comedy Routine http://www.

independent.co.uk/news/world/americas/
charleston-shootings-australian-comedian-
jim-jefferies-standup-routine-on-gun-con-
trol-seems-particularly-apposite-at-the-mo-
ment-10334007.html
(WARNING: Jeffries uses offensive language throughout, so beware. Even gun
owners might find this hilarious, however.)

2. *Identification Strategies:* Stephen Colbert in
   Iraq, Operation Iraqi Stephen
   http://thecolbertreport.cc.com/videos/
   wy7a2l/operation-iraqi-stephen---
   john-mccain

3. *Cognitive Dissonance:* Jon Stewart, Bad
   Credit
   http://www.thedailyshow.com/watch/tue-
   may-8-2012/bad-credit

4. *Framing:* Jon Stewart, The GOP Whisper
   http://www.thedailyshow.com/watch/tue-
   february-5-2013/the-gop-whisperer

5. *Graphic Fear Appeals:* Montana Meth Project
   TV Ads
   http://www.youtube.com/
   watch?v=QYlwSepW7Bs

Interviewing

Interviewing, a common communication event, is defined as "a purposeful, planned conversation, characterized by extensive verbal interaction" (Peterson, 1997, p. 288). In every instance, communication competence is a central element of effective job interviewing.

The principal purpose of this appendix is to offer ways to improve your interviewing skills. By the end of this appendix, you should be able to:

1. Identify and avoid common mistakes made during job interviews.

2. Improve your own interviewing skills.

The informational interview conducted for research purposes is discussed in Chapter 12.

Preinterview Mistakes

We live in the Age of Technology. Thus, you must be cognizant that prospective employers may use technology to investigate your background and gain an impression of you from sources other than your résumé or in-person interview. An increasingly common research tool used by employers is to access your social networking sites. Much can be learned from viewing photos, comments, humor, and so forth posted there. A survey by CareerBuilder reported that 52% of employers research candidates by accessing their social networking sites. Of the employers surveyed, 41% responded that they had found content on social networking sites that had caused them not to hire a candidate. The most frequently cited examples of objectionable content that caused rejection included provocative or inappropriate photos or information (46%), content that revealed drinking and using drugs (40%), candidate bad-mouthed a previous employer (34%), candidate showed poor communication skills (30%), and candidate made discriminatory comments (29%) (Grasz, 2015a).

Conversely, 32% of employers who responded to the same CareerBuilder survey noted that they had also hired a candidate based primarily on information found on the candidate's social networking site. The most frequently cited examples included: the profile on the social networking site supported professional qualifications (42%), candidate's personality came across as a good fit with the company's culture (38%), the site conveyed a professional image (38%), the site showed that the candidate had strong communication skills (37%), and the site showed the candidate was creative (36%). The moral of this story is clean up your social networking site before submitting any job applications. If you don't have an online presence, create one because the CareerBuilder survey also reported that 35% of employers are less likely to interview applicants who do not appear online.

Job Interview Mistakes

Few events are as anxiety producing and as significant to our lives as a job interview. So much can be riding on such a brief encounter. Communicating competently during a job interview can be crucial to securing a job. This section addresses common mistakes and effective communication strategies

There is probably no such thing as a perfect interview. Communication strategies that work in one interview may not work as well in another. Nevertheless, some behaviors seem destined to torpedo any chance of success in an interview for a job. Another CareerBuilder survey (Lorenz, 2015) listed the following actual candidate blunders reported by employers:

The candidate tried to Google the answer to a question.

The candidate sat in the yoga position during the interview.

In answer to a question about diversity, the individual used the phrase "off the boat."

The candidate asked if he could offer religious advice to the employees.

The candidate gave "kicking someone's butt that really needed it" as the reason for leaving a previous job.

The candidate asked how much money everyone else was making.

These examples are clearly cases of clueless communication behavior on the part of interviewees. Another CareerBuilder survey (Ricker, 2014) listed more common problems displayed by candidates as witnessed by employers. These common mistakes include:

Seeming disinterested (55%)

Dressing inappropriately (53%)

Appearing arrogant (53%)

Answering a cell phone or texting during the interview 49%)

Appearing uninformed about the company or role (39%).

Common nonverbal mistakes reported by employers to CareerBuilders that interviewees make include:

Failing to make eye contact (65%)

Failing to smile (36%

Playing with something on the table (33%)

Having bad posture (30%)

Crossing their arms over their chest (26%)

Having a weak handshake (22%)

In addition to making these specific mistakes, interviewees commonly err in more general ways during the interview. First, they approach the interview as though it were a sales pitch and they were the product. Most people are mildly, and sometimes profoundly, repelled by a hard sell, no matter what the product. Using a hard sell to land a job will likely produce a similar response from an interviewer or hiring panel. Second, interviewees sometimes attempt to relate their entire life story when answering a question. Too much detail can make interviewers weary and

cause their attention to fade. Third, interviewees sometimes try to fake their knowledge and experience by inflating the importance of relatively minor background experience and accomplishments. If an interviewing committee senses that you are unreasonably padding your résumé, they may doubt your credibility across the board. Fourth, interviewees who are obviously unprepared to answer tough questions have little hope of being chosen for the job (Ricker, 2014).

Competent Interviewing Skills

Rob Anderson and G. Michael Killenberg (1999) identify three qualities that are necessary for an interview to be a success: empathy, honesty, and respect. *Empathy* puts us in the position of seeing from the other person's perspective. This is a vital quality for an interviewee. Empathy allows you to anticipate questions that will be asked and to frame answers that will speak to the concerns of those interviewing you. *Honesty* is vital because no one is likely to hire a person he or she does not perceive to be candid and straightforward. If a person lies on his or her résumé and the lie is discovered, it can be grounds for immediate dismissal from the position. Embellishing minor accomplishments walks close to the precipice of dishonesty. *Respect*, the final quality, shows sensitivity and concern. It is a two-way street. Interviewers should show respect by addressing the applicant in a manner that is not demeaning. Similarly, interviewees should show respect for interviewers. Some of the previous examples of clueless behavior during interviews show disrespect for the interviewer. Taking cell phone calls during the interview, for example, communicates that your priority is not first and foremost landing the job for which you are interviewing.

There are several ways to improve your interviewing skills. First, *be prepared*. Do research on the job you seek. Most job announcements specify what experience, skills, and knowledge are essential to the performance of the job. Be ready to adapt your background to the specific requirements of the job. If the job calls for knowledge of specific software or computer technology, be able to describe your experience with such software and technology. If the job announcement expressly identifies "effective interpersonal skills" as desirable in an applicant, have a list ready that speaks to this qualification directly. For example, if you have taken a college course in interpersonal communication, if communication is your college major or minor, if you have taken any workshops in conflict management or couples communication, or if you have conducted workshops or classes in interpersonal communication, list these on your résumé. Have these examples ready in case you are asked questions on such background during the interview.

Second, *rehearse for your interview*. Have a friend ask typical interview questions:

What are your strengths and weaknesses?

Why did you apply for this particular job?

Why did you leave your previous job?

Have you ever had difficulty working for a boss or supervisor?

What problems did you encounter at your last position?

Where would you like to be professionally in five years?

What's the worst job you've ever had?

Would you have difficulty contradicting your boss if you thought he or she was about to make a bad decision?

Do you work well on a team?

Have you had good or bad experiences working in groups?

Frame your answers as positive reflections of your work ethic and determination to excel. For example, the question "Have you ever had difficulty working for a boss?" could be answered this way: "Yes, and it taught me a lot about how to deal with difficult people . . ." "Where would you like to be professionally in five years?" could be answered this way: "I'd like to have my work recognized and receive a promotion because of it." You certainly don't want to answer such a question by indicating that the job you are seeking is merely a steppingstone to a better position elsewhere. Honesty doesn't require an answer that wasn't sought.

Third, *look and act the part of a credible candidate for the job*. Professional jobs require professional attire. Show that you care about the position by arriving on time, appearing well groomed and neat, and dressing in professional clothing. During the interview, speak so everyone can easily hear you. Listen carefully to all questions, and if in doubt, ask for clarification or elaboration. Answer questions directly, and eliminate nervous mannerisms (e.g., tapping fingers on the table, cracking knuckles, twirling hair, tapping a pen or pencil, or biting nails). Humor is often welcome, but avoid sarcasm or ethnic humor. Self-deprecating humor often works well as long as it doesn't diminish your qualifications for the position. Establish direct eye contact with the interviewer. If a panel conducts the interview, establish initial eye contact with the panel member who asks you the questions and then gradually direct your eyes to all panel members as you develop your answer. Do not express anger or hostility for previous bosses that have "done you wrong." Interviewers are looking for composure as an indicator of credibility. Speak fluently. Avoid long vocal pauses and dysfluencies (e.g., *um, uh, you know*, and *like*). Don't be reticent, fail to smile, look unfriendly, or demonstrate a lack of enthusiasm for the position.

Fourth, *provide sufficient elaboration when answering questions*. Very brief answers ("Yes, I did that") with no detail leave interviewers guessing about your qualifications for the position. Successful applicants for jobs use focused elaboration when asked questions. This means they provide considerable detail when answering questions, and the detail is always directly relevant to the questions asked. Unsuccessful applicants usually provide no elaboration, or their answers drift to irrelevant experiences, stories, or knowledge. When providing detail, look for signals from interviewers that you've answered the question sufficiently. When interviewers glaze over, fidget, glance around the room, stare at a pencil, look at the clock, or shift in their chairs, it is usually time to wrap up your answer.

Fifth, *organize your answers*. If you have prepared sufficiently for the interview, you should be able to answer most questions clearly and in an organized fashion. "What experience do you have working with people from diverse cultural backgrounds?" might be one question asked. A possible answer is "I've worked with three very diverse groups. At Datacom West, a third of the workers were Asian. When I worked at Silicon Software, several of the workers I supervised were from India and Pakistan. When I ran my own printing business, most of my workers were either African American or Jewish. As you can see, I've worked with a rich mixture of ethnic groups, and I feel such diversity has produced synergy."

Sixth, *provide sufficient evidence of your qualifications for the job.* **Behavioral interviewing** has become increasingly popular, especially in the business world (Hansen, 2015). It involves asking interviewees for specific examples of behavior that illustrates an answer. Here are some typical behavioral interviewing questions (Hansen & Hansen, 2015a):

> Describe a situation in which you were able to use persuasion to successfully convince someone to see things your way.
>
> Describe a time when you were faced with a stressful situation that demonstrated your coping skills.
>
> Give me a specific example of a time when you used good judgment and logic in solving a problem.
>
> Tell me about a time when you had to use your presentational skills to influence someone's opinion.
>
> What is your typical way of dealing with conflict? Give me an example.
>
> Give me an example of a time when something you tried to accomplish failed.
>
> Tell me about a time when you were forced to make an unpopular decision.

All of these questions seek evidence of your skills on the job. Answers to these behavioral questions reveal an applicant's knowledge of real-life situations. Be prepared to provide specific evidence of your talents and abilities. Brainstorm examples that illustrate your strengths. Use the STAR interviewing method for answering such behavioral questions: *ST* stands for *situation/task*, *A* for *action*, and *R* for *result* (Hansen,

2015). Thus, you identify the situation or task, explain what action you took, and describe what resulted from that action.

Seventh, *be prepared to ask relevant questions of interviewers.* An interview is a conversation, not an interrogation. Unlike a witness in a court trial, you have a right to ask questions of your interviewers. Your interviewers want to know if you are right for the job, but they also want to know if the job is right for you. Use the behavioral interviewing technique when asking questions of your interviewers. Don't ask "Do people get promoted in this company?" Instead, ask "Can you give me an example of the last person to receive a promotion and how that person earned it?"

Finally, **video interviewing** has become increasingly popular because it saves money for the candidate in travel expenses and may save the employer money if it is common practice to reimburse candidates' expenses. It also can winnow the list of promising candidates more easily and efficiently by serving as a kind of short, preinterview before final selection of candidates to interview in person is determined. A Career-Builder survey reported that almost half (49%) of employers know within the first five minutes of an interview whether a candidate fits the job well, and 87% know within the first 15 minutes (Ricker, 2014). Creating a strong, positive first impression is challenging when the interview is conducted using Skype or other video chat services. Besides advice already presented on effective interviewing, conduct a tech check to avoid distracting video glitches with the equipment, dress as you would for in-person interviews, be certain that there is no clutter or distracting objects in the background, and make sure that you look directly into the camera, not at the screen while talking (Brooks, 2014).

Answering Illegal Questions

Employers may ask you an illegal question, such as requesting your marital status, national origin, religion, sexual orientation, age, or the cause of a disability. Such questions can all be sources of potential discrimination against a candidate.

Illegal questions usually result not from malicious intent, however, but from carelessness, misplaced curiosity, or ignorance of legal restrictions. A CareerBuilder survey found that 20% of employers unknowingly asked an illegal question during an interview (Grasz, 2015b).

Despite legal restrictions on what interviewers may ask of a candidate, you may be asked questions that are out of bounds. How should you respond? You have several options. First, you could view the question as relatively harmless and answer it directly: "What is your marital status?"—"I've been married for 10 years! You aren't going to hold that against me are you?" Second, you could ask for clarification: "How old are you?"—"Perhaps you could clarify why that is relevant for this job? Are you seeking further detail about my experience?" Third, you could simply refuse to answer the question: "Are you a religious person?"—"I consider my religious views and status a personal matter unrelated to the description of this job." Fourth, you could simply terminate the interview: "These questions are inappropriate, and I can see that I would not feel comfortable working here. I thank you for your time." There is no correct option. You have to decide how uncomfortable the illegal questions make you, what these questions say about the place of employment, how much you want the job, and the degree of objection you have to specific questions.

You may also be asked seemingly out-of-bounds questions that are not actually illegal, although they may seem odd at best. The Career-Builder survey on illegal questions list several actual questions asked of candidates that seem strange:

> Do you believe in life on other planets? (Seeking to determine attitude about anything is possible)
>
> What superpower would you like to have? (Seeking candidate's view of strengths and weaknesses)
>
> If you were trapped in a blender, what would you do to get out? (Seeking candidate's creativity potential)

Most Human Resources departments would nix such questions, not because they are illegal, but because they may not seem entirely fair to the candidates. They do test, however, a candidate's mental agility and ability to think quickly under pressure.

🌐 Summary

Interviews are important events in our lives. An interview is a purposeful, planned conversation characterized by extensive verbal interaction. Empathy, respect, and honesty should imbue every interview. Preparation is a major element of an interview from the standpoint of both the interviewee and the interviewer. The interview should be focused. Questions and answers should be direct, relevant, and purposeful. Anticipate how you will respond if illegal questions are asked.

Speeches for Special Occasions

Speeches for special occasions should, of course, be special. They are different from informative and persuasive speeches. Although a special occasion speech may impart knowledge and information or briefly persuade, that is not its main purpose. Audience expectations are critical to the effectiveness of a special occasion speech. The occasion sets the expectation for the audience, and your primary goal is to meet your audience's expectations. An inspirational occasion requires an inspirational speech. Listeners want to be moved, not merely informed. Listeners at a roast expect to laugh heartily and often. Little effort should be made to offer deep insights or persuade anyone to action. *The primary purpose of this appendix is to explore ways to give effective and appropriate special occasion speeches.*

By the end of this appendix, you should be able to:

1. Recognize a variety of special occasion speeches, including eulogies, tributes, commencement addresses, after-dinner speeches, introductions, and award ceremony presentations.
2. Identify guidelines for delivering effective special occasion speeches.

Eulogies

Comedian George Carlin once remarked, "I'm always relieved when someone is delivering a eulogy and I realize I'm listening to it." Eulogies pay tribute to someone who has died. Given the sadness that typically surrounds a funeral, your challenge is to show respect for those grieving and provide a sense of closure for those feeling the profound loss of a loved one. The word *eulogy* originates from the Greek word that means "to praise." A **eulogy** is a speech delivered in praise of a deceased friend or family member. You want to capture the essence of the person eulogized. For years, I required my speech students to deliver their own eulogy, to play the role of someone paying tribute to them after their death. It offered a way of getting in touch with how my students saw themselves, who they wanted to become, and what they would want others to say about them after they died. The assignment was always instructive and often quite moving and insightful.

Eulogies do not have to be somber speeches, or as newscaster Tom Brokaw said at the funeral of his colleague Tim Russert, there would be "some tears, some laughs and the occasional truth" (quoted in Wilson, 2008, p. 2D). Capturing the essence of the person may mean paying tribute to their infectious sense of humor and their uniqueness as a human being. My father was just such a person. In my eulogy, I wanted to capture who my father was in life without excessively diminishing his faults or magnifying his admirable qualities. He could be irascible and enormously impatient, yet he could exhibit random acts of stunning kindness. I described not just my father's many acts of kindness, but I also tried to transform his legendary impatience into moments of gentle humor that all could appreciate. For example:

> Dad hated to get behind slow drivers (which was anyone obeying the speed limit). When Dad was in his 70s, he barely slowed down. I remember Mom and Dad picking me up at the airport one time. Dad was driving his Thunderbird. The freeways were jammed so Dad took a back

route home. At one point he was flying down the boulevard. From the back seat I gently inquired: "Dad, when exactly will our flight be leaving the ground?" He reduced his speed only slightly.

Using humor in a eulogy can be tricky, however. You want to show the utmost respect for the deceased, and you certainly don't want to cause offense for the grieving. Listeners typically welcome gentle humor that humanizes and explores the principal personal characteristics of the deceased.

In constructing an effective and appropriate eulogy, follow these guidelines:

1. *Your opening should capture attention and set the theme.* A few possibilities are a relevant quotation, a short story that reflects the core characteristics of the deceased, or a novel example from the life of the lost loved one. I began my father's eulogy this way: "There's a Jewish saying, 'The only truly dead are those who have been forgotten.' My dad won't be forgotten. One reason is that he was such an unforgettable character."

2. *Your organizational pattern is typically narrative.* You're briefly telling a story of the person's life, capturing the important plot lines about this individual. This is not a mere biography of the person. Don't simply list the person's résumé of awards, degrees, professional publications, and the like. Tell a story about what this person was like. Personal attributes are more important and heartfelt than personal accomplishments unless those accomplishments illustrate important and personal laudatory attributes.

3. *Strive for emotional control.* Your audience doesn't need to feel grief more than comes naturally from the loss of a loved one. A eulogy is a tribute. It should offer uplifting praise. You want the audience to feel a little better after your speech, not worse.

4. *Be balanced and realistic in your praise.* Senator Ted Kennedy's eulogy of his brother Robert, who was assassinated during his California campaign for president in 1968, included the perfect line to make this point: "My brother need not be idealized, or enlarged in death beyond what he was in life; to be remembered simply as a good and decent man, who saw wrong and tried to right it, saw suffering and tried to heal it, saw war and tried to stop it" (quoted in "Ted Kennedy's Eulogy," 1968).

5. *Relate what you will most remember and miss about the person.* Here are a few things I related about my father: "I will miss his puns—most of them real groaners. I will miss him teaching me golf, or trying to. I will miss Dad and Mom dancing to the big bands played on their stereo. I will remember Dad getting up in restaurants, grabbing the coffee pot and serving himself and other customers because the service was too slow. I will remember Dad hip deep in the Oxford Canal, saying 'Dammit Dorothy Mae,' as if Mom had something to do with his falling into the British muck. Most of all, I will remember Dad's unconditional love, unfailing support, and boundless generosity."

6. *Finish strong.* After telling several stories about my father that illustrated his uniqueness, the final line of my eulogy said this: "Heaven will be a more interesting place now that Dad has entered the Kingdom." This closing statement reflects again on the theme of my father as a unique and unforgettable character, and offers mild comfort to those grieving. Ted Kennedy finished his eulogy for his brother Robert this way: "As he [Robert] said many times, in many parts of this nation, to those he touched and who sought to touch him: 'Some men see things as they are and say why. I dream things that never were and say why not'" (quoted in "Ted Kennedy's Eulogy," 1968). After the space shuttle *Challenger* exploded in 1986 with the loss of the entire crew, Ronald Reagan delivered a nationally televised eulogy commemorating the fallen heroes who had risked their lives to explore space. Delivering one of the most powerful, touching eulogies ever presented by a President of the United States—a speech ranked

eighth on a list of the top-100 American speeches of the 20th century (Lucas & Medhurst, 2008)—Reagan captured the essence of the moment with these final few sentences:

> The crew of the space shuttle *Challenger* honored us by the manner in which they lived their lives. We will never forget them, nor the last time we saw them, this morning, as they prepared for their journey and waved goodbye and "slipped the surly bonds of earth" to "touch the face of God."

Using the words from a sonnet entitled "High Flight," a poem many pilots know well and some keep on their person, Reagan gave nobility to the deaths of our astronauts in the moving, eloquent finish to his eulogy.

Tribute Addresses

Although eulogies are tribute addresses, they are specifically related to the death of someone. There are other types of tribute speeches, however. **Tribute speeches** praise or celebrate a living person. They honor the person. You hear tribute speeches at retirement parties, birthdays, anniversaries, going-away parties, and award ceremonies. Brief tribute speeches can be *roasts* or *toasts*.

A **roast** is a purposely humorous tribute to a person. Although the humor can be sarcastic, ribald, even wildly exaggerated, everyone in attendance knows and expects that the entire affair is meant to praise the honoree. You poke fun at the honoree as a way of expressing your admiration and affection for the person. Here are some guidelines:

1. *Humor is the key ingredient of any roast.* This is not meant to be a serious event. It is supposed to be lighthearted and amusing. Follow the guidelines in Chapter 13 on using humor appropriately and effectively.

2. *Keep the tone positive.* A roast is meant to be a good-natured kidding of the honoree, not an opportunity to embarrass the person in front of friends and relatives.

3. *Be brief.* This is not an opportunity for you to audition for stand-up comedian of the year. Usually, each speaker at a roast addresses the audience for about three to five minutes. Stick to the time limit.

4. *Finish on a heartfelt, serious note.* Playfully making fun of the honoree should be amusing, but don't forget that a roast is meant to express admiration and affection for the person roasted. "All kidding aside, you know how much I respect and admire my dear friend. He is a beacon of light in a sometimes dark world, and I will miss his smiling face at work every day" is one way to close your roast on a serious note.

Another type of tribute is the **toast**—a brief tribute to a person or couple. Weddings usually have several toasts offered by the best man and maid of honor, and sometimes by bridesmaids and groomsmen, or even friends and family members. Keep toasts brief. A well-known, oft-quoted Irish toast goes:

> May the road rise to meet you.
> May the wind be always at your back.
> May the sun shine warm upon your face.
> And rains fall soft upon your fields.
> And God hold you in the hollow of
>   His hand.

If so inclined, you could play off this well-known toast and give it your own unique twist, such as:

> May the road rise to meet you, and may
>   you avoid the potholes of life.
> May the wind be always at your back,
>   unless a cool breeze in the face offers
>   refreshment.
> May the sun shine warm on your face, but
>   never burn you.
> And may rain fall softly, washing away any
>   sadness you may feel

Because a toast is often accompanied by a drink of wine or other alcoholic beverage, be cautious about the effect alcohol can have on your ability to offer a coherent and effective toast. Your toast may follow many others. I have heard some head-shaking, profoundly embarrassing toasts offered by those already toasted by excessive alcohol consumption. You don't want to make a fool of yourself and make others uncomfortable. Always be appropriate. Remember, weddings almost always have young children present. Your humor should be playful but PG rated—"To keep your marriage brimming, with love in the wedding cup, whenever you're wrong, admit it; whenever you're right, shut up" (Ogden Nash) or "If I'm the best man, why is she marrying him?" (Jerry Seinfeld) or "Love is an electric blanket with someone else in control of the switch" (Cathy Carlyle). Your toast should also be addressed to the couple. You stand and deliver the toast while everyone else remains seated. At the finish, you raise your glass and salute the couple.

A tribute to someone leaving due to retirement or moving to another place of employment has its own expectations and requirements. Such a tribute is very similar to a eulogy except the person is still living and is present for the tribute. The departure may not be welcome by the audience because a good colleague and friend is leaving, but it should be a cause for a happy send-off. This type of tribute speech should be lighthearted and emphasize the contributions made by the person who is leaving and any notable qualities that everyone will miss.

Recently, I was asked to give a tribute speech for a friend and long-time colleague. I began:

> I'd like to begin this tribute to Jack with a short poem I've written for this occasion. I apologize in advance.
> There is a professor named Jack.
> Who deserved a most elegant plaque.
> With flattering comments and a turn of a phrase.
> Abundant awards and plentiful praise.
> But instead he must settle for this sorry rhyme.
> Knowing full well that he'll be teaching part-time.
> Because try as he might; no matter what he may say.
> Old teachers never die, they just grade away.

The point of this opening was to create a lighthearted tone and to be a bit playful. The last line is a glancing reference to the famous line from Gen. Douglas MacArthur in his April 19, 1951, address to the U.S. Congress, "Old soldiers never die, they just fade away." I continued by reflecting on some of my friend's accomplishments during his long career as a teacher and administrator. I finished as I began, with a "bit of doggerel" or bad poetry (a lighthearted finish):

> The power of one is so often unclear.
> But let voices be raised and perhaps a dark beer.
> To proclaim across campus for all to hear.
> There's one special man whose impact is felt.
> And although his physique is no longer so svelte.
> Our dear friend and colleague will surely be missed.
> But let's all make a vow to steadfastly resist.
> Dwelling long on Jack's parting, no need for redundance.
> And instead wish he and Diane joy in abundance.

No one in the audience expected great poetry from me—and they certainly didn't hear any—but listeners were amused and attentive to hear something a bit different than the previous tribute speeches. Don't be afraid to take a small risk and produce a speech that tries something different. My attempt was greatly appreciated by my friend, who recognized immediately that I had put some effort into constructing the tribute. It's the apparent effort that you put into a tribute speech that sends the message "I care about you and you will be missed."

Commencement Addresses

A **commencement address** is an inspirational speech that occurs at graduation ceremonies. You want to move your listeners to think in new ways, to participate in a cause, or to help your community solve problems. The primary focus is on engaging your listeners and imparting wisdom. This is no small task. Celebrities, comedians, actors, CEOs of major corporations, politicians, members of the news media, and individuals who have overcome great obstacles in life are invited every year to give commencement addresses at colleges and universities all across the United States. Even presidents of the United States give commencement addresses. As a student, you may be asked to give one type of commencement address, the valedictory speech.

Commencement addresses usually have a serious message to impart to graduates, but the best such addresses blend abundant humor with a serious theme. Barack Obama gave a commencement address at the University of Michigan on May 1, 2010, before 92,000 people. He began: "It is great to be here in the Big House, and may I say 'Go Blue!' I thought I'd go for the cheap applause line to start things off." Obama continued by quoting letters he received from a kindergarten class in Virginia. These youngsters asked him a number of questions, such as "Do you work a lot?" "How do you do your job?" and "Do you live next to a volcano?" The last question he read, however, was more serious and became the theme of his address: "Are people being nice?" The rest of his speech developed the theme of the proper role of government in a democracy and the inability to succeed as a democracy when incivility reigns supreme in our political discourse ("Obama Michigan," 2010).

Harry Potter author J. K. Rowling, in her 2008 Harvard commencement address, began this way: "The first thing I would like to say is 'thank you.' Not only has Harvard given me an extraordinary honor, but the weeks of fear and nausea I have endured at the thought of giving this commencement address have made me lose weight" ("The Fringe Benefits," 2008). Her amusing opening tapped beautifully into her theme—fear of failure and the fringe benefits of experiencing failure.

Rock star Bono began his commencement address to graduates at the University of Pennsylvania on May 17, 2004, this way: "My name is Bono, and I am a rock star. Don't get me too excited because I use four-letter words when I get excited. I'd just like to say to the parents, your children are safe, your country is safe . . . Doctor of Laws, wow! I know it's an honor, and it really is an honor, but are you sure? I never went to college, I've slept in some strange places, but the library wasn't one of them." Bono identified the central theme of his speech this way: "So

what's the problem that we want to apply all this energy and intellect to? Every era has its defining struggle, and the fate of Africa is one of ours" ("Because We Can," 2004).

Stephen Colbert delivered a commencement address to graduates at Wake Forest University on May 18, 2015. Not surprisingly, there was abundant humor throughout his presentation. He began with this introduction: "Congratulations to you, the class of 2015. You did it and you look amazing. Although it's a little embarrassing you all showed up in the same outfit. Really, even all of the accessories are the same. Everyone has a black and gold tassel—or is it blue and white?" He later launched into his theme: "I hope you find the courage to decide for yourself what is right and what is wrong, and then please, expect as much of the world around you" (quoted by Mosbergen, 2015).

Colbert had given previous commencement addresses. He delivered one at at Knox College on June 3, 2006. At one point, he said, somewhat mocking a cliché heard at so many commencements, "It has been said that children are our future. But does that not also mean that we are their past? You are here to replace us. I don't understand why we're here helping and honoring them. You do not see union workers holding benefits for robots." On a more serious note, Colbert remarked, "Cynicism masquerades as wisdom, but it is the farthest thing from it. Because cynics don't learn anything. Because cynicism is a self-imposed blindness, a rejection of the world because we are afraid it will hurt us or disappoint us. Cynics always say no. But saying yes begins things." He finished on a humorous note, offering advice (sort of) to graduates, as is traditional in commencement addresses: "And lastly, the best career advice I can give you is to get your own TV show. It pays well, the hours are good, and you are famous. And eventually some very nice people will give you a doctorate in fine arts for doing jack squat" ("Stephen Colbert's Address," 2006).

Inspirational commencement addresses should appeal to our better nature. You want to touch deep feelings in your audience, encouraging pure motives and greater effort to achieve a common good. This is a commencement, a new beginning.

After-Dinner Speeches

An **after-dinner speech** is a presentation that typically occurs at a formal gathering of some group. After-dinner speeches are not always presented after dinner. Developed in England in the 19th century as a formal type of presentation, such speeches were literally delivered right after a dinner, usually to a large gathering for some occasion. More recently, these presentations may occur after a luncheon or even a breakfast gathering of business or civic groups. They probably should be renamed *after-meal speeches* or *postprandial public speeches* (eh, maybe not), but *after-dinner speech* remains the common term.

An after-dinner speech is meant to entertain. Although your topic can be a serious one, you need to take an amusing approach to it. For example, a speech on vegetarianism could be informative if you describe the pros and cons of eschewing meat, it could be persuasive if you argue forcefully that we should convert to vegetarianism, and it could be an after-dinner speech if you made light of the vegetarian substitutes for meat (e.g., lentil loaf and soy burgers). The tone should be whimsical, not serious. This makes some topics more appropriate than others. AIDS doesn't lend itself easily to whimsy, for example, nor does child abuse, terminal illness, or torture. "The Most Ridiculous Things People Do with Cell Phones" or "My Top 10 List of Irritating Behaviors in Restaurants" or "The World's Most Pointless Signs" all suggest humorous potential, however. Again, review the guidelines in Chapter 13 for using humor effectively and appropriately.

Despite the whimsical nature of after-dinner speeches, this is not stand-up comedy. Skip the canned jokes. Telling lawyer jokes to a group of attorneys, for example, would likely backfire anyway; they probably have heard every lawyer joke ever made. Be original and creative. Don't deliver a series of one-liners unrelated to any theme or thoughtful point. Your after-dinner speech should have a central theme, and a serious point relevant to that theme, even though you accomplish this with humor. Often the topic and theme are your choice, or the group that invites you to speak considers you an authority on certain topics and wants you to speak about one of them. The occasion and makeup of your audience may also dictate certain topic choices. If you're speaking before an environmental group, for instance, there should be an environmental flavor to your theme (e.g., common mistakes the public makes about the environmental movement in America).

Speeches of Introduction

A **speech of introduction** prepares an audience for a speech that is about to be presented. Sometimes an audience is very familiar with the speaker, requiring a very brief introduction. You want to create enthusiasm for the speaker, but remember that you are not the main focus. Identify who you are if the audience is unfamiliar with you, but place the focus on the speaker being introduced.

If I were introducing American humorist Dave Barry, a well-known personality in most circles, I would keep the introduction very brief because the audience isn't excited to hear me speak. They have gathered to hear the featured speaker. I would mostly quote his own self-description taken from his website (www.davebarry.com) because it is so amusing, places the focus squarely on him, and sets the mood for his speech. For example:

> Thank you for attending this anxiously anticipated event. It is my great honor to introduce to you a man who describes himself in these words: Dave Barry is a humor columnist. In 1988 he won the Pulitzer Prize for Commentary. Many people are still trying to figure out how this happened. Dave has also written a total of 30 books, although virtually none of them contain useful information. In his spare time, Dave is a candidate for President of the United States. If elected, his highest priority will be to seek the death penalty for whoever is responsible for making Americans install low-flow toilets. Anything else I might add about Dave Barry would pale in comparison to his own self-description, so without further ado, please welcome Dave Barry.

Notice that the last statement asks the audience to welcome the speaker. This cues the audience to applaud the speaker as a welcoming gesture.

Less familiar speakers require a bit more information for an audience. You may need to build the speaker's credibility by briefly listing awards, titles, accomplishments, and the like: "Jerald Grayson has advanced degrees in geotechnical engineering and has investigated some of the worst natural disasters in our recent history, including our own all-too-familiar and tragic collapse of the county's earthen dam. He is a recognized geological expert internationally, and he has won numerous awards for his service to our country." Remember, the audience doesn't assemble to hear you speak, so keep the credential building short. Also, make sure that you pronounce the speaker's name correctly. If you are unsure, ask the speaker before introducing him or her. Finally, never provide any potentially embarrassing details about the speaker. Making a speaker and the audience uncomfortable at the outset sets an awful tone for the ensuing speech.

As a featured speaker, responding well to an introduction, especially an effusively positive one, can ingratiate you to your audience. Gen. Henry Shelton, when Chairman of the Joint Chiefs of Staff, responded to just such an effusive introduction this way: "Thank you, Mr. Secretary, for that incredible introduction. If I had known you were going to eulogize me, I would have done the only decent thing and died" ("Victory, Honor," 2000). For more standard introductions, simply offer a gracious thanks, express enthusiasm for appearing before this audience, and then begin your speech.

Speeches of Presentation

Awards ceremonies have become commonplace. It's hard to find a week on television that has a total absence of some award program. As journalist and editor Joanne Lipman noted, "Hollywood has its Oscars. Television has its Emmys. Broadway has its Tonys. And advertising has its Clios. And its Andys, Addys, Effies, and Obies. And 117 other assorted awards. And those are just the big ones" (quoted in Foley, 2010). This list doesn't even include the awards in the music entertainment industry, which seem to grow uncontrollably.

As a student, you may not have many opportunities to present an award, but you may find occasions, on campus and off, when you are responsible for giving a presentation speech. A **speech of presentation** must communicate to the audience the meaning and importance of the award. "The Floyd Younger Award for Excellence in Teaching is offered each year to the one instructor on our campus, chosen by committee from nominations made by his or her colleagues, who has exhibited outstanding effectiveness as a teacher" is an example. Also, a presentation speech should identify why the recipient has earned the award: "Karen Follett has taught creative writing on this campus for 15 years. Her students adore her. One student remarked, 'I've never had a teacher who was so enthusiastic, so encouraging, so down right fun in class.' Another student said, 'Professor Follett rocks! She's simply the best instructor in the universe.' It is my great pleasure to give the Floyd Younger Award for Excellence in Teaching to Karen Follett." Present the award to the recipient with your left hand so you are free to shake the recipient's right hand.

Speeches of Acceptance

How many times have you watched the Academy Awards and heard a winner begin an acceptance speech with "I didn't think I would win so I didn't prepare a speech"? Every time I hear that, I cringe. It's false humility, and it's lame. Actors especially should have a prepared script. It is the essence of their business. Some of the worst, most cringe-inducing acceptance speeches have occurred at the Oscars. If you have any inkling that you might win an award, large or small, prepare a brief acceptance speech. Don't embarrass yourself.

Your acceptance speech should be appreciative, genuine, and humble. No one wants to hear the winner gloat. "I knew I would win this" or "Boy, I deserve this" doesn't endear you to the audience. Express your pleasure at receiving the award: "This is such an honor. I am so happy to receive it." Show your appreciation with a simple statement: "Thank you so much for this great honor." Thank the most important people who helped you and those who gave you the award. Thanking your parents for conceiving you is not usually appropriate or effective. Keep the list of those you wish to thank short. When Kim Basinger won the best actress Oscar in 1998, she said, "I just want to thank everybody I've ever met in my entire life!" Thankfully, she didn't proceed to list each person by name. In 2004, after a series of Oscar winners gave acceptance speeches for *The Lord of the Rings: The Return of the King*, host Billy Crystal remarked, "It's now official. There is no one left to thank in New Zealand." An audience easily grows restless when a laundry list of people, most of whom may be unknown to audience members, is presented by the award recipient.

Summary

Special occasion speeches are different from informative and persuasive speeches. Each type has its own guidelines to be effective and appropriate. In most cases, such speeches work best when they are relatively brief, heartfelt, entertaining, and well suited to audience expectations. Make your special occasion speeches truly special.

Glossary

Abstracting The process whereby we formulate increasingly vague, general conceptions of our world by leaving out details associated with objects, events, and ideas.

Accommodating style Yielding to the needs and desires of others during a conflict.

Acculturation The process of adapting to a culture different from one's own.

Active listening Mindful not mindless listening that is effortful and focused on what others are saying.

Ad hominem fallacy A personal attack on the messenger to avoid the message.

Ad populum fallacy Basing a claim on popular opinion.

Advising response Listeners telling individuals how they should act.

After-dinner speech An entertaining presentation that typically occurs at a formal gathering of some group.

Agenda A list of topics to be discussed in a group meeting presented in the order in which they will be addressed.

Aggression Any physical or verbal communication that is intended to inflict harm.

Alliteration The repetition of the same sound, usually a consonant sound, at the start of several words in a sentence.

Amalgamating Addressing both contradictory forces (dialectics) without compromising on either impulse.

Ambushing When we listen for weaknesses and ignore strengths of a speaker's message.

Amplitude Variation of sound that is perceived as loudness.

Anchor attitude A preexisting attitude on an issue that serves as a reference point for how close or distant other attitudes and positions are.

Anecdote A short, entertaining story.

Anger Activism Model Helps explain the relationship between anger and persuasion; posits that anger provokes desired behavioral changes.

Antithesis A stylistic device that uses opposites to create impact.

Appropriateness Behavior that is viewed as legitimate for, or fitting to, the context.

Argument An implicit or explicit presentation of a claim and support for that claim with reasoning and evidence.

Articulation Speaking words clearly and distinctly.

Assertiveness The ability to communicate the full range of thoughts and emotions with confidence and skill.

Attachment theory Children raised in families whose communication is supportive learn to join in conversations with new people and read social signals accurately, while those raised in families whose communication is threatening and fear arousing learn to be withdrawn or overaggressive.

Attitude A learned predisposition to respond favorably or unfavorably toward some attitude object.

Attribution Assigning a cause, either situations or personal characteristics, to people's behavior.

Avoiding style Sidestepping or ignoring conflict.

Bad apples Disruptive group members who poison the group.

Beauty bias A perceived advantage accorded those who are viewed as physically attractive.

Behavioral interviewing Interviewers asking for specific examples of behavior by an applicant that illustrate an answer given to a question.

Beliefs What we think is true or probable.

Benevolent sexism A subtle form of discrimination that embraces the "positive" stereotype of women as "pure creatures" who deserve to be protected and shown affection, but only as long as they behave in a conventional manner.

Bilateral symmetry The right and left sides of the human body match: eyes are straight across from each other, not one higher than the other, and so forth.

Binge drinking Consuming five or more drinks for men and four or more for women in a two-hour period.

Bound morpheme Unit of meaning that has no meaning of its own until attached to a stand-alone word.

Brainstorming The creative problem-solving process characterized by encouragement of even zany ideas, freedom from initial evaluation of potential solutions, and energetic participation by all group members.

Breadth (of self-disclosure) The range of subjects discussed.

Burden of proof The obligation of the claimant to support a claim with evidence and reasoning; whoever makes the claim has the burden to prove it.

By-passing Assuming that everyone assigns the same meaning to a word without checking to see if it is true.

Channel Medium through which a message travels, such as oral or written.

Channel lean A single channel devoid of the richness of nonverbal cues.

Channel rich Incorporates multiple channels besides words, such as gestures, facial expressions, tone of voice, posture, and other nonverbal cues.

Charisma Constellation of personal attributes that people find attractive and that causes them to accord influence to a person perceived to have such attributes.

Claim A generalization that remains to be proven.

Cliché A once-vivid expression that has been overused to the point of seeming commonplace.

Closedness An unwillingness to communicate with others.

Coalitions Temporary alliances formed by individuals to enhance their power relative to others.

Co-culture Any group that is part of a dominant culture yet often has a common history and shares some differences in values, beliefs, and practices from the dominant culture.

Cognitive dissonance The unpleasant feeling produced by seemingly inconsistent thoughts.

Cohesiveness The degree to which members identify with the group and wish to remain in the group.

Collaborating style Style of conflict management in which parties work together to maximize the attainment of goals for all involved in the conflict.

Collectivist culture A culture that has a "we" consciousness; individuals see themselves as being closely linked to one or more groups and are primarily motivated by the norms and duties imposed by these groups.

Commencement address An inspirational speech that occurs at graduation ceremonies.

Commitment A passion for excellence; accepting nothing less than the best that you can be and dedicating yourself to achieving excellence.

Communication A transactional process of sharing meaning with others.

Communication climate The emotional atmosphere; the pervading or enveloping tone that we create by the way we communicate with others.

Communication competence Engaging in communication that is perceived to be both effective and appropriate in a given context.

Communication orientation A focus on making your message clear and interesting to listeners to assuage anxiety.

Communication skill The ability to perform a communication behavior effectively and repeatedly.

Communication style of conflict management The typical way an individual addresses a conflict.

Competence (of speaker) An audience's perception of a speaker's knowledge and experience on a topic.

Competing style (of conflict management) Exhibited by threats, criticism, contempt, hostile remarks and jokes, sarcasm, ridicule, intimidation, fault finding and blaming, and denials of responsibility. This style tries to "win" the argument.

Competition A process of mutually exclusive goal attainment (MEGA); for you to win, others must lose.

Competitive interrupting Dominating the conversation by seizing the floor from others who are speaking.

Composure A speaker's emotional stability, confidence, and degree of control over himself or herself when under stress.

Comprehension Shared meaning between and among parties in a transaction.

Compromising style Attempting to resolve a conflict by giving up something to get something in return.

Confirmation bias The tendency to seek information that supports, and to ignore information that contradicts, our beliefs and values.

Confirming response A response that enhances the person's self-esteem and confidence.

Conflict The expressed struggle of interconnected parties who perceive incompatible goals and interference from one or more parties in attaining those goals.

Conformity The inclination of group members to think and behave in ways that are consistent with group norms.

Confrontation A strategy of the collaborating style of conflict management in which there is an overt recognition of a conflict and a direct effort to find creative ways to satisfy all parties involved.

Connecting bid An attempt to engage another person in a positive transaction, sometimes at a deep and enduring level and other times at a superficial and fleeting level.

Connection-autonomy dialectic The desire to come together with another person (connection) yet remain apart, independent, and in control of one's own life (autonomy).

Connotation The volatile, personal, subjective meaning of words; composed of three dimensions: evaluation, potency, and activity.

Consensus A state of mutual agreement among members of a group in which all legitimate concerns of individuals have been addressed to the satisfaction of the group.

Constructive communication climate Composed of two general elements: (1) a pattern of openness, or a willingness to communicate, and (2) a pattern of supportiveness, or a confirmation of the worth and value of others and a willingness to help others be successful.

Constructive competition Occurs when competing against others produces a positive, enjoyable experience and promotes increased efforts to achieve victory without jeopardizing positive interpersonal relationships and personal well-being.

Constructive conflict Conflict characterized by communication that is cooperative, supportive, and flexible.

Contact theory Predicts that interacting and becoming more familiar with members of stereotyped groups can diminish prejudice and discrimination resulting from stereotyping.

Contempt Communication intended to insult and emotionally abuse a person.

Content dimension (of messages) What is actually said and done.

Content-only response A response that focuses on the content of a message and ignores the emotional side of the communication.

Context The environment in which communication occurs; the who, what, where, when, why, and how of communication.

Contingencies of self-worth Those things that are perceived as most important to you feeling good about yourself.

Contrast effect A persuasive strategy beginning with a large request that makes a later, smaller request seem more palatable.

Control Communication that seeks to regulate or direct a person's behavior.

Conventionality-uniqueness dialectic Wanting your relationship to be perceived as the same yet different from other relationships.

Convergence Similarities that connect us to others.

Conversational narcissism The tendency of listeners to turn the topics of ordinary conversation to themselves without showing sustained interest in others' topics.

Cooperation A process of mutually inclusive goal attainment (MIGA); for you to achieve your goals, others must also achieve their goals.

Cooperative argumentation Engaging in a process of deliberation with understanding and problem solving as the ultimate goals.

Correlation A consistent relationship between two variables.

Counterpersuasion Attacks from an opposing side on an issue of controversy.

Credibility (of evidence) Believability of supporting material determined by its reliability and validity.

Credibility (of speaker) Judgments made by listeners concerning the believability of a communicator.

Critical listening The process of evaluating the merits of claims as they are heard.

Cultural relativism The view that cultures are merely different, not deficient, and that each culture's norms and practices should be assessed only from the perspective of the culture itself, not based on standards embraced by another culture.

Culture A learned set of enduring values, beliefs, and practices that are shared by an identifiable, large group of people with a common history.

Culture shock The stressful transition stage after you move to unfamiliar cultural surroundings characterized by different rules, norms, and practices, with a corresponding challenge to adapt to these new circumstances.

Cynic Someone who unthinkingly mocks, ridicules, and tears down other people and their ideas.

Cynicism Nay-saying, fault finding, and ridiculing the beliefs and values of others.

Dead-level abstracting The practice of freezing on one level of abstraction; getting stuck using mostly very vague or very concrete words.

Deep diversity Substantial variation among members in task-relevant skills, knowledge, abilities, beliefs, values, perspectives, and problem-solving strategies.

Defensiveness A protective reaction to a perceived attack on our self-esteem and self-concept.

Defiance Unambiguous, overt, purposeful non-compliance with the dictates of others who exercise greater power.

Demographics Characteristics of an audience, such as age, gender, culture, ethnicity, and group affiliations.

Denotation The socially agreed-upon meaning of words; the meaning shared by members of a speech community.

Depth (of self-disclosure) How personal you become when discussing a particular subject that reveals something about yourself.

Description (supportive communication) A first-person report of how you feel, what you perceive to be true in specific situations, and what behaviors you desire from others.

Descriptions (sensory experience) Verbal reports that sketch what you perceive from your senses.

Destructive communication climate Composed of two general elements: a pattern of closedness and a pattern of defensiveness.

Destructive conflict Conflict characterized by escalation, retaliation, domination, competition, cross-complaining, defensiveness, and inflexibility.

Development Composed of the ability of group members, their motivation, and their experience with relevant tasks.

Dialectics Impulses that simultaneously push and pull us in opposite directions within our relationships with others.

Direct aggression Hostile communication that targets the victim openly, such as pushing, shoving, physically assaulting, or shouting insults.

Direct questions Inquiries that seek overt responses from listeners.

Directive style (of leadership) Leaders tell group members what to do and expect compliance.

Directory An Internet tool in which humans edit indexes of webpages that match, or link with, keywords typed in a search window.

Disconfirming responses Responses that diminish the person and reduce his or her confidence.

Discrimination Any behavior that manifests negative feelings about members of a group.

Disinhibiting Less restrained, impersonal, abrupt, even offensive communication from lean channels of communication.

Displacement The human ability to use language to talk about objects, ideas, events, and relations that don't just exist in the here and now and may not exist at all except in our minds.

Display rules Culture-specific prescriptions that dictate the appropriateness of behaviors.

Disruptive roles Group roles that serve individual needs at the expense of group needs and goals.

Divergence Differences that separate people.

Dominance The exercise of power over others.

Door-in-the-face strategy The contrast effect used as a persuasive strategy.

Downward communication Messages that flow from superordinates to subordinates in a hierarchical organization.

Dyad A couple or two-person, interpersonal relationship.

Dynamism The enthusiasm and energy exhibited by a speaker.

Dysfunctional speech anxiety When the intensity of the fight-or-flight response prevents a person from performing a speech appropriately and effectively.

Effectiveness How well an individual progresses toward the achievement of his or her goal.

Ego involvement The degree to which an issue is relevant or important to a person.

Elaboration likelihood model (of persuasion) Theory of how persuasion works that posits two routes to persuasion: the central route that requires mindfulness and the peripheral route that is relatively mindless.

Emblems Gestures that have a precise meaning separate from verbal communication and are usually recognized across an entire culture or co-culture, sometimes even across cultures.

Emoticons Graphic notations that indicate emotional information.

Emotional contagion Feeling the emotion communicated by speaker's tone of voice.

Emotional intelligence The ability to perceive, glean information from, and manage one's own and others' emotions.

Emotionally restrictive Having difficulty and fears about expressing one's feelings and difficulty finding words to express basic emotions.

Empathic listening Requires listeners to take the perspective of the other person and to listen for what that person needs and wants.

Empathy Thinking and feeling what you perceive another to be thinking and feeling.

Empowerment Power derived from enhancing the capabilities, choices, and influence of individuals and groups.

Equivocation Using language that permits more than one plausible meaning, often as a substitute for outright lying.

Ethics (in communication) A system for judging moral correctness by using an agreed-upon set of standards to determine what constitutes right and wrong behavior.

Ethnocentrism Seeing our own culture as the center of the universe and other cultures as insignificant or even inferior.

Ethos Aristotle's version of credibility, characterized by "good sense, good moral character, and good will" of the speaker.

Eulogy A speech delivered in praise of a deceased friend or family member.

Euphemisms Forms of linguistic Novocain whereby word choices numb us to or camouflage unpleasant or offensive realities.

Evaluations Value judgments made about individuals and their performance; exhibited as praise, recognition, admiration, criticism, contempt, or blame.

Evaluative response A judgment by a listener about a person's conduct.

Evidence Statistics, testimony of experts and credible sources, and verifiable facts.

Exchange theory An analysis that weighs the benefits of a particular relationship against any costs incurred.

Explicit norms Norms that specifically and overtly identify acceptable and unacceptable behavior in groups.

Extemporaneous (extemp) speech A speech delivered from a prepared outline or notes.

Extended example A detailed story or illustration.

Extrinsic reward An external inducement, such as money, grades, recognition, awards, or prestige.

Fallacies Errors in evidence and reasoning.

False analogies When a significant point or points of difference exist despite some superficial examples of similarities between the two things being compared.

False dichotomy Using either-or language to frame a choice as though only two opposing possibilities exist when at least a third option is clearly available.

Feedback The receiver's verbal and nonverbal responses to a message.

Feminine culture A culture that exhibits stereotypic feminine traits, such as affection, nurturance, sensitivity, compassion, and emotional expressiveness.

Fields of experience Cultural background, ethnicity, geographic location, extent of travel, and general personal experiences accumulated over the course of a lifetime that influence messages.

Fight-or-flight response Myriad physiological changes that are activated by a threat prepare both animals and humans either to fight the foe or flee the threat; the physiological defense alarm process triggered by stress.

Flaming A cyberterm for sending an abusive, attacking message (a *flame*) electronically to others.

Flooding When you can no longer think clearly because conflict triggers intense emotional reactions.

Forgetting curve The rate at which we no longer retain information in our memory.

Forgiveness Letting go of feelings of revenge and desires to retaliate.

Formal roles Roles that assign position, usually in an organizational structure.

Framing The influence wording has on our perception of choices.

Free morpheme A stand-alone word.

Friendship-warmth touch Touch communication that can be ambiguous but is intended to express friendship.

Functional-professional touch Instrumental touch communication that is limited to the requirements of the situation.

Functional speech anxiety When the fight-or-flight response is managed and stimulates an optimum speech presentation.

Fundamental attribution error Overemphasizing personal characteristics and underemphasizing situational causes of other people's behavior.

Gender The cultural construction of beliefs and behaviors considered appropriate for each sex; social role behavior that is learned from communicating with others.

Gender-biased language Language variants that make women virtually invisible and tacitly brand them as less powerful and less important than men.

Gender differences hypothesis The view that men and women communicate in vastly divergent ways.

Gender role stereotypes The set of expectations defined by each culture that specifies what is appropriate behavior for men and women (what is considered "masculine" or "feminine").

Gender similarities hypothesis The view that men and women communicate in mostly similar ways.

General purpose (of speech) Identifies the overall goal of a speech (to inform, describe, explain, demonstrate, persuade, celebrate, memorialize, entertain, or eulogize).

Glass ceiling An invisible barrier of subtle discrimination that excludes women and ethnic minorities from top leadership positions in corporate and professional America.

Glazing over When listeners' attention wanders and daydreaming occurs.

Grammar The set of rules that specify how the units of language can be meaningfully combined.

Group Three or more individuals, interacting for the achievement of some common purpose(s), who influence one another.

Grouphate The significant dissatisfaction, even dread, many people experience when working in groups.

Groupthink A mode of thinking that people engage in when they are deeply involved in a cohesive in-group, when the members' strivings for unanimity override their motivation to realistically appraise alternative courses of action.

Halfalogue Hearing only half the conversation, such as cell phone calls by others; often produces irritation in outside listeners.

Haptics The study of touch.

Hasty generalization A broad claim based on too few or unrepresentative examples.

Hearing The physiological process of registering sound waves as they hit the eardrums.

Hierarchy The rank ordering of members of an organization.

High-context communication style Indirect verbal expression; significant information is derived from contextual cues, such as relationships, situations, setting, and time; typically found in collectivist cultures.

High power-distance cultures Cultures with a relatively strong emphasis on maintaining power differences.

Hindsight bias The tendency to look back after a fact or outcome has been revealed and say to yourself, "I knew that all along."

Horizontal communication Messages that flow between individuals with equal power in organizations.

Hostile environment sexual harassment Insult, ridicule, humor, or intimidation of a sexual nature that makes the work environment an unpleasant, even threatening, place to remain.

Hostile sexism Antipathy toward women who are viewed as usurping men's power.

Hypercompetitiveness The excessive emphasis on beating others to achieve one's goals.

Hypothetical examples Instances that describe imaginary situations; concocted to make a point, illustrate an idea, or identify a general principle.

Identification (in persuasion) The affiliation and connection between speaker and listeners.

Illusion of transparency The overestimation of the extent to which audience members detect a speaker's nervousness.

Illustrators Gestures that help explain what one person says to another.

Immediacy The perception of closeness and involvement with others.

Implicit norms Observable patterns of behavior, exhibited by group members, that identify acceptable and unacceptable conduct.

Impromptu speech A speech delivered off-the-cuff, without notes.

Inattentional blindness Lack of attention to an unexpected object.

Inclusion-seclusion dialectic The desire to spend time alone with one's partner and also spend time together with others outside the relationship.

Indirect aggression Hostile communication that intends to harm a targeted person while avoiding identification as an aggressor, such as gossiping, spreading malicious rumors, or sabotaging behind the victim's back.

Individual achievement The realization of personal goals without having to defeat an opponent.

Individualist culture A culture that has a "me" consciousness; individuals see themselves as loosely linked to each other and largely independent of group identification.

Inferences Conclusions about the unknown based on the known.

Inferential error A mistaken conclusion that results from the assumption that inferences are factual descriptions of reality instead of interpretations of varying accuracy made by individuals.

Informal roles Roles that identify functions, not positions; usually emerge naturally from group transactions.

Informational listening Attempting to comprehend the message of a speaker.

Integration A collaborative strategy that finds alternatives that meet the goals of all parties in a conflict.

Intensity Concentrated stimuli used to gain and maintain audience attention.

Internal summary Restates a key point or points of a speech in the body of the speech.

Interpersonal relationship A connection two people have to each other because of kinship (e.g., brother-sister), attraction (e.g., lovers and friends), or power distribution (e.g., boss-employee).

Interpreting response A listener expressing what he or she thinks is the underlying meaning of a situation presented by another person.

Interrupting When one person stops speaking when another person starts speaking.

Interviewing A purposeful, planned conversation characterized by extensive verbal interaction.

Intimate relationship A type of interpersonal relationship characterized by strong emotional bonding, closeness, and interdependence in which individuals meaningfully influence each other.

Intimate terrorism The most extreme form of relationship violence; a violent attempt to control a relationship completely, or at least to dominate a relationship generally.

Intrinsic reward Enjoyment from what one does for its own sake and because it gives pleasure.

Jargon The specialized language of a profession, trade, or group.

Judgments Subjective evaluations of objects, events, or ideas.

Kinesics The study of both facial communication and gestures.

Label A name or a descriptive word or phrase.

Laissez-faire style (of leadership) A sit-on-your-derrière approach to leadership, which is to say no leadership at all is exercised.

Language A structured system of symbols for communicating meaning.

Latitude of acceptance Positions a person finds acceptable or at least tolerable.

Latitude of noncommitment Positions that provoke only a neutral or ambivalent response from people.

Latitude of rejection Positions a person finds objectionable because they are too far from his or her anchor attitude.

Law of Very Large Numbers With large enough numbers, almost anything is likely to happen to *somebody*.

Leadership A leader-follower influence process with the goal of producing positive change that reflects mutual purposes of group members and is largely accomplished through competent communication.

Legitimate authority Someone who is perceived to have a right to direct others' behavior because of his or her position, title, role, experience, or knowledge.

Lexicon The total vocabulary of a language.

Linguistic determinism The claim that we are prisoners of our native language, unable to think certain thoughts or perceive in certain ways because of the grammatical structure and lexicon of our language.

Linguistic relativity The claim that the grammar and lexicon of our native language powerfully influence but do not imprison our thinking and perception.

Listening The process of receiving, constructing, and reconstructing meaning from, and responding to, spoken and/or nonverbal messages.

Logos Aristotle's conception of building arguments based on logic and evidence.

Love and intimacy touch Touch reserved for a very few, special individuals that is not sexual but does express tenderness.

Low-context communication style Verbally precise, direct, assertive, self-enhancing, and explicit method of communication usually found in individualistic cultures.

Low power-distance cultures Culture whose people value relatively equal power sharing and discourage attention to status differences and ranking in society.

Magic ratio Five positive for every one negative act are needed to sustain a relationship.

Maintenance roles Group roles that address the social dimensions of small groups.

Manipulative communication An attempt by one person to maneuver another toward the manipulator's goal.

Manipulators Gestures made by one part of the body, usually the hands, that rub, pick, squeeze, clean, or groom another part of the body, and have no specific meaning.

Margin of error A measure of the degree of sampling error accounted for by imperfections in sample selection.

Masculine culture A culture that exhibits stereotypic masculine traits, such as male dominance, ambitiousness, assertiveness, competitiveness, and drive for achievement.

Masculine-feminine dimension Degree to which a culture expects rigid adherence to or is flexible about gender role expectations.

Masculine-generic gender references The use of masculine nouns and pronouns to include references to both women and men.

Meaning The conscious pattern humans create out of their interpretation of experience; making sense of our world.

Message Stimulus that produces meaning.

Metaphor An implied comparison of two seemingly dissimilar things.

Metasearch engine An Internet tool that will send your keyword request to several search engines at once.

Mindfulness Thinking about one's communication with others and persistently working to improve it.

Mindlessness Not being cognizant of one's communication with others and putting little or no effort into improving it.

Mixed messages Inconsistencies or outright contradictions between verbal and nonverbal messages.

Mixed metaphor The use of two or more vastly different metaphors in a single expression.

Morpheme The smallest unit of meaning in a language.

Morphology The part of grammar that describes how morphemes are constructed meaningfully from phonemes.

Multiculturalism Social-intellectual movement that promotes the value of diversity as a core principle and insists that all cultural groups be treated with respect and as equals.

Murphy's Law The assertion that anything that can go wrong likely will go wrong.

Muscle dysmorphia A preoccupation with one's body size and a perception that, though very muscular, one actually looks puny.

Myth A belief that is contradicted by fact.

Negativity bias A strong tendency to weigh negative information more heavily than positive information, especially when forming perceptions of others.

Netiquette Etiquette (rules of proper conduct) when using the Internet.

Noise Any interference with effective transmission and reception of a message.

Nominal group technique Creative problem-solving method in which team members work alone to generate ideas, those ideas are announced to the group, and team members' ranking of those ideas result in the group's top preferences.

Nonverbal communication Sharing meaning with others nonlinguistically.

Norm of reciprocity You give back what you get from others.

Norms Rules that indicate what group members have to do (obligation), should do (preference), and cannot do (prohibition) if they want to accomplish specific goals.

Oculesics The study of eye contact in human communication.

Openness A willingness to communicate.

Openness-closedness dialectic The tension in relationships between accessibility and privacy.

Operational definition Specifies measurable behaviors or experiences that indicate what a word means to the user; what is included and what is excluded.

Paralanguage Vocal cues.

Parallel processing Using both central and peripheral routes to persuasion.

Paraphrasing A concise response that states the essence of the speaker's content but in the listener's words.

Participative style (of leadership) Leaders encourage all group members to engage meaningfully in discussions and decision making.

Pathos Aristotle's conception of emotional appeals used for persuasion.

Perception The process of selecting, organizing, and interpreting sensory data.

Perception checking A description of a behavior followed by an interpretation of the behavior and finishing with a request for verification of your interpretation.

Performance orientation An attempt to satisfy an audience of critics whose members are focused on evaluating your presentation.

Persuasion A communication process of converting, modifying, or maintaining the attitudes, beliefs, and/or behavior of others.

Phonemes The individual units of sounds that compose a specific spoken language.

Phonology A part of grammar that describes the patterns of sound in a language.

Physical noise External environmental distractions, such as startling sounds, poorly heated rooms, and the like, that divert our attention from the message sent by a source.

Physiological noise Biological influences, such as sweaty palms, pounding heart, and butterflies in the stomach induced by speech anxiety or feeling sick or exhausted at work, that interfere with sending and receiving messages.

Picture Superiority Effect When text alone is presented, audience members usually remember only about 10% of the information three days later, but if you combine brief text with relevant, interesting images, retention increases dramatically

Pitch How frequency is perceived; how high or low the sound is (e.g., how high or low a human voice is during conversation).

Power The ability to influence the attainment of goals sought by oneself or others.

Power-distance dimension Cultural variations in the acceptability of unequal distribution of power in relationships, institutions, and organizations.

Power resource Anything that enables individuals to achieve their goals, assist others to achieve their goals, or interferes with others achieving their goals.

Predictability-novelty dialectic The desire for both stability and change in interpersonal relationships.

Prejudice Negative feelings about members of a group.

Prevention Power used to thwart the influence of others.

Primacy effect The tendency to be more influenced by initial information about a person than by information gathered later.

Principle of least interest The person who cares less about continuing a relationship usually has more power.

Probability Likelihood of an occurrence.

Probing response Seeking more information from others by asking questions.

Productivity (in groups) The degree to which a group accomplishes its work efficiently and effectively.

Productivity (in language) The capacity of a language to transform a small number of phonemes into whatever words, phrases, and sentences that we require to communicate our abundance of thoughts, ideas, and feelings.

Proposition The primary overriding claim for a persuasive speech.

Proposition of fact The primary overriding claim in a persuasive speech that alleges a truth.

Proposition of policy The primary overriding claim in a persuasive speech that calls for a significant change from how problems are currently handled.

Proposition of value The primary overriding claim in a persuasive speech that calls for a judgment assessing the worth or merit of an idea, object, or practice.

Prototype The most representative or "best" example of something.

Provisionalism Qualifying our statements with words such as *possibly, probably, perhaps, maybe,* and *could be* and avoiding absolutes such as *always, never, must, can't,* and *won't.*

Proxemics The study of the influence of distance and territoriality on human communication.

Pseudolistening When someone pretends to listen.

Psychological noise Preconceptions, biases, and assumptions that interfere with effective message transmission and reception.

Psychological reactance The more someone tries to control our behavior and restrict our choices, the more we are inclined to resist such efforts, or even to do the opposite behavior.

Quid pro quo sexual harassment When the more powerful person requires sexual favors from the less powerful person in exchange for keeping a job, getting a high grade in a class, landing an employment promotion, and the like.

Random sample A portion of a population chosen in such a manner that every member of the entire population has an equal chance of being selected.

Rationalization of disconfirmation Inventing superficial, even lame, alternative explanations for contradictory evidence.

Real examples Actual occurrences used to illustrate an idea, make a point, or identify a general principle.

Reasoning Thought process of drawing conclusions from evidence.

Rebid An attempt to connect with another person after an initial bid has been ignored.

Rebuttal Exceptions or a refutation that diminishes the force of a claim.

Receiver The decoder of a message.

Referents The objects, events, ideas, or relationships referred to by words.

Reflective thinking model John Dewey's sequence of logical steps that incorporates the scientific method of defining, analyzing, and solving problems.

Reframing (problem-solving technique) The creative process of breaking rigid thinking by placing a problem in a different frame of reference.

Refutation The process of answering opposing arguments in a debate or disagreement.

Relationship dimension (of messages) How the message defines or redefines the association between individuals.

Relevance Evidence used to support claims must relate directly to those claims.

Reliability Consistency of a source of information.

Resistance Covert, ambiguous noncompliance with the dictates of more powerful individuals.

Response styles The types of initial verbal reactions we make when another person comes to us with a problem, reveals a frustrating event, or experiences an emotional crisis.

Revelation-concealment dialectic The dilemma you face when you want to share information about a relationship with those outside the relationship yet also want to conceal the relationship for various reasons.

Rhetorical question A question asked by a speaker that the audience answers mentally but not out loud.

Roast A purposely humorous tribute to a person.

Role fixation Playing a group role rigidly, with little or no inclination to try other roles.

Roles Patterns of behavior that group members are expected to exhibit.

Rule A prescription that indicates what behavior is obligated, prohibited, or preferred in a given context.

Sapir-Whorf hypothesis The claim that we are either prisoners of our native language, unable to think certain thoughts or perceive in certain ways (linguistic determinism), or that our language powerfully influences but does not imprison our thinking and perceptions (linguistic relativity).

Schemas Mental frameworks that create meaningful patterns from stimuli.

Script A predictable sequence of events that indicates what we are expected to do in a given situation.

Search engine An Internet tool that computer generates indexes of webpages that match, or link with, keywords typed in a search window.

Segmenting A strategy to manage dialectics in which certain parts of a relationship are divided into separate domains and some of these domains are declared off-limits.

Selecting A strategy for managing dialectics in which one contradictory impulse is given attention and another is ignored.

Self-concept The sum total of everything that encompasses the self-referential term *me*; your identity or self-perception.

Self-deprecation Humor that makes gentle fun of one's own failings and limitations.

Self-disclosure The process of purposely revealing to others information about ourselves that is significant and that others would not know unless we told them.

Self-enhancement Engaging in personal promotion, such as in a job interview.

Self-esteem The evaluative element of self-perception; self-appraisal or your perception of self-worth, attractiveness, and social competence.

Self-fulfilling prophecy An erroneous expectation that produces an action that in turn causes the expected behavior and confirms the original impression.

Self-humbling Downplaying oneself via modest talk, restraint, hesitation and the use of a self-deprecation message concerning one's performance and effort.

Self-managing work teams Teams that regulate their own performance free from outside interference while completing an entire task.

Self-reflexiveness The ability to use language to talk about language.

Self-selected sample A collection of individuals, usually the most committed, aroused, or motivated, who have chosen themselves to participate in a survey, poll, or study.

Self-serving bias The tendency to attribute our successful behavior to ourselves (personal traits) but to assign external circumstances (situations) to our unsuccessful behavior.

Semantic noise Confusing or distracting word choice that interferes with accurate message transmission and reception.

Semantic reaction A delayed, thoughtful response to language that seeks to decipher the user's intended meaning of a word.

Semantics The set of rules that governs the meaning of words and sentences.

Sender The initiator and encoder of messages.

Sensation The process by which our sense organs (eyes, ears, nose, skin, tongue) that contain sense receptors change physical energy (light, sound waves, chemical substances) into neural impulses that are sent to our brains.

Sensitivity Receptive accuracy whereby we can detect, decode, and comprehend signals in our social environment.

Sensory acuity The level of sensitivity of our senses.

Serial arguments Recurring arguments that never get resolved.

Servant leaders Those who place the good of followers over their own self-interests and demonstrate strong moral behavior toward followers.

Severity (of feared occurrences) Extent of rational/irrational fear of public speaking.

Sex Biological differences between males and females.

Sexting Sending sexually suggestive text messages, nude, or nearly nude photos and videos via a smartphone.

Sexual harassment Verbal or nonverbal communication of a sexual nature that is unwelcome by the recipient and likely to interfere with the victim's work.

Sexual touch Intimate touch between individuals.

Shift response A competitive vying for attention and focus on oneself by shifting topics.

Shifting the burden of proof Inappropriately assuming the validity of a claim unless it is proven false by another person who never made the original claim.

Signal reaction An automatic, unthinking, emotional response to a symbol (usually a word).

Signposts Organizational markers that indicate the structure of a speech and notify listeners a particular point is about to be addressed.

Similarity attraction theory The idea that we are drawn to those who are similar to us.

Simile An explicit comparison of two seemingly dissimilar things using the word *like* or *as*.

Situational couple violence Individuals quarrel with their partners, anger and frustration erupt, and an assault occurs.

Skepticism The process of listening to claims, evaluating evidence and reasoning supporting those claims, and drawing conclusions based on probabilities.

Slang Highly informal words not in standard usage but that are used by a group with a common interest.

Smoothing A collaborative strategy that attempts to calm the agitated feelings of those involved in a conflict.

Social cohesion That which binds us together in mutual liking.

Social comparison Evaluating yourself by comparing yourself to other people.

Social dimension (of groups) Relationships between group members and the impact these relationships have on the group.

Social judgment theory A theory of persuasion that focuses on how close or distant an audience's position on a controversial issue is from its anchor attitude.

Social loafing The tendency of individuals to reduce their work effort when they join groups.

Social-polite touch Touch communication that occurs during introductions, business relationships, and formal occasions.

Socialization The communication of shared cultural practices, beliefs, and values from generation to generation.

Spamming Sending unsolicited email, especially advertisements for products or activities.

Specific purpose statement (of speech) A concise, precise infinitive phrase composed of simple, clear language that encompasses both the general purpose and the central idea and that indicates what the speaker hopes to accomplish.

Speech anxiety Fear of public speaking and the nervousness that accompanies that fear.

Speech of introduction Prepares an audience for a speech that is about to be presented.

Speech of presentation A brief speech that must communicate to an audience assembled the meaning and importance of an award being conferred.

Speech segmentation Process of discerning breaks between recognizable words.

Stages of relationship model The five "coming together" stages and five "coming apart" stages of relationships.

Standard Agenda Structured method of decision making and problem solving based on the reflective thinking model.

Stereotype A generalization about a group or category of people.

Stonewalling A form of the avoiding style of conflict management exhibited by refusing to discuss problems or by physically leaving when the other person is complaining, disagreeing, or attacking.

Stratification Various levels of cultural division based on power, spanning the extremes of the haves and the have-nots.

Structure A form or shape characterized by an interrelationship among its parts.

Style (of speaking) Words chosen to express your thoughts and the ways you use language to bring your thoughts to life for an audience.

Stylistic similarity An identification strategy of persuasion in which a speaker tries to look and act similarly to listeners.

Substantive similarity Creates identification between a speaker and an audience by establishing common ground between the two.

Superordinate goal A goal that requires mutual effort by both groups to achieve a desired end.

Support response A cooperative effort to focus attention on the other person, not oneself, during conversation.

Supporting materials Examples, statistics, and testimony used to bolster a speaker's theme or viewpoint.

Supporting response A response that acknowledges the feelings of the speaker and tries to boost the person's confidence.

Supportiveness A confirmation of the worth and value of others and a willingness to help others succeed.

Symbols Arbitrary representations of objects, events, ideas, or relationships.

Synergy By individuals working together as a group, the work of group members yields a greater total effect than the sum of the individual members' efforts could have produced.

Syntax The rules that govern appropriate combinations of words into phrases and sentences.

Systematic desensitization A technique of incremental exposure to increasingly threatening stimuli coupled with relaxation techniques; used to control anxiety, even phobias, triggered by a wide variety of stimuli.

Task dimension (of groups) The work performed by a group and its impact on the group.

Task roles Group roles that advance the attainment of group goals.

Team A small number of people with complementary skills who are equally committed to a common purpose, goals, and working approach for which they hold themselves mutually accountable.

Territoriality A predisposition to defend a fixed geographic area, or territory, as one's exclusive domain.

Testimony A first-hand account of events by witnesses or the conclusions offered publicly by experts on a topic

Thesis Identifies the central idea that you want the audience to understand, believe, or feel

Threshold (of human senses) Minimum amount of energy that triggers a sensation for each human sensory system.

Toast A brief tribute to a person or couple.

Toulmin structure of argument The six elements that constitute an argument: claim, grounds, warrant, backing, rebuttal, and qualifier.

Traits Relatively enduring characteristics of a person that highlight differences between people and are displayed in most situations.

Transitions Connect what was said in a speech with what will be said.

Triangular theory of love The interaction among three elements of love—intimacy, passion, and commitment—that determines seven different types of love between people.

Tribute speeches Speeches that praise or celebrate a living person.

True belief A willingness to accept claims without solid reasoning or valid evidence and to hold these beliefs tenaciously even if a googol of contradictory evidence disputes them.

True believers Those who willingly accept claims by authorities or valued sources without question and protect beliefs based on these claims by embracing confirmation bias.

Trustworthiness How truthful or honest an audience perceives a speaker to be.

Turning-against response An overtly negative rejection of a connecting bid.

Turning-away response Ignoring a connecting bid or acting preoccupied when a bid is offered.

Turning point (in relationships) A key moment that changes a relationship, such as sharing an interest, disclosing a personal secret, or lending something important.

Turning-toward response Reacting positively to a connecting bid.

Twenty Percent Rule Discrimination decreases when at least 20% of group membership is composed of women or minorities.

Uncertainty Reduction Theory Posits that when strangers first meet, their principal goal is to reduce uncertainty and to increase predictability.

Understanding response A listener checking his or her perceptions for comprehension of the speaker's message or paraphrasing the message to check for accuracy.

Upward communication Messages that flow from subordinates to superordinates in an organization.

Validity Accuracy of a source of information.

Value dimensions Varying degrees of importance placed on those deeply felt views of what is right, good, and worthwhile; deep structure of cultures.

Values The most deeply felt, generally shared views of what is good, right, or worthwhile behavior or thinking.

Variable Anything that can change.

Virtual groups Groups whose members communicate electronically and rarely, if ever, meet face-to-face.

Virtual library An Internet search tool that combines Internet technology and standard library techniques for cataloguing and appraising information.

Visualization Countering negative thoughts of catastrophe with positive images of success.

Vividness effect When outrageous, shocking, controversial, and dramatic events distort our perceptions of the facts.

Vocal fillers The insertion of *uhm, ah, like, you know, know what I mean, whatever,* and additional variants that substitute for pauses during speech and often draw attention to themselves.

Waist-to-hip ratio Universal measure of female attractiveness; the smaller the waist is compared to the hips (hourglass figure), the greater the perception of attractiveness.

Wedge shape Relatively broad shoulders and narrow waist and hips in men; used as a measure of male attractiveness.

Workplace bullying Persistent verbal and nonverbal aggression at work that includes public humiliation, constant criticism, ridicule, gossip, insults, and social ostracism.

References

A survey of LGBT Americans. (2013, June 13). *Pew Research Center*. Retrieved from http://www.pewsocialtrends.org/2013/06/13/a-survey-of-lgbt-americans/

Ackerman, R. A., Kashy, D. A., Donnellan, M. B., Neppl, T., Lorenz, F. O., & Conger, R. D. (2013). The interpersonal legacy of a positive family climate on adolescence. *Psychological Science, 24*, 243–250.

Ackrill, C. (2012, October 5). 6 thought patterns of the stressed: No. 3—catastrophizing. *The American Institute of Stress*. Retrieved from http://www.stress.org/6-thought-patterns-of-the-stressed-no-3-catastrophizing/

Adler, J. E. (1998, January/February). Open minds and the argument from ignorance. *Skeptical Inquirer*, pp. 41–44.

Adler, R. (1977). *Confidence in communication: A guide to assertive and social skills*. New York: Holt, Rinehart & Winston.

Adler, R., & Elmhorst, J. M. (2008). *Communicating at work: Principles and practices for business and the professions*. New York: McGraw-Hill.

Adler, R., & Proctor, R. F. (2007). *Looking out, looking in*. Belmont, CA: Thomson/Wadsworth.

Adorbs new words added to OxfordDictionaries.com. (2014, August 13). *Oxford Dictionaries*. Retrieved from http://blog.oxforddictionaries.com/2014/08/oxford-dictionaries-update-august-2014/

Afifi, T. D., McManus, T., Steuber, K., & Coho, A. (2009). Verbal avoidance and dissatisfaction in intimate conflict situations. *Human Communication Research, 35*, 357–383.

Afifi, W. A., Guerrero, L. K., & Egland, K. L. (1994, June). *Maintenance behaviors in same- and opposite-sex friendships: Connection to gender, relational closeness, and equity issues*. Paper presented at the annual meeting of the International Network on Personal Relationships, Iowa City, IA.

Aggarwal, P., & O'Brien, C. L. (2008). Social loafing on group projects: Structural antecedents and effects on student satisfaction. *Journal of Marketing Education, 30*, 255–264.

Agthe, M., Sporrle, M., & Maner, J. K. (2011). Does being attractive always help? Positive and negative effects of attractiveness on social decision making. *Personality and Social Psychology Bulletin, 37*, 1042–1054.

Ahn, Y.-Y., Ahnert, S. E., Bagrow, J. P., & Barabasi, A.-L. (2011). Flavor network and the principles of pairing. *Scientific Reports*. Retrieved from http://www.barabasilab.com/pubs/CCNR-ALB_Publications/201112-15_Nature-Flavor/201112-15_Nature-Flavor.pdf

Ahrons, C. (1994). *The good divorce: Keeping your family together when your marriage comes apart*. New York: Harper Perennial.

Albada, K. F., Knapp, M. L., & Theune, K. E. (2002). Interaction Appearance Theory: Changing perceptions of physical attractiveness through social interaction. *Communication Theory, 12*, 8–40.

Albers, H. (2012). Pediatric bipolar disorder: A psychological misnomer. In L. G. Schnoor, L. Mayfield, & K. Young (Eds.), *Winning orations*. Mankato, MN: Interstate Oratorical Association.

Allan, K., & Burridge, K. (1991). *Euphemism and dysphemism: Language used as shield and weapon*. New York: Oxford University Press.

Alejo, L. A. (2014, September 22). Washington's NFL team name is offensive. *San Jose Mercury News*, p. A7.

Allen, G. (1996). Military drug testing. In L. G. Schnoor (Ed), *Winning orations*. Mankato, MN: Interstate Oratorical Association.

Allen, M. (1998). Comparing the persuasive effectiveness of one- and two-sided messages. In M. Allen & R. W. Preiss (Eds.), *Persuasion: Advances through meta-analysis*. Cresskill, NJ: Hampton Press.

Allen, M., Bruflat, R., Fucilla, R., Kramer, M., McKellips, S., Ryan, D. J., & Spiegelhoff, M. (2000). Testing the persuasiveness of evidence: Combining narrative and statistical forms. *Communication Research Reports, 17*, 331–336.

Allen, M., Hunter, J. E., & Donohue, W. A. (2009). Meta-analysis of self-report data on the effectiveness of public speaking anxiety treatment techniques. *Communication Education, 38*, 54–76.

Alley, M. (2005). *The craft of scientific presentations: Critical steps to succeed and critical errors to avoid*. Warren, MI: Springer.

Almendrala, A. (2015, April 8). College kids text during showers, sex and class. We're doomed. *Huffington Post*. Retrieved from http://www.huffingtonpost.com/2015/04/08/college-kids-text_n_7014214.html

Altman, I., & Taylor, D. (1973). *Social penetration: The development of interpersonal relationships*. New York: Holt, Rinehart & Winston.

Amanatullah, E. T., & Morris, M. W. (2010). Negotiating gender roles: Gender differences in assertive negotiating by women's fear of backlash and attenuated when negotiating on behalf of others. *Journal of Personality and Social Psychology, 98,* 256–267.

Ambady, N., & Rosenthal, R. (1992). Thin slices of expressive behavior as predictors of interpersonal consequences: A meta-analysis. *Psychological Bulletin, 111,* 256–274.

Ambady, N., & Rosenthal, R. (1993). Half a minute: Predicting teacher evaluations from thin slices of nonverbal behavior and physical attractiveness. *Journal of Personality and Social Psychology, 64,* 431–441.

Ambady, N., Bernieri, F. J., & Richeson, J. A. (2000). Toward a histology of social behavior: Judgmental accuracy from thin slices of the behavioral stream. In M. P. Zanna (Ed.), *Advances in experimental social psychology*. San Diego, CA: Academic Press.

Amen, D. G. (2007). *The brain in love*. New York: Three Rivers Press.

American Civil Liberties Union. (2009). The persistence of racial and ethnic profiling in the United States. Retrieved from http://www.aclu.org/files/pdfs/humanrights/cerd_finalreport.pdf

American College Health Association. (2012). *National college health assessment II: Undergraduate reference group executive summary*. Hanover, MD: American College Health Association.

Ames, D., Maissen, L. B., & Brockner, J. (2012). The role of listening in interpersonal influence. *Journal of Research in Personality, 46,* 345–349.

Andersen, P. (1999). *Nonverbal communication: Forms and functions*. Mountain View, CA: Mayfield.

Andersen, P. A. (2006). The evolution of biological sex differences in communication. In K. Dindia & D. J. Canary (Eds.), *Sex differences and similarities in communication*. Mahwah, NJ: Erlbaum.

Andersen, P. A., Guerrero, L. K., & Jones, S. M. (2006). Nonverbal behavior in intimate interactions and intimate relationships. In V. Manusov & M. L. Patterson (Eds.), *The Sage handbook of nonverbal communication*. Thousand Oaks, CA: Sage.

Anderson, C. A. (1999). Attributional style, depression, and loneliness: A cross-cultural comparison of American and Chinese students. *Personality and Social Psychology Bulletin, 25,* 482–499.

Anderson, J. L., Crawford, C. B., Nadeau, J., & Lindberg, T. (1992). Was the Duchess of Windsor right? A cross-cultural review of the socioecology of ideals of female body shape. *Ethology and Sociobiology, 13,* 197–227.

Anderson, K., & Leaper, C. (1998). Meta-analyses of gender effects on conversational interruption: Who, what, when, where, and how. *Sex Roles, 39,* 225–252.

Anderson, R., & Killenberg, G. (1999). *Interviewing: Speaking, listening, and learning for professional life*. Mountain View, CA: Mayfield.

Anderson, R., & Ross, V. (1994). *Questions of communication: A practical introduction to theory*. New York: St. Martin's Press.

Andeweg, B. A., de Jong, J. C., & Hoeken, H. (1998). May I have your attention? Exordial techniques in informative oral presentations. *Technical Communication Quarterly, 7,* 271–284.

Angier, N. (2002, March 5). One lifetime is not enough for a trip to distant stars. *The New York Times*. Retrieved from http://www.nytimes.com/learning/teachers/featured_articles/20020305tuesday.html

Ann Landers learns that most women would rather be hugged than you-know-what. (1985, January 21). *People*. Retrieved from http://www.people.com/people/archive/article/0,20089743,00.html

Antisweatshop activist brings delegates to their feet. (2002, March/April). *California Teacher*, p. 4.

Archer, D. (2000a). *A world of food: Tastes and taboos in different cultures* [videotape]. Berkeley: University of California Extension Center of Media and Independent Learning.

Archer, J. (2000b). Sex differences in aggression between heterosexual partners: A meta-analytic review. *Psychological Bulletin, 126,* 651–680.

Archer, J. (2002). Sex differences in physically aggressive acts between heterosexual partners: A meta-analytic review. *Aggression and Violent Behavior, 7,* 213–351.

Arkowitz, H., & Lilienfeld, S. O. (2009, April/May). Road warriors. *Scientific American Mind*, pp. 64–65.

Aronson, E. (2012). *The social animal*. New York: Worth.

Aronson, E., Fried, C., & Stone, J. (1991). Overcoming denial and increasing the intentions to use condoms through the induction of hypocrisy. *American Journal of Public Health, 81,* 1636–1638.

Arranged marriage: CNN examines the age-old practice in India. (2013, May 31). *Huffington Post*. Retrieved from http://www.huffingtonpost.com/2012/05/31/arranged-marriage_n_1560049.html

Arrillaga, P. (2001, August 15). Trauma of "civilizing." *San Jose Mercury News*, p. 13A.

Atkinson, C. (2008). *Beyond bullet points: Using Microsoft Office PowerPoint 2007 to create presentations that inform, motivate, and inspire*. Redmond, WA: Microsoft Press.

Aube, C., & Rousseau, V. (2005). Team goal commitment and team effectiveness: The role of task interdependence and supportive behaviors. *Group Dynamics: Theory, Research, and Practice, 9,* 189–204.

Aune, K. S., Kim, M., & Hu, A. (2000). *"Well I've been talking long enough about me. . . . What do you think of my accomplishments?" The relationship between self-construals, narcissism, compulsive talking, and bragging.* Paper presented at the meeting of the National Communication Association, Seattle, WA.

Avolio, B. J. (2007). Promoting more integrative strategies for leadership theory-building. *American Psychologist, 62,* 25–33.

Axtell, R. E. (1998). *Gestures: The do's and taboos of body language around the world.* New York: Wiley.

Ayres, J. (2005). Performance visualization and behavioral disruption: A clarification. *Communication Reports, 18,* 55–63.

Babcock, J. C., Graham, K., Canady, B., & Ross, J. M. (2011). A proximal change experiment testing two communication exercises with intimate partner violent men. *Behavior Therapy, 42,* 336–347.

Babcock, L. (2002). *Do graduate students negotiate their job offers?* Unpublished manuscript, Carnegie Mellon University.

Babcock, L., & Laschever, S. (2009). *Women don't ask: The high cost of avoiding negotiation--and positive strategies for change.* New Jersey: Princeton University press

Babcock, L. M., Gelfand, M., Small, D., & Stayn, H. (2002). *Propensity to initiate negotiations: A new look at gender variation in negotiation behavior.* Unpublished manuscript, Carnegie Mellon University.

Babiak, P., & Hare, R. D. (2006). *Snakes in suits: When psychopaths go to work.* New York: Bantam.

Bach, G., & Goldberg, H. (1972). *Creative aggression.* New York: Avon.

Bachman, G. F., & Guerrero, L. K. (2006). Forgiveness, apology, and communicative responses to hurtful events. *Communication Reports, 19,* 45–56.

Bailey, J. M., Gauline, S., Agyei, Y., & Gladue, B. A. (1994). Effects of gender and sexual orientation on evolutionarily relevant aspects of human mating psychology. *Journal of Personality and Social Psychology, 66,* 1081–1093.

Ball, A. L. (2010, May 28). Are 5001 Facebook friends one too many? *The New York Times.* Retrieved from http://www.nytimes.com/2010/05/30/fashion/30FACEBOOK.html

Banaji, M. (2011, February). Harnessing the power of *Wikipedia* for scientific psychology: A call to action. *APS Observer,* pp. 5–6.

Baram, M. (2009, June 8). Stephen Colbert Iraq show: Gen. Odierno shaves his head. *Huffington Post.* Retrieved from http://www.huffingtonpost.com/2009/06/08/stephen-colbert-iraq-show-n_212388.html

Bargh, J. A., & McKenna, K. Y. A. (2004). The Internet and social life. *Annual Review of Psychology, 55,* 573–590.

Barker, L., & Watson, K. (2000). *Listen up: How to improve relationships, reduce stress, and be more productive by using the power of listening.* New York: St. Martin's Press.

Barnes, S. B. (2001). *Online connections: Internet interpersonal relationships.* Cresskill, NJ: Hampton Press.

Baron, N. S. (2008). *Always on: Language in an online and mobile world.* New York: Oxford University Press.

Baron, R. A. (1990). Countering the effects of destructive criticism: The relative efficacy of four interventions. *Journal of Applied Psychology, 75,* 235–243.

Barrabi, T. (2015, March 24). Despite Germanwings flight 4U 9525 crash, odds of dying in plane accident are low. *IBT Media Inc.* Retrieved from http://www.ibtimes.com/despite-germanwings-flight-4u-9525-crash-odds-dying-plane-accident-are-low-1857216

Barron, L. A. (2003). Ask and you shall receive: Gender differences in negotiators' beliefs about requests for a higher salary. *Human Relations, 56,* 635–662.

Baruah, J., & Paulus, P. B. (2008). Effects of training on idea generation in groups. *Small Group Research, 39,* 523–541.

Bass, B. M., & Bass, R. (2008). *The Bass handbook of leadership: Theory, research, and managerial applications.* New York: Free Press.

Bauer, B. (1996, February 24). Undue pride tied to violence. *San Jose Mercury News,* p. 20A.

Baumeister, R. F., Campbell, J. D., Krueger, J. I., & Vohs, K. D. (2003). Does high self-esteem cause better performance, interpersonal success, happiness, or healthier lifestyles? *Psychological Science in the Public Interest, 4,* 1–44.

Baumeister, R. F., Catanese, K. R., & Vohs, K. D. (2001). Is there a gender difference in strength of sex drive? Theoretical vies, conceptual distinctions, and a review of relevant evidence. *Personality and Social Psychology Review, 5,* 242–273.

Baumeister, R., Smart, L., & Boden, J. (1996). Relation of the threatened egotism to violence and aggressions: The dark side of high self-esteem. *Psychological Review, 103,* 5–33.

Baxter, L. (1990). Dialectical contradictions in relationship development. *Journal of Social and Personal Relationships, 7,* 69–88.

Baxter, L. (1994). A dialogic approach to relationship management. In D. Canary & L. Stafford (Eds.), *Communication and relational maintenance.* New York: Academic Press.

Baxter, L. (2011). *Voicing relationships: A dialogic perspective.* Thousand Oaks, CA: Sage.

Baxter, L., & Montgomery, B. (1996). *Relating: Dialogues and dialect*. New York: Guilford Press.

Baxter, L. A., & Bullis, C. (1986). Turning points in developing romantic relationships. *Human Communication Research*, 12, 469–494.

Baxter, L. A., & Erbert, L. A. (1999). Perceptions of dialectical contradictions in turning points of development in heterosexual romantic relationships. *Journal of Social and Personal Relationships*, 16, 547–569.

Baxter, L. A., & Wilmot, W. W. (1984). "Secret tests": Social strategies for acquiring information about the state of the relationship. *Human Communication Research*, 11, 171–201.

Bazarova, N. N., & Choi, Y. H. (2014). Self-disclosure in social media: Extending the functional approach to disclosure motivations and characteristics on social network sites. *Journal of Communication*, 64, 635–657.

Bazil, L. G. D. (1999). The effects of social behavior on fourth- and fifth-grade girls' perceptions of physically attractive and unattractive peers. *Dissertation Abstracts International*, 59, 4533B.

Beal, D. J., Cohen, R. R., Burke, M. J., & McLendon, C. I. (2003). Cohesion and performance in groups: A meta-analytic clarification of construct relations. *Journal of Applied Psychology*, 88, 989–1004.

Beal, V. (2014, August 26). Twitter dictionary: A guide to understanding Twitter lingo. *Webopedia*. Retrieved from http://www.webopedia.com/quick_ref/Twitter_Dictionary_Guide.asp

Beating the odds. (2002, August 5). *People*, pp. 78–79.

Because we can, we must. (2004, May 17). *Almanac Between Issues*. Retrieved from http://www.upenn.edu/almanac/between/2004/commence-b.html

Bechler, C., & Johnson, S. (1995). Leadership and listening: A study of member perceptions. *Small Group Research*, 26, 77–85.

Beck, A. J. (2010, August 26). Sexual victimization in prisons and jails reported by inmates. *Bureau of Justice Statistics*. Retrieved from http://bjs.ojp.usdoj.gov/index.cfm?ty=pbdetail&iid=2202

Becker, J, & Wright, S. (2011). Yet another dark side of chivalry: Benevolent sexism undermines and hostile sexism motivates collective action for social change. *Journal of Personality and Social Psychology*, 101, 62–77.

Behnke, R. R., & Sawyer, C. R. (1999a). Milestones of anticipatory public speaking anxiety. *Communication Education*, 48, 1–8.

Belbin, R. (1996). *Team roles at work*. London: Butterworth-Heinemann.

Bell, M. M., & Ashwood, L. L. (2016). *An invitation to environmental sociology*. Thousand Oaks, CA: Sage.

Belle, D. (1987). Gender differences in the social moderators of stress. In R. C. Barnett, L. Biener, & G. K. Baruch (Eds.), *Gender and stress*. New York: Free Press.

Belle, D. (1989). Gender differences in children's social networks and supports. In D. Belle (Ed.), *Children's social networks and social supports*. New York: Wiley.

Belser, A. (2015, May 15). CEO pay 373 times workers' pay. *San Jose Mercury News*, p. B9.

Benfield, K. (2010, January 14). "Gated communities" are not necessarily safer. *National Resources Defense Fund*. Retrieved from http://switchboard.nrdc.org/blogs/kbenfield/gated_communities_are_not_nece.html

Benne, K., & Sheats, P. (1948). Functional roles of group members. *Journal of Social Issues*, 4, 41–49.

Bennis, W. (2007). The challenges of leadership in the modern world. *American Psychologist*, 62, 2–5.

Bennis, W., & Biederman, P. (1997). *Organizing genius: The secrets of creative collaboration*. New York: Addison-Wesley.

Berdahl, J., & Moore, C. (2006). Workplace harassment: Double jeopardy for minority women. *Journal of Applied Psychology*, 91, 426–436.

Bergeson, L. (2014). The truth about hair loss and baldness cures. *Huffington Post*. Retrieved from http://www.huffingtonpost.com/2014/11/08/hair-loss-baldness-cure_n_6101528.html

Bergner, R. M., & Holmes, J. R. (2000). Self-concepts and self-concept change: A status dynamic approach. *Psychotherapy: Theory, Research, Practice, Training*, 37, 36–44.

Berlo, D. (1960). *The process of communication*. New York: Holt, Rinehart & Winston.

Berman, J. (2015, January 29). Soon, not even 1 percent of Fortune 500 companies will have black CEOs. *Huffington Post*. Retrieved from http://www.huffingtonpost.com/2015/01/29/black-ceos-fortune-500_n_6572074.html

Bernieri, F. J. (2001). Toward a taxonomy of interpersonal sensitivity. In J. A. Hall & F. J. Bernieri (Eds.), *Interpersonal sensitivity: Theory and measurement*. Mahwah, NJ: Erlbaum.

Berns, N. (2001). Degendering the problem and gendering the blame: Political discourse on women and violence. *Gender and Society*, 15, 262–281.

Bernstein, E. (2013, June 25). The perils of giving advice. *The Wall Street Journal*. Retrieved from http://www.wsj.com/articles/SB10001424127887324637504578565350148621048

Berry, J. W. (1994). Acculturative stress. In W. J. Lonner & R. Malpass (Eds.), *Psychology and culture*. Boston: Allyn & Bacon.

Berry, J. W. (1997). Immigration, acculturation, and adaptation. *Applied Psychology: An International Review, 46,* 5–34.

Berscheid, E., & Walster, E. (1974). Physical attractiveness. In L. Berkowitz (Ed.), *Advances in experimental social psychology* (Vol. 7). New York: Academic Press.

Billingsley, K. L. (2010, August 15). Twenty years later, self-esteem report looks foolish. *San Jose Mercury News,* p. A10.

Bingham, S. (1991). Communication strategies for managing sexual harassment in organizations: Understanding message options and their effects. *Journal of Applied Communication Research, 19,* 88–115.

Birditt, K. S., Brown, E., Orbuch, T. L., & Mcllvane, J. M. (2010). Marital conflict behaviors and implications for divorce over 16 years. *Journal of Marriage and Family, 72,* 1188–1204.

Birdwhistell, R. (1970). *Kinesis and context.* Philadelphia: University of Pennsylvania Press.

Bitton, M. S., & Shaul, D. B. (2013). Perceptions and attitudes to sexual harassment: An examination of sex differences and the sex composition of the harasser-target dyad. *Journal of Applied Social Psychology, 43,* 2136–2145.

Bjorkqvist, K., Osterman, K., & Lagerspetz, K. (1994). Sex differences in covert aggression among adults. *Aggressive Behavior, 20,* 27–33.

Black, J. (2014, September). Native American mascotting reveals neocolonial logics. *Spectra,* pp. 14–17.

Black, K. (1990a, March). Can getting mad get the job done? *Working Women,* pp. 86–90.

Black, K. (1990b, March). The matter of tears. *Working Women,* p. 88.

Blake, R., & Mouton, J. (1964). *The managerial grid.* Houston, TX: Gulf Publishing.

Blakely, E. J. (2012, April 6). In gated communities, such as where Trayvon Martin died, a dangerous mindset. *The Washington Post.* Retrieved from http://www.washingtonpost.com/opinions/in-gated-communities-such-as-where-trayvon-martin-died-a-dangerous-mind-set/2012/04/06/gIQAwWG8zS_story.html

Blass, T. (2009). From New Haven to Santa Clara: A historical perspective on the Milgram obedience experiments. *American Psychologist, 64,* 37–45.

Blenko, M. W., Mankins, M. C., & Rogers, P. (2010). *Decide & deliver: 5 steps to breakthrough performance in your organization.* Boston: Harvard Business Review Press.

Bleske-Rechek, A., Somers, E., Micke, C., Erickson, L., Matteson, L., Stocco, C., Schumacher, B., & Ritchie, L. (2012). *Journal of Social and Personal Relationships, 29,* 569–596.

Blood, toil, tears, and sweat. (2015). The Churchill Centre. Retrieved from http://www.winstonchurchill.org/resources/speeches/1940-the-finest-hour/blood-toil-tears-and-sweat

Bodie, G. D. (2010). A racing heart, rattling knees, and ruminative thoughts: Defining, explaining, and treating public speaking anxiety. *Communication Education, 59,* 70–105.

Bodie, G. D., Vickery, A. J., Cannava, K., & Jones, S. M. (2015). The role of "active listening" in informal helping conversations: Impact on perceptions of listener helpfulness, sensitivity, and supportiveness and discloser emotional improvement. *Western Journal of Communication, 79,* 151–173.

Bogart, K. R. (2014). People are all about appearances: A focus group of teenagers with Moebius syndrome. *Journal of Health Psychology.* Retrieved from http://hpq.sagepub.com/content/early/2014/01/09/1359105313517277.abstract

Bogart, K. R., Tickle-Degnen, L., & Ambady, N. (2012). Compensatory expressive behavior for facial paralysis: Adaptation to congenital or acquired disability. *Rehabilitation Psychology, 57,* 43–51.

Bok, S. (1978). *Lying: Moral choice in public and private life.* New York: Random House.

Bolton, R. (1979). *People skills: How to assert yourself, listen to others, and resolve conflicts.* New York: Simon & Schuster.

Bond, C. F., & DePaulo, B. M. (2006). Accuracy of deception judgments. *Personality and Social Psychology, 10,* 214–234.

Bond, C., & Uysal, A. (2007). On lie detection "wizards." *Law and Human Behavior, 31,* 109–115.

Boone, R. (2009, September 5). Court: Ashcroft can be held liable. *San Jose Mercury News,* p. A5.

Bor, J. (2001, January 3). Canadian smokers get stark warning: New labels depict harsh consequences. *San Jose Mercury News,* p. 6A.

Borkenau, P., Mauer, N., Riemann, R., Spinath, F. M., & Angleitner, A. (2004). Thin slices of behavior as cues of personality and intelligence. *Journal of Personality and Social Psychology, 86,* 599–614.

Bormann, E. (1990). *Small group communication: Theory and practice.* New York: Harper & Row.

Boroditsky, L. (2011, February). How language shapes thought. *Scientific American.* Retrieved from https://psych.stanford.edu/~lera/papers/sci-am-2011.pdf

Bostrom, R. (1970). Patterns of communicative interaction in small groups. *Speech Monographs, 37,* 257–263.
Boudreau, J. (2007, August 12). Beijing brushes up on its English skills. *San Jose Mercury News,* p. 17A.

Bower, S., & Bower, G. (1976). *Asserting yourself.* Reading, MA: Addison-Wesley.

Bowles, H. R. (2012, October). Psychological perspectives on gender in negotiation. *Harvard Kennedy*

School. Retrieved from https://research.hks.harvard.edu/publications/getFile.aspx?Id=862

Boyes, A. (2013a, March 13). 6 tips for overcoming anxiety-related procrastination. *Psychology Today.* Retrieved from https://www.psychologytoday.com/blog/in-practice/201303/6-tips-overcoming-anxiety-related-procrastination

Boyes, A. (2013b, January 10). What is catastrophizing? Cognitive distortions. *Psychology Today.* Retrieved from https://www.psychologytoday.com/blog/in-practice/201301/what-is-catastrophizing-cognitive-distortions

Bradbury, T. N., & Fincham, F. D. (1990). Attributions in marriage: Review and critique. *Psychological Bulletin*, 107, 3–33.

Bradbury, T. N., & Fincham, F. D. (1992). Attributions and behavior in marital interaction. *Journal of Personality and Social Psychology*, 63, 613–628.

Branan, N. (2007, November). Celebrating the bizarre. *Scientific American Mind*, p. 85.

Brehm, J. (1972). *Responses to loss of freedom: A theory of psychological resistance.* Morristown, NJ: General Learning Press.

Brescoll, V. L., & Uhlmann, E. L. (2008). Can an angry woman get ahead? *Psychological Science*, 19, 268–275.

Brewer, C. S., Kovner, C. T., Obeidat, R. F., & Budin, W. C. (2013). Positive work environments of early-career registered nurses and the correlation with physician verbal abuse. *Nursing Outlook*, 61, 408–416.

Bricker, B. J. (2014). Feigning environmentalism: Anti-environmental organizations, strategic naming, and definitional argument. *Western Journal of Communication*, 78, 636–652.

Bridge that gap: Analyzing the student skill index (2013, Fall). *Chegg.* Retrieved from https://www.insidehighered.com/sites/default/server_files/files/Bridge%20That%20Gap-v8.pdf

Brislin, R. (1993). *Understanding culture's influence on behavior.* Fort Worth, TX: Harcourt Brace Jovanovich.

British Association for the Advancement of Science. (2002). *LaughLab: The scientific quest for the world's funniest joke.* London: Arrow Books.

Brooks, D. (2011). *The social animal.* New York: Random House.

Brossart, A. (2009). Don't trust your life to a ratio. In L. G. Schnoor & D. Cronn-Mills (Eds.), *Winning orations.* Mankato, MN: Interstate Oratorical Association.

Brown, A., Henningsen, D. D., Kartch, F., & Orr, N. (2009). The perceptions of verbal and nonverbal flirting cues in cross-sex interactions. *Human Communication*, 12, 371–381.

Brown, T. (2014). Untitled. In L. G. Schnoor, K. Young, & L. Mayfield (Eds.), *Winning orations.* Mankato, MN: Interstate Oratorical Association.

Brown, W. (2009). Listen up. *Professional Safety*, 54, 8.

Brownell, C. A., Svetlova, M., Anderson, R., Nichols, S. R., & Drummond, J. (2013). Socialization of early prosocial behavior: Parents' talk about emotions is associated with sharing and helping in toddlers. *Infancy*, 18, 91–119.

Brownell, J. (2013). *Listening: Attitudes, principles, and skills.* New York: Pearson.

Brownlow, S. (2003). Gender-linked linguistic behavior in television interviews. *Sex Roles: A Journal of Research*, 49, 121–132.

Bruess, C. J., & Pearson, J. C. (1996). Gendered patterns in family communication. In J. Wood (Ed.), *Gendered relationships.* Newbury Park, CA: Sage.

Brummett, E. A., & Steuber, K. R. (2015). To reveal or conceal? Privacy management processes among interracial romantic partners. *Western Journal of Communication*, 79, 22–44.

Bruskin & Goldring. (1993). America's number 1 fear: Public speaking. In Bruskin & Goldring (Eds.), *Bruskin & Goldring report.* Edison, NJ: Bruskin-Goldring.

Brustein, M. (2014, July 23). Should you offer advice to a friend who is in crisis? *Good Therapy.org.* Retrieved from http://www.goodtherapy.org/blog/should-you-offer-advice-to-friend-in-crisis-072314

Bryson, B. (1990). *The mother tongue: English and how it got that way.* New York: Avon Books.

Budziszewska, M., Hansen, K., & Bilewicz, M. (2014). Backlash over gender-fair language: The impact of feminine job titles on men's and women's perception of women. *Journal of Language and Social Psychology*, 33, 681–691.

Buller, D., & Aune, K. (1992). The effects of speech rate similarity on compliance: Application of communication accommodations theory. *Western Journal of Communication*, 56, 37–53.

Bumiller, E. (2010, April 26). We have met the enemy and he is PowerPoint. *The New York Times.* Retrieved from http://www.nytimes.com/2010/04/27/world/27powerpoint.html?partner=rss&emc=rss&pagewanted=print

Bureau of Labor Statistics (2015, April 2). Employment projection. *United States Department of Labor.* Retrieved from http://www.bls.gov/emp/ep_chart_001.htm

Burfeind, M., & Witkemper, T. (2010, July 14). TeleNav-commissioned survey suggests both genders have similar views on abiding by and breaking the rules of the road. *TeleNav.* Retrieved from http://www.telenav.com/about/pr/pr-20100714.html

Burger, J. M. (2009). Replicating Milgram: Would people still obey today? *American Psychologist*, 64, 1–11.

Burgoon, J. K., & Dunbar, N. E. (2006). Nonverbal expressions of dominance and power in human relationships. In V. Manusov & M. L. Patterson (Eds.), *The Sage handbook of nonverbal communication*. Thousand Oaks, CA: Sage.

Burgoon, J. K., Buller, D. B., & Woodall, W. G. (1996). *Nonverbal communication: The unspoken dialogue*. New York: McGraw-Hill.

Burleson, B. R. (2003). Emotional support skills. In J. O. Greene & B. R. Burleson (Eds.), *Handbook of communication and social interaction skills*. Mahwah, NJ: Erlbaum.

Burleson, B. R., & Samter, W. (1996). Similarity in the communication skills of young adults: Foundations of attraction, friendship, and relationship satisfaction. *Communication Reports*, 9, 127–139.

Burleson, B. R., Holmstrom, A. J., & Gilstrap, C. M. (2005). "Guys can't say that to guys": Four experiments assessing the normative motivation account for deficiencies in the emotional support provided by men. *Communication Monographs*, 72, 468–501.

Burnette, J. L., Davisson, E. K., Finkel, E. J., Van Tongeren, D. R., Hui, C. M., & Hoyle, R. H. (2013). Self-control and forgiveness: A meta-analytic review, *Social Psychological and Personality Science*, 5, 443–450.

Burnley, W. (2015, February 5). Voices: In college, the racial politics of dating are complicated. *USA Today*. Retrieved from http://college.usatoday.com/2015/02/05/voices-in-college-the-racial-politics-of-dating-are-complicated/

Burns, J. (1978). *Leadership*. New York: Harper & Row.

Bushman, B. J. (2013, September 25). Anger management: What works and what doesn't. *Psychology Today*. Retrieved from https://www.psychologytoday.com/blog/get-psyched/201309/anger-management-what-works-and-what-doesnt

Bushman, B. J., & Baumeister, R. F. (1998). Threatened egotism, narcissism, self-esteem, and direct and displaced aggression: Does self-love or self-hate lead to violence? *Journal of Personality and Social Psychology*, 75, 219–229.

Buss, D. M. (2003). *The evolution of desire: Strategies of human mating*. New York: Basic Books.

Byers, E. S., & Heinlein, L. (1989). Predicting initiations and refusals of sexual activities in married and cohabiting heterosexual couples. *Journal of Sex Research*, 26, 210–231.

Byrne, D. (1997). An overview (and underview) of research and theory within the attraction paradigm. *Journal of Social and Personal Relationships*, 14, 417–431.

Cacioppo, J. T., Cacioppo, S., Gonzaga, G. C., Ogburn, E. L., & VanderWeele, T. J. (2013). Marital satisfaction and break-ups differ across on-line and off-line meeting venues. *Proceedings of the National Academy of Sciences*, 110 (25), 10135–10140. doi: 10.1073/pnas.1222447110

Callahan, D. (2004). *The cheating culture: Why more Americans are doing wrong to get ahead*. New York: Harcourt.

Cameron, D. (2007). *The myth of Mars and Venus: Do men and women really speak different languages?* New York: Oxford University Press.

Campbell, S. (2008). Perceptions of mobile phone use in public: The roles of individualism, collectivism, and focus of the setting. *Communication Reports*, 21, 70–81.

Canary, D. J., & Hause, K. S. (1993). Is there any reason to research sex differences in communication? *Communication Quarterly*, 41, 129–144.

Canary, D. J., Cupach, W. R., & Messman, S. J. (1995). *Relationship conflict: Conflict in parent-child, friendship, and romantic relationships*. Thousand Oaks, CA: Sage.

Canary, D. J., Stafford, L., Hause, K. S., & Wallace, L. A. (1993). An inductive analysis of relational maintenance strategies: Comparisons among lovers, relatives, friends, and others. *Communication Research Reports*, 10, 5–14.

Canfield, J., Hansen, M. V., & Kirberger, K. (1997). *Chicken soup for the teenage soul*. Deerfield Beach, FL: Health Communications.

Cannon, W. B. (1932). *The wisdom of the body*. New York: Norton.

Caplan, M., & Goldman, M. (1981). Personal space violations as a function of height. *Journal of Social Psychology*, 114, 167–171.

Card, N. A., Stucky, B. D., Sawalani, G. M., & Little, T. D. (2008). Direct and indirect aggression during childhood and adolescence: A meta-analytic review of gender differences, intercorrelations, and relations to maladjustment. *Child Development*, 79, 1185–229.

Carey, B. (2010, February 23). Evidence that little touches do mean so much. *The New York Times*. Retrieved from http://www.nytimes.com/2010/02/23/health/23mind.html?_r=1&pagewanted=print

Carey, H. R., & Laughlin, P. R. (2012). Groups perform better than the best individual on letters-to-numbers problems: Effects of induced strategies. *Group Process and Intergroup Relations*, 15, 231–242.

Carl, D., Gupta, V., & Javidan, M. (2004). Power distance. In R. J. House, P. J. Hanges, M. Javidan, P. W. Dorfman, & V. Gupta (Eds.), *Culture, leadership, and organizations*. Thousand Oaks, CA: Sage.

Carli, L. L. (2001). Gender and social influence. *Journal of Social Issues*, 57, 725–742.

Carnevale, A. (1996). *Workplace basics: The skills employers want*. Washington, DC: U.S. Department of Labor Employment and Training Administration.

Carnevale, P., & Probst, T. (1998). Social values and social conflict in creative problem solving. *Journal of Personality and Social Psychology*, 74, 1300–1309.

Carothers, B. J., & Reis, H. T. (2013). Men and women are from Earth: Examining the latent structure of gender. *Journal of Personality and Social Psychology*, 104, 385–407.

Carpenter, C. J. (2012). Narcissism on Facebook: Self-promotional and anti-social behavior. *Personality and Individual Differences*, 52, 482–486.

Carrier, J. R. (2013, November 6). Rand Paul admits his plagiarism "is my fault." *USA Today*. Retrieved from http://www.usatoday.com/story/news/politics/2013/11/06/rand-paul-plagiarism/3451991/

Carrillo, J. (2014). The other war. In L. G. Schnoor, K. Young, & L. Mayfield (Eds.), *Winning orations*. Mankato, MN: Interstate Oratorical Association.

Carroll, R. T. (2014, September 12). Alien abduction. *The Skeptic's Dictionary*. Retrieved from http://skepdic.com/aliens.html

Cass, C., & Agiesta, J. (2011, September 21). Online slurs seen as jokes. *San Jose Mercury News*, p. A5.

Catala, P. (2015, April 23). AP curbside recycling continues to be popular. *Tampa Tribune*. Retrieved from http://highlandstoday.com/hi/local-news/ap-curbside-recycling-continues-to-be-popular-20150423/

Catchpole, K., Mishra, A., Handa, A., & McCullough, P. (2008). Teamwork and error in the operating room: Analysis of skills and roles. *Annals of Surgery*, 247, 699–706.

Cepeda, E. J. (2015, May 17). Hispanics are assimilating like other immigrant groups. *San Jose Mercury News*, p. A19.

Chabris, C., & Simons, D. (2010). *The invisible gorilla: And other ways our intuitions deceive us*. New York: Crown.

Chammah, M. (2015, February 25). Rape in the American prison. *The Atlantic*. Retrieved from http://www.theatlantic.com/features/archive/2015/02/rape-in-the-american-prison/385550/

Chamorro-Permuzic, T. (2013, August 26). Why do so many incompetent men become leaders? *Today*. Retrieved from http://www.todayonline.com/business/management/why-do-so-many-incompetent-men-become-leaders

Chao, G. T., & Moon, H. (2005). The cultural mosaic: A metatheory for understanding the complexity of culture. *Journal of Applied Psychology*, 90, 1128–1140.

Chatman, J., & Barsade, S. (1995). Personality, organizational culture, and cooperation: Evidence from a business simulation. *Administrative Science Quarterly*, 40, 423–443.

Chatter box. (2007, July 1). *San Jose Mercury News*, p. 2C.

Chemaly, S. (2013, September 13). "Smile, baby": The words no woman wants to hear. *Salon*. Retrieved from http://www.salon.com/2013/09/13/smile_baby_the_words_no_woman_wants_to_hear/

Chen, G., & Starosta, W. J. (1998b). Chinese conflict management and resolution: Overview and implications. *Intercultural Communication Studies*, 7, 1–16.

Chen, S., Geluykens, R., & Chong, J. C. (2006). The importance of language in global teams: A linguistic perspective. *Management International Review*, 46, 679–695.

Chen, Y., & Nakazawa, M. (2009). Influences of culture on self-disclosure as relationally situated in intercultural and interracial friendships from a social penetration perspective. *Journal of Intercultural Communication Research*, 38, 77–98.

Chen, Y., Tjosvold, D., & Fang, S. S. (2005). Working with foreign managers: Conflict management for effective leader relationships in China. *International Journal of Conflict Management*, 16, 265–286.

Chen, Z. (1996). Lying is part of everyday life, new research confirms. (1996). *Nando.net*. Retrieved from https://news.google.com/newspapers?nid=1988&dat=19960608&id=_G0iAAAAIBAJ&sjid=w6wFAAAAIBAJ&pg=3460,3662811&hl=en

Chesebro, J. L. (2003). Effects of teacher clarity and nonverbal immediacy on student learning, receiver apprehension, and affect. *Communication Education*, 52, 135–147.

Cheung, B. Y., Chudek, M., & Heine, S. J. (2011). Evidence for a sensitive period for acculturation: Younger immigrants report acculturating at a faster pace. *Psychological Science*, 22, 147–152.

Chew, J. (2015, August 31). Ashley Madison: Site is "still growing," despite hack. *Fortune*. Retrieved from http://fortune.com/2015/08/31/ashley-madison-site-growing-despite-hack/

Chew, P. K., & Kelley-Chew, L. K. (2007). Subtly sexist language. *Columbia Journal of Gender and Law*, 16, 643–680.

Chidambaram, L., & Tung, L. L. (2005). Is out of sight, out of mind? An empirical study of social loafing in technology-supported groups. *Information Systems Research*, 16, 149–160.

Chillot, R. (2013, March 11). The power of touch. *Psychology Today*. Retrieved from https://www.psychologytoday.com/articles/201302/the-power-touch

Cho, H., & Witte, K. (2004). A review of fear-appeal effects. In J. S. Seiter & R. H. Gass (Eds.), *Perspectives on persuasion, social influence, and compliance gaining*. New York: Pearson.

Christensen, A. J. (2004). *Patient adherence to medical treatment regimens: Bridging the gap between behavioral science and biomedicine.* New Haven, CT: Yale University Press.

Christopher, F. S., & Lloyd, S. A. (2000). Physical and sexual aggression in relationships. In C. Hendrick & S. Hendrick (Eds.), *Close relationships: A sourcebook.* Thousand Oaks, CA: Sage.

Cialdini, R. (1993). *Influence: Science and practice.* New York: HarperCollins.

Cialdini, R., & Trost (1998). Social influence: Social norms, conformity, and compliance. In D. T. Gilbert, S. T. Fiske, & G. Lindzey (Eds.), *Handbook of social psychology* (Vol. 2). Boston: McGraw-Hill.

Clark, D. G., Mendez, M. F., Farag, E., & Vinters, H. V. (2003). Clinicopathologic case report: Progressive aphasia in a 77-year-old man. *Journal of Neuropsychiatry and Clinical Neurosciences, 15,* 231–238.

Clark, H. H. (1996). *Using language.* New York: Cambridge University Press.

Clark, J., & Barber, B. (1994). Adolescents in postdivorce and always married families: Self-esteem and perceptions of father's interest. *Journal of Marriage and the Family, 56,* 608–614.

Clawson, L. (2014, July 11). Company tracks worker bathroom visits so it can punish people who need to pee too much. *Daily Kos.* Retrieved from http://www.dailykos.com/story/2014/07/11/1313307/-Company-tracks-worker-bathroom-visits-so-it-can-punish-people-who-need-to-pee-too-much#

Clay, R. A. (2002). Advertising as science. *Monitor on Psychology, 33,* 38–41.

Clayson, D. E., & Haley, D. A. (2013). An introduction to multitasking and texting: Prevalence and impact on grades and GPA in marketing. *Journal of Marketing Education, 35,* 26–40.

Clinton, H. (2011, December 6). Remarks in recognition of International Human Rights Day. *U. S. Department of State.* Retrieved from http://www.state.gov/secretary/rm/2011/12/178368.htm

Coach known best for 1980 hockey classic. (2003, August 19). *ESPN.* Retrieved from http://espn.go.com/classic/obit/s/2003/0811/1594173.html

Cohen, A. B., & Tannenbaum, I. J. (2001). Lesbian and bisexual women's judgments of the attractiveness of different body types. *Journal of Sex Research, 38,* 226–232.

Cohen, L. J., & DeBenedet, A. T. (2012, July 17). Penn State cover-up: Groupthink in action. *Time.* Retrieved from http://ideas.time.com/2012/07/17/penn-state-cover-up-group-think-in-action/

Cohen, S., & Bailey, D. (1997). What makes teams work: Group effectiveness research from the shop floor to the executive suite. *Journal of Management, 23,* 239–291.

Cohen, S., Janicki-Deverts, D., Turner, R. B., & Doyle, W. J. (2015). Does hugging provide stress-buffering social support? A study of susceptibility to upper respiratory infection and illness. *Psychological Science, 26,* 135–147.

Coleman, J. (2001, February 8). India's traditional social system is complicating distribution of relief to earthquake survivors. *San Jose Mercury News,* p. 7A.

Collins, G. (2015, May 14). Wow, Jeb Bush is awful. *The New York Times.* Retrieved from http://www.nytimes.com/2015/05/14/opinion/gail-collins-wow-jeb-bush-is-awful.html

Collins, R., & Cooper, P. J. (1997). *The power of story: Teaching through storytelling.* Boston: Allyn & Bacon.

Colt, G. (1997, August). The magic of touch. *LIFE,* pp. 53–62.

Columbia Accident Investigation Board. (2003, August). *Columbia accident investigation report* (Vol. 1). Retrieved from http://www.nasa.gov/columbia/caib/html/VOL1.html.

Compton, J., & Ivanov, B. (2012). Untangling threat during inoculation-conferred resistance to influence. *Communication Reports, 25,* 1–13.

Conlon, T. (2007, July 26). E-mail addiction: Battle of the sexes! *Switched.com.* Retrieved from http://www.switched.com/2007/05/24/rise-of-the-blackberry-addicted

Connaughton, S. L., & Daly, J. A. (2005). Leadership in the new millennium: Communication beyond temporal, spatial, and geographical boundaries. In P. Kalbfleisch (Ed.), *Communication yearbook 29.* Mahwah, NJ: Erlbaum.

Cools, C. (2011). Relational dialectics in intercultural couples' relationships. *Jyvaskyla Studies in Humanities.* Retrieved from https://jyx.jyu.fi/dspace/bitstream/handle/123456789/37189/9789513945732.pdf?sequence=1

Coontz, S. (1997). *The way we really are: Coming to terms with America's changing families.* New York: Basic Books.

Coontz, S. (2009, January 18). Intimacy unstuck. *Boston Globe Sunday.* Retrieved from http://www.stephaniecoontz.com/articles/article43.htm

Cooper, C. (2008). Elucidating the bonds of workplace humor: A relational process model. *Human Relations, 61,* 1087–1115.

Cooper, L. (1960). *The rhetoric of Aristotle: An expanded translation with supplementary examples for students of composition and public speaking.* New York: Appleton Century Crafts.

Cooper, M. L., Shapiro, C. M., & Powers, A. M. (1998). Motivations for sex and risky sexual behavior among adolescents and young adults: A functional perspective. *Journal of Personality and Social Psychology*, 75, 1528–1558.

Cooper, V. W. (1994). The disguise of self-disclosure: The relationship ruse of a Soviet spy. *Journal of Applied Communication Research*, 22, 338–347.

Corbett, W. R. (2013). An outrageous response to "You're fired!" *North Carolina Law Review*, 92, 17–56.

Cordero-Guzman, H. (2014, July 15). The "majority-minority" America is coming, so why not get ready? *MSNBC*. Retrieved from http://www.msnbc.com/melissa-harris-perry/the-majority-minority-america-coming-so-why-not-get-ready

Correll, J., Park, B., Judd, C. M., Wittenbrink, B. (2002). The police officer's dilemma: Using ethnicity to disambiguate potentially threatening individuals. *Journal of Personality and Social Psychology*, 83, 1314–1329.

Cotton, G. (2013, August 13). Gestures to avoid in cross-cultural business: In other words, "Keep your fingers to yourself." *Huffington Post*. Retrieved from http://www.huffingtonpost.com/gayle-cotton/cross-cultural-gestures_b_3437653.html

Coutu, D. (2009). Why teams don't work: An interview with J. Richard Hackman. *Harvard Business Review*. Retrieved from http://hbr.org/2009/05/why-teams-dont-work

Covey, S. J. (1991). *The seven habits of highly effective people*. New York: Simon & Schuster

Covin, R. (2011, September 18). What makes a person likeable? *Huffington Post*. Retrieved from http://www.huffingtonpost.ca/roger-covin/likeable_b_901191.html

Cowan, R. L., & Horan, S. M. (2014). Love at the office? Understanding workplace romance disclosures and reactions from the coworker perspective. *Western Journal of Communication*, 78, 238–253.

Cox, F. D., & Demmitt, K. (2014). *Human intimacy: Marriage, the family, and it's meaning*. Boston, MA: Cengage.

Craig, K., & Rand, K. (1998). The perceptually "privileged" group member: Consequences of solo status for African Americans and whites in task groups. *Small Group Research*, 29, 339–358.

Cramer, D. (2002). Satisfaction with romantic relationships and a four-component model of conflict resolution. In S. P. Shohov (Ed.), *Advances in psychological research*. Hauppauge, NY: NOVA Science.

Cramton, C. (2001). The mutual knowledge problem and its consequences for dispersed collaboration. *Organizational Science*, 12, 346–371.

Cramton, C. (2002). Attribution in distributed work groups. In P. J. Hinds & S. Kiesler (Eds.), *Distributed work*. Cambridge, MA: MIT Press.

Crane, D. R. (1987). Diagnosing relationships with spatial distance: An empirical test of a clinical principle. *Journal of Marital and Family Therapy*, 13, 307–310.

Crary, D. (2010, May 7). Over 45 sex: Approval up, activity down. *San Jose Mercury News*, p. A6.

Crawford, J. (1996, March 21). *Anatomy of the English-only movememt: Social and ideological sources of language restrictionism in the United States*. Paper presented at a conference at University of Illinois at Urbana–Champaign, IL.

Crawford, J. (2012, February 1). Language legislation in the U.S.A. *LanguagePolicy.net*: Retrieved from http://www.languagepolicy.net/archives/langleg.htm

Crawford, M., & Kaufman, M. R. (2006). Sex differences versus social processes in the construction of gender. In K. Dindia & D. J. Canary (Eds.), *Sex differences and similarities in communication*. Mahwah, NJ: Erlbaum.

Crawford, W., & Gorman, M. (1996). Coping with electronic information. In J. Dock (Ed.), *The press of ideas: Readings for writers on print culture and the information age*. Boston: St. Martin's Press.

Crescenzo, S. (2005). It's time to admit the hard truth: We're not photographers. *Communication World*, 22, 12–14.

Crime in the Unites States. (2013). *U. S. Department of Justice, Federal Bureau of Investigation, Criminal Justice Information Services Division*. Retrieved from http://www.fbi.gov/about-us/cjis/ucr/crime-in-the-u.s/2013/crime-in-the-u.s.-2013/persons-arrested/persons-arrested

Crocker, J. (2006). What is optimal self-esteem? In M. H. Kernis (Ed.), *Self-esteem: Issues and answers*. New York: Psychology Press.

Crocker, J., & Carnevale, J. J. (2013, September/October). Letting go of self-esteem. *Scientific American Mind*, pp. 27–33.

Crocker, J., & Knight, K. M. (2005). Contingencies of self-worth. *Current Directions in Psychological Science*, 14, 200–203.

Crocker, J., & Park, L. E. (2004). The costly pursuit of self-esteem. *Psychological Bulletin*, 130, 392–414.

Crocker, J., & Wolfe, C. (2001). Contingencies of self-worth. *Psychological Review*, 108, 593–623.

Crocker, J., Brook, A. T., Niija, Y., & Villacorta, M. (2006). The pursuit of self-esteem: Contingencies of self-worth and self-regulation. *Journal of Personality*, 744, 1749–1772.

Cross, S. E., & Madson, L. (1997). Models of the self: Self-construals and gender. *Psychological Bulletin*, 122, 5–37.

Croucher, S. M. (2004). I uh know what like you are saying: An analysis of discourse markers in limited preparation events. *National Forensic Association Journal.* Retrieved from http://www.researchgate.net/profile/Stephen_Croucher/publication/275041050_I_uh_know_what_like_you_are_saying_An_analysis_of_discourse_markers_in_limited_preparation_events/links/55310e9d0cf2f2a588abffe1.pdf

Crown, D. F. (2007). The use of group and group-centric individual goals for culturally heterogeneous and homogeneous task groups: An assessment of European work teams. *Small Group Research, 38,* 489–508.

Crystal, D. (1997). *The Cambridge encyclopedia of language.* New York: Cambridge University Press.

Crystal, D. (2005). *How language works: How babies babble, words change meaning, and languages live or die.* New York: The Overlook Press.

Crystal, D. (2008). *Txtng: The gr8 db8.* New York: Oxford University Press.

Cuddy, A. J. C., Norton, M. I., & Fiske, S. T. (2005). This old stereotype: The pervasiveness and persistence of the elderly stereotype. *Journal of Social Issues, 61,* 267–285.

Cunningham, V, Lefkoe, M., & Sechrest, L. (2006). Eliminating fears: An intervention that permanently eliminates the fear of public speaking. *Clinical Psychology and Psychotherapy, 13,* 183–193.

Cupach, W. R., & Spitzberg, B. H. (Eds.). (2011). *The dark side of close relationships II.* New York: Routledge.

Current numbers. (2015). *Center for American Women and Politics.* Retrieved from http://www.cawp.rutgers.edu/current-numbers

Curseu, P. L., & Schruijer, S. G. L. (2010). Does conflict shatter trust or does trust obliterate conflict? Revisiting the relationships between team diversity, conflict, and trust. *Group Dynamics: Theory, Research, and Practice, 14,* 66–79.

Curtis, K. (2002, March 8). Critics nip at attorney's trial tactics. *Santa Cruz Sentinel,* pp. A1, A4.

Czech translation. (2015). *Spectrum Translation.* Retrieved from http://www.spectrumtranslation.com/czech-translation/

Czopp, A. M., Monteith, M. J., & Mark, A. Y. (2006). Standing up for a change: Reducing bias through interpersonal confrontation. *Journal of Personality and Social Psychology, 90,* 784–803.

Czopp, A. M., Kay, A. C., & Cheryan, S. (2015). Positive stereotypes are pervasive and powerful. *Perspectives on Psychological Science, 10,* 451–463.

Dahlberg, T. (2001, June 3). Violence in youth sports reaching an ugly point. *Santa Cruz Sentinel,* pp. C1, C2.

Dailey, R. M., McCracken, A. A., Jin, B., Rossetto, K. R., & Green, E. W. (2013). Negotiating breakups and renewals: Types of on-again/off-again dating relationships. *Western Journal of Communication, 77,* 382–410.

Dainton, M. (2003). Equity and uncertainty in relational maintenance. *Western Journal of Communication, 67,* 164–186.

Damasio, A. R., & Damasio, H. (1999). Brain and language. In A. R. Damasio (Ed.), *The Scientific American book of the brain.* New York: Lyons Press.

Daniel, D. K. (2008, January 23). Bush falsehoods about war counted. *San Jose Mercury News,* p. 15A.

Davidowitz, M., & Myricm, R. D. (1984). Responding to the bereaved: An analysis of "helping" statements. *Death Education, 8,* 1–10.

Davidson, C. (2007, March 19). We can't ignore the influence of digital technologies. *Chronicle of Higher Education,* p. B20.

Davidson, K. (2014, April 25). Major League baseball's unspoken problem. *BloombergView.* Retrieved from http://www.bloombergview.com/articles/2014-04-25/major-league-baseball-s-unspoken-problem

Davies, J. W. (2011, September 25). Is there any real evidence that people are more afraid of public speaking than dying? *Quora.* Retrieved from http://www.quora.com/Is-there-any-real-evidence-that-people-are-more-afraid-of-public-speaking-than-dying

Dawn (2014). Dawn, R. (2014, December 15). Frankly, my dear, I don't give a straw: The secret history of "Gone with the Wind's" curse. *Today Pop Culture.* Retrieved from http://www.today.com/popculture/frankly-my-dear-i-dont-give-straw-gone-winds-secret-1D80341776

De Araujo, I. E., Rolls, E. T., Velazco, M. I., Margot, C., & Cayeux, I. (2005). Cognitive modulation of olfactory processing. *Neuron, 4,* 671–679.

De Dora, M. (2015, July/August). Homeopathy "unsupported, ineffective, dangerous": CFI testimony to FDA. *Skeptical Inquirer,* pp. 32–33.

De Graaf, A., Hoeken, H., Sanders, J., & Beentjes, J. W. J. (2012). Identification as a mechanism of narrative persuasion. *Communication Research, 39,* 802–823.

De Waal, F. (2010). *The age of empathy: Nature's lessons for a kinder society.* New York: Three Rivers Press.

Dean, J. (2009, May 29). Social loafing: When groups are bad for productivity. *PsyBlog.* Retrieved from http://www.spring.org.uk/2009/05/social-loafing-when-groups-are-bad-for-productivity.php

DeAndrea, D. C., Tong, S. T., & Walther, J. B. (2011). Dark sides of computer-mediated communication. In W. R. Cupach & B. H. Spitzberg (Eds.), *The dark side of close relationships II.* New York: Routledge.

DeBono, E. (1992). *Sur/petition: Going beyond competition.* New York: HarperCollins.

Decenteceo, N. (2014). Tax lien abuse: The other foreclosure crisis. In L. G. Schnoor, K. Young, & L. Mayfield (Eds.), *Winning orations*. Mankato, MN: Interstate Oratorical Association.

DeChurch, L. A., Hamilton, K. L., & Haas, C. (2007). Effects of conflict management strategies on perceptions of intragroup conflict. *Group Dynamics: Theory, Research, and Practice*, 11, 66–78.

Den Hartog, D. N. (2004). Assertiveness. In R. J. House et al. (Eds.), *Culture, leadership, and organizations*. Thousand Oaks, CA: Sage.

Denworth, L. (2015, July/August). The social power of touch. *Scientific American Mind*, pp. 30–39.

Derber, C. (1979). *The pursuit of attention: Power and individualism in everyday life*. New York: Oxford University Press.

Devine, P. G. (1989). Stereotypes and prejudice: Their automatic and controlled components. *Journal of Personality and Social Psychology*, 56, 5–18.

DeVito, J. (1970). *The psychology of speech and language: An introduction to psycholinguistics*. New York: Random House.

DeVito, J. (1990). *Messages: Building interpersonal communication skills*. New York: Harper & Row.

Devos-Comby, L., & Salovey, P. (2002). Applying persuasion strategies to alter HIV-relevant thoughts and behavior. *Review of General Psychology*, 6, 287–304.

DeWall, C. N., Lambert, N. M., Slotter, E. B., Pond, R. S., Deckman, T., Finkel, E. J., Luchies, L. B., & Fincham, F. D. (2011). So far away from one's partner, yet so close to romantic alternatives: Avoidant attachment, interest in alternatives, and infidelity, *Journal of Personality and Social Psychology*, 101, 1302–1316.

Dewey, J. (1910). *How we think*. Lexington, MA: D. C. Heath.

Diamond, D. (1997, January 31). Behind closed gates. *USA Weekend*, pp. 4–5.

Diamond, R. (1997, August 1). Designing and assessing course and curricula. *Chronicle of Higher Education*, p. B7.

Dicker, R. (2015, February 7). Chipper Jones apologizes after claiming FBI confirmed Sandy Hook didn't happen. *Huffington Post*. Retrieved from http://www.huffingtonpost.com/2015/02/07/chipper-jones-sandy-hook_n_6636622.html

DiClaudio, D. (2006). *The hypochondriac's pocket guide to horrible diseases you probably already have*. New York: Bloomsbury.

DiDonato, T. E. (2014, August 11). How to spot a flirt. *Psychology Today*. Retrieved from https://www.psychologytoday.com/blog/meet-catch-and-keep/201408/how-spot-flirt

Dieckmann, L. E. (2000). Private secrets and public disclosure: The case of battered women. In S. Petronio (Ed.), *Balancing the secrets of private disclosures*. Mahwah, NJ: Erlbaum.

DiGangl, C. (2015, May 10). D.C.: Biggest income inequality in U.S. *USA Today*. Retrieved from http://www.usatoday.com/story/money/personalfinance/2015/05/10/credit-dotcom-states-income-inequality/25718549/

Dillard, J. (1994). Rethinking the study of fear appeals: An emotional perspective. *Communication Theory*, 4, 195–323.

Dillard, J. P., & Nabi, R. L. (2006). The persuasive influence of emotion in cancer prevention and detection messages. *Journal of Communication*, 56, 123–139.

Dindia, K. (2000). Sex differences in self-disclosure, reciprocity of self-disclosure, and self-disclosure and liking: Three meta-analyses reviewed. In S. Petronio (Ed.), *Balancing the secrets of private disclosures*. Mahwah, NJ: Erlbaum.

Dindia, K. (2002). Self-disclosure research: Knowledge through meta-analysis. In M. Allen, R. W. Preiss, B. M. Gayle, & N. A. Burrell (Eds.), *Interpersonal communication research: Advances through meta-analysis*. Mahwah, NJ: Erlbaum.

Dindia, K. (2006). Men are from North Dakota, women are from South Dakota. In K. Dindia & D. J. Canary (Eds.), *Sex differences and similarities in communication*. Mahwah, NJ: Erlbaum.

Dindia, K., & Canary, D. J. (Eds.). (2006). *Sex differences and similarities in communication*. Mahwah, NJ: Erlbaum.

DiSalvo, D. (2010, January/February). Are social networks messing with your head? *Scientific American Mind*, pp. 48–55.

Dixson, B. J., Grimshaw, G. M., Linklater, W. L., & Dixson, A. F. (2010). Watching the hourglass: Eye tracking reveals men's appreciation of the female form. *Human Nature*, 21, 355–370.

Dodd, C. (2012). *Managing business and professional communication*. Boston: Allyn & Bacon.

Domagalski, T. (1998). *Experienced and expressed anger in the workplace*. Unpublished doctoral dissertation, University of South Florida.

Donald and Rosie. (2007, January 8). *Newsweek*, p. 55.

Donald Trump tells FNC: "Rosie O'Donnell's a loser." (2007). *FoxNews.com*. Retrieved from http://www.foxnews.com/printer_friendly_story/0,3566,237997,00.html

Donohue, W. A., & Kolt, R. (1992). *Managing interpersonal conflict*. Newbury Park, CA: Sage.

Dorman, N. (2014). Triclosan. In L. G. Schnoor, K. Young, & L. Mayfield (Eds.), *Winning orations*. Mankato, MN: Interstate Oratorical Association.

Dotan-Eliaz, O., Sommer, K. L., & Rubin, Y.S. (2009). Multilingual groups: Effects of linguistic ostracism on felt rejection and anger, coworker attraction, perceived team potency, and creative performance. *Basic and Applied Social Psychology*, 31, 363–375.

Dougherty, T., Turban, D., & Collander, J. (1994). Conforming first impressions in the employment interview. *Journal of Applied Psychology*, 79, 659–665.

Douglas, K. M., & Sutton, R. M. (2014). "A giant leap for mankind" but what about women? The role of system-justifying ideologies in predicting attitudes toward sexist language. *Journal of Language and Social Psychology*, 33, 667–680.

Douglas, W. (1987). Affinity-testing in initial interactions. *Journal of Social and Personal Relationships*, 4, 3–16.

Dovidio, J. F., Saguy, T., & Shnabel, N. (2009). Cooperation and conflict within groups: Bridging intragroup and intergroup processes. *Journal of Social Issues*, 65, 429–449.

Dowd, E. T., Hughes, S., Brockbank, L., Halpain, D., Seibel, C., & Seibel, P. (1988). Compliance-based and defiance-based intervention strategies and psychological reactance in the treatment of free and unfree behavior. *Journal of Counseling Psychology*, 35, 363–369.

Doyle, M. (2015, January 21). Supreme Court OKs inmate's beard. *San Jose Mercury News*, p. A6.

Drager, T. (2013). *Clostridium Difficile*: "The killer bacterium." In L. G. Schnoor, K. Young, & L. Mayfield (Eds.), *Winning orations*. Mankato, MN: Interstate Oratorical Association.

Dressler, C. (1995, December 31). Please! End this meeting madness! *Santa Cruz Sentinel*, p. D1.

Drew, T., Vo, M. L. H., & Wolfe, J. M. (2013). The invisible gorilla strikes again: Sustained inattentional blindness in expert observers. *Psychological Science*, 24, 1848–1853.

Driscoll, R., Davis, K., & Lipetz, M. (1972). Parental interference and romantic love: The Romeo and Juliet effect. *Journal of Personality and Social Psychology*, 24, 1–10.

Driskell, J., Radtke, P., & Salas, E. (2003). Virtual teams: Effects of technological mediation on team performance. *Group Dynamics: Theory, Research, and Practice*, 7, 297–323.

Droesch, K. (2013, September 29). Wedding traditions from around the world. *Huffington Post*. Retrieved from http://www.huffingtonpost.com/2013/09/29/wedding-traditions_n_3964844.html

Druskat, V. U., & Wolff, S. B. (1999). Effects and timing of developmental peer appraisals in self-managing work groups. *Journal of Applied Psychology*, 84, 58–74.

Duck, S. (1991). Some evident truths about conventions in everyday relationships: All communications are not created equal. *Human Communication Research*, 18, 228–269.

Duck, S. W., & Pittman, G. (1994). Social and personal relationships. In M. L. Knapp & G. R. Miller (Eds.), *Handbook of interpersonal communication*. Thousand Oaks, CA: Sage.

Duggan, M., Ellison, N. B., Lampe, C., Lenhart, A., & Madden, M. (2015, January 9). Demographics of key social networking platforms. *Pew Research Center*. Retrieved from http://www.pewinternet.org/2015/01/09/demographics-of-key-social-networking-platforms-2/

Dugosh, K. L, Paulus, P. B., Roland, E. J., & Yang, H. (2000). Cognitive stimulation in brainstorming. *Journal of Personality and Social Psychology*, 79, 722–735.

Dunleavy, K. N., Martin, M. M., Brann, M., Booth-Butterfield, M., Myers, S. A., & Weber, K. (2008). Student nagging behavior in the college classroom. *Communication Education*, 57, 1–19.

Duran, R. L., Kelly, L., & Keaton, J. A. (2005). College faculty use and perceptions of electronic mail to communicate with students. *Communication Quarterly*, 53, 159–176.

Dyer, J. (2001, June 10). Ethics and orphans: The monster study. *San Jose Mercury News*, pp. 1A, 14A–16A.

Eagan, K., Stolzenberg, E. B., Ramirez, J. J., Aragon, M. C., Suchard, M. R., & Hurtado, S. (2014). The American freshman: National norms fall 2014. *Cooperative Institutional Research Program at the Higher Education Research Institute at UCLA*. Retrieved from http://www.heri.ucla.edu/monographs/theamericanfreshman2014.pdf

Eagly, A. H. (1995). The science and politics of comparing women and men. *American Psychologist*, 50, 145–158.

Eagly, A. H. (2007). Female leadership advantage and disadvantage: Resolving the contradictions. *Psychology of Women Quarterly*, 31, 1–12.

Eagly, A. H., & Carli, L. L. (2007). *Through the labyrinth: The truth about how women become leaders*. Boston: Harvard Business School Press.

Eagly, A. H., Ashmore, R. D., Makhijani, M. G., & Kennedy, L. C. (1991). What is beautiful is good, but . . . : A meta-analytic review of research on the physical attractiveness stereotype. *Psychological Bulletin*, 110, 109–128.

Eagly, A., Johannesen-Schmidt, M. C., & van Engen, M. L. (2003). Transformational, transactional, and laissez-faire leadership styles: A meta-analysis comparing women and men. *Psychological Bulletin*, 129, 569–591.

Earnest, W. (2007). Save our slides: PowerPoint design that works. Dubuque, IA: Kendall Hunt.

Earthquake facts & earthquake fantasy. (2015, May 28). *USGS*. Retrieved from http://earthquake.usgs.gov/learn/topics/megaqk_facts_fantasy.php

Eastwick, P. W., Luchies, L. B., Finkel, E. J., & Hunt, L. L. (2014). The predictive validity of ideal partner preferences: A review and meta-analysis. *Psychological Bulletin, 140*, 623–665.

Ebrahim, N. A., Ahmed, S., & Taha, Z. (2009). Virtual teams: A literature review. *Australian Journal of Basic and Applied Science, 3*, 2653–2669.

Edwards, J. (2002, May 8). Songwriter Otis Blackwell, "Don't Be Cruel" among hits. *Santa Cruz Sentinel*, p. A8.

Edwards, K., & Smith, E. E. (1996). A disconfirmation bias in the evaluation of arguments. *Journal of Personality and Social Psychology, 71*, 5–24.

Egas, M., Kats, R., Van der Sar, X., Reuden, E., & Sabelis, M. W. (2013). Human cooperation by lethal group competition. *Scientific Reports, 3*, 1373–1384.

Eggert, D. (2012, September 7). Jennifer Granholm: "I probably shouldn't have gotten so worked up" in convention speech. *Michigan Live*. Retrieved from http://www.mlive.com/politics/index.ssf/2012/09/jennifer_granholm_i_probably_s.html

Ehrlich, P. (2000). *Human natures: Genes, culture, and the human prospect*. Washington, DC: Island Press.

Ehrlinger, J., Johnson, K., Banner, M., Dunning, D., & Kruger, J. (2008). Why the unskilled are unaware: Further explorations of (absent) self-insight among the incompetent. *Organizational Behavior and Human Decision Process, 105*, 98–121.

Eighteen-24-year-old smartphone owners send and receive almost 4K texts per month. (March 21, 2013). *Marketing Charts*. Retrieved from http://www.marketingcharts.com/online/18-24-year-old-smartphone-owners-send-and-receive-almost-4k-texts-per-month-27993/

Einarsen, S., Hoel, H., Zapf, D., & Cooper, C. L. (2003). The concept of bullying at work. In S. Einarsen, H. Hoel, D. Zapf, & C. L. Cooper (Eds.), *Bullying and emotional abuse in the workplace: International perspectives in research and practice*. London: Taylor & Francis.

Eisenchias, S. A. (2013, October 7). Gender roles and expectations: Any changes online? *Sage Open*. Retrieved from http://sgo.sagepub.com/content/3/4/2158244013506446

Ekman, P. (1992). *Telling lies: Clues to deceit in the marketplace, politics, and marriage*. New York: Norton.

Ekman, P. (1993). Facial expression and emotion. *American Psychologist, 48*, 384–393.

Ekman, P., & Friesen, W. (1987). Universal and cultural differences in the judgment of facial expressions of emotion. *Journal of Personality and Social Psychology, 53*, 712–717.

Ekman, P., & Keltner, D. (2014, March 12). Are facial expressions universal? *The Greater Good: The Science of a Meaningful Life*. Retrieved from http://greatergood.berkeley.edu/article/item/are_facial_expressions_universal

Ekman, P., & O'Sullivan, M. (1991). Who can catch a liar? *American Psychologist, 46*, 913–920.

Ekman, P., Friesen, W., & Bear, J. (1984, May). The international language of gestures. *Psychology Today*, pp. 64–69.

El Nasser, H. (2002, December 15). Gated communities more popular, and not just for the rich. *USA Today*. [Online]. Available at: http://www.usatoday.com/news/nation/2002-12-15-gated-usat_x.htm

Eldridge, N. S., & Gilbert, L. A. (1990). Correlates of relationship satisfaction in lesbian couples. *Psychology of Women Quarterly, 14*, 43–62.

Elfenbein, H. A., & Ambady, N. (2002). On the universality and cultural specificity of emotion recognition: A meta-analysis. *Psychological Bulletin, 128*, 203–235.

Elgin, S. H. (1989). *Success with the gentle art of verbal self-defense*. Englewood Cliffs, NJ: Prentice Hall.

Ellis, A. (1995). Thinking processes involved in irrational beliefs and their disturbed consequences. *Journal of Cognitive Psychotherapy, 9*, 105–116.

Ellis, A. (1996). How I learned to help clients feel better and get better. *Psychotherapy, 33*, 149–151.

Ellison, S. (2009). *Taking the war out of our words*. Deadwood, OR: Wyatt-MacKenzie.

Emanuel, R., Adams, J., Baker, K., Daufin, E. K., Ellington, C., Fitts, E., Himsel, J., Holladay, L., & Okeowo, D. (2008). How college students spend their time communicating. *International Journal of Listening, 22*, 13–28.

Emberson, L. L., Lupyan, G., Goldstein, M. H., & Spivey, M. J. (2010). Overheard cell-phone conversations: When less speech is more distracting. *Psychological Science, 21*, 1383–1388.

Emmons, M. (2005, April 10). Scholarship pressure changes youth sports. *San Jose Mercury News*, pp. 1A, 12A–13A.

Enforcement guidance. (2010, June 28). *U.S. Equal Opportunity Commission*. Retrieved from http://www.eeoc.gov/eeoc/publications/upload/currentissues.pdf

Eng, S. (1997, May 14). Cover story. *San Jose Mercury News*, pp. 1, 8.

Engleberg, I. (2002). Presentations in everyday life: Linking audience interest and speaker eloquence. *American Communication Journal*. Retrieved from http://ac-journal.org/journal/vol5/iss2/special/engleberg.htm

English, T., & Chen, S. (2007). Culture and self-concept stability: Consistency across and within contexts among Asian Americans and European Americans. *Journal of Personality and Social Psychology, 93*, 478–490.

Enough is enough": Elizabeth Warren launches fiery attack after Congress weakens Wall Street regs. *The Washington Post.* Retrieved from http://www.washingtonpost.com/news/wonkblog/wp/2014/12/12/enough-is-enough-elizabeth-warrens-fiery-attack-comes-after-congress-weakens-wall-street-regulations/

Enrollment in distance education courses, by state: Fall 2012. (2014, June). *U.S. Department of Education.* Retrieved from http://nces.ed.gov/pubs2014/2014023.pdf

Epstein, R. (2006, February/March). Do gays have a choice? *Scientific American Mind*, pp. 51–57.

Epstein, R. (2007, February/March). The truth about online dating. *Scientific American Mind*, pp. 28–35.

Epstein, R. (2010, January/February). How science can help you fall in love. *Scientific American Mind*, pp. 26–33.

Erb, S. E., Renshaw, K. D., Short, J. L., & Pollard, J. W. (2014). The importance of college roommate relationships: A review and systemic conceptualization. *Journal of Student Affairs Research and Practice, 51*, 43–55.

Erbert, L. A. (2000). Conflict and dialectics: Perceptions of dialectical contradictions in marital conflict. *Journal of Social and Personal Relationships, 17*, 638–659.

Ernst, E. (2010). Homeopathy: What does the "best" evidence tell us? *The Medical Journal of Australia, 192*, 458–460.

Escera, C., Alho, K., Winkler, I., & Naatanen, R. (1998). Neural mechanisms of involuntary attention to acoustic novelty and change. *Journal of Cognitive Neuroscience, 10*, 590–604.

Eshbaugh, E. M., & Gute, G. (2008). Hookups and sexual regret among college women. *Journal of Social Psychology, 148*, 77–90.

Estrada, R. (2014, September). 2014 corporate recruiters survey report. *GMAC.* Retrieved from http://www.gmac.com/market-intelligence-and-research/research-library/employment-outlook/2014-corporate-recruiters.aspx

Evans, C. R., & Dion, K. L. (2012). Group cohesiveness and performance: A meta-analysis. *Small Group Research, 43*, 690–701.

Exline, J. J., & Baumeister, R. F. (2000). In M. E. McCullough, K. I. Pargament, & C. E. Thoresen (Eds.), *Forgiveness: Theory, research, and practice.* New York: Guilford Press.

Fadiman, C. (Ed.). (1985). *The Little, Brown book of anecdotes.* Boston: Little, Brown.

Fairhurst, G. T., & Sarr, R. A. (1996). *The art of framing: Managing the language of leadership.* San Francisco: Jossey-Bass.

Famous quotes and authors. (2009). Retrieved from http://www.famousquotesandauthors.com/authors/albert_einstein_quotes.html

Fang, F. C., & Casadevall, A. (2013, May/June). Why we cheat. *Scientific American Mind*, pp. 31–37.

Farrell, E. (2005, February 4). More students plan to work to help pay for college. *Chronicle of Higher Education*, pp. A1, A34.

Farris, C., Treat, T. A., & Viken, R. J. (2008). Perceptual mechanisms that characterize gender differences in decoding women's sexual intent. *Psychological Science, 19*, 348–354.

Fathi, N. (2009, June 23). Woman's death creates symbol of Iran protests. *San Jose Mercury News*, pp. 1A, 6A.

FDA's graphic cigarette labels rule goes up in smoke after U.S. abandons appeal. *CBS News.* Retrieved from http://www.cbsnews.com/news/fdas-graphic-cigarette-labels-rule-goes-up-in-smoke-after-us-abandons-appeal/

Fear. (2015, February 2). *FearExit.* Retrieved from http://fearexit.com/index.php/category/fear/

Feeley, T. H., Anker, A. E., & Aloe, A. M. (2012). The door-in-the-face persuasive message strategy: A meta-analysis of the first 35 years. *Communication Monographs, 79*, 316–343.

Feeley, T. H., Marshall, H. M., & Reinhart, A. M. (2006). Reactions to narrative and statistical written messages promoting organ donation. *Communication Reports, 19*, 89–100.

Feeney, R. L. (2013). Value-focused brainstorming. *Decision Analysis.* Retrieved from http://pubsonline.informs.org/doi/abs/10.1287/deca.1120.0251

Fein, M. L. (1993). *I. A. M. A common sense guide to coping with anger.* Westport, CT: Praeger.

Feingold, A. (1992). Good-looking people are not what we think. *Psychological Bulletin, 111*, 304–341.

Feldman, R., Rosenthal, S., & Eldelman, A. (2014). Maternal-preterm skin-to-skin contact enhances child physiologic organization and cognitive control across the first 10 years. (2014). *Biological Psychiatry, 75*, 56–64.

Felps, W., Mitchell, T. R., & Byington, E. (2006). How, when, and why bad apples spoil the barrel: Negative group members and dysfunctional groups. *Research in Organizational Behavior, 27*, 175–222.

Female body shape men prefer most. (2015, June 7). *Netscape.* Retrieved from http://webcenters.netscape.compuserve.com/love/package.jsp?name=fte/curvywomen/curvywomen

Fenell, D. L. (1993). Characteristics of long-term first marriages. *Journal of Mental Health Counseling*, 15, 446–460.

Fenelon, J. V. (2014). Survey on Redskins team name found most American Indians believe it to be offensive and racist. *Center for Indigenous Peoples Studies at California State University, San Bernardino.* Retrieved from http://cips.csusb.edu/docs/PressRelease.pdf

Ferris, S. H., & Farlow, M. (2013). Language impairment in Alzheimer's disease and benefits of acetylcholinesterase inhibitors, *Clinical Intervention & Aging*, 8, 1007–1014.

Festinger, L. (1957). *A theory of cognitive dissonance.* Stanford, CA: Stanford University Press.

Festinger, L. (1977). Cognitive dissonance. In E. Aronson (Ed.), *Readings about the social animal.* San Francisco: Freeman.

Fiedler, F., & House, R. (1988). Leadership theory and research: A report of progress. In C. Cooper & I. Robertson (Eds.), *International review of industrial and organizational psychology.* New York: Wiley.

Field, A. E., Sonneville, K. R., Crosby, R. D., Swanson, S. A., Eddy, K. T., Camargo, C. A., Horton, N. J., & Micali, N. (2014). Physique and the development of obesity, binge drinking, and drug use among adolescent boys and young adult me. *JAMA Pediatrics*, 168, 34–39.

Field, T. (2003). *Touch.* Providence, RI: Bradford Books.

Final report of the California task force to promote self-esteem and personal and social responsibility. (1990). Sacramento: California State Department of Education.

Fincham, F. D., Beach, S. R. H., & Davila, J. (2008). Forgiveness and conflict. *American Psychological Association.* Retrieved from http://www.apa.org/international/resources/publications/forgiveness.pdf

Fincham, F. D., Harold, G. T., & Gano-Phillips, S. (2000). The longitudinal association between attributions and marital satisfaction: Direction of effects and role of efficacy expectations. *Journal of Family Psychology*, 14, 267–285.

Finding love at work is more acceptable than ever. (2015, February 11). *Vault.* Retrieved from http://www.vault.com/blog/workplace-issues/2015-office-romance-survey-results/

Fingerman, K. L., & Charles, S. T. (2010). It takes two to tango. *Current Directions in Psychological Science*, 19, 172–176.

Finkel, E. J., Eastwick, P. W., Karney, B. R., Reis, H. T., & Sprecher, S. (2012). Online dating: A critical analysis from the perspective of psychological science. *Psychological Science in the Public Interest*, 13, 3–66.

Finn, A. N., Sawyer, C. R., & Schrodt, P. (2009). Examining the effect of exposure therapy on public speaking state anxiety. *Communication Education*, 58, 92–109.

Firestone, J. D. (2011, April 12). The Moth radio hour wins Peabody award. *The Moth.* Retrieved from http://themoth.org/posts/the-moth-radio-hour-wins-peabody-award

Fisher, A. (2007, February 13). Cupid at work: 3 tips for office romances. *Fortune.* Retrieved from http://money.cnn.com/2007/02/12/news/economy/cupid.fortune/index.htm

Fisher, H. E., Brown, L. L., Aron, A., Strong, G., & Mashek, D. (2010). Reward, addiction, and emotional regulation systems associated with rejection in love. *Journal of Neurophysiology*, 104, 51–60.

Fisher, K. (2000). *Leading self-directed work teams: A guide to developing new team leadership skills.* New York: McGraw-Hill.

Fisher, R., & Brown, S. (1988). *Getting together: Building a relationship that gets to yes.* Boston: Houghton Mifflin.

Fisher, R., & Shapiro, D. (2005). *Beyond reason: Using emotions as you negotiate.* New York: Penguin Books.

Fisher, R. M. (2003, January/February). Beliefs on trial, and the legality of reasonableness. *Skeptical Inquirer*, pp. 29–34.

Fitzhenry, R. I. (1993). *The Harper book of quotations.* New York: HarperCollins.

Fletcher, G., & Fincham, F. (1991). Attribution in close relationships. In G. Fletcher & F. Fincham (Eds.), *Cognition in close relationships.* Hillsdale, NJ: Erlbaum.

Flowers, B. J., & Richardson, F. C. (1996). Why is multiculturalism good? *American Psychologist*, 51, 609–621.

Floyd, K. (2006). An evolutionary approach to understanding nonverbal communication. In V. Manusov & M. L. Patterson (Eds.), *The Sage handbook of nonverbal communication.* Thousand Oaks, CA: Sage.

Foley, K. (2010, February 5). The award machine. *IN-Business.* Retrieved from at: http://www.in-business.co.nz/the-award-machine/

Foley, R. J. (2012, December 22). Iowa court: Bosses can fire workers for being attractive. *San Jose Mercury News*, p. A4.

Folger, J., Poole, M., & Stutman, R. (1993). *Working through conflict: Strategies for relationships, groups, and organizations.* New York: HarperCollins.

Forbes, A. (2012). Prioritize children. In L. G. Schnoor, L. Mayfield, & K. Young (Eds.), *Winning orations.* Mankato, MN: Interstate Oratorical Association.

Forest, A. L., & Wood, J. V. (2012). When social networking is not working: Individuals with low self-esteem recognize but do not reap the benefits of self-disclosure on Facebook. *Psychological Science*, 23, 295–302.

Ford, H. (2003). *My life and work.* Whitefish, MT: Kessinger Publishing.

Forsyth, D. R. (2014). *Group dynamics*. Boston, MA: Wadsworth Cengage.

Foulke, E. (2006). Listening comprehension as a function of word rate. *Journal of Communication*, 18, 198–206.

Fowler, G. (1991). Iben Browning, 73; researcher studied climate and quakes. *The New York Times*. Retrieved from http://www.nytimes.com/1991/07/20/obituaries/iben-browning-73-researcher-studied-climate-and-quakes.html

Fragale, A. R. (2006). The power of powerless speech. The effects of speech style and task interdependence on status conferral. *Organizational Behavior and Human Decisions Processes*, 101, 243–261.

Frederick, D. A., Buchanan, G. M., Sadeghi-Azar, L., Peplau, L. A., Haselton, M. G., & Berezovskaya, A. (2007). Desiring the muscular ideal: Men's body satisfaction in the United States, Ukraine, and Ghana. *Psychology of Men & Masculinity*, 8, 103–117.

Fredrickson, B. (2009b). *Positivity: Groundbreaking research reveals how to embrace the hidden strength of positive emotions, overcome negativity, and thrive*. New York: Crown.

Freed, A. (1992). We understand perfectly: A critique of Tannen's view. In *Locating power* (Proceedings of the 1992 Berkeley Women and Language Conference). Berkeley: University of California Press.

Frerking, B. (1995, March 15). Question authority, parents say. *San Jose Mercury News*, p. A4.

Frey, W. H. (2014, December 12). New projections point to a majority minority nation in 2044. *Brookings*. Retrieved from http://www.brookings.edu/blogs/the-avenue/posts/2014/12/12-majority-minority-nation-2044-frey?utm_campaign=Brookings+Brief&utm_source=hs_email&utm_medium=email&utm_content=15281320&_hsenc=p2ANqtz-_qpt4RD--793M0n_ewCTTCDdvJIS4jif_Y0V2lXp1wesPjvJ9inK5IpVTcZUEp6USYvbg7pQ-KOTCzdB3pA4IGDTsjqMrLoV_x0OJRmZTPsHWkYsI&_hsmi=15281320

Froomkin, D. (2010, August 26). Inmate sexual victimization persists, while feds stall on new rules. *Huffington Post*. Retrieved from http://www.huffingtonpost.com/2010/08/26/sexual-victimization-of-i_n_695640.html

Frye, N. E., & Karney, B. R. (2006). The context of aggressive behavior in marriage: A longitudinal study of newlyweds. *Journal of Family Psychology*, 20, 12–20.

Fulwiler, M. (2012, July 2). Managing conflict: Solvable vs. perpetual problems. *The Gottman Relationship Blog*. Retrieved from http://www.gottmanblog.com/archives/2014/10/28/managing-conflict-solvable-vs-perpetual-problems

Furnham, A., McClellan, A., & Omer, L. (2003). A cross-cultural comparison of ratings of perceived fecundity and sexual attractiveness as a function of body weight and waist-to-hip ratio. *Psychology, Health and Medicine*, 8, 219–230.

Gagne, F. (2004). Bias and accuracy in close relationships: An integrative review. *Personality and Social Psychology Review*, 8, 322–338.

Galanter, E. (1962). Contemporary psychophysics. In R. Brown, E. Galanter, E. H. Hess, & G. Mendler (eds.), *New directions in psychology*. New York: Holt, Rinehart & Winston.

Gallo, C. (2014, September 25). New survey: 70% say presentational skills are critical for career success. *Forbes*. Retrieved from http://www.forbes.com/sites/carminegallo/2014/09/25/new-survey-70-percent-say-presentation-skills-critical-for-career-success/

Galloway, L. (2014). Untitled. In L. G. Schnoor, K. Young, & L. Mayfield (Eds.), *Winning orations*. Mankato, MN: Interstate Oratorical Association.

Gamer, M. (2009, February/March). Portrait of a lie. *Scientific American Mind*, pp. 50–55.

Gantz, J., & Reinsel, D. (2012, December). The digital universe in 2020. Big data, bigger digital shadows, and biggest growth in the Far East. *International Data Corporation*. Retrieved from http://idcdocserv.com/1414 .

Garcia, J. R., Reiber, C., Massey, S. G., & Merriwether, A. M. (2013, February). Sexual hook-up culture. *Monitor*. Retrieved from http://www.apa.org/monitor/2013/02/ce-corner.aspx

Garcia-Navarro, L. (2014, December 29). Same-sex couples have more egalitarian relationships. *NPR*. Retrieved from http://www.npr.org/2014/12/29/373835114/same-sex-couples-may-have-more-egalitarian-relationships

Garfield, C. (1986). *Peak performers*. New York: Avon Books.

Garland-Thomson, R. (2009). *Staring: How we look*. New York: Oxford University Press.

Garofoli, J. (2015, May 13). Gavin Newsom crowdsourcing his commencement speech for SF State University. *SFGATE*. http://blog.sfgate.com/nov05election/2015/05/13/gavin-newsom-crowdsourcing-his-commencement-speech-for-sf-state-university/

Gaschler, K. (2005, November 21). Judging Amy and Andy. *Scientific American Mind*, pp. 52–57.

Gass, R., & Seiter, J. (2011). *Persuasion, social influence, and compliance gaining*. Boston: Allyn & Bacon.

Gastil, J. (1994). A meta-analytic review of the productivity and satisfaction of democratic and autocratic leadership. *Small Group Research*, 25, 384–410.

Gaulin, S. J. C., & Lassek, W. (2012, February 25). Do men find very skinny women attractive? *Psychology Today*. Retrieved from https://www.psychologytoday.com/blog/why-women-need-fat/

201202/do-men-find-very-skinny-women-attractive

Gelles, R., & Straus, M. (1988). *Intimate violence: The causes and consequences of abuse in the American family.* New York: Simon & Schuster.

Gender equality universally embraced, but inequalities acknowledged. (2010, July 1). *Pew Research Center.* Retrieved from http://www.pewglobal.org/2010/07/01/gender-equality/

Gentner, D., & Goldin-Meadow, S. (2003). *Language in mind: Advances in the study of language and thought.* Cambridge, MA: MIT Press.

George, D. S. (2008, September 26). Women are gaining ground in family decision making. *Washington Post.* Retrieved from http://www.washingtonpost.com/wp-dyn/content/article/2008/09/25/AR2008092504167.html

Gershon, I. (2010). *The breakup 2.0: Disconnecting over new media.* Ithaca, NY: Cornell University Press.

Getter, H., & Nowinski, I. (1981). A free response test of interpersonal effectiveness. *Journal of Personality Assessment,* 45, 301–308.

Getting to know us. (2015, April 25). *About McDonalds.* Retrieved from http://www.aboutmcdonalds.com/mcd/our_company/mcdonalds_history_timeline.html

Gibb, J. (1961). Defensive communication. *Journal of Communication,* 11, 141–148.

Gibson, C. B., & McDaniel, D. M. (2010). Moving beyond conventional wisdom: Advancements in cross-cultural theories of leadership, conflict, and teams. *Perspectives on Psychological Science,* 5, 450–462.

Giles, H., & Le Poire, B. A. (2006). The ubiquity and social meaningfulness of nonverbal communication. In V. Manusov & M. L. Patterson (Eds.), *The Sage handbook of nonverbal communication.* Thousand Oaks, CA: Sage.

Gilligan, J., & Lee, B. (2004). Beyond the prison paradigm: From provoking violence to preventing it by creating "anti-prisons" (residential colleges and therapeutic communities). *Annals of the New York Academy of Sciences.* Retrieved from https://groups.yahoo.com/neo/groups/evolutionary-psychology/conversations/messages/35810

Girion, L. (2000, December 20). Americans losing their cool at work. *San Jose Mercury News,* pp. 1C, 6C.

Gladwell, M. (2005). *Blink: The power of thinking without thinking.* New York: Little, Brown.

Glassner, B. (1999). *The culture of fear: Why Americans are afraid of the wrong things.* New York: Basic Books.

Gleicher, F., & Petty, R. (1992). Expectations of reassurance influence the nature of fear-stimulated attitude change. *Journal of Experimental Social Psychology,* 28, 86–100.

Glick, P., & Fiske, S. T. (2001). An ambivalent alliance: Hostile and benevolent sexism as complementary justifications for gender inequality. *American Psychologist,* 56, 109–118.

Glick, P., Lameriras, M., Fiske, S. T., et al. (2004). Bad but bold: Ambivalent attitudes toward men predict gender inequality in 16 nations. *Journal of Personality and Social Psychology,* 86, 713–728.

Glinski, N. (2015, July 30). Women on boards. *Bloomberg Quick Take.* Retrieved from http://www.bloombergview.com/quicktake/women-boards

Global study on homicide. (2013). *United Nations Office on Drugs and Crime.* Retrieved from http://www.unodc.org/documents/gsh/pdfs/2014_GLOBAL_HOMICIDE_BOOK_web.pdf

Glomb, T. M. (2002). Workplace anger and aggression: Informing conceptual models with data from specific encounters. *Journal of Occupational Health Psychology,* 7, 20–36.

Goldenberg, O., Larson, J. R., & Wiley, J. (2013). Goal instructions, response formats, and idea generation in groups. *Small Group Research,* 44, 227–256.

Goldfarb, B. (2015). The militarization of police departments. In L. G. Schnoor & L. Mayfield, (Eds.), *Winning orations of the Interstate oratorical Association.* Mankato, MN: Interstate Oratorical Association

Goldsmith, D. J. (2000). Soliciting advice: The role of sequential placement in mitigating face threat. *Communication Monographs,* 67, 1–19.

Goldsmith, D. J., & MacGeorge, E. L. (2000). The impact of politeness and relationship on perceived quality of advice about a problem. *Human Communication Research,* 26, 234–263.

Goldston, L. (2007, June 8). Men test their best lines as women eat up attention. *San Jose Mercury News,* pp. 1B, 7B.

Goleman, D. (1998). *Working with emotional intelligence.* New York: Bantam.

Goleman, D. (2013). *Focus: The hidden driver of excellence.* New York: HarperCollins.

Gonzaga, G. C., Turner, R. A., Keltner, D., Campos, B., & Altemus, M. (2006). Romantic love and sexual desire in close relationships. *Emotion,* 6, 163–179.

Goodboy, A. K., & Brann, M. (2010). Flirtation rejection strategies: Toward an understanding of communicative disinterest in flirting. *The Qualitative Report,* 15, 268–278.

Goodboy, A. K., Myers, S. A., & Members of Investigating Communication. (2010). Relational quality indicators and love styles as predictors of negative relational maintenance behaviors in romantic relationships. *Communication Reports,* 23, 65–78.

Goodman, E. (2009, July 16). Sotomayor takes one for the supreme team. *San Jose Mercury News,* p. A13.

Goodwin, E. (2010, February 21). Primary reasons why kids drop out of community sports programs. *Youth Sports Quality Institute*. Retrieved fromhttp://ysqi4ed.wordpress.com/2010/02/

Gopnik, A., Meltzoff, A. N., & Kuhl, P. (2001). *The scientist in the crib: What early learning tells us about the mind*. New York: Perennial.

Gordon, A. M. (2012, October 12). You be the judge: Are you making bad attributions? *Psychology Today*. Retrieved from https://www.psychologytoday.com/blog/between-you-and-me/201210/you-be-the-judge-are-you-making-bad-attributions

Gordon, R. A., Crosnoe, R., & Wang, X. (2014). *Physical attractiveness and the accumulation of social and human capital in adolescence and young adulthood: Assets and distractions*. New York: Wiley.

Gorman, S. (2015, January 12). Bobby Scott: After WWII U.S. executed Japanese for war crimes including waterboarding. *PolitiFact*. Retrieved from http://www.politifact.com/virginia/statements/2015/jan/12/bobby-scott/bobby-scott-after-wwii-us-executed-japanese-war-cr/

Gottman couples & marital therapy. (2015). *Couples Training Institute*. Retrieved from http://couplestraininginstitute.com/gottman-couples-and-marital-therapy/

Gottman, J. M. (1994a). *What predicts divorce? The relationship between marital processes and marital outcomes*. Hillsdale, NJ: Erlbaum.

Gottman, J. M. (1994b, May/June). Why marriages fail. *Family Therapy*, pp. 40–48.

Gottman, J. M., & Carrere, S. (1994). Why can't men and women get along? Developmental notes and marital inequities. In D. Canary & L. Stafford (Eds.), *Communication and relational maintenance*. New York: Academic Press.

Gottman, J. M., & DeClaire, J. (2001). *The relationship cure: A five-step guide for building better connections with family, friends, and lovers*. New York: Crown.

Gottman, J. M., Levenson, R. W., Swanson, C., Swanson, K., Tyson, R., &Yoshimoto, D. (2003). Observing gay, lesbian and heterosexual couples' relationships: Mathematics modeling and conflict interactions. *Journal of Homosexuality*, 45, 65–91.

Gottman, J. M., & Gottman, J. S. (2006). *10 lessons to transform your marriage*. New York: Crown.

Gottman, J. M., & Levenson, R. W. (1999). Dysfunctional marital conflict: Women are being unfairly blamed. *Journal of Divorce and Remarriage*, 31, 1–7.

Gottman, J. M., & Silver, N. (1994). *Why marriages succeed and fail: And how you can make yours last*. New York: Simon & Schuster.

Gottman, J. M, & Silver, N. (1999). *The seven principles for making marriage work*. New York: Crown.

Gottman, J. M., Coan, J., Carrere, S., & Swanson, C. (1998). Predicting marital happiness and stability from newlywed interactions. *Journal of Marriage and the Family*, 60, 5–22.

Govier, T. (2010). *A practical study of argument*. New York: Wadsworth Cengage.

Grace, K. (2000). Unsanitary hotels. In L. G. Schnoor & B. Wickelgren (Eds.), *Winning orations*. Mankato, MN: Interstate Oratorical Association.

Grasz, J. (2012, July 25). Swearing at work can harm your career prospects, finds CareerBuilder survey. *CareerBuilder*. Retrieved from http://www.careerbuilder.com/share/aboutus/pressreleasesdetail.aspx?sd=7%2f25%2f2012&sc_cmp1=cb_pr709_&siteid=cbpr&id=pr709&ed=12%2f31%2f2012

Grasz, J. (2015a, May 14). 35 percent of employers less likely to interview applicants they can't find online, according to annual CareerBuilder social media recruitment survey. *CareerBuilder*. Retrieved from http://www.careerbuilder.com/share/aboutus/pressreleasesdetail.aspx?sd=5%2F14%2F2015&id=pr893&ed=12%2F31%2F2015

Grasz, J. (2015b, April 9). 1 in 5 employers has unknowingly asked an illegal interview question, CareerBuilder survey finds. *CareerBuilder*. Retrieved from http://www.careerbuilder.com/share/aboutus/pressreleasesdetail.aspx?sd=4%2F9%2F2015&id=pr877&ed=12%2F31%2F2015

Grasz, J. (2011, January 12). Employers reveal outrageous and common mistakes candidates make in job interviews. *CareerBuilder*. [Online]. Available at: http://www.careerbuilder.com/share/aboutus/pressreleasesdetail.aspx?id=pr614&sd=1/12/2011&ed=12/31/2011

Gray, J. (1992). *Men are from Mars, Women are from Venus: A practical guide to improving communication and getting what you want in your relationships*. New York: Harper Collins.

Graybar, S. R., Antonuccio, D. O., Boutilier, L. R., & Varble, D. L. (1989). Psychological reactance as a factor affecting patient compliance to physician advice. *Scandinavian Journal of Behavior Therapy*, 18, 43–51.

Green, A. (2011, August 16). Can my employer stop me from using the bathroom? *Ask A Manager*. Retrieved from http://www.askamanager.org/2011/08/employer-is-monitoring-my-bathroom-breaks.html

Green, M. C., & Brock, T. C. (2000). The role of transportation in the persuasiveness of public narratives. *Journal of Personality and Social Psychology*, 79, 701–721.

Greenberg, J. (1981, June/July). An interview with David Rosenhan. *APA Monitor*, pp. 4–5.

Greengross, G., & Miller, G. F. (2008). Dissing oneself versus dissing rivals: Effects of status, personality, and sex on the short-term and long-term attractiveness of self-deprecating and other-deprecating humor. *Evolutionary Psychology Journal*, 6, 393–408.

Gregoire, C. (2013, September 28). How technology is killing eye contact. *Huffington Post*. Retrieved from http://www.huffingtonpost.com/2013/09/28/why-youre-not-making-eye-_n_4002494.html

Grenny, J. (2009). Crucial conversations: The most potent force for eliminating disruptive behavior. *Physician Executive Journal*, 35, 30–33.

Grewal, D. (2012, July August). When nice guys finish first. *Scientific American Mind*, pp. 62–65.

Griffin, E. (2006). *A first look at communication theory*. New York: McGraw-Hill.

Grim, R. (2014, July 2). Two lesbians raised a baby and this is what they got—A White House intern. *Huffington Post*. Retrieved from http://www.huffingtonpost.com/2014/07/02/zach-wahls_n_5551300.html

Grohol, J. M. (2013). What is catastrophizing? *Psych Central*. Retrieved from http://psychcentral.com/lib/what-is-catastrophizing/1276/

Gronbeck, B., German, K., Ehninger, D., & Monroe, A. (1998). *Principles of speech communication*. New York: Longman.

Grossmann, I., & Varnum, M. E. W. (2015). Social structure, infectious diseases, disasters, secularism, and cultural change in America. *Psychological Science*, 26, 311–324.

Gruber, J. (2001). Heart disease in women. In L. G. Schnoor & B. Wickelgren (Eds.), *Winning orations*. Mankato, MN: Interstate Oratorical Association.

Grusec, J. E., & Redler, E. (1980). Attribution, reinforcement, and altruism: A developmental analysis. *Developmental Psychology*, 16, 525–534.

Grusec, J. E., Kuczynski, L., Rushton, J. P., & Simutis, Z. M. (1978). Modeling, direct instruction, and attributions: Effects on altruism. *Developmental Psychology*, 14, 51–57.

Grusky, O., Bonacich, P., & Webster, C. (1995). The coalition structure of the four-person family. *Current Research in Social Psychology*, pp. 16–29.

Gudykunst, W. B. (2005). An anxiety/uncertainty management (AUM) theory of effective communication: Making the mesh of the net finer. In W. B. Gudykunst (Ed.), *Theorizing about intercultural communication*. Thousand Oaks, CA: Sage.

Gudykunst, W. B., & Kim, Y. Y. (Eds.). (1992). *Readings on communicating with strangers*. New York: McGraw-Hill.

Guerrero, L. K. (1992). "I'm so mad I could scream": The effects of anger expression on relational satisfaction and communication competence. *Southern Communication Journal*, 59, 125–141.

Guerrero, L. K., & Chavez, A. M. (2005). Relational maintenance in cross-sex friendships characterized by different types of romantic intent: An exploratory study. *Western Journal of Communication*, 69, 339–358.

Gully, S. M., Devine, S., & Whitney, D. (2012). A meta-analysis of cohesion and performance: Effects of level of analysis and task interdependence. *Small Group Research*, 43, 702–725.

Gurrie, C. (2013, November 20). Group work: A Millennial myth? Improving group communication in traditional undergraduate settings. Paper presented at the National Communication Association convention, Washington, D.C.

Haas, S. M., & Stafford, L. (1998). An initial examination of maintenance behaviors in gay and lesbian relationships. *Journal of Social and Personal Relationships*, 15, 846–855.

Hackman, M., & Johnson, C. (2013). *Leadership: A communication perspective*. Prospect Heights, IL: Waveland Press.

Haefner, P. T., Notarius, C. I., & Pellegrini, D. S. (1991). Determinants of satisfaction with marital discussions: An exploration of husband-wife differences. *Behavioral Assessment*, 13, 67–82.

Hagensick, M. E. (2008). In L. G. Schnoor & D. Cronin-Mills (Eds.), *Winning orations*. Mankato, MN: Interstate Oratorical Association.

Hair care services industry profile. (2015, February 9). *First Research*. Retrieved from http://www.firstresearch.com/industry-research/Hair-Care-Services.html

Haleta, L. L. (1996). Student perceptions of teachers' use of language: The effects of powerful and powerless language on impression formation and uncertainty. *Communication Education*, 45, 16–28.

Halfaker, A., Geiger, R. R., Morgan, J. T., & Riedl, J. (2013). The rise and decline of an open collaboration system: How *Wikipedia's* reaction to popularity is causing its decline. *American Behavioral Scientist*, 57, 664–688.

Hall, E. (1969). *The hidden dimension*. New York: Doubleday

Hall, E. (1981). *Beyond culture*. New York: Doubleday.

Hall, E. V., Phillips, K. W., & Townsend, S. M. A rose by any other name? The consequences of subtyping "African-American" from "Blacks."(2015). *Journal of Experimental Social Psychology*, 56, 183–190.

Hall, J., & Watson, W. (1970). The effects of normative intervention on group decision making. *Human Relations*, 23, 299–317.

Hall, J. A. (2006b). Women's and men's nonverbal communication. In V. Manusov & M. L. Patterson (Eds.), *The Sage handbook of nonverbal communication*. Thousand Oaks, CA: Sage.

Hall, J. A. (2013). Humor in long-term romantic relationships: The association of general humor styles and relationship-specific functions with relationship satisfaction. *Western Journal of Communication, 77*, 272–292.

Hall, J. A., & Bernieri, F. J. (2001). *Interpersonal sensitivity: Theory and measurement.* Mahwah, NJ: Erlbaum.

Hall, J. A., Coats, E. J., & LeBeau, L. S. (2005). Nonverbal behavior and the vertical dimension of social relations: A meta-analysis. *Psychological Bulletin, 131*, 898–924.

Hall, J. A., Xing, C., & Brooks, S. (2014). Accurately detecting flirting: Error management theory, the traditional sexual script, and flirting base rate. *Communication Research.* Retrieved from http://crx.sagepub.com/content/early/2014/05/25/00936502145349 72.abstra

Hamachek, D. (1982). *Encounters with others: Interpersonal relationships and you.* New York: Harcourt Brace.

Hamachek, D. (1992). *Encounters with the self.* Fort Worth, TX: Harcourt Brace Jovanovich.

Hamel, J. (2012, November). The Partner Abuse State of Knowledge project manuscripts and online database: Overview of findings. *Partner Abuse.* Retrieved from http://www.springerpub.com/media/springer-journals/OverviewofFindings.pdf

Hamermesh, D. S. (2013). *Beauty pays: Why attractive people are more successful.* Princeton, NJ: Princeton University Press.

Hamermesh, D. S., & Parker, A. M. (2005). Beauty in the classroom: Professors' pulchritude and putative pedagogical productivity. *Economics of Education Review, 24*, 369–376.

Hample, D. (2006). Anti-comfort messages. In K. M. Galvin & P. J. Cooper (Eds.), *Making connections: Readings in relational communication.* Los Angeles: Roxbury.

Hampton, D., Rainie, L., Lu, W., Shin, I., & Purcell, K. (2015, January 15). Social media and the cost of caring. *Pew Research Center.* Retrieved from http://www.pewinternet.org/2015/01/15/social-media-and-stress/

Han, M. (2003). Body image dissatisfaction and eating disturbance among Korean college female students: Relationships to media exposure, upward comparison, and perceived reality. *Communication Studies, 34*, 65–78.

Han, S., & Shavitt, S. (1994). Persuasion and culture: Advertising appeals in individualistic and collectivistic societies. *Journal of Experimental Social Psychology, 30*, 326–350.

Hancock, A. B., & Rubin, B. A. (2015). Influence of communication partner's gender on language. *Journal of Language and Social Psychology, 34*, 46–64.

Haney, W. (1967). *Communication and organizational behavior.* Homewood, IL: Irwin.

Hannah, M. (2009, June 26). How will Iranian protests change Twitter? *Mediashift.* Retrieved from http://www.pbs.org/mediashift/2009/06/how-will-Iranian-protests-change-twitter177.html

Hansen, K. (2015, June 3). Quintessential careers: Behavioral job interviewing strategies. *Quintessential Careers.* Retrieved from http://www.quintcareers.com/behavioral_interviewing.html

Hansen, K., & Hansen, R. (2015a, June 3). Free sample behavioral interview questions for job-seekers. *Quintessential Careers.* Retrieved from http://www.quintcareers.com/sample_behavioral.html

Hansen, R. S., & Hansen, K. (2015b, February 13). What do employers *really* want? Top skills and values employers seek from job-seekers. *Quintessential Careers.* Retrieved from http://www.quintcareers.com/job_skills_values.html

Hanson, R. (2010, October 26). Confronting the negativity bias. *Psychology Today.* Retrieved from http://www.psychologytoday.com/blog/your-wise-brain/201010/confronting-the-negativity-bias

Hardy, J., Eys, M. A., & Carron, A. V. (2005). Exploring the potential disadvantages of high cohesion in sports teams. *Small Group Research, 36*, 166–187.

Hare, W. (2009, March/April). What open-mindedness requires. *Skeptical Inquirer,* pp. 36–39.

Harris, J. (2009, November 16). Fact-checking critics of President Obama's bowing controversy. *San Diego City Buzz Examiner.* Retrieved from http://www.examiner.com/city-buzz-in-san-diego/fact-checking-critics-on-president-obama-s-bowing-controversy

Harrison, D. A., Price, K. H., Gavin, J. H., & Florey, A. T. (2002). Time, teams, and task performance: Changing effects of surface- and deep-level diversity on group functioning. *Academy of Management Journal, 45*, 1029–1045.

Harrison, L. E. (2000). Introduction. In L. E. Harrison & S. P. Huntington (Eds.), *Culture matters: How values shape human progress.* New York: Basic Books.

Harrison, L. E., & Huntington, S. P. (Eds.). (2000). *Culture matters: How values shape human progress.* New York: Basic Books.

Hart, J. W., Bridgett, D. J., & Karau, S. J. (2001). Coworker ability and effort as determinants of individual effort on a collective task. *Group Dynamics: Theory, Research, and Practice, 5*, 181–190.

Hartshorne, J. K. (2011, March/April). Where are the talking robots? *Scientific American Mind,* pp. 44–51.

Hartwell-Walker, M. (2013, February 15). Signs you are verbally abused: Part I. *Psych Central.* Retrieved from http://psychcentral.com/lib/signs-you-are-verbally-abused-part-i/00015267

Harvey, S. (2013). A different perspective: The multiple effects of deep level diversity on group creativity. *Journal of Experimental Social Psychology*, 49, 822–832.

Harwell, D. (2014, October 17). More women play video games than boys, and other surprising facts lost in the mess of Gamergate. *The Washington Post*. Retrieved from http://www.washingtonpost.com/blogs/the-switch/wp/2014/10/17/more-women-play-video-games-than-boys-and-other-surprising-facts-lost-in-the-mess-of-gamergate/

Haslam, S. A., & Reicher, S. D. (2012, July/August). In search of charisma. *Scientific American Mind*, pp. 42–49.

Haslam, S. A., Reicher, S. D., & Platow, M. J. (2011). *The new psychology of leadership: Identity, influence and power*. New York: Psychology Press.

Haslett, B. (1992). *The organization woman: Power and paradox*. Norwood, NJ: Ablex.

Hausmann, R., Tyson, L. D., Bekhouche, Y., & Zahidi, S. (2013). The global gender gap report 2013. *World Economic Forum*. Retrieved from http://www3.weforum.org/docs/WEF_GenderGap_Report_2013.pdf

Hawkins, K. (1995). Effects of gender and communication content on leadership emergence in small task-oriented groups. *Small Group Research*, 26, 234–249.

Hayes, J. (2008). Workplace conflict and how businesses can harness it to thrive. *CPP Global*. Retrieved from https://www.cpp.com/pdfs/CPP_Global_Human_Capital_Report_Workplace_Conflict.pdf

Hecht, M., Collier, M., & Ribeau, S. (1993). *African American communication: Ethnic identity and cultural interpretation*. Newbury Park, CA: Sage.

Hellweg, S., Samovar, L., & Skow, L. (1994). Cultural variations in negotiation styles. In L. Samovar & R. Porter (Eds.), *Intercultural communication: A reader*. Belmont, CA: Wadsworth.

Hendricks, W., Holliday, M., Mobley, R., & Steinbrecher, K. (1996). *Secrets of power presentations*. Franklin Lakes, NJ: Career Press.

Henley, N. (1995). Body politics revised: What do we know today? In P. Kalbfleisch & M. Cody (Eds.), *Gender, power, and communication in human relationships*. Hillsdale, NJ: Erlbaum.

Henningsen, D. D., Kartch, F., Orr, N., & Brown, A. (2009). The perceptions of verbal and nonverbal flirting cues in cross-sex interactions. *Human Communication*, 12, 371–381.

Henry, J. (1963). *Culture against man*. New York: Random House.

Herring, S. C. (2003). Gender and power in on-line communication. In J. Holmes & M. Meyerhoff (Eds.), *The handbook of language and gender*. Maiden, MA: Blackwell Publishing.

Hersey, P., Blanchard, K. H., & Johnson, D. E. (2007). *Management of organizational behavior: Leading human resources*. Upper Saddle River, NJ: Prentice Hall.

Hershey, T. (2000). *Soul gardening: Cultivating the good life*. Minneapolis, MN: Augsburg.

Hertenstein, M. J. (2002). Touch: Its communicative functions in infancy. *Human Development*, 45, 70–95.

Hertenstein, M. J., Holmes, R., McCullough, M., & Keltner, D. (2009). The communication of emotion via touch. *Emotion*, 9, 566–573.

Heslin, R. (1974, May). *Steps toward a taxonomy of touching*. Paper presented to the annual convention of the Midwestern Psychological Association.

Hess, A. (2014, June 3). Smile, baby! A new study shows how often women and gay men are sexually harassed on the street. *Slate*. Retrieved from http://www.slate.com/blogs/xx_factor/2014/06/03/stop_street_harassment_study_how_often_women_gay_men_and_people_of_color.html

Hicks, T. (2015, January 28). Benedict Cumberbatch apologizes for racist remark. *San Jose Mercury News*, p. A2.

Hingson, R. W., Zha, W., & Weitzman, E. E. (2009). Magnitude of and trends in alcohol-related mortality and morbidity among U. S. college students ages 18–24, 1998–2005. *Journal of Studies on Alcohol and Drugs*, 16, 12–20.

Historic earthquakes: Magnitude 7.7 India. (2012, October 30). USGS, Retrieved from http://earthquake.usgs.gov/earthquakes/eqarchives/year/2001/2001_01_26.php

Hitlan, R. T., Kelly, K. M., Schepman, S., Schneider, K. T., & Zarate, M. A. (2006). Language exclusion and the consequences of perceived ostracism in the workplace. *Group Dynamics: Theory, Research, and Practice*, 10, 56–70.

Hitsch, G. J., Hortacsu, A., & Ariely, D. (2010). Matching and sorting in online dating. *American Economic Review*, 100, 130–163.

Hodson, G. (2011). Do ideologically intolerant people benefit from intergroup contact? *Current Directions in Psychological Science*, 20, 154–159.

Hoffeld, D. (2015, April). The science of effective PowerPoint presentations. *Hoffeld Group*. Retrieved from https://www.hoffeldgroup.com/wp-content/uploads/2015/04/Science-of-Effective-PowerPoint-Presentations.pdf

Hoffman, S. (2014, October 7). Why students forget what they've learned & how to increase learning retention. *Reading Horizons*. Retrieved from http://www.readinghorizons.com/blog/review---is-it-worth-it

Hofstede, G. (2012). Dimensionalizing cultures: The Hofstede model in context. In L. A. Samovar, R. E.

Porter, & E. R. McDaniel (Eds.), *Intercultural communication: A reader.* Boston: Wadsworth/Cengage.

Hofstede, G., & Hofstede, G. J. (2010). *Cultures and organizations: Software of the mind.* New York: McGraw-Hill.

Hogan, P. C. (2003). *The mind and its stories: Narrative universals and human emotion.* Cambridge, UK: Cambridge University press.

Hoigaard, R., Safvenbom, R., & Tonnessen, F. E. (2006). The relationship between group cohesion, group norms, and perceived social loafing in soccer teams. *Small Group Research, 37,* 217–232.

Holahan, P., Mooney, A., Mayer, R. C., & Paul, L. F. (2008). Do debates get more heated in cyberspace? Team conflict in the virtual environment. *Current Issues in Technology Management, 12,* 1–4.

Holan, A. D. (2009, December 18). PolitiFact's Lie of the Year: "Death panels." Retrieved from http://www.politifact.com/truth-o-meter/article/2009/dec/18/politifact-lie-year-death-panels/

Hollander, E. (1985). Leadership and power. In G. Lindzey & E. Aronson (Eds.), *Handbook of social psychology.* New York: Random House.

Hollander, E., & Offerman, L. (1990, February). Power and leadership in organizations. *American Psychologist,* pp. 179–189.

Holley, S. R., Haase, C. M., & Levenson, R. W. (2013). Age-related changes in demand-withdraw communication behaviors. *Journal of Marriage and Family, 75,* 822–836.

Holman, T. B., & Jarvis, M. O. (2003). Hostile, volatile, avoiding, and validating couple-conflict types: An investigation of Gottman's couple-conflict types. *Personal Relationships, 10,* 267–282.

Holstein, L. (2012). Slavery in the sunshine state. In L. G. Schnoor, L. Mayfield, & K. Young (Eds.), *Winning orations.* Mankato, MN: Interstate Oratorical Association.

Holtgraves, T., & Dulin, J. (1994). The Muhammad Ali effect: Differences between African Americans and European Americans in their perceptions of a truthful braggart. *Language and Communication, 14,* 275–285.

Hoppes, S. (2008). Cross at your own risk: America's bridge safety neglect. In L. G. Schnoor & D. Cronin-Mills (Eds.), *Winning orations.* Mankato, MN: Interstate Oratorical Association.

Horan, S. (2012, June 20). Speed dating: Brief impressions are lasting impressions. *Psychology Today.* Retrieved from https://www.psychologytoday.com/blog/adventures-in-dating/201206/speed-dating-brief-impressions-are-lasting-impressions

Horn, D. (1999, May 26). Road rage driver freed. *The Cincinnati Enquirer.* Retrieved from http://www.enquirer.com/editions/1999/05/26/loc_road_rage_driver.html

Hornsey, M. J., Robson, E., Smith, J., Esposo, S., & Sutton, R. M. (2008). Sugaring the pill: Assessing rhetorical strategies designed to minimize defensive reactions to group criticism. *Human Communication Research, 34,* 70–98.

Horowitz, B. (2002). *Communication apprehension: Origins and management.* Albany, NY: Singular.

Hoshino-Browne, E., Zanna, A. S., Spencer, S. J., Zanna, M. P., Kitayama, S., & Lackenbauer, S. (2005). On the cultural guises of cognitive dissonance: The case of Easterners and Westerners. *Journal of Personality and Social Psychology, 89,* 294–310.

Hosman, L. A. (2002). Language and persuasion. In J. P. Dillard & M. Pfau (Eds.), *The persuasion handbook: Developments in theory and practice.* Thousand Oaks, CA: Sage.

House, R. J., & Javidan, M. (2004). Overview of GLOBE. In R. J. House, P. J. Hanges, M. Javidan, P. W. Dorfman, & V. Gupta (Eds.), *Culture, leadership, and organization: The GLOBE study of 62 societies.* Thousand Oaks, CA: Sage.

How we got from 1 to 162 million websites on the Internet. (2008, April 4). *Royal Pingdom.* Retrieved from http://royal.pingdom.com/2008/04/04/how-we-got-from-1-to-162-million-websites-on-the-internet

Howell, W. S. (1982). *The empathic communicator.* Belmont, CA: Wadsworth.

Hsu, J. (2008, August/September). The secrets of storytelling: Our love for telling tales reveals the workings of the mind. *Scientific American Mind,* pp. 46–51.

Huffington, A. (2011, November 28). Mitt Romney brazenly lies and the media lets him slide. *Huffington Post.* Retrieved from http://www.huffingtonpost.com/arianna-huffington/mitt-romney-ad_b_1117288.htmlHughes, S. M., & Gallup, G. G. (2003). Sex differences in morphological predictors of sexual behavior: Shoulder to hip and waist to hip ratios. *Evolution and Human Behavior, 24,* 173–178.

Hui, C. H., & Triandis, H. C. (1986). Individualism-collectivism: A study of cross-cultural researchers. *Journal of Cross-Cultural Psychology, 17,* 225–248. Humphrys, J. (2007, September 24). I h8 txt msgs: How texting is wrecking our language. *Daily Mail.* Retrieved from http://www.dailymail.co.uk/news/article-483511/I-h8-txt-msgs-How-texting-wrecking-language.html

Hunt, L. L., Eastwick, P. W., & Finkel, E. J. (2015). Leveling the playing field: Longer acquaintance predicts reduced assortive mating on attractiveness. *Psychological Science.* Retrieved from http://pss.sagepub.com/content/early/2015/06/11/0956797615579273

Hurst, N. (2011, August 17). Extreme negative anti-smoking ads can backfire, MU experts find. *News*

Bureau, University of Missouri. Retrieved from http://munews.missouri.edu/news-releases/2011/0817-extreme-negative-anti-smoking-ads-can-backfire-mu-experts-find/

Husband, R. (1992). Leading in organizational groups. In R. Cathcart & L. Samovar (Eds.), *Small group communication.* Dubuque, IA: Brown.

Huspek, M. (2000). Oppositional codes: The case of the penitentiary of New Mexico riot. *Journal of Applied Communication Research, 28,* 91–116.

Hutchinson, S. (2002, March 22). Jury's verdicts reaffirm court of public opinion. *San Jose Mercury News,* p. 9A.

Hyatt, J. (2010, May 20).David Kelley of IDEO: Reinventing innovation. *Newsweek.* Retrieved from http://www.newsweek.com/david-kelley-ideo-reinventing-innovation-72611 http://www.newsweek.com/2010/05/21/smarter-by-design.print.html

Hyde, J. S. (2005). The gender similarities hypothesis. *American Psychologist, 60,* 581–592.

Icon, E. (2011). Tattoos and piercings in the workplace. *Working World.* Retrieved from http://www.workingworld.com/articles/Tattoos-and-Piercings-in-the-Workplace

Impett, E. A., & Peplau, L. A. (2000, August). *Saying "yes" but thinking "no": Consensual participation in unwanted sex.* Paper presented at the annual meeting of the American Psychological Association, Washington, D.C.

Impett, E. A., & Peplau, L. A. (2003). Sexual compliance: Gender, motivational, and relationship perspectives. *Journal of Sex Research, 40,* 87–100.

Impett, E. A., Gable, S. L., & Peplau, L. A. (2005). Giving up and giving in: The costs and benefits of daily sacrifice in intimate relationships. *Journal of Personality and Social Psychology, 89,* 327–344.

Inch, E., & Warnick, B. (1998). *Critical thinking and communication: The use of reason in argument.* Boston: Allyn & Bacon.

Internet seen as positive influence on education but negative on morality in emerging and developing nations. *Pew Research Center.* Retrieved from http://www.pewglobal.org/2015/03/19/internet-seen-as-positive-influence-on-education-but-negative-influence-on-morality-in-emerging-and-developing-nations/

Irvin, M. (2013, September 16). The hazards of email, text messages & social media in a divorce. *Family Law Blog.* Retrieved from http://www.mckinleyirvin.com/Family-Law-Blog/2013/September/The-Hazards-of-Email-Text-Messages-038-Social-Me.aspx

Is sign language the same the world over? (2015). *DCAL.* Retrieved from http://www.ucl.ac.uk/dcal/faqs/questions/bsl/question6

Isenhart, M. W., & Spangle, M. (2000). *Collaborative approaches to resolving conflict.* Thousand Oaks, CA: Sage.

Italie, L. (2010, June 28). Facebook is divorce lawyers' new best friend. *MSNBC.* Retrieved from http://www.nbcnews.com/id/37986320/ns/technology_and_science-tech_and_gadgets/

Ito, R. (2015, March 6). In the documentary "GTFO," female video gamers fight back. *The New York Times.* Retrieved from http://www.nytimes.com/2015/03/08/movies/in-the-documentary-gtfo-female-video-gamers-fight-back.html

Jackson, B., Gore, D., Farley, R., & Robertson, L. (2015, June 17). Donald Trump tramples facts in 2016 campaign kickoff. *FactCheck.org.* Retrieved from http://www.huffingtonpost.com/2015/06/17/donald-trump-2016_n_7602754.html

Jacobson, N., & Gottman, J. (1998, March/April). Anatomy of a violent relationship. *Psychology Today,* pp. 61–65.

Jacobson, R. (2014, September/October). Should you tell your boss about a mental illness? *Scientific American Mind,* pp. 28–29.

Jaffe, C. (1998). *Public speaking: Concepts and skills for a diverse society.* Belmont, CA: Wadsworth.

Jaffe, E. (2010). The psychological study of smiling. *Observer.* Retrieved from http://www.psychologicalscience.org/index.php/publications/observer/2010/december-10/the-psychological-study-of-smiling.html.

Jaksa, J., & Pritchard, M. (1994). *Communication ethics: Methods of analysis.* Belmont, CA: Wadsworth.

James, D., & Clarke, S. (1993). Women, men, and interruptions: A critical review. In D. Tannen (Ed.), *Gender and conversational interaction.* New York: Oxford University Press.

James, J. (2013). A new, evidence-based estimate of patient harm associated with hospital care. *Journal of Patient Safety, 9,* 122–128.

Jamieson, K. H. (1988). *Eloquence in an electronic age.* New York: Oxford University Press.

Janis, I. (1982). *Groupthink: Psychological studies of policy decisions and fiascoes.* Boston: Houghton Mifflin.

Janis, I. (1989). *Crucial decisions: Leadership in policy-making and crisis management.* New York: Free Press.

Jarc, R. (2012, October 31). Survey finds half of high school boys admit to hitting a person in the past year because they were angry. *Josephson Institute Center for Youth Ethics.* Retrieved from http://charactercounts.org/programs/reportcard/2012/installment_report-card_bullying-youth-violence.html

Jaschik, S. (2015, January 20). Well-prepared in their own eyes. *Inside Higher Ed.* Retrieved from https://

www.insidehighered.com/news/2015/01/20/study-finds-big-gaps-between-student-and-employer-perceptions

Jay, T., & Janschewitz, K. (2012). The science of swearing. *The Observer*, 25, 21, 40–41.

Jeffries, V. (2002). The structure and dynamics of love: Toward a theory of marital quality and stability. *Humboldt Journal of Social Relations*, 27, 42–72.

Jemmott, J. B., Jemmott, L. S., & Fong, G. T. (2010). Efficacy of a theory-based abstinence-only intervention over months. *Archives of Pediatrics and Adolescent Medicine*, 164, 152–159.

Jensen-Campbell, L., Graziano, W., & West, S. (1995). Dominance, prosocial orientation, and female preferences: Do nice guys really finish last? *Journal of Personality and Social Psychology*, 68, 427–440.

Jill Bolte Taylor: Neuroanatomist. (2008, March). *TED*. Retrieved from http://www.ted.com/speakers/jill_bolte_taylor.html

Jin, B., & Pena, J. F. (2010). Mobile communication in romantic relationships: Mobile phone use, relational uncertainty, love, commitment, and attachment styles. *Communication Reports*, 23, 39–51.

Jodie Foster speech: Retirement speculation at Golden Globes. (2013, January 13). *Huffington Post*. Retrieved from http://www.huffingtonpost.com/2013/01/13/jodie-foster-speech-retirement-_n_2469530.html

Johnson, A. J., Kelley, K. M., Liu, S.-J., Averbeck, J. M., King, S. D., & Bostwick, E. N. (2014). Family serial arguments: Beliefs about the argument and perceived stress from the srgument. *Communication Reports*, 27, 116–128.

Johnson, C. (2009). Bad blood: Doctor-nurse behavior problems impact patient care. *Physician Executive Journal*, 35, 6–10.

Johnson, C. (2006, December 21). Trump vs. Rosie: the war continues. *CBSNews*. Retrieved from http://www.cbsnews.com/news/trump-vs-rosie-the-war-continues/

Johnson, D. W. (1971). Role-reversal: A summary and review of the research. *International Journal of Group Tensions*, 1, 318–334.

Johnson, D. W. (2003). Social interdependence: Interrelationships among theory, research, and practice. *American Psychologist*, 58, 934–945.

Johnson, D. W., & Johnson, R. T. (2000a, June). Teaching students to be peacemakers: Results of twelve years of research. *National Criminal Justice Reference Service*. Retrieved from https://www.ncjrs.gov/App/Publications/abstract.aspx?ID=198362

Johnson, D. W., & Johnson, R. T. (2000, May). Civil political discourse in a democracy: The contribution of psychology. *Peace and Conflict: Journal of Peace Psychology*, 6, 291–317.

Johnson, D. W., & Johnson, R. T. (2003a). Field testing integrative negotiations. *Peace and Conflict: Journal of Peace Psychology*, 9, 39–68.

Johnson, D. W., & Johnson, R. T. (2003b). Training for cooperative group work. In M. A. West, D. Tjosvold, & K. G. Smith (Eds.), *International handbook of organizational teamwork and cooperative working*. New York: Wiley.

Johnson, D. W., & Johnson, R. T. (2005). Learning groups. In S. A. Wheelan (Ed.), *The handbook of group research and practice*. Thousand Oaks, CA: Sage.

Johnson, D. W., & Johnson, R. T. (2009). An educational psychology success story: Social interdependence theory and cooperative learning. *Educational Researcher*, 38, 365–379.

Johnson, K. G., Senatore, J. J., Liebig, M. C., & Minor, G. (1974). *Nothing never happens: Exercises to trigger group discussions and promote self discovery*. New York: Glencoe Press.

Johnson, M. P. (1995). Patriarchal terrorism and common couple violence: Two forms of violence against women. *Journal of Marriage and the Family*, 57, 283–294.

Johnson, M. P. (2006a). Conflict and control: Gender symmetry and asymmetry in domestic violence. *Violence Against Women*, 12, 1003–1018.

Johnson, M. P. (2006b). Gendered communication and intimate partner violence. In B. J. Dow & J. T. Wood (Eds.), *The Sage handbook of gender and communication*. Thousand Oaks, CA: Sage.

Johnson, M. P. (2008). *A typology of domestic violence: Intimate terrorism, violent resistance, and situational couple violence*. Boston: Northeastern University Press.

Johnson, S. (2009, June 18). Survey: Users irked by gadget gaffes. *San Jose Mercury News*, p. 13B.

Johnson, S., & Bechler, C. (1998). Examining the relationship between listening effectiveness and leadership emergence: Perceptions, behaviors, and recall. *Small Group Research*, 29, 452–471.

Johnson, W. (1946). *People in quandaries*. New York: Harper.

Johnston, L. D., O'Malley, P. M., Bachman, J. G., Schulenberg, J. E., & Miech, R. A. (2014). *Monitoring the future: National results on drug use, 1975–2013: Volume II, college students and adults ages 19–55*. Ann Arbor, MI: Institute for Social Research, The University of Michigan. Retrieved from http://www.monitoringthefuture.org/pubs/monographs/mtf-overview2013.pdf

Jonas, E., Schultz-Hardt, S., Frey, D., & Thelen, N. (2001). Confirmation bias in sequential information search after preliminary decisions: An expansion of dissonance theoretical research on selective exposure to information. *Journal of Personality and Social Psychology*, 80, 557–571.

Jonas, K. J., & Sassenberg, K. (2006). Knowing how to react: Automatic response priming from social categories. *Journal of Personality and Social Psychology, 90*, 709–721.

Jones, E. E., & Kelly, J. R. (2007). Contributions to a group discussion and perceptions of leadership: Does quantity always count more than quality? *Group Dynamics: Theory, Research, and Practice, 11*, 15–30.

Jones, J. (2011). The facts about for-profit universities. In L. G. Schnoor, L. Mayfield, & K. Young (Eds.), *Winning orations*. Mankato, MN: Interstate Oratorical Association.

Jones, S. (1994). *The right touch: Understanding and using the language of physical context*. Cresskill, NJ: Hampton Press.

Josephson, M. (2002). *Making ethical decisions*. Los Angeles: Josephson Institute of Ethics.

Judge, T. A., & Piccolo, R. F. (2004). Transformational and transactional leadership: A meta-analytic test of their relative validity. *Journal of Applied Psychology, 89*, 755–768.

Just, M. A., Keller, T. A., & Cynkar, J. (2008). A decrease in brain activation associated with driving when listening to someone speak. *Brain Research, 1205*, 70–80.

Kalbfleisch, P., & Cody, M. (Eds.). (1995). *Gender, power, and communication in human relationships*. Hillsdale, NJ: Erlbaum.

Kalbfleisch, P. J., & Herold, A. L. (2006). Sex, power, and communication. In K. Dindia & D. J. Canary (Eds.), *Sex differences and similarities in communication*. Mahwah, NJ: Erlbaum.

Kameda, N. (2003). Miscommunication factors in Japanese-US trade relationships. Retrieved from https://doors.doshisha.ac.jp/duar/repository/ir/17894/038005020002.pdf

Kameda, N. (2007). *Communicative challenges for Japanese companies: Strategies in the global marketplace*. Proceedings of the Association for Business Communication Seventh Asia-Pacific Conference.

Kane, M. J., Brown, L. H., McVay, J. C., Silvia, P. J., Myin-Germeys, I., & Kwapil, T. R. (2007). For whom the mind wanders, and when: An experience-sampling study of working memory and executive control in daily life. *Psychological Science, 18*, 559–656.

Kanner, B. (March/April, 1995). Ideal couples and romance. *Psychology Today*, pp. 46–49.

Kaplowitz, R. A. (1986). *Selecting college and university personnel: The quest and the questions* (ASHE-ERIC Higher Education Report No. 8). Washington, DC: Association for the Study of Higher Education.

Karau, S., & Williams, K. (1993). Social loafing: A meta-analytic review and theoretical integration. *Journal of Personality and Social Psychology, 65*, 681–706.

Karau, S. J., & Elsaid, A. M. M. K. (2009). Individual differences in beliefs about groups. *Group Dynamics: Theory, Research, and Practice, 13*, 1–13.

Karau, S. J., & Williams, K. D. (2001). Understanding individual motivation in groups: The collective effort model. In M. E. Turner (Ed.), *Groups at work: Theory and research*. Mahwah, NJ: Erlbaum.

Katzenbach, J., & Smith, D. (1993a). *The wisdom of teams*. Boston: Harvard Business School Press.

Katzenbach, J., & Smith, D. (1993b, March/April). The discipline of teams. *Harvard Business Review*, pp. 111–120.

Kauffeld, S., & Lehmann-Willenbrock, N. (2012). Meetings matter: Effects of team meetings on team and organizational success. *Small Group Research, 43*, 130–158.

Kawatsu, H. (2009, May 25). *A mixed jury system for Japan*. Paper presented at the annual meeting of The Law and Society, Las Vegas, NV. Retrieved from http://www.allacademic.com/meta/p18168_index.html

Kay, K., & Shipman, C. (2014, April 14). The confidence gap. *The Atlantic*. Retrieved from http://www.theatlantic.com/features/archive/2014/04/the-confidence-gap/359815/

Keats, J. (2011). *Virtual words*. New York: Oxford University Press.

Kehoe, R. L., Halley, R., & Wolvin, A. (2015, March 13). Where is listening instruction today: A research proposal to survey of colleges and state universities. Retrieved from http://listeningandcommunication.com/uploads/Research_Paper_revised.pdf

Kell, J. (2014, September 17). Corporate dress codes relax in an age of tattoos, piercings. *Fortune*. Retrieved from http://fortune.com/2014/09/17/walmart-starbucks-dress-code/

Kellas, J. K., Cunningham, C., & Cheng, K. Y., (2008). The ex-files: Trajectories, turning points, and adjustments in the development of post-dissolutional relationships. *Journal of Social and Personal Relationships, 25*, 23–50.

Keller, P. A. (1999). Converting the unconverted: The effect of inclination and opportunity to discount health-related fear appeals. *Journal of Applied Psychology, 84*, 403–415.

Kelley, T., & Littman, J. (2001). *The art of innovation: Lessons in creativity from IDEO, America's leading design firm*. New York: Doubleday.

Kelley, T., & Littman, J. (2005). *The ten faces of innovation: IDEO's strategies for beating the devil's advocate & driving creativity throughout your organization*. New York: Doubleday.

Kelly, J. R. (2005). The effect of nonverbal behaviors associated with sexual harassment proclivity on women's performance. *Sex Roles: A Journal of Research*, 53, 689–701.

Kelly, L., & Keaten, J. A. (2000). Treating communication anxiety: Implications of the communibiological paradigm. *Communication Education*, 49, 45–57.

Kelly, R. (2009, August 12). Twitter study reveals interesting results about usage—40% is "pointless babble." *Pear Analytics*. Retrieved from http://www.pearanalytics.com/blog/2009/twitter-study-reveals

Kelsey, B. (1998). The dynamics of multicultural groups: Ethnicity as a determinant of leadership. *Small Group Research*, 29, 602–623.

Keltner, D. (2007). The power paradox. *Greater good.* Retrieved from http://greatergood.berkeley.edu/article/item/power_paradox/

Keltner, D., Gruenfeld, D. H., & Anderson, C. (2003). Power, approach, and inhibition. *Psychological Review*, 110, 265–284.

Kemp, N., & Bushnell, C. (2011). Children's text messaging: Abbreviations, input methods and links with literacy. *Journal of Computer Assisted Learning*, 27, 18–27.

Kennedy, T. L. M., Smith, A., Wells, A. T., & Wellman, B. (2008, October 19). Networked families. *Pew Internet & American Life Project*. Retrieved from http://www.pewinternet.org/~/media//Files/Reports/2008/PIP_Networked_Family.pdf.pdf

Kernis, M. H. (2003). High self-esteem: A differentiated perspective. In E. C. Chang & L. J. Sanna (Eds.), *Virtue, vice, and personality: The complexity of behavior*. Washington, DC: APA Books.

Kertesz, S. (2010, August 20). Physician's errors: How our health care system is failing us. *Huffington Post*. Retrieved from http://www.huffingtonpost.com/stefan-kertesz/quality-eludes-doctors-wi_b_684221.html?view=print

Kertscher, T. (2011, March 10). Michael Moore says 400 Americans have more wealth than half of all Americans combined. *PolitiFact*. Retrieved from http://www.politifact.com/wisconsin/statements/2011/mar/10/michael-moore/michael-moore-says-400-americans-have-more-wealth-/

Key findings of work and power survey. (2007, January). *MSNBC.com*. Retrieved from http://www.msnbc.msn.com/id/17407725/

Keysar, B., & Henly, A. S. (2002). Speakers' overestimation of their effectiveness. *Psychological Science*, 13, 207–212.

Kidder, R. M., Mirk, P., & Loges, W. E. (2002). Maricopa values & ethics survey. *The Institute for Global Ethics*. Retrieved from https://administration.maricopa.edu/sites/default/files/Values%20%26%20Ethics%20Survey.pdf

Kifer, Y., Heller, D., Perunovic, W. Q. E., & Galinsky, A. D. (2013). The good life of the powerful: The experience of power and authenticity enhances subjective well-being. *Psychological Science*, 24, 280–288.

Kiken, L. G., & Shook, N. J. (2011). Mindfulness increases positive judgments and reduces negativity bias. *Social Psychological and Personality Science*, 2, 425–431.

Killion, A. (1996, July 5). VanDerveer ordeal proves worth it for well-drilled team. *San Jose Mercury News*, pp. D1, D3.

Killion, A. (2004, August 16). Yet another "wake-up call" won't rouse this U.S. team. *San Jose Mercury News*, pp. 1D, 3D.

Kilmann, R., & Thomas, K. (1977). Developing a force-choice measure of conflict handling behavior: The "mode" instrument. *Educational Psychological Measurement*, 37, 309–325.

Kim, H. S. (2010). Cultural differences in verbal expression lead to distinctive patterns of cognitive performance, stress responses, and social support. *Psychological Science Agenda*. Retrieved from http://www.apa.org/science/about/psa/2010/06/sci-brief.aspx

Kim, M. S. (1992). A comparative analysis of nonverbal expressions as portrayed by Korean and American print-media advertising. *Howard Journal of Communication*, 3, 321.

Kim, R. K., & Levine, T. R. (2011). The effect of suspicion on deception detection accuracy: Optimal level of opposing effects? *Communication Reports*, 24, 51–62.

Kim, S. J., & Niederdeppe, J. (2014). Emotional expressions in antismoking television advertisements: Consequences of anger and sadness framing on pathways to persuasion. *Journal of Health Communication*, 19, 692–709.

Kinard, B., & Webster, C. (2010). The effects of advertising, social influence, and self-efficacy on adolescence tobacco use and alcohol consumption. *The Journal of Consumer Affairs*, 44, 24–43.

King, E. B., Hebl, M. R., & Beal, D. J. (2009). Conflict and cooperation in diverse work-groups. *Journal of Social Issues*, 65, 261–285.

King, M. L., (1963). "I Have a Dream" speech. Retrieved from: http://www.archives.gov/press/exhibits/dream-speech.pdf

Kirkman, B. L., Rosen, B., Gibson, C. B., Tesluk, P. E., & McPherson, S. O. (2002). Five challenges to virtual team success: Lessons from Sabre, Inc. *Academy of Management Executive*, 16, 67–79.

Kissell, R. (2015, February 23). Update: Oscar ratings down 16%, lowest in six years. *Variety*. Retrieved from http://variety.com/2015/tv/ratings/oscar-ratings-abc-telecast-down-10-in-overnights-to-four-year-low-1201439543/

Kjerulf, A. (2012, September 12). The top 5 ways not to praise people at work. *The Chief Happiness Officer Blog*. Retrieved from http://positivesharing.com/2012/09/the-top-5-ways-not-to-praise-people-at-work/

Klaas, T. (2015, July 1). Top 3 benefits and challenges of going to college online. *StemJobs*. Retrieved from http://stemjobs.com/top-3-benefits-challenges-going-college-online/

Klapp, O. (1978). *Opening and closing: Strategies of information adaptation in society*. New York: Cambridge University Press.

Klein, C., Diaz Granados, D., Salas, E., Le, H., Burke, C. S., & Goodwin, G. F. (2009). Does team building work? *Small Group Research*, 40, 181–222.

Klein, R. C. A., & Johnson, M. P. (1997). Strategies of couple conflict. In S. Duck (Ed.), *Handbook of personal relationships*. New York: Wiley.

Klein, S. (1996). Work pressure as a determinant of work group behavior. *Small Group Research*, 27, 299–315.

Kleinman, A. (2013, July 12). Nearly 20 percent of young adults use their smartphones during sex: Survey. *Huffington Post*. Retrieved from http://www.huffingtonpost.com/2013/07/12/smartphones-during-sex_n_3586647.html

Klopf, D. (1998). *Intercultural encounters: The fundamentals of intercultural communication*. Englewood, CO: Morton.

Knapp, M., & Vangelisti, A. (1992). Stages of relationships. In M. Knapp & A. Vangelisti (Eds.), *Interpersonal communication and human relationships*. Needham Heights, MA: Allyn and Bacon.

Knapp, M., & Vangelisti, A. (2005). *Interpersonal communication and human relationships*. New York: Allyn & Bacon.

Knapp, M. L. (2006). Lying and deception in close relationships. In A. Vangelisti & D. Perlman (Eds.), *The Cambridge handbook of personal relationships*. New York: Cambridge University Press.

Knoll, K., & Jarvenpaa, S. L. (1998). Working together in global virtual teams. In M. Igbaria & M. Tan (Eds.), *The virtual workplace*. Hershey, PA: Idea Group.

Knutson, T. J., & Posirisuk, S. (2006). Thai relational development and rhetorical sensitivity as potential contributors to intercultural communication effectiveness: JAI YEN YEN. *Journal of Intercultural Communication Research*, 35, 205–217.

Knutson, T. J., Komolsevin, R., Chatiketu, P., & Smith, V. R. (2002). A comparison of Thai and U.S. American willingness to communicate. *Journal of Intercultural Communication Research*, 31, 3–12.

Knutson, T. J., Komolsevin, R., Chatiketu, P., & Smith, V. R. (2003). A cross-cultural comparison of Thai and US American rhetorical sensitivity: Implications for intercultural communication effectiveness. *International Journal of Intercultural Relations*, 27, 63–78.

Ko, V. (2013, April 14). Can you cope with criticism at work? *CNN*. Retrieved from http://www.cnn.com/2013/04/14/business/criticism-praise-feedback-work-life/

Koenig, A. M., Eagly, A. H., Mitchell, A. A., & Ristikari, T. (2011). Are leader stereotypes masculine? A meta-analysis of three research paradigms. *Psychological Bulletin*, 137, 616–642.

Kohn, A. (1992). *No contest: The case against competition*. Boston: Houghton Mifflin.

Kohn, A. (1993). *Punished by rewards*. New York: Houghton Mifflin.

Korzybski, A. (1958). *Science and sanity*. Lakeville, CT: International Non-Aristotelian Literary.

Kotter, J. P. (1990). *A force for change: How leadership differs from management*. New York: Free Press.

Kotzman, M., & Kotzman, A. (2008). *Listen to me, listen to you: A step-by-step guide to communication skills training*. Sydney, Australia: Australian Council for Education Research.

Kouri, K., & Lasswell, M. (1993). *Black–white marriages*. Binghamton, NY: Hayworth Press.

Kozlowski, S. W. J., & Ilgen, D. R. (2006). Enhancing the effectiveness of work groups and teams. *Psychological Science in the Public Interest*, 7, 77–124.

Kramer, T. J., Fleming, G. P., & Mannis, S. M. (2001). Improving face-to-face brainstorming through modeling and facilitation. *Small Group Research*, 32, 533–557.

Kraul, C. (2006, December 20). Renowned for longevity, Ecuadorian town changing. *San Jose Mercury News*, p. 16A.

Kraus, M. W., & Keltner, D. (2009). Signs of socioeconomic status: A thin slicing approach. *Psychological Science*, 20, 99–106.

Kraus, M. W., Huang, C., & Keltner, D. (2010). Tactile communication, cooperation, and performance: An ethological study of the NBA. *Emotion*, 10, 745–749.

Krauss, R. M. (2001). The psychology of verbal communication. In N. Smelser & P. Baltes (Eds.), *International encyclopedia of the social and behavioral sciences*. London: Elsevier.

Krauss, R. M., & Chiu, C.-Y. (1998). Language and social behavior. In D. T. Gilbert, S. T. Fiske, & G. Lindzey (Eds.), *The handbook of social psychology* (Vol. 2). New York: Oxford University Press.

Kraut, R. E. (1973). Effects of social labeling on giving to charity. *Journal of Experimental Social Psychology*, 9, 551–562.

Kraut, R., Patterson, M., Lundmark, V., Kiesler, S., Mukopadhyay, T., & Scherlis, W. (1998). Internet paradox: A social technology that reduces social involvement and psychological well-being? *American Psychologist*, 53, 1017–1031.

Krebs, D. L., & Denton, K. (1997). Social illusions and self-deception: The evolution of biases in person perception. In J. A. Simpson & D. T. Kenrick (Eds.), *Evolutionary social psychology*. Mahwah, NJ: Erlbaum.

Krieger, L. M. (1999, February 5). Mystery rock injures woman asleep at home. *San Jose Mercury News*, pp. 1B, 4B.

Krieger, L. M., & Mattson, S. (2015, July 2). Water usage drops 29%. *San Jose Mercury News*, p. A1.

Kruger, J. (2009, October 8). Survey finds 3 out of 10 city residents would give up sex before cellphones. *PMA Newsline*. Retrieved from http://pmanewsline .com/2009/10/08.survey-finds-3-out-of-10-city-residents-would-give-up-sex-before-cellphones/

Kuchinskas, S. (2008, January/February). Conquering fear of public speaking. *WebMD*. Retrieved from http://www.webmd.com/anxiety-panic/features/conquering-fear-public-speaking?print=true

Kuhl, P. K. (1994). Speech perception. In F. D. Minifie (Ed.), *Introduction to communication sciences and disorders*. San Diego, CA: Singular.

Kuhl, P. K. (2004). Early language acquisition: Cracking the speech code. *Nature Reviews Neuroscience*, 5, 831–843.

Kuhl, P. K., Conboy, B. T., Padden, D., Nelson, T., & Pruitt, J. (2005). Early speech perception and later language development: Implications for the "critical period." *Language Learning and Development*, 3, 237–264.

Kuhn, T., & Poole, M. S. (2000). Do conflict management styles affect group decision making? Evidence from a longitudinal field study. *Human Communication Research*, 26, 558–590.

Kuipers, G (2006). *Good humor, bad taste: A sociology of the joke*. Boston, MA: De Gruyter Mouton

Kunkel, A. W., & Burleson, B. R. (2006). Revisiting the different cultures thesis: An assessment of sex differences and similarities in supportive communication. In K. Dindia & D. J. Canary (Eds.), *Sex differences and similarities in communication*. Mahwah, NJ: Erlbaum.

Kuo, F. E., & Sullivan, W. C. (2001). Aggression and violence in the inner city: Effects of environment via mental fatigue. *Environment and Behavior*, 33, 543–571.

Kurtzman, D. (2015). Ronald Reagan quotes. *About Entertainment*. Retrieved from http://politicalhumor.about.com/cs/quotethis/a/reaganquotes.htm

Kushner, H. (1981). *When bad things happen to good people*. New York: Avon.

Kwang, T., Crockett, E. E., Sanchez, D. T., & Swann, W. B. (2013). Men seek social standing, women seek companionship: Sex differences in deriving self-worth from relationships. *Psychological Science*, 24, 1142–1150.

Lacohee, H., & Anderson, B. (2001). Interacting with the telephone. *Journal of Human-Computer Studies*, 54, 665–699.

LaFasto, F., & Larson, C. (2001). *When teams work best: 6,000 team members and leaders tell what it takes to succeed*. Thousand Oaks, CA: Sage.

Lamb, C. (2008). Political comebacks: The art of the putdown. (2008, May 12). *NPR*. Retrieved from http://www.npr.org/templates/story/story .php?storyId=90337494

Lamberth, J. (1998, August 6). Driving while black: A statistician proves that prejudice still rules the road. *Washington Post*, p. C1.

Landers, A. (1995, February 25). Low-income families need fire protection too. *Santa Cruz Sentinel*, p. D5.

Lane, K., Balleweg, B. J., Suler, J. R., Fernald, P. S., & Goldstein, G. S. (2000). Acquiring skills-undergraduate students. In M. E. Ware & D. E. Johnson (Eds.), *Handbook of demonstrations and activities in the teaching of psychology. Vol. 3: Personality, abnormal, clinical-counseling, and social*. Mahwah, NJ: Erlbaum.

Lang, N. (2015, February 27). John Travolta, Joe Biden, and why men touch women's bodies without asking. *The Daily dot*. Retrieved from http://www .dailydot.com/opinion/mantouching-john-travolta-joe-bide

Langer, E. (1989). *Mindfulness*. Reading, MA: Addison-Wesley.

Langer, E., & Abelson, R. (1974). A patient by any other name . . . : Clinical group differences in labeling bias. *Journal of Consulting and Clinical Psychology*, 42, 4–9.

Langfred, C. (1998). Is group cohesiveness a double-edged sword? An investigation of the effects of cohesiveness on performance. *Small Group Research*, 29, 124–143.

Langlois, J. H., Kalakanis, L., Rubenstein, A. J., Larson, A., Hallam, M., & Smoot, M. (2000). Maxims and myths of beauty? A meta-analytic and theoretical review. *Psychological Review*, 126, 390–423.

Lanka, B. (1989). *I dream a world: Portraits of black women who changed America*. New York: Stewart, Tabori, & Chang.

Lapakko, D. (1997). Three cheers for language: A closer examination of a widely cited study of nonverbal communication. *Communication Education*, 46, 63–69.

Larson, C. (1992). *Persuasion: Reception and responsibility*. Belmont, CA: Wadsworth.

Larson, C., & LaFasto, M. (1989). *Teamwork: What must go right/what can go wrong*. Newbury Park, CA: Sage.

Larson, C. U. (2007). *Persuasion: Reception and responsibility.* Belmont, CA: Thomson/Wadsworth.

Larson, J. R. (2007). Deep diversity and strong synergy: Modeling the impact of variability in members' problem-solving strategies on group problem-solving performance. *Small Group Research, 38,* 413–436.

Laughlin, P. R., Hatch, E. C., Silver, J. S., & Boh, L. (2006). Groups perform better than the best individuals on letters-to-numbers problems: Effects of group size. *Journal of Personality and Social Psychology, 90,* 644–650.

Laurin, K., Kay, A. C., & Fitzsimons, G. J. (2012). Reactance versus rationalization: Divergent responses to policies that constrain freedom. *Psychological Science, 23,* 205–209.

Lavenda, R. H., & Schultz, E. A. (2015). *Anthropology: What does it mean to be human?* New York: Oxford University Press.

Lazar, J. (1991). Ensuring productive meetings. In R. Swanson & B. Knapp (Eds.), *Innovative meeting management.* Austin, TX: Minnesota Mining and Manufacturing.

Lazarus, R. S. (1991). *Emotion and adaptation.* New York: Oxford University Press.

Leaders CEOs most admire. (2014). *PWC.* Retrieved from http://www.pwc.com/gx/en/ceo-survey/2013/key-findings/admired-leaders-leadership-attributes.jhtml

Leaper, C., & Ayres, M. M. (2007). A meta-analytic review of gender variations in adults' language use: Talkativeness, affiliative speech, and assertive speech. *Personality and Social Psychology Review, 11,* 328–363.

Leaper, C., & Robnett, R. D. (2011). Women are more likely than men to use tentative language, aren't they? A meta-analysis testing gender differences and moderators. *Psychology of Women Quarterly, 35,* 129–142.

Leathers, D. (1970). The process effects of trust-destroying behaviors in the small group. *Speech Monographs, 37,* 181–187.

Leathers, D. (1979). The impact of multichannel message inconsistency on verbal and non verbal decoding behavior. *Communication Monographs, 46,* 88–100.

Leathers, D. (1986). *Successful nonverbal communication: Principles and applications.* New York: Macmillan.

Ledbetter, A. M., & Keating, A. T. (2015). Maintaining Facebook friendships: Everyday talk as a mediator of threats to closeness. *Western Journal of Communication, 79,* 197–217.

Lee, B. (1997). *The power principle: Influences with honor.* New York: Simon & Schuster.

Lee, Y.-T., Jussim, L. J., & McCauley, C. R. (1995). *Stereotype accuracy: Toward appreciating group differences.* Washington, DC: American Psychological Association.

Lehmann-Willenbrock, N., Allen, J. A., & Kauffeld, S. (2013). A sequential analysis of procedural meeting communication: How teams facilitate their meetings. *Journal of Applied Communication Research, 41,* 365–388.

Lehrer, J. (2012, January 30). Groupthink. *The New Yorker.* Retrieved from http://www.newyorker.com/magazine/2012/01/30/groupthink

Leit, L., Jabovitz, D., & Hazen-Swann, N. (2008). *Conversational narcissism in marriage: Narcissistic attention seeking behaviors in face-to-face interactions: Implications for marital stability and partner mental health.* Saarbrucken, Germany: Verlag.

Lenbuck, J. (2013, April 26). How does sex differ from intimacy? *PsychCentral.* Retrieved from http://psychcentral.com/blog/archives/2013/04/26/how-does-sex-differ-from-intimacy/

Lenckus, D. (2005, November 28). Physician apologies, listening skills found to reduce medical malpractice claims. *Business Insurance,* p. 4.

Lenhart, A. (2015, April 9). Teens, social media & technology overview 2015. *Pew Research Center.* Retrieved from http://www.pewinternet.org/2015/04/09/teens-social-media-technology-2015/

Lenhart, A., & Duggan, M. (2014, February 11). Couples, the Internet, and social media. *Pew Research Center.* Retrieved from http://www.pewinternet.org/2014/02/11/couples-the-internet-and-social-media/

LePort, A. K. R., Mattfeld, H. D., Fallon, C. E. L., Kruggel, F., Cahill, L., & McGaugh, J. L. (2012). Behavioral and neuroanatomical investigation of highly superior autobiographical memory (HSAM). *Neurobiology of Learning and Memory, 98,* 78–92.

Lerner, J. S., & Tetlock, P. E. (1999). Accounting for the effects of accountability. *Psychological Bulletin, 125,* 255–275.

Lese, K. (2012). The kid who cried "Mine": Patent trolls greedy takeover of the technology industry. In L. G. Schnoor, L. Mayfield, & K. Young (Eds.), *Winning orations.* Mankato, MN: Interstate Oratorical Association.

Lese, K. (2014). First responder training and police misinterpretation of health crisis cases. In L. G. Schnoor, K. Young, & L. Mayfield (Eds.), *Winning orations.* Mankato, MN: Interstate Oratorical Association.

Less support for death penalty, especially among Democrats. (2015, April 16). *Pew Research Center.* Retrieved from http://www.people-press.org/2015/04/16/less-support-for-death-penalty-especially-among-democrats/

Levine, K. (2001). The dentist's dirty little secret. In L. G. Schnoor & B. Wickelgren (Eds.), *Winning orations.* Mankato, MN: Interstate Oratorical Association.

Levine, K., Muenchen, R., & Brooks, A. (2010). Measuring transformational and charismatic leadership. Why isn't charisma measured? *Communication Monographs, 77,* 576–586.

Levine, M., & Shefner, J. (1991). *Fundamentals of sensation and perception.* Pacific Grove, CA: Brooks/Cole.

Levine, M. P., & Murnen, S. K. (2009). "Everybody knows that mass media are/are not [pick one] a cause of eating disorders": A critical review of evidence for a causal link between media, negative body image, and disordered eating in females. *Journal of Social and Clinical Psychology, 28,* 9–42.

Lewin, K., Lippitt, R., & White, R. K. (1939). Patterns of aggressive behavior in experimentally created social climates. *Journal of Social Psychology, 10,* 271–299

Lewin, M. R., McNeil, D. W., & Lipson, J. M. (1996). Enduring without avoiding: Pauses and verbal dysfluencies in public speaking fear. *Journal of Psychopathology and Behavioral Assessment, 18,* 387–402.

Lewis, M. (2013, January 30). Why I hate Twitter. *The Week.* Retrieved from http://theweek.com/articles/468264/hate-twitter

Lewis, P. (2015, February 21). Welcome to the 18th edition. *Ethnologue: Languages of the World.* Retrieved from http://www.ethnologue.com/ethnoblog/m-paul-lewis/welcome-18th-edition

Lewis, R. D. (1996). *When cultures collide: Managing successfully across cultures.* London: Brealey.

Li, C. (1975). *Path analysis: A primer.* Pacific Grove, CA: Boxwood Press.Li, N. P., Bailey, J. M., Kenrick, D. T., & Linsenmeier, J. A. W. (2002). The necessities and luxuries of mate preferences: Testing the tradeoffs. *Journal of Personality and Social Psychology, 82,* 947–955.

Lieberman, M. D. (2013). *Social: Why our brains are wired to connect.* New York: Broadway Books.

Lilienfeld, S. O., & Arkowitz, H. (2010, May/June). Are men the more belligerent sex? *Scientific American Mind,* pp. 64–65.

Lilienfield, S. O., Ammirati, R., & Landfiled, K. (2009). Giving debiasing away: Can psychological research on correcting cognitive errors promote human welfare? *Perspectives on Psychological Science, 4,* 390–398.

Lim, S.-J., & Holt, L. L. (2011). Learning foreign sounds in an alien world: Videogame training improves non-native speech categorization. *Cognitive Science, 35,* 1390–1405.

Linder, M., & Nygaard, I. (1998). *Void where prohibited: Rest breaks and the right to urinate on company time.* Ithaca, NY: Cornell University Press.

Lindsey, A. E., & Zakahi, W. R. (2006). Perceptions of men and women departing from conversational sex-role stereotypes. In K. Dindia & D. J. Canary (Eds.), *Sex differences and similarities in communication.* Mahwah, NJ: Erlbaum.

Lindsey, L. L. M., & Yun, K. A. (2003). Examining the persuasive effect of statistical messages: A test of mediating relationships. *Communication Studies, 54,* 306–322.

Linville, P. W., Fischer, G. W., & Fischoff, B. (1992). Perceived risk and decision-making involving AIDS. In J. B. Pryor & G. D. Reeder (Eds.), *The social psychology of HIV infection.* Hillsdale, NJ: Erlbaum.

Lipman, V. (2013, June 13). New employee study shows recognition matters more than money. *Psychology Today.* Retrieved from https://www.psychologytoday.com/blog/mind-the-manager/201306/new-employee-study-shows-recognition-matters-more-money

Lipnack, J., & Stamps, J. (1997). *Virtual teams: Reaching across space, time, and organizations with technology.* New York: Wiley.

Lithwick, D. (2013, September 12). Parents left behind: How public school reforms are turning American parents into dummies. *Slate.* Retrieved from http://www.slate.com/articles/life/low_concept/2013/09/school_jargon_for_parents_i_can_t_understand_what_my_child_s_teacher_is.html

Little, A. C., Burt, D. M., & Perrett, D. I. (2006). What is good is beautiful: Face preference reflects desired personality. *Personality and Individual Differences, 41,* 1107–1118.

Littlejohn, S. W., & Foss, K. A. (2011). *Theories of human communication.* Belmont, CA: Thomson/Wadsworth.

Liu, A., Sharkness, J., & Pryor, J. H. (2008). *Findings from the 2007 administration of your first college year (YFCY): National aggregates.* Los Angeles, CA: Higher Education Research, University of California, Los Angeles.

Liu, M. (2009). The intrapersonal and interpersonal effects of anger on negotiation strategies: A cross-cultural investigation. *Human Communication Research, 35,* 148–169.

Livingston, G. (2014, November 14). Four-in-ten couples are saying "I do" again: Growing number of adults have remarried. *Pew Research Center.* Retrieved from http://www.pewsocialtrends.org/2014/11/14/four-in-ten-couples-are-saying-i-do-again/

Lock, C. (2004, July 31). Deception detection: Psychologists try to learn how to spot a liar. *Science News, 166,* 72–76.

Lodge, M., & Taber, C. S. (2005). The automaticity of affect for political candidates, parties, and issues: An experimental test of the hot cognition hypothesis. *Political Psychology, 26,* 455–482.

Lohr, J. M., Olatunji, B. O., Baumeister, R. F., & Bushman, B. J. (2007). The pseudopsychology of anger venting and empirically supported alternatives that do no harm. *Scientific Review of Mental Health Practice, 5,* 54–65.

Longo, J. (2010). Combating disruptive behaviors: Strategies to promote a healthy work environment. *The Online Journal of Issues in Nursing.* Retrieved from http://www.nursingworld.org/MainMenu Categories/ANAMarketplace/ANAPeriodicals/ OJIN/TableofContents/Vol152010/No1Jan2010/ Combating-Disruptive-Behaviors.html

Loots, G., & Devise, I. (2003). The use of visual-tactile communication strategies by deaf and hearing fathers and mothers of deaf infants. *Journal of Deaf Studies and Deaf Education, 8,* 31–43.

Lopez-Guimera, G., Levine, M. P., Sanchez-Carracedo, D., & Fauquet, J. (2010). Influence of mass media on body image and eating disordered attitudes and behaviors in females: A review of effects and processes. *Media Psychology, 13,* 387–416.

Lopez-Zafra, E., Garcia-Retamero, R., & Landa, J. M. A. (2008). The role of transformational leadership, emotional intelligence, and group cohesiveness on leadership emergence. *Journal of Leadership Studies, 2,* 37–49.

Lorenzo, G. L., Biesanz, J. C., & Human, L. J. (2010). What is beautiful is good and more accurately understood: Physical attractiveness and accuracy in first impressions of personality. *Psychological Science, 21,* 1777–1782.

Loretto, p. (2015). The top 10 skills employers want. *About careers.* Retrieved from http://internships .about.com/od/internshipsuccess/a/The-Top-10-Skills-Employers-Want.htm

Lovett, F. (1997). Thinking about values. *Responsive Community, 7,* 87.

Lowry, P. B., Roberts, T. L., Romano, N. C., & Cheney, P. D. (2006). The impact of group size and social presence on small-group communication: Does computer-mediated communication make a difference? *Small Group Research, 37,* 631–661.

Lucas, S. E., & Medhurst, M. J. (2008). *Words of a century: The top 100 American speeches, 1900–1999.* New York: Oxford University Press.

Luckmann, J. (1999). *Transcultural communication.* Albany, NY: Delmar.

Luckow, A., Reifman, A., & McIntosh, D. N. (1998, August). *Gender differences in coping: A meta-analysis.* Presented to the annual meeting of the American Psychological Association, San Francisco.

Lukianoff, G. (2013, August 15). Speech codes: Alive and well, 10 years later. *Huffington Post.* Retrieved from http://www.huffingtonpost.com/greg-lukianoff/speech-codes-alive-and-we_b_3762031 .html

Lulofs, R. (1994). *Conflict: From theory to action.* Scottsdale, AZ: Gorsuch Scarisbrick.

Luong, A., & Rogelberg, S. G. (2005). Meetings and more meetings: The relationship between meeting load and the daily well-being of employees. *Group Dynamics: Theory, Research, and Practice, 9,* 58–67.

Lustig, M. W., & Koester, J. (2013). *Intercultural competence: Interpersonal communication across cultures.* New York: Pearson.

Lutgen-Sandvik, P. (2006). Take this job and . . . : Quitting and other forms of resistance to workplace bullying. *Communication Monographs, 73,* 406–433.

Lutgen-Sandvik, P., & Sypher, B. D. (2009). Workplace bullying: Causes, consequences, and corrections. In P. Lutgen-Sandvik & B. D. Sypher (Eds.), *Destructive organizational communication.* New York: Routledge.

Lutgen-Sandvik, P., Tracy, S., & Alberts, J. (2005, February). *Burned by bullying in the American workplace: A first time study of U.S. prevalence and delineation of bullying "degree."* Paper presented at the Western States Communication Convention, San Francisco, CA.

Lutgen-Sandvik, P., Tracy, S. J., & Alberts, J. K. (2007). Burned by bullying in the American workplace: Prevalence, perception, degree, and impact. *Journal of Management Studies, 44,* 837–862.

Lynch, J. (2014, February 14). No, one billion people do not watch the Oscars. *Quartz.* Retrieved from http:// qz.com/182355/no-one-billion-people-do-not-watch-the-oscars/

Lyubomirsky, S. (2012, December 1). New love: A short shelf life. *The New York Times.* Retrieved from http:// www.nytimes.com/2012/12/02/opinion/sunday/ new-love-a-short-shelf-life.html?_r=0

Maass, A., Cadinu, M., Guarnieri, G., & Grasselli, A. (2003). Sexual harassment under social identity threat: The computer harassment paradigm. *Journal of Personality and Social Psychology, 85,* 853–870.

Maccoby, E. E. (1998). *The two sexes: Growing up apart, coming together.* Cambridge, MA: Harvard University Press.

MacDonald, L. (2014). What is a self-managed team? *Chron.* Retrieved from http://smallbusiness.chron. com/selfmanaged-team-18236.html

Maheshvaranda, D. (2012, October). Is human nature competitive or cooperative? *Prout Globe.* Retrieved from http://proutglobe.org/2012/10/is-human-nature-competitive-or-cooperative/

MacInnis, C. C., MacKinnon, S. P., & MacIntyre, P. D. (2010). The illusion of transparency and normative beliefs about anxiety during public speaking. *Current Research in Social Psychology.* Retrieved from http://www.academia.edu/5388931/The_

illusion_of_transparency_and_normative_beliefs_about_anxiety_during_public_speaking

Mack, D. (2015, February 17). Joe Biden got a little handsy with the new defense secretary's wife. *BuzzFeed News*. Retrieved from http://www.buzzfeed.com/davidmack/say-heyyyyy-miss-carter#.lqBJ5Ooxwg

Maddieson, I. (1984). *Patterns of sound*. Cambridge, UK: Cambridge University

Madison, L. & Boxer, A. B. (2012, January 9). Mitt Romney: "I like being able to fire people" for bad service. *CBS News*. Retrieved from http://www.cbsnews.com/8301=50344_162-57355212-503544/mitt-romney-i-like-being-able-to-fire-people-for-bad-service/

Maher, S. (2011, May 24). Saturday was spiritual Rapture, predictor says. *San Jose Mercury News*, B1, B5.

Major, B., Kaiser, C. R., & McCoy, S. K. (2003). It's not my fault: When and why attributions to prejudice protect self-esteem. *Personality and Social Psychology Bulletin, 29*, 772–781.

Makau, J. M., & Marty, D. L. (2001). *Cooperative argumentation: A model for deliberative community*. Prospect Heights, IL: Waveland Press.

Makau, J. M., & Marty, D. L. (2013). *Dialogue & deliberation*. Long Grove, ILL: Waveland Press.

Malec, B. (2015, February 24). John Travolta's creepy face-touching was planned! Story behind his awkward Oscars moment with Idina Menzel. *Eonline*. Retrieved from http://www.eonline.com/news/629145/john-travolta-s-creepy-face-touching-was-planned-story-behind-his-awkward-oscars-moment-with-idina-menzel

Mallicoat, S. L. (2015). *Women and crime*. Thousand Oaks, CA: Sage.

Mancini, M. (2003). *Selling destinations: Geography for the travel professional*. Clifton Park, NY: Thomson/Selmar Learning.

Mandelbaum, D. G. (Ed.). (1949). *Selected writings of Edward Sapir*. Los Angeles: University of California Press.

Mannix, E., & Neale, M. A. (2005). What differences make a difference: The promise and reality of diverse teams in organizations. *Psychological Science in the Public Interest, 6*, 31–55.

Mansfield, M. (1990). Political communication in decision-making groups. In D. Swanson & D. Nimmo (Eds.), *New directions in political communication: A resource book*. Newbury Park, CA: Sage.

Marano, H. E. (2014, January 1). Love and power. *Psychology Today*. Retrieved from https://www.psychologytoday.com/articles/201312/love-and-power

Marantz, A. (2005, November 21). The dreaded middle seat. *Scientific American Mind*, p. 9.

March 2010 web server survey. (2010, March). *Netcraft* Retrieved from http://news.netcraft.com/archives/2010/03/17/march_2010_web_server_survey.html

Marcus-Newhall, A., Miller, N., Holtz, R., & Brewer, M. B. (1993). Cross-cutting category membership in role assignment: A means of reducing intergroup bias. *British Journal of Social Psychology, 32*, 125–145.

Marek, C. I, Wanzer, M. B., & Knapp, J. L. (2004). An exploratory investigation of the relationship between roommates' first impressions and subsequent communication patterns. *Communication Research Reports, 21*, 210–220.

Marie, E. (2014, October 2). 58 funny and romantic chat-up lines that actually work. *WeLoveDates*. Retrieved from http://www.welovedates.com/blog/229/top-58-pickup-lines/

Markey, C. N. (2005). Relations between body image and dieting behaviors: An examination of gender differences. *Sex Roles: A Journal of Research, 53*, 519–530.

Markoe, L. (2014, May 13). Survey: One-quarter of the world harbors anti-Semitic sentiment. *Religion News Service*. Retrieved from http://www.religionnews.com/2014/05/13/survey-one-four-globally-infected-anti-semitism/

Marshall, E. (2014, August). An experiment in zero parenting, *Science*, pp. 752–754.

Martell, R. F., Lane, D. M., & Emrich, C. (1996). Male-female differences: A computer simulation. *American Psychologist, 51*, 157–158.

Martin, J., & Nakayama, T. (2010). *Intercultural communication in contexts*. New York: McGraw-Hill.

Martin, J., & Nakayama, T. (2013). *Experiencing intercultural communication: An introduction*. New York: McGraw-Hill.

Martin, M. M., & Hemphil, P. (2013). *Taming disruptive behavior*. Tampa, FL: American College of Physician Executives.

Masland, S. R., Hooley, J. M., Tully, L. M., Dearing, K., & Gotlib, I. H. (2015). Cognitive-processing biases in individuals high on perceived criticism. *Clinical Psychological Science, 3*, 3–14.

Mason, M. F., & Morris, M. W. (2010). Culture, attribution and automaticity: A social cognitive neuroscience view. *Social Cognitive and Affective Neuroscience, 5*, 292–306.

Matos, K. (2014). Modern families: Same- and different-sex couple negotiating at home. *Families and Work Institute*. Retrieved from http://www.familiesandwork.org/downloads/modern-families.pdf

Matsumoto, D. (1990). Cultural influences on facial expressions of emotion. *Southern Communication Journal, 56*, 128–137.

Matthew, E. (2012, September 6). Sexism in video games [study]: There is sexism in gaming. *Price*

Charting. Retrieved from http://blog.pricecharting.com/2012/09/emilyami-sexism-in-video-games-study.html

Mattingly, B. (2012, September 27). "We can still be friends": Six ways you can stay friends after a breakup. *Science of Relationships.* Retrieved from http://www.scienceofrelationships.com/home/2012/9/27/we-can-still-be-friends-six-ways-you-can-stay-friends-after.html

Mattioli, D. (2010, March 23). More men make harassment claims. *The Wall Street Journal.* Retrieved from http://online.wsj.com/article/SB10001424052748704117304575137881438719028.html#printMode

Maxfield, D., Grenny, J., McMillan, R., Patterson, K., & Switzler, A. (2005). Silence kills: The seven crucial conversations in healthcare. Retrieved from http://www.silencekills.com/UPDL/SilenceKillsExecSummary.pdf

May, P. (2002, March 22). Jury says it's murder. *San Jose Mercury News,* p. 18A.

May, P. (2009, June 22). What's next for Twitter now it's on world stage? *San Jose Mercury News,* p. 6A.May, P. (2014, October 23). Internet users say bullying is common. *San Jose Mercury News,* pp. B1, B8.

May, P. (2015, April 9). Teens diversify their social media use. *San Jose Mercury News,* pp. B1, B6.

Mayer, R. E. (Ed.). (2005). *The Cambridge handbook of multimedia learning.* Cambridge, MA: Cambridge University Press.

Mazer, J. P., & Hunt, S. K. (2008a). Cool communication in the classroom: A preliminary examination of student perceptions of instructor use of slang. *Qualitative Research Reports in Communication, 9,* 20–28.

Mazer, J. P., & Hunt, S. K. (2008b). The effects of instructor use of positive and negative slang on student motivation, affective learning, and classroom climate. *Communication Research Reports, 25,* 44–55.

Maznevski, M. L., & Chudoba, K. M. (2000). Bridging space over time: Global virtual team dynamics and effectiveness. *Organization Science, 11,* 473–492.

McBain, K. A., Hewitt, L., Maher, T., Sercombe, M., Sypher, S., & Tirendi, G. (2013). Is this seat taken? The importance of context during the initiation of romantic communication. *International Journal of Humanities and Social Science, 3,* 79–89.

McBride, B. (2015, June 9). BLS: Jobs openings increased to 5.4 million in April, highest on record. *Calculated Risk.* Retrieved from http://www.calculatedriskblog.com/2015/06/bls-jobs-openings-increased-to-54.html

McCabe, M. P., & Ricciardelli, L. A. (2004). Weight and shape concerns of boys and men. In J. K. Thompson (Ed.), *Handbook of eating disorders and obesity.* Washington, DC: American Psychological Association.

McCallum, N. L., & McGlone, M. S. (2011). Death be not profane: Mortality salience and euphemism use. *Western Journal of Communication, 75,* 565–584.

McLaren, C., Null, J., & Quinn, J. (2005). Heat stress from enclosed vehicles: Moderate ambient temperatures cause significant temperature rise in enclosed vehicles. *Pediatrics, 116,* 109–112.

McClintock, E. A. (2014, December 19). Why breakups are actually tougher on men. *Psychology Today.* Retrieved from https://www.psychologytoday.com/blog/it-s-man-s-and-woman-s-world/201412/why-breakups-are-actually-tougher-men

McCoy, S. L., Tun, P. A., Cox, L. C., & Wingfield, A. (2005, July 12). Aging in a fast-paced world: Rapid speech and its effect on understanding. *ASHA Leader,* pp. 12, 30–31.

McCrae, R. R., Martin, T. A., Hrebickove, M., Urbanek, T., Willemsen, G., & Costa, P. T. (2008). Personality trait similarity between spouses in four cultures. *Journal of Personality, 76,* 1137–1163.

McCroskey, J. C., & Richmond, V. P. (1992). Communication apprehension and small group communication. In R. S. Cathcart & L. A. Samovar (Eds.), *Small group communication: A reader.* Dubuque, IA: Brown.

McCullough, M., Rochal, K. C., & Worthington, E. L. (1997). Interpersonal forgiving in close relationships. *Journal of Personality and Social Psychology, 73,* 321–336.

McDaniel, E. R. (2000). In L. A. Samovar & R. E. Porter (Eds.), *Intercultural communication: A reader.* Belmont, CA: Wadsworth.

McDonald, H. (2015, May 23). Ireland becomes first country to legalise gay marriage by popular vote. *The Guardian.* Retrieved from http://www.theguardian.com/world/2015/may/23/gay-marriage-ireland-yes-vote

McDonald, P., & Thompson, P. (2015). Social media(tion) and the reshaping of public/private boundaries in employment relations. *International Journal of Management Reviews.* Retrieved from http://onlinelibrary.wiley.com/doi/10.1111/ijmr.12061/abstract

McGee, D. S., & Cegala, D. J. (1998). Patient communication skills training for improved competence in the primary care medical consultation. *Journal of Applied Communication Research, 26,* 412–430.

McGirk, J. (1998, February). You're not fat, you're in the wrong country. *Marie Claire,* pp. 52–56.

McGrath, M. (2007, January). Methamphetamine in Montana: A preliminary report on trends and impact. *Montana Meth Project.* Retrieved from http://www.fvgroup.com/news/MT_AG_Report_Final.pdf

McGrath, M. (2008, April). *Methamphetamine in Montana: A follow-up report on trends and progress.*

Retrieved from http://www.doj.mt.gov/news/releases2008/20080331report.pdf

McGuinnies, E., & Ward, C. (1980). Better liked than right: Trustworthiness and expertise as factors in credibility. *Personality and Social Psychology Bulletin, 6*, 467–472.

McKay, M., Rogers, P., & McKay, J. (1989). *When anger hurts: Quieting the storm within*. Oakland, CA: New Harbinger.

McKimmie, B. M., Terry, D. J., Hogg, M. A., Manstead, A. S. R., Spears, R., & Doosje, B. (2003). I'm a hypocrite, but so is everyone else: Group support and the reduction of cognitive dissonance. *Group Dynamics: Theory, Research, and Practice, 7*, 214–224.

McLaughlin, S. (1996). The dirty truth about your kitchen: Using common sense to prevent food poisoning. In L. G. Schnoor (Ed.), *Winning orations*. Northfield, MN: Interstate Oratorical Association.

McNatt, D. B. (2000). Ancient Pygmalion joins contemporary management: A meta-analysis of the result. *Journal of Applied Psychology, 85*, 314–322.

McNeil, B. J., Pauker, S. G., Sox, H. C., & Tversky, A. (1982). On the elicitation of preferences for alternative therapies. *New England Journal of Medicine, 306*, 1259–1262.

McQuaid, M. (2015, March 6). The strengths revolution transforming our workplaces. *Psychology Today*. Retrieved from https://www.psychologytoday.com/blog/functioning-flourishing/201503/the-strengths-revolution-transforming-our-workplaces

McVay, J. C., & Kane, M. J. (2009). Conducting the train of thought: Working memory capacity, goal neglect, and mind wandering in an executive-control task. *Journal of Experimental Psychology: Learning, Memory, and Cognition, 35*, 196–204.

Meacham, J. (2009, August 14). Hitler and health care don't mix. *Newsweek*, p. 9.

Measles: Q&A about disease & vaccine. (2015, April 7). *Center for Disease Control & Prevention*. Retrieved from http://www.cdc.gov/vaccines/vpd-vac/measles/faqs-dis-vac-risks.htm

Medina, J. (2014). *Brain rules*. Seattle, WA: Pear Press. Mehl, M., & Pennebaker, J. (2002). *Mapping students' natural language use in everyday conversations*. Paper presented at the third annual meeting of the Society for Personality and Social Psychology, Savannah, GA.

Mehrabian, A. (1971). *Silent messages*. Belmont, CA: Wadsworth.

Mehrabian, A. (1995). *Intercultural encounters: The fundamentals of intercultural communication*. Englewood, CO: Morton.

Meleis, A. F., & Meleis, M. (1998). Egyptian-Americans. In L. D. Purnell & B. J. Paulanka (Eds.), *Transcultural health care: A culturally competent approach*. Philadelphia: Davis.

Menon, M., Tobin, D. D., Corby, B. C., Menon, M., Hodges, E. V., & Perry, D. G. (2007). The developmental costs of high self-esteem for antisocial children. *Child Development, 78*, 1627–1639.

Merolla, A. J. (2008). Communicating forgiveness in friendships and dating relationships. *Communication Studies, 59*, 114–131.

Meslow, S. (2015, March 6). Why Hollywood needs to stop treating prison rape as a punchline. *The Week*. Retrieved from http://theweek.com/articles/542707/why-hollywood-needs-stop-treating-prison-rape-punchline

Message of hope. (1998, July 24). *USA Weekend*, pp. 9–10.

Messman, S. J., Canary, D. J., & Hause, K. S. (2000). Motives to remain platonic, equity, and the use of maintenance strategies in opposite-sex friendships. *Journal of Social and Personal Relationships, 17*, 67–94.

Metts, S., Cupach, N., & Imahori, T. (1992). Perceptions of sexual compliance resisting messages in three types of cross-sex relationships. *Western Journal of Communication, 56*, 1–17.

Michelle Obama: Power fashion. (2015, June 17). *Harper's Bazaar*. Retrieved from http://www.harpersbazaar.com/fashion/trends/g813/michelle-obama-fashion/

Migdol, E. (2015, February 27). 9 things all people in long-distance relationships know to be true. *Connections.Mic*. Retrieved from http://mic.com/articles/111504/9-important-things-you-learn-after-being-in-a-long-distance-relationship

Milgram, S. (1974). *Obedience to authority*. New York: Harper & Row.

Miller, A. N. (2011, February). Men and women's communication is different—sometimes. *Communication Currents*. Retrieved from https://www.natcom.org/CommCurrentsArticle.aspx?id=749

Miller, C. (1989). The social psychological effects of group decision rules. In P. Paulus (Ed.), *Psychology of group influence*. Hillsdale, NJ: Erlbaum.

Miller, J. (2013, January 14). Ten wildly varying interpretations of Jodie Foster's Golden Globes speech. *Vanity Fair*. Retrieved from http://www.vanityfair.com/hollywood/2013/01/jodie-foster-golden-globe-speech-coming-out-reviews

Miller, K. (2005). *Communication theories: Perspectives, processes, and contexts*. New York: McGraw-Hill.

Mitchell, T. R., & Lee, T. W. (2001). The unfolding model of voluntary turnover and job embeddedness: Foundations for a comprehensive theory of attachment. In B. M. Staw & R. I. Sutton (Eds.), *Research in Organizational Behavior*. Greenwich, CT: JAI Press.

Miura, A., & Hida, M. (2004). Synergy between diversity and similarity in group-idea generation. *Small Group Research*, 35, 540–564.

Mobius, M. M., & Rosenblat, T. S. (2006). Why beauty matters. *American Economic Review*, 96, 222–235.

Moghaddam, F. M. (1998). *Social psychology: Exploring universals across cultures*. New York: Freeman.

Mohamed, A., & Wiebe, F. (1996). Toward a process theory of groupthink. *Small Group Research*, 27, 416–430.

Mole, P. (2002, November/December). Are skeptics cynical? Popular misunderstandings of skepticism. *Skeptical Inquirer*, pp. 44–48.

Moncur, B., Bailey, B. W., Lockhart, B. D., LeCheminant, J. D., & Perkins, A. E. (2013). The relationship of body size and adiposity to source of self-esteem in college women. *American Journal of Health Education*, 44, 299–305.

Mongeau, P. A., Serewicz, M. C., Henningsen, M. L., & Davis, K. L. (2006). Sex differences in the transition to a heterosexual romantic relationship. In K. Dindia & D. J. Canary (Eds.), *Sex differences and similarities in communication*. Mahwah, NJ: Erlbaum.

Monmaney, T. (1993, September 20). Marshall's hunch. *The New Yorker*, pp. 64–72.

Montana Meth Project (2015).*Meth Project Organization*. Retrieved from http://www.montanameth.org/Results/index.php

Moody, C. (2015, June 6). Donald Trump thinks pretty much everyone is a loser. *CNN*. Retrieved from http://www.cnn.com/2015/06/16/politics/donald-trump-2016-election-loser/

Moore, A. S. (2010). Failure to communicate. *The New York Times*. Retrieved from http://www.nytimes.com/2010/07/25/education/edlife/25roommate-t.html

Moreland, R. L. (2010). Are dyads really groups? *Small Group Research*, 41, 251–267.

Morreale, S. P., & Pearson, J. C. (2008). Why communication education is important: The centrality of the discipline in the 21st century. *Communication Education*, 57, 224–240.

Morris, D. (1977). *Manwatching: A field guide to human behavior*. New York: Abrams.

Morris, D., Collett, P., Marsh, P., & O'Shaughnessy, M. (1979). *Gestures: Their origins and distribution*. New York: Stein & Day.

Morris, M. W., & Peng, K. (1994). Culture and cause: American and Chinese attributions for social and physical events. *Journal of Personality and Social Psychology*, 67, 949–971.

Morris, T., & Gorham, J. (1996). Fashion in the classroom: Effects of attire on student perceptions of instructors in college classes. *Communication Education*, 45, 135–148.

Morse, C. R., & Metts, S. (2011). Situational and communicative predictors of forgiveness following a relational transgression. *Western Journal of Communication*, 75, 239–258.

Morton, J. B., & Trehub, S. E. (2001). Children's understanding of emotion in speech. *Child Development*, 72, 834–843.

Mosbergen, D. (2015, May 19). "Have your own standards": Stephen Colbert offers spot-on life advice in Wake Forest commencement speech. *Huffington Post*. Retrieved from http://www.huffingtonpost.com/2015/05/19/stephen-colbert-commencement-speech-wake-forest_n_7310848.html

Motley, M. T. (1995). *Overcoming your fear of public speaking: A proven method*. New York: McGraw-Hill.

Motley, M.T. (1997). COM therapy. In J.A. Daly, J. C. McCroskey, J. Ayres, T. Hopf, & D. M. Ayres (Eds.), *Avoiding communication*. Cresskill, NJ: Hampton Press.

Motley, M. T. (2009). COM therapy. In J. A. Daly, J. C. McCroskey, J. Ayres, T. Hopf, & D. M. Ayers Sonandre (Eds.), *Avoiding communication: Shyness, reticence, and communication apprehension*. Creskill, NJ: Hampton Press.

Mudrack, P., & Farrell, G. (1995). An examination of functional role behavior and its consequences for individuals in group settings. *Small Group Research*, 26, 542–571.

Muehlenhard, C., Koralewski, M., Andrews, S., & Burdick, C. (1986). Verbal and nonverbal cues that convey interest in dating: Two studies. *Behavior Therapy*, 17, 404–419.

Mulac, A. (2006). The gender-linked language effect: Do language differences really make a difference? In K. Dindia & D. J. Canary (Eds.), *Sex differences and similarities in communication*. Mahwah, NJ: Erlbaum.

Mulac, A., & Bradac, J. (1995). Women's style in problem solving interaction: Powerless, or simply feminine? In P. Kalbfleisch & M. Cody (Eds.), *Gender, power, and communication in human relationships*. Hillsdale, NJ: Erlbaum.

Mulgrew, K. E., Volcevski-Kostas, D., & Rendell, P. G. (2014). The effect of music video clips on adolescent boys' body image, mood, and schema activation. *Journal of Youth and Adolescence*, 43, 92–103.

Murray, B. (1997, May). How important is teaching style to students? *APA Monitor*, p. 103.

Murray-Johnson, L., Witte, K., Liu, W., Hubbell, A., Sampson, J., & Morrison, K. (2001). Addressing cultural orientations in fear appeals: Promoting AIDS-protective behaviors among Mexican immigrant and African American adolescents and American and Taiwanese college students. *Journal of Health Communication*, 6, 335–358.

Myatt, M. (2012, April 12). 8 tips for using workplace humor. *Forbes*. Retrieved from http://www.forbes.com/sites/mikemyatt/2012/04/12/8-tips-for-using-workplace-humor/

Myers, D. G. (2002). *Intuition: Its power and perils.* New Haven, CT: Yale University Press.

Myers, D. G. (2012). *Psychology.* New York: Worth Publishers.

Na, J., & Kitayama, S. (2011). Spontaneous trait inference is culture-specific: Behavioral and neural evidence. *Psychological Science*, 20, 1–8.

Nabi, R. L. (2002). Discrete emotions and persuasion. In J. P. Dillard & M. Pfau (Eds.), *The persuasion handbook: Developments in theory and practice.* Thousand Oaks, CA: Sage.

Namie, G., Christensen, D., & Phillips, D. (2014). 2014 WBI U.S. workplace bullying survey. *Workplace Bullying Institute*. Retrieved from http://workplacebullying.org/multi/pdf/WBI-2014-US-Survey.pdf

Narcisco, J., & Burkett, T. (1975*). Declare yourself.* Englewood Cliffs, NJ: Prentice Hall.

Nasar, J. L., & Troyer, D. (2013). Pedestrian injuries due to mobile phone use in public places. *Accident Analysis and Prevention*, 57, 91–95.

Nataatmadja, I., Sixsmith, A., & Dyson, L. E. (2007). Improving class participation by Asian students. *IRMA International Conference*. Retrieved from http://www.irma-international.org/viewtitle/33025/

National Survey of Student Engagement. (2012). *Preparing student learning and institutional improvement: Lessons from NSSE at 13.* Retrieved from http://nsse.indiana.edu/NSSE_2012_Results/pdf/NSSE_2012_Annual_Results.pdf

National Survey of Student Engagement. (2014). *2014 topic module: Development of transferable skills.* Retrieved from http://nsse.indiana.edu/2014_institutional_report/pdf/Modules/NSSE14%20Module%20Summary-Development%20of%20Transferable%20Skills.pdf

Navigating today's complex dating scene. (2011, June). *Spirit*, 61–63.

Neal, T., & Brodsky, M. S. (2008). Warmth and competence on the witness stand: Implications for the credibility of male and female expert witnesses. *Journal of the American Academy of Psychiatry and the Law Online*, 40, 488–497.

Neff, K. D., & Harter, S. (2002). The authenticity of conflict resolutions among adult couples: Does women's other-oriented behavior reflect their true selves? *Sex Roles*, 47, 403–412.

Nelson, T. F., Xuan, A., Lee, H., Weitzman, E. R., & Wechsler, H. (2009). Persistence of heavy drinking and ensuing consequences at heavy drinking colleges. *Journal of Studies on Alcohol and Drugs*, 70, 726–734.

Neuliep, J. W. (2012). The relationship among intercultural communication apprehension, ethnocentrism, uncertainty reduction, and communication satisfaction during initial intercultural interaction: An extension of anxiety and uncertainty management (AUM) theory. *Journal of Intercultural Communication Research*, 41, 1–16.

Neumann, R., & Strack, F. (2000). "Mood contagion": The automatic transfer of mood between persons. *Journal of Personality and Social Psychology*, 79, 211–223.

Nevid, J. S. (2011, May/June). Teaching the Millennials. *APS Observer*, 24, 53–56.

Newman, D., Hocking, J., & Turk, D. (2000, February 27). *At last, redemption for the physically unattractive: An updated examination of physical attractiveness as a dependent variable.* Paper presented at the Western Communication Convention, Sacramento, CA.

Newport, F. (2010, November 8). In U.S., 64% support death penalty in cases of murder. *Gallup*. Retrieved from http://www.gallup.com/poll/144284/Support-Death-Penalty-Cases-Murder.aspx

Newport, F. (2012, May 22). Americans, including Catholics, say birth control is morally OK. *Gallup Politics*. Retrieved from http://www.gallup.com/poll/154799/americans-including-catholics-say-birth-control-morally.aspx#

Newton, M. (2002). *Savage girls and wild boys: A history of feral children.* New York: St. Martin's Press.

Ng, S. H. (2001). Influencing through the power of language. In J. P. Forgas & D. W. Kipling (Eds.), *Social influence: Direct and indirect processes.* Philadelphia: Psychology Press.

NHMRC releases statement and advice on homeopathy. (2015, March 11). *NHMRC*. Retrieved from https://www.nhmrc.gov.au/media/releases/2015/nhmrc-releases-statement-and-advice-homeopathy

Nichols, N. B., Backer-Fulghum, L. M., Boska, C. R., & Sanford, K. (2015). Two types of disengagement during couples' conflicts: Withdrawal and passive immobility. *Psychological Assessment*, 27, 203–214.

Nicholson, C. (2010, May/June). The humor gap. *Scientific American Mind*, pp. 38–45.

Noguchi, S. (2008, June 25). Lifted lines in grads' speeches. *San Jose Mercury News*, pp. 1B, 5B.

Nonnemaker, S. E. (2009). Living behind bars? An investigation of gated communities in New Tampa, Florida. *Theses and Dissertations*. Paper 2121. Retrieved from http://scholarcommons.usf.edu/etd/2121

Noonan, P. (1998). *Simply speaking: How to communicate your ideas with style, substance, and clarity.* New York: HarperCollins.

Nordin, K. (2015). 911's deadly flaw. In L. G. Schnoor & L. Mayfield, (Eds.), *Winning orations of the Interstate oratorical Association*. Mankato, MN: Interstate Oratorical Association.

Northouse, P. (2013). *Leadership: Theory and practice*. Thousand Oaks, CA: Sage.

Notarius, C., & Markman, H. (1993). *We can work it out: Making sense of marital conflict*. New York: Putnam's.

Number of words in the English language: 1,025,109.8. (2014). *Global Language Monitor*. Retrieved from http://www.languagemonitor.com/number-of-words/number-of-words-in-the-english-language-1008879/

Nunberg, G. (2003, June 8). In Mideast, language of compromise does exist. *San Jose Mercury News*, pp. 1P, 3P.

Nurok, M., Sundt, T. M., & Frankel, A. (2011). Teamwork and communication in the operating room: Relationship to discrete outcomes and research challenges. *Anesthesiology Clinics*, 29, 1–11.

Nussbaum, B. (2004, May 17). The power of design. *Business Week*, pp. 86–94.

Nye, J. (2013, July 2). Farewell to freshman—Washington state to remove 40,000 pieces of legislation of "gender biased language" . . . but manhole survives. *Daily Mail*. Retrieved from http://www.dailymail.co.uk/news/article-2353938/Farewell-freshman--Washington-State-remove-40-000-pieces-legislation-gender-biased-language--manhole-survives.html

Obama approval inches up, tied with Putin as leader, Quinnipiac University national poll finds; voters say Putin is not Hitler, but fear military action. (2014, April 2). *Quinnipiac University*. Retrieved from http://www.quinnipiac.edu/news-and-events/quinnipiac-university-poll/national/release-detail?ReleaseID=2027

Obama Michigan graduation speech: Full text. (2010, May 20). *Huffington Post*. Retrieved from http://www.huffingtonpost.com/2010/05/01/obama-michigan-graduation_n_559688.html

Obama shoe photo seen as "insult" by some Israelis. (2009, June 10). *Huffington Post*. Retrieved from http://www.huffingtonpost.com/2009/06/10/obama-phone-seen-as_n_213693.html?view=print

Obeidallah, D. (2014, September 11). 13 years after 9/11, anti-Muslim bigotry is worse than ever. *The Daily Beast*. Retrieved from http://www.thedailybeast.com/articles/2014/09/11/13-years-after-9-11-anti-muslim-bigotry-is-worse-than-ever.html

O'Brien, T. (1995, November 5). No jerks allowed. *West*, pp. 8–14.

O'Donohue, W. T., & Fisher, J. E. (2008). *Cognitive behavior therapy: Applying empirically supported techniques in your practice*. Hoboken, NJ: Wiley.

O'Keefe, D. J. (2016). *Persuasion: Theory and research*. Thousand Oaks, CA: Sage.

Okrent, A. (2014, September 22). Why is Y sometimes a vowel? *JustEnglish*. Retrieved from http://justenglish.me/tag/why-is-y-a-vowel/

Olivola, C. Y., & Todorov, A. (2010). Elected in 100 milliseconds: Appearance-based trait inferences and voting. *Journal of Nonverbal Behavior*, 34, 83–110.

Olympic basketball/2008 Olympics. (2008). *InsideHoops.com*. Retrieved from http://www.insidehoops.com/olympics.shtml

Omarzu, J. (2000). A disclosure decision model: Determining how and when individuals will self-disclose. *Personality and Social Psychology Review*, 4, 174–185.

One in five U.S. adults now has a tattoo. (2012, February 23). *Harris Interactive*. Retrieved from http://www.harrisinteractive.com/NewsRoom/HarrisPolls/tabid/447/mid/1508/articleId/970/ctl/ReadCustom%20Default/Default.aspx

O'Neil, J. M., Good, G. E., & Holmes, S. (1995). Fifteen years of theory and research on men's gender role conflict: New paradigms for empirical research. In R. Levant & W. Pollock (Eds.), *The new psychology of men*. New York: Basic Books.

Onishi, N. (2001, February 17). Fat is the ideal body shape in West Africa. *San Jose Mercury News*, p. 2A.

Onishi, N. (2007, July 16). Japanese wary as they prepare to join juries. *San Jose Mercury News*, p. 8A.

Oprah: A heavenly body? Survey finds talk-show host a celestial shoo-in. (1997, March 31). *U.S. News & World Report*, p. 18.

Ortutay, B. (2014, November 6). Drivers know dangers of texting, do it anyway. *San Jose Mercury News*, p. A5.

Osgood, G. (1969). The nature of measurement of meaning. In J. Snider & C. Osgood (Eds.), *The semantic differential technique*. Chicago: Aldine.

O'Sullivan, L. F., & Byers, E. S. (1992). College students' incorporation of initiator and restrictor roles in sexual dating interactions. *Journal of Sex Research*, 29, 435–446.

O'Sullivan, M. (2005). Emotional intelligence and deception detection: Why most people can't "read" others, but a few can. In R. E. Riggio & R. S. Feldman (Eds.), *Applications of nonverbal communication*. Mahwah, NJ: Erlbaum.

O'Sullivan, M. (2009, March 23). Are there any "natural" lie detectors? *Psychology Today*. Retrieved from https://www.psychologytoday.com/blog/deception/200903/are-there-any-natural-lie-detectors

Otterson, J. (2015, March 18). Jimmy Kimmel tricks SXSW attendees into saying they like fake bands. *The Wrap*. Retrieved from http://www.thewrap.com/jimmy-kimmel-tricks-sxsw-attendees-into-saying-they-like-fake-bands-video/

Oveis, C. (2010, January). *Thin slices of touch reveal affective style and relationship dynamics.* Paper presented at the 11th annual meeting of the Society for Personality and Social Psychology, Las Vegas, NV.

Owen, W. F. (1987). The verbal expression of love by women and men as a critical communication event in personal relationships. *Women's Studies in Communication, 10,* 15–24.

Oyserman, D., Coon, H. M., & Kemmelmeier, M. (2002). Rethinking individualism and collectivism: Evaluation of theoretical assumptions and meta-analyses. *Psychological Bulletin, 128,* 3–72.

Oyerserman, D., & Uskul, A. K. (2008). Individualism and collectivism: Societal-level processes with implications for individual-level and society-level outcomes. *The Selected Works of Ayse K. Uskul.* Retrieved http://works.bepress.com/cgi/viewcontent.cgi?article=1007&context=ayse_uskul&sei-redir=1&referer=http%3A%2F%2F

Paivio, A. (1969). Mental imagery in associative learning and memory. *Psychological Review, 76,* 241–263.

Park, D. C., & Huang, C.-M. (2010). Culture wires the brain: A cognitive neuroscience perspective. *Perspectives on Psychological Science, 5,* 391–400.

Park, H., & Antonioni, D. (2007). Personality, reciprocity, and strength of conflict resolution strategy. *Journal of Research in Personality, 41,* 110–125.

Park, H. S., Levine, T. R., McCornack, S. A., Morrison, K., & Ferrara, M. (2002). How people really detect lies. *Communication Monographs, 69,* 144–157.

Park, R. (2000). *Voodoo science: The road from foolishness to fraud.* New York: Oxford University Press.

Parker, E. S., Cahill, L., & McGaugh, J. I. (2006). A case of unusual autobiographical remembering. *Neurocase, 12,* 35–49.

Parker, S. K., & Griffin, M. A. (2002). What is so bad about a little name-calling? Negative consequences of gender harassment for over-performance demands and distress. *Journal of Occupational Health Psychology, 7,* 195–210.

Parkins, R. (2012). Gender and emotional expressiveness: An analysis of prosodic features in emotion. *Griffith Working Papers in Pragmatics and Intercultural Communication, 5,* 46–54.

Parks, C., & Vu, A. (1994). Social dilemma of individuals from highly individualist and collectivist cultures. *Journal of Conflict Resolution, 3,* 708–718.

Parks, M. R. (2007). *Personal relationships and personal networks.* Mahwah, NJ: Erlbaum.

Pashler, H. E. (1998). *The psychology of attention.* Cambridge, MA: MIT Press.

Passer, M. W., & Smith, R. E. (2011). *Psychology: The science of mind and behavior.* New York: McGraw-Hill.

Patrick, S., & Beckenbach, J. (2009). Male perceptions of intimacy: A qualitative study. *The Journal of Male Studies, 17,* 47–56.

Paulos, J. A. (1988*). Innumeracy: Mathematical illiteracy and its consequences.* New York: Hill & Wang.

Pausch, R., & Zaslow, J. (2008). *The last lecture.* New York: Hyperion.

Pavitt, C., & Curtis, E. (1994). *Small group discussion.* Scottsdale, AZ: Gorsuch Scarisbrick.

Pearson, C. M., Andersson, L. M., & Porath, C. L. (2000). Assessing and attacking workplace incivility. *Organizational Dynamics, 29,* 123–137.

Pearson, P. (1997). *When she was bad: Women and the myth of innocence.* Toronto: Random House.

Penn, M. J., & Zalesne, E. K. (2007). *Microtrends: The small forces behind tomorrow's big changes.* New York: Twelve Press.

Peplau, L. A., & Spalding, L. R. (2000). The close relationships of lesbians, gay men, and bisexuals. In C. Hendrick & S. S. Hendrick (Eds.), *Close relationships: A sourcebook.* Thousand Oaks, CA: Sage.

Perez-Pena, R. (2012, September 7). Studies find more students cheating with high achievers no exception. *The New York Times.* Retrieved from http://www.nytimes.com/2012/09/08/education/studies-show-more-students-cheat-even-high-achievers.html

Perkins-Munn, T. (2012, October 1). Do pick-up lines actually work? *Examiner.* Retrieved from http://www.examiner.com/article/do-pick-up-lines-actually-work

Perloff, R. M. (2013). *The dynamics of persuasion: Communication and attitudes in the 21st century.* New York: Routledge.

Perman, C. (2011, September 2). Think your boss is a psychopath? That may be true. *CNBC.* Retrieved from http://www.cnbc.com/id/44376401

Perret, G. (1994). *Classic one-liners.* New York: Sterling.

Perry, S., & Tauber, M. (2014, December 22). Kate & William take New York. *People,* pp. 21–22.

Pertaub, D., Slater, M., & Barker, C. (2002). An experiment on public speaking anxiety in response to three different types of virtual audiences. *Presence: Teleoperators and Virtual Environments, 11,* 670–678.

Peterson, C. (2000). The future of optimism. *American Psychologist, 55,* 44–55.

Peterson, M. S. (1997). Personnel interviewers' perception of the importance and adequacy of applicants' communication skills. *Communication Education, 46,* 287–291.

Petrovic, K. (2013, March/April). Closing the book on "open-mindedness." *Skeptical Inquirer,* p. 53.

Pettigrew, T., & Martin, J. (1987). Shaping the organizational context for black American inclusion. *Journal of Social Issues, 43,* 41–78.

Pettigrew, T. F., & Tropp, L. R. (2006). A meta-analytic test of intergroup contact theory. *Journal of Personality and Social Psychology, 90,* 751–783.

Petty, R., & Cacioppo, J. (1984). The effects of involvement on responses to argument quantity and quality: Central and peripheral routes to persuasion. *Journal of Personality and Social Psychology, 46,* 69–81.

Petty, R., & Cacioppo, J. (1986a). The elaboration likelihood model of persuasion. In L. Berkowitz (Ed.), *Advances in experimental social psychology* (Vol. 19). New York: Academic Press.

Petty, R., & Cacioppo, J. (1986b). *Communication and persuasion: Central and peripheral routes to attitude change.* New York: Springer-Verlag.

Petty, R., Kasmer, J., Haugtvedt, C., & Cacioppo, J. (1987). Source and message factors in persuasion: A reply to Stiff's critique of the elaboration likelihood model. *Communication Monographs, 54,* 233–249.

Petty, R. E., Rucker, D. D., Bizer, G. Y., & Cacioppo, J. T. (2004). The elaboration likelihood model in persuasion. In J. S. Seiter & R. H. Gass (Eds.), *Perspectives on persuasion, social influence, and compliance.* New York: Pearson.

Pew Research Center. (2009, June 29). *Growing old in America: Expectations vs. reality.* Retrieved from http://pewresearch.org/pubs/1296/aging-survey-expectations-versus-reality

Pfau, M., & Van Bockern, S. (1994). The persistence of inoculation in conferring resistance to smoking initiation among adolescents: The second year. *Human Communication Research, 20,* 413–430.

Pfau, M., Ivanov, B., Houston, B., Haigh, M., Sims, J., Gilchrist, E., Russell, J., Wigley, S., Eckstein, J., & Richert, N. (2005). Inoculation and mental processing: The instrumental role of associative networks in the process of resistance to counterattitudinal influence. *Communication Monographs, 72,* 414–441.

Pfau, M., Szabo, E. A., Anderson, J., Morrill, J., Zubric, J., & Wan, H. (2001). The role and impact of affect in the process of resistance to persuasion, *Human Communication Research, 27,* 216–252.

Phanor-Faury, A. (2010, June 24). "Nude" doesn't translate in fashion. *Essence.* Retrieved from http://www.essence.com/fashion_beauty/fashion/nude_dresses_racial_bias_fashion_world.php

Philpot, C. (2008). Forgiveness—definitions and effects (pp. 5–7). *American Psychological Association.* Retrieved from http://www.apa.org/international/resources/publications/forgiveness.pdf

Piezon, S. L., & Ferree, W. D. (2008). Perceptions of social loafing in online learning groups: A study of public university and U.S. Naval War College students. *The International Review of Research in Open and Distributive Learning.* Retrieved from http://www.irrodl.org/index.php/irrodl/article/view/484/1034

Pileggi, S. (2010, January/February). The happy couple. *Scientific American Mind,* pp. 34–39.

Pinel, E. C. (1999). Stigma consciousness: The psychological legacy of social stereotypes. *Journal of Personality and Social Psychology, 76,* 114–128.

Pinel, E. C. (2002). Stigma consciousness in intergroup contexts: The power of conviction. *Journal of Experimental Social Psychology, 38,* 178–185.

Pinker, S. (1997). *How the mind works.* New York: Norton.

Pinker, S. (1999). *Words and rules: The ingredients of language.* New York: HarperCollins.

Pinker, S. (2007). *The stuff of thought: Language as a window into human nature.* New York: Viking Penguin.

Pinkley, R. L., & Northcraft, G. B. (2000). *Get paid what you're worth.* New York: St. Martin's Press.

Pinola, M. (2012, May 16). What employers look for in entry-level job candidates. *Lifehacker.* Retrieved from http://lifehacker.com/5910871/what-employers-look-for-in-entry-level-job-candidates

Pitts, L. (2011, March 6). Prominent blogger dismisses accuracy as "no big deal." *San Jose Mercury News,* p. A13.

Plester, B., Wood, C., & Joshi, P. (2009). Exploring the relationship between children's knowledge of text message abbreviations and school literacy outcomes. *British Journal of Developmental Psychology, 27,* 145–161.

Pogrebin, L. C. (1987). *Among friends.* New York: McGraw-Hill.

Political bias affects brain activity, study finds. (2006, January 24). *MSNBC.com.* Retrieved from http://www.msnbc.msn.com/id/11009379/

Politics. (2007). Informal MSNBC Poll: 87% of respondents believe Bush should be impeached. (2007, January 28). *WikiNews.* Retrieved from https://en.wikinews.org/wiki/Informal_MSNBC_Poll:_87%25_of_respondents_believe_Bush_should_be_impeached. Source: http://www.nbcnews.com/id/10562904/from/ET/#.VgsCxU1FAdU

Poll. (2012, April 9). *Daily Kos.* Retrieved from http://www.dailykos.com/

Poll: College students feel pressure to drink. (2000, June 20). *San Jose Mercury News,* p. 9A.

Pollack, I., & Pickett, J. M. (1964). Intelligibility of excerpts from fluent speech: Auditory vs. structural context. *Journal of Verbal Learning and Verbal Behavior, 3,* 79–84.

Pomerantz, E. M., & Wang, Q. (2009). The role of parents' control in children's development in Western and East Asian countries. . *Current Directions in Psychological Science, 18,* 285–289.

Pomery, E. A., Gibbons, F. X., & Stock, M. L. (2012). Social comparison. *Encyclopedia of Human Behavior*, 2, 463–469.

Poole, M. (2009, July 27). A's great Henderson cool at Cooperstown. *San Jose Mercury News*, pp. 1A, 6A.

Poole, M. S., & Zhang, H. (2005). Virtual teams. In S. A. Wheelan (Ed.), *The handbook of group research and practice*. Thousand Oaks, CA; Sage.

Pope, H. G. (2004, March 28). The pressures behind steroid abuse: Young men-not just athletes-take risks for a big build. *San Jose Mercury News*, p. 1P.

Pope, H. G., Gruber, A. J., Mangweth, B., Bureau, B., deCol, C., Jouvent, R., & Hudson, J. I. (2000). Body image perception among men in three countries. *American Journal of Psychiatry*, 157.

Pope, H.G., Phillips, K.A., & Olivardia, R. (2002). *The Adonis complex: How to identify, treat, and prevent body obsession in men and boys*. New York: Free Press.

Pornpitakpan, C. (2004). The persuasiveness of source credibility: A critical review of five decades' evidence. *Journal of Applied Social Psychology*, 34, 243–281.

Porter, S., & ten Brinke, L. (2010). Truth about lies: What works in detecting high-stakes deception? *Legal and Criminological Psychology*, 15, 57–76.

Powell, T. (2012). It's not the addict, it's the drug: Redefining America's War on Drugs. In L. G. Schnoor, L. Mayfield, & K. Young (Eds.), *Winning orations*. Mankato, MN: Interstate Oratorical Association.

PowerPoint turns 20, as its creators ponder a dark side to success. (2007, June 20). *The Wall Street Journal*, p. B1.

Pratkanis, A., & Aronson, E. (2001). *Age of propaganda: The everyday use and abuse of persuasion*. New York: Freeman.

President George W. Bush to the 300th graduating class of Yale University. (2001, May 22). *Everything2.com*. Retrieved from http://www.everything2.com/index.pl?node_id=1056073

Price, J., & Davis, B. (2008). *The woman who can't forget: The extraordinary story of living with the most remarkable memory known to science*. New York: Free Press.

Pronovost, P. J., & Freischlag, J. A. (2010). Improving teamwork to reduce surgical mortality. *Journal of the American Medical Association*, 304, 1721–1722.

Provine, R. R. (2000). *Laughter: A scientific investigation*. New York: Viking.

Pruitt, D., & Rubin, J. (1986). *Social conflict: Escalation, stalemate, and settlement*. New York: Random House.

Przybylski, A. K., & Weinstein, N. (2012). Can you connect with me now? How the presence of mobile communication technology influences face-to-face conversation quality, *Journal of Social and Personal Relationships*, 30, 237–246.

Public Support for Impeaching," 2014. Public support for impeaching Obama is no higher than it was for Bush seven years ago. (2014, July 15). *Pekin Daily Times*. Retrieved from http://www.pekintimes.com/article/20140715/BLOGS/307159981/10141

Purcell, K., Rainie, L. (2014, December 30). Technology's impact on workers. *Pew Research Center*. Retrieved from http://www.pewinternet.org/2014/12/30/technologys-impact-on-workers/

Purdy, M., & Borisoff, D. (1997). *Listening in everyday life*. Lanham, MD: University Press of America.

Putnam, F. W. (2010). Beyond sticks and stones. *American Journal of Psychiatry*, 167, 1422–1424.

Radmacher, K., & Azmitia, M. (2006). Are there gendered pathways to intimacy in early adolescents' and emerging adults' friendships? *Journal of Adolescent Research*, 21, 415–448.

Radosh (2005, February 28). The pictures: One billion. *The New Yorker*, p. 32.

Rainie, L., Purcell, K., & Smith, A. (2011, January 18). The social side of the Internet. *Pew Internet*. Retrieved from http://www.pewinternet.org/Reports/2011/The-Social-Side-of-the-Internet.aspx

Rains, S. A., & Young, V. (2009). A meta-analysis of research on formal computer-mediated support groups: Examining group characteristics and health outcomes. *Human Communication Research*, 35, 309–336.

Raizada, R. D. S., Tsao, F.-M., Liu, H.-M., & Kuhl, P. (2010). Quantifying the adequacy of neural representations for a cross-language phonetic discrimination task: Prediction of individual differences. *Cerebral Cortex*, 20, 1–12.

Raja, R. H. (2014, July 9). Burqah ban, multiculturalism and secularism. *Huffington Post*. Retrieved from http://www.huffingtonpost.com/raza-habib-raja/burqah-ban-multiculturali_b_5551825.html

Ramirez, A., & Broneck, K. (2009). IM me: Instant messaging as relational maintenance and everyday communication. *Journal of Social and Personal Relationships*, 26, 291–315.

Ratini, M. (2014, December 1). What is *H. pylori*? *WebMD*. Retrieved from http://www.webmd.com/digestive-disorders/h-pylori-helicobacter-pylori

Ravitch, D. (2007). *EdSpeak: A glossary of education terms, phrases, buzzwords, and jargon*. Alexandria, VA: ASCD.

Rawson, C. (2013). The dreaded "S" word. In L. G. Schnoor, K. Young, & L. Mayfield (Eds.), *Winning orations*. Mankato, MN: Interstate Oratorical Association.

Ray, J. (2005, July 12). Censorship: Do teens bow to school control? *Gallup*. Retrieved from http://www.gallup.com/poll/17281/censorship-teens-bow-school-control.aspx

Reason, J., & Mycielska, K. (1982). *Absent-minded? The psychology of mental lapses and everyday errors*. Englewood Cliffs, NJ: Prentice Hall.

Reed, L. (2013, October 23). UNL study shows college students are digitally distracted in class. Retrieved from http://newsroom.unl.edu/releases/2013/10/23/UNL+study+shows+college+students+are+digitally+distracted+in+class

Reicher, S. D., Haslam, S. A., & Platow, M. J. (2007, August/September). The new psychology of leadership. *Scientific American Mind*, pp. 22–29.

Reid, S. A., Byrne, S., Brundidge, J. S., Shoham, M. D., & Marlow, M. L. (2007). A critical test of self-enhancement, exposure, and self-categorization explanations for first-and third-person perceptions. *Human Communication Research*, 33, 143–162.

Reilly, K. (2013, July 3). A generational gap in American patriotism. *Pew Research Center*. Retrieved from http://www.pewresearch.org/fact-tank/2013/07/03/a-generational-gap-in-american-patriotism/

Remarks of Senator Barack Obama. (2008, January 3). *Obama News & Speeches*. Retrieved from http://www.barackobama.com/2008/01/03/remarks_of_senator_barack_obam_39.php

Remarks of Senator Barack Obama on New Hampshire primary night. (2008, January 8). *Wikisource*. Retrieved from https://en.wikisource.org/wiki/Remarks_of_Senator_Barack_Obama_on_New_Hampshire_Primary_Night

Report: The media have debunked the death panels more than 40 times. (2009, August 15). *MediaMatters for America*. Retrieved from http://mediamatters.org/research/200908150001

Rettner, R. (2011, November 9). 6 ways sexual harassment damages women's health. *Live Science*. Retrieved from http://www.livescience.com/16949-sexual-harassment-health-effects.html

Reynolds, G. (2012). *Presentation Zen: Simple ideas on presentation design and delivery*. San Francisco, CA: New Riders.

Reynolds, R. A., & Reynolds, J. L. (2002). Evidence. In J. E. Dillard & M. Pfau (Eds.), *The persuasion handbook: Developments in theory and practice*. Thousand Oaks, CA: Sage.

Rhode, D. L. (2011). *The beauty bias: The injustice of appearance in life and law*. New York: Oxford University Press.

Rhodes, G., Yoshikawa, S., Clark, A., Lee, K., McKay, R., & Akamatsu, S. (2001). Attractiveness of facial averageness and symmetry in non-Western cultures: In search of biologically based standards of beauty. *Perception*, 30, 611–625.

Rhodes, N. (2015). Fear-appeal messages: Message processing and affective attitudes. *Communication Research*. Retrieved from http://crx.sagepub.com/content/early/2015/01/08/0093650214565916.abstract

Rhodes, T. (2010, November). Learning across the curriculum: Communication departments hold a vital role. *Spectra*, pp. 12–15.

Richards, G. (2010, September 26). Total cell phone ban in works for drivers? *San Jose Mercury News*, B1, B7.

Ricker, S. (2014, January 16). What not to do in the interview. *CareerBuilder*. Retrieved from http://advice.careerbuilder.com/posts/what-not-to-do-in-the-interview

Ricks, D. (2000, February 4). Cancer likely to become leading U.S. killer. *San Jose Mercury News*, p. 10A.

Rieke, R. D., Sillars, M. O., & Peterson, T. R. (2005). *Argumentation and critical decision making*. New York: Pearson.

Rietzschel, E. F., Nijstad, B. A., & Strobe, W. (2006). Productivity is not enough: A comparison of interactive and nominal brainstorming groups on idea generation and selection. *Journal of Experimental Social Psychology*, 42, 244–251.

Riggio, R. E. (2012, November 30). The nonverbal power cues of men and women. *Psychology Today*. Retrieved from https://www.psychologytoday.com/blog/cutting-edge-leadership/201211/the-nonverbal-power-cues-men-and-women

Riggio, R. E., Riggio, H. R., Salinas, C., & Cole, E. J. (2003). The role of social and emotional communication skills in leader emergence and effectiveness. *Group Dynamics: Theory, Research, and Practice*, 7, 83–103.

Risk of crime in gated communities. (2013, March 20). *Science Daily*. Retrieved from http://www.sciencedaily.com/releases/2013/03/130320115113.htm

Robb, D. (2015, May 30). STX's Sophie Watts: "Money is not the "issue" but good ideas are. *Deadline*. Retrieved from http://deadline.com/2015/05/sophie-watts-stx-entertainment-produced-by-1201435044/

Roby, D. E. (2009, Summer). Teacher leadership skills: An analysis of communication apprehension. *Education*, 129, 608–614.

Rochlen, A. B., & Mahalik, J. R. (2004). Women's perception of male partners' gender role conflict as predictors of psychological well-being and relationship satisfaction. *Psychology of Men and Masculinity*, 5, 147–157.

Rodriguez, J. (1995). *Confounds in fear arousing persuasive messages: Do the paths less traveled make all the difference?* Unpublished doctoral dissertation, Michigan State University, East Lansing.

Roediger, H., Capaldi, E., Paris, S., & Polivy, J. (1991). *Psychology*. New York: HarperCollins.

Roese, N. J., & Vohs, K. D. (2012). Hindsight bias. *Perspectives on Psychological Science*, 7, 411–426.

Roethel, K. (2014, September 10). College students spending hours daily on smartphones. *SFGATE*. Retrieved from http://www.sfgate.com/health/article/College-students-spending-hours-daily-on-5745673.php

Rogelberg, S. G., Leach, D. J., Warr, P. B., & Burnfield, J. L. (2006). "Not another meeting!" Are meeting time demands related to employee well-being? *Journal of Applied Psychology*, 91, 83–96.

Rogelberg, S. G., Shanock, L. R., & Scott, C. W. (2012). Wasted time and money in meetings: Increasing return on investment. *Small Group Research*, 43, 236–245.

Rogers, C., & Roethlisberger, F. (1952, July/August). Barriers and gateways to communication. *Harvard Business Review*, pp. 28–35.

Romano, D. (1988). *Intercultural marriage: Promises and pitfalls*. Yarmouth, ME: Intercultural Press.

Romig, D. (1996). *Breakthrough teamwork: Outstanding results using structured teamwork*. Chicago: Irwin.

Rosen, D., Stefanone, M. A., & Lackaff, D. (2010). Online and offline social networks: Investigating culturally-specific behavior and satisfaction. In *Proceedings of IEEE's Hawaii International Conference on Systems Science*. Los Alamitos, CA: IEEE Press.

Rosenbaum, J. E. (2009). Patient teenagers? A comparison of the sexual behavior of virginity pledgers and matched nonpledgers. *Pediatrics*, 123, 110–120.

Rosenbaum, L., & Rosenbaum, W. (1985). Morale and productivity consequences of group leadership style, stress, and type of task. *Journal of Applied Psychology*, 55, 343–358.

Rosenfeld, L. (1983). Communication climate and coping mechanisms in the college classroom. *Communication Education*, 32, 169–174.

Rosenhan, D. L. (1973). On being sane in insane places. *Science*, 179, 250–258.

Rosenthal, D. B., & Hautaluoma, J. (1988). Effects of importance of issues, gender, and power of contenders on conflict management style. *Journal of Social Psychology*, 128, 699–701.

Rosenthal, N. (1997, July 15). How to prevent that "us vs. them" feeling within the family. *San Jose Mercury News*, p. E4.

Ross, C. C., (2012). Why do women hate their bodies? *PsychCentral*. Retrieved from http://psychcentral.com/blog/archives/2012/06/02/why-do-women-hate-their-bodies/

Rost, J. C. (1991). *Leadership for the twenty-first century*. New York: Praeger.

Rothwell, J. D. (1982). *Telling it like it isn't: Language misuse and malpractice*. Englewood Cliffs, NJ: Prentice Hall.

Rothwell, J. D. (2016). *In mixed company: Communicating in small groups and teams*. Boston: Wadsworth/Cengage.

Rotundo, M., Nguyen, D., & Sackett, P. R. (2001). A meta-analytic review of gender differences in perceptions of sexual harassment. *Journal of Applied Psychology*, 86, 914–922.

Rovio, E., Eskola, J., Kozub, S. A., Duda, J. L., & Lintunen, T. (2009). Can high group cohesion be harmful? A case study of a junior ice-hockey team. *Small Group Research*, 40, 421–435.

Ruback, B. R., & Jweng, D. (1997). Territorial defense in parking lots: Retaliation against waiting drivers. *Journal of Applied Social Psychology*, 27, 821–834.

Ruch, W. (1989). *International handbook of corporate communication*. Jefferson, NC: McFarland.

Rucker, D. D., & Petty, R. E. (2004). When resistance is futile: Consequences of failed counterarguing for attitude certainty. *Journal of Personality and Social Psychology*, 86, 219–235.

Ruet, B. (2006). Sudan's forgotten war. In L. G. Schnoor & B. Wickelgren (Eds.), *Winning orations*. Mankato, MN: Interstate Oratorical Association.

Ruggeiro, V. (1988). *Teaching thinking across the curriculum*. New York: Harper & Row.

Ruining it for the rest of us. (2008, December 19). *This American Life*. Retrieved from http://www.thisamericanlife.org/radio-archives/episode/370/transcript

Ruiter, R. A. C., Kessels, L. T. E., Jansma, B. M., & Brug, J. (2006). Increased attention for computer-tailored health communications: An event-related potential study. *Health Psychology*, 25, 300–306.

Rupp, R. (2014, September 30). Are you a supertaster? *The Plate*. Retrieved from http://theplate.nationalgeographic.com/2014/09/30/are-you-a-supertaster/

Rusbult, C. E., & Van Lange, P. A. M. (2003). Interdependence, interaction, and relationships. *Annual Review of Psychology*, 54, 351–375.

Rusting, C. L., & Nolen-Hoeksema, S. (1998). Regulating responses to anger: Effects of rumination and distraction on angry mood. *Journal of Personality and Social Psychology*, 74, 790–803.

Rutkowski, A.-F., Saunders, C., Vogel, D., & van Genuchten, M. (2007). "Is it already 4 A.M. in your time zone?" Focus immersion and temporal dissociation in virtual teams. *Small Group Research*, 38, 98–129.

Sabatini, P. (2015, March 26). 75% say we're a nation of smartphones. *San Jose Mercury News*, p. B8.

Sabourin, T. C. (1995). The role of negative reciprocity in spouse abuse: A relational control analysis. *Journal of Applied Communication Research*, 23, 271–283.

Sacks, O. (1990). *Seeing voices: A journey into the world of the deaf*. New York: Vintage Books.

Sagan, C. (1996). *The demon-haunted world: Science as a candle in the dark*. New York: Random House.

Sagrestano, L. M. (1992). Power strategies in interpersonal relationships. *Psychology of Women Quarterly*, 16, 481–495.

Sahlstein, E. M. (2006). Making plans: Praxis strategies for negotiating uncertainty-certainty in long-distance relationships. *Western Journal of Communication*, 70, 147–165.

Said, C., Sebe, N., & Todorov, A. (2009). Structural resemblance to emotional expressions predicts evaluation of emotionally neutral faces. *Emotion*, 9, 260–264.

Saint, S., & Lawson, J. (1997). *Rules for reaching consensus*. San Diego, CA: Pfeiffer.

Salazar, A. (1995). Understanding the synergistic effects of communication in small groups. *Small Group Research*, 26, 169–199.

Samovar, L., & Porter, R. (2004). *Communication between cultures*. Belmont, CA: Thomson-Wadsworth.

Samovar, L. A., Porter, R. E., & McDaniel, E. R. (2010). *Communication between cultures*. Boston: Cengage Learning.

Sampson, J., Witte, K., Morrison, K., Liu, W. Y., Hubbell, A. P., & Murray-Johnson, L. (2000). Addressing cultural orientations in fear appeals: Promoting AIDS-protective behaviors among Hispanic immigrant and African-American adolescents, and American and Taiwanese college students. *Journal of Health Communication*, 6, 335–358.

Sanford, K., & Wolfe, K. L. (2013). What married couples want from each other during conflicts: An investigation of underlying concerns. *Journal of Social and Clinical Psychology*, 32, 674–699.

Sapir, E. (1931). Conceptual categories in primitive languages. *Science*, 74, 572–578.

Savage, D. G. (2011, March 3). Court: Speech that offends still protected. *San Jose Mercury News*, p. A3.

Savitsky, K., & Gilovich, T. (2003). The illusion of transparency and the alleviation of speech anxiety. *Journal of Experimental Social Psychology*, 39, 618–625.

Sawyer, K. (2007). *Group genius: The creative power of collaboration*. New York: Basic Books.

Sayer, L. C., Endgland, P., & Kangas, N. (2011). She left, he left: How employment and satisfaction affect men's and women's decisions to leave marriages. *American Journal of Sociology*, 116, 1982–2018.

Scheer, R., & Moss, D. (2012, December 20). After 40 years, has recycling lived up to its billing? *Scientific American*. Retrieved from http://www.scientificamerican.com/article/has-recycling-lived-up-to-its-promises/

Scherer, K. R. (2003). Vocal communication of emotion: A review of research paradigms. *Speech Communication*, 40, 227–256.

Schiller, S. Z., & Mandviwalla, M. (2007). Virtual team research: An analysis of theory use and a framework for theory applications. *Small Group Research*, 38, 12–59.

Schimmack, U., Oishi, S., & Ciener, E. (2005). Individualism: A valid and important dimension of cultural differences between nations. *Personality and Social Psychology Review*, 9, 17–31.

Schittekatte, M., & Van Hiel, A. (1996). Effects of partially shared information and awareness of unshared information on information sampling. *Small Group Research*, 27, 431–449.

Schlosser, E. (2002). *Fast food nation*. New York: Penguin Books.

Schmidt, F. L., & Hunter, J. E. (1998). The validity and utility of selection methods in personnel psychology: Practical and theoretical implications of 85 years of research findings. *Psychological Bulletin*, 124, 262–274.

Schmitt, D. P., & Allik, J. (2005). Simultaneous administration of the Rosenberg Self-Esteem Scale in 53 nations: Exploring the universal and culture-specific features of global self-esteem. *Journal of Personality and Social Psychology*, 89, 623–642.

Schmitt, D. P., & Buss, D. M. (2001). Human mate poaching: Tactics and temptations for infiltrating existing mateships. *Journal of Personality and Social Psychology*, 80, 894–917.

Schoenbachler, D. D., & Whittler, T. E. (1996). Adolescent processing of social and physical threat communications. *Journal of Advertising*, 25, 37–54.

Schoettler, J. (1998, September 25). Minister shoots himself in church. *The Florida Times-Union*. Retrieved from http://jacksonville.com/tu-online/stories/092698/met_2a1MINIS.html

Scholz, M. (2005, June). A "simple" way to improve adherence. *RN*, 68, 82.

Schrodt, P., Witt, P. I., Myers, S. A., et al. (2008). Learner empowerment and teacher evaluations as functions of teacher power use in the college classroom. *Communication Education*, 57, 180–200.

Schubert, S. (2006, October/November). A look tells all. *Scientific American Mind*, pp. 26–31.

Segall, M. H., Dasen, P. R., Berry, J. W., & Poortinga, Y. H. (1990). *Human behavior in global perspective: An introduction to cross-cultural psychology*. New York: Pergamon.

Seidman, G. (2014, July 23). Can you really trust the people you meet online? *Psychology Today*. Retrieved fromhttps://www.psychologytoday.com/blog/close-encounters/201407/can-you-really-trust-the-people-you-meet-online

Seligman, M. (1991). *Learned optimism*. New York: Knopf.

Sell, J., Lovaglia, M. J., Mannix, E. A., Samuelson, C. D., & Wilson, R. K. (2004). Investigating conflict, power, and status within and among groups. *Small Group Research*, 35, 44–72.

Senate Select Committee on Intelligence (2004). U.S. intelligence community's prewar intelligence assessments on Iraq: Conclusions. *Report of the 108th Congress*. Retrieved from http://intelligence.senate.gov

Senthilingam, M. (2015). E-cigarettes: Helping smokers quit, or fueling a new addiction? *CNN*. Retrieved from http://www.cnn.com/2015/03/23/health/e-cigarettes-smoking-addiction-nicotine/index.html

Serico, C. (2015, February 22). Neil Patrick Harris hosts the Oscars: Catch up on all his best lines. *Today Pop Culture*. Retrieved from http://www.today.com/popculture/neil-patrick-harris-hosts-oscars-all-his-best-lines-academy-2D80504883

Seubert, J., & Regenbogen, C. (2012, March/April). I know how you feel. *Scientific American Mind*, pp. 54–57.

Sex in the digital age. (2010). *Men's Fitness*. Retrieved from http://www.mensfitness.com/women/sex-tips/sex-digital-age

Sexual harassment: What is it? (2015). *FindLaw*. Retrieved from http://employment.findlaw.com/employment-discrimination/sexual-harassment-what-is-it.html

Shadel, W. G., Niaura, R., & Abrams, D. B. (2001). How do adolescents process smoking and antismoking advertisements? A social cognitive analysis with implications for understanding smoking initiation. *Review of General Psychology*, 5, 429–444.

Shaffner, G. (1999). *The arithmetic of life and death*. New York: Ballantine Books.

Shearman, S. (2014, February 24). Stop telling women to "smile": New York street art says it how it is. *Telegraph*. Retrieved from http://www.telegraph.co.uk/women/womens-life/10653324/Stop-telling-women-to-smile-New-York-street-art-says-it-how-it-is.html

Sheldon, P. (2013). Examining gender differences in self-disclosure on Facebook versus face-to-face. *The Journal of Social Media in Society*, 2, 88–105.

Sheldon, P., Gilchrist-Petty, E., & Lessley, J. A. (2014). You did what? The relationship between forgiveness tendency, communication of forgiveness, and relationship satisfaction in married and dating couples. *Communication Reports*, 27, 78–90.

Shenk, D. (1997). *Data smog: Surviving the information glut*. New York: HarperCollins.

Sheppard, N. (2010, January 22). Stewart blasts Olbermann for Brown rants, defends Michelle Malkin. *NewsBusters*. Retrieved from http://newsbusters.org/blogs/noel-sheppard/2010/01/22/stewart-blasts-olbermann-brown-rants-defends-michelle-malkin

Sheridan, C., & King, R. (1972). Obedience to authority with an authentic victim. *Proceedings of the 80th Annual Convention, American Psychological Association*, 7, 165–166.

Sherif, C. W., Kelly, M., Rodgers, H. L., Sarup, G., & Tittler, B. I. (1973). Personal involvement, social judgment and action. *Journal of Personality and Social Psychology*, 27, 311–328.

Sherif, M., Sherif, C., & Nebergall, R. (1965). *Attitude and attitude change: The social judgment-involvement approach*. Philadelphia: Saunders.

Sherman, M. (2014, January 20). Why we don't give each other a break. *Psychology Today*. Retrieved from https://www.psychologytoday.com/blog/real-men-dont-write-blogs/201406/why-we-dont-give-each-other-break

Sherrin, N. (1996). *The Oxford dictionary of humorous quotations*. New York: Oxford University Press.

Shilling, D. (2000, September). How to find and keep top talent in today's tight labor market. *Medical Marketing & Media*, 35, 125.

Shimanoff, S. B. (2009). Rules theory. In S. W. Littlejohn & K. A. Foss (Eds.), *Encyclopedia of communication theory*. Beverly Hills, CA: Sage.

Shimanoff, S., & Jenkins, M. (1996). Leadership and gender: Challenging assumptions and recognizing resources. In R. Cathcart, L. Samovar, & L. Henman (Eds.), *Small group communication: Theory and practice*. Dubuque, IA: Brown & Benchmark.

Siebel, T. M., & Mange, S. A. (2009). The Montana Meth project: "Unselling" a dangerous drug. *Stanford Law and Policy Review*, 20, 405–416.

Sifferlin, A. (2012, February 16). Is online gaming messing up your marriage? *Time*. Retrieved from http://healthland.time.com/2012/02/16/is-online-gaming-messing-up-your-marriage/

Sillars, M. L., Weisberg, J., Burggraf, C. S., & Zietlow, P. H. (1990). Communication and understanding revisited: Married couples' understanding and recall of conversations. *Communication Research*, 17, 500–532.

Silver, N. (2012). *The signal and the noise: Why so many predictions fail-but some don't*. New York: The Penguin Press.

Simmons, H. (2014). Sexual abuse of male juvenile inmates. In L. G. Schnoor, K. Young, & L. Mayfield (Eds.), *Winning orations*. Mankato, MN: Interstate Oratorical Association.

Simonite, T. (2013, October 22). The decline of Wikipedia. *MIT Technology Review*. Retrieved from http://www.technologyreview.com/featuredstory/520446/the-decline-of-wikipedia/

Simons, L., & Zielenziger, M. (1996, March 3). Culture clash dims U.S. future in Asia. *San Jose Mercury News*, pp. A1, A22.

Simon-Thomas, E. R., Keltner, D. J., Sauter, D., Sinicropi-Yao, L., & Abramson, A. (2009). The voice conveys specific emotions: Evidence from vocal burst displays. *Emotion, 9*, 838–846.

Simpson, B., & Macy, M. W. (2001). Collective action and power inequality: Coalitions in exchange networks. *Social Psychology Quarterly, 64*, 88–100.

Simpson, P. A., & Stroh, L. K. (2004). Gender differences: Emotional expression and feelings of personal inauthenticity. *Journal of Applied Psychology, 89*, 715–721.

Sine, R. (2013, August 22). Sex drive: How do men and women compare? *WebMD*. Retrieved from http://www.webmd.com/sex/features/sex-drive-how-do-men-women-compare

Singh, D. (1993). Adaptive significance of female physical attractiveness: Role of waist-to-hip ratio. *Journal of Personality and Social Psychiatry, 65*, 293–307.

Singh, D. (1995). Female judgment of male attractiveness and desirability for relationships: Role of waist-to-hip ratio and financial status. *Journal of Personality and Social Psychology, 69*, 1089–1101.

Singh, D, & Singh, D. (2011). Shape and significance of feminine beauty: An evolutionary perspective. *Sex Roles, 64*, 723–731.

Signs (2015). Retrieved from http://www.liberalamerica.org/2014/04/15/the-teabonics-hall-of-fame-60-iconic-misspelled-protest-signs-photos/ accessed September 23, 2015.

Sinha-Roy, P. (2013, February 25). Hollywood's elite mingle at glitzy post-Oscar party. *Reuters*. Retrieved from http://www.reuters.com/article/2013/02/25/us-oscars-parties-idUSBRE91O0DS20130225

Sion, M. (2011, February 11). In matters of the heart, it's all about the green. *San Jose Mercury News*, p. A11.

Slater, M., Antley, A., Davison, A., Swapp, D., Guger, C., Barker, C., Pistrang, N., & Sanchez-Vives, M. V. (2006). A virtual reprise of the Stanley Milgram obedience experiments. *PloS ONE*. Retrieved from http://www.ncbi.nlm.nih.gov/pmc/articles/PMC1762398/

Smedes, L. B. (1984). *Forgive and forget: Healing the hurts we don't deserve.* New York: Harper & Row.

Smell. (2011, February 1). *Science Learning Hub.* Retrieved from http://sciencelearn.org.nz/Science-Stories/Our-Senses/Smell

Smith, A., & Duggan, M. (2013, October 21). Online dating & relationships. *Pew Research Center.* Retrieved from http://www.pewinternet.org/files/old-media/Files/Reports/2013/PIP_Online%20Dating%202013.pdf.

Smith, A. (2014, January 2). More than half of cell owners affected by "distracted walking." *Pew Research Center.* Retrieved from http://www.pewresearch.org/fact-tank/2014/01/02/more-than-half-of-cell-owners-affected-by-distracted-walking/

Smith, C. (2015, January 30). By the numbers: 200+ amazing Facebook user statistics. *DMR.* Retrieved from http://expandedramblings.com/index.php/by-the-numbers-17-amazing-facebook-stats/

Smith, E. E. (2014, June 12). Masters of love. *The Atlantic.* Retrieved from http://www.theatlantic.com/health/archive/2014/06/happily-ever-after/372573/

Smith, N. K., Larsen, J. T., Chartrand, T. L., Cacioppo, J. T., Katafiasz, H. A., & Moran, K. E. (2006). Being bad isn't always good: Affective context moderates the attention bias toward negative information. *Journal of Personality and Social Psychology, 90*, 210–220.

Smith, P. B., Dugan, S., & Trompenaars, F. (1997). Locus of control and affectivity by gender and occupational status: A 14-nation study. *Sex Roles, 36*, 51–57.

Smith, S. M., & Shaffer, D. R. (1995). Speed of speech and persuasion: Evidence for multiple effects. *Personality and Social Psychology Bulletin, 21*, 1051–1060.

Snyder, M. (2001). Self-fulfilling stereotypes. In A. Branaman (Ed.), *Self and society: Blackwell readers in sociology.* Malden, MA: Blackwell.

Snyder, K. (2014, July 14). Do men interruptt more than women? Yes, they do. *Jenga One Week at a Time.* Retrieved from http://jengaoneweekatatime.tumblr.com/post/91743154369/do-men-interrupt-more-than-women-yes-they-do.

Social networking sites in our lives (2011, June 16). *Pew Internet.* Retrieved from http://www.pewinternet.org/Reports/2011/Technology-and-Social-networks/summary.aspx

Solomon, C. (2010). The challenge of working in virtual teams: Virtual teams survey report-2010. *RW3 Culture Wizard.* Retrieved from http://static1.1.sqspcdn.com/static/f/616450/11590299/1302056653533/VTSReportv7.pdf?token=rHxzxFN1LEz3Hvndgtx65zNlfsk%3D

Sommer, R. (1969). *Personal space: The behavioral basis of design.* Englewood Cliffs, NJ: Prentice Hall.

Sommers, S. (2011, August 3). Study: When being beautiful backfires. *Huffington Post.* Retrieved from http://www.huffingtonpost.com/sam-sommers/beauty-advantage-study_b_906392.html

Sorensen, S. (1981, May). *Grouphate.* Paper presented at a meeting of the International Communication Association, Minneapolis, MN.

Sorokowski, P., Koscinski, K., & Sorokowska, A. (2013). Is beauty in the eye of the beholder but ugliness culturally universal? Facial preferences of Polish and Yali (Papua) people. *Evolutionary Psychology, 11*, 907–925.

Sparrow, B., Liu, J., & Wegner, D. M. (2011). Google effects on memory: Cognitive consequences of having information at our fingertips. *Science*. Retrieved from http://www.sciencemag.org/content/early/2011/07/13/science.1207745

Spitzberg, B. H. (2000). A model of intercultural communication competence. In L. A. Samovar & R. E. Porter (Eds.), *Intercultural communication: A reader*.

Spitzberg, B. H. (2011). Intimate partner violence and aggression: Seeing the light in a dark place. In W. R. Cupach & B. H. Spitzberg (Eds.), *The dark side of close relationships II*. New York: Routledge.

Sprecher, S., & Regan, P. C. (1998). Passionate and companionate love in courting and young married couples. *Sociological Inquiry*, 68, 163–185.

Sprecher, S., Schmeeckle, M., & Felmlee, D. (2006). The principle of least interest: Inequality in emotional involvement in romantic relationships. *Journal of Family Issues*, 27, 1255–1280.

Springen, K. (1997, June 3). The biology of beauty. *Newsweek*, pp. 61–66.

Sriussadaporn-Charoenngam, N., & Jablin, F. M. (1999). An exploratory study of communication competence in Thai organizations. *Journal of Business Communication*, 36, 382–418.

Sroufe, L. A., Egeland, B., Carlson, E. A., & Collins, W. A. (2005). *The development of the person: The Minnesota study of risk and adaptation from birth to adulthood*. New York: Guilford Press.

Stallings, H. (2009). Prosecution deferred is justice denied. In L. G. Schnoor & D. Cronn-Mills (Eds.), *Winning orations*. Northfield, MN: Interstate Oratorical Association.

Stanovich, K. E., West, R. F., & Toplak, M. E. (2013). Myside bias, rational thinking, and intelligence. *Current Directions in Psychological Science*, 22, 259–264.

Stefanone, M. A., Lackaff, D., & Rosen, D. (2011). Contingencies of self-worth and social-networking-site behavior. *Cyberpsychology, Behavior, and Social Networking*, 14, 41–49.

Stephen Colbert's address to the graduates. (2006, June 5). *AlterNet*. Retrieved from http://www.alternet.org/story/37144/stephen_colbert's_address_to_the_graduates

Stephens, K. K., Houser, M. L., & Cowan, R. L. (2009). R U able to meat me: The impact of students' overly casual email messages to instructors. *Communication Education*, 58, 303–326.

Stern, N. (2004). Just say no to PowerPoint: Enough is enough. Retrieved from http://www.eitforum.com/696.php

Sternberg, R. J. (1986). A triangular theory of love. *Psychological Review*, 93, 119–135.

Sternberg, R. J. (1988). *The triangle of love*. New York: Basic Books.

Sternberg, R. J. (1997). Construct validation of a triangular love scale. *European Journal of Social Psychology*, 27, 313–335.

Steward, C. (2009a, July 24). Rickey takes his speech to school. *San Jose Mercury News*, pp. C1, C5.

Steward, C. (2009b, July 27). With the pressure on, Henderson once again steals the show. *San Jose Mercury News*, pp. 1A, 3A.

Stewart, M. (2009). *The management myth: Debunking modern business philosophy*. New York: Norton.

Stone, D., Patton, B., & Heen, S. (1999). *Difficult conversations: How to discuss what matters most*. New York: Viking Press.

Stone, J., Cooper, J., Wiegard, A. W., & Aronson, E. (1997). When exemplification fails: Hypocrisy and the motive for self-integrity. *Journal of Personality and Social Psychology*, 72, 54–65.

Storytelling tips. (2015, June 1). *The Moth*. Retrieved from http://themoth.org/tell-a-story/storytelling-tips

Stout, J. G., & Dasgupta, N. (2011). When *he* doesn't mean *you*: Gender-exclusive language as ostracism. *Personality and Social Psychology Bulletin*, 37, 757–769.

Stovall, S. (2012). Juvenile crime from deleterious environmental conditions. In L. G. Schnoor, L. Mayfield, & K. Young (Eds.), *Winning orations*. Mankato, MN: Interstate Oratorical Association.

Straus, M. A. (2001). Prevalence of violence against dating partners by male and female university students worldwide. *Violence Against Women*, 10, 790–811.

Straus, M. A. (2008). Dominance and symmetry in partner violence by male and female university students in 32 nations. *Children and Youth Services Review*, 30, 252–275.

Straus, M. (2010). Thirty years of denying the evidence on gender symmetry in partner violence: Implications for prevention and treatment. *Partner Abuse*, 1, 332–363.

Straus, M. A., & Sweet, S. (1992). Verbal/symbolic aggression in couples: Incidence rates and relationship to personal characteristics. *Journal of Marriage and the Family*, 54, 346–357.

Strayer, D. L., Cooper, J. M., Turrill, J., Coleman, J., Medeiros-Ward, N., & Biondi, F. (2013). Measuring cognitive distraction in the automobile. *AAA Foundation for Traffic Safety*. Retrieved from https://www.aaafoundation.org/sites/default/files/MeasuringCognitiveDistractions.pdf

Street, M. (1997). Groupthink: An examination of theoretical issues, implications, and future research suggestions. *Small Group Research*, 28, 72–93.

Streich, L. (2012). 4-H four-gotten. In L. G. Schnoor, L. Mayfield, & K. Young (Eds.), *Winning orations*. Mankato, MN: Interstate Oratorical Association.

Stromberg, J. (2012, November 14). Images on cigarette packs are scarier to smokers than text warnings. *Smithsonian Magazine*. Retrieved from http://www.smithsonianmag.com/science-nature/images-on-cigarette-packs-are-scarier-to-smokers-than-text-warnings-122605824/?no-ist

Study indicates college students prefer casual dress. (2015, June 17). *University of Arkansas News*. Retrieved from http://news.uark.edu/articles/21304/study-indicates-college-students-prefer-casual-dress

Sudweeks, S., Gudykunst, W., Ting-Toomey, S., & Nishida, T. (1990). Developmental themes in Japanese–North American relationships. *International Journal of Intercultural Relations, 14*, 207–233.

Sumter, S. R., Valkenburg, P. M., & Peter, J. (2013). Perceptions of love across the lifespan: Differences in passion, intimacy, and commitment. *International Journal of Behavioral Development*. Retrieved from http://jbd.sagepub.com/content/early/2013/07/15/0165025413492486.abstract

Sunstein, C. R. (2006). *Infotopia: How many minds produce knowledge*. New York: Oxford University Press.

Sunwolf & Frey, L. R. (2005). Facilitating group communication. In S. A. Wheelan (Ed.), *The handbook of group research and practice*. Thousand Oaks, CA: Sage.

Superhuman heroes. (1998, June 6). *Economist*, pp. 10–12.

Surinder, K. S., & Cooper, R. B. (2003). Exploring the core concepts of media richness theory: The impact of cue multiplicity and feedback immediacy on decision quality. *Journal of Management Information Systems, 20*, 263–299.

Surk, B. (2008, October 16). Couple accused of sex on beach expose Dubai's cultural clash. *San Jose Mercury News*, p. 4A.

Surowiecki, J. (2005). *The wisdom of crowds: Why the many are smarter than the few and how collective wisdom shapes business, economics, societies, and nations*. New York: Anchor.

Surprenant, J. (2012). ALEC: Stopping the puppet master. In L. G. Schnoor, L. Mayfield, & K. Young (Eds.), *Winning orations*. Mankato, MN: Interstate Oratorical Association.

Sutton, R. (2011, October 24). How a few bad apples ruin everything. *The Wall Street Journal*. Retrieved from http://www.wsj.com/articles/SB10001424052970203499704576622550325233260

Svoboda, E. (2009, February/March). Avoiding the big choke. *Scientific American Mind*, pp. 36–41.

Swaine, J., Laughland, O., & Lartey, J. (2015, June 1). Black Americans killed by police twice as likely to be unarmed as white people. *The Guardian*. Retrieved from http://www.theguardian.com/us-news/2015/jun/01/black-americans-killed-by-police-analysis

Swaminathan, N. (2007, August 3). The sound track of our minds. *Scientific American*. Retrieved from http://www.sciam.com/article.cfm?articleID=2CE5B31C-E7F2-99DF-3D96DEA33C219680

Swann, W. B., Rentfrow, P. J., & Gosling, S. D. (2003). The precarious couple effect: Verbally inhibited men + critical, disinhibited women = bad chemistry. *Journal of Personality and Social Psychology, 85*, 1095–1106.

Swift, J. S., & Huang, Y. (2004). The changing nature of international business relationships and foreign language competence. *International Journal of Management Practice, 1*, 21.

Szivos, F. (2010, June 24). Anger in the workplace erupting. *Minuteman News Center*. Retrieved from http://minutemannewscenter.com/articles/2010/06/24/westport/business/doc4c22643adebba882851574.txt

Tafoya, M. A., & Spitzberg, B. H. (2007). The dark side of infidelity: Its nature, prevalence, and communicative functions. In B. H. Spitzberg & W. R. Cupach (Eds.), *The dark side of interpersonal communication*. Mahwah, NJ: Erlbaum.

Taibi, C. (2014, September 25). Rosie O'Donnell: Donald Trump's comments were "most bullying I ever experienced in my life." *Huffington Post*. Retrieved from http://www.huffingtonpost.com/2014/09/25/rosie-odonnell-donald-trump-weight-bullying-people-view_n_5884188.html

Talbot, M. M. (1998). *Language and gender: An introduction*. Malden, MA: Blackwell.

Tallmadge, A. (2007, Winter). When, not if. *Oregon Quarterly*, pp. 21–25.

Tannenbaum, M. (2013), April 2). The problem when sexism just sounds so darn friendly. *Scientific American*. Retrieved from http://blogs.scientificamerican.com/psysociety/2013/04/02/benevolent-sexism/

Tannen, D. (1990). *You just don't understand: Women and men in conversation*. New York: Ballantine.

Tannen, D. (1994). *Talking from 9 to 5*. New York: Avon.

Tannen, D. (1998). *The argument culture: Moving from debate to dialogue*. New York: Random House.

Tannen, D. (2003, January 5). Hey, did you catch that? Why they're talking as fast as they can. *Washington Post*, pp. B1, B4.

Tannen, D. (2010, May/June). He said, she said. *Scientific American Mind*, pp. 55–59.

Tannen, D. (2014, March 11). "Bossy" is more than a word to women. *USA Today*. Retrieved from http://www.usatoday.com/story/opinion/2014/03/11/sandberg-bossy-hillary-clinton-sotomayor-women-column/6302371/#

Taps, J., & Martin, P. (1990). Gender composition, attributional accounts, and women's influence and likability in task groups. *Small Group Research, 4,* 471–491.

Tapscott, D., & Williams, A. D. (2006). *Wikinomics: How mass collaboration changes everything.* New York: Penguin Group.

Taraban, C. B., Hendrick, S. S., & Hendrick, C. (1998). In P. A. Andersen & L. K. Guerrero (Eds.), *Handbook of communication and emotion.* New York: Academic Press.

Tarter, J. (2006, May/June). The cosmic haystack is large. *Skeptical Inquirer,* pp. 31–32.

Tavris, C. (1989). *Anger: The misunderstood emotion.* New York: Simon & Schuster.

Tavris, C. (1992). *The mismeasure of women.* New York: Simon & Schuster.

Tavris, C., & Aronson, E. (2007). *Mistakes were made (but not by me).* New York: Harcourt.

Taylor, J. B. (2006). *My stroke of insight: A brain scientist's personal journey.* New York: Viking.

Taylor, S. (2002). *The tending instinct: Women, men, and the biology of relationships.* New York: Holt.

Tecce, J. J. (2004). Body language in presidential debates as a predictor of election results: 1960–2004. Unpublished report, Boston College.

Tecce, J. J. (2012). The functional significance of eyeblinks. *International Journal of Psychophysiology, 85,* 336.

Ted Kennedy's eulogy of brother Robert, St. Patrick's Cathedral, New York City, June 8, 1968. (2009, August 8). *New York Daily News.* Retrieved from http://nydailynews.com/news/politics/2009/ 08/26/2009-08-26_ted_kennedys_eulogy_of_ brother_robert_1968.html

Teicher, M. H., Samson, J. A., Polcari, A., & McGreenery, C. E. (2006). Sticks, stones, and hurtful words: Relative effects of various forms of childhood maltreatment. *American Journal of Psychiatry, 163,* 993–100.

Teicher, M. H., Samson, J. A., Sheu, Y.-S., Polcari, A., & McGreenery, C. E. (2010). Hurtful words: Association of exposure to peer verbal abuse with elevated psychiatric symptom scores and corpus callosum abnormalities. *American Journal of Psychiatry, 167,* 1464–1471.

Teven, J. J., & Comadena, M. E. (1996). The effects of office aesthetic quality on students' perceptions of teacher credibility and communicator style. *Communication Research Reports, 13,* 101–108.

Thalheimer, W. (2010, December). How much do people forget? Retrieved from http://www .willatworklearning.com/2010/12/how-much-do-people-forget.html

The Chapman University survey on American fears. (2015, May 17). *Chapman University.* Retrieved from http://www.chapman.edu/wilkinson/research-centers/babbie-center/survey-american-fears.aspx

The fringe benefits of failure, and the importance of imagination. (2008, June 5). *Harvard Magazine.* Retrieved from http://harvardmagazine.com/ commencement/the-fringe-benefits-failure-the-importance-imagination

The top 20 most annoying buzzwords and phrases in the workplace. (2014, September 4). *Accountemps.* Retrieved from http://www.prnewswire.com/news-releases/the-top-20-most-annoying-buzzwords-and-phrases-in-the-workplace-accountemps-survey-reveals-dynamic-deep-dive-and-leverage-among-most-overused-buzzwords-273919931.html

The week in perspective. (2006, December 31). *San Jose Mercury News,* p. 2P.

Thomaes, S., Bushman, B. J., Orobio de Castro, B., Cohen, G. L., & Denissen, J. J. A. (2009). Reducing narcissistic aggression by buttressing self-esteem. *Psychological Science, 20,* 1536–1542.

Thomas, L. S., Tod, D. A., & Lavallee, D. E. (2011). Variability in muscle dysmorphia symptoms: The influence of weight training. *Journal of Strength and Conditioning Research, 25,* 846–851.

Thompson, L., & Nadler, J. (2002). Negotiating via information technology: Theory and application. *Journal of Social Issues, 58,* 109–124.

Thompson, M. (2015, January 10). Jackson tries to play it cool, but Oracle ovation gets to him. *San Jose Mercury News,* p. C1.

Thompson, M., Zimbardo, P., & Hutchinson, G. (2005, March 9). *Consumers are having second thoughts about online dating.* Retrieved from www.weattract.com/

Thomson, J. (2008, October 24). A quarter of people fear public speaking more than dying-here's how to beat your fear. *Smartcompany.* Retrieved from http://www .smartcompany.com.au/technology/information-technology/5453-a-quarter-of-people-fear-public-speaking-more-than-dying-here-s-how-to-beat-your-fear.html

Ting-Toomey, S., & Chung, L. C. (2012). *Understanding intercultural communication.* New York: Oxford University Press.

Ting-Toomey, S., Yee-Jung, K. K., Shapiro, R. B., Garcia, W., Wright, T. J., & Oetzel, J. G. (2000). Ethnic/ cultural identity salience and conflict styles in four U.S. ethnic groups. *International Journal of Intercultural Relations, 24,* 47–81.

Tipping. (2015, June 9). *Wikitravel.* Retrieved from http://wikitravel.org/en/Tipping

Titsworth, B. S. (2004). Students' notetaking: The effects of teacher immediacy and clarity. *Communication Education, 53,* 305–320.

Tjosvold, D., Johnson, D. W., Johnson, R. T., & Sun, H. (2003). Can interpersonal competition be constructive within organizations? *Journal of Psychology, 137,* 63–84.

Tjosvold, D., Johnson, D. W., Johnson, R. T., & Sun, H. (2006). Competitive motives and strategies: Understanding constructive competition. *Group Dynamics: Theory, Research, and Practice,* 10, 87–99.

Today in labor history Oct 9 Smith Barney a tentative sexual harassment settlement (never finalized). (2010, October 9). *Democratic Underground.* Retrieved from http://www.democraticunderground.com/discuss/duboard.php?az=view_all&address=367x28815

Tolhuizen, J. H. (1989). Communication strategies for intensifying dating relationships: Identification, use and structure. *Journal of Social and Personal Relationships,* 6, 413–434.

Top 15 most popular search engines. (2015, May). *EBizMBA.* Retrieved from http://www.ebizmba.com/articles/search-engines

Total number of websites. (2015, May 28). *Internet Live Stats.* Retrieved from http://www.internetlivestats.com/total-number-of-websites/

Toulmin, S. E. (1958). *The uses of argument.* Cambridge, UK: Cambridge University Press.

Trask, R. L. (1999). *Language: The basics.* New York: Routledge.

Trends in U.S. study abroad. (2015). *NAFSA.* Retrieved from http://www.nafsa.org/Explore_International_Education/Advocacy_And_Public_Policy/Study_Abroad/Trends_in_U_S__Study_Abroad/

Triandis, H. C. (1990). Cross-cultural studies of individualism and collectivism. In J. J. Berman (Ed.), *Cross-cultural perspective.* Lincoln: University of Nebraska Press.

Triandis, H. C. (1994). *Culture and social behavior.* New York: McGraw-Hill.

Triandis, H. C. (1995). *Individualism and collectivism.* Boulder, CO: Westview Press.

Triandis, H. C. (2009). Ecological determinants of cultural variations. In R. S. Wyer, C. Chiu, Y. Hong, & D. Cohen (Eds.), *Understanding culture: Theory, research and applications.* New York, NY: Psychology Press.

Triandis, H. C. (2012). Culture and conflict. In L. A. Samovar, R. E. Porter, and E. R. McDaniel (Eds.), *Intercultural communication: A reader.* Boston, MA: Wadsworth Cengage Learning.

Trosser, C. (1998, September/October). Obstacles to open discussion and critical thinking: The Grinnell College study. *Change Magazine,* pp. 44–49.

Tsapelas, I., Aron, A., & Orbuch, T. (2009). Marital boredom now predicts less satisfaction 9 years later. *Psychological Science,* 20, 543–545.

Tsapelas, I., Fisher, H. E., & Aron, A. (2011). Infidelity: When, where, why. In W. R. Cupach & B. H. Spitzberg (Eds.), *The dark side of close relationships.* New York: Routledge.

Tufte, E. (2003, September). PowerPoint is evil: Power corrupts, PowerPoint corrupts absolutely. *Wired News.* Retrieved from http://www.wired.com/wired/archive/11.09/ppt2_pr.html

Tulshyan, R. (2013, September 13). Millennials have the power to banish workplace bullying. *Forbes.* Retrieved from http://www.forbes.com/sites/ruchikatulshyan/2013/09/13/millennials-have-the-power-to-banish-workplace-bullying/

Turnage, A. K. (2007). Email flaming behaviors and organizational conflict. *Journal of Computer-Mediated Communication.* Retrieved from http://onlinelibrary.wiley.com/doi/10.1111/j.1083-6101.2007.00385.x/pdf

Turner, M. (2014, September 10). Anger appeals. *Encyclopedia of Health Communication.* Retrieved from http://knowledge.sagepub.com/view/encyclopedia-of-health-communication/n29.xml

Turner, M., Bessarabova, E., Sipek, S., & Hambleton, K. (2007, May 23). *Does message-induced anger facilitate or debilitate persuasion? Two tests of the Anger Activism Model.* Paper presented at the annual meeting of the International Communication Association, San Francisco, CA.

Turner, M. M., Bessarabova, E., Hambleton, K., Weiss, M., Sipek, S., & Long, K. (2013, December 17). Does anger facilitate or debilitate persuasion? A test of the Anger Activism Model. Retrieved from http://citation.allacademic.com/meta/p_mla_apa_research_citation/0/9/3/2/0/p93201_index.html

Turner, S. A., & Silvia, P. J. (2006). Must interesting things be pleasant? A test of competing appraisal structures. *Emotion,* 6, 670–674.

TV or not TV. (1993, April 19). *San Jose Mercury News,* p. 5E.

2014 national recycling survey. (2014, April). *National Waste & Recycling Association.* Retrieved from http://beginwiththebin.org/resources/for-communities/2014-national-recycling-survey

Uggen, C., & Blackstone, A. (2004). Sexual harassment as a gendered expression of power. *American Sociological Review,* 69, 64–92.

Ury, W. (1993). *Getting past no: Negotiating your way from confrontation to cooperation.* New York: Bantam.

U.S. and world population clock. (2015, April 1). *United States Census Bureau.* Retrieved from http://www.census.gov/popclock/

U.S. Equal Employment Opportunity Commission. (2015). Charges alleging sexual harassment FY 2010–FY 2014. Retrieved from http://www.eeoc.gov/eeoc/statistics/enforcement/sexual_harassment_new.cfm

U.S. Geological Survey. (2015). Retrieved from http://earthquake.usgs.gov/earthquakes/world/world_deaths.php

Van der Heijden, A. H. C. (1991). *Selective attention in vision*. New York: Routledge.

Van der Kleij, R., Schraagen, J. M., & De Dreu, C. K. W. (2009). How conversations change over time in face-to-face and video-mediated communication. *Small Group Research*, 40, 355–381.

Van Dijke, M., & Poppe, M. (2004). Social comparison of power: Interpersonal versus intergroup effects. *Group Dynamics: Theory, Research, and Practice*, 8, 13–26.

Van Kleef, G. A., Homan, A. C., Beersman, B., & Van Knippenberg, D. (2010). On angry leaders and agreeable followers: How leaders' emotions and followers' personalities shape motivation and team performance. *Psychological Science*, 21, 1827–1834.

Van Kleef, G. A., De Creu, C. K. W., & Manstead, A. S. R. (2004). The interpersonal effects of anger and happiness in negotiations. *Journal of Personality and Social Psychology*, 86, 57–76.

Van Mierlo, H., & Kleingeld, A. (2010). Goals, strategies, and group performance: Some limits of goal setting in groups. *Small Group Research*, 41, 524–555.

Van Oostrum, J., & Rabbie, J. (1995). Intergroup competition and cooperation within autocratic and democratic management regimes. *Small Group Research*, 26, 269–295.

Vandello, J. A., & Cohen, D. (1999). Patterns of individualism and collectivism across the United States. *Journal of Personality and Social Psychology*, 77, 279–292.

Vangelisti, A. L. (1994). "Couples" communication problems: The counselor's perspective. *Journal of Applied Communication Research*, 22, 106–126.

Vangelisti, A., Knapp, M., & Daly, J. (1990). Conversational narcissism. *Communication Monographs*, 57, 251–274.

Vaugh, D. (2013). The problem with homeless LGBT youth. In L. G. Schnoor, K. Young, & L. Mayfield (Eds.), *Winning orations*. Mankato, MN: Interstate Oratorical Association.

Vecchio, R. P., Bullis, R. C., & Brazil, D. M. (2006). The utility of situational leadership theory. *Small Group Research*, 37, 407–424.

Vennochi, J. (2006, July 23). Bush, Merkel, and the quickie neck rub. *The Boston Globe*. Retrieved from http://www.boston.com/news/globe/editorial_opinion/oped/articles/2006/07/23/bush_merkel_and_the_quickie_neck_rub/

Verlinden, J. (2005). *Critical thinking and everyday argument*. Belmont, CA: Wadsworth.

Vesselinov, E. (2008). Members only: Gated communities and residential segregation in metropolitan U.S. *Sociological Forum*, 23, 536–555.

Victor, D. A. (2007, March 27–31). *What is the language of business? Affecting business outcome before you say a word*. Proceedings of the Association for Business Communication, Seventh Asia-Pacific Conference, City University of Hong Kong.

Victory, honor, sacrifice. (Henry H. Shelton address) (transcript) (2001, August 1). *Vital Speeches of the Day*. Retrieved from http://connection.ebscohost.com/c/speeches/3391427/victory-honor-sacrifice

Vigen, T. (2015, May 28). Spurious correlations. Retrieved from http://www.tylervigen.com/spurious-correlations

Violence against women. (2014, November). *World Health Organization*. Retrieved from http://www.who.int/mediacentre/factsheets/fs239/en/

Vitanza, S., & Marshall, L. (1993). *Dimensions of dating violence, gender and personal characteristics*. Unpublished manuscript.

Vrij, A. (2000). *Detecting lies and deceit: The psychology of lying and its implications for professional practice*. Chichester, UK: Wiley.

Vrij, A. (2006). Nonverbal communication and deception. In V. Manusov & M. L. Patterson (Eds.), *The Sage handbook on nonverbal communication*. Thousand Oaks, CA; Sage.

Vrij, A., Granhad, P. A., & Porter, S. (2010). Pitfalls and opportunities in nonverbal and verbal lie detection. *Psychological Science in the Public Interest*, 11, 89–121.

Vroom, V. H., & Jago, A. G. (2007). The role of the situation in leadership. *American Psychologist*, 62, 17–24.

Wachsmuth, I. (2006, October/November). Gestures offer insight. *Scientific American Mind*, pp. 20–25.

Wade, C., & Tavris, C. (2008). *Invitation to psychology*. New York: Longman.

Wade, N. G., & Worthington, E. L. (2005). In search of a common core: A content analysis of interventions to promote forgiveness. *Psychotherapy: Theory, Research, Practice, Training*, 42, 160–177.

Wade, T. J. (1996). An examination of locus of control/fatalism for blacks, whites, boys, and girls over a two-year period of adolescence. *Social Behavior and Personality*, 24, 239–248.

Wade, T. J. (2010). The relationship between symmetry and attractiveness and mating relevant decisions and behavior: A review. *Symmetry*, 2, 1081–1098.

Wagner, N. (2011, April 1). Medicalese turns patients' perception of common conditions into serious diseases. *TheDoctorWillSeeYouNow.com*. Retrieved from http://www.thedoctorwillseeyounow.com/content/public_health/art2445.html

Wahr, J. A., Prager, R. L., Abernathy, J. H., et al. (2013). Patient safety in the cardiac operating room: Human factors and teamwork. *American Heart Association Statement*. Retrieved from http://circ.ahajournals.org/

content/early/2013/08/05/CIR.0b013e3182a38efa.full.pdf

Waldron, J. J. (2015). When building muscle turns into muscle dysmorphia. *Association for Applied Sport Psychology*. Retrieved from http://www.appliedsportpsych.org/resource-center/health-fitness-resources/when-building-muscle-turns-into-muscle-dysmorphia/

Wallace, D. S., Paulson, R. M., Lord, C. G., & Bond, C. F. (2005). Which behaviors do attitudes predict? Meta-analyzing the effects of social pressure and perceived difficulty. *Review of General Psychology, 9*, 214–227.

Wallace, P. (1999). *The psychology of the Internet*. New York: Cambridge University Press.Walsh, M. W. (2000, November 27). Many workers barred from trip to bathroom. *San Jose Mercury News*, p. 6E.

Walsh, M., & Vivona, M. (2010, October). International workplace productivity survey: Legal highlights. *LexisNexis*. Retrieved from http://www.multivu.com/players/English/46619-LexisNexis-International-Workplace-Productivity-Survey/flexSwf/impAsset/document/231ecd9b-fc56-4548-a061-b11156970873.pdf

Walter, C. (2006, December/January). Why do we cry? *Scientific American Mind*, pp. 44–51.

Walther, J. B. (2008). Computer-mediated communication and virtual groups. In E. A. Konijn, S. Utz, M. Tanis, & S. B. Barnes (Eds.), *Mediated interpersonal communication*. New York: Routledge.

Wang, W. (2014, September 24). Record share of Americans never have married. *Pew Research Center*. Retrieved from http://www.pewsocialtrends.org/2014/09/24/record-share-of-americans-have-never-married/

Wanzer, M. B., Frymier, A. B., Wojtaszczyk, A. M., & Smith, T. (2006). Appropriate and inappropriate uses of humor by teachers. *Communication Education, 55*, 178–196.

Ward, A. F. (2012, October 23). Men and women can't be "just friends." *Scientific American*. Retrieved from http://www.scientificamerican.com/article/men-and-women-cant-be-just-friends/

Warren, C., & McGraw, A. P. (2013). When humor backfires: Revisiting the relationship between humorous marketing and brand attitude. *Marketing Science Institute Working Paper Series*. Retrieved from http://cn.cnstudiodev.com/uploads/document_attachment/attachment/529/msi_report_13-124__1_.pdf

Warters, B. (2005, November). Changing patterns of roommate conflict fueled by the net. *Conflict Management in Higher Education Report*. Retrieved from http://www.campus-adr.org/CMHER/ReportEvents/Edition6_1/roommates.html

Wasserman, D. (2013). 2012 national popular vote tracker. Retrieved from https://docs.google.com/spreadsheet/lv?key=0AjYj9mXElO_QdHpla01oWE1jOFZRbnhJZkZpVFNKeVE&toomany=true

Watts, T. (2014). Financial aid leveraging. In L. G. Schnoor, K. Young, & L. Mayfield (Eds.), *Winning orations*. Mankato, MN: Interstate Oratorical Association.

Watzlawick, P., Beavin, J., & Jackson, D. (1967). *Pragmatics of human communication*. New York: Norton.

Weber, S. N. (1994). The need to be: The sociocultural significance of black language. In L. A. Samovar & R. E. Porter (Eds.), *Intercultural communication: A reader*. Belmont, CA: Wadsworth.

Wechsler, H., & Nelson, T. F. (2008). What we have learned from the Harvard School of Public Health College Alcohol Survey: Focusing attention on college student alcohol consumption and the environmental conditions that promote it. *Journal of Studies on Alcohol and Drugs, 69*, 481–490.

Wei, F.-Y. F., Wang, Y. K., & Klausner, M. (2012). Rethinking college students' self-regulation and sustained attention: Does text messaging during class influence cognitive learning? *Communication Education, 61*, 185–204.

Weiner, B., Graham, S., Peter, D., & Zmuidinas, M. (1991). Public confession and forgiveness. *Journal of Personality, 59*, 281–312.

Weiner, R. (2009, December 27). Death panels lie on Factcheck.org's "Whoppers of 2009." *Huffington Post*. Retrieved from http://www.huffingtonpost.com/2009/12/27/death-panels-lie-on-factc_n_404284.html

Weiner, S., Schwartz, A., Weaver, F., et al. (2010). Contextual errors and failures in individualizing patient care: A multicenter study. *Annals of Internal Medicine, 153*, 69–75.

Weingarten, G. (1994, September 27). I'm absolutely sure: You need a marshmallow enema. *San Jose Mercury News*, p. B7.

Weinrich, M., & Simpson, A. (2014). Differences in acoustic vowel space and the perception of speech tempo. *Journal of Phonetics, 43*, 1–10.

Weinrich, M., Simpson, A., Fuchs, S., Winkler, R., & Perrier, P. (2014). Mumbling is morphology? *ResearchGate*. Retrieved from http://www.researchgate.net/profile/Susanne_Fuchs2/publication/261322998_Mumbling_is_morphology/links/00b49533dc4e887e33000000.pdf

Wellen, J. M., & Neale, M. (2006). Deviance, self-typicality, and group cohesion: The corrosive effects of the bad apples on the barrel. *Small Group Research, 37*, 165–186.

Wells, G. I., Wright, E. F., & Bradfield, A. L. (1999). Witnesses to crime: Social and cognitive factors governing the validity of people's reports. In R. Roesch, S. D., Hart, & J. R. P. Ogloff (Eds.), *Psychology and the law: The state of the discipline*. New York: Kluwer.

Wener, R. (2006). Effectiveness of the direct supervision system of correctional design and management. *Criminal Justice and Behavior*, 33, 392–410.

Wener, R. (2015). *The environmental psychology of prisons and jails: Creating humane spaces in secure settings*. Cambridge, UK: Cambridge University Press.

Wener, R., Frazier, W., & Farberstein, J. (1987, June). Building better jails. *Psychology Today*, pp. 40–49.

Werking, K. (1997). *We're just friends: Women and men in nonromantic relationships*. New York: Guilford Press.

Werner, S. (2005). Mandatory minimum sentencing. In L. G. Schnoor & B. Wickelgren (Eds.), *Winning orations*. Mankato, MN: Interstate Oratorical Association.

West, R., & Turner, L. H. (2007). *Introducing communication theory: Analysis and application*. New York: McGraw-Hill.

Westen, D. (2007). *The political brain: The role of emotion in deciding the fate of the nation*. New York: Public Affairs Press.

Westlake, A. (2012, June 29). The view of tattoos in Japanese society. *Japan Daily Press*. Retrieved from http://japandailypress.com/the-view-of-tattoos-in-japanese-society-295623/

What social science can tell you about flirting and how to do it. (2007, March 16). *Social Issues Research Centre*. Retrieved from http://www.sirc.org/publik/flirt.html

Wheelan, S. A. (2009). Group size, group development, and group productivity. *Small Group Research*, 40, 247–262.

Whitbourne, S. K. (2012, March 13). 11 ways that active listening can help your relationships. *Psychology Today*. Retrieved from https://www.psychologytoday.com/blog/fulfillment-any-age/201203/11-ways-active-listening-can-help-your-relationships

White, A., & Hingson, R. (2013). The burden of alcohol use: Excessive alcohol consumption and related consequences among college students. *Alcohol Research: Current Review*, 35, 201–218.

Who was Neda? Slain woman an unlikely martyr. (2009, June 24). *CNN.com*. Retrieved from http://www.cnn.com/2009/WORLD/meast/06/23/iran.neda.profile/

Wieselquist, J., Rusbult, C. E., Agnew, C. R., & Foster, C. A. (1999). Commitment, pro-relationship behavior, and trust in close relationships. *Journal of Personality and Social Psychology*, 77, 942–966.

Wikipedia stats. (2015, May). *Wikimedia*. Retrieved from https://stats.wikimedia.org/EN/TablesArticlesTotal.htm

Willer, E. K., & Cupach, W. R. (2011). The meaning of girls' social aggression: Nasty or mastery? In W. R. Cupach & B. H. Spitzberg (Eds.), *The dark side of close relationships II*. New York: Routledge.

Williams, C. L., & Berry, J. W. (1991). Primary prevention of acculturative stress among refugees. *American Psychologist*, 46, 632–641.

Williams, K. D. (2011, January/February). The pain of exclusion. *Scientific American Mind*, pp. 30–37.

Williams, R., & Williams, V. (1993). *Anger kills*. New York: Random House.

Willis, J., & Todorov, A. (2006). First impressions: Making up your mind after a 100-ms exposure to a face. *Psychological Science*, 17, 592–598.

Wilmot, W., & Hocker, J. (2014). *Interpersonal conflict*. New York: McGraw-Hill.

Wilms, T. (2012, September 18). It is time for a "parental control, no texting while driving" phone. *Forbes*. Retrieved from http://www.forbes.com/sites/sap/2012/09/18/it-is-time-for-a-parental-control-no-texting-while-driving-phone/

Wilson, C. (2008, June 19). Russert gets a final toast from Washington. *USA Today*, p. 2D.

Wilson, J. P., & Rule, N. O. (2015). Facial trustworthiness predicts extreme criminal-sentencing outcomes. *Psychological Science*, Retrieved from http://pss.sagepub.com/content/early/2015/07/10/0956797615590992.abstract

Wilson, S. (2012, July 21). Where English is a whole different language. *San Jose Mercury News*, p. C3.

Wilson, T. D. (2002). *Strangers to ourselves: Discovering the adaptive unconscious*. Cambridge, MA: Harvard University Press.

Winchester, S. (2011, May 28). A verb for our frantic times. *The New York Times*. Retrieved from http://www.nytimes.com/2011/05/29/opinion/29winchester.html

Wingnut history: (2015, March 25). The Warren G. Harding miracle. *Daily Kos*. Retrieved from http://www.dailykos.com/story/2015/03/26/1373338/-Are-we-ready-for-the-Warren-G-Harding-miracle#

Witherall, S., & Clayton, E. (2014, November 17). Open doors: International students in the United States and study abroad by American students are at all-time high. *Institute of International Education*. Retrieved from http://www.iie.org/Who-We-Are/News-and-Events/Press-Center/Press-Releases/2014/2014-11-17-Open-Doors-Data

Witt, C., & Fetherling, D. (2009). *Real leaders don't do PowerPoint: How to sell yourself and your ideas*. New York: Crown Forum.

Witt, P. L., & Behnke, R. R. (2006). Anticipatory speech anxiety as a function of public speaking assignment type. *Communication Education*, 55, 167–177.

Witt, P. L., Brown, K. C., Roberts, J. B., Weisel, J., Sawyer, C. R., & Behnke, R. R. (2006). Somatic anxiety patterns before, during, and after giving a public speech. *Southern Communication Journal, 71,* 87–100.

Witte, K. (1998). In P. A. Andersen & L. K. Guerrero (Eds.), *Handbook of communication and emotion.* New York: Academic Press.

Witte, K., & Allen, M. (1996, November). *When do scare tactics work? A meta-analysis of fear appeals.* Paper presented at the annual meeting of the Speech Communication Association, San Diego, CA.

Witte, K., Murray-Johnson, L., Hubbell, A. P., Liu, W. Y., Sampson, J., & Morrison, K. (2000). Addressing cultural orientations in fear appeals: Promoting AIDS-protective behaviors among Hispanic immigrant and African-American adolescents, and American and Taiwanese college students. *Journal of Health Communication, 6,* 1023.

Witvliet, C. V., Ludwig, T. E., & Wade, N. G. (2001). Granting forgiveness or harboring grudges: Implications for emotion, physiology, and health. *Psychological Science, 12,* 117–123.

Wnek, A. (2012). Untitled. In L. G. Schnoor, L. Mayfield, & K. Young (Eds.), *Winning orations.* Mankato, MN: Interstate Oratorical Association.

Wojciszke, B., Baczynska, R., & Jaworski, M. (1998). On the dominance of moral categories in impression formation. *Personality and Social Psychology Bulletin, 24,* 1245–1257.

Women CEOs of the S & P 500. (2015, April 3). *Catalyst.* Retrieved from http://www.catalyst.org/knowledge/women-ceos-sp-500

Wondrak, I., & Hoffman, J. (2007, April/May). A personal obsession: What drives stalkers to pursue their victims? *Scientific American Mind,* pp. 76–81.

Wong, Y. J., Pituch, K. A., & Rochlen, A. B. (2006). Men's restrictive emotionality: An investigation of associations with other emotion-related constructs, anxiety, and underlying dimensions. *Psychology of Men and Masculinity, 7,* 113–126.

Wood, C., Kemp, N., & Plester, B. (2014). *Text messaging and literacy: The evidence.* New York: Routledge.

Wood, J. (1994). *Gendered lives: Communication, gender, and culture.* Belmont, CA: Wadsworth.

Wood, J. (2014, August 31). College students in study spend 8 to 10 hours daily on cell phone. *PsychCentral.* Retrieved from http://psychcentral.com/news/2014/08/31/new-study-finds-cell-phone-addiction-increasingly-realistic-possibility/74312.html

Wood, J. T. (1998). *But I thought you meant . . . : Misunderstandings in human communication.* Mountain View, CA: Mayfield.

Wood, J. T. (2004). *Communication theories in action: An introduction.* Belmont, CA: Wadsworth/ Thomson Learning.

Wood, J. T. (2015). *Gendered lives: Communication, gender, and culture.* Belmont, CA: Cengage.

Wood, J. T., & Inman, C. (1993). In a different mode: Recognizing male models of closeness. *Journal of Applied Communication Research, 21,* 279–295.

Woodrow, L. (2006). Anxiety and speaking English as a second language. *RELC: Journal of Language Teaching and Research.* Retrieved from http://rel.sagepub.com/content/37/3/308.abstract

Woodzicka, J. A., & LaFrance, M. (2005). Working on a smile: Responding to sexual provocation in the workplace. In R. E. Riggio & R. S. Feldman (Eds.), *Applications of nonverbal communication.* New York: Lawrence Erlbaum.

World Baseball Classic. (2015). *Wikipedia.* Retrieved from https://en.wikipedia.org/wiki/World_Baseball_Classic

Wright, D. B., Memon, A., Skagerberg, E. M., & Gabbert, F. (2009). When eyewitnesses talk. *Current Directions in Psychological Science, 18,* 174–178.

Wright, R. (2000). *Nonzero: The logic of human destiny.* New York: Vintage Books.

Xiao, X., & Chen, G.-M. (2009). A Confucian perspective of communication competence. *Journal of Multicultural Discourse, 4,* 61–74.

Yadegaran, J. (2013, August 11). Dorm diplomacy: Mutual respect is key to getting along. *San Jose Mercury News,* p. D1.

Yang, J. L. (2006, June 12). The power of number 4.6. *Fortune,* p. 122.

Yela, C. (2006). The evaluation of love: Simplified version of the scales for Yela's tetrangular model based on Sternberg's model. *European Journal of Psychological Assessment, 22,* 21–27.

Yen, H. (2010, May 27). Growth of interracial marriage slowing. *San Jose Mercury News,* p. A5.

Yerman, M. G. (2015, January 30). "She's Beautiful When She's Angry" highlights grassroots feminists. *Womens Media Center.* Retrieved from http://www.womensmediacenter.com/feature/entry/shes-beautiful-when-shes-angry-highlights-grassroots-feminists

Yoder, J. D. (2002). 2001 Division 35 presidential address: Context matters: Understanding tokenism processes and their impact on women's work. *Psychology of Women Quarterly, 26,* 108.

Yogi Berra quotes. (2015). *BrainyQuote.* Retrieved from http://www.brainyquote.com/quotes/authors/y/yogi_berra.html

Yoo, Y., & Alavi, M. (2004). Emergent leadership in virtual teams: What do emergent leaders do? *Information and Organization, 14,* 27–58.

Young, A. (2013, February 25). Oscars 2013: A billion people did not watch the Academy Awards, so stop saying they did. *IBTimes*. Retrieved from http://www.ibtimes.com/oscars-2013-billion-people-did-not-watch-academy-awards-so-stop-saying-they-did-1102263

Young, S. L. (2015, February 25). Workplace bullying: Its impact goes beyond hurt feelings. *Huffington Post*. Retrieved from http://www.huffingtonpost.com/s-l-young/workplace-bullying-its-im_b_6753992.html

Yu, X. (1997). The Chinese "nature" perspective on mao-dun (conflict) and mao-dun resolution strategies: A qualitative investigation. *Intercultural Communication Studies*, 7, 63–82.

Yukl, G. (2006). *Leadership in organizations*. Upper Saddle River, NJ: Prentice Hall.

Zenger, J., & Folkman, J. (2012, March 15). Are women better leaders than men? *Harvard Business Review Blog Network*. Retrieved from https://hbr.org/2012/03/a-study-in-leadership-women-do

Zernike, K., & Thee-Brenan, M. (2010, April 14). Poll finds Tea Party backers wealthier and more educated. *The New York Times*. Retrieved from http://www.nytimes.com/2010/04/15/us/politics/15poll.html

Zhang, Q. (2010). Asian Americans beyond the Model Minority stereotype: The nerdy and the left out. *Journal of International and Intercultural Communication*, 3, 20–37.

Zhang, Y., Kong, F., Zhong, Y., & Kou, H. (2014). Personality manipulations: Do they modulate facial attractiveness ratings? *Personality and Individual Differences*, 70, 80–84.

Zillman, C. (2014, February 4). Microsoft's new CEO: One minority exec in a sea of white. *Fortune*. Retrieved from http://fortune.com/2014/02/04/microsofts-new-ceo-one-minority-exec-in-a-sea-of-white/

Zillmann, D. (1993). Mental control of angry aggression. In D. Wegner & J. Pennebaker (Eds.), *Handbook of mental control* (Vol. 5). Englewood Cliffs, NJ: Prentice Hall.

Zimbardo, P. (1992). *Psychology and life*. New York: HarperCollins.

Zormeier, S. M., & Samovar, L. A. (2000). Language as a mirror of reality: Mexican-American proverbs. In L. A. Samovar & R. E. Porter (Eds.), *Intercultural communication: A reader*. Belmont, CA: Wadsworth.

Zornoza, A., Ripoll, P., & Peiro, J. M. (2002). Conflict management in groups that work in two different communication contexts: Face-to-face and computer-mediated communication. *Small Group Research*, 33, 481–508.

Credits

Photo Credits

Index